A Visitor's Guide
to
CHINA

ELIZABETH MORRELL

Michael Joseph
LONDON

To Philip

First published in Great Britain by Michael Joseph Ltd
44 Bedford Square, London WC1
1983

Cased edition ISBN 0 7181 1905 3
Paperback edition ISBN 0 7181 2201 1

Typeset by Rowland Phototypesetting Ltd,
Bury St Edmunds, Suffolk
Printed and bound in Great Britain by
Billings and Son Ltd, Worcester

Contents

List of Illustrations

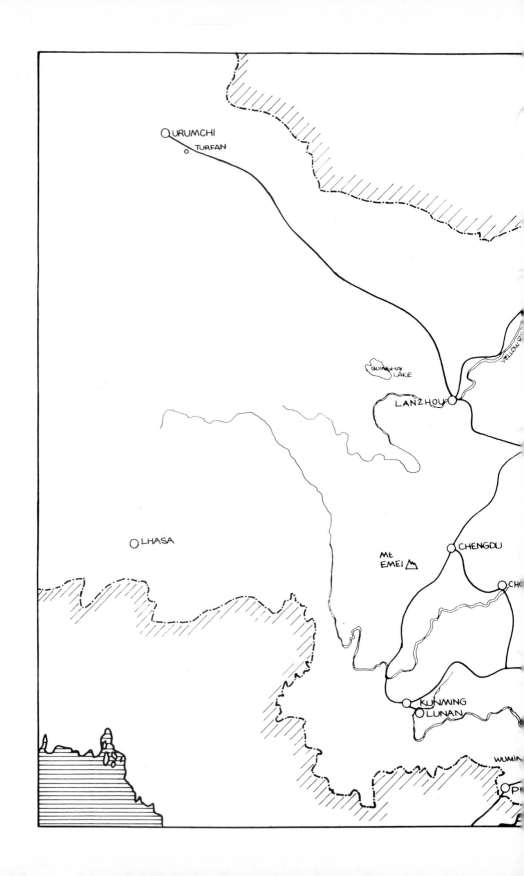

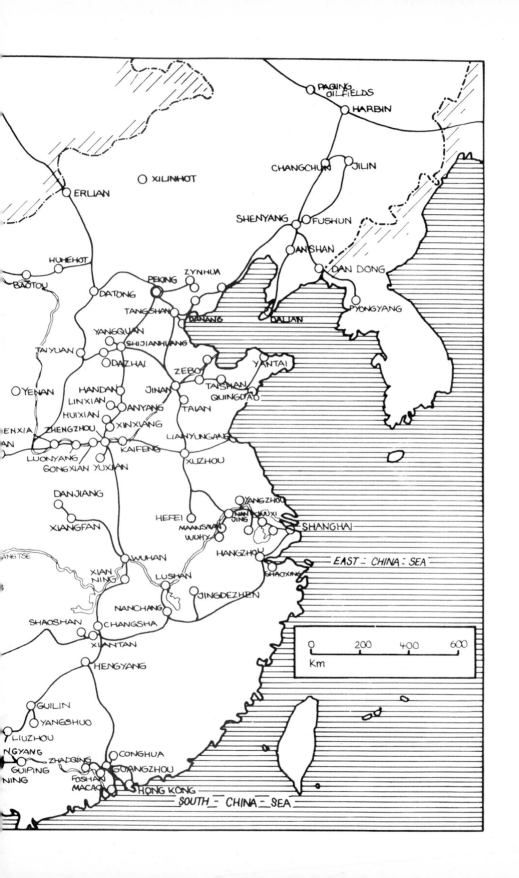

Acknowledgments

This guidebook has been written against a background of constant change and development in China, in both the socio-political and touristic spheres. It would have been impossible to keep abreast of these changes without the valuable help and assistance of many people.

In this respect my thanks are due particularly to the directors and staff of the First European Department of China International Travel Service in Peking. They have assisted me throughout, keeping me apprised of new developments, suggesting amendments and facilitating contacts with branch offices, where managers and staff enthusiastically applied their own expertise to the sections on each locality with their profound sense of local pride and history.

At home, I wish to thank Eleni Pohani for her constant support and assistance with typing the awesome manuscript, as well as Adele Bis, Angela Newsome, Georgie Katzen and Prue Stern. I am extremely grateful to Nick Thompson, Miles Flint, Richard Byron and Colin Thomas, who all provided photographs. Philip Morrell, Graham Hutt, Jennie Davies, my editor, and Bridget Harris, her assistant, deserve ten thousand thanks for their considered advice and patience.

With the help of all these people, I have sought to provide a practical and up-to-date introduction to China, and any inconsistencies or inaccuracies are my own.

PART ONE

An Introduction to China

An Introduction to China

Limpid lakes, soaring mountains, swift-flowing rivers, sheer gorges, ancient cities buried in deserts, ornate palaces, wooded hills, hot springs, ancient tombs, terracotta warriors, leaning pagodas, elaborate temples, memorials to modern heroes, steam trains, bicycles, exotic cuisine, embroidered silk, intricate ivory, translucent jade, multifarious bamboo, gnarled pines, sweeping calligraphy, walls – great walls, city walls, courtyard walls, babes in padded suits, old men in teahouses, dark-suited cadres, silk-skirted girls, nimble acrobats, Friendship Stores, noodle shops . . . and over 120 cities and resorts await the visitor to China.

Having made the decision to go to China the prospective traveller will no doubt nurture a few misgivings. Given the distance that must be covered and the resulting cost, few people will travel to China more than once in their lifetime. All the more reason to choose the itinerary with due care and to prepare well for the journey. The purpose of this book is twofold: to provide a background to China's history and culture, and an orientation of the places to be visited. As the sense of provincial identity is strong in China, I have subdivided the gazetteer by municipality, province or autonomous region, concentrating on those areas which are officially 'open' to the overseas visitor. Personal experience in organizing and accompanying tours to the People's Republic of China has shown that for many people China is still as inscrutable as ever, and that although they have come to China because it is unlike any other place in the world, they are unprepared for the unexpected.

When this book was first conceived it was at the beginning of a period of great change in China, marking the end of the Cultural Revolution and the beginning of the drive towards modernization of this enormous and populous country. Although most Chinese knew that the so-called downfall of the Gang of Four in 1976 would have far-reaching effects on their daily lives, the exact direction was difficult to predict and foreign observers were even less apprised of the implications of this change. In early 1977 an extensive modernization programme was announced in China, encouraging the Chinese to look for example to the experience and technology of the western world.

Major changes and adjustments have taken place in the drive to update and strengthen the economy. Bonus systems have been reintroduced into factories, free markets flourish in the countryside, higher standards are being set in the educational field, and the traditional arts of China have been revived. Modernization has brought contact with the rest of the world – through the expansion of tourism to China, through Chinese delegations travelling to all parts of the world on trade missions, visits by Chinese leaders to the West, or the admission of the Chinese to

3

the Olympic movement. In the topmost ranks of Chinese society 7 September 1980 saw the peaceable transfer of power from the gerontocracy to younger, business-minded hands, and the separation of 'party' and 'government' – a process which has been reflected in every level of industrial, agricultural and cultural administration.

Since 1977 the requirements of China's modernization plans have meant that China urgently needs to increase her foreign currency earnings, hence the rapid expansion of tourism and the large investments in hotel building and refurbishment, excursion buses, guides, souvenir shops and all the accoutrements of a developing tourist infrastructure. The Chinese tourist authorities have recently announced that 220,000 tourists visited China in 1982, and 440,000 are expected in 1983, increasing to one million by 1985.

It remains to be seen whether China can easily absorb this rapid increase by providing adequate hotel accommodation, aircraft seats, trains and fully trained guides and interpreters. The logistics of organizing tourism in China are among the most complex in the world. People do not go to China to stay in one resort: they follow multi-centred itineraries travelling the length and breadth of China in a matter of days, taxing the limited transportation system to its limit. Scheduled itineraries are frequently subject to unpredictable changes and, with the plans for rapid expansion, the situation is unlikely to change in the near future. It would be better to visit China sooner rather than later, as no doubt the pollutant effects of tourism will tarnish the freshness and sense of uniqueness which makes travel to China such a pleasurable and rewarding experience.

Elizabeth Morrell
London, May 1982

Geography and Population

China is the third largest country in the world, and its vast area includes the extremes of climate, vegetation, topography and population. They range from the permafrost of Heilongjiang in the north to the monsoons of Guangdong Province in the south, from the Himalayas in the south-west to the East China plain or the Turfan depression in the north-west, from the typhoons of the eastern seaboard to the sandstorms of the Gobi Desert, from Shanghai with its 12 million population to the scantily populated north-west.

SIZE

AREA: Approximately 9.6 million km^2
DISTANCES: East to west over 5000 km
              North to south over 5500 km
              Coastline 14,000 km
              Border 20,000 km
              Islands – over 5000
LATITUDE: Nansha Islands 4° N
              Hainan Island 18° N
              Guangzhou – Tropic of Cancer
              Shanghai 31° N
              Peking 40° N
              Heilongjiang (Amur River) 54° N
LONGITUDE: East – where the Heilongjiang meets the Ussuri River 136° E
              West – the Pamirs on the western edge of the Xinjiang Autonomous
                 Region 73° E

ADMINISTRATIVE DIVISIONS

China has twenty-two provinces, Anhui, Fujian, Gansu, Guangdong, Guizhou, Hebei, Heilongjiang, Henan, Hubei, Hunan, Jiangsu, Jiangxi, Jilin, Liaoning, Qinghai, Shandong, Shanxi, Shaanxi, Sichuan, Yunnan, Zhejiang and Taiwan; five autonomous regions – Xinjiang-Uighur, Tibet (Xizang), Ningxia-Hui, Inner Mongolia (Nei Menggu) and Guangxi-Zhuang; and three municipalities which are under the authority of the central government – Peking, Shanghai and Tianjin. Many of the provinces take their names from their geographical positions: Henan means south of the (Yellow) river, Hubei means north of the (Dongting) lake, etc., while the name of each autonomous region usually includes that of its majority nationality.

TOPOGRAPHY

Broadly speaking, China slopes downwards from west to east; there are three steps – from mountain to plateau to the plains of the eastern seaboard. Mountains cover 66 per cent of Chinese territory.

Mountains and Basins

Drawing a north–south line between Lanzhou and Kunming divides the country into the mountainous west and the east, where the land rarely rises above 3000 m and 2000 m passes for a mountain. West of this line stand the peaks of the Himalayas, with Everest or Jolmolungma (its Tibetan name, meaning The Goddess) soaring to 8848 m on the Sino–Nepalese border, the extensive Qinghai–Tibet plateau which averages 4000 m above sea-level, and the Kunlun mountain ranges. In the far north-west are the ranges of Xinjiang Autonomous Region – the Altai Mountains and the Tianshan (the Heavenly Mountains); here also are found desert and basin areas – the Tarim and Dzungari Basins in Xinjiang, and the Tsaidam Basin in Qinghai Province.

Major ranges east of the imaginary Lanzhou–Kunming line are the Greater Xing'an Mountains and the Changbai of Manchuria, the Taihang Mountains of Shanxi, and the Wu Mountains which isolate the Sichuan Basin. In the south lie the Wuyi Mountains, on the borders of Jiangxi and Fujian Provinces, and the Nan ling Mountains of southern Hunan.

Hills

The coastal provinces contain hilly regions – the gentle eastern China landscape of undulating hills around 500 m above sea-level. In east China are the famous Five Sacred Mountains – Tai shan in Shandong (1524 m), Heng shan in Hunan, Hua shan in Shaanxi (2600 m), Heng shan in Shanxi and Song shan in Henan, where gods and goddesses are reputed to have lived and emperors came to worship. The famous Buddhist mountain shrines are Emei Mountain in Sichuan, Jiuhua shan in Anhui, Putuo shan in Zhejiang and Wutaishan in Shanxi.

Plateau Areas

Apart from the Qinghai–Tibet plateau in the west there is also the Inner Mongolian plateau 1–2000 m above sea-level, which is renowned for stock-raising. South of this is a loess plateau, formed from the silt of the Yellow River which covers parts of Gansu, Shaanxi, Shanxi and Hebei. The soil is fertile but liable to erosion and water loss; extensive land reclamation has been carried out here since 1949, as well as terracing, tree-planting and irrigation projects. In southern China lies the limestone Yunnan–Guizhou plateau, again 1–2000 m above sea-level; it is an area of contrasting pinnacles, caverns and valleys.

Rivers, Waterways and Lakes

China's rivers are legendary, the best-known being the Yellow and Yangtse Rivers, and through the ages work has constantly been carried out to tame them and redirect them for irrigation; today they form a major potential source of energy. Many of the major rivers rise in the Qinghai–Tibet plateau and drain into the East China Sea. The Yangtse is 6300 km long and has its source in the Tangla Mountains in Qinghai. The Yellow River, named for its silt content, is 4800 km long, rises in the Bayankala Mountains in Qinghai, and flows into the Bohai Sea. The arid desert zones of the north-west have a system of interior drainage – the rivers are formed by melting snow from the surrounding mountain areas. The longest river of this kind is the Tarim, which flows 2179 km eastward along the northern periphery of the basin.

The Grand Canal, begun in 486 BC, was made by dredging existing river beds as well as digging new channels. The major construction period took place during the Sui dynasty; eventually the canal linked Peking and Hangzhou, a distance of 1794 km, passing through Hebei, Shandong, Jiangsu and Zhejiang. During the mid-nineteenth century it became blocked, when the Yellow River changed course; parts of it are at present being cleared so that it can be put to full use.

The major rivers of north China are the Heilongjiang (Amur), the Sungari and the Liao he, the Yellow River and the Hai he. They are all important for irrigation and potential hydro-electric power, although they tend to freeze in winter; they flow slowly, with the water at its highest level in July and August, and have a high silt content.

South China is fed by the Huai River, the Yangtse, the Qiantang, the Minjiang and the Pearl, which flow through humid zones. The water level of these rivers is high and the flood season comes between April and September; they contain little sediment and are ice-free. The Mekong, the Salween and the Brahmaputra rivers flow across the Chinese border into Vietnam, Burma and Bangladesh.

The country contains some 370 large lakes, the best known of which are the Poyang in Jiangxi, the Dongting in Hunan and the Tai hu in Jiangsu. The largest salt lake is the Kokonor in Qinghai.

CLIMATE

The climate ranges from tropical to freezing, although in most of the country it is temperate. January is usually the coldest month throughout China: in the far north the temperature drops to $-20°$ C, while in the south it can be a relatively mild 8° C. High pressure in central Asia and Siberia brings constant north-westerly winds and sandstorms to the northern parts of China, where it is very dry; by spring most of northern China often suffers from drought, followed by flooding.

In the summer the extremes of temperature between north and south are less acute; in July the countrywide average is 25°C. The high pressure shifts to the Pacific, bringing monsoons and south and south-easterly winds and typhoons in August and September. Eighty per cent of the rainfall throughout the country falls between May and October. The north-west and western parts of China, including Tibet and Qinghai, receive less than 250 mm of rainfall per annum, while in the area south of the Yellow River and east of the Qinghai–Tibet plateau the rainfall is over 1000 mm, rising to above 2000 mm. The growing season in the south lasts all year, while in the north it is short and usually only one crop can be harvested.

POPULATION

The figure usually quoted for China's population is 1 billion, or one-quarter of the population of the entire world. The most recently published figure shows the population standing at 996.2 million at the end of 1981. Population control has become one of the most pressing issues of the new era; a member of the Politburo, Chen Muhua, has been appointed to monitor population growth, and the theories of the Chinese population expert Ma Yinchu are the object of discussion.

Throughout the ages China has had a large population checked at different periods by war and famine. By the middle of the nineteenth century the population stood at over 400 million, and in 1949 it was 548 million. The annual growth rate has since been reduced from twenty per thousand to twelve per thousand; the current target is to bring it down even further, and not to exceed a total population of 1.2 billion by the year 2000. China had a baby boom in the 1960s, and today half the population is under twenty-one.

Every effort is being made, using all the machinery of party and government, to emphasize the importance of birth control and one child per couple is considered the ideal; material incentives are offered to those who agree to have one child only, and penalties are exacted on those who exceed this limit. Contraception advice and abortion are both available, and at street or commune team level charts are prepared to work out who can have babies in any one year. The Chinese constitution even includes these words: 'The State advocates and encourages family planning.' The revival of emphasis on population control is in keeping with China's current efforts to ensure an improved standard of living for everyone, better education, and fair distribution of basic goods. However it will be interesting to see the effects on family life of the small nuclear family in a country where traditionally more children have meant more wealth and happiness.

Distribution

China's population is concentrated in the eastern half of the country. The enormous land mass of the border areas of Xinjiang, Qinghai, Tibet, Ningxia and Inner Mongolia, which together make up half of China, contain only around 3 per cent of the total population; many areas here are uninhabited, and those parts that are inhabited are lived in by minority nationalities.

The remainder of China has been farmed and settled for centuries, and is densely populated. Most of eastern China has a population of over 80 per square kilometre; around the fertile reaches of the Yangtse, in Sichuan and Guangdong, this figure increases to 193 per square kilometre. Today approximately 80 per cent of the population works on 11% of the land, while the remaining 20 per cent form the urban population.

Very often the population of any one province is large enough to form the basis of a respectable-sized country. Indeed Sichuan Province, whose latest population figure is 97 million, is larger than France. China has seventeen cities with a population exceeding 1 million; these are mostly on the eastern seaboard and in Manchuria, but include several inland cities, such as Xi'an and Chongqing, which have developed since the mid-1950s. It is in the cities where visitors will perhaps be most aware of the strain on resources. Here there are cramped living conditions, overcrowded public transport, and a large youthful population which must be found work and which is now reluctant to work in the countryside.

Peoples

The ethnic fabric of China consists of 94 per cent Han Chinese and 6 per cent 'fraternal nationalities' or national minorities who inhabit over half of China's

Chinese children in a kindergarten clapping their welcome

A bamboo pram

A noodle shop in Luoyang

Old man eating an ice-lolly

territory, particularly the immense border areas which are vital for defence and for potential mineral and agricultural wealth. The title 'Han' for ethnic Chinese comes from the Han dynasty (206 BC–AD 220), during which many of the enduring institutions of Chinese life were established. Until recently there were fifty-four minority nationalities; Chinese ethnographers have recently discovered another small tribe – the Jinuo – in south-west China, making the total fifty-five.

At Minority Institutes, such as the Palace in Peking, cadres are trained. Much is made of the importance of unity and equality, the colourful dancing and singing, costumes and customs, and the historic precedents for unity – plays and stories about marriages between Han princesses and foreign potentates, and the part that was played by the minority nationalities in the Revolution, aiding and joining the communist guerrillas. Since the end of the Cultural Revolution the different nationalities have been able to resume their traditional religions, customs and means of livelihood, and several areas have been specifically opened to tourists. In minority areas the official language is the one spoken by the local ethnic population, and the minority nationalities are exempt from current population control programmes.

There are several important minority groups. Tibetans live in south-west China – Tibet, Qinghai and part of Sichuan. Dominated by Lamaism, the Tibetan Autonomous Region was founded in 1965. The Turkic peoples live in the north-west – Xinjiang, Gansu and Qinghai; they are all Moslem and the majority are Uighur, although there are also some nomadic Kazakhs and Kirghiz. The Mongolians live along the border with the People's Republic of Mongolia. They are organized into leagues and banners (tribal groups), their life is nomadic and pastoral, and Lamaism is the religious influence. The Tungusic peoples, of whom the dominant group were the Manchus (who from 1644–1911 were rulers of China – the so-called Qing dynasty), live in north-east China and have become assimilated into the Chinese population. Koreans are found in the north-east.

In south-west China, along the borders in Yunnan and Guangxi, are several minority populations. Living in the uplands are Dais, Zhuang and the Puyi; the Miao and Yao live in southern Guizhou and Yunnan. The Zhuang is the largest group, numbering some 8 million; the smallest group comprises the Hezhe, of whom there are only 700.

Most of the minority nationalities live in autonomous regions or districts, where they have control of their own internal affairs, although Han Chinese also play an administrative role. China contains five autonomous regions (see page 5), twenty-nine autonomous prefectures and sixty-nine autonomous counties.

NATURAL RESOURCES

China's natural resources, from minerals to energy, are enough to support even her growing industrial requirements. Many resources remain unexploited: China's capacity for producing hydro-electric power is immense, and her inadequate transport system has slowed down the progress of mining and distribution. There are oilfields in Heilongjiang, Xinjiang, Qinghai, Shandong and Sichuan, and extensive unexplored off-shore reserves, making China the tenth largest oil producer in the world. There are also large supplies of natural gas.

Coal reserves are thought to be the third largest after the USSR and USA. Most of the mining is carried out in north-west China, and Shaanxi and Sichuan provinces have extensive coalfields. Coal-fired thermal plants provide most of China's generating capacity; the electricity is used largely by industry.

The country has large deposits of iron ore, with major iron and steel works at Anshan, supplied from nearby Penchi in Liaoning Province. Shijingshan outside Peking is supplied from Luoyang, which also supplies the Taiyuan and Baotou steelworks. The Wuhan steelworks are supplied from Daye in Hubei Province. There are other major iron and steel works at Maanshan, Chongqing, in the Gansu corridor. Iron ore is found on Hainan Island.

China also has deposits of copper, aluminium, tungsten (15.4 per cent of the world's supply), tin, molybdenum, manganese, lead, zinc, mercury, antimony, refractory clay, quartz, dolomite, phosphorus, sulphur, salt and gypsum.

History

INTRODUCTION

The span of recorded Chinese history covers 4000 years and this was preceded by a prehistoric era of 600,000 years; archaeologists are making new discoveries all the time. Given such a long timespan, as well as China's great size and variety, it is impossible to condense the history into a few paragraphs. However certain themes recur and help establish a pattern.

For centuries the origins of Chinese history were reputed to be in the mythical Xia and Shang dynasties whose people lived in the Yellow River Basin. Archaeologists have discovered a few fossilized forms of early man – Yuanmou man thought to be 1 million years old, Lantian man and Peking man both over 500,000 years old. Nearer to the dynastic period more and more details are being provided of prehistoric China and it has now been established that the Shang dynasty did exist.

The dynastic era lasted from the Shang to the Qing dynasty – c.2000 BC to 1911. During this time the Chinese empire expanded and contracted: sometimes parts of it were overrun by aliens and twice China was ruled entirely by a non-Chinese people. The rise and fall of dynasties followed a pattern. Early in the Han dynasty the principle of the 'mandate of heaven' was established, this being the right of an emperor to his throne and title. If there were peasant uprisings caused by poverty and heavy tax burdens, this evidence of misrule would lead to the emperor's downfall.

The end of a dynasty would often be followed by a period of division into several smaller states or kingdoms. In a country as vast as China there exists a perennial tension between the centre and the periphery, between strong centralized administration and devolved power. Consequently when a dynasty was in decline, the power of local leaders increased as they plotted to stake a claim to local power and independence. Every province and city in China has a very strong sense of local history, the course of which may have had little to do with the mainstream of events.

The secret societies usually played a decisive role in the downfall of a dynasty. They were semi-political underground organizations of 'bandits', who operated in the remote, mountainous forests of the provincial borderlands. Like the heroes of the Chinese classic *The Water Margin* they were often fugitives from the law, and they also often had religious affiliations – to branches of Buddhism or Daoism (Taoism) and in the nineteenth century to Christianity.

Another important influence in Chinese history was the role of the non-Han border peoples. Their incursions into Chinese territory caused the Chinese to retreat southwards and at various times in Chinese history they controlled the whole of northern China. The most notable groups were the Huns, Xiongnu, Jurchen, Jinzhen, Mongolians and Manchus. Being of nomadic origins they found it difficult to deal with the day-to-day running of a country at peace, and so the Chinese were called upon to act as administrators, peacekeeping armies or pioneer farmers of the new territories. Gradually the border groups absorbed the Chinese language and customs. This delicate relationship with the border territories was one of the principle reasons for the shifting of the capital: at the beginning of the Chinese empire it was in the Yellow River Valley, shifting between Zhengzhou, Luoyang and later further west to Xi'an. As the cultural and economic ascendancy of the Yangtse delta area developed it might have seemed natural to move in that direction, but apart from the Song dynasty when northern China was overrun and it was forced southwards to Hangzhou, it stayed in the north. Finally, in the early Ming, the capital was established at Peking – a good vantage point from which to monitor border activities. Access to and control of the south were assured by the construction of a good transport system – canals and roads – and a strong centralized administration.

Some people believe that China has always been isolationist, cutting herself off from the western world, but this only became true during the Qing dynasty when an already non-Chinese dynasty felt threatened by approaches from western nations. Cultural and economic links with the countries nearest to China – with Japan, Vietnam and Nepal, for example – have always been strong. During the great dynasties – the Han, Tang, Song and even Yuan – there were substantial cosmopolitan communities to be found in all the major cities.

Both China's material culture and her system of social relations evolved at a very early stage in the country's history. Mining, paper-making, transportation, farming methods, spinning and weaving, iron smelting, pottery and porcelain, medicine, irrigation and metallurgy all developed to a highly sophisticated degree in the Han dynasty. Wood-block printing was developed in the eighth century and gunpowder in the Song dynasty.

There were four main classes in traditional Chinese society: the nobles, the peasants, the craftsmen and the merchants. The administrators and officials were drawn from the noble classes; the peasants formed the mainstay of the Chinese economy; the craftsmen represented the earliest origins of the industrial classes – their skills were hereditary and they were often employed in state enterprises. The merchants were regarded with suspicion and disdain, often being forced to live outside the city walls and even obliged to wear special forms of dress.

Consciousness of her past has always been an important element in Chinese culture. The central tenet of Confucianism looked to the exemplary rule of the early Zhou dynasty, and Confucius established the tradition of dynastic histories. Today, while it seems that many young people have lost this strong sense of history, it lives on among people of an older generation.

PREHISTORY AND THE BEGINNINGS OF CHINESE CULTURE

Until the present century the origins of Chinese culture were rooted in mythology and peopled with kings and heroes who bestowed on the indigenous population the skills of farming, fishing, irrigation, silkworm breeding and silk weaving. Legend has it that at the very beginning the god Pan gu created the universe and the goddess Nuwa created mankind. Then some four to five thousand years ago the age of the five mythical emperors began. Shen Nong was the patron and teacher of the agricultural skills on which the Chinese economy has always been based. Huang Di – the Yellow Emperor – united the tribal groups living in the Yellow River valley. His legacies to Chinese culture were the cart, the boat, the first calendar and medical knowledge, while his wife imparted the skills of sericulture and weaving. Other legendary figures developed early pictographs, the twelve-tone musical scale, measuring instruments and the forerunner of the compass – the south-pointing cart. During this time accession to the throne was not hereditary and the most notable emperors after the Yellow Emperor were Yao, who developed clothing, musical instruments and domestic animals, Shun, who initiated the system of exchange with his surplus grain, and finally Yu, who was accredited with taming the great flood which covered the land. He broke with the tradition of election to the throne by handing the succession to his son Hou Ji – founder of the Zhou. Although all these figures are legendary, even today they may often be alluded to, particularly during visits to sites of historic interest. All the events, personalities and social developments of this period have been given a new perspective in the twentieth century by the archaeological discoveries that have taken place all over China, which have often verified the writings of the early historians. Indeed archaeology is probably one of the most exciting areas of research and study in modern China, and is dominated by personalities and scholars who are respected all over the world. Archaeologists are beginning to piece together the story of the origins of the Chinese people and their culture, with the striking possibility that a culture which could be called 'Chinese' existed not only in the Yellow River Basin area, but all over the region known today as China.

The first exciting archaeological find, in the 1920s, was Peking Man, who was discovered at Zhoukoudian outside Peking (see page 120 for further details). Peking Man was estimated to have lived in the area some 500,000 years ago, and used flaked stone tools. Lantian Man, whose remains were first discovered in Shaanxi Province in 1963, is 100,000 years older than Peking Man. In Yuanmou in Yunnan Province two teeth were discovered in 1965; they were established as the teeth of *Homo erectus*, an early form of man, and in 1976 the Research Institute of Geomechanics of the Academy of Geological Sciences announced that palaeomagnetic dating methods indicated that the fossils were 1.7 million years old.

Extensive work has also been carried out in China on the Neolithic period or late Stone Age, which is characterized by the development of farming for food, pottery and polished stone implements. The many sites discovered all over China have been classified into three main types and eras, named after the place where each was first identified: Yangshao in the Yellow River valley in central China; Dapenkeng in south-east China (including Taiwan); and Qinliangang, comprising the eastern seaboard of the Huai and lower Yangtse River valleys.

The Yangshao and Dapenkeng cultures began in China around the fifth millennium BC, with the Qinliangang culture appearing slightly later. The

Yangshao culture is probably the best known, and the best-excavated site is at Banpo near Xi'an. Yangshao itself is a village in north-west Henan where peasant farmers first discovered some tools in 1920. Archaeologists have decided that the culture at Yangshao does not strictly speaking belong to that era, but have continued to use the name. Sites of the Yangshao period have been found in western Shandong to the east, and as far west as Qinghai and Gansu. At this time millet was cultivated, stone farming implements were used, and the pottery was characterized by a red base, often with black designs. Dogs and pigs were the earliest domesticated animals. This is the period of social development which Marxist historians would call primitive communes – people lived in temporary small village settlements, moving as often as necessitated by their farming system of 'slash and burn'. Dwellings were circular or rectangular, and sometimes semi-subterranean. The Banpo site contains graves for both single and group burials – the latter were probably for people from the same family or clan. The pottery was often coiled rather than made on a wheel, and decorative impressions found on excavated shards suggest that the people of that era had developed the techniques of basket-weaving.

The geographically extensive Longshan culture, distributed along the major rivers of China – the Yellow River, the Yangtse, the Han and the Huai, represented the next great advance in the development of Chinese society. Named after the site discovered in Shandong Province in 1928, this era, which began about 3200 BC, was the forerunner of the earliest dynasties. The pottery had now reached a new stage of refinement – it was thin, hard, shiny and black; more sophisticated stone tools were used, as well as tools made from shells. Gradually through this era more permanent settlements, with stamped earth (hangtu) walls, grew up. There is evidence of oracle bones being used for rituals, and an incipient ancestor cult. Cattle and sheep were domesticated, and in Longshanoid sites in south China evidence of rice cultivation has been found.

An archaeological discovery at Anyang in 1899 established that the Shang dynasty was not mythical, that it covered the period between about 1750 and 1100 BC, and that it reached a high level of civilization. The court had its own scribes and there was a written culture; the writing was done on bamboo strips, which have not survived, but evidence of writing and records has been taken from oracle bones and bronze vessels which often bore the insignia of the maker or owner. (Oracle bones were used by court shamans for purposes of divination: the shoulder blades of sheep or tortoise shell were heated until cracks appeared. The patterns made by these cracks were interpreted and the interpretations were then scratched on to the bones so that records were kept.) The Shang state covered modern Henan, southern Hebei, western Shandong and northern Anhui, although sites with similar traits and levels of civilization are found all over China.

The Shang dynasty was established by King Tang, who overthrew the Xia dynasty (unfortunately archaeologists and historians are still unable to establish the veracity of the Xia) and set up his capital at Po in 1766 BC. Po is thought to have been at or near the sites excavated near Yenshi in western Henan. In true Chinese fashion the capital was moved seven times, at one stage to Ao (present-day Zhengzhou), and by the end of the Shang dynasty it was established at Yin (present-day Anyang). Anyang remained the capital for twelve Shang kings. Excavations show the settlements at the time to be large and walled. There was a royal quarter and a quarter for craft workers, and outside the city confines people were served by the surrounding farming settlements. The king was seen as having access to the heavens, and shamans made predictions based on the burning of the shoulder bones of sheep or tortoise shells. The pottery was richly decorated with animal designs, and bronze vessels used for ceremonial purposes were also made. Tombs are an important source of information: in some cases a man's slaves were obviously buried alive with him, while other tombs contain remains of horse-drawn chariots. At the time there were three 'classes' – aristocracy, farmers and craftsmen. At this time lineage was gradually becoming established through the eldest son of the first wife.

As the Shang expanded their political and cultural influence they were increasingly involved in warlike campaigns. To the west in the Wei River valley, near present-day Xi'an, the kingdom of Zhou was gaining in power and strength. The origins and cultural development of the Zhou seem to have been separate from those of the Shang; they have different mythological bases, and their legendary ancestor was Hou Ji, although it was Wu Wang who finally conquered the Shang around 1027 BC.

The Shang at first continued to be ruled by their own prince, but the situation was rife with divided loyalties not just among the Shang but among the family of Wu Wang, as all the brothers sought supreme power. When there was a rebellion in the Shang areas the Duke of Zhou, who was acting as regent, was forced to subjugate the Shang once and for all. The next expedient was to move the capital eastward to the area of Luoyang – this occurred in 771 BC under the reign of Ping Wang, and marked the founding of the Eastern Zhou or Spring and Autumn period. A characteristic of the Zhou regime was the creation of ducalities – each duke owed allegiance to the king, but had sufficient power and independence to run his own army. Ample proof of their power is provided by the lavish tombs which were prepared not only for the royal family but also for the dukes.

The Warring States period, as this time is known, dated from around 450 BC. While the states were engaged in internecine warfare, philosophers scurried from one state to another to advise the dukes, and to try to bring about peace by recalling the upright character and rule of the Duke of Zhou. The state of permanent warfare and the need for defence was reflected in the way cities were strengthened and fortified at this time. Communications were improved and cities became more sophisticated and self-sufficient, with specialized quarters which were interdependent. Iron was used more and more for weapons and ploughs, while bronze was kept for use by the ruling class.

Meanwhile the highly militaristic state of Qin encroached on the Zhou ducalities from the west. First the state of Ba-Shu was over-run in 329 BC, then in 256 BC the royal Zhou was taken, and by 221 BC the states of Chu, Yan, Zhao, Wei, Han and Qi had been united under the Qin. The Qin dynasty, although short-lived because of its brutality, marked a turning-point in Chinese history as this was the first time that China had been united, and the word 'China' is derived from 'Qin'.

After the death of Qin Shi Huangdi (whose name means First Emperor of China) in 210 BC, his line was continued for only another four years, until after much intrigue and fighting Liu Bang, a man of peasant origins, became the first emperor of the Han dynasty. The Han dynasty was to last for four hundred years, during which time many aspects of Chinese culture were established and the empire flourished and expanded. There was a renewed reliance on the gentry, the land-owning classes who became the arm of governmental administration.

The death of the first Han emperor, whose reign title was Gao Zu, was followed by a period of rule by his wife the empress dowager Lü – the first of the three infamous women rulers in Chinese history. Under the second emperor, Wen Di, the Chinese empire was at peace. The 'civil service' expanded and the arts and scholarship developed. Confucian morals were discussed and revived and the scholar Dong Zhongshu (179–104 BC) propounded that Confucius's teachings embodied a set of legal ethics by which the ruling classes should be judged. Confucianism became the official doctrine, as did the principles of the mandate of heaven and the three relationships – between ruler and subject, father and son, and husband and wife.

During the latter half of the second century BC, under Emperor Wu of the Han, campaigns were launched against the border tribes – the Xiongnu in the north and the Yuezhi to the west – in an attempt both to contain the tribes and to keep the profitable trade routes to the west open. The generals Huo Qubing and Zhang Qian are both heroic figures in this saga. Reconciliation was also attempted through the marriage of royal Han princesses to the sons of the ruling families of the Xiongnu.

At the turn of the millennia a hiatus occurred in the Han rule. The dynasty had gradually weakened: the treasury had been drained by the campaigns against the border tribes and tributes to the 'barbaric' alliances, and Wang Mang from one of the powerful land-owning families who had now grown up took the throne and confirmed his rule with the ritual of the assumption of the imperial seal. His original intentions were to reform many aspects of the state, but he was unable to maintain control and a series of uprisings led by the 'Red Eyebrows' brought about his death and the restoration of the old line of the Han dynasty. The new capital of the eastern Han was established at Luoyang. The lands to the west were kept open for trade and within China there followed a period of relative prosperity. The power of individual families and generals grew until three parties gained dominance – Cao Cao in the north, Liu Bei in Sichuan and Sun Quan in the south east. The ordinary populace was neglected, leading to the famous 'Yellow Turban Uprising' with its exotic religious overtones in 184. Cao Cao took over northern China and established the Wei dynasty in 220.

The Han dynasty saw many developments in the arts and culture: recent tomb excavations have revealed a high level of technology in the production of silk, lacquer ware and sculpture, and in smelting; encyclopedias were written, and the famous *Shi ji* – the book of history – was compiled by Sima Qian in 125 BC. AD 65 marks the official introduction of Buddhism into China, a religion which was to find a welcome among the ordinary people.

The last Han emperor was forced to abdicate in favour of Cao Pei, son of Cao Cao, and China was then divided among the 'Three Kingdoms': Wei, Shu-Han and Wu. This era has been romanticized as an age of chivalry and heroic adventure in the Ming dynasty novel, *Tales of the Three Kingdoms*. To the west, in the area equivalent to modern Sichuan, the kingdom of Shu-Han had a small population and excellent natural defences. The outstanding emperor of the kingdom was Liu Bei, whose Prime Minister, Zhu Geliang, was a brilliant tactician. Through Zhu Geliang's ruses and battle strategy Shu-Han was able to defeat Cao Cao of Wei in the battle of Red Cliff in 208. However, by 263 Shu-Han had been annexed by Wei.

Sun Quan of Wu had his capital at Nanking. Of the three kingdoms Wu was the least aggressive: its aims were to fortify the land they possessed already and occasionally to engage in diplomatic manoeuvres with either Wei or Shu-Han. By 280 they too had been annexed by Wei.

The powerful state of Wei had come to prominence with its capital at Xi'an and Luoyang with the aid of the Xiongnu. The Xiongnu demanded payment for this assistance, which added to the area's financial burdens: Wei also had to maintain a lavish court, the garrisons along the silk route and the campaigns against the south. The rich and powerful families of Wei intrigued among themselves and eventually Sima Yan usurped the throne of Wei, established the Jin dynasty and completed the annexation of Wu. In the interests of restoring peace and a sound economy, in 280 he ordered a general amnesty and demobilization. Instead of returning to the king, many weapons found their way into the hands of rich families or the non-Han peoples to the north.

Hereafter followed one of the most complex periods of Chinese history. Between 304 and 580 — the founding of the Sui dynasty — there were twenty dynasties in northern China, which frequently overlapped. They were mostly non-Chinese, being established by Xiongnu, Tibetans, Xianbi and Toba. The south was more stable but less significant. The Jin dynasty was forced southwards to establish the Eastern Jin 317–419, with its capital at Nanking, followed by four 'southern' dynasties — the Song, Qing, Liang and Chen. During this period of stability the south grew wealthier, the immigrants from the north learnt to grow rice and cash crops, and links were still maintained with the north. There were selective campaigns against the north and some of the wealthier families formed into cliques.

In the north the dominant and most enduring state was that of the Toba who ruled from 385–543 and whose base was around present-day Datong, although with the expansion of their domain it was eventually moved to Luoyang in 494. The Toba were a nomadic people, warfaring and dependent on cattle-rearing for their livelihood; they were unused to the administration of a large state and the cultivation of the land. The Chinese were called upon to an increasing extent to handle the day-to-day administration of the empire and finally gained access to the reins of power.

The Toba adopted Buddhism as their official religion and the Toba emperor was declared the reincarnation of Buddha. One of the great legacies of this period are the Buddhist grottoes at Datong, Luoyang and Dunhuang. However, this adherence to Buddhism conflicted with the Confucian ethics of the Chinese administrators and by this time the Chinese were strong enough to split off and form their own empire to the east — the Northern Qi. A new threat from the Turkic tribes of the west then reunited the Toba and the Chinese, but the Toba ascendancy was by this time on the wane. One of the most powerful Chinese families was the Yang and in 581 Yang Jian declared himself ruler and established the Sui dynasty, at the same time bringing the south under his control.

China was reunited and the tangible legacies of the short-lived Sui dynasty reflect the preoccupation with unity and stability. The Great Wall was strengthened in the north and under the second Sui emperor, Yang Di, work was started on the Grand Canal with the intention of facilitating communications and transport between north and south. In the north east there were campaigns against Korea, but a more serious threat came from the Turks to the west who in 615 came close to capturing the emperor. He was saved by the quick thinking of a young general, Li Shimin, who frightened the Turks away with rumours of relief forces. Li Shimin was of mixed origin, almost certainly connected to one of the old Toba families, and he later joined forces with the Turks to try and defeat the Sui. A series of uprisings enabled his forces to take Chang'an; in 618 the Sui emperor was assassinated and Li Shimin established his father on the throne as the first emperor of the Tang.

The Tang dynasty (618–907) is regarded as a golden age in Chinese history. Poetry and literature reached new heights of perfection, porcelain was produced, and the renewed interest in Buddhism contributed to the development of wood-block printing, enabling the publication of many translations of Buddhist works. Buddhism also exerted an influence on Chinese art. This was a period of overseas trade by land and sea and many foreign merchants came to China.

For all its glory, the Tang dynasty was by no means completely stable. The Turkish threat was ever present and there were internal power struggles. At the beginning of the Tang there was a major redistribution of land in favour of the peasant, the local reserve militias were disbanded and large permanent armies were set up instead to patrol the border provinces. Li Shimin assumed the throne in 627 as the emperor Tai Zong. The country prospered and the total population was around 50 million. In 639 when the Turks attacked the garrison city of Gaochang in present-day Xinjiang, the Chinese routed them with the assistance of the Uighurs, and the area was brought under Chinese dominion. Korea was annexed and this was a time of close economic and cultural ties between Japan and China.

At the turn of the seventh century a woman came to power for the second time in Chinese history. The empress dowager Wu Zetian had been the concubine and later the wife of the third Tang emperor, Gao Zong. After his death she acted as regent and in 690 she founded her own dynasty – the Zhou – and had the capital moved to Luoyang. She was a devout Buddhist and sought to invest the throne with spiritual significance, at the same time giving no small amount of financial assistance to the monasteries. Internal political struggles continued during her reign, and it was only the encroaching of the Turks from the west which finally convinced her to cede the throne and allow Xuan Zong to assume power (713–755).

Xuan Zong's reign began magnificently. He was a patron of the arts and the country prospered under his rule; however, his downfall is traditionally blamed on his infatuation for the concubine Yang Guifei and his consequent neglect of affairs of state. This allowed An Lushan, a non-Chinese military governor to march from the borders to Chang'an. The emperor abdicated and his son, Su Zong, fled. Reinforcements and aid came to the royal family from central Asia and the Uighurs and in 757 An Lushan was forced to retreat. He was assassinated by one of his eunuchs. His successor continued to dominate the east, and once more the Uighurs assisted in quelling the rebellious forces. Naturally the Tang had to pay heavily for this aid from the Uighurs, particularly as they were constantly embroiled in campaigns against the Khitans and Tibetans. The central government was weak and the court degenerated into cliques and power struggles played off against each other by wily eunuchs. In the middle of the ninth century there was a clamp down on the wealth and existence of Buddhist monasteries and their large estates.

In 874 there was a succession of peasant uprisings in Hebei under Huang Chao, a former salt merchant, and Wang Xianzhi. By 881 the emperor was overthrown and Huang Chao established the Qi dynasty at Chang'an. He was killed in 884 and the emperor restored the Tang dynasty. His generals and governors with their large armies were continually involved in power struggles, each setting up his own dynasty – leading to a short period when there were five dynasties in the north and the ten kingdoms in the south (906–960).

The first emperor of the Song – Tai Zu – had been a successful general whose men elected him emperor in 960 with his capital at Kaifeng. From the north he was harassed by the Khitans who had set up their Liao dynasty with the capital at Shenyang and eventually Peking. Tai Zu's major concern was to the south where he intended to absorb the wealthy states whose power now extended into Vietnam – by 980 he had succeeded. To the north the Khitans were contained for the time being by the payment of tribute. There was an administrative reorganization with the military affairs being brought under centralized governmental supervision and for the first time soldiers were voluntary and salaried. This created an enormous new expense for the government, which led to inflation and the first use of paper money. Heavy taxes were imposed and many people saw fit to invest in land. Civil service exams were developed.

In the north west on the borders of Shaanxi the Western Xia Dynasty, which was of Turko–Tibetan origin, was established at the turn of the tenth century. Under emperor Shen Zong (1068–86), the legalist Prime Minister Wang Anshi, who could be described as an interventionist in favour of state control, was called upon to revitalize the economy and increase revenue. His reforms brought relief to the small man – there were credits and higher salaries, but a fall in prices. In 1085 his place was taken by Sima Guang who repealed his reforms.

During the Song dynasty there was a revival of Confucianism led by Zhu Xi (1130–1200). His influence was conservative: he repressed women in society and insisted on the natural order and hierarchy.

The Song was a great age of poetry – Su Dongpo (1036–1101) was famous for his poems in the vernacular. This dynasty is also noted for its landscape painting and the development of celadonware. Less romantically it is seen as a commercial age when the seeds of capitalism were sown.

Meanwhile there were new threats from the north. The Jurchen overran the Liao and by 1126 had captured Kaifeng and the emperor, bearing him off into humiliating captivity. The Song dynasty was forced southwards, where it established its capital at Hangzhou under the former emperor's brother. The Southern Song dynasty (1127–1278) was a period of calm, partly due to the fact that the Song paid tribute to the Jin whose capital was at Peking. The growing power of the Mongols was welcomed by the Song as support in fending off the Jin (Jurchen). In 1227 Chinggis Khan conquered the Western Xia and in 1234 the Jin. By 1260 Khubilai Khan had his capital at Peking and he captured Hangzhou in 1276. For the first time China was united under alien rule.

The Mongolian empire extended far to the west and contacts with other civilizations had helped them to develop an advanced armoury with which the Chinese could not compete. Their role in China as a minority, alien race was a delicate one and laws were introduced to make sure everyone kept their place. The Mongols were to be the most privileged group in society, followed by the Central Asians, northern Chinese and finally the southern Chinese who had few rights. All Chinese officials were disenfranchised and many turned their hand to playwriting, in order to be able to make veiled criticisms of the ruling classes. This made the Yuan dynasty the age of the Chinese theatre.

During the Yuan dynasty the military had little to do as the country was stable; they became flaccid and out of practice in the art of warfare. The capital was at

Dadu – Peking – a convenient site from which to control the north and the rest of the Mongolian empire as well as China. It was a time characterized by lavish building projects, imposing heavy burdens on the peasantry in the form of corvée and taxes, and leading to the gradual decrease of Chinese resources. There were constant uprisings, not so much against Mongol rule but in protest against poverty and taxes.

The decisive uprising was led by Guo Zixing in 1352 and he was joined by Zhu Yuanzhang in 1353. As a monk he had had connections with the secret society known as the 'White Lotus' sect and his own band was known as the 'Red Turbans'. By 1356 he had established a base at Nanking, going on to take Peking in 1368, forcing the last emperor of the Yuan dynasty to flee to Xanadu. Zhu Yuanzhang established the Ming dynasty, with his capital at Nanking. Thus began an era of Chinese rule, and although Zhu Yuanzhang had come from a very ordinary background his style was that of the absolute ruler. When he died in 1398 his place was taken by the son of the former heir apparent. However the emperor Cheng Zu, the son of Zhu Yuanzhang who had been given command of the Peking area, was resentful at having been bypassed in the succession and marched on Peking, razing the city and its fine palaces. He returned to Peking and, calling himself the emperor Yong le,* he set about building the grand Peking – parts of which may still be seen today. Initially the Ming dynasty was very wealthy and under Yong le the Great Wall was carefully rebuilt.

External relations were peaceful although the southern coastal waters and the mouth of the Yangtse were troubled by Japanese pirates, and Chinese control of Xinjiang was occasionally troubled by the Mongolians. It was an era of exploration with the Chinese Muslim Zheng He leading expeditions to Indo-China, Arabia and Africa, and an era of agricultural development: new strains of rice gave double cropping, and there were new methods of fish farming, irrigation, and crop rotation, with cotton being grown as a major cash crop. The merchants of the middle Yangtse river enjoyed a reputation as astute businessmen. Due to improved farming methods the population increased and a larger administration was required. The usual source of administrators was the gentry, but the pool was widened by means of the examination system, which was now opened to a broader section of the community. During the Ming the craftsman's skills flourished: there were state-run kilns, and cloisonné was prized. It was also the age of the novel. In court the eunuchs were powerful and led cliques – one of the most ferocious was Wang Zhen who had his own secret police force and fought for control over young rulers.

During the late fifteenth century and early sixteenth century there were uprisings. In the north-east the Manchus were establishing their power, but the main blow came from the uprising led by Li Zicheng in protest against famine and poverty which began in Shanxi and reached Peking by 1544. For a short while Li Zicheng became emperor, but he gradually lost support and General Wu Sangui, who had been sent to campaign against the Manchus, gave the Manchus access to establish the second and last period of a non-Chinese people ruling China.

The Manchus absorbed many aspects of Chinese culture, in return imposing some of their own customs on the Chinese – such as the wearing of pigtails. Initially the Qing dynasty was an era of stability and prosperity. The population expanded

*Apart from his personal name each emperor took a reign title after consulting the court soothsayers.

rapidly, but this expansion was not matched by increased agricultural production giving rise to famine and consequent unrest. The last seventy years of the dynasty saw a gradual decline into 'semi-colonialism' and wars with the western powers. The two most notable emperors were Kangxi (1662–1723) and Qian long (1736–96), both of them patrons of Chinese art and culture. Early in the dynasty there were campaigns with the Mongols, in Xinjiang and Tibet. Disputes with Russia over the Amur river led to the Treaty of Nerchinsk in 1689; this was revised in 1727 and allowed the first foreign church and legation to be established in Peking. Towards the end of the eighteenth century there were uprisings led by adherents of the 'White Lotus' sect. Lord Macartney's first mission to the court of Qian long in 1793 met with a sharp rebuttal and British and foreign merchants were subsequently only allowed to trade in restricted zones in Guangzhou and Macao. It is at this point that the direction of Chinese history began to change rapidly – not only was the dynasty weak, and famines and uprisings on the increase, but there were new ideas coming from the west and being adopted by Chinese who felt that the source of China's weakness was her backwardness.

THE OPIUM WARS TO THE REPUBLIC

The Manchus, who came to power in 1644, were cautious about foreigners. They were, after all, a foreign power themselves in China. Although during the previous great dynasties foreign traders had had access to China, under the Manchus at first only the Russians were allowed to establish a commercial post, church and legation in Peking in 1727, as a result of the Treaty of Nerchinsk which had established the Sino–Russian border. However during the eighteenth century China was wealthy and stable and her foreign trade was allowed to grow. Foreigners were permitted to buy silk and tea at Canton and Macao through special trading organizations known as *hongs*. Goods were paid for in silver, as the self-sufficient Chinese required nothing from overseas traders; previously the British had brought cotton to China from India, but it was no longer needed. The British, at the height of their empire-building, sent in 1793 a mission under Lord Macartney to apply for permission to trade directly with Peking or at other ports. This importunate request was rejected by the emperor Qian long.

The British wanted another commodity which would not place a strain on their cash resources, and found it in opium; it was easy to transport and could be paid for in silver, all of which was detrimental to the Chinese treasury, giving rise to inflation and tax increases. In 1800 an official decree banned the import and sale of opium, but to little effect. It was not until 1839 that Lin Zexu, the governor of Hubei and Hunan who had taken effective measures in his own areas to stop the use of opium, was sent to Guangzhou. He ordered a blockade of the small residential quarter set aside for the foreign merchants, and forced the British to hand over to the Chinese their opium stocks, which were burnt before their very eyes. The British, unused to being thwarted in their attempts to increase trade and develop diplomatic relations, prepared for war. In London Gladstone spoke out against the futility and injustice of war in the name of opium, but in 1840 British ships attacked the south-east coast of China. Despite his brave efforts Lin Zexu was dismissed, and the British encroached as far as Nanking.

In 1842 the Treaty of Nanking gave Britain Hong Kong, and other treaty ports were opened to the European powers; compensation was extorted; and the Chinese customs were to be controlled by the Europeans. Shanghai was opened to foreigners in 1843 and its population expanded rapidly; opium-smuggling continued and the foreign powers gained many advantages. In 1856 the British declared war again – the so-called Arrow War. Joined by the French, they attacked Guangzhou, Tianjin and Peking, forcing the Emperor to flee to Jehol. The Treaty of Tianjin afforded more concessions to the foreign powers, allowed access to missionaries and the sale of opium. China was now a semi-colony, prevented from becoming completely colonized only by the squabbles of the various powers who tried to gain footholds there. In the 1860s France acquired Cochin-China and Cambodia, and by 1884 had control of Tongking and Annam (modern Vietnam).

Japan too wanted a part of China, for the Japanese state was becoming rapidly modernized and saw great potential in Chinese land and raw materials. Initial relations were friendly, but in the 1870s Japan took over the Ryukyu Islands and Taiwan. War broke out in 1894, after which Korea and Taiwan were ceded to Japan, and the Japanese took over Manchuria from the Russians.

As for internal problems, unrest had been growing since the end of the eighteenth century and had resulted in a series of uprisings. The population had expanded rapidly but agricultural production had not kept pace; famine and flood, hatred of corrupt government, and strong anti-Manchu and later anti-foreign feeling all fuelled the people's discontent.

In the middle of the nineteenth century the Taiping rebellion broke out. It began in the south, in Guangxi Province, which had been subject to devastating famines. Hong Xiuquan, a failed scholar and mystic, proclaimed himself a brother of Christ and promised his followers 'Heaven on earth' when he established the 'heavenly kingdom of great peace'. A combination of Christian and primitive communist reforms – love and equality – led the people's army to take Hankou in 1852 and in 1853 Nanking, where they proclaimed their capital. During their ten-year stay in Nanking they enacted many of their reforms: women were treated as equals and participated in government and army affairs, the men cut off their pigtails as a sign of defiance against the Manchus, foreigners were regarded as equals, property was communal, and opium, tobacco and alcohol were outlawed.

The foreign powers were undecided about whom to support – the Taiping did purport to be Christian – but they had recently concluded favourable business deals with the Manchus. Several generals were called upon to quell the Taipings, the most notable being Zeng Guofan (1811–92) and Li Hongzhang (1823–1901). The former took Nanking in 1863 after a fifteen-day battle; Hong Xiuquan and many of his followers committed suicide.

In 1855 the Yellow River had changed course, which had damaging effects on Henan and Anhui Provinces; famine led to a further series of uprisings. Between 1855 and 1868 a number of Mohammedan uprisings took place in the border areas of Xinjiang and Yunnan. Some sought local independence, others were anti-foreign, while yet others were against poverty and corruption; all were speedily quelled.

It was through the south that the Chinese first came into contact with foreigners. Though many suffered, others benefited, particularly the commercial classes, who by the late nineteenth century had begun sending their children to Japan or Europe to be educated. Those children came back with new ideas and visions, and the south modernized itself more quickly. Up in the northern capital life continued in its traditional way.

From 1862 when the Manchu throne was restored until the beginning of the twentieth century the throne was run by the Empress Dowager Ci xi (1835–1908). All those who advocated reforms or war to defend China against her aggressors had to contend with Ci xi's stubbornness and scheming. The first attempt at reform came in the form of the 1862 Restoration and Self-strengthening Policy, aimed at modernizing defence.

Progressive forces were also represented by Kang Youwei, and Liang Qichao. The latter advocated a modern army, a telegraph system, the need to study western technology, and an expansion of coal- and iron-mining; he was also responsible for the first cotton mill in Shanghai. Influenced by such men, when the emperor Guang xu came of age in 1898 he introduced the Hundred Days' Reform, which was rapidly quashed by Empress Ci xi and led to his imprisonment in the Summer Palace.

Rebellion threatened China once more as the Boxer movement arose in the south against the gentry and the Manchus. The Boxers often accredited themselves with special powers, and their original anti-Manchu feeling was turned on the foreign population in China, culminating in the siege of Peking of 1899, with the quiet connivance of the imperial court. However when an eight-nation army contingent advanced on Peking to liberate the besieged, the Empress Dowager and Guang xu fled to Shaanxi, not returning until 1902.

The peace treaty extracted more concessions from the Chinese, and the so-called Boxer Indemnity Fund was set up to be used for buildings and services in China, such as schools and hospitals. A few modest reforms were passed, but half-heartedly enacted. Kang Youwei went to Europe in despair. The warlord Yuan Shikai, in command of the first modern Chinese army, was gaining power and came to be regarded by foreign powers as a progressive force. In 1908 Ci xi died, having first arranged for the assassination of Guang xu. The new emperor, Pu yi, was two years old. A new era was dawning in China.

Sun Yatsen, the founder of modern China, was born in 1866 in Guangdong Province and was eventually sent to England to study. In 1894 he formed in Hunan a reforming and nationalist movement called Xingzhong hui, the Chinese Resurrection Society. By 1895 he was active in Guangzhou. However, because of his political activities he lived in Japan, travelling to the USA and Europe to gather support for his cause. In 1905 the Tongmeng hui (United League) was formed. They summarized their aim as the three people's principles: 'Nationalism, Democracy and People's Livelihood in an Independent Republic'.

In 1906 a constitutional government was proclaimed and in 1910 the first national assembly was held. The provinces were becoming more independent under the sway of governors. A growing class of urban proletariat building the railways, working in the cotton mills or in the army formed key elements in the uprisings of Sichuan and Wuchang in 1911. These uprisings spread, and in December 1911 when Sun Yatsen returned from exile, he established a provisional government at Nanking, and was elected President. In Peking the Qing cabinet resigned and appointed Yuan Shikai Prime Minister. So China was now ruled by two governments, of which Yuan Shikai's was more acceptable to the foreign community. After intense negotiations, Sun Yatsen was forced to step down and Yuan Shikai became President. In March 1912 Sun Yatsen formed the Nationalist

Party. While some people felt the revolution – known as the Xinhai (double tenth) – was over, there was still unrest and many changes remained to be made. The Xinhai Revolution took its name from the Chinese calendar, occurring on the tenth day of the tenth month.

REPUBLIC TO PEOPLE'S REPUBLIC

The years immediately following the Xinhai Revolution were characterized by confusion, little recorded fact, weak government, the power of provincial warlords and their battles, and a growing and new-found social and political awareness among different classes of Chinese people. Although there was a constitution of sorts and the power of the royal family had been curtailed, discussion was still continuing on the relative merits of a constitutional and a parliamentary republic. Many political parties were formed, of which two eventually came to the fore – the Nationalist Party, which had its origins in Sun Yatsen's United League, and the Progressive Party on the right. Both gave their support to Yuan Shikai, who schemed and plotted until he was supreme dictator, and in 1915 began preparations for his investiture as emperor. He died a natural death in 1916 and was replaced by his Vice-President, Li Yuanhong, who was so weak that the warlords were able to continue fighting unabated, and gradually increased their territorial influence. Sun Yatsen and other leftists went underground or into exile.

During these years China enjoyed a certain prosperity. Although old debts from the Boxer Rebellion were still being repaid, Chinese industry and her economy were able to develop independently since the Allies were concentrating on their war against the Germans. The bourgeoisie flourished, and new banking organizations grew up, as did a new urban proletariat and intelligentsia. Although the Republic could hardly be said to have succeeded, the seeds of democracy and a sense of national identity had been sown.

All these elements paved the way for the May Fourth Movement, joined by students who had returned from Japan, France, Britain and Germany burning with new ideas. In 1915 Chen Duxiu founded the magazine *New Youth*, which discussed science, politics and culture. It started the *baihua* movement when Hu Shi discussed in an article the importance of using the vernacular for writing, as opposed to the impenetrable classical forms. Li Dazhao, a librarian at Peking University, wrote about Bolshevism. There was an atmosphere of intellectual excitement, influenced by world events – not least the Bolshevik Revolution. However it was the news that Chinese claims at Versailles had been ignored, and that Germany's rights in Shandong had been passed to Japan instead of being returned to China, which sparked off the 4 May 1919 demonstrations in Peking. The demonstrations were echoed all round the country; student unions were organized, and young people – intellectuals, the bourgeoisie and workers – were all drawn into the movement. Japanese goods were boycotted and the Chinese representative in Versailles refused to sign the treaty. From now on there was to be no turning back to the feudal age of empire and Confucianism.

In the country as a whole the government was weak, there were devastating famines on the north China plain between 1920 and 1921, and opium continued to have its damaging effect. Among the many ideas discussed at the time there came a new demand for a federal China, and slogans called for the independence of each province; such a system would of course have been beneficial to the warlords. In 1920 Chen Qiongming, the warlord of Guangdong, called Sun Yatsen back to Guangzhou. In 1919 Sun Yatsen had reformed his party on the basis of the three people's principles (independence, democracy and wellbeing of the people) and started publishing a magazine called *Reconstruction*. In 1921 he was declared President of the Republic and the 1912 constitution was resuscitated. At the same time the first Communist cells were holding meetings. New Soviet Russia had disowned her concessions in China, and in 1921 the first Soviet delegation came to China and met the Nationalists and Communists. In 1921 the first meeting of the Chinese Communist Party was convened in Shanghai and Chen Duxiu was elected Secretary General *in absentia*.

Following the Moscow mould the Communist Party began to make contact with China's small industrial proletariat, of whom there were approximately 1½ million concentrated in the coastal cities, and a trade union secretariat was formed. The new organization of the industrial workers gave rise to a spate of strikes between 1921 and 1922, and at Zhengzhou in 1923 the warlord Wu Peifu brutally crushed the railway workers who had struck in protest at not being allowed to form their own union. It was some years before Mao was to publish his articles on the role of the peasant in the revolutionary process, and before the Chinese peasantry were to be seen as the key to the Revolution. For the time being flood, famine and expropriation of land were driving the peasantry off the land to the cities, to the north-east of China, or overseas.

The warlords continued their power games in the north; the main protagonists were Wu Peifu in Henan and Hubei, Cao Kun in Zhili and Hebei, Zhang Zuolin in north-east China, Feng Yuxiang in the Peking area, and Yan Xishan in Shanxi. They fought with each other, were represented by factions in Peking, and subjected their local population to enormous tax burdens to support their armies. After much manoeuvring Cao Kun was elected President in Peking in 1923.

Sun Yatsen had to give up hopes of starting an expedition to the north to quell the warlords when his uneasy relationship with Chen Qiongming disintegrated. Sun was gaining support among the bourgeoisie, who saw him as the only possible saviour of China, and by 1924 Sun re-emerged in Guangzhou as head of a Nationalist government. The first alliance between the Communists and the Nationalists was engineered by Maring and Joffe, two Soviet agents who helped found the CCP. Their common programme was the unification of China achieved by overthrowing the warlords and acquiring independence from the foreign powers. The doctrine of the Nationalists was based on Sun's three people's principles, and their aims would be realized through alliance with the Communists, the workers and the peasants. Out of this alliance the Whampoa Military Academy was formed – Chiang Kaishek was the commanding officer and Zhou Enlai was political commissar; the Nationalist government also established the peasant cadre training institute. At the end of 1924, at Feng Yuxiang's invitation (he was now in control in Peking), Sun Yatsen went to Peking for discussions about a conference which would include representatives of every political hue in China, but while there he became ill and died.

Sun Yatsen's personality had held the united front of the Nationalists and Communists together, but by 1926 this alliance was destroyed and the Right was in control under Chiang Kaishek. The year 1925 saw a strengthening of the workers' movements. On 30 May English police fired on protestors in Shanghai, as a result of which the whole International Concession was closed down by a general strike involving workers and chamber of commerce members. The strike spread, and was supported all over China. In Guangzhou English and French guards again fired on a supporting demonstration; this led to a year-long blockade of Hong Kong and Guangzhou.

In the middle of 1926 the Northern Expedition finally moved off from Guangzhou, meeting with support and assistance from workers and peasants. Chiang Kaishek, based in Nanchang, was busy consolidating his relationship with the northern warlords and the bourgeoisie. In March 1927 the unions took Shanghai; Chiang Kaishek's forces were to back up the victory, but on 12 April he used his troops to attack the union headquarters. There followed a purge of Communists from the Nationalist Party; workers' and peasants' organizations were outlawed; Li Dazhao was executed in the north by Zhang Zuolin; and by 18 April Chiang Kaishek had established his government at Nanking.

Twenty years of military dictatorship were to follow. Lip-service was paid to Sun's three people's principles, but the model for government was the Fascist regimes of Italy and Germany. During this period China was dominated by the 'four great families' – Chiang, Song, Chen and Kong. Banking and financial investment were developed at the expense of heavy industry. Chiang made his peace with the warlords, allowing them relative independence in the form of regional political councils. He courted the foreign powers, particularly the Americans and Japanese, and gained the support of the Chinese business community and the landowners. The unity of China was still unstable, and alternative governments were occasionally declared in Peking or Guangzhou. In September 1931 the Japanese took Mukden (Shenyang) and put Puyi, the last Qing emperor, on the throne of Manzhouguo in the mineral-rich north-east. The Nationalist government seemed unperturbed by this incursion on to Chinese soil, since they regarded the Communists as their main threat.

After the débâcle of Shanghai in 1927, the Communists were forced underground, to re-emerge in the Jiangxi soviets, their first 'red bases' and attempts at independent government. The road to revolution was reappraised and argued over. Following a period of fieldwork, Mao published his article 'Investigation into the Peasant Movement in Hunan', which gave priority to the role of the peasant movement in the Communist struggles.

At this stage the Revolution must have seemed to have little chance of success, and it required great vision and tenacity to see the hitherto uneducated, uninvolved, unpoliticized peasantry as the key to the Revolution – even though they were the largest social group in China. The Maoist prescription was a slow but thorough one: starting in the countryside, the Communists would establish strong local bases, with a view to a protracted struggle against their opponents. The Bolshevists had a more orthodox view, based on the Russian experience, which felt the proletariat were the key to the Revolution and sought to bring it about rapidly.

On 1 August 1927 the Communists, led by Zhou Enlai, attempted to take Nanchang under the banner of the fight against imperialism and the warlords, and for the rights of workers and peasants and agrarian reform. Although the attack began successfully they were forced to retreat by the Nationalist army; however this occasion is commemorated as the founding of the People's Liberation Army. Zhu De, Ye Ting and Peng Dehuai had now joined the Communists, bringing their armies, and in 1928 they were also joined by Chen Yi and Lin Biao. Further attempts were made to gain Changsha and Guangzhou, but in the end the Communists were forced to retreat into the hilly and remote border areas of Jiangxi and Hunan.

At Jinggang shan they set up their own army and first bases; Zhu De was commander-in-chief and Mao was the party representative. This army was governed by a code of conduct and respect for the local populace previously unknown in China, beginning a tradition which has been more or less maintained until the present day. The army was a political as well as a military organization, and it was this sense of political purpose which would enable the Red Army to achieve the Long March, the defeat of Japan and finally the respect of the whole country and the defeat of Chiang Kaishek's disillusioned and maltreated forces.

Red bases were established in the following years in many parts of Central China. Between June and September 1928 the Sixth Party Conference was held in Moscow, out of reach of the Nationalists. The central controversy of the congress raged between on the one hand Li Lisan, Zhou Enlai and Qu Qiubai, and on the other hand Zhang Guodao – the first three saw the moment for renewed uprising as imminent, while the last-named was pessimistic about the Revolution ever being achieved. A compromise choice of Secretary-General was arrived at in Xiang Zhongfa; Li Lisan and Zhou Enlai were given important positions in the Politburo, and the role of the industrial proletariat was reaffirmed. It was decided that Peng Dehuai was to take Changsha, Mao and Zhu De were to concentrate on Nanchang, and He Long was to take Wuhan, sparking off uprisings in other cities. Peng Dehuai was the first to move against Changsha, in July 1930; he was quickly driven back, and the others decided to flout orders and not attempt the attacks on Wuhan and Nanchang. Li Lisan was completely discredited.

In 1929 the Jinggang shan base had been moved south to the Ruijin area of Jiangxi. The Central Committee was headed by Moscow-reared Bolshevists such as Wang Ming and Bo Ku. Some agrarian reform was introduced, but the urban worker was still defined as the key to the Revolution. In November 1931 the first Congress of the Soviets was held; representatives came from the ten soviets which had been established from Hainan in the south to Shaanxi in the north-west. In each soviet the peasants had been organized, the landlords had been dispossessed of their lands, and there was a full political organization.

Although the Communists were few in number, Chiang Kaishek continued to see them as the biggest threat to his stability. In 1931 he launched an attack on the soviets, pushing those based in the Yangtse River area westwards. He was interrupted when the Japanese attacked Shenyang to start the Sino–Japanese War, but returned to blockade the Jiangxi soviet, forcing them eventually to break through the Nationalist lines in 1939, and begin what is known as the Long March, a massive manoeuvre taking a whole year and covering 6000 miles to the north-west in the search for a new base.

The rift between the Maoists and Bolshevists had been growing, and in January 1934 Mao was left out of the leadership altogether. When the army reached Zunyi in Guizhou they stopped to discuss strategy, routes and destination. Mao, Zhu De, Peng Dehuai and Lin Biao regained control, the Bolshevists went off to Shanghai and Zhou Enlai came over to the Maoists. Their destination was the north-west, where they would be in a better position to fight the Japanese; following a tortuous route, often breaking into small groups and having to deal with hostile minority groups in the border areas, they crossed the Yangtse, the Dadu River and the mountains of Tibet. They met the Fourth Army in Sichuan, split with Zhang Guodao who went over to the Nationalists, and finally reached Baoan in Shaanxi Province in 1936, where a new phase was to begin and the rallying call of the Communists was to become the united front against Japan.

Following their installation of Pu Yi as puppet king of Manzhouguo, by 1935 the Japanese had occupied Jehol, Chahar, Hebei and Inner Mongolia. The Nationalist government did nothing. The Chinese people were getting impatient and indignant, and on 9 December 1935 students led a massive demonstration against the Japanese. The All-China Federation of Associations for National Salvation was formed, and joined by intellectuals, clerks and business people; a similar movement was inaugurated in Xi'an.

That month Chiang Kaishek was in fact in Xi'an, but planning his next move against the Communist bases. Zhang Xueliang, son of the infamous Zhang Zuolin of Manchuria, headed a large army; he took up the cause of the united front against the Japanese and held talks with the Communists and Zhou Enlai. Chiang dismissed him, and arrested students who were demonstrating. Zhang turned the tables on the Generalissimo and, together with Yong Hucheng, arrested Chiang Kaishek at the Huaqing hot springs, threatening him with his life. There followed several days of intense and secret negotiations, but the united front was formed. The Communist Party were allowed to keep their own troops, and the Eighth Route and New Fourth Army were formed. The Communists in turn guaranteed that they would not try to overthrow the Nationalist government, stopped their agrarian reform programme, and dissolved their alternative government in the north-west. The united front was always delicate. The Communists set up commission offices close to the seat of government, and they ran their own newspapers. Chiang was still interested in their defeat, and the Americans were to become involved in mediating between the two parties.

In 1937 the affair known as the Marco Polo Bridge incident was used as an excuse for the Japanese to invade the whole of China, and by October the country was occupied as far south as Guangzhou. 'Free China' was forced westwards, first to Wuhan and then to Chongqing; industry and the universities were uprooted too. The Japanese invasion brought many tragedies, such as the breaching of the Yellow River, the burning of Changsha and the massacre at Nanking. In 1941 the opportunistic Wang Jingwei became Prime Minister of the puppet government established by the Japanese in Nanking. Between 1938 and 1941 aid came to Free China from the United States, Britain, France and the USSR, though it was not in fact until Pearl Harbor in 1941 that China officially declared war on Japan. General 'Vinegar Joe' Stilwell was sent to Chongqing from the United States as Chiang's chief of staff. Stilwell favoured the united front, and became frankly disillusioned with Chiang's obstinacy and mismanagement of the war effort; he was later replaced by Ambassador Patrick Hurley and Wedemeyer. Chiang's China was becoming more authoritarian, governed by political and military cliques, the Blue Shirts (an imitation of Hitler's Brown Shirts) and the secret service operated by Dai Li; some democratic groups were tolerated – to keep up the flow of US aid – but Chiang kept in constant touch with Nanking.

It was largely the efforts of the Communist armies which defeated the Japanese; they worked behind the enemy lines from bases in Shandong and north-east China, and in areas of difficult terrain such as the Wutai Mountains and the Taihang Mountains. The Communists relied on guerrilla tactics and mobility – close knowledge with the area, and the assistance of the local population against the cumbersome armies of the Japanese who were in unfamiliar territory. In 1940 the New Fourth Army undertook a successful campaign in the Yangtse areas, forcing the Japanese to retreat; as this was an independent action the Nationalists took their revenge by attacking the New Fourth Army. From 1941 to 1943 the Japanese conducted a 'kill all, burn all, destroy all' campaign. Between 1944 and 1945 the Chinese renewed their attack; by 1945 the Japanese were surrounded in all the major cities, and after Hiroshima they surrendered, on 14 August 1945.

From Baoan the Communists moved their base to Yan'an where life was established on socialist lines. In the rest of China rumours were rife about life in the 'liberated zones', and some foreign journalists, notably Edgar Snow, were able to go behind the lines and bring back enthusiastic reports about life at Yan'an. The base at Yan'an was the headquarters of the Northwest zone; it was run by the Central Committee of the Communist Party with its own People's Congress. It had its own university, known as the Japanese Resistance University. The leaders enjoyed a simple life, making their homes in caves formed in the loess earth; elections were held, newspapers were produced, wall posters provided material for discussion, and industrial co-operatives were organized. There were also other liberal and democratic political groups there of a left-wing or independent nature. Many controversies raged – Mao wrote his article on 'New Democracy' defining the role in the Revolution of the workers, poor and middle peasants, petit-bourgeoisie, intellectuals and capitalists. Liu Shaoqi wrote his document 'How to Be a Good Communist', and Mao held his famous forum on the role of art and literature in the Revolution. The leaders participated in physical labour, such as farming or construction work.

Their success against the Japanese gave the Communists a new standing in China and people sought peace and unity. Talks were held in Chongqing, with Ambassador Hurley as mediator, to establish a coalition of the Communists and Nationalists and avoid the dreadful consequences of a civil war in a country already war-weary. The coalition convened in Yan'an in March 1945. In the same month Chiang Kaishek called a national assembly, from which the Communists were excluded. Finally a formula was arrived at for a People's Consultative Conference. A ceasefire was called in June 1946 and the conference was convened, but once more the unity was short-lived.

The Russians, who had occupied Manchuria in 1945 under the Yalta agreement, were scheduled to withdraw in winter 1946. The Nationalists wanted their own troops to replace them; however under the terms of the ceasefire no troop movements were allowed. Nevertheless the Americans were prepared to provide planes for an airlift. But the Communists positioned themselves to the north of Shenyang and surrounded all the main cities of the north-east, so that when the Russians withdrew they were able to take all the cities. Civil war broke out once more. The national assembly gave Chiang Kaishek absolute power, but in January 1948 the revolutionary committee of the Nationalists pledged their support to the Communists. The Communist troops made their way southwards through China, beating back the Nationalists, who often surrendered to them: by 1948 membership of the Communist Party had reached 3 million. On 21 September 1949 the Consultative Conference met again, with representatives from the many different democratic parties in attendance. On 1 October the founding of the People's Republic was announced, and by December Chiang Kaishek and the Nationalists had retreated to Taiwan (then known as Formosa). The Communists now faced the daunting tasks of rebuilding the country's war-battered economy and services, of establishing workable forms of government, and of allaying the anxieties of the bourgeoisie.

THE PEOPLE'S REPUBLIC

The founding of the People's Republic in 1949 marked a new phase in Chinese history: the task of reconstruction was to be undertaken and the Chinese had to consider how to achieve this reconstruction and modernization within a socialist framework. At Yan'an the Communist Government had been responsible for a population of a few million; now, under the 'common Programme for Reconstruction' proposed by Mao Zedong, they had to unite the varying strands of opinion in China, set up a sound administrative system, and deal with industrialization as well as foreign and diplomatic relations. The Consultative Political Conference acted as a 'parliament'. Ordinary people became involved in the running of the new society through numerous campaigns of a practical nature. In commerce and industry nationalized and private industries co-existed and the formation of co-operatives was encouraged. In the countryside agrarian reform ensured the distribution of land to men and women alike; the marriage law gave women a more independent status; the currency was stabilized; and the army was put to large-scale construction tasks such as dike building and railway construction.

In 1950 the Korean War interrupted the government's formidable programme, the result of this engagement being the division of Korea. China suffered many casualties and her resulting alienation from the rest of the world brought her closer to the USSR.

The first five-year plan was initiated in 1953. Cities such as Xi'an, Lanzhou or Luoyang in China's interior were singled out for accelerated industrial development, and new hierarchical management structures were introduced. New products were evolved and the army was ordered to concentrate on its technical development. There was a movement away from the countryside to the cities as the government refused to pay the peasants good enough prices for their produce. In 1954 political campaigns were waged against the intellectual Hu Feng and provincial governors who were wielding too much individual power.

1956 saw the collectivization of the economy – independent small businesses and craft workshops were grouped into co-operatives and the state took over enterprises belonging to national capitalists. There was a move towards the re-establishment of co-operatives in the countryside. At around the same time, in 1956, Khrushchev denounced Stalin and there were uprisings in Poland and Hungary. This unrest, coupled with China's own internal problems of inflation, meant that the government needed renewed impetus and support from the intellectuals. The aim of the Hundred Flowers Campaign in 1956 was to give intellectuals freedom to express their opinions and ideas. At the Eighth Party Congress, one of the principle topics of discussion was the need to develop and modernize production. These were the views held by Liu Shaoqi, Deng Xiaoping and others, while Mao Zedong advocated that the emphasis should be on political work as only a politically conscious people could begin to modernize.

The Rectification Movement of 1957 sought to stamp out bureaucracy, sectarianism and subjectivism and quieten the controversies raised by the Hundred Flowers Campaign. Equal emphasis was laid on being 'red and expert', i.e., politically conscious as well as knowledgeable. The following year, the Great Leap Forward inspired by Mao Zedong aimed at politically mobilizing and motivating China's greatest natural resource – manpower – to undertake a rapid modernization programme. Under the slogan 'walking on two legs' agriculture was declared as important as industry and administrative organs were to be decentralized. The 'three banners' of the mass line, the people's communes and the Great Leap Forward called for universal involvement in the political process – the formation of communes and the move to bring industry to the countryside. Communes set up their own small industrial enterprises; in industry management structures were changed to involve cadres, workers and technicians. Study was to be divided between the classroom and the factory floor or the farm, and intellectuals and cadres were expected to do a stint of manual labour. However the Great Leap Forward foundered in the wake of bad harvests and floods between 1959 and 1962 and faced considerable general opposition. This was also the era of the split with the USSR and the withdrawal of Soviet Russian experts and technicians. In 1962 Mao made speeches criticizing Khrushchev and the Soviet policy of revisionism, and in the same vein alluded to the problems of the internal situation in China.

There followed an extremely difficult period between 1962 and 1966. Differences of opinion among the leadership were so acute that the Central Committee of the Chinese Communist Party did not meet at all during this period. While the more pragmatic members of the leadership advocated modernizing the forces of production, others recognized the need to change people's way of thinking before modernization could be achieved. Following a directive which gave agriculture priority over industry, the Socialist Education Movement, begun in 1963, initiated a drive to send work teams of political activists to the countryside where, as well as working with the peasants and giving political instruction, they would also inspect accounting systems and wipe out corruption. In the army Lin Biao called for the study of Mao's writings. Rank was abolished and the soldiers of the People's Liberation Army were sent to the countryside armed with their little red books containing the main tenets of Mao Zedong thought. They were urged to emulate the socialist morals of Lei Feng, a young soldier who had died an untimely death and whose posthumously published diaries had revealed a character dedicated to serving others and the socialist cause.

In the cultural field, as well as in education and medicine, there were new developments. Ordinary people were encouraged to write their own personal histories, and work/study schemes were set up in schools and colleges. During this period Jiang Qing, Mao's wife, began producing some of her revolutionary ballets and operas. Following a tradition which has existed in the Chinese theatre since the Yuan dynasty, drama was often used to make political points. In 1961 Wu Han, the deputy mayor of Peking, wrote a play called *Hai Rui Dismissed from Office*, which was interpreted as an allegory of Peng Dehuai's dismissal from his government posts subsequent to his critical remarks about the Great Leap Forward. Yao Wenyuan – later one of the Gang of Four – wrote a critical review of the play at the end of 1965. While sympathizers in the government ranks sought to suppress further discussion on this theme, a seminar was held in Shanghai by Mao Zedong, Lin Biao and Jiang Qing which related the contents of the play to the broader issues of bourgeois ideology and the need to eradicate the 'four olds' in Chinese society –

ideas, habits, customs and culture. These ideas were taken up in the *Liberation Daily* – the army newspaper. On 6 May 1966 a circular was issued within the Communist Party attacking revisionists in the party – and particularly Liu Shaoqi. *Dazibao* – big character posters began to appear threatening leaders and cadres who followed the so-called black line. At Peking university a movement was set up to change methods of education and teaching and Red Guard groups were formed in many institutions. In Peking Mao incited rebellion with the poster he pinned on the door of the Central Committee's Offices exhorting the Red Guards to bombard the headquarters. A meeting of the Central Committee in August 1966 ratified the movements for change in education and the attacks on the cadres. During this year nearly all normal transport services and schooling were suspended, and students were allowed free travel across China; in August one million young people converged on Peking where they were reviewed by Chairman Mao. However there were growing problems of factionalism and the rebellion was getting out of control. In order to control the situation wage increases and various incentive schemes were set up. In 1967 rallies were held in Shanghai and the short-lived Shanghai commune was set up. It was based on the Paris Commune, but its socialist principles were too advanced for the time; eventually the army was called in to calm the situation through political education and revolutionary committees were formed. The situation persisted and eventually exploded in outright attacks on Liu Shaoqi and the surrounding of the British embassy – there was a strong current of anti-foreign feeling.

Finally the situation was brought back to normal by a campaign against the original instigators of the Cultural Revolution who were accused of planning a coup. Liu Shaoqi was deprived of office and party membership and disappeared from public life. Revolutionary committees were set up to administer the provinces and regions, cadre schools were established, and many young people went to work in the countryside.

In April 1969 Lin Biao was established as the successor to Mao. Jiang Qing, Yao Wenyuan and Wang Hongwen were in the Politburo, but although unity was sought there were many tensions between Lin Biao's group and Zhou Enlai's veteran cadres. In 1970, during a conference at Lu shan, Lin Biao made a bid for the state chairmanship, which was blocked. He made plans for a coup d'etat but his plot failed and he was killed when his plane crashed as he tried to escape to Mongolia.

News of Lin Biao's death was not revealed until 1972. He was identified with Confucius and there was a succession of campaigns against him until the death of Mao.

During these years Mao gradually receded from political life. There were constant differences between the more pragmatic policies of Zhou Enlai and the radical faction led by Jiang Qing, Yao Wenyuan, Zhang Chunqiao, and Wang Hongwen, later to be dubbed as the Gang of Four. In 1974 and 1975 Zhou Enlai and Deng Xiaoping worked together to introduce modernization policies. In 1972 President Nixon visited China, and in 1971 she once again took up membership of the United Nations. In January 1976 Zhou Enlai died; the funeral ceremonies and mourning were kept to the minimum and, as he had requested, his ashes were scattered to the wind by his wife, Deng Yingchao. On 5 April 1976 the young people of Peking congregated spontaneously at Tianan men Square to mourn the death of Zhou Enlai at the festival of Qingming, traditionally the time for commemorating the dead. The demonstration was brutally stopped; at the same time Deng Xiaoping disappeared from public life and a campaign of criticism was begun. A new face appeared – Hua Guofeng, a compromise choice between moderates and radicals – and he was designated Mao's successor. Hua had been governor of Hunan province and in charge of the Bureau of Public Security, and a careful campaign was launched to secure his tenure when Mao died at the beginning of September.

The press was still controlled by Mao's wife, Jiang Qing, and her entourage. Finally in the middle of October the arrest of the 'Gang of Four' was announced; posters appeared all over the cities proclaiming their downfall, rallies were held everywhere, and a vigorous campaign was begun to expose their wrongdoings.

Hua Guofeng presided over the reinstatement of the Four Modernizations Policy and a relaxation on the cultural front. By the middle of 1977, Deng Xiaoping reappeared in public and there was a flurry of activity in every sphere of life. Wage increases were announced, delegations went overseas in search of technology, businessmen were invited to China and an expansion plan for tourism was drawn up.

At the Fifth National People's Congress held in 1978, a new Constitution was ratified and the modernization programme was reaffirmed. These years were astonishing for observers – it was as though the country drew a sigh of relief as former dogma was upended. The Science and Technology Conference acknowledged the essential role of skilled technicians and scientists in the building of a modern state: 'seek truth from facts' was the catch phrase. Both new and old faces appeared in government, political outcasts were rehabilitated and a new legal code and system were drawn up.

By 1979 this open atmosphere had erupted into the Democracy Wall Movement. For a few heady months a modest wall near a bus station in Peking became a forum for radical ideas, underground papers were printed and there were many contacts between Chinese and foreigners. However, by the end of the year the pace had slowed, arrests were made and there were readjustments in the earlier economic targets.

At the beginning of 1980 Liu Shaoqi was posthumously rehabilitated. At the third session of the Fifth People's Congress the role of Party and State were separated and Zhao Ziyang formally took over the premiership from Hua Guofeng. In December of that year the 'Gang of Four' were brought to trial and convicted of counter revolutionary crimes.

A document was released in the early months of 1981 by the Central Committee. Its theme was the History of the Chinese Communist Party and it assessed in particular Mao's enormous contribution in founding the new China and his one great mistake – the Cultural Revolution. In June, Hua Guofeng ceded his post as chairman to Hu Yaobang.

Under Hu Yaobang there has been a streamlining of Ministries and state Organs in the first half of 1982. A determined effort has been made to retire the veterans and allow younger blood to take up managerial and executive posts as China moves towards the end of the millennium. The Twelfth National Congress of the Communist Party of China, held in September 1982, put the seal on these trends and the position of Party Chairman was replaced with that of General Secretary.

Chinese Art

In Chinese the term *meishu* (fine arts) is often used to refer not only to painting and calligraphy, but also to the applied arts – ivory and jade carving, sculpture, porcelain, cloisonné and embroidery. In the past painting and calligraphy were the domain of the scholar officials, while the applied arts were executed by artisans, who inherited skills from their families. They were often employed by the state to supply the imperial household. In tracing the history and development of Chinese art it is often to the applied arts that one must turn for information. For example, the pottery shards of the Neolithic period show how the throwing and firing of pots developed and that they were decorated with both symbolic and representational designs.

With the Shang dynasty came the discovery of bronze, which was used for ceremonial vessels or tripods. These have shown not only that the people of the Shang had command of sophisticated casting techniques, but that recurring stylized animal motifs were used, such as the *taotie* – a stylized monster mask. The vessels and oracle bones were inscribed with early forms of writing. By the Zhou dynasty the designs of these bronze vessels were more elaborate, bird motifs were often used and the inscriptions were longer and more detailed. Jade *bi* discs – symbols of power and status – found in tombs from this era show that the precious qualities of jade had been discovered by this time.

With the unification of China under the Qin and Han dynasties the arts began to reflect more aspects of daily life and developed a strong representational content. Writing was at first done on bamboo strips, then silk. Paper was developed by Cai Lun and used from 106 onwards, and brushes made of animal bristles and ink made from soot and glue were used as writing materials. With these new materials scribes were able to experiment with brush and ink and the absorbency of the paper to develop the main styles of calligraphy which have been used to this day. The seal script was derived from inscriptions found on the early bronzes. The *li* script was developed from inscriptions on stone tablets and characterized by the heavy stroke endings – this is the most legible script and it is the basis of the printed character forms. While these two scripts were derived from the carved character, the 'grass' script took advantage of the special properties of the brush and was used to develop a form of speed writing. It was also known as the 'running hand' script.

Tombs are a rich source of information about the high level of attainments in the arts in the Han dynasty. Wall and brick paintings and bas reliefs depict scenes from daily life: musicians, acrobats, spinning, farming and hunting. The silk funeral hanging found at Mawangdui in Changsha is an excellently preserved work of art, reflecting the Han vision of the universe. The funerary figures to be found in the tombs of the Qin and Han were made from clay or wood and were painted. They depicted armies, ladies-in-waiting, acrobats and musicians. Other finds which reflect developments in the applied arts include early lacquer ware, musical instruments and the jade burial suits from Hebei province.

One of the major outside influences on the development of Chinese art in the first millennium was Buddhism. The styles and forms of Indian Buddhist iconography and architecture were gradually transformed to conform to Chinese aesthetic standards. The introduction of Buddhism was a motivating force in the development of paper and later (in the eighth century) wood block printing to facilitate the distribution of Buddhist writings. The influence of Buddhism was also reflected in the building of pagodas based on the Indian stupa, temples, and the great Buddhist grottoes of Dunhuang, Luoyang and Datong – magnificent pieces of devotional art, where both giant and miniscule Buddhist figures are carved into the rock face and the walls are painted with murals. Paintings on paper or silk from this period depict either the Buddhist paradise or the single figure of a Buddhist saint.

When the Buddhist purges occurred at the end of the Tang Dynasty, the pace of development slowed down. There was also a body of secular art produced during this millennium, which has survived through copies made by later generations: in China 'copying' is thought to benefit the artist's technical development. The works of the fourth-century painter Gu Kaizhi have survived in this way.

In the field of art criticism and theory, in the sixth century Xie He produced a treatise emphasizing the importance of painting with 'vitality', using the brush to create form and colour for the composition of a painting. This was as important for the improvement of one's technique as the need to copy. During this time the hand scroll was more popular than the hanging scroll: this was unfurled horizontally revealing scenes which, while complete in their own right, formed part of a whole.

Towards the end of the first millennium landscape painting was introduced when, in the ninth century, Wang Wei began to use ink to create monochromatic paintings which were redolent with atmosphere. In the applied arts developments in glazing techniques gave a new status to ceramics and the classical pottery of Yue, Ru and Dingzhou was highly acclaimed. Sculpture was at its most vital and realistic in the Tang dynasty and artisans worked in precious metals and hard stone.

The Song dynasty saw the apogee of Chinese art: artists enjoyed imperial patronage and there was an Art Academy. Painters experimented with perspective – a mountain painting would take the spectator upwards through the different levels of the mountain – and both ink and coloured paint were used. By way of contrast to the bold landscape painting a new miniature style of 'bird and flower' painting was developed: this depicted in accurate and delicate detail a single bird poised on a branch of blossom. When the capital of the Song dynasty was forced to move southwards to Hangzhou, the gentler landscape of this area and the different artistic traditions exerted their influence on painting, making it more romantic. There was great interest in brush techniques and strokes and during the Song period the different strokes were named. The devices of 'bird and flower' painting were combined with landscape painting in the 'one corner' technique – in the corner of a painting a group of rocks, buildings or trees would be painted in detail, while in the broad expanse of the rest of the picture a few strokes of the brush would be used to denote the background giving a new sense of perspective and depth to the landscape painting. A growing interest in the Chan (Zen) sect of Buddhism also brought a very simple but inspired form of art in the painting of everyday items: objects such as pieces of fruit or fish would be brought to life in a few witty bold brush strokes. During the Southern Song dynasty the great potteries of the south produced their fine glazed porcelain: from Jingde zhen came white Yingqing ware with its pale blue glaze; from Longquan came the famous jade-like celadon which was supplied to the court; from Fujian Province came a black glazed tea ware which was adopted by the Japanese. The natural resources of the south – bamboo, ivory and lacquer – meant that these materials predominated in the applied arts during the Southern Song, and the design used reflected a taste for uncluttered elegance.

During the Yuan dynasty there was greater individualism in art and more is known about the lives of the painters who experimented with different genres and brush strokes. Qian Xuan (1235–1301) developed an archaistic style, based on the late Tang, while Zhao Mengfu (1254–1322) served as secretary on the Board of War under the Mongols and produced highly realistic work. There was also a group known as the Four Great Masters: Huang Gongwang (1269–1354) experimented with brush techniques and light; Wu Zhen (1280–1354) was known for his genre paintings of Lake Taihu; Ni Zan (1301–74) painted many scenes with water as the main subject, using light brush strokes, and Wang Meng (1308–1385) was admired for his mountain scenes and the use of a stippling brush stroke.

In the same period the kilns at Jingde zhen began experimenting with the use of cobalt and copper to etch designs under the Yingqing glaze, while the kilns of Guangdong and Fujian were also developing rapidly and exporting their ware overseas.

During the Ming, although the capital was now in the north, the area south of the Yangtse continued to be the centre for the arts. The cities of Nanking, Suzhou and Yangzhou were flourishing and the wealthy families and merchants of the area patronized art in its many forms – from the laying out of gardens to the purchase of fine porcelain. In painting there was a certain rivalry between the court painters and the scholar painters. The former painted decorative subjects on demand – birds, flowers, children, kittens and puppies, for example – while the scholar painters drew on the great masters of the past to develop their skills. They gradually introduced colour into their painting and at the same time techniques of multi-coloured wood block printing were developed. During this period it became fashionable to complete a painting with a short poem, and a painting came to be judged not only on the representation of the subject matter, but on the poem, the calligraphy and the painter's seal.

The new-found taste for colour was also reflected in the applied arts and at Jingde zhen the use of the overglaze produced more vivid hues of red, yellow and green. Pictorial designs were used, and this was the period that saw the development of the bright blue and white porcelain which is now famed throughout the world. Cloisonné, which was made from brightly coloured enamels fired on to intricate metalwork designs, was produced in Peking, and filigree work inlaid with precious stones and richly carved lacquer were all sought after by the wealthy.

The Manchu taste was flamboyant and many different kinds of art flourished during the Qing dynasty. Bada shanren (1626–1705) was the great exponent of the Chan (Zen) style of art which has influenced Chinese and Japanese artists up to the present day. Shi Tao (1630–1707) was a landscape and genre painter who used a kind of pointilliste technique to achieve different effects of light and shade.

Emperor Kang xi was a great patron of the arts. He had workshops and studios opened in the grounds of the Forbidden City in Peking and he also patronized the Jingde zhen kiln. During his reign the blue and white porcelain was produced in vast quantities, many articles being painted with landscapes or scenes from daily life in the style of the time, producing the *famille rose* and *verte* styles of porcelain.

During the eighteenth century, chinoiserie was becoming popular in Europe and designs were adapted to European taste. During the reign of Qian long there were further exchanges between Europe and China – his collection of clocks and musical boxes can still be seen in the Forbidden City, and Giuseppe Castiglione (1688–1766), whose Chinese name was Lang Shining, worked as a painter in Qian long's court combining Italian styles and techniques of drawing and perspective with features of Chinese painting. In southern China the Eight Eccentrics were typical of the many schools and styles of painting which flourished in the eighteenth century. They sold their paintings, this being the first time that artists had actually used their work for commercial gain. During the nineteenth century there were no great developments in the arts apart from a short flourish under the patronage of the Empress Dowager. Styles tended to be cumbersome and over fussy. However, the work of two painters has survived to the present day: Qi Baishi (1863–1957), who came from Changsha, had a highly individual style, based loosely on the Chan traditions. His favourite subjects were prawns, fruit and even cabbages! Xu Beihong (1896–1953) was best known for his paintings of horses.

In the 1920s and '30s the wood block print in the style of the German artist Käthe Kollwitz was favoured by writers such as Lu Xun for depicting revolutionary themes, and the form was further developed in Yan'an.

In modern China there are several different kinds of painting which are fashionable: there is renewed interest in classical Western styles of painting and sculpture, while other artists continue to paint in the traditional style. A revolutionary romantic style derived from Soviet Russian art is prevalent in propaganda posters and in the massive granite sculptures of young people, soldiers and peasants typified by those standing guard at Chairman Mao's Memorial Hall in Peking or the bas reliefs on the Monument to the People's Heroes on Tianan men Square. In the applied arts the traditional skills of the old artisans are encouraged. In the late 'fifties many artisans who had worked alone or in small workshops were co-opted into larger state-run studios. Many of the great old kilns continue to operate at Jingde zhen, Foshan, Yixing and Yu xian, producing pottery that is suitable for daily use as well as fine art pieces which may form part of a state gift. The traditional arts and crafts are one of China's major exports and a valuable source of revenue, but the drive to export, as well as to increase production for the home market, has had a detrimental effect on the quality of work produced.

Architecture

The visitor to China will encounter several styles of architecture. In the former residences of the royal families there is the imposing palace style. The gardens typical of southern China are a synthesis of the work of man and nature – pavilions, belvederes, corridors and lattice windows all contrive to focus the attention on a particular natural scene. Religious architecture features pagodas and temples. Domestic architecture reflects the many regional differences to be found in every section of life in China – the private courtyard houses of the northern cities contrast with the open-fronted, two-storeyed houses of the southern cities. In the country-side the monochromatic mud-built houses of the north give way to airy whitewashed farmhouses with elaborate eaves. While modern architecture is more starkly functional in style – red brick housing, high-rise flats, wide boulevards and massive squares – some administrative buildings and hotels retain features of traditional Chinese architecture – glazed roof tiles or balustrades with cloud designs, for example.

Due largely to the extensive use of wood as the primary building material, few really ancient buildings have survived to the present day – the massive bronze water containers placed in the Forbidden City bear witness to the constant risk of fire. Where buildings have been damaged or burnt, they have generally been rebuilt on the same site, giving continuity.

Information about China's past architecture is to be found largely in the ancient writings and records of the work of archaeologists. The Neolithic site at Banpo in Xi'an reveals several types of dwelling which were prevalent 6000 years ago, most of them round and some semi-subterranean. Shang dynasty excavations have shown that palaces and royal buildings already existed on a grand scale, also that most cities were surrounded by walls. In the dynastic period tombs provide the most clues to architectural forms and development. The tombs themselves are often impressive constructions – either as tumuli or underground 'palaces' – and the funerary objects which they contain include clay-built models of houses, farms and towers.

The essential features of Chinese palace architecture were established in the Han dynasty. Ceremonial buildings were invariably built on a raised platform surrounded by decorative balustrades and approached by a wide staircase, the added height making them more imposing. For decoration red was the colour most often used and beams, pillars, doors and walls could be elaborately carved or gilded.

It is perhaps the roofs which provide the most distinctive feature of Chinese architecture. Initially thatch was used as a roofing material, but gradually porcelain tiles were introduced with a complex system of levers and brackets to bear the added loads. Their cunning design often meant that whole buildings could be supported without a single nail.

The curved roof was an innovation of the Song dynasty and was adopted eagerly in the south of China. Just as the Song dynasty saw the greatest flowering of art, so it was the age of the finest architecture. The architect Li Jiayi compiled a book about architectural techniques which has been reprinted regularly.

Another feature of the Chinese roof is the acreterion – the ornament to be found at either end of the ridge of the roof – which became more complex and extravagant in the Ming and Qing dynasties. The animal figures which surmount the eaves of many Qing buildings were added partly for decorative reasons, and partly to ward off evil spirits. In the south the eaves and the areas under them were often decorated with vivid scenes of people, animals and plants, modelled from plaster and gaudily painted.

One of the keys to ancient Chinese buildings is the art of *fengshui* or geomancy. The literal meaning of *fengshui* is wind and water, and before construction of any building could commence, the local geomancer would be called upon to select the most propitious site. As with so many ancient speculative arts, the practical and the mystical were intertwined. Among other considerations the front of a building should be facing southwards, the nearest source of water was vital, and a stone screen would be built inside the courtyard entrance to prevent evil spirits and draughts entering (evil spirits can only move in straight lines). On entering most old Chinese buildings one has to climb over the threshold as a precaution against evil spirits, floods, draughts and vermin. In order to relate the temporal and the heavenly, ceremonial buildings, palaces, and even the design of whole cities, particularly after the Han dynasty, were centred on a north–south axis, with the epicentre at the emperor's throne room, for example. Symbolism would also be prevalent in other forms – e.g., the Hall of Prayer for a Good Harvest in the Temple of Heaven in Peking is supported by four beams representing the four seasons, twelve beams for the months of the year, a further twelve for the two-hourly divisions of the day, and the total of twenty-four representing the divisions of the solar year which regulated farming.

Examples of religious architecture are to be found in the many Buddhist temples. The earliest temple was built on the site of the White Horse temple at Luoyang, and before the purges of the ninth century, tens of thousands of temples were to be found all over China. One of the oldest extant buildings in China is the Foguang Temple on Wutai Mountain in Shanxi Province which dates from around 850.

Pagodas were also an important feature of Buddhism. Initially they reflected Indian styles of architecture, but they were gradually sinicized. Built of wood or brick they were square, circular or polygonal, and they invariably had an uneven number of storeys – from three to seventeen. The Indian influence was revived with the introduction of Lamaism in the Yuan dynasty – so in Peking, Inner Mongolia and Tibet one finds examples of the dagoba with its broad round base and tapering top, and the diamond throne pagoda consisting of a square base surmounted by two or more highly decorated conical turrets. The pagoda was the focal point of the temple – and later they were used as reliquaries, store houses for Buddhist scriptures (sutras) and tombs.

Religion and Philosophy

INTRODUCTION

The visitor's first contact with China's religious and philosophical past will be a visit to one of the temples or shrines in which China abounds, such as the Longmen Grottoes at Luoyang, the Sacred Mountain of Tai shan in Shandong Province, the Temple of Heaven in Peking, or the Yimin Mosque at Turfan. The panoply of deities is unfamiliar and often confusing, and sometimes it is impossible to be sure which religious sect the temple or shrine in question belongs to. Many religious sites will be swarming with Chinese and foreign visitors and are often in very attractive surroundings. Others are being restored, or are still functioning, while some have been put to use as workshops or offices. Many visitors to China are also interested to find out about the place of religion in modern China and whether the popular view of the Confucian gentleman still holds true.

The main indigenous systems of belief in China were Confucianism and Daoism. Buddhism was an import which became thoroughly sinicized and many Chinese practised elements of all three religions in the belief that there were 'three ways to one goal'. Confucianism is perhaps more of a moral code than a religion, and therefore made little appeal to the mystical needs of human nature. Buddhism and Daoism fulfilled this requirement, and were a reaction against the orthodoxy of Confucianism. Confucianism was the doctrine of the ruling classes, while Buddhism and Daoism were adapted by the ordinary people and combined with elements of folk cults to create a heaven inhabited by deities and immortals who would promise a better life and instruct people how to attain salvation. Islam, and much later Christianity, were also imported to China.

ANCESTOR WORSHIP

Before the arrival of all these religions the Chinese practised the cult of ancestor worship, characterized by clan ancestral temples, the care and maintenance of graves, and the duty to continue the family line; the Qingming Festival, the traditional day for commemorating the dead, is a relic of this cult. Another feature of ancestor worship was the fertility cult of grain and the soil – at the imperial level these were part of the solemn rituals performed at temples of Heaven, Earth, Moon and Sun, while the peasants had their own gods of the soil to whom they prayed for a bountiful harvest.

DAOISM

The founder of Daoism was Laozi who lived around 590 BC and who wrote the *Daode jing* ('The Book of the Way'). He advocated harmony between man's life and the 'way of the universe', choosing to become one with nature or the way *(dao)* through 'non-action' *(wuwei)* and passive acceptance of life's vagaries. Zhuangzi developed these ideas in the third century BC. In many ways Daoism was the rich man's creed, for he could afford to 'drop out' and commune with nature; it was also the anarchic creed of poets, painters and bohemians.

During the Qin and Han Dynasties different interpretations of the *Daode jing* gave rise to the practices of seeking immortality through the elixir of life and of changing cinnabar into gold. These were the roots of science and medicine, but the Daoist necromancer was regarded as a charlatan and the studies never developed, though during the third and fourth centuries Daoism enjoyed the patronage of some of the emperors. To ordinary people Daoism supplied magical rites and gods.

CONFUCIANISM

Confucius was born in 551 BC in the state of Lu – present-day Shandong – and was tutor to the children of noble families. He moved from one family to the next with a small retinue of followers, and eventually returned to Lu where he taught his disciples until his death in 479 BC. After his death his pupils collected his teachings into the *Analects*; he also annotated the *Spring and Autumn Annals* – the history of the state of Lu – which became the source book on correct behaviour for later Confucians.

Confucius looked to the golden age of the mythical rulers Yao and Shun, and to the Zhou dynasty and their cult of heaven. His main tenet was to achieve harmony with the *dao* – the way. In his humanistic doctrine, harmony on earth came from loyalty in the hierarchy of relationships between son and father, younger brother and elder brother, wife and husband, subject and ruler, and ruler and Heaven. It meant a society where each knew his place and no two people were equal. Anyone could become a gentleman by cultivating virtue and self-control.

During the Han dynasty Confucianism gained in importance. Scholars sought to relate Confucian morality and natural phenomena, drawing on the concepts of *yin* and *yang* – the force of opposites – and the five relationships related to the five elements, based on the *Yi jing* ('The Book of Changes'), the Zhou dynasty manual of divination which was annotated by the disciples of Confucius.

After this period Buddhism flourished until the Song dynasty, when Neo-Confucianism gained a hold through the works of Zhu Xi (1130–1200). The main tenet of his dogma was the concept of *qi*, a unifying force in the universe which is corrupted by birth and which can only be regained through being good and benevolent, and he sought guidance in the ancient writings. His strict interpretation led to the curtailing of women's freedom and the rigid requirements of chastity, and the popular view of the orthodox Confucian gentleman.

The far-reaching influence of Confucian thought lives on today in strongly held family ties and respect for old age and position.

BUDDHISM

This was the only foreign religion to be absorbed into and changed by Chinese culture, contributing in many ways to the country's cultural development. Legend has it that the emperor Ming Di of the Han dynasty dreamt he saw the Buddha, and he despatched envoys to India to bring back the scriptures. They returned with two monks on a white horse, and he set up the first Buddhist temple in AD 65 at Luoyang. The more realistic interpretation is that Buddhism came to China along the Silk Route in the first century AD, and by the third and fourth centuries was well established particularly among the non-Han Wei and Toba emperors, who created the famous grottoes at Datong, Luoyang and Dunhuang. Fa Xian in the fourth century and Xuan Zang (602–44) are famous pilgrims who made their way to the west to seek the Buddhist scriptures.

Buddhism was founded in India in the fifth century BC. It holds that life is a cycle of sin and suffering, and that the only way to break the cycle is through attaining *nirvana* or the state of absence of desire through years of leading an ascetic life as a monk.

There were several branches of Buddhism. Hinayana Buddhism (the Lesser Vehicle) acknowledged only one Buddha – Sakyamuni. Mahayana Buddhism acknowledged that Sakyamuni was one Buddha in an infinite number of Buddhas – this branch of Buddhism is called the Greater Vehicle. The Buddhist hierarchy also contains a layer of Boddhisattvas, who are destined for enlightenment and *nirvana*, but have chosen to remain on earth to relieve the suffering of mankind; they are therefore accessible to the prayers of the ordinary human being. There is also the promise of the Buddha to come – the Maitreya Buddha or Laughing Buddha.

Chan Buddhism – or Zen as it is more commonly known – was a development peculiar to China. Based on the teachings of Boddhidarma, an Indian monk who lived in Luoyang in the sixth century, it taught that the road to enlightenment lay through contemplation and the discovery of the germ of Buddhahood in each person. Close in kind to Daoists, the followers of Chan scorned the scriptures, in favour of meditation and repetition of *koans*.

During the Tang dynasty Buddhism flourished in China, and made enormous contributions to Chinese culture. Temples became very rich and used their wealth to erect bronze statues whose weights and sizes were noted down as a record of their value. Great contributions were made to the oral tradition in literature by the stories told to illustrate the scriptures – another reason for the popularity of Buddhism. Since the translation and copying of texts were considered beneficial to one's *karma*, this led to the development of printing. However by the end of the Tang dynasty, when the power and strength of the empire were somewhat diminished, resentment and anti-clerical feeling grew, temples were closed down, and monks and nuns returned to lay life.

Eventually the most widespread form of Buddhism was to be Amidism, which revolved around Amitabha, a deity born from a lotus in Heaven – Western Paradise. There was no need for contemplation or asceticism; merely invoking his name would bring salvation and pave the way to paradise. Those with loftier ideals could devote their lives to doing good for others. It is not hard to understand why this form of instant *nirvana* was to become the most popular among the ordinary people. Most of the temples visited by tourists are devoted to this branch of Buddhism and peopled by its deities – for example the goddess of mercy, Guanyin;

or the *arhats* – 'saints' who have attained enlightenment and have special powers just as a Christian might pray to St Anthony if he loses something. The Ming dynasty novel by Wu Chengen, translated by Arthur Waley as *Monkey* provides a lively, readable introduction to the figures which inhabit the Buddhist Paradise.

Buddhism was absorbed not only by the Han Chinese but by the Manchus. The Tibetans and Mongolians, as well as the Tu, Qiang and Dai nationalities, took it in as Lamaistic Buddhism.

Relics of Buddhism are found all over China today. Many of them are now under the protection of the state. Monks and nuns still practise their religion in some of the temples, and many have been reopened only recently. The Association of Chinese Buddhists was formed in 1953; a library of *sutras* and a novitiate were set up, and rubbings were made at the Jinling scripture-carving house in Nanking of the complete collection of Buddhist scriptures, carved on over 15,000 stone tablets. The association publishes a magazine called *Modern Buddhism*. During the early 1960s the 2,500th anniversary of the death of Sakyamuni was celebrated, as well as the 1,300th anniversary of the death of Xuan Zang, and the Buddha's Tooth Pagoda was rebuilt in the Western Hills. Today the Association of Chinese Buddhists has been reconvened, new research centres have been set up, and renewed contacts have been made with Buddhists throughout the world.

ISLAM

The Moslem religion came to China along the Silk Route during the Tang dynasty. Persian and Arab merchants worshipped in their own mosques in Chang'an, and in 651 an envoy of the Caliph Othman Ibn-affan journeyed to Chang'an and expounded the principles of Islam to the court; his visit is regarded as the official introduction of Islam to China.

There are approximately 10 million Moslems in China today. The main Islamic nationality is the Hui, who have their own autonomous region in Ningxia. Many of the nationalities in Xinjiang, including the Uighurs, are Moslem, as are those living in Qinghai and Gansu. Nearly every major city has special shops and restaurants for Moslems, and there are mosques dating from the ancient Guang ta in Guangzhou – the oldest mosque in China – to the South Mosque in Shenyang, built in 1661. Geographically they are found from Shanghai in the east to Kashgar in the far west.

The China Islamic Association convened its fourth National Congress in April 1980 – the first since 1963 – and there are plans to publish more editions of the Koran. Chinese Moslems are taking part in the World Islamic Movement and have recently journeyed to the Hajj. The magazine *Moslems in China* is being reissued, and the China Institute of Islamic has been reopened. Moslems are also represented at the Fifth National People's Congress and on the Chinese People's Political Consultative Conference.

CHRISTIANITY

In the collection of steles in the Provincial Museum in Xi'an is a tablet recording the presence of Nestorian Christianity in China in the seventh century. From the Yuan dynasty there are records of the presence of a Franciscan monk in Peking at the end of the thirteenth century. At the end of the sixteenth century Matteo Ricci (1552–1610) came to the Ming court, bringing Catholicism and western astronomy and even converting some of the court. The first church was erected at Xuanwu men in Peking in the mid-seventeenth century; the present church on the same site was built in 1906.

It was only after the Opium Wars in the 1840s that Christianity made much impression in China, because of the influx of foreign missionaries. It made such an impact that the banner of the Taiping rebellion was raised in the name of Christianity. By 1949 China contained some 3 million Catholics, 700,000 Protestants and a small number of Eastern Orthodox Christians. In 1951 the Patriotic Society of Chinese Catholics was formed, which was independent of the Vatican – at the time it was felt that the Vatican was inciting Catholics to oppose the new order, and in addition the Vatican had in the past recognized the states of Manchuria and Taiwan. Since that time the Catholic Church has elected its own bishops and ordained its own priests. During the Cultural Revolution, the last aging missionaries were expelled from China, and the church in Xuanwu men was closed between 1966 and 1971, when it was reopened for use by the foreign community. Since the late 1970s Chinese Catholics have been able to practise their faith more openly; a new bishop was elected in Nanking, and the church there and in Shanghai reopened. The Bible has been scheduled for republishing, and Christmas and Easter are openly celebrated by many Chinese Christians.

RELIGION IN CHINA TODAY

Since 1977 the government has gone to great lengths to reaffirm the constitutional right to freedom of religious belief, the equality between religions, and the need for them to coexist peacefully. In January 1980 a law came into effect making it a punishable offence for a state official to impede the right of an individual to follow his chosen religion, or to interfere with the customs of a minority nationality. However a 'sorcerer or witch who uses superstition to spread rumours or fraudulently acquire money' is liable to imprisonment or public surveillance. Temples, churches and mosques, and various religious associations have been reconstituted, as mentioned above, and the Department of Religious Affairs is the watchdog body of the State Council which keeps an eye on freedom of worship.

Although Marxism is a system of thought which has no place for religion or god, being based on materialism and science, at the present stage of development in Chinese society the government recognizes that religion cannot be eradicated by harsh means. It realizes that such methods only lead to resentment and covert practices, and prefers to allow people to practise religion, believing that changes in society will gradually make religion unnecessary, and that religious belief will not necessarily impede the creation of a healthy state and economy.

In the early 1950s religious organizations needed to affirm their allegiance to the New China, landowning monasteries were dispossessed under the land reform movement, and patriotic religious associations were established which maintained links with world organizations. The beginning of the Cultural Revolution saw a fierce movement to eradicate religion altogether: all religious practice was impossible, and there was wholesale burning and destruction of religious buildings and artefacts – damage which the government is now repairing, recognizing these buildings and objects as part of China's cultural heritage. Today in China few young people will profess to having a religion, which is seen as something for the elderly. The only recollections the young have are perhaps the rites and prayers of a parent or grandparent, although there is a renewed curiosity about different religions and once more religion and philosophy are subjects which may be studied and discussed.

AN OUTLINE OF CHINESE PHILOSOPHY

'Let a hundred flowers blossom and a hundred schools of thought contend' – since 1949 this phrase has been invoked on two notable occasions: first in 1956, in an attempt to draw the sting of the intellectuals, and then in 1977, to signal a genuine liberalization of the arts. It is an allusion to the many schools of philosophy and thought which flourished in the Warring States period between 476 and 221 BC, before China was unified. This was a period of political upheaval, when the emperor lost the allegiance of the feudal lords, who fought among themselves and were often dispossessed of their lands.

At this time itinerant scholars moved from state to state, advising and lobbying princes with new stratagems and formulas for achieving and holding on to power, and providing advice on a social philosophy which could bring stability to a large, unified state. Philosophers argued about whether man's basic nature was good or evil. Mencius (376–289 BC) developed the ideas of Confucius – that all good in a country sprang from the emperor following the way of kings and providing sound and benevolent government. Mo zi (479–381 BC) advocated universal love and the simple life. Zhuang zi developed the ideas of Lao Zi in the third century BC: rejecting the ceremonial constraints of court life, he sought communion with nature and passive acceptance of change.

By 221 BC Legalism and its pragmatism had given enough brute strength to the state of Qin to take over the other states and unite China; the main exponents of this school of thought were the Lord of Shang and Han Fei zi from the state of Qin. Dismissing Confucianism as ineffectual, the Legalists held that man was evil by nature, and that he should be controlled by a strong body of law with administrative power coming from the chancellor. Ideological opposition was stamped out in 213 BC by the burning of all books, except for one copy from each school of thought which was kept in the imperial library. In 206 BC the Qin was overthrown and the Han dynasty established. During the Cultural Revolution the Legalists enjoyed a renewed status as the progressive force in history, and all history was seen in terms of the struggle between Legalists and Confucianists, a restrictive view which has been discredited as a hobby horse of the Gang of Four.

Contemporary Life

POLITICAL, MILITARY AND LEGAL STRUCTURES

Even the most politically disinterested visitor must wonder how it is possible to administer such a large country as China with its diverse and scattered population, and what the relationship must be between central and local government. Then there are the political questions – is it the Communist Party who actually make all the decisions? Are there any other political parties in China? It is useful to know of a few terms before visiting China, and for those who are interested the constitution and party policies are always available in translation.

There are four principal administrative and political levels, as shown in the tree.

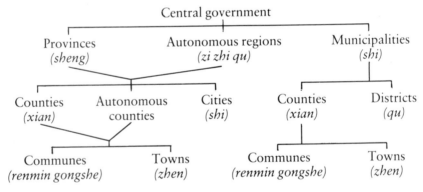

Between the second and third levels, autonomous regions and provinces are also divided into prefectures *(zhou)* for administrative purposes, but they do not have rights in the People's Congresses. In Inner Mongolia a league is equivalent to a prefecture, and a banner to a county.

The National People's Congress (Quanguo renmin daibiao dahui)
The function of the National People's Congress is roughly equivalent to that of Parliament in Britain or Congress in the United States; it is responsible for the ratification of laws, the election of the government (the State Council), the choice of premier, financial affairs, administration, and matters of war. The National People's Congress is convened once a year and its term lasts for five years. The first session of the Fifth National People's Congress was held at the beginning of 1978.

There are approximately 3 500 deputies to the National People's Congress, made up as follows: workers 26.7 per cent, peasants 20.6 per cent, soldiers 14.4 per cent, revolutionary cadres 13.4 per cent, intellectuals 15 per cent, patriotic personages 8.9 per cent (ie those who co-operated with the Chinese Communist Party before 1948, but belonged to other parties), and returned overseas Chinese 1 per cent.

How the Deputies Are Elected
Most people over the age of eighteen have the right to vote and to stand for election; direct secret ballot elections are held at commune, town and municipal district levels every two years. Elections at county and city level are held every three years. These elected deputies are then responsible for electing deputies to higher levels, ie to the provincial National People's Congress and to the National People's Congress.

The Standing Committee of the National People's Congress
The Standing Committee, the permanent organ of the National People's Congress, has some 175 members. Its role is supervisory: it can convene sessions of the National People's Congress as far as State Council, people's court and procuratorate (see page 49) are concerned, and if the National People's Congress is not in session it has certain powers of decision concerning provincial resolutions and members of the State Council. It has its own chairman and several vice-chairmen.

The State Council
This is the name given to the 'cabinet', which is responsible for all affairs of state and is accountable to the National People's Congress and the Standing Committee. It consists of the Premier (Prime Minister), the Vice-Premiers, and the ministers of the various commissions and ministries such as State Planning, Foreign Trade, Water Conservancy and Public Health.

The Communist Party in China
The Communist Party held its first ever congress in Shanghai on 21 July 1921, when it had a membership of seventy. By 1947 it had a membership of 1.2 million and today the membership is around 39 million. The Communist Party operates at all levels of Chinese society, down to the commune and the individual factory. At Party Congresses the current line of policy is established; at the Eleventh Party Congress, held in August 1977, the key was 'modernization' in a socialist context. At the Twelfth Party Congress, held in September 1982, important organizational changes were made. The People's Congress and the State Council use the policy agreed at Party Congress as a guideline for their decisions and actions.

Since 1982 the central organization of the Chinese Communist Party consists of the general secretary, the secretariat and about twenty-five members of the Politburo, with alternate members and a standing committee and a central advisory commission. Members of the central organization of the Communist Party are frequently also on the Standing Committee or State Council of the National People's Congress.

Becoming a member of the Communist Party is a hard-won privilege. A young candidate must have been a diligent and active member of the Communist Youth League (Qingnian tuan), and needs two sponsors to recommend his or her formal application. Even so, being a member of the Qingnian tuan does not guarantee entry into the Party.

Other Political Parties

Since 1977 the former 'patriotic and democratic' parties have been able to resume their activities. All these parties were founded before 1948 and worked closely with the Communist Party in the united front against the right-wing faction of the Guomin dang (Nationalist Party or KMT). Such parties have a membership consisting largely of 'intellectuals' and some businessmen. They joined the Chinese People's Political Consultative Conference in 1948 and participated in its first plenary session which established a programme, organized a central people's government, and announced the founding of the People's Republic. Some members have places in the People's Congresses at local levels.

The Chinese People's Political Consultative Conference

The Chinese People's Political Consultative Conference was the forerunner to the National People's Congress, which was formed in 1954. Before that date it had been the body which established the first government of the People's Republic of China. Nowadays it combines elements in modern Chinese society which do not necessarily fit into the socialist mould, but for whom there is nonetheless a role in modern China; it is supervised by the Communist Party.

The People's Liberation Army

Contrary to most people's expectations there is no compulsory military conscription in China. It is generally considered a duty and an honour to join the army at the age of eighteen, and there is an annual levy for which stringent qualifications are required. The period of enlistment for ground forces is three years, and during this period a monthly allowance is received. A soldier may extend his service for up to fifteen years as a volunteer, and will receive a full salary. During the three years as a conscript he may be posted to any part of China and will probably learn a skill such as driving which will enable him to find a job when he returns to civilian life. Many of the taxi drivers in the major cities learned to drive in the army!

The army uniform is khaki green (the navy wears blue) with red felt flashes on the collar and a red star on the cap. The distinguishing signs of rank were for several years the number of pockets on the jacket; however the army is now being reorganized, and more traditional marks of rank are to be reintroduced.

There is also a reserve or auxiliary force called the People's Militia which operates in communes, factories, schools, government offices and so on. It is for men between the ages of sixteen and forty and women from sixteen to thirty-five.

The origins of the People's Liberation Army are in the Chinese Workers' and Peasants' Red Army, founded on 1 August 1927. In 1937, during the war against the Japanese, it was renamed the Eighth Route and New Fourth Route National Revolutionary Army. In 1946 it was reorganized as the People's Liberation Army. The success of the People's Liberation Army is often attributed to their conduct when billeted in rural areas. Unlike armies of the imperial past, or enemy forces, they were governed by the 'eight rules and three disciplines', which forbade them even to take a needle and cotton from the ordinary people, much less to go to the excesses which armies tend to regard as their right.

Today national defence is one of the priorities of the four modernizations. The political and romanticized role the army enjoyed previously is giving way to a rather more businesslike attitude as contracts are discussed with many foreign countries.

The Legal System

The application of the law is at an experimental stage in China today, as the code of criminal law and procedure adopted at the second session of the Fifth National People's Congress on 1 July 1979 has only been in effect since 1 January 1980. This code was enacted in the current spirit of modernization and as part of the policy which recognized that a 'sound socialist democracy' could not be realized without a 'sound socialist legal system'. In the light of this the second session of the Fifth National People's Congress examined not only the criminal law, but its procedure and the judicial structure which would supervise it, as well as laws concerning joint investment with foreign companies and electoral reforms dealing with the organization of local government. The catch-all notion of the 'counter-revolutionary' was re-examined, and the period between arrest and trial was limited to between four and five and a half months at the most. A body of 'economic' law was also established regarding such matters as embezzlement of wages, breaking of contracts, shoddy work etc., at the level of manufacturing organizations.

Up till 1979 the system of law enforcement seems to have been somewhat arbitrary; certainly legal consultants had shut up shop and the law and jurisprudence departments of universities had closed down. The whole gamut of crimes was seen in a political light as counter-revolutionary and harmful to the masses, part of the class struggle, to be dealt with by 're-education', 'struggle', 'criticism' and 'reform through labour'. Today penalties range from 'public surveillance' (equivalent to the British system of probation) through detention for short periods to imprisonment and the death sentence – with a system of two years' reprieve.

The administration of justice is supervised by the 'procuratorate' which operates at every level of contemporary Chinese society from the supreme or national – the chief procurator – to the district and county levels which have local people's courts. Special courts exist for transport and the railways. There are civil and criminal divisions at all levels of the courts, and at the higher levels an economic division. Cases are heard publicly unless they involve state secrets, people's intimate private lives or those under the age of eighteen. The court will have a president, two or more vice-presidents, chief and associate judges who will have been elected by the local people's congresses. The accused has the right to call on legal defence or to defend himself or obtain the assistance of a referee from his place of work. Recently the departments of jurisprudence have been reopened in the universities, as have the lawyers' associations and legal consultants' offices. Charges range from less than one *yuan* for advice to 30 *yuan* for legal defence, with 'legal aid' if defendants are unable to pay. The courts and the procuratorate are subject to the law only, and not to any political body.

AGRICULTURE AND THE COMMUNES

Introduction

Travelling through China by train from Guangzhou to Peking and beyond, few visitors fail to be impressed by the fact that every inch of land seems to be cultivated. In fact about 15% of China's land mass provides for the whole nation (a billion hectares of land are under food and cash crop cultivation), the areas to the west being almost entirely uncultivable. China has always been an agrarian society, with 80 per cent of the population living on and working the land, and the development and organization of agriculture quickly became a central feature of the Communist Party's policy, since this was considered essential to a new and stable society in China. The development of agricultural organization is thus a vital part of modern Chinese history, and a visit to an agricultural commune is not be missed during a tour of China.

By western standards farming methods will seem backward and labour-intensive, but the organization provides scope for development and mechanization is being achieved in a step-by-step programme. New farming methods have in every case sought to increase production and yield.

In the fertile eastern China basin stretching from north to south, arable farming is most important. North of the Yangtse the major crops are wheat and coarse grains such as millet, gaoliang, maize, soya beans. This crop pattern is of course reflected in the people's diet: traditionally rice has always had to be transported from the south of China, though now it can be cultivated as far north as Heilongjiang. South of the Yangtse rice becomes predominant, with some winter wheat and cash crops such as tea and cotton. Tobacco is grown in several areas of China. In the outlying regions of Tibet, Inner Mongolia and Xinjiang sheep farming and cattle breeding are predominant. Vegetables are the most important crops in the areas near the cities.

The nationwide co-ordination and planning of agriculture are supervised by the Ministry of Agriculture and related bodies who draw up quotas for the staple crops – rice, wheat, cotton and so on. They also supervise developments in irrigation, fertilizing techniques, soil, mechanization, pest control and seed strains, disseminating information and providing research facilities. Quotas and distribution for many cash crops, meat and vegetables are decided at local level. While a good grain harvest is the mainstay of agricultural policy in China, cultivation of cash crops and diversification are encouraged increasingly.

There is also a very close link between agriculture and industry: agriculture provides the raw materials for light industry; as more people are released from farm work they provide a source of labour for industry; and the rural areas form the market for about two-thirds of all manufactured goods.

Agriculture since 1949

Mao realized at a very early date – in 1924 he was already conducting work among the peasants in Hunan – that the peasants were to be the mainstay of the Revolution, both economically and politically. The existing ancient base of rural villages and hamlets was used to build the new and extensive collective form of agriculture.

The priority of the new government in 1949 was to feed and clothe the population and to establish a new social order out of the tatters of the defeated one, without help from outside and relying on the country's own resources. In a bankrupt country people and land were the most vital assets, but they had to be organized into units which could engage in cost-effective farming – before liberation high costs and low yields had made farming uneconomic. Additionally this kind of organization would enable more people to be mobilized for essential projects such as road building and irrigation.

Before 1949 10 per cent of the population owned 70 per cent of the land. Between 1949 and 1952, under the land reform processes and following the precedent which had already been established in the north-west before 1949, land was distributed among the previously landless masses. At this stage the government could not afford to alienate certain sectors of the peasants by making indiscriminate and blanket redistribution of land, so the peasants were divided into categories. While the great landlords were dealt with severely, losing their land and political rights and condemned to execution or a term of imprisonment, rich and middle-income peasants who both owned and worked their land were allowed to retain most of their property – the Communists needed their support since they owned the tools and livestock needed for the next stage of collectivization. The rest of the land was divided among the poor peasants, who were either tenant farmers or labourers; 300 million peasants, including women, benefited from this reform. However the new plots of land were very small, often only about 2000 m², and the new landowners had no capital. It was clearly not the right time to expropriate the new landowners and enforce collectivization, so the formation of mutual aid teams was encouraged as a means of pooling labour, draft animals and tools, and state loans were readily awarded to those who established such teams. The mutual aid teams begun in Yan'an were developed into co-operatives: land, animals and tools were pooled in exchange for a share in the co-operative's income relative to the size of one's contribution; each peasant's labour contribution was also included when calculating wages. By 1956 advanced co-operatives were being formed: one or more villages consisting of about two hundred families would combine, electing a local council and managers, and the income would be collectively owned and invested for the whole village. These larger organizations enabled machinery to be purchased and large-scale projects such as irrigation works to be completed.

With the enthusiastic call of the Great Leap Forward to 'go all out, aim high, to achieve greater, faster and better and more economical results in building social-ism', and with the mobilization of thousands of people in the construction of public works, a spontaneous movement towards the merging of co-operatives into larger units came about. In an attempt to combine both government and management of agriculture, co-operatives merged into communes about three times their original size. Impossible quotas were set, and the zeal with which some cadres pursued pure Communism by establishing communal canteens and pooling all private property resulted in chaos and hardship and led to the intervention of the Central Committee who at the end of 1958 issued guidelines on the running of communes.

Qiliying commune in Henan Province was the first to receive the personal approval of Mao. According to the principle behind commune organization, which still applies today, people should be rewarded according to the work they contri-bute and peasants have the right to their private property. The commune itself is the lowest level of state power and integrates local government and management of agriculture, embracing local industry, commerce, education and home defence. It is an economically self-sufficient unit. Communes vary in size and wealth, according to their distance from the nearest city. China today has over 90,000 communes, which usually have between 10,000 and 20,000 members. The commune itself corresponds to a small township; the production brigade corresponds to a group of villages; and the production team to a village where often, as in the past, everyone has the same surname. The production team consists of fifteen to thirty families and is the lowest accounting unit; it has responsibility for the allocation of work within the larger plan of the commune and is in charge of its own accounts.

During the late 1960s and early 1970s the slogan 'In agriculture learn from Dazhai' could be heard everywhere to encourage the peasants to work hard and with revolutionary spirit. Dazhai was a model brigade in Shanxi Province which, against the odds of stony and almost barren terrain, worked to terrace the land and farm it. However, by the end of the 1970s Dazhai's agricultural efforts had been discredited.

Today, as part of the effort to revitalize the economy, greater emphasis is being laid on diversification – the cultivation of cash crops and development of sideline industries – and on giving greater power of decision and independence to the production team. Alongside the commune as a unit of agricultural production and organization, the role of the state farm has been given renewed emphasis. There are 2000 state farms in China with a work force of 5 million. State farms, whose workers receive a salary, are generally larger than communes, and are more highly mechanized. Many are to be found in the border regions of China.

A Typical Commune

The commune does not represent a static or regimented organization, a fact which may be difficult to realize during a half-day visit when facts and impressive figures will be bandied around. It can be hard to appreciate in these circumstances that every evening the commune members return to their homes and families, and that profit and the improvement in the peasants' standard of living is the result of the sum of individual efforts. Progress can be measured not only in terms of doubled and trebled crop yields, but also in the fact that the individual peasant can afford a new house or sewing machine. What follows is a description of a commune near Wuxi in Jiangsu Province, explaining how one production team's funds are allocated and something of their daily life and plans for the future (as in 1978).

The Helie commune is situated 3 km from Wuxi and lies on Lake Tai, a very fertile area which is intensively cultivated and also has the many advantages of being close to the city. The commune has a population of 15,000 – or 4500 households – and is as such a medium-size commune subdivided into eight production brigades and eighty production teams.

Most of the land is taken up in the cultivation of rice and wheat – since 1966 this commune has worked a triple-crop system with two rice crops and one wheat crop per year. Fish farming is important and takes up 2600 *mu* of water surface. This is an area famous for its silk, and the commune has 800 *mu* of mulberry groves; silkworms are bred from May to October every year. Being near Wuxi, the commune provides the city with vegetables, for which 2100 *mu* of land are set apart. Pigs, dairy cattle and poultry are reared. About 600 *mu* of the remaining hilly land is used to produce tea and fruit trees, particularly peach trees; in addition cedar trees have recently been planted as they grow quickly and can be used for building, making the commune more self-sufficient.

Mechanization has been a major aim in the development of agriculture; though every commune will detail to the visitor its number of rice transplanters or hand tractors, in reality much of the work is still done by sheer physical labour. In the Helie commune, a fairly advanced and wealthy one, about 30–40 per cent of the work was still done by hand in 1978. Their major objectives were to solve 'three back-breaking' tasks through mechanization – picking rice seedlings, harvesting rice and maize, and digging ditches. In pisciculture they were preparing a vacuum pump for collecting snails and weeding the bottom of Lake Tai – snails and weed provide foodstuff for the fish. The commune members also required dredgers for the ponds, and granulators for making fodder. In their vegetable farming they

Tea-sorting at Dragon Well in
Hangzhou

Tea-pickers

A water buffalo in the paddyfields of an agricultural commune

A room in a commune member's house in the vicinity of Shanghai

wanted pumps for spreading fertilizer and sprays for watering. In sericulture they were trying to develop a disease-resistant strain of mulberry tree and needed machines for shredding the leaves which are fed to the silkworms. The commune has a technological research and development station where work is carried out on new strains of seeds, and where education in modern methods is provided, which is essential since the peasants tend otherwise to cling to tradition.

As already mentioned, the commune economy includes industry. Three principles decide the kind of industry that a commune should have. First, the needs of commune production and mechanization are considered, so that many commune factories are repair and maintenance shops, while others make agricultural machinery such as pumps, or process the products of the commune. The second principle is that the industry 'serves the needs of the people'. This covers carpentry workshops or craft industries such as basket making. Thirdly it serves heavy industry in the city, such as small machine toolshops making spare parts for the factories. The proceeds of the work carried out in commune factories are part of the yearly final account of the commune or brigade, and most of the workers are paid in work points in the same way as the people working in the fields.

The production and distribution of fertilizer is a vital factor in the economic equation of the commune. Organic fertilizer is the most important kind and in Helie consists of silt from the fishponds (50 per cent), pig and goat droppings and human waste (30 per cent) and green fertilizer – alfalfa (20 per cent). Fields are never allowed to lie fallow. There is also a chemical fertilizer plant in Wuxi producing ammonia, and Helie uses as much as 80 kg of chemical fertilizer per *mu*, which is higher than in many other places in China. The building of chemical fertilizer plants has been one of the priorities in industrial expansion.

Distribution of Profits
As the team is the basic accounting unit, here is a breakdown of the distribution of the annual profits of a team in the Helie commune. These profits come from the sale of grain to the state and also from the sale of other crops such as tea or fruit and vegetables. In a typical year the breakdown was as follows:

58.02 per cent: commune members' wages. During the year each peasant accumulates work points based on the amount and type of work that he does. The value of each work point is arrived at by dividing the 58.02 per cent by the total number of work points, which means that the income of each peasant can vary from year to year according to the relative success of the harvest – the average income is between 400 and 650 *yuan*. Within each team are small work groups of twenty people, who usually work together. There are three scales of work points – the strongest earning twelve points a day, the middle grade ten points and the lowest eight points; this last group usually consists of the elderly and weakest. It is possible to be promoted from the middle to the top grade. In principle men and women can earn the same for equal work. The work points are evaluated every month by the whole team and each member keeps a record of the number he has earned. As the major reckoning only takes place once a year, commune members are entitled to a monthly advance. Recently a system of quotas and incentives has been introduced in some communes.

26.1 per cent: production costs, ie seeds, insecticide, fertilizer, water and electricity, and machine maintenance;

9.3 per cent: public funds, ie new tractors and irrigation projects;

3.9 per cent: public welfare, ie the co-operative medical service, which is free apart from a 5 *fen* registration fee, and the care of old people without families; under the Five Guarantees the old are assured of a place to live, food, clothes, sickness benefits and a decent burial. As yet in the rural areas pension schemes are not the norm, and if an old person's family is still alive it is responsible for them, which usually means that the elderly continue working for as long as possible. Where communes or teams have pension schemes the average contribution is 15 *yuan* per month. This particular team hoped to be able to introduce pensions by 1985, enabling women to retire at sixty and men at sixty-five. Primary school education was provided free of charge in this commune, although in some other communes members had to pay a small fee.

1.49 per cent: agricultural tax. This was fixed in 1956, and relative to production figures at that time the amount payable has decreased from 6 per cent to 1.49 per cent. The government is generally lenient, and in the event of a bad harvest payment is deferred. In return for this tax the government gives financial assistance in projects such as the installation of overhead wires or purchasing a rice transplanter.

0.56 per cent public reserve fund, in case of war or natural disaster. This money may be used for the construction of underground tunnels or for some kinds of military training.

Housing, Social Services and Leisure

In most communes houses are privately owned. If sons and daughters marry they can apply for land, which the team usually gives free of charge, the major expenses being the actual building costs. Building is usually carried out by the commune construction team. The average cost is 600 *yuan* for 30 m², ie one room, and new couples usually build two rooms. Every person is entitled to a private plot of land of approximately 20 m², and can breed pigs, goats or poultry. This produce is mainly for private consumption, and any surplus may be sold to the supply and marketing co-operative in the commune or in the 'free market'. Grain is usually free, although it sometimes forms part of the wage.

The commune is also responsible for education. Helie contains nine primary and three middle schools; from eight weeks to six years children can attend nurseries provided by the team, after which they attend the primary schools set up by the brigade. Teachers are paid by the state and come from the county teaching bureau. At the moment upper middle school education (see page 59) is not yet available unless the commune is near the city, in which case the children may attend schools there.

Medical care is provided by the commune. Helie has a hospital with twenty-four qualified medical workers – doctors, nurses and technicians. Complicated illnesses can be treated in the city hospitals. Every brigade has a clinic with thirty-two barefoot doctors (see page 61). And in each team there are medical workers responsible for family planning and preventive medicine.

The commune as a whole is managed by the party committee, which passes on and determines the correct party line from central government. It is administered by committee members who at Helie have held their positions since the commune was set up. Leisure time is limited for most peasants – they are entitled to two days off per month, though in the busy season they will often work right through. Most teams have access to a television set, and films will sometimes be shown in the brigade. During the slack season commune members' attention and energy will be turned to various construction projects such as levelling the land and dam building.

INDUSTRY

Foreign visitors are not generally impressed by their first visit to a Chinese factory. Working conditions will seem Dickensian and the machinery outdated; there seem to be few safety precautions, and stacks of rusting spare parts in the yard may arouse suspicions that there are distribution problems. Nowadays the Chinese quickly recognize these shortcomings and list what is being done to remedy them; on the other hand western businessmen in the medical equipment field leave China depressed that there is no market for their wares because they are already being produced to high standards and in good conditions.

Since 1976 industry has prospered and enjoyed a new lease of life – it is the second priority after agriculture in the Four Modernizations. Although industry occupies 20 per cent of the workforce, it provides less than 45 per cent of the gross national product. Many efforts are being made to increase productivity. New management structures have been installed and the old 'revolutionary committee' abolished. The technician has been reinstated to his former standing. Wage increases and bonus and incentive schemes have been introduced. New forms of co-operation with overseas companies are being sought, from buying machinery to introducing and translating overseas technical material, as well as joint investment projects.

Industry first came to China during the 'self-strengthening' movement of the 1860s, when the Chinese began to construct their own arsenals and shipyards – a move prompted by their increasing contact with foreign powers and their superiority in warfare. After 1896 foreign industry was allowed to establish itself in the treaty ports, and later when the Japanese established themselves in Manchuria industry was developed there.

The immediate task after the Revolution was to get basic services such as transport and coal production moving again. By 1953 the Communist government was ready to introduce the First Five-year Plan, which relied heavily on the Russian model, emphasizing heavy industry and a rigid, centrally planned structure. In the north-east at Anshan the iron and steel industry was built up; oil was found in Xinjiang; a bridge was constructed over the Yangtse at Wuhan; and an ambitious hydroelectric power station was begun on the Yellow River at the Sanmen gorge. Several key cities in the interior were chosen for special assistance in industrial development.

In 1956 the collectivization of industrial enterprises took place – the state took over those large enterprises which the national capitalists had been allowed to keep, and individual handicraft and cottage industries were collectivized. Between 1956 and 1958 economists led by Chen Yun discussed decentralization and self-management plans. The Great Leap Forward was Mao's attempt to accelerate this process: powers of decision were allowed at provincial, municipal and factory level.

Under the banner of 'walking on two legs' small factories in the countryside were encouraged. These were the years of the so-called 'backyard furnaces', producing inferior steel from old pots and pans. The movement foundered because of the poor quality of the goods and the general inexperience of the people in charge of these enterprises, coupled with the detrimental effect of bad harvests. In 1961 and 1962 ideas about decentralization and self-management were again introduced, with an emphasis on self-reliance after the withdrawal of the Russian presence.

Oil drilling was developed: in the wastes of the north-east Daqing grew from a minor pioneering settlement of 1000 people into today's important township of 500,000 inhabitants. China is now almost self-sufficient in oil; her largest customer is Japan.

Although industrial development continued during the Cultural Revolution, industry, like every other walk of life in China, was affected by politics: factories were run by revolutionary committees, the triple alliance of workers, technicians and cadres. Creativity in the technical field was branded as 'following the capitalist road', and the over-assiduous book-keeper was accused of placing too much emphasis on profit. The over-riding effect was stagnation, because people became unwilling to exert themselves.

In the early 1970s the pragmatists in the Chinese leadership opened up trade links with the West. In 1975 the State Council issued three documents which made recommendations for the recovery of industry and the economy as a whole. When Deng Xiaoping came under attack in 1976 they were attributed to him and dubbed 'The Three Poisonous Weeds'. These documents called for the importation of advanced technology, the need to reallocate labour and raw materials, improvement in the quality and quantity of goods, and changes in management structure and wages. He had to wait until 1977 before he could begin to put these ideas into practice. In that year, when the Four Modernizations programme was announced, emphasis was placed on capital construction projects such as iron and steel works and dams.

However, by late 1979 readjustment was taking place – ambitious foreign contracts went unsigned and the emphasis lay on operating existing heavy industry more economically. The old economists – such as Chen Yun, Hu Qiaomu and Xue Muqiao – have reintroduced the discussions on decentralization, self-management, horizontal relationship between enterprises, and market forces with a socialist structure.

The State Planning Commission and the State Economic Commission are responsible for drawing up five-year and annual plans respectively. Under their aegis are ministries with responsibility for special areas such as mining, oil and light industry. They oversee investment, supplies, planning, research, their own large scale enterprises and purchases from overseas. Bureaux and corporations in the major cities act as local co-ordinators, in direct contact with the manufacturers. This rather centralized structure has proved problematical for smaller enterprises, and direct sales and supply contacts are being encouraged between factories. The rapid expansion of light industry is encouraged to boost the economy by supplying more consumer goods for the home market and for export. Overseas companies, hoping to do business with China, should contact the bureaux and corporations in Peking or in the relevant city if they are familiar with the market. It is only at an advanced stage of contracting that the Ministry will become involved.

The factory worker has seen several changes to his advantage – 1977, for instance, saw the first salary increases since 1963. At the factory level salaries are divided into eight grades (there are similar grades for other categories, such as cadres, teachers and engineers). The grade is based on job title, length of service, technical skill and conduct. New management structures – not always linked to the Party hierarchy – allow the worker greater say, and bonus and incentive schemes have been introduced.

Most factories operate three shifts a day, seven days a week. Each worker is allocated to a section which has two leaders, one of whom is a member of the appropriate trade union. The function of trades unions is basically one of welfare, although they also arrange the execution of incentive schemes and recreational activities. On a visit to a factory you will usually come across colourful charts recording each worker's progress. The unions organize crèche and nursery facilities, a clinic or first aid post, depending on the size of the factory; here medical treatment, which is also available to children and elderly parents, is free. The unions organize the canteen. Each factory usually has wash and shower facilities. The trades unions organize factory libraries, visits by theatre troupes, tickets for sports matches and youth activities. The factory may also provide accommodation in dormitories for young people, or they may own property which is at the disposal of the workers.

For the time being the extent of freedom to be allowed in the economy is still in the experimental stage. However, the goal is fixed – an acceptable increase in the standard of living by the year 2000 which will bring the Chinese worker to a level near that of his counterpart in western countries.

EDUCATION

When the Communist government took over in 1949 they were confronted with the task of rebuilding the shattered economy in a country where almost 90 per cent of the population was illiterate. Educational facilities were concentrated along the east coast and were run either by missionaries or by teachers steeped in Confucian notions of book learning and examinations. The government had to find the right balance between popularizing education and training a band of specialists who could make a major contribution in the reconstruction of China's economy. Indeed this dilemma has been at the heart of every educational policy adjustment or upheaval since 1949.

In the early 1950s the two went hand in hand. Specialized schools were set up and care was taken to accommodate intellectuals to win their support for the new government. Continuing in the style begun in Yan'an, mass literacy campaigns were implemented in the countryside; basic reading and instruction were given in the newly formed co-operatives, and the trade unions organized reading classes in factories. By the late 1950s during the Great Leap Forward the need to combine learning and labour was both a political ideal and a necessary expedient, and students participated in various building projects and in agricultural and factory work.

In the mid-1960s the Cultural Revolution was fomented in the schools and universities; the children of the Revolution were felt to be complacent: their educational ideas did not relate to the new economic and socialist system and were elitist. Schools erupted into chaos as teachers and intellectuals were harangued and assaulted by their pupils. The whole educational system and traditional beliefs and customs were attacked. During this period public transport and accommodation were free, and young people, often only thirteen or fourteen years of age, set off across China to attend massive rallies or follow revolutionary routes without consulting their parents. While many realized with the passing of time that they did not know what they were doing, it is also true that this period was often the only opportunity in a young person's life to travel across China.

By 1967 the schools and universities had been reopened in a new format – run by revolutionary committees made up of workers or peasants, the People's Liberation Army, teachers and students. For the next ten years the priority was politics – hours were spent in political study, the curriculum was steeped in political content, and the range and scope of subjects was reduced to a minimum. Examinations were regarded as revisionist, and the student who spoiled his exam paper was held up as a good example to all. Young people spent time working in factories or in the countryside, learning from the workers and peasants.

Since 1977 the priorities have been reversed and the political emphasis in education has shifted. Intellectuals have been reinstated as workers with the mind, and education is regarded as essential in the drive towards modernizing China. Examinations and degrees have been reintroduced; a wider range of subjects may be studied; there is now access to libraries which had been closed; research is encouraged, particularly in science; time spent in labour in the countryside or factories has been drastically reduced, and attention is given to relating it to the student's major subjects; and 'key schools' have been established at every level.

The delicate balance between educating the masses and training technicians for the new China now appears therefore to have swung in favour of the latter, with better facilities and prospects in the cities than in the countryside. Nonetheless an educational infrastructure exists, ranging from pre-school to university, by which the majority of children, even in remote areas, can look forward to eight years of education, even though facilities may often seem spartan to the visitor.

At the age of eight weeks children may be taken to crèches attached to factories or production brigades in communes, or organized by neighbourhood committees. (As an incentive to decrease the population growth, those intending to have only one child may have up to six months' maternity leave.) A fee is payable to cover board and childcare, and if medical attention is required the parents are usually asked to contribute 50 per cent of the expenses incurred – the total cost is around 13 *yuan* per month. It is also possible for children to spend all week at the nursery, returning home on their parents' day off. Informal teaching begins in the nursery schools at the age of three, with games, singing and dancing; art, Chinese and arithmetic are also introduced. Visitors are always charmed by the quality of the performances given at kindergartens. A watchful eye is kept on the children's health, and attention is given to their 'social education': children are taught to 'love the motherland, the people, labour, science and public property'.

Children progress at the age of six and a half to seven to primary school, where they stay for five years. Primary schools are organized on a district-to-district basis. The subjects begun at nursery school level are continued and developed; by the third year politics and nature studies are introduced, and in some schools English is taught too. In the fourth and fifth years children spend the equivalent of two weeks a year taking part in manual labour, usually of a very unstrenuous form such as working in a school workshop or weeding the school garden. Learning to 'love manual labour' is part of the education.

Middle school is divided into two levels – junior secondary for three years, and senior secondary for two years; in many rural areas education finishes after the junior secondary level. The *Peking Review* of 7 January 1980 quotes a figure of 4 per cent who will continue from middle school to some form of further education. Middle-school standards have been tightened and the scope of subjects broadened to include politics, Chinese, mathematics, chemistry, physics, biology, foreign languages, history, geography, hygiene, physical education, music and drawing. After the chaos of the Cultural Revolution discipline and respect for teachers and fellow-students are emphasized, as well as the importance of studying hard. One month a year is given over at this level to 'manual labour'.

The process of choosing a career or finding a job is the result of a combination of factors: while the state, in the form of the local authority, is responsible for allocating students to jobs, the kind of job given depends on the student's natural abilities, recommendation, availability at the time of graduation, and personal contacts. Alternatively students may put themselves forward for senior school and the prospect of college or university. For those who leave school at the age of sixteen after junior secondary level, there are opportunities for part-time courses for apprentices in classes attached to their factory or other place of work.

There are stiff entrance examinations for university places. At the end of the 1970s competition was particularly fierce. Many young people had missed their opportunity to enter university earlier because they had had to spend long years working in factories or in the countryside. Particularly talented students are sent to 'key schools', where standards are higher and the quality of teaching is better, and to which the government have allocated extra funds. University courses last a minimum of three years and discussion is taking place about lengthening this period. Recently the 'television university' has become extremely popular in an atmosphere where all young people are eager to learn now that the possibilities of better jobs and even study abroad have increased.

From the point of view of extra-curricular activities, the major cities have children's palaces where the young can go after school for activities such as sports and music. Political organizations include the Young Pioneers who can be joined at primary school level and wear red scarves around their necks; membership is awarded to those who behave well and show that they are well adjusted. At secondary level there is the Communist Youth League which organizes various social and political activities; membership of this group is harder to obtain. Active membership is a good qualification for future entry into the Communist Party, but no guarantee of membership.

MEDICAL CARE

Modern Medicine
From less than one fully trained doctor per 10,000 people in 1949, China now has one medical worker per 100 people. From a situation where most medical facilities were concentrated in the cities, a countrywide network of healthcare has been established from city and county hospitals down to health workers in commune production teams and urban neighbourhood committees. Diseases endemic in most underdeveloped countries have been brought under control by the combined efforts of extensive vaccination and immunization campaigns and educational work on basic hygiene and sanitation. In many ways a model for other Third World countries, China has tackled the problem of modernization of the health services through a band of highly trained specialists and dissemination of a basic knowledge of medical care to a wider number of people.

When the Communists came to power in 1949 they were confronted with a population of 500 million ignorant on matters of health, some 10,000–12,000 western-style doctors, and over 300,000 doctors trained in traditional Chinese medicine and capable of treating a host of endemic diseases. The priorities decided by the National Health Care Conference held in 1950 were first, the direction of health work towards the masses and the poor; second, the development of a preventive medicine programme of inoculation and education; third, the retraining of the traditional Chinese doctors, who despite their reputation as charlatans were familiar with the people and could be retrained, and indeed in the liberated areas had been the only people to provide some kind of treatment for wounded soldiers; and fourth, the 'mass campaigns', involving ordinary people up and down the country in campaigns to eradicate pests and disease. The first 'mass campaigns' were against venereal disease and the Four Pests – flies, mosquitoes, bedbugs and rats – with an inoculation programme against smallpox, bubonic plague, cholera and typhus.

Short-term training programmes were begun for assistant doctors, to last not more than three years, and in the meantime local cadres or village leaders were called to meetings held by mobile medical demonstration teams and given illustrated lectures on the effects, symptoms and causes of diseases, first venereal disease and later other common skin diseases such as kalahazar, schistosomiasis, filariasis, hookworm, ringworm and leprosy. A simplified system of identification was worked out based on a twelve-point questionnaire, armed with which the village leaders returned to their homes. Often a competitive spirit was fostered in an attempt to break down the fears and prejudices of the ordinary people.

In 1956 the controversy over the value of Chinese medicine was sparked off again by Chairman Mao, and by 1958 medical students were required to spend six months of their training course studying Chinese medicine. After the enthusiasm of the Great Leap Forward and the stress on self-reliance the emphasis changed in the direction of modernization and research, concentrated in the eastern cities, which gave rise to Mao's Instruction on Public Healthwork of 25 June 1959. He called for medical personnel to concentrate on the rural areas since medicine was not reaching the peasantry, and declared that medical courses were long and too theoretical – a training period of three years was adequate and should be combined with practical sessions. The priority was to find cures for common ailments.

In response to this directive some 10,000 medical mobile units were formed to go to the countryside; they were to work in the spheres of preventive and therapeutic medicine, health education and family planning. They served several communes at once and lived with the peasants in the spirit of the times, participating in their daily routine of fetching and carrying and even tending the land; at this stage they still received salaries. They carried out immunization programmes, educated people on the dangers of waterborne diseases, eliminated lice, set up sanitation systems in the villages, visited people in their homes and villages and began to train paramedical personnel from among the local people.

During the slack season – usually in the winter months – members of the production brigade and team were selected by their fellow-members for their 'political attitude', 'good general knowledge', and willingness and ability, to attend courses at the mobile medical unit centre. The title 'barefoot doctor' was first coined around 1968 as an affectionate nickname given by the peasants on the outskirts of Shanghai to these health workers who spent part of their time working barefoot in the paddy fields and part in their role as medical workers. Indeed the popular image of the barefoot doctor shows him or her working in the fields with a doctor's kit at the ready or visiting peasants working in the fields in order to treat them. Several popular films in the ten years following the Cultural Revolution were based on the theme of barefoot doctors – fighting in bad weather to find the correct medicinal herb and reach a sick patient with it, struggling to train as a doctor, dealing with the prejudices of traditional-style doctors.

In the mood of the time here were peasants among peasants, understanding the problems and fears of peasants, dealing with their particular recurrent illnesses. The first winter months of study are followed by a summer's practical experience with a return for more advance training in the winter. The courses concentrate on prevention, diagnosis, treatment and nursing. Barefoot doctors are usually attached to the commune brigade; two work on a part-time basis, and they are paid on work points. At the commune level there is a hospital with fully trained staff. At the production team level there are two health workers, who will have followed shorter courses in first aid and sanitation, and are in charge of the family planning rota and immunization programmes; they also act as local midwives.

In 1956 the co-operative medical scheme was set up: each member of a brigade pays around 1 *yuan* a year, and the public welfare fund contributes a lump sum to pay for maintenance costs and supplies at the clinic, as well as medicine and treatment; each patient pays about 5 *fen* per consultation. Serious or complicated cases are passed on to the commune hospital and if necessary to the town or city hospital, and if heavy expenses are incurred for serious operations the brigade will assist. The growth and use of medicinal herbs is encouraged as an economic matter and as part of the self-sufficiency programme. Often each clinic will have a small plot attached, and the barefoot doctors' teaching manual devotes a large section to the types and use of medicinal herbs.

Today there are over 1,300,000 barefoot doctors and some 3,600,000 health workers. In densely populated areas and around the cities students may go to city hospitals to study as barefoot doctors or spend time in their commune clinic. The role of the mobile medical teams has been shifted to the outlying border regions, where they will work for periods of six months to two years. The role of the barefoot doctors is currently being reappraised.

The cities offer medical facilities at every level. Most factories have their own clinic; workers can participate in the government labour insurance scheme and receive free medical care with reductions for members of their immediate family. On the factory floor is the equivalent of the St John's Ambulance man – worker doctors who have followed short courses in first aid and the rudiments of acupuncture, and who help in prevention work. At the neighbourhood committee level there are again clinics dealing with common illnesses and first aid stations run by volunteers – usually women who monitor family planning and the immunization programme.

To the western eye, used to the comforts and excessive cleanliness of a highly developed medical service, the Chinese facilities may seem somewhat primitive – you will look in vain for central heating, and the equipment, not to mention some of the tests used, is outdated. Having established a base, it seems the Chinese are now poised to go on to modernization and more specialization. In 1977 the length of medical courses was increased to six years again. Researchers and surgeons who went into hiding during the Cultural Revolution have been invited to take up their old positions, continue with their work, and pass their knowledge on to the younger generation.

Today the 'patriotic health campaign' is revived at least once a year to ensure that not only the Four Pests but also the epidemic diseases, such as cholera, smallpox and tuberculosis, are kept under control by intensive inoculation programmes. In a city such as Shanghai the average life expectancy has increased from 42 years for men and 45.6 years for women in 1951 to 70.6 for men and 75.5 for women in 1979. At the other end of the scale infant mortality has been reduced from 56.5 per cent in 1949 to 9.37 per cent in 1979. Population experts aim to bring the growth of China's population down to 5 per 1000 by 1985. With government approval late marriage is advocated and financial incentives are awarded to those couples who pledge to have only one child. Contraception advice and abortion are available to young married couples.

In some centres pioneering work has been carried out in the field of cancer research, the treatment of burns and reimplantation of limbs. However at a more mundane level the priorities remain those of increasing the number and quality of hospital beds and general medical facilities, and until the problem of bringing a clean water supply to every household in the cities has been solved certain associated diseases will be difficult to eradicate.

Traditional Medicine
'Chinese medicine and pharmacology are a great treasure-house,' wrote Chairman Mao, 'and efforts should be made to explore them and raise them to a higher level.' Chinese traditional medicine differs from western medicine in that its application is based on years of experience and precedent rather than a strictly scientific approach. In the West it is now seen as either a magical cure-all or the gimmick of a Communist regime. Every pharmacy in China today has a range of both Chinese and western-style drugs. The concept of Chinese versus western medicine only arose in the nineteenth century with the foreign presence, when China was faced with the choice of following western courses of treatment or doing things her own familiar way. The general policy of the new Republic in 1911 was to follow western techniques, and to discard Chinese medicine which represented yet another facet of China's backwardness. However, some people began to explore Chinese medicine, developing it and linking it to modern techniques in a move to preserve national identity and self-esteem.

In 1921 Yan Xishan, the warlord of Shanxi Province, set up a Society for the Reform of Chinese Medicine, whose chief task was to develop a system of medicine which was both scientific and Chinese. In 1927 the Nationalist government wanted to do away with Chinese traditional methods of medicine altogether; this provoked such an outcry from articulate and involved members of the government and public that a token gesture, the Institute of National Medicine, was set up. Several people took up the cause of establishing a scientific foundation for Chinese medicine, seeking a rationale for the concepts of *yin* and *yang*.

As a forward-thinking force the Communists would have been expected to disapprove of Chinese medicine; however they soon recognized that any kind of medical facilities were better than none. In the early 1950s while the methods of medicine used were based on the Russian model, improvement classes were held for traditional-style doctors who would then be able to participate in the new health movements. The concept of Chinese medicine was to be a political weapon as an example of the accumulated wisdom of the masses vis-à-vis the elitist medical knowledge of the bourgeois-trained doctors, and as a nationalistic example of .

China's rich heritage. After 1954 schools and hospitals specializing in Chinese medicine were opened; hospital wards often had one traditional Chinese doctor attached, and the study of Chinese medicine was included in medical courses.

Major areas of success have been in the field of acupuncture anaesthesia, the treatment of burns, deaf mutes, and a non-invasive alternative to surgery, as for example in the treatment of gallstones. The use of Chinese traditional medicine is also an economic measure: in the countryside, where supply is always a problem, 'home-grown' medicine ensures a well-stocked pharmacy, and treatment by acupuncture does not require complex machinery.

Whereas western medical history can be traced somewhat tenuously to Hippocrates, the sources of Chinese medicine are found in the *Yellow Emperor's Classic of Internal Medicine*, a treatise on medicine published in the third century BC. The wisdom it contains is attributed to the mythical 'Yellow Emperor', who is said to have lived in the third millennium BC. It is in nature more a philosophical treatise than a practical guide, relating the harmony of the world order, the *yin* and *yang*, to the body. The *Book of History* of the historian Sima Qian, written in the Han dynasty, includes biographies of two famous physicians, Bian Jue and Zang Gong. It records how the former used acupuncture to bring a man out of a coma, and reveals his diagnostic methods, which placed particular emphasis on the pulse, the patient's environment, face colour, tongue and odours, and on asking the patient questions about himself.

Acupuncture itself is thought to have developed from massage — applying pressure on or near inflamed areas. Massage is one of the oldest forms of therapy in China. Its use ranges from relieving lumbago to relaxing children's eyes — children at school usually pause for several minutes to massage their eyes during lesson time. The first acupuncture needles were made of stone, and gold and silver needles have been found in Han dynasty tombs dating back to the second century BC. An illness was seen as a temporary imbalance in the relationship between *yin* and *yang* by the accumulation or uneven distribution of *qi*, a kind of life force which flowed along twelve *jing* or abstract 'paths' in the body. Along these abstract lines lay some 360 points, where by applying the acupuncture needle this imbalance could be restored.

Moxibustion is a type of cauterization process whereby moxa wool sticks (moxa is a Chinese wormwood) are slowly burned over an affected area or on acupuncture points; the technique can also be used in conjunction with acupuncture needles. While all the various acupuncture points are still known, the barefoot doctor is usually acquainted with only around seventy points. There are nine different kinds and sizes of needles in three categories — for insertion into the skin, for use on the surface, and for blood letting. The area to be injected is cleaned with alcohol and the needles are inserted rapidly, with slower movement as they penetrate the tissues; the needles may be inserted at different angles and to different depths. Certain points are recognized as being beneficial in the case of different ailments, and the needle is generally twirled or vibrated on the spot for a short period until the pain is alleviated somewhat and the required numbing sensation is experienced in the area where the needle was inserted.

The major development in the use of acupuncture has of course been acupuncture anaesthesia, which was developed in the late 1950s after being used to reduce pain in post-operative cases. Now acupuncture is regularly used for all kinds of operations as an alternative to standard anaesthetics. An important part of the preparation involves gaining the patient's confidence and selecting the correct sites for insertion of the needles. Usually a light sedative is given beforehand. At the pioneering stage up to eighty needles were inserted and had to be vibrated constantly for a period of twenty minutes at 120 twirls a minute. The art has now been refined with practice and seven needles are usually enough; they are inserted for twenty minutes or until the patient has the sensation of *de qi* – a slight soreness, distension, heaviness and numbness at the place where the needle has been inserted – and the acupuncturist has a sensation that his hand is being sucked in. Nowadays the needles are connected to a small battery of six to nine volts. There are varying interpretations of how acupuncture anaesthesia works, but the many advantages are obvious – the patient does not have to recover from the after-effects of a standard anaesthetic, and the internal organs continue to function during the operation.

The pharmocopia of Chinese medicine is exotic, and a visit to a Chinese pharmacy is a bewildering experience as one gazes at drawers and piles of strange roots, deer's tails, snakes and so on. The standard *materia medica* which is still referred to today was compiled in the Ming dynasty by Li Shizhen (1518–93), and in recent years many folk remedies have been collected from among the people. Chinese herbal medicine works perhaps more slowly than western medicine, and its main tenet is to cure the cause rather than the symptom, thus avoiding surgery. Research is being carried out on combining Chinese and western medicine, which can mean compounding herbal medicine into pill or capsule form instead of the traditional infusion; in the case of heart attacks, while strong, western-style drugs or methods of resuscitation may be given, Chinese medicine will be given to stimulate blood circulation. There is evidence that it has been possible to expel gallstones without resorting to surgery, and some progress has been made in reducing the size of malignant tumours and the side-effects of radiotherapy. Serious burn cases have been treated with *Ilex chinensis*, which helps the burn to heal, reducing shock and loss of fluid. A wealth of work remains to be done on traditional Chinese medicine – from exploring the ancient classics to finding new adaptations of old methods and researching a scientific base to acupuncture.

FAMILY LIFE

Many people are under the impression that the family unit has been destroyed in China; in fact it is as vital an economic and social force today as it ever was. Based on reciprocity and respect, it ensures that the elderly are cared for and that the younger and more able-bodied can go out to work, certain that there will be somebody at home to cook meals and look after the very young. Morality in China is very strict: pre-marital sex is frowned upon, there are harsh penalties for rape, and the mother of an illegitimate child will suffer a cut in wages.

While there are always exceptions, young people tend to marry close to home – from the same district or village. Once two young people are seen out together it is taken for granted that they will marry each other. While by the standards of many western countries this may seem rather backward, it is a far cry from the days of arranged marriages and go-betweens, when young people were pledged to another family at a very early age; this arrangement was seen above all as an economic one – losing an extra mouth to feed or gaining an additional pair of hands to help in the house. During the Cultural Revolution all mention of love and the problems that

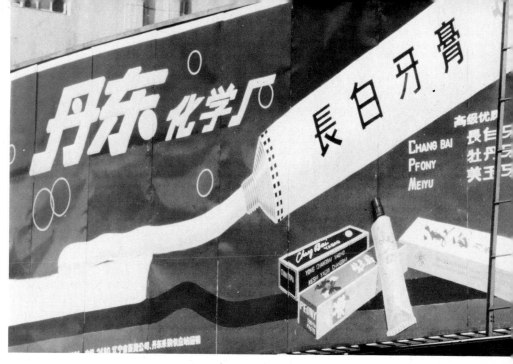

A toothpaste advert

Left Bamboo chairs, baskets and shoots.
Right Open-fronted shops, typical of southern China

An English lesson: English is the second language in China and children start studying it at primary school

Traditional domestic architecture in southern China

A typical northern-style house

Northern farmhouses and hand-ploughs

Houseboats on a canal – another form of accommodation

young people face were eradicated from films, books and plays, but fortunately the balance has now been restored. When two people decide that they want to marry they apply to their respective places of work, who then check that there is no impediment to the marriage. When permission has been granted the young people then go to the district headquarters to register, or, in the countryside, to the commune.

The wedding is usually celebrated with a special meal in a restaurant. Gifts such as silk bedspreads form part of the trousseau, and the couple's parents will have saved up to help them buy furniture. In the city, where space is precious and living conditions often cramped, the couple may have to live with one or other set of parents until a flat becomes available. In the countryside a separate house, or an extension on an existing house, is built to accommodate the newly-weds. Traditionally it is the bride who goes to live with her husband's family, a custom which is slowly being changed. Nursery facilities enable both parents to work; nurseries have week-long living-in facilities, but the day nursery is more commonly used. If in the bigger cities one of the partners works in a factory a long way from home, he or she will stay there for the week, coming home on the day off. Sometimes husbands and wives are separated for a year at a time at opposite ends of the country, although this situation is now being rectified. Divorce is legal but frowned upon, and everything is done by society to keep marriages together for the sake of the children.

The average individual wage is around 60 *yuan* per month, and most categories of work have an eight-grade wage scale from 30 to 120 *yuan*. Income and expenditure will vary, depending on the number of working people in a household, which may consist of the nuclear family of two adults and two children or include grandparents, single young people, a married couple and their children. Rent in the city is usually around 3–5 per cent of the total family income, and food costs about 15 *yuan* per person per month. A small amount goes in electricity, nursery fees have to be paid, and there are bus fares to work; if there are elderly people in the household who have not worked and are therefore not entitled to a pension, they have to be supported. Food markets usually open very early in the morning, and it is quite common for the wife to get up early in order to shop before going to work; equally the husband may do the shopping on his way home from work on his bicycle. If children come home from school before their parents they are often responsible for preparing a meal. Many basic items of food, and soap, are rationed; this subject, and Chinese home cooking, are discussed on pages 77–8. Cotton too is rationed, allowing each person one new outfit of clothes per year.

The standard of living is very simple – only newly-built apartment blocks in the cities have gas and running water; elsewhere water is taken from a tap in the courtyard or some other central point. Food is cooked over small, free-standing stoves fuelled by coal cakes made of coal dust and glue, which can often be seen spread out to dry on the pavement.

The major consumer items are bicycles and watches. Luxury goods are relatively expensive – a watch starts at 100 *yuan*, bicycles are from 180, and radios from 30 to 40 *yuan*. Some families have their own televisions, although there is usually one in the quarter or in the production team for communal watching. In the north of China the traditional bed is the *kang*, made of stone and heated underneath. In the daytime the bedding is neatly folded away and the *kang* is used for sitting on. There is a growing mood of consumer-consciousness in China today – foreign and

Chinese-made electrical goods are beginning to appear in the shops, and there is more freedom and variety in dress than there used to be.

After the day's work is over, listening to the radio or watching television are popular activities. Groups of men will often be seen playing cards or chess. There is no institution similar to the bar, and all-night snack bars serving noodles or *jiaozi* (a kind of ravioli) and beer are largely for the benefit of shift workers; the Chinese prefer to gather in each other's houses to drink and talk. In many cities the tea house is still popular, particularly with retired men. Women and girls will usually take advantage of their spare time in the evenings to knit the brightly coloured jumpers worn under the cotton jackets which give rise to the impression that Chinese people all wear the same clothes. Embroidery is also popular, for pillow cases and the lace crochet mats which adorn every dressing table. Sundays and holidays can mean a day out to a park or a visit to a historic monument, an opportunity to take photographs posing in one's best clothes. The cinema and theatre are also popular, although one of the main problems is obtaining tickets.

Culture

ENTERTAINMENT AND THE ARTS

The briefest trip to China will bring the visitor into contact with a wide range of aspects of modern China's cultural life. They might include daring acrobatics shows, endearing song and dance performances by schoolchildren, a visit to the Palace Museum in Peking to admire some examples of classical Chinese art, or an evening at the opera to meet the heroes of the most popular Chinese novels. Visits by western tourists to the theatre or the acrobatics will be arranged when possible by Luxing she guides.

The late 1970s and early 1980s have seen a revival and blossoming in every sphere of Chinese cultural life. From a very young age Chinese children are taught the arts of calligraphy, dancing and singing. Copying – a cardinal sin in the West – has long been a traditional method of learning in China; most schoolchildren can turn out a passable poem or painting, and young peasants or workers will try their hand at a poem to commemorate some political event. Old painters are taking up their brushes again, and can make a painting of plum blossom without an electric pylon in the background. Famous singers return to the stage, acclaimed by the masses, to pass on their skills to the younger generation. The colourful costumes of valiant heroes from popular operas have been taken out of their mothballs, films made before the Cultural Revolution are on show again, and people flock to see exhibitions of Chinese arts and crafts from seals to handicrafts and consumer items.

It is hard for westerners to understand how politics and art can be so closely linked that a change of personalities in the government can mean liberalization in the arts, or the reverse. In socialist philosophy 'bourgeois art' is seen as the prerogative of those with education and leisure, a minority interest which is imposed on the majority as the criterion of what is good and pleasing. Since the early twentieth century Chinese artists and politicians have been discussing how art and culture could and should reflect the life of ordinary people, and the role of art as an educational tool.

After the Republic was established in 1911, intellectuals gradually realized that no great changes could be made in Chinese society unless ordinary people could read and write. For 2000 years written Chinese had existed mostly in a classical form which bore no relation to the way people spoke, and was therefore an obstacle to the achievement of universal literacy. These intellectuals sought to overthrow the old tenets of Confucianism, and championed votes for women and the use of the vernacular (ie *baihua*, the language as spoken) in contemporary writing and newspapers. In 1919 the May Fourth Uprising of students took place, revolting against the Treaty of Versailles and the weak government who had acceded to its unfair conditions (see page 24). This uprising brought the students and ordinary people closer together, and by 1920 publishing companies were producing books in vernacular Chinese.

The 1920s and 1930s was a period of experimentation in the arts, centred on Shanghai. Novels were produced, that had been influenced by French Naturalist writers such as Zola and Hugo, or by the Russians, particularly Gorki. Western-style spoken drama was experimented with, and Shanghai became the centre of a flourishing film industry. Writers and artists involved themselves in the political controversies of the time, such as the need to unite against Japanese invasion.

Yan'an was the next landmark in modern Chinese culture. By the time the Communists reached their base at Yan'an in Shaanxi Province and established a base with its own universities, arts workshops and newspapers, these largely town-bred intellectuals were faced with attempting to make contact with the peasants. Drama and music became the most important forms to be developed, and the ancient dance of the north-west, the *yangge*, and local opera were adapted to revolutionary themes. At this period were sown the seeds of such famous plays as *The White-haired Girl*, and many of the plays and operas which people flock to see today were first performed then. In 1942 Mao conducted a 'Forum on Arts and Literature', which has been used ever since as the guideline for artistic policies in modern China. In it he coined the phrase 'Art should serve the people', and expanded on Lenin's notion that art was the cog-wheel of the Revolution.

The post-liberation era used the arts as a tool of propaganda, but considerable freedom was allowed and traditional forms of the arts were used as much as new ones. This gave rise to Mao's criticism in 1963 that too many Chinese plays were peopled with 'ghosts, emperors and princes, generals and ministers, gifted scholars and beauties', and as such had little to do with the problems of a modern China tracing the road to socialism. In 1964, therefore, a festival of Peking operas on contemporary themes was held.

Since the Yuan dynasty theatrical productions had often been used as a way of highlighting some dissatisfaction with the government of the day, and it was in this spirit that Wu Han, the Mayor of Peking, wrote in 1965 a play called *Hai Rui* ('Dismissed from Office'). Yao Wenyuan (number three in the Gang of Four) wrote articles interpreting the play as an attack on the recent dismissal of the Defence Minister, Peng Dehuai. In this way the seeds of the Cultural Revolution were sown; it was a factional struggle which used the arts, among other things, as a weapon, and in its efforts to purify the Revolution and bring about a levelling down of society it led to the suicide, imprisonment or enforced retirement of many artists, while others were sent to do forced labour in the fields.

During the turmoil of 1965 and 1966 Jiang Qing, Mao's wife, was establishing herself as doyenne of the arts. In 1966 she persuaded Lin Biao, commander-in-chief of the armed forces, to let her hold a forum on arts and literature in Shanghai, where she encouraged the soldiers to take up pens and start writing themselves. She gradually expanded her base and went on to develop her revolutionary model opera and ballet. The people lived on this cultural diet for ten years. The best-known ballets were *The Red Detachment of Women* and *The White-haired Girl*, and among the operas were *Taking Tiger Mountain by Storm* and *Sha Jia Bang*, the latter set in a guerrilla base area. She also took credit for the Yellow River

Symphony. In these works all life and realism were taken out of the original storyline and replaced by fiercely determined heroes and heroines with flashing eyes, motivated only by the call of the Chairman or the Revolution.

Now that the Gang of Four have gone and the excesses of the Cultural Revolution have been repudiated the Chinese people can engage in the arts with a new sense of excitement. Chinese audiences are by no means as reverential as western ones. During a performance there may be a hubbub of chatter or desultory clapping, and the Chinese will laugh mercilessly at any slip. The political content of the current spate of revivals in the performing arts is much less than before, and to the foreign visitor may not be apparent at all. It is a long-standing tradition of the Chinese theatre that a play should have a moral.

Chinese theatre first came into its own in the Yuan dynasty when the Chinese scholar classes went out of business under the Mongol rule and turned to playwriting as a means of livelihood and of criticizing the government. Most traditional Chinese theatre is more aptly termed opera, since it is largely sung – the songs encapsulate the main events of the story. The spoken play is a twentieth-century borrowing from the West. The most famous form of opera is the Peking opera. Local operas are given in the local dialect and often the music will be of a different quality – for example in the south it is usually described as being higher and gentler than the more strident music of the north. Traditionally all parts were played by men who would specialize in interpreting one kind of role, such as a clown, a female role or an official.

For the foreigner, unattuned to the music and at a loss to understand the words, the most attractive aspect of the opera will be the spectacle of the costumes. The painted faces quickly enable one to distinguish heroes from villains. The musical accompaniment comes from a small ensemble at the side of the stage, often visible behind a net screen, who perform on traditional Chinese instruments: the gong is particularly important and used very evocatively, and other instruments include the Chinese violin and the Chinese lute. A battle scene provides an excellent excuse for a lively display of martial arts. The subject matter of recent productions has ranged from stories taken from popular novels such as *The Water Margin* and *Monkey*, to the Opium Wars or the secret societies of the Taiping Rebellion, or more modern themes such as the struggle of a young girl to marry the man of her choice, or the saga of Mao's first wife, now brought into the limelight by way of contrast with Jiang Qing.

Films have followed a similar trend with the revival of pre-Cultural Revolution favourites; they cover all topics from the underground in Shanghai to the classic novel *The Dream of the Red Chamber*. The major film studios are in Shanghai and Changchun. Some imaginative work has been done in the field of cartoons, and in adapting Chinese traditional painting to this form.

Acrobatics are perhaps the most universally popular form of entertainment, since their displays of agility and verve make no demands on people's linguistic capabilities, technical knowledge or intellectual capacity. Acrobatics used to be a family business – passed from generation to generation and performed in the streets – right up to the Cultural Revolution. They date back 2000 years to the Han dynasty, according to the evidence of Han tombstones, and had reached a high degree of sophistication by the Tang dynasty. Most big towns today boast their own acrobatics troupe, and children start training as early as seven years old. The acts range from the lion dance to balancing piles of plates on the end of a baton from a monocycle, and there will usually be a couple of comic interludes such as clowns mimicking the skills of the artistes.

Chinese concert programmes usually mix western-influenced orchestral-type music and Chinese folk music – folk tunes adapted and given revolutionary titles. After a long silence Mozart was heard again on Chinese radio in the spring of 1977, and since that time many western orchestras have paid visits. Chinese musical instruments are versatile and easy on the ear. The main ones are the *er hu* – a kind of two-stringed violin; the *pipa* – the Chinese lute; the *qin*; and the *zheng* – two instruments similar to the zither. The *sheng* is a kind of mouth organ, and the *suo na* a trumpet, while the *dizi* is the Chinese flute. Gongs and drums are also used to good dramatic effect. Nowadays young people are showing more interest in modern western music, and particularly the pop music of Taiwan and Hong Kong.

A section on culture cannot be complete without some mention of Chinese literature; the Chinese are avid readers, and the Chinese word for civilization embodies the notion of literacy. The golden age of poetry was during the Tang dynasty. Until this period poetry was written according to very strict rules governing concordance of tone and rhyme, and the subject matter was often impersonal; the most famous poets of this period were Du Fu, Li Bai and Bai Ju Yi.

The Ming and Qing Dynasties saw the development of the novel: the characters in these classic works are all well known and loved by the Chinese, and usually embody certain distinctive vices or virtues. *The Romance of the Three Kingdoms*, with its heroes Zhu Geliang and Cao Cao, records the exploits of the 'Three Kingdom Period'. *The Journey to the West* or *Monkey* has already been mentioned; needless to say Monkey himself is a very popular and amusing stage figure, playing this role requires special interpretative skills. *The Water Margin* is a kind of Robin Hood saga about thirty-six wrongfully outlawed heroes, forced into hiding on Liang shan in Shandong Province by corrupt officialdom in the Song dynasty. This book was loved and often quoted by Mao.

The Dream of the Red Chamber by Cao Xueqin, variously translated as *The Story of the Stone* or *A Dream of Red Mansions*, charts the rise and fall of a wealthy family in the Qing Dynasty; thought to be semi-autobiographical, it was the first Chinese novel to pay attention to characterization and psychology. Today it is held up as an example of life in the feudal era, and people will discuss avidly the merits of the different characters – the hero Bao Yu, a revolutionary force rejecting his feudal background, and his cousin Bao Chai, the force of reaction.

Lu Xun, who died in 1936, is often referred to as China's Gorki; he was certainly influenced by him, and is considered China's leading modern writer. Lu Xun's work consists of short stories and essays which are often satirical in tone and highlight the evils of Chinese society. Many of his works have been translated into English. Recently other leading modern writers have been reinstated, such as Ba Jin, author of sagas such as *Family*, Mao Dun, who wrote about Shanghai life in *Midnight*, and Ding Ling, a woman writer and polemicist who had not enjoyed favour since the days of Yan'an. Translations of foreign authors, among them Cervantes and Shakespeare, have also been republished. The revival in literature is further emphasized by the number of local literary journals produced in universities and by youth groups.

The plastic arts, which reached their high point in the Song dynasty, have enjoyed a similar revival, and old masters may again practise traditional styles of painting or the art of the seal. Qi Baishi's works are once more reproduced by block printing –

Left A member of the Peking ballet applying his make-up: each character type has his own mask. *Right* A scene from the opera

A song and dance troupe in an elegant tableau

Scene from a modern Chinese opera

The individual figures of Arhats
(disciples) which are to be found in
many temples

Suzhou embroidery

Fan-painting

Some of the 77 million bicycles in China

he was particularly renowned for the lifelike quality of his paintings of everyday subjects such as prawns and cabbages. Other artists such as Xu Beihong, famous for his renderings of horses, are also enjoying renewed favour. Exhibitions of western art have been held in China in recent years, and students are being trained in western methods of painting and sculpture. The tradition of naive paintings of Hu xian is being continued, and experimental work is being done with woodcuts and wood block printing. The connoisseur looks for four elements in a traditional Chinese painting: how nature is reflected in the object or scene which has been painted, the contents of the couplet or poem, the calligraphy, and the painter's seal.

LANGUAGE AND ROMANIZATION

As in most foreign countries, English-speakers do not need to know the language of the country being visited. Today in China English is one of the most avidly studied languages; pupils start at an early age, and those who missed out when they were younger are busily trying to catch up. The Chinese language has always seemed impossibly difficult to outsiders, but it is by no means impenetrable. The word order is similar to that of English, and the tense system is far less complicated. The characters are difficult to memorize at first, but the learner gradually builds up a core of basic characters, which enables him or her to start making reasoned interpretations of new characters. However, in order to speak good Chinese the most important element to grasp from the beginning is the tone system.

Standard Chinese contains 400 monosyllables, each of which can be pronounced with four different tones or inflections of the voice, which changes the meaning of the syllable completely. Take the word *ma*, for instance: pronounced with a level inflection it means 'mother'; with a rising one, 'hemp'; with both a rising and a falling one, 'horse'; and with a falling inflection it means 'curse' or 'scold'.

mother 妈 mā
hemp 麻 má
horse 马 mǎ
curse or scold 骂 mà

There are many homophones in Chinese, and in spite of the differentiating inflections the Chinese often have to clarify which word they mean by drawing it in the air or 'spelling' the shape of the character.

Generally speaking, every character has at least two parts. The first is the radical – in classical Chinese there are 214 of these, classified from one to twenty-four in order of number of strokes, and these often provide clues to the meaning or classification of a character.

water 水 shuǐ
wood 木 mù
heart 心 xīn

In the case of *mǎ*, the word for 'horse' is also a radical. Its pictographic origins are clear. It recurs in the word for 'mother' and 'scold' as a phonetic element, indicating how the character should be pronounced. The character for 'mother' combines the radical for 'woman', indicating the meaning, and the element *ma*, indicating the pronunciation.

By no means all characters lend themselves to such simple analysis. Some do not contain a phonetic element, which means that one must just learn the pronunciation, and the meaning is derived by association, eg:

Sun 日 + moon 月 = bright 明   míng
or
woman 女 + child 子 = good 好 hǎo

Different systems have been sought to provide an alphabetic or phonetic rendering of Chinese. Apart from the difficulties it causes the foreigner, Chinese does not lend itself to computer programming, portable typewriters or teleprinters. To this end the Chinese Written Language Reform Committee was set up after 1949 to monitor the standardization of Chinese pronunciation, to simplify the characters and develop the system of romanization known as *Hanyu pinyin* which it is hoped will eventually replace characters.

In 1958 the *pinyin* system of romanization was adopted by the First National People's Congress. It became on 1 January 1979 the official transcription for Chinese names as used in diplomatic documents and foreign-language publications. Peking is now transcribed as Beijing, Canton as Guangzhou, and Teng Hsiao Ping has become Deng Xiaoping. *Pinyin* is taught in primary schools even before pupils start to tackle characters; road signs in major cities will be written in characters and *pinyin*, and both forms are also used on packaging. More and more filing systems and dictionaries are now listed according to the Roman alphabet.

Another daunting aspect of the Chinese language is the number of characters – some 60,000. The Chinese Written Language Reform Committee have identified 7000 characters in current use, of which 2000 constitute 90 per cent of the words to be found in a newspaper; 700–800 of these are the most commonly used characters, and they form the basis of both the primary school course and adult literacy classes.

Chinese has many dialects which are mutually unintelligible. There are eight major dialect regions in the country: north China, Jiangsu, Zhejiang (Shanghai/Hangzhou area), north Fujian, south Fujian, Guangdong (Cantonese) and Hakka. The last-named is an ancient form of Chinese brought to the south of China several centuries ago by émigrés from the north.

For centuries the written language was the unifying force in Chinese. One of the first measures of the Emperor Qin Shi Huang, who unified China in 221 BC, was to order the standardization of the language and style of writing by introducing the seal script which has given China linguistic continuity through the ages. The sources of standard Chinese or *putonghua* lie in the early Qing dynasty when the Manchus took control and needed a lingua franca for the purpose of government. They selected the Chinese spoken in and around Peking; this language was to become the language of the official class, and was known as Mandarin Chinese. It was also declared the official language of the Republican government in 1912, and in 1955 was again declared the universal language, *putonghua*. Today the major broadcasting stations use *putonghua*, and it is meant to be the medium for teaching and for use on all official occasions. Needless to say, most people speak their local dialect at home and with friends, and standard Chinese is kept for work and officialdom. Even then it is strongly tinged with inflections from the local dialect.

Romanization

The *pinyin* system has been used for transliterating Chinese words throughout this book. Here alternative spellings are given for all major resorts and cities in the Wade-Giles system and where there is a familiar anglicized version of a place or personal name, this has been used in preference to the *pinyin* version e.g., Sun Yatsen instead of Sun Zhongshan, Nanking instead of Nanjing.

Wade-Giles (or familiar spelling)	*Pinyin*
Amoy	Xiamen
Anhwei	Anhui
Canton	Guangzhou
Chekiang	Zhejiang
Chengchou	Zhengzhou
Chengteh (Jehol)	Chengde
Chengtu	Chengdu
Chingtehchen	Jingde zhen
Chungking	Chongqing
Foochow	Fuzhou
Fukien	Fujian
Hangchow	Hangzhou
Hofei	Hefei
Honan	Henan
Hopei	Hebei
Hupeh	Hubei
Kansu	Gansu
Kiangsu	Jiangsu
Kirin	Jilin
Kwangtung	Guangdong
Kweilin	Guilin
Lanchow	Lanzhou
Loyang	Luoyang
Mukden (Shenyang)	Shenyang
Nanking	Nanjing
Ningpo	Ningbo
Peking	Beijing
Shansi	Shanxi
Shensi	Shaanxi
Shantung	Shandong
Shaohsing	Shaoxing
Shichiachuang	Shijia zhuang
Sian	Xi'an
Sinkiang	Xinjiang
Soochow	Suzhou
Szechwan	Sichuan
Tatung	Datong
Tibet	Xizang
Tientsin	Tianjin
Tsinan	Jinan
Tsingtao	Qingdao

Urumchi	Wulumuqi
Hankow	Hankou (Wuhan)
Wuhsi	Wuxi
Yenan	Yan'an
Yihsing	Yixing

People

Mao Ts'e-tung	Mao Zedong
Teng Hsiao-P'ing	Deng Xiaoping
Chiang Ch'ing	Jiang Qing
Chou En-lai	Zhou Enlai

The *pinyin* is the simplest of all the romanization systems to follow as the letters correspond quite closely to their usual pronunciation in standard English. However there are a few vowels and consonants that require some explanation:

Pin yin	IPA	Corresponding Sound in English Word
j	[tɕ]	jeep
q	[tɕʻ]	cheer
x	[ɕ]	she
z	[ts]	reads
c	[tsʻ]	hats
ie	[iɛ]	yes
iu	[iou]	yoke

SPORTS AND GAMES

As yet there are few sporting holidays available in China. Hotels may provide table tennis or badminton facilities, and one or two hotels have swimming pools, but this situation will no doubt improve as more hotels are built and resort holidays are developed. Apart from this one may need a medical pass to use any of the swimming pools attached to clubs for foreigners or public swimming pools. North-east China has a potential for winter sports which is being explored, and trekking- and mountaineering-type holidays and expeditions may sometimes be arranged through the Chinese Mountaineering Association.

The tradition of physical fitness and alertness is an ancient one, and in recent years it has inevitably become caught up in the world of politics – from the days of 'ping-pong diplomacy' in the early 1970s to the admittance in 1980 of China into the Olympic Association. Physical fitness also forms part of the general awareness of civil defence; at intervals throughout the day in factories, offices and schools everyone will down tools and follow the call of the radio to 'keep fit and defend the mother country'. If an energetic visitor to China gets up at first light and goes to the nearest square or open patch of land he or she will find both young and old exercising – practising the ancient martial arts, *wushu*, from shadow boxing to sword fighting, or running and volleyball.

Every school and place of work has some kind of sports facilities; children will often stay on after normal lessons have finished for 'group activities' – sports of some kind or other. Apart from the energetic, fast-moving game of ping-pong, volleyball, basketball, badminton, swimming in the summer and ice sports in the winter are also popular, and football is increasing in popularity. *Taijiquan* is practised mostly by elderly people. Nowadays it means the slow-moving, graceful art of shadow boxing, but its origins lie in preparation for combat: controlled breathing ensures that all the limbs are used and all the internal organs exercised. There are two main sequences, one lasting four minutes and the other twenty minutes. Younger people prefer the faster-moving forms of the martial arts which entail the use of a wooden sword or knife. A demonstration of martial arts is often given during a visit to a school or children's palace.

Apart from games which require physical exertion, there are several ancient Chinese games which exercise the mental faculties – groups of men will often be seen seated on low cane chairs beneath the glow of a street lamp, engrossed in one of these or more modern card games. *Wei qi*, which the Japanese call *go*, dates back some two thousand years and involves understanding a situation and foreseeing likely moves; together with poetry writing, it used to be considered one of the essential skills of the all-round educated Chinese gentleman. The Chinese also have their own vernacular version of chess, which probably originated in Persia, as well as playing standard international chess. Recently bridge has been reintroduced into China, and majong sets are being sold to foreigners.

CUISINE

Chinese cuisine is not all shark's fin soup and bird's nests. From north to south every region has its share of delicacies – be it braised bear's paw or grouse in north-east China; dog in Guangzhou; or on a more mundane level noodles as wide as belts in the province of Shaanxi. All the different nationalities have also, of course, brought their specialities to the Chinese menu. The different types of cuisine, or a special oil, or famous soy sauce, are always one of the main things the traveller looks for when visiting another region in China. Haute cuisine to the Chinese is a delicate art – the skilled chef will produce a banquet which not only delights the olfactory senses and fills the stomach, but which pleases the eye by its presentation – hors d'oeuvres presented in the shape of a flower basket, carefully garnished fish, prawns in two sauces forming a peacock's tail design, or soup on which float egg-white ducks! The dish names themselves often have an imaginative ring. With their penchant for classification, the Chinese recognize four major culinary regions: Peking, the lower Yangtse, Sichuan and Guangzhou.

Peking-style cuisine is generally characterized as 'rich in flavour and well-seasoned'; the food of the north is generally saltier than that of the south. As the capital of China for ten centuries, Peking has assimilated the influence of the different nationalities who ruled or lived there; this is reflected in the many different types of restaurants, among them Mongolian, Manchu and Uighur, for whom lamb is the main meat. If you eat in a Moslem restaurant you will not find any pork at all, only lamb and beef. One of the great delicacies is *shuan yang rou*, like Japanese *sukiyaki* or French *fondue bourguignonne*, prepared at the table from wafer-thin slices of lamb which are dipped in a bowl of water in a charcoal-heated pot in the middle of the table. This dish was introduced to Peking some seventy years ago. In the same pot diners also cook cabbage, rice noodles and beancurd, while for flavour they make a sauce with soy, chilli, mustard, chopped shallots and parsley; and the meat is accompanied by sesame seed buns. Lamb is also eaten roasted, and in a version of the eastern European dish called shashlik. However for most Han Chinese pork is the favourite meat. In Peking this will be served boiled *(bai zhu)*, fried and stewed *(shao)* or roasted.

Peking-style cooking, also known as 'Tan family' cuisine, after a famous family of Peking chefs, has also been influenced by the Shandong style of cuisine, particularly in the preparation of seafood and soups. The best-known refinement of Peking-style cuisine is the Peking duck *(kaoya)*. The life of the Peking duck is short – about sixty-five days, during the latter part of which time they are force-fed on carbohydrate-rich grain until they weigh between 2.5 and 3 kg. Preparation for roasting involves inserting a sorghum stalk for support inside the cavity of a cleaned duck. Hot water is then poured over the duck to close the pores so that the fat will not escape during roasting. A malt sugar solution is painted over the bird, which gives it its characteristic golden colour and helps to make the skin crisper; then the duck is hung up to dry. The duck is then suspended in a wood-burning oven so that the heat does not fall directly on to it but radiates out from the oven wall. Special varieties of wood are used, such as jujube date, pear and peach, which all exude a pleasant aroma and produce relatively little smoke. When the duck is ready it is usually brought to the table and presented, to applause from the diners; then it is taken away to be sliced.

A Peking duck banquet will consist of dishes made from duck – there are over a hundred recipes to choose from. The hors d'oeuvres will consist of meat from the wing, marinaded in mustard sauce or set in gelatine; raw, marinaded gizzard; boiled, sliced duck liver; fried duck liver cooked with bamboo shoots and peppers; and so on. The roast duck itself is returned to the table sliced, to be accompanied by platefuls of thin pancakes *(bao bing)* or piles of sesame buns, saucers of scallions (small onions) and fermented sweet sauce. One chooses a piece of duck, dips the scallion in the sauce and rolls all three ingredients in a pancake, or inserts them in the bun. The tang of the scallion and sauce complements the fattiness of the duck. This course will be followed by a delicious duck soup. *Basi pingguo* (toffee apples) or fresh fruit in season will be the dessert.

Sichuanese-style cuisine is renowned throughout China for being hot and peppery. The late Chairman Mao was known to be fond of hot food – his home province of Hunan also favours the use of chillies in cooking, which is probably the origin of the saying 'If it's not hot, it's not revolutionary.' The climate and soil of Sichuan have provided a wide range of food and vegetables through the ages. Snack shops selling two hundred varieties of snacks such as rice dumplings and ravioli, and tea houses, still flourish, while the free markets offer a wide range of prepared foods such as sausages and the traditional Sichuan salted vegetables, which are popular throughout China. Unlike the cuisine of Peking, which has often emanated originally from the royal kitchens, it is perhaps a reflection of the natural wealth of Sichuan that the renowned dishes are to be found at every level of society and could perhaps best be described as farmhouse-style. A typical dish is the simple *dan dan mian* or 'pole-carried noodles' which are served cold and in a hot chilli sauce; their name comes from the way they were sold by street vendors, on trays hung from shoulder poles. Another is *Chen mapo doufu* – 'Old Mother Chen's beancurd'; for foreigners, who are usually disappointed by the blandness of beancurd, this dish, in a hot sauce, is probably one of the most acceptable ways to eat it. Other popular dishes are *gongbao rouding* – cubed meat, pork or chicken, served with peanuts and yet more chillies. Sichuanese food isn't laced only with chillies – *guai wei ji*, 'strange-tasting chicken', for instance, is piquant but combines salty and sweet flavours as well.

The influence of the lower Yangtse-style cuisine is to be found in the Shanghai area and Jiangsu Province. Yangzhou was one of China's great cultural centres, famous for its school of painting and sophisticated local style of opera, as well as being a wealthy river port. Jiangsu Province is often referred to as 'a land of fish and rice' because of its rich agricultural resources. Crabs, prawns, freshwater fish and eels are particularly popular, according to season. Yangzhou-style cuisine is prepared in such a way that it is oily but not greasy. Traditionally well done, without being overdone, the cooking method brings out the natural flavour of the main ingredients.

Of the four types of cuisine Guangzhouese (Cantonese), the style best known in the West, is probably the most exotic, because the area is semi-tropical, with a wide range of flora and fauna. Its main characteristic is that it is sweet and lightly cooked; the rest of China often looks askance at some of the eating habits of the Guangzhouese. From choice of ingredients to preparation Guangzhouese cuisine probably requires more skill than any type of Chinese cookery, and the Guangzhouese also pay great attention to the health-giving properties of their diet. Visitors may sample frog, snake or dog – indeed there are restaurants specializing in the latter. One of the specialities of Guangzhouese cuisine is the *dim sum* breakfast – steamed pastries with sweet and savoury fillings.

Eating in the Average Chinese Household

The Chinese household has few of the conveniences which westerners take for granted: there are few refrigerators, for instance, so shopping must be done daily, and the diet follows the seasons – from a glut of cabbage through the winter months to aubergines, tomatoes, peppers and water melons in the summer, with prices varying according to supply. The reintroduction of the free market in the last few years has meant that a wider variety of foods is available, even if at times they are slightly more expensive. During the week most people eat their main meals at their place of work. Where meals are to be cooked at home the Chinese exhibit an extraordinary degree of family co-operation – one will do the shopping, another will put the rice on before mother comes home, and so on; and if a grandparent lives with the family it often falls to him or her to prepare the food for the wage-earners.

The kitchen is a simple affair – the best-off have gas to cook by and cold running water, while others have to collect water and cook on a small, coal-fired stove. People living in the countryside, in areas not too far from major cities, are generally regarded as the best-off from the point of view of variety, freshness and availability of food. Nonetheless Chinese families can put on a superb spread when time permits, and produce food with all the skill of a chef in a restaurant. On average 15 *yuan* per person is spent on food monthly. Rice, grain, and oil are rationed – so whether a person eats at home or at work he or she will have to present coupons. The rice and grain allowance is substantial – nearly 14 kg per person per month, and some people boast about how many *liang* of rice they can eat in a sitting.

Generally speaking, the people north of the Yangtse prefer grain-based staples – so they eat steamed bread *(mantou)*, noodles, dumplings, or *wowotou* made from corn meal, whereas south of the river, where the conditions are more favourable for rice growing, rice is the staple diet and the people eat rice gruel for breakfast, have rice with their main meals and make many rice dishes. Brown rice is never served; the rice is always the polished kind, and there are great variations in quality. Much is made in the West of how protein-rich beancurd – *doufu* – is. It is one of the favourite Chinese dishes, but is often difficult to obtain.

The Chinese eat few dairy products – milk is for children and cheese and yogurt are generally indigestible, although there are shops which stock both, catering for the Moslem section of the community and to the national minorities such as Mongolians, Tibetans and Uighurs. Pork and chicken are the favourite meats – beef and lamb, regarded with distaste by many Chinese, are the food of the Moslem and national minorities.

Breakfast, if eaten at home, is generally a bowl of rice gruel with a few salted vegetables, or a fried pancake, steamed bread etc. The main meals of the day consist of rice plus a meat and vegetable dish. The Chinese generally drink tea throughout the day. Food is either eaten in the canteen or brought back to one's workplace in tins, and eaten more often than not with a spoon.

There are several traditions and festivals which call for special food. The arrival of a guest or the Spring Festival or just a day off are often an excuse to prepare *jiaozi* – a kind of ravioli consisting of a flour-and-water dough rolled very thin and filled with minced pork and vegetables. The preparation of *jiaozi* is a social occasion in itself. They are lightly boiled in water and eaten with soy sauce or vinegar; uncooked ones will be left for the following day, while cooked leftover ones will be fried the next day. Again much is made of how many one can eat in a session. The spring festival sees the same flurry of activity as the pre-Christmas rush in the West. Suddenly everyone in the city seems to have a chicken scratching around the yard, sweet things containing sesame seeds appear in the shops, and families prepare other sweets with glutinous rice flour and fillings of bean paste. The Dragon Boat Festival in May, commemorating the death of the poet Qu Yuan, is an excuse to prepare *zongzi* – glutinous rice with red beans or nuts wrapped in bamboo leaves. Later on, in late August and September, the mid-autumn festival provides an excuse to eat moon cakes and admire the full moon.

To sum up, the diet of the average Chinese still leaves a lot to be desired from the western dietician's point of view. Anaemia is common, particularly among young women, although there seems little evidence of rickets or other illnesses which are associated with a poor diet. There are constant problems of supply and distribution to the big cities and to the outlying areas. However, agriculture and food production are still the priority of the central government, which is constantly seeking ways to improve production and quality.

Eating Out
A Luxingshe group inclusive tour generally includes one evening meal in a Chinese restaurant. It is of course possible, with the help of your local guide, to book at a restaurant outside your hotel. While you may not be visiting the centres of the four main styles of cuisine, the main towns will certainly have restaurants serving the different types of cuisine. At the time of writing 25–30 *yuan* will buy an excellent meal with drinks included. It is generally best to let the chef choose the menu, based on what he has in stock and the style of cuisine in which he specializes. If you do go out to eat, and book a table, in order to have the best value for money the minimum

number should be four and the maximum about ten. If you are determined to eat in a masses' restaurant then you should go in groups of no more than two to four people, be prepared to brave the crowds and wait or suffer the embarrassment of a table cleared especially for you, and decipher the menu which will be scribbled on a blackboard.

Opening hours are generally earlier and shorter than in the West – lunch will begin at 11.30 am and no food will be served after 1.30 pm. In the evening you cannot hope to order much after 7 pm, and the restaurant is well and truly closed by 8.30. In the summer and in the south – in Guangzhou, for instance – restaurants may stay open later. Most ordinary restaurants have little to offer in the way of decor. They contain masses of small tables with benches or stools; side rooms are reserved for family parties, weddings or foreigners.

Banquets

If you are in China as the guests of a particular organization or on business, at some stage your Chinese counterparts may invite you to a banquet. The banquet will usually begin at around 6.30 in the evening. On arrival at the restaurant you will probably be brought a cup of jasmine tea and a perfumed towel, and will exchange pleasantries with your hosts. Then you will be invited to the table; the guest of honour is usually seated on the right of the host.

The table will be set with carefully arranged cold hors d'oeuvres, and each place setting will consist of one saucer-sized dish and possibly a small bowl, a pair of chopsticks, a china spoon and a table napkin. There will be three glasses – one thimble-sized one with a stem, filled with a spirit such as *maotai*, which is used for toasting; a larger, stemmed glass containing a red sweetish wine or rice wine, which is also used for toasting; and a tumbler, which is kept filled with beer or orangeade.

Invariably the host will serve the guest with some choice morsel from the hors d'oeuvres, a precedent which will continue through the meal, although you will also be invited to help yourself. Dishes will be brought in one by one, so that each may be appreciated on its own merits. Sometimes a soup will be served after a few courses, or some small cakes, and the plates from which you are eating will be changed regularly. Rice is only served if specially requested. Apart from the local specialities which may be served, there are several special dishes which demonstrate hospitality – they include sea cucumber, abalone and silver ear, *yiner* which is a fungus prepared in a fruit syrup and thought to be very good for the health.

After the first couple of courses the host will propose a toast as appropriate to the common interests of host and guest. The table will rise, clink glasses and wish each other *gan bei* – usually translated by enthusiastic young interpreters as 'Bottoms up' or 'Down the hatch'. After this the guest may return the toast. If the number of dishes seems endless, the serving of a whole steamed fish will indicate the final course before the last soup is served – soup is considered an aid to digestion and is served last. This may be followed by either *yiner* or almond jelly, served with fruit, and fresh fruit in season. After this the meal will finish quite quickly, and the guests will leave first.

Tourist Information

CHINA INTERNATIONAL TRAVEL SERVICE

China International Travel Service (Zhongguo guoji luxingshe, usually abbreviated to Luxingshe or CITS) is the state body under the Tourism Administration Bureau responsible for co-ordinating travel arrangements for all visitors to China.

The function of the Head Office in Peking is to draw up the overall plan for tourism each year, based on the facilities available in each locality, to liaise with overseas tour operators concerning the allocation of space and visas, and to notify local branches concerning precise details of the passengers arriving in each city. The local sub-branches of Luxingshe which are to be found in every tourist city and resort in China come under the local government authority and act as ground handling agents. The Luxingshe branch offices will arrange transfers, accommodation, excursion programmes and guides and finalize onward travel arrangements. Apart from dealing specifically with group inclusive tours, the local branches of Luxingshe also handle conference and exhibition arrangements, travel arrangements for delegations hosted by other organizations and ministries in China, and arrangements for the individual traveller.

Zhongguo Luxingshe (China Travel Service) deals specifically with Overseas Chinese and the All China Youth Federation has its own travel service.

Between 1981 and 1982 Luxingshe has set up tourist offices in Hong Kong, New York, Tokyo, Paris and London.

Changes to your Itinerary
The prospective traveller to China may often be perturbed by the lack of concrete information that is available before his journey begins. Even the most reliable travel agent cannot supply names of hotels or give exact times and details of transportation between cities. The traveller must wait until he reaches China for these final details, and then he must be prepared for the unexpected – a curtailed stay in one city, travel by rail instead of by air, accommodation a long way from the city centre, and even the omission of a city from one's tour. Such changes arise out of the complex nature of tourism in China – visitors want to see as much as possible within a relatively short space of time and this poses a strain on the means of transportation, which are required not only to service tourists but the local population as well. A delayed flight may mean a rail journey instead, a return to the hotel where another group of travellers was hoping to stay, and loss of time at your place of destination. Until the number of hotels in the major tourist centres has been

increased and there is a concomitant increase in the means of transportation available between these cities, such occurrences are to be expected.

Group Inclusive Tours

There are now many tour operators in Europe and the United States offering group inclusive tours to China. The tour cost will usually include the international flight to and from China, full board accommodation in China, excursions, internal travel in China, transfers, the services of local guides and interpreters, and probably a couple of nights stay in Hong Kong at the end of the trip.

The minimum group size is ten, but the group size favoured most by Luxingshe is around twenty-four, although in certain circumstances group sizes may be much larger than this.

Excursions in China

One of the outstanding features of the group inclusive tour in China is the intensive excursion programme which is arranged in each city. A well briefed tour escort and national guide will have put every effort into ensuring that the programme is balanced and that visitors have some free time. You are not obliged to participate in every visit and it is important to have sufficient rest. Your Chinese guides will encourage you to adopt the custom of the midday siesta, especially in the height of summer. However such luxuries are not always feasible: your time in China is short, the most interesting places always seem to entail a long drive and an early start . . . and you can rest when you reach Hong Kong. Apart from visits to places of historic or scenic interest, the visit to a commune, a factory, hospital or school is one of the opportunities which make the visit to China rather special. The institutions visited are not *de rigueur* showplaces and you will receive an enthusiastic welcome wherever you go. Following an introduction and some facts and figures over a cup of Chinese tea, you will be conducted on a guided tour, with time at the end of your visit for further questions and a vote of thanks.

Most excursions are included in the tour price, but local branches sometimes offer extra excursions – such as a river trip, or an evening meal in a restaurant, and if an unscheduled trip is taken which exceeds the daily mileage limit travellers may be asked to pay a supplement. While visitors are not encouraged to use their visit to China for business purposes – frankly, too many changes occur to make this a reliable proposition – if you have a special minority interest your guide will often try to arrange a visit with the relevant state body or enterprise – but success cannot always be guaranteed.

Evening Entertainment

Contrary to the general impression there is plenty to do in the evening in China, although most of the local population go by the motto 'early to bed, early to rise'. Your local guide may arrange a theatre visit – to see opera, ballet, acrobatics, a musical, a concert or puppets. There are bars in most hotels, and some hotels will organize dances, a film or a show.

INDEPENDENT TRAVEL

The high season for tourism in China lasts from mid-March to the end of November. All the resources at the disposal of Luxingshe – guides, buses and hotel beds – and until recently independent travel was not encouraged. In October 1982 a relaxation in the regulations governing travel permits between cities has not only made life easier for long term overseas residents, but also reflects a willingness to accept more independent travellers, although travellers are still expected to liaise through Luxingshe branch offices (see also p.86).

To obtain the necessary visa you should contact your local specialist tour operator, who will in turn contact the Miscellaneous Department at the Head Office of Luxingshe to obtain authorization. Transit passengers not spending more than five days in China can also apply directly to the Chinese Embassy or Tourist Office for a visa. If you travel to China independently, a Luxingshe guide will meet you and take you to your hotel and, if required, make arrangements for your stay in the city and your onward travel. You will be required to pay for all services on the spot in cash.

Overseas Chinese visiting relatives may travel independently in China, making any necessary arrangements through China Travel Service.

Specialist Tours

There are endless possibilities for specialist tours: for those interested in medicine and acupuncture a visit to Nanking is essential; snuff bottle collectors should visit Boshan in Shandong Province; lovers of arts and crafts will want to visit many of China's cities, including Suzhou, Yangzhou and Luoyang; porcelain and ceramics collectors should go to Henan Province, to Jingde zhen in Jiangxi Province, to Yixing near Wuxi in Jiangsu and to Foshan near Guangzhou. Those interested in the development of Chinese art should visit one of the famous grottoes at Luoyang, Dunhuang or Datong, and the art collections at the Palace Museum in Peking and the Shanghai Museum, but please bear in mind that at most museums in China there are, as yet, no introductions to the exhibits or explanatory catalogues in English. Gourmets should visit the four main centres of regional cooking – Peking, Shanghai, Chengdu in Sichuan and Guangzhou. Historians and archaeologists should visit the Yellow River, Luoyang and Zhengzhou in Henan Province, and of course Xi'an. Botanists and seekers of wild life should visit Emei Mountain in Sichuan and Yunnan Province. Steam engine enthusiasts should go to Datong – where the steam train is still produced – and then chug around China, stopping at junction cities such as Xuzhou, Zhengzhou and Taiyuan.

The arrangements for tours of a specialist nature will be made by your specialist tour operator together with Luxingshe, and where necessary the relevant state organizations will be contacted to arrange meetings and visits.

GUIDES AND INTERPRETERS

If you are visiting China as part of a group inclusive tour arrangement, you will invariably be accompanied by a national guide or escort appointed by the Head Office of Luxingshe. He will remain with you throughout your stay in China and attend to your arrangements – travel between cities, any special requirements, and liaison with the escort sent by the company with whom you have arranged your visit, as well as liaison with local guides. In each city you will be met by a local or city guide who will introduce the main sights of his city.

The first criterion for the selection of a guide-interpreter is his knowledge of a foreign language. However, there are few specific training courses for guides and misunderstandings sometimes occur when a young and inexperienced guide is required to handle the demands of a group from overseas.

TRAVEL TO AND FROM CHINA

The number of airlines flying into China is increasing all the time, and the Chinese national airline, CAAC, has also expanded its routes to many parts of the world. The following airlines now operate directly to Peking and have offices there: Aeroflot, Air France, British Airways, Iran Air, JAL (also flies to Shanghai), Jugoslav Airlines, Lufthansa, Pakistan International Airways, Panam, Philippine Airlines (via Guangzhou), Swissair and Tarom. The other main gateway to China is via Hong Kong through Guangzhou. In Hong Kong you can obtain a visa and arrange a tour to China with transport by hovercraft, express train or boat to Guangzhou or by air to the major cities. There are also cruise ships which visit Shanghai and other ports.

TRAVELLING WITHIN CHINA

If you visit China as part of a group tour all the internal travel arrangements will be made for you. You don't have to worry about tickets, your luggage arrives separately and on time in a luggage van at the station or airport, and you don't have to bother yourself with travel passes between cities.

The main forms of transport between cities are rail and air. China does not have the kind of road network to enable visitors to travel for more than short distances by bus, and distances which may seem short to the overseas visitor are viewed quite differently by the Chinese. When there is no alternative – such as travelling through the desert from Liuyuan to the Dunhuang grottoes in Gansu Province – the journey by road is exciting, often bumpy, and not always in air-conditioned vehicles, but there are more opportunities to stop to take photographs or to enjoy the view.

By Air
CAAC, which stands for the General Administration of Civil Aviation of China, covers an extensive network of internal as well as international routes. On major routes within China the SP747 is used, as well as Tridents, Boeing 707s and Ilyushin 62s. On lesser routes smaller aircraft are used, such as IL18s and AN24s.

Except on the 747 service between Canton and Peking there are no in-flight catering facilities. You will be served jasmine tea, a biscuit, orangeade and sometimes an ice cream, and generally the air hostesses will hand out a souvenir such as a notebook, key ring or sweets. If the flight is long and has to make stops en route, you will often be given a meal at the transit airport; alternatively your Luxingshe guide may arrange for a lunch box to be taken with you.

All the major cities have CAAC ticket offices. If you are travelling alone in China on an international flight, you will be required to reconfirm your flight at the CAAC office, presenting your passport and visa, seventy-two hours before departure, and if you are flying on international flights you will have to pay an airport tax of 10 *yuan.*

By Rail
The railway network, both for freight and for passengers, is vital to China's economy. The first railway was constructed in 1876 by the British, and was added to by many of the foreign interests in China. Since 1949 over 30,000 km of new line have been added, and today Tibet is the only area which is not accessible by rail.

Travelling by train in China is a must for the first-time visitor, particularly for those who yearn nostalgically for the age of steam; the atmosphere of excitement and adventure is enhanced by the rousing martial music often played as the train pulls out of the station. There are two categories on Chinese trains – hard and soft class – and there is usually one soft-class carriage per train.

Foreign visitors, high-ranking Chinese officials and army personnel travel in soft class, which is equivalent to western first class. If you are travelling overnight, accommodation in soft class will be in four-berth compartments with quilt and bedding, adequate space for luggage, lace curtains, and supplies of boiled water for making tea. An electric fan keeps the compartment cool in summer, and the trains are usually well heated in winter. Washing and toilet facilities are situated at either end of the carriage.

In hard class people travel for several days sitting on benches, or they may be privileged enough to obtain a bunk berth – the bunks are three-tiered and the sleeping compartments are open. Among visitors, usually only foreign students and overseas Chinese will be called upon to travel hard class.

On main routes, such as Guangzhou–Peking, Nanking–Peking and Guangzhou–Shanghai, the restaurant car facilities are excellent. Eggs and coffee will be served for breakfast, and a wide variety of Chinese dishes made with fresh ingredients will be offered at other meals. On inland routes the dining car service can become erratic, and it is worth taking supplies of fruit, chocolate, instant coffee and biscuits.

Trains also have public address systems, which play popular music and announce approaching stations and important sights. Chinese trains also travel on international routes – to Pyongyang in North Korea, to Hanoi in Vietnam via Nanning (closed at present), and to Moscow via Manzhouli or via Ulan Bator in Mongolia. The last-mentioned have operated continuously in spite of the vagaries of international relations, and one may book a ticket from Peking to points on the border of the eastern bloc countries. It is essential to obtain all necessary visas beforehand from the embassies in Peking – working backwards from your ultimate destination. There are now specialist tour operators who will do all the work for you, arranging accommodation en route, as well as visas and train tickets between Hong Kong and London.

Public Transport Within Cities
If you have time, are armed with a map and can say where you want to go in Chinese, then you may like to take a bus or trolley bus. The fare will rarely exceed 20 *fen* and the buses are often crowded, although a great deal of courtesy is shown to foreign visitors and seats will be given up for you.

Transporting produce from the commune into the towns

Bamboo shoots on bicycles

A typical Chinese scene: horse-drawn carts moving along the road

Carrying-poles are still in regular use

Manpower is one of China's greatest assets

Rail travel is the best way to see China

The entrance to a Friendship Hotel

Taxis and Car Hire

Self-drive car hire is not yet available in China; regulations concerning driving by foreign residents are still very strict, and it is often a lengthy process to obtain permission. It is possible to hire a car and driver by the day for travel within the vicinity of a city. In some cities it is now also possible to hire a bicycle.

Taxis cannot be hailed on the streets except in Guangzhou. In all other cities they can be obtained from the hotel reception desk and it is often best to keep the driver with you. If you go to a restaurant or friendship store, you may order a taxi from there. Drivers generally give receipts and don't accept tips. The average minimum fare is 2 *yuan*, which covers distances up to 4 km; about 50 *fen* is paid for every extra kilometre, and waiting time is about 2 *yuan* per hour. Pedicabs and three-wheeled taxis will also be seen, but they are generally not available for use by foreigners.

ACCOMMODATION AND HOTELS

By 1985 there will be 40,000 more hotel beds available in China than there are today, removing one of the greatest causes of concern for prospective visitors, travel agents and the Chinese tourist authorities alike. Already joint venture hotels and motels, financed by both Chinese and overseas finance and furnished with imported fixtures and fittings, have been built in a number of cities, including Peking, Guilin, Nanking and Suzhou, but these only go some of the way towards relieving the pressure and for the next few years the visitor to China will be using the existing accommodation. This falls into four main types: hotels built before 1949, which were summer villas or sanatoria, or were built in the grand style of the '20s and '30s in the treaty ports where there were large foreign communities; hotels built in the 1950s during the era of Sino-Soviet co-operation to accommodate Russian technicians and experts – these are large and comfortable in a lugubrious way; hotels built by the Chinese in the '60s and '70s, which mostly conform to international standards while maintaining an essentially Chinese style; finally guesthouses which were previously reserved for visiting state dignitaries have now been opened for general use. The current shortage of hotel accommodation gives rise to two recurring problems: the visitor to China rarely knows which hotels he will be staying in before his arrival in China, and single rooms are difficult to obtain.

Most hotels have a post office counter, exchange facilities, shops and a hairdresser. A choice of western and Chinese cuisine is usually available and special dietary requirements can also be catered for. Western-style breakfast is served unless otherwise requested.

In multi-storeyed hotels the floor numbering system used is the same as in America – ie the 'ground floor' is the first floor. There is usually a service counter on each floor which will look after keys, room service, laundry and small repairs, and early morning calls. The hotel staff will often have some command of a foreign language, and many are eagerly studying one.

In large hotels the bedrooms will be twin-bedded with a bathroom en suite supplied with soap and towels. Flasks of boiled hot water, often a carafe of boiled cold water, slippers, writing paper and desks are also provided. Some hotel rooms have telephones. Further details are given in the gazetteer.

As in restaurants, mealtimes are often slightly earlier than westerners are used to – breakfast between 7 am and 8.30, lunch from noon to 2 pm, and dinner between 6 pm and 8.30. If the hotel doesn't have a bar, the restaurant will usually serve drinks and snacks until later in the evening. Hotels used by foreigners have central heating which is switched on in mid-November. More and more hotels are installing air-conditioning systems; alternatively they will supply electric fans.

Hotels outside the main centres are better classed as hostels: there may be no running water in the building, but only a pump in the yard; the lavatories will be outside too, and only Chinese-style food will be available. These situations only arise for maybe two nights at the most, and the sights that the visitor has come to see and the atmosphere of hospitality more than compensate for the lack of facilities.

PASSPORTS AND VISAS

Foreigners wanting to travel to China should hold a valid full passport and a validating visa. For the time being holders of South African and Israeli passports are not allowed entry into China. If you are travelling with a tour operator he will be responsible for obtaining your visa through the Consular section of the Chinese embassy or China Travel Service in Hong Kong. The visa for group tours is usually a group visa held by the tour manager or leader, although in some cases the visa may be stamped in your passport. If you are going to China on business or individually, the relevant organization will notify your local Chinese embassy to issue the visa.

Following an announcement by the Ministry of Public Security on 23 October 1982, travel permits are no longer required for the following 28 cities: Peking, Tianjin, Shanghai, Qinhuangdao, Taiyuan, Shengyang, Changchun, Harbin, Nanking, Suzhou, Wuxi, Hangzhou, Jinan, Qingdao, Zhengzhou, Kaifeng, Luoyang, Wuhan, Changsha, Guangzhou, Foshan, Zhaoqing, Nanning, Guilin, Xian, Chengdu, Chongqing, and Lunan. Permits should be obtained for all other areas.

MONEY

The currency in China is the *renminbi*, the 'people's money,' denominated in *yuan*:
10 *jiao* = 1 *yuan*   £1 sterling = 3.30 *yuan*
10 *fen* = 1 *jiao* $1 US dollar = 1.7 *yuan*
There are 1, 2, 5, 10 and 50 *yuan* notes, and 1, 2 and 5 *jiao* notes. *Fen* are in coins only – 1, 2 and 5.

Foreign visitors are issued with foreign currency exchange certificates, which are in the same denominations as local currency and have the same value, but their use is restricted to overseas Chinese and visitors. They are used for all transactions in hotels, restaurants and Friendship Stores (see page 91) and on imported goods, and usually in local shops.

Foreign currency exchange certificates may be exported from the country and brought back at a later date, but may not be exchanged or obtained outside China. Cheques in *renminbi* can be obtained from the Bank of China in Hong Kong. At present visitors are not required to declare how much money they have brought into the country. However, you should retain exchange receipts for possible inspection and to present in case you need to re-exchange money before leaving China. Travellers' cheques issued by all the well-known banks and by American Express are accepted in China, as are all the hard currencies in cash. Most hotels have exchange facilities – the rate of exchange is the same as in the banks, and in small cities sometimes a representative will come from the local bank to the hotel at a fixed time to change money. Credit cards are now accepted in some of the major centres in China, but their use is not very widespread as yet. There are also exchange counters in friendship stores, in some antique stores, and in stores reserved for foreigners.

CUSTOMS

Foreign visitors are requested to present their baggage and other possessions of inspection on arrival in China. They must also fill out a customs declaration form stating how many pieces of baggage they have, and giving details of jewellery, precious metals and wrist-watches, radio sets, cameras, ciné cameras, calculators, tape recorders and typewriters for personal use. This form should be kept until you leave China; if you lose it you may have to pay a fine of up to 50 *yuan*. Visitors are entitled to bring in up to 600 cigarettes and four bottles of alcoholic beverage.

Goods such as cultural relics, old handicrafts, antiques, jewellery made from precious stones and metals, and articles in jade and ivory may be taken out of China providing they are marked with the government's wax seal. However you should keep for inspection by the customs the receipts issued by the friendship store or antique shop where the goods were purchased.

PHOTOGRAPHY

Photographic opportunities in China are abundant, but it is vital to take adequate supplies of film, flash bulbs and batteries – although imported film is now available in China, supplies cannot always be guaranteed. Ciné cameras should not exceed 8 mm; if you want to take a larger camera special dispensation must be applied for. Some hotels now have good fast film developing services.

There are relatively few restrictions on photography, apart from the constraints of courtesy: always, for instance, obtain a person's assent before pointing your camera at him, as the Chinese generally like to be photographed at their best. The major restrictions are that photography is not allowed from planes, of naval or military installations, of soldiers on duty, and of some bridges. As in many countries, when visiting cultural sites and some musuems, such as the excavations at Xi'an or the caves in Datong, photography is either forbidden or you have to pay a fee to photograph.

HEALTH AND VACCINATIONS

As the journey both to and within China is often strenuous, if you suffer from a particular complaint requiring regular treatment you should consider carefully the kind of tour you are going to take and its duration. Some tour operators ask prospective passengers to provide a medical certificate if they are over seventy.

If you fall ill in China you can be assured of the best available treatment. Many hospitals in the major cities have wards for foreigners, the doctors have command of a foreign language, and treatment facilities are of a perfectly good standard. Though you will be required to pay for treatment and hospitalization, charges are by no means high, and everything is done to facilitate your rejoining your group or returning home when you are well enough to travel.

The most common minor ailments are the 'Peking throat' and colds which often afflict the first-time visitor to China, particularly in late autumn or early spring. Arm yourself beforehand with your favourite cold antidotes. In the summer months there is a risk of stomach complaints, so take a good prophylactic, as well as insect repellent and ointments for bites.

For visitors from northern Europe and America neither smallpox nor cholera vaccinations are mandatory. People travelling from other countries should check the rulings prevalent at the time of travel. Sometimes yellow fever inoculations will be required. If you are travelling at the height of summer and into the interior of China a course of anti-malaria tablets can be a wise precaution.

WATER

It is not advisable to drink water straight from the tap. You will soon get used to the ubiquitous flasks of *kāishŭi*, which means boiled water. You may even get used to drinking hot water 'neat' – an antidote strongly recommended by the Chinese for 'Peking throat'. Probably by the end of your stay you will be considering whether to take one of those brightly coloured flasks home with you. *Lĕng kāishŭi* (cold boiled water) can be ordered in hotel dining-rooms, though not always in restaurants. Bottled mineral water from Shandong Province is also available – it is called *laóshānshŭi*.

POST AND TELECOMMUNICATIONS

Postcards are usually bought in packets of ten, and an airmail stamp for a postcard to Europe or the USA costs 6 *jiao*. The stamp for an airmail letter to the same destinations costs 7 *jiao*, and aerogrammes are 6 *jiao*. Postage to Australia, New Zealand and Hong Kong is cheaper. Letters and postcards usually take about six days to reach Europe or the US.

Most envelopes and some stamps in China do not have any glue on them, but there is usually a big pot of glue and brush on the post office counter. Commemorative stamps are colourful.

Freight of any large goods which you may purchase during your stay can be arranged through the friendship stores in Peking, Shanghai, Guangzhou and elsewhere in China. The charge is usually 5 per cent of the value of the goods purchased.

Telephone calls may be made free of charge from hotels to other places within the same city. Small shops and department stores often have telephones for public use, and sometimes make a small charge of about 4 *fen*. Long distance calls within China have to be connected by the operator. Overseas calls can be made from most places in China and connections are usually quick and clear. Reversed-charge (collect) calls can be made. If there is a telephone in your hotel room the boys at the service desk will give you booking forms for long distance calls. If there isn't a telephone in your room, then apply to the post office counter. The charge for a call to Europe is around 28 *yuan* for three minutes, and you rarely have to wait more than half an hour.

Telegrams can often be sent from the hotel. To Europe the cost is 1.3 *yuan* per word, and within China the tariff is cheaper. The telex is not widely used in China, although there are telex facilities in Peking, Shanghai and Guangzhou; the major corporations which have dealings overseas can usually supply a telex number.

PUBLIC HOLIDAYS

There are four major public holidays during the year, as well as other feast days which don't merit a day off, but are commemorated in some time-honoured fashion. The four major public holidays are as follows.

1 January – New Year
The Spring Festival (Chinese New Year)
This is as important to the Chinese as Christmas is to westerners. It usually falls in February, and commemorates the lunar New Year; it is celebrated by extensive food preparations and the purchase of new clothes. Since it is a family occasion, people are given time off to return to their homes. Friends are visited, dragon dances are performed, and many traditional local customs associated with the festival, such as the Flower Fair in Canton and lantern festivals, still survive.

1 May – Labour Day
During the Cultural Revolution, International Labour Day was marked by political meetings, concerts, etc. Nowadays it is a more low-key festival and an opportunity for family gatherings.

1 October – National Day
National Day or *guoqing* commemorates the founding of the Republic on 1 October 1949. These holidays are often accompanied by the appearance of red-and-gold greetings signs over factory and school entrances, firework displays, concerts and at least one day off work.

The other types of feast days which occur during the year fall into two categories: they are either traditional feasts, based on the lunar calendar, or 'revolutionary' feasts, commemorating some aspect of modern life or recent history, with cultural and political activity the focal point of the celebration in question.

Other Modern Festivals
Although these are not holidays as such, they are usually commemorated by newspaper articles and various cultural activities.
8 March – International Women's Day
1 June – Children's Day
1 July – Founding of the Chinese Communist Party
1 August – Founding of the People's Liberation Army

Other Traditional Festivals

As these are based on the lunar calendar, they do not always fall on the same day.

Qingming, at the beginning of April, is traditionally the day when families would go to sweep the graves of their ancestors. In recent years, it has become a day for commemorating the revolutionary heroes, as in 1976 when people turned out to mourn the recent death of Zhou Enlai and the Tianan men incident occurred.

In May or June Duanwu – the fifth day of the fifth lunar month – commemorates the death of the poet Qu Yuan with the eating of *zongzi*, cakes of glutinous rice wrapped in bamboo leaves and cooked with dates or nuts. It is also traditionally the day of the dragon boat race, which was revived in grand style in 1980 at Miluo in Hunan Province.

Late September or early October is the time of the Mid-autumn Festival, when the moon is full and people turn out to admire it and eat moon cakes, which have sweet or savoury fillings. The day was also traditionally one for wishing for a good harvest.

ELECTRICITY

Voltage all over China is 220. Socket sizes and types do vary from place to place, although the most common type are two-pin. Some form of adaptor can usually be obtained from the service desk on your floor in the hotel. It's probably best to take as few plug-in electrical gadgets as possible; pack a good supply of batteries for tape recorders and shavers, or else take mechanical alternatives where they exist.

CLIMATE AND CLOTHING

The climate of a foreign country can influence your opinion of the place and prevent you enjoying your holiday if you don't go properly prepared for extremes of temperature or unfamiliar weather conditions. The other option, if there are no restrictions on your time or finance, is to choose a time of year when the weather is reasonably good, and no Chinese will hesitate to inform you that the best times of year to visit China are spring and autumn. At these seasons you will not only find good weather, but will see nature at its most glorious – be it the blossoms of spring or the colours of autumn – an aspect most important to the Chinese eye. There will be less mist and rain obscuring fine views, although, particularly in spring, you will find the lakes and rivers low. While you may still need some sort of coat in spring and autumn, you need not be cocooned in padding like a Chinese baby. These spring and autumn periods last respectively from late March until the end of May, and from September to mid-November.

For those who have less choice in the matter, however, certain precautions can be taken before embarking on the journey. In winter warm, comfortable clothing must be the order of the day; take a warm hat, gloves, boots and overcoat, with trousers or thick tights for women. One cannot do any harm in taking a tip from the Chinese and dressing in layers. Moisturizing creams and throat lozenges are a must against the drying effects of the winds which will blow down from the Gobi Desert, particularly in January and February. One word of warning – the area south of the Yangtse River is generally considered to enjoy a mild climate in winter. This means that public buildings are usually not heated, and while some hotels do have central heating there are many which don't, particularly in the smaller tourist centres. The bedding usually consists of warm quilts and blankets, but if you like to remove the chill from your bed you would be well advised to pack a hot water bottle, particularly if you are travelling extensively in the south of China. Trains travelling southwards from Peking do not as a rule turn on the heating until 15 November, the official beginning of winter.

In the height of summer the main problems for northern European visitors are heat and humidity. Clothing should be loose and cool, preferably made of cotton, and your shoes should be comfortable ones. If you are staying in one place for any length of time, air your clothes regularly to prevent the growth of mildew. Drink plenty, and possibly take salt tablets. Air conditioning is still something of a luxury and electric fans will often be placed in your hotel room. Mosquito nets are supplied in many hotels.

What To Take

Some of these articles are mentioned in other sections, but a quick checklist all in one place is useful. Though many of the items are now available in some parts of China, they won't be on sale everywhere so it is worth having an adequate supply with you.

All cosmetics, shampoo, moisturizer, paper tissues and toiletries.

Proprietary or recommended brands of medicine and treatment for colds and stomach disorders; insect repellents.

Effervescent vitamin C tablets to counteract dehydration on the long outward and return flights.

Instant coffee.

Films, batteries, spare parts for electrical equipment, cassettes.

Favourite cigarettes and spirits.

Tailoring

Unlike Hong Kong and Bangkok it is not possible to have silk suits etc. run up in a matter of 24 hours. However, if you are a long-term resident most friendship stores have good tailoring departments and will make up copies of clothes you have already, adapt patterns, or make Chinese-style padded jackets and 'qipaos' – the famous slit-skirted dress known in Hong Kong as the 'cheongsam'. Prices are reasonable and the minimum time is usually 2 weeks.

SHOPPING

When you visit China as part of a tourist group you will not be called upon to pay for many extras, so the money you take with you is mainly for souvenir shopping. There are two possibilities – on the one hand you can purchase many unusual and typically Chinese goods for very little, or you may prefer to buy the more expensive and elaborately worked goods, antiques and objets d'art.

Goods in the first category include cotton or velveteen shoes, 'Mao' caps and jackets, lidded mugs, handkerchiefs, bamboo objects, silk scarves, brocade- or plastic-covered notebooks, tracksuits, canvas holdalls with the name of a Chinese city emblazoned across the side, silk socks, Chinese brushes and inkstones, teapots, children's clothes, small silk paintings, stone rubbings, batik ware, posters from bookshops, records, papercuts, thermos flasks, tea, basketware, soft toys, puppets, small embroidered tablecloths, silk, plant pots, clay figures, and padded jackets. All these goods may be obtained in local department stores as well as in the friendship stores. Purchasing goods in local department stores will often mean that you gather a curious audience.

The Friendship Store is designed for the convenience of all foreign visitors and residents and there is one in every major city. Goods are paid for in foreign currency exchange certificates and prices are the same as in local stores. The goods are basically the same, but quality and design are often better in the Friendship Stores. Goods for sale include jade, ivory, precious jewellery, cloisonné enamel, elaborately embroidered silk blouses, brocade dressing-gowns, nightwear, cashmere knitwear and fabric, fur, leather goods, acupuncture charts and needles, wood carvings, musical instruments, furniture, chests, screens, chairs and tables, rattan suites, lacquerware, high-quality embroidered linen tablecloths, silk crêpe, hand-cut silk and wool carpets, high-quality and antique porcelain, antiques in general, dinner services, scrolls, snuff bottles, and embroidered panels from mandarins' robes. Many local friendship stores also sell the best of local handicrafts. Shops are open seven days a week, from 8.30 am – 6 pm, with some regional variations.

If you are shopping for goods in local stores, you may acquire cotton coupons – check with your guide before setting out. Smaller shops may not be used to accepting foreign currency exchange certificates. When buying material in local stores you will often find the price is given in units of feet (the Chinese 'chi' foot and yard is virtually the equivalent of the Imperial foot). There seems to be great variation in the clothing sizes used, so it is best to try things on before buying them. In friendship stores the metric system is used. Similarly, when purchasing fruit, tea, biscuits etc. in local shops goods will be priced by the 'jin' or 'catty' (equivalent to one pound in the Imperial system).

Weights and Measures

Length
1 kilometre (1000 m) = 2 *li* = 0.621 mile = 0.540 nautical mile
1 metre (m) = 3 *chi* = 3.281 feet
1 *li* = 0.5 kilometre = 0.311 mile = 0.270 nautical mile
1 *chi* = 0.333 metre = 1.094 feet
1 mile = 1.609 kilometres = 3.219 *li* = 0.868 nautical mile
1 foot = 0.305 metre = 0.914 *chi*
1 nautical mile = 1.852 kilometres = 3.704 *li* = 1.150 miles

Area
1 hectare = 15 *mu* = 2.47 acres
1 *mu* = 6.667 ares = 0.164 acre
1 acre = 0.405 hectare = 6.070 *mu*

Weight
1 kilogramme = 2 *jin* = 2.205 pounds
1 *jin* = 0.5 kilogramme = 1.102 pounds
1 pound = 0.454 kilogramme = 0.907 *jin*

Capacity
1 litre (metric system) = 1 *sheng* = 0.220 gallon
1 gallon (English system) = 4.546 litres = 4.546 *sheng*

Time and Dates
Peking is 8 hours ahead of Greenwich Mean Time. Dates are written as follows:
year/month/day, ie, 49/10/01 = 1 October 1949.

ETIQUETTE

Tipping is not expected in China. If you want to express gratitude to your guide it is best conveyed by the gift of an English or foreign-language classical novel or a dictionary. Chocolates and calendars are also popular gifts.

Generally speaking, the visitor to China will feel like an honoured guest. When you visit a commune or school, for instance, a reception committee will often greet you with clapping, which should be returned by the visitors. At the end of question-and-answer sessions the group leader or a member of the group is often called upon to give a vote of thanks. As guests, it is essential that you phrase your questions tactfully and do not appear to be making a personal attack on the system.

China has earned a reputation for great honesty: some small article discarded by a visitor has often been known to follow him or her to the next city, so in order not to waste people's time it is best to make certain that an unwanted article is properly discarded in the waste bin.

PART TWO

Gazetteer

Gazetteer

PEKING

The first time I flew into Peking I looked in vain for the sprawling conurbation which one associates with a capital city. Mountains and desert gave way to cultivated land and paddyfields and suddenly we were landing at the airport, greeted by outsize portraits of Mao and the ubiquitous slogans proclaiming 'We have friends all over the world.' The atmosphere in the terminal was no less welcoming as passport and customs formalities were dealt with in a friendly and efficient manner and suitcases were flung through a hole in the wall – a sharp contrast to other airports. That was in 1976: Peking airport is now much busier and streamlined.

Alternatively your first contact with Peking may be as you spill out of the station into the bustle of the city centre – you will see people with bundles watching and waiting, a line of three-wheeler taxis, a queue waiting for the buses trundling by throwing up dust, and someone bringing a pile of steaming *baozi* to his travelling companions. The station is an ornate yellow building from the 1950s, topped with green tiles, Chinese turrets and a big clock by which everyone sets their watches as the bus passes along Chang'an Avenue at the bottom of the road running up to the station.

Peking's grace and charm lie in the fact that it is not like a typical capital city. For hundreds of years it was on the periphery of the cultural and political centres of China, be they Xi'an or Nanking. In the end expediency dictated that the capital should be in the north, and the Chinese name Beijing means northern capital.

It is a city where change seems to come in cycles. It is not yet a city of prestigious skyscrapers, but rows of apartment blocks and office buildings along the main boulevards, as well as flyovers and ring roads, have been appearing in recent years. For the moment, however, Peking's traffic problem is not too many cars but too many bicycles, and visitors never fail to be astounded at just how noisy a herd of bike bells can be. The last big change took place in the late 1950s, when Peking's city wall with its towering gates was demolished, ostensibly to reduce traffic congestion but perhaps also as a symbolic gesture. These years also saw the construction of the modern symbols of Peking – the Great Hall of the People, museums, and administration and telecommunication buildings.

While there is much that is new and much that has gone, Peking retains some of its essential characteristics. The old city can still be described today as Marco Polo characterized it 600 years ago – a 'chess board' of wide boulevards, behind which lies a maze of alleys or *hutong* as they are called in Peking. Each old-style house has its courtyard surrounded by an anonymous wall, the occasional peeling red-painted door allowing a glimpse of once-elegant carved façades, and someone doing their washing or preparing vegetables. Peking, in contrast with other big Chinese cities, is frustratingly private and discreet – something to do with its years of being the seat of government. Perhaps it is rendered even more elusive by the fact that buildings which were once used for government purposes have now become ghostly museums where people wander and gaze and try in vain to reconstruct an image of life and activity in the Summer Palace, say, or in the Forbidden City.

Peking is situated on the north-west frontiers of the North China Plain, in the north of Hebei Province. On latitude 40°N, it is level with Rome, New York and Ankara; it is 150 km from the Bohai Gulf and Tianjin. The area to the north and west of Peking is mountainous – to the west lie the Western Hills and to the north the Yan Mountains, which form part of the plateau which stretches into Inner Mongolia; the mountains in this area are no more than 1000–1500 m above sea level. Peking itself is 43 m above sea level. The major rivers serving Peking are the Yongding and the Chaobai and the Northern Canal (Bei yunhe), which at Tong xian, south of Peking, becomes the famous Imperial Canal.

While Peking is actually in Hebei Province, it shares with Tianjin and Shanghai the distinction of being a municipality directly under the central government, with a status and autonomy not unlike English metropolitan boroughs. The whole area covers 16,800 km² and is about 150 km long at its longest edge. The population of the city proper is 4 million; the city is two and a half times bigger than it was in 1949 and has spread out along an east–west axis. There are four main city districts, five suburban districts and eleven rural districts or counties, with a total population of 8.7 million.

Naturally enough, Peking's main role is as an administrative and political centre. All government offices have their headquarters here, and without their approval provincial offices often cannot take independent actions, although recent efforts have been made to decentralize.

Climate

Each of the four seasons makes its mark in Peking. The winters are cold and dry. The early morning smog caused by fuel stoves and factory chimneys usually gives way to clear, sunny days. January is the coldest month, with average temperatures around −4°C and at the coldest −22°C. Winter usually begins suddenly in mid-November, when the first snow falls. In January and February sandstorms blow in from the Gobi Desert, and there is a tendency to drought in early spring until the rains come. Spring breaks the monochrome of winter with fruit blossom and new leaves. Spring and autumn are the most pleasant seasons to visit Peking. The spring is mild, with some wind; the average temperature is 12–15°C. July is the hottest and wettest month of the year, the average temperature being in the mid- to high twenties (23–26°C). September and October are the best months – mild and sunny but not too dry.

Agriculture

There are 275 communes around Peking, many of which serve the city as market garden-type communes, providing those mountains of cabbage which are seen around Peking in the winter months. They also produce a wide variety of fruit including grapes, persimmons (September and October), pears and dates. Further from the city, cotton and grain are most important – the latter includes rice. Regular cultivation of rice has been made possible by an improved irrigation system; previously it was only grown near the Summer Palace to provide the imperial family with rice. There are now 300 reservoirs in the Peking area. Apart from rice, wheat, corn, millet, sweet potatoes and *gaoliang* (sorghum) are the staples, and two crops per year may be harvested. Before the ground freezes it is prepared for winter – ditches with low protective walls are dug, bamboo and reed matting form windshields or are used to cover the earth.

Industry

Peking's industrial area has been built since 1949, in its eastern and south-eastern suburbs, so that the smoke and fumes from factory chimneys would blow away from the city. Heavy industry includes iron and steel, coal, petrochemicals, electricity generation and machinery manufacture; other industries include electronics, textiles and handicrafts.

History

The story of Peking begins as much as 500,000 years ago with Peking Man, whose remains were discovered in 1929 at Zhoukoudian 40 km south of Peking. There is a gap in the story until the Warring States period, when under the name of Ji Peking was the capital of the state of Yan, the last state to resist the warmongering Qin, until it succumbed in 221 BC. Until the end of the tenth century it remained relatively unimportant, on the periphery of the cultural and political centres of Xi'an, Luoyang and Kaifeng; it was a trading post when relations with the northern tribes were good, and a barracks when they deteriorated.

During the turmoil of the tenth and eleventh centuries, while the Song dynasty flourished in the south, Peking became the southern capital of the Khitan or Tartars. It was called Nanjing or Yanjing – 'the swallow capital' – and Yan is still one of the names used for Peking today. In 1125 the Khitan were driven out by the Jin and Peking became their capital; it was known then as Zhongdu – the central capital. Although nothing remains of that city, archaeologists know that it was a walled city built to the south-west of the later city.

In 1215 Zhongdu was razed to the ground by the Mongols under Chinggis Khan, and in 1261, with the whole of China under the Mongols, Khubilai Khan established his capital at Peking, calling it Dadu – the great capital. Marco Polo left detailed and lively descriptions of Khanbalik – the Khan's City. Dadu, a strategic point from which Khubilai Khan could command his vast empire, was a cosmopolitan city receiving traders from all corners of the globe. Khubilai Khan adopted many of the Chinese customs and habits, to the extent of building a walled and turreted Chinese city. According to Marco Polo, he took the advice of his court astrologers in choosing a new site for the city. He played a part in furnishing some of the parks which still remain in modern Peking. Marco Polo describes a city of magnificent proportions – a city within a city, with vast halls which could hold 6000 men, arsenals and stores, a 'chess board' which enabled one to see along the wide, straight streets to the gate at the opposite end of the city. He gives some sociological details – merchants, prostitutes and foreigners had their quarters outside the city wall; curfew and the watches were all for the protection and welfare of the citizens, and no crime or act of violence was ever committed within the city walls. Marco Polo admired the use of paper money, and speaks of the imperial welfare service providing for the poor.

At the end of the dynasty the palace fell into disrepair and was badly damaged as the Khan fled from the uprisings which were to establish the Ming dynasty. While the Xizhi men city gate was being demolished in 1969, traces of this former Mongol capital were discovered in the north-west suburbs of Peking.

The first two emperors of the Ming dynasty had their capital at present-day Nanking, and during this period Peking was called Beiping – Northern Peace. The third emperor, Yong le, moved the capital to Peking. He came to power in 1402 and, having decided in 1406 to establish his capital there, sent ministers all over China to find the best materials. In 1407 they started work on the Imperial Palace, and Yong le moved there on its completion in 1420. This was to a certain extent a strategic move, enabling the Chinese to keep a watchful eye over the Mongols and the Tartars; later on it was to be an ideal situation for the Manchus, enabling them to rule China and still be close to their own homeland, though as far as internal affairs were concerned it was a long way from the prosperous centres of the south. Under Yong le the city took on the form that it was to keep at least until the downfall of the empire in 1912.

The new centre of the city was to be the present Forbidden City, with its 'vermilion' walls forbidding all but those on imperial business to enter the city; the main entrance was to be used only by the emperor himself when he went to the Temple of Heaven to pray for a good harvest. In accordance with the principles of *fengshui* (geomancy) it was built on a north–south axis running 8 km from Yongding men in the south, through the Forbidden City and out to the Drum Tower at the north; a climb to the top of Coal Hill today will still reveal this axis. Within the high walls of the Inner City was the Imperial City, containing the area which is now called Beihai Park, and at the centre of the Imperial City was the Forbidden City – the royal residence. To the south of this was the Outer City, also surrounded by walls, which was where the ordinary people lived. When the Manchus took over Peking in 1644 they settled their troops in the Inner City, which was often referred to as the Tartar City. In 1727 the first foreign legation was granted to the Russians, in the area to the south-east of the Forbidden City, opposite today's Peking Hotel.

While the city wall can no longer be seen, a quick glance at the map will reveal its former site, and most of the quarters once adjacent to the city gates retain their old names. The southern confines of the Outer or Chinese City were just south of the Temple of Heaven at the end of Qian men Street. Yongdingmen, the northern part of the city, ended at Anding men, just north of the Drum Tower. The entrance to the Inner City was at Qian men, which means 'front gate'. The former eastern limit of the city was near the new flyover, just by the friendship store; the western boundary was Xidan for the Inner City and Fuxing men for the Outer City.

After the fall of the empire Yuan Shi-kai continued to use the Imperial City as a palace. The area in front of Tiananmen Gate which was destroyed during the Boxer Rebellion became the meeting place of Peking and the site of momentous protests in China's recent history – from the May Fourth demonstrations in 1919 to the demonstrations of April 1976 to commemorate Zhou Enlai's death. After 1937 and the Japanese invasion, when the Nationalists moved the capital to Nanking and later to Chongqing, the city was once more known as Beiping – Northern Peace.

Modern Peking offers much to the short- or long-stay visitor, from historical sights to art exhibitions, picnics at the Ming tombs or the Great Wall, an evening meal at one of the many excellent restaurants, or a shopping expedition to Wangfujing. The people of Peking are reasonably phlegmatic about foreigners, so one can mingle much more easily.

Peking is the seat of Chinese government – most of the ministries are to be found along the western side of the city and are recognizable by the red star on the roof. Most of the universities and colleges are in the west and north-western quarters of the city, and the south-east has become the industrial centre, while in the east and north-east are situated the two major embassy quarters of Sanlitun and the area around the friendship store. The southern part of the city (Front Gate) was traditionally the 'red light' and entertainments quarter of the city, and while it now by no means bears the infamous name of former years it is a popular and bustling shopping area. Here was the site of the antique market of Liuli chang, which still continues on a reduced scale with promises of refurbishment and restoration. Many of the streets bear names which reveal their former trade or occupants, such as lantern selling or the pig market; and Niujie or Ox Street denotes the road where Peking's Moslems have traditionally lived. Where once Peking was built on a north–south axis it now extends on an east–west axis along Chang'an Avenue, which stretches for 40 km through Peking. The horse and cart are still one of the most common forms of transport in the area around Peking and traffic jams will be made up equally of lorries and carts. In winter passengers are covered up to the eyes in warm goatskin-lined coats.

Tianan men Square

The new centre of Peking is Tianan men Square. The first nursery rhyme children learn is 'I love Tianan men in Peking', and everyone's most prized photograph is taken on Tianan men Square.

The place takes its name from the 'Gate of Heavenly Peace', the entrance to the Forbidden City (or the Palace Museum as it is now known). The gate itself now forms part of the national emblem; where once the emperor issued edicts, it is now honoured as the spot from which Mao announced the founding of the Republic in October 1949, and during rallies held on Tianan men Square it is from here that members of the Central Committee make speeches.

Before 1949 the square covered an area of approximately 11 ha. On 30 November 1949 the First Plenary Session of the Chinese People's Political Consultative Conference recommended the building of the Monument to the People's Heroes which now stands in the centre of Tianan men Square. Work on this and the general expansion of the square began in 1952 and was completed in 1958, by which time the square was enlarged to 40 ha.

The most recent addition to the square has been Chairman Mao's Memorial Hall, built behind the Monument to the People's Heroes. The square is flanked by the History Museum and the Great Hall of the People. At the southern end of the square is Qian men – Front Gate – behind this is the Arrow Tower or the Zhengyang men, built to be directly beneath the sun at mid-day and distinguished by its elegant balustrade. At the northern end of the square is the Gate of Heavenly Peace itself, with the entrance to the Sun Yatsen Park – Zhongshan gongyuan on the west side and the Workers' Cultural Palace on the other side. The northern end is delimited by the red wall of the former palace. Portraits of Marx,

Engels, Lenin and Stalin guard either side of the square.

The square is reputedly the largest in the world, and in Chinese the most common epithets for it are words like grand and imposing. Chang'an Avenue also passes along the northern edge. For rallies it can hold up to 1 million people.

Chairman Mao's Memorial Hall
The decision to build the Memorial Hall was announced shortly after Mao's death as the wish of the ordinary people. It was begun on 24 November 1976, when Hua Guofeng laid the foundation stone, and it was completed behind fences and under floodlights within nine months so that the opening ceremony could coincide with the first anniversary of his death, on 9 September 1977. Taking up much of the southern half of Tianan men Square, it is 33.6 m high and has 20,000 m² of floor space. The architecture, with its pillars and flat roof and the two-tiered cornices of yellow-glazed tiles, combines modern Chinese and Roman. It is guarded by large sculptures of the heroic peasant and soldier. A wide marble staircase leads into the ante-chamber, which contains an enormous seated marble statue of Mao in front of a tapestry. Behind this is the room containing his embalmed body encased in a crystal coffin, and the last hall has one of his poems engraved in the wall. Visits to the Memorial Hall (it is never referred to as a mausoleum) can be arranged on certain days of the week for foreign visitors. Silence is usually requested, as is the removal of hats, and cameras are not allowed.

Monument to the People's Heroes
Work on this edifice started in 1952 and was completed in 1958. It is an obelisk of white stone bearing an inscription by Chairman Mao: 'The people's heroes are immortal.' Around the base are eight bas-reliefs in white marble depicting the major events in China's liberation struggle – the triumphant burning of opium by Lin Zexu in 1840; the uprising at Jiutian village which triggered the Taiping Rebellion in 1858; the Wuchang Uprising of 1911 which signalled the end for the Manchus; the rally held in Tianan men Square on 4 May 1919 to protest at the Treaty of Versailles; the 30 May Movement – the demonstration in Shanghai which ended in bloodshed when the police turned on the protestors; the Nanchang Uprising of 1927 against Jiang Kaishek; the war against Japan from 1937 to 1945; and finally the crossing of the Yangtse by the People's Liberation Army to liberate Nanking on 21 April 1949.

Great Hall of the People
The Great Hall of the People, on the west side of the square, was completed in 1959 in ten months; it is an imposing building with a sweeping staircase and pillars, plus two-tiered cornices of yellow-glazed tiles. This is the venue of all important conferences and meetings, including the National Assembly; the main conference hall holds 10,000 people. There is also an enormous dining-room where banquets in honour of foreign guests are held. Small side rooms each decorated with the materials and craftmanship of one of the various provinces, are used for meetings, banquets and overseas conferences.

Museum of Chinese History
The museum, completed in 1959, stands on the east side of the square facing the Great Hall of the People. It provides an extensive tour through the ages from Peking Man to the Opium Wars and is well worth a visit with a good guide. The exhibits include some excellent reconstructions of the earliest Chinese scientific inventions, such as

the south-pointing cart, and some of China's best archaeologists and historians work in the archives.

To the north is the Museum of the Chinese Revolution. Smaller exhibition rooms will contain temporary exhibitions introducing the life of a major revolutionary or contemporary figure. While the southern side of Tianan men Square leads to the shopping quarter of Qian men, the north leads into another world – the once Forbidden City and Palace Museum. However on either side of the main entrance are two less imposing gates, leading into Zhongshan Park on the left and the Workers' Cultural Palace on the right. (see p.121)

Zhongshan Park
The park was first named after Sun Yatsen in 1928. Originally, under the Liao dynasty in the tenth century, it was the Temple of the Renaissance of the Country (Xingguosi). Inside the entrance is a gallery and the memorial arch to peace – white with blue tiles. Built to commemorate the German Baron Kettler for his role during the Boxer Rebellion, it was moved to the park in 1919 and assumed its present role after a world peace conference held in Peking in the early 1950s. The Lan ting pei ting (the Orchid and Stele Pavilion) was moved from the old Summer Palace and contains eight pillars carved with the work of China's great calligraphers, such as Wang Yizhe. In 1421 Emperor Yong le built the Sheji tan, the Altar of Earth and Harvest. The three-storeyed, square altar, now in the northern part of the park, contains five different coloured soils – blue, red, white, yellow and black – as an indication of the emperor's far-reaching power and the fact that everything in the world belonged to him. The emperor would come here twice a year to pray to the god of the soil and the god of grain. To the north of the altar is the Hall of

Prayer, built over five hundred years ago. One of the finest remaining examples of Ming architecture, it has been renamed in memory of Sun Yatsen. The garden also contains cypress trees which are almost a thousand years old, a nursery famous for Chinese medicinal herbs and peonies, a series of exhibition pavilions and a concert hall. The Tongzi moat borders the park, over which the walls of the Forbidden City and its watchtowers loom high. Both this park and the one surrounding the Workers' Cultural Palace (below) adjoin the Forbidden City and can be visited during opening hours on payment of a small entrance fee.

Workers' Cultural Palace
The entrance is on the eastern side of the Palace Museum. During the Ming and Qing dynasties this was the site of the imperial ancestral temple, first built by Yong le in 1420 and rebuilt in 1544. The emperor would come here on the first day of each quarter to sacrifice to his ancestors. Caretakers and crows were the only inhabitants of this imposing temple. The Workers' Cultural Palace was opened in 1950 by the municipal trade union organization. It contains a cinema, an open air theatre, exhibition pavilions, a library, sports grounds and a boating lake.

Forbidden City (Palace Museum)
This part of Peking has known many names during its history. It was forbidden because the ordinary people could not enter it, and its name in Chinese meant the Polar Forbidden City. Astrologists believe the pole star is the star around which all the other planets revolve, so it became a metaphor for the Imperial Palace, which was considered the centre of all earthly activity. Some people interpret the Chinese to mean the Purple Forbidden City, after the colour of the walls. Its size meant that it

was often called the Imperial City. Now it is known as the Former Palace or the Palace Museum (Gugong).

The Forbidden City is one of the jewels of Peking. Its contents cover the history of the past 500 years, including the most glorious days of the Ming dynasty, some of the more enlightened rulers of the Qing, and finally the decay of the dynastic order, the incursion of foreign troops in 1900, the intrigues of the Empress Ci xi and the fate of Guang xu and Xuan tong, the last emperors.

Yong le, the third emperor of the Ming dynasty, had it built between 1407 and 1420 when he moved the capital to Peking. Fires caused by lightning have caused parts of the palace to be rebuilt at later dates, and after falling into total disrepair and neglect after the demise of the empire it was restored on the basis of the original plans in the 1950s. Many of China's great old palaces have been lost because they were largely built of wood and in the dry air of Peking the risk of fire is increased.

The palace was built according to the ancient traditions of geomancy, which ensured that the emperor faced south and his people faced north to pay homage to him. The style of the building – or rather group of buildings, for in no way is it one large, solid stately home – is very similar to that of the palaces in the former capital of Chang'an.

After the establishment of the Republic in 1912, the child Pu yi, son of the last Qing emperor's brother-in-law, remained in the palace, nominally at least emperor. President Yuan Shikai used the palace as the seat of government. Pu Yi was educated in western style, and there are stories that he had the

PALACE MUSEUM

Key to plan of Palace Museum
 1 Meridian Gate (Wu men)
 2 Gate of Supreme Harmony (Taihe men)
 3 Hall of Supreme Harmony (Taihe dian)
 4 Hall of Complete Harmony (Zhonghe dian)
 5 Hall for Preserving Harmony (Baohe dian)
 6 Gate of Purity (Qianqing men)
 7 Hall of Purity (Qianqing gong)
 8 Hall of Heavenly and Earthly Intercourse (Jiaoy dian)
 9 Hall of Earthly Tranquillity (Kunning gong)
10 Imperial Garden
11 Qin an dian
12 Longzong men Gate
13 Office of the Grand Council
14 Palace of Mental Cultivation (Yangxin dian)
15 Taiji dian
16 Tiyuan dian
17 Palace of Eternal Spring (Changchun gong)
18, 19, 20 The quarters of the imperial seraglio
21 Shunzhen Gate
22 Shenwu men Gate
23 Jade Room
24 Ming and Qing craftsmanship – wood, ivory, bamboo, lacquerware
25 Bronzes
26 Dragon Screen
27 Art Gallery
28 Imperial jewels

} The quarters of Ci xi and other imperial wives

104

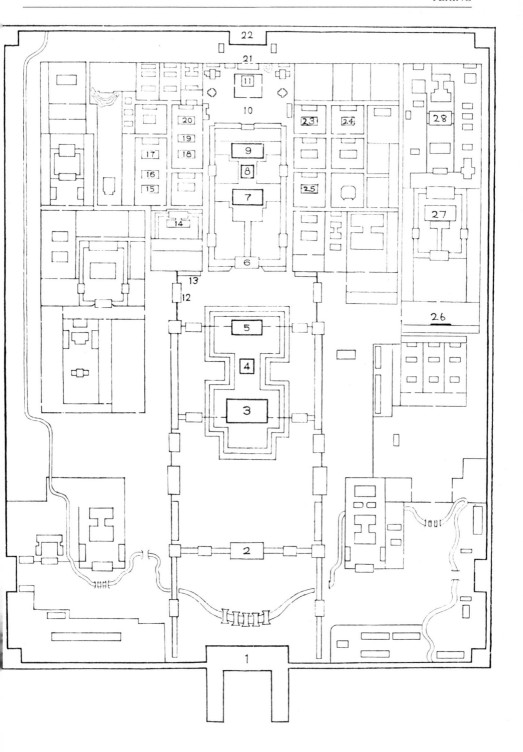

threshold steps removed so that he could ride around the palace on his tricycle. Pu yi later became puppet emperor of Manchuria under the Japanese, and was taken away by the Russians after Hiroshima. On his return to the palace in 1959 he declared it to be in a far better state of repair than he remembered it as a child. He spent the last years of his life working in the Palace Museum and died in the early 1970s. He confessed his 'bourgeois' sins and wrote a book called *The First Half of My Life*, which has been translated as *From Prince to Commoner* and is available from the Foreign Languages Press in Peking.

After Pu yi left, a cursory inventory was made of the contents of the palace and in 1928 it was opened to the public as a museum. The entrance fee was by no means cheap, being equivalent to the cost of about 13.5 kg of flour – 5 *yuan* 3 *jiao*. With the invasion of the Japanese many of the contents were moved to Nanking and Shanghai for safe keeping. After the end of the Sino-Japanese War some of the objets d'art were brought back to Peking, and when the Nationalist Party fled to Taiwan they took a very large portion of the palace treasures with them.

As one of the most complete remaining examples of Ming architecture it is not surprising that the Palace Museum is considered one of the major national monuments, and a great deal of time and money is spent on its restoration and upkeep. The entrance fee is now 1 *jiao*, and tickets can be bought from the front entrance (Wu men) or the back entrance (Shenwu men). Many people say that as with all fine palaces one visit is not enough, and advise going through the front entrance on the first occasion to explore the major buildings and the living quarters, and returning for a second visit, via the back entrance this time, to admire the treasures in the ex-hibition quarters in the north-eastern quarter of the palace.

Before you visit the Forbidden City for the first time you will probably have glimpsed en route to another destination its faded vermilion walls – a mysterious contrast to the strident modernity of Tianan men Square, or you may have gazed down from the highest point on Coal Hill at the palace's myriad golden roofs. To get to it from Tianan men Square you pass over stone bridges, past two carved ceremonial pillars and lions, and through the dark tunnel of the Tianan men Gate. There are still two gates to be passed through and a long approach before you reach the Forbidden City proper. In the area between the Duan men Gate and the Meridian Gate (Wumen), the soaring gate to the palace itself, there are now snack shops, souvenir shops and photograph booths. The Meridian Gate was built in 1647 and is sometimes called the Five Phoenix Pavilion. This central approach was in fact formerly only used by the emperor when he left the palace on ceremonial occasions.

Encircling the palace are a 10-m-high wall and the Tongzi moat, which is 52 m wide. At each corner is a watchtower; there is a back entrance in the north and there are two side entrances. The palace contains 9000 rooms. From north to south it is 960 m long, and from east to west 760 m.

The palace is redolent with symbolism pertaining to the ancient Chinese notion of imperial power. The emperor was the 'Son of Heaven', so the scale of the imperial palace and ceremonial halls were intended to reflect grandeur and majesty, so that the emperor was distanced from the man in the street. The dragon is the symbol of the emperor, the phoenix that of the empress, while the turtle and the crane are symbols of longevity. Be prepared for the rich reds, blues, greens and golds; the low,

A hall in the Forbidden City

Left Throne room in the Forbidden City. *Right* Balustrades and parapets in the Forbidden City. The dragon-head gargoyles assist drainage – the Chinese word for tap literally means 'dragon's head'

Left View from the Forbidden City to Coal Hill. *Right* An unusual pagoda in the Forbidden City, showing Tibetan influence

Left The Imperial Stairway. *Right* Details of the phoenix carved on the stone over which the Empress's palanquin would be carried in the Forbidden City

sweeping roofs; and the rows of eave ornaments, usually of wild or mythical beasts but sometimes human likenesses, whose main function was to ward off evil spirits but which often also had specific functions such as lightning conductors. Standing guard here, as at the gates of many imperial buildings, are a pair of lions – the king of beasts and a lioness with a cub under her paw. The palace is divided into two main sections – ceremonial halls on the grand scale and the intimate living quarters of the emperor and his court in the north of the palace; while the north-west section still presents the appearance of living quarters, the north-east section has been turned into a fascinating museum.

Entering through the Meridian Gate, you cross five bridges over the winding Jin River. In the ceremonial quarter with the three great halls there are no trees or shrubs, which might have detracted from the majesty of the emperor. Now you are approaching the Gate of Supreme Harmony (Taihemen), the gate to the main ceremonial quarter, the San da dian or three great halls. These comprise the throne room of the emperor – the hall of Supreme Harmony (Taihe dian) – the hall of Complete Harmony (Zhonghe dian) and the hall of Preserving Harmony (Baohe dian). They are all raised on a three-tiered terrace, surrounded by an intricately carved white stone balustrade featuring dragons' heads, which are a drainage device. On either side of this major courtyard are two lesser halls – on the left the Hall of Military Splendour, and on the right the Hall of Literary Splendour, the seat of vital ministries of the emperor's court.

There are three stairways to the Hall of Supreme Harmony: the central one is a flat carved slab up which the emperor would be carried. In front of the hall you will find a standard bushel measure on your left, a sundial on your right, and

various incense burners, including ones shaped like turtles or cranes and constructed so that the smoke issued from their mouths, and large bronze cauldrons which were filled with water in preparation for fires.

The Hall of Supreme Harmony was the throne room, built in 1609 by Emperor Wan li; it was where the coronations took place, where New Year was celebrated, where important decrees were issued and where the emperor came on his birthday. The throne, made of gold lacquered wood, stood on a raised dais in front of an intricate carved screen, and was positioned at the centre of old Peking.

Behind this is the smaller Hall of Complete Harmony, an ante-chamber where the emperor would rest before coming out into the throne room, and where he received some of his courtiers. The Hall of Preserving Harmony was a banqueting hall. Its main architectural feature is the absence of supporting pillars over an area of 400 m^2; degrees were awarded here for successful candidates in the imperial examinations. The famous jade suit and terracotta warriors are now displayed here. Behind the Hall of Preserving Harmony is an enormous slab over which the emperor would be borne; carved with clouds and dragons, it is 16 m long and weighs 200 tonnes.

On leaving the ceremonial or outer section for the six palaces of the inner or living quarters, the scale and atmosphere change, becoming more intimate with small buildings clustered round courtyards and a maze of paths running between them. Here there are gardens, quarters for the empress, concubines and eunuchs, storehouses, temples, and the palace to which the old emperor would retire.

First you will reach Qianjing men, the Gate to the Hall of Heavenly Purity. Just to the left of the gate is a long, low, rather insignificant-looking building. This was the office of the Grand Council, conveniently placed close to the Hall of Heavenly Purity where the emperor carried out most of his day-to-day work. After 1735 state affairs were run from the Yangxing dian, the Hall of Mental Cultivation, which was where the Empress Dowager hatched many of her intrigues. On the approach to the Hall of Heavenly Purity are two rows of persimmon trees in pots; behind them lay the Hall of Heavenly and Earthly Intercourse (Jiaoyi dian) where the imperial seals were kept, and also where offerings were made to Buddha. The Hall of Earthly Tranquillity (Kunning gong), immediately behind, was the sleeping quarters of the empress, where in the Qing dynasty weddings were also held. The Empress Dowager lived in the Palace of Gathering Excellence (Chuxiu gong). In the north-west quarter of the palace, which has been retained to reflect the daily lives of the imperial family and court, are some of the clocks and clockwork paraphernalia presented by foreign kings (among them George III of England) to the Qing emperors.

There were three gardens in the palace, including one for the women in the west and one in the east built by Qian long for his retirement in the Palace of Peaceful Old Age (Ningshou gong). The one which has remained tended and open is the imperial garden at the northern extremity of the palace, where plants, rockeries and waterfalls will be found. Adjacent is the theatre stage in the Lodge of Fresh Fragrance (Shufang zhai). In keeping with Chinese ideas of harmony and symmetry the pavilions have complementary names – such as the Pavilion of Endless Autumns (Wanqiu ting) and the Pavilion of Ceaseless Springs (Qianchun ting). In the eastern section of the palace is the Nine Dragon Screen, and here the

palaces have been formed into exhibition rooms, for which a small entrance fee is often payable. The Palace of Peaceful Old Age contains the finest collection of paintings in China; the oldest and most interesting paintings are generally displayed only once a year – in October, when the climate is not too harsh. Behind this, in the Palace of Mental Cultivation, is the Treasure Room, containing ornate swords, costumes, jewellery, gold and silver, and flowers made from semi-precious stones. Other rooms contain bronzes, jade, arts and crafts from the Ming and Qing, wood lacquer, ivory, bamboo and porcelain.

You leave the Palace Museum via the Shenwu Gate at the back. A fitting end to the visit is to climb Coal Hill Park, directly opposite, for a view over the Forbidden City.

Coal Hill Park or Prospect Hill Park (Jing shan gongyuan)

Jing shan, one of the highest spots in Peking, is the best place for an aerial picture of the Forbidden City. As you stand on the top you should look both north and south and recall that this was the axis of Peking; looking north you will see the Drum Tower. The hill has changed its name several times. In the Yuan dynasty there was already a small hill here; it formed part of the imperial garden and, since it was covered with every possible plant and tree brought from all over China by Khubilai Khan, it was called Green Hill. During the construction of the Forbidden City, while the moat was being dug, the earth was piled up here to make the hill higher – it is now 43 m in height. The popular name for the hill is Coal Hill. Though some people thought that there actually was coal in the hill, kept there in case the palace or the city were ever under siege, it seems that coal was piled near here during the construction of the palace and this has stuck as the popular name. In 1751 Emperor Qian long had five pavilions built here; he also built some other buildings behind the hill and generally improved the layout and the garden, and so the name was changed to Prospect Hill Park. If you enter the park on the east side you will come upon the stump of the locust tree where Zhong zhen, the last emperor of the Ming dynasty, hanged himself when Li Zicheng led his peasant army against the imperial house.

The buildings at the back of the hill were originally imperial ancestral temples which were repaired and restored after liberation and are now used as the Peking Children's Palace. The main feature of this park, though, is the five pavilions ranged along the side of the hill. The pavilion on top of the hill is called Wanchun (Ten Thousand Springs); the roof is three-tiered and it is rectangular in shape, with green-glazed tiles. Further down the hill are two smaller pavilions on either side – Zhoushang on the east and Fulan on the west. They have octagonal double-tiered roofs with glazed tiles of jade green. Lower down on either side are two pavilions with double-deckered round roofs; they are called Guan miao and Ji fang.

Each pavilion formerly contained a buddha, four of which were looted by the Allied troops in 1900; the last one was removed some time during the Cultural Revolution. Both this park and the Bei hai Park were closed for several years before the spring of 1978. Inside the main entrance is the Qiwang lou (Fine View Pavilion) which was a temple to Confucius and now houses a shop selling some interesting souvenirs – stones for seals, batik and calligraphy. Naturally one also can climb to the top of the hill from this entrance, but the climb is rather steep.

Bei hai Park or Northern Lake Park

To the west of the Forbidden City is a series of lakes which end in the north-west suburbs – most of this area was once marshland which has been drained. The northern lake is part of this series and the southern and middle lake, separated from the northern lake by a road bridge, are part of the grounds of the State Council. The whole area used to be part of the Imperial Palace. The entrance to the State Council is on Chang'an Avenue, where you will see two guards and an ornate red gate.

In the tenth century the Liao dynasty had their summer palace in Bei hai Park, in the Jin dynasty Emerald Island (Qionghuadao) was dug out, and the famous Guanhan dian, the Palace in the Moon was built here along with the Yaoguang Palace. The concept and style of these summer and leisure palaces differ from those of the Imperial Palace – they are more natural and informal. Khubilai Khan was the next to enlarge the island, making it the centre of his city.

The main entrance to the park is on Wenjin jie, to the west of the back exit of the Forbidden City. The park has four main sections – the Round City, the Emerald Island with the distinctive White Dagoba, the lake itself which occupies about half of the available space of 68 ha, and the north-west corner.

To the left of the entrance is the so-called Round City (Tuan cheng), built from the earth of the lake. In the Jin dynasty it formed a resting place for the emperor. The high wall around it was built at the beginning of the fifteenth century, giving a fortress-like appearance. In the centre of the 'city' is the Chengguan dian, built in 1746 by the Emperor Qian long. It is a rectangular building reminiscent of the corner towers of the Forbidden City. The Chengguan dian contains one of the three jade buddhas presented to the Empress Dowager by Burma. Made of fine white jade, it is 1.5 m high; unfortunately one of its arms was broken off when the Allied troops entered Peking in 1900. A small pavilion with a blue roof and white pillars contains a famous Yuan dynasty wine pitcher, used by Khubilai Khan at banquets, made from dark jade and carved with dragons and sea animals. It is 0.7 m high, 1.35 m in diameter, and 4.55 m in circumference. The Round City also contains some pine trees which are seven hundred years old. Today exhibitions are often held in the Tuan cheng.

To reach the Emerald Island you enter the park by the main gate and cross the Yongan qiao, the Bridge of Everlasting Peace, which dates back to the thirteenth century, passing under the arches known as Duiyun and Jizui. In the summer the lake is usually covered with lotus flowers. The island has several features: exhibition halls, goldfish, and a pavilion where old and young come to play *weiqi*. The island is dominated by the White Dagoba. At the foot of the hill is the Temple of Everlasting Peace, built in 1651 in honour of the Lama, where he read the sutras. A bell and a drum tower stand on either side of the temple, which contains a statue of Sakyamuni and his disciples. Behind this is the Temple of Universal Peace.

Finally you reach the dagoba itself, with a small square shrine in front of it covered in tiles carved with various buddhas. It was built in 1651 by the first Qing emperor, Shun zhi, as a gesture of conciliation and honour to the Dalai Lama who came to Peking then. It contains relics of the Dalai Lama's clothes and some scriptures, and is 35.9 m high. A dagoba usually has a wide base with a smaller structure on top; at the very pinnacle of this one is a kind of golden sphere. The dagoba has several times been damaged by earthquakes, the last time being in 1976.

Most visitors descend to the eastern side of the island, where there is a stone tablet bearing Qian long's calligraphic inscription claiming this as one of the eight ancient scenic spots of Peking with the words: 'The spring moon over Emerald Isle'. The northern side of the island is bordered by a long gallery, similar to the one in the Summer Palace, with paintings on the ceiling.

Behind the gallery is a famous restaurant – the Bei hai fang shang – which serves food in the style of the imperial kitchens and where you may sample some of the dishes which the Empress Dowager used to enjoy – best known are the *wowo tou*, usually made of corn meal, but prepared for the imperial palate with chestnut paste. Crossing a small bridge you come to the eastern shores of the lake, a small exit, where there is a children's park. In the north-eastern corner where formerly the Hall of Sericulture stood, there is now a kindergarten and a model of a hydro-electric power station.

Time permitting, you can hire a rowing boat or take the ferry across to the north-west shores of the lake to take a look at the famous Nine Dragon Screen – the finest and one of the three most famous screens in China. On disembarking, you come first to the Iron Screen, made of a dark rock and decorated with mythical animals and clouds. It was transferred in 1937 from the garden of a high-ranking official in another part of the city, and is six hundred years old. These screens were usually found in the entrances to courtyards, where their purpose was to keep out evil spirits. The Nine Dragon Screen lies behind the Iron Screen and is covered with glazed five-colour tiles depicting nine dragons frolicking in the waves playing with pearls. Nine (the highest single number) was considered the imperial number. At 27 m long, 5 m high and 1.2 m thick the screen is the second largest in China.

Returning in a southerly direction along the western shore of the river you will pass the Five Dragon Pavilions, built in 1651, where the emperor would come to watch fireworks, to gaze at the moon or to fish. The way the pavilions are linked resembles a dragon. Behind in the corner are two buildings – the Hall of the Ten Thousand Buddhas and the Small Western Paradise; the former was built by Qian long in 1771 to celebrate his mother's eightieth birthday. Now they are both rather decrepit, presenting an exterior of bare wood, since they were damaged in 1900.

Continuing along the shore you can exit by the western gate, on the other side of Bei hai bridge. Adjacent to the park is the Peking Library, recognizable by its traditional Chinese-style entrance, it contains 9.8 million volumes. First set up in 1910 by the imperial court, it holds the complete collection of Chinese classical works compiled under Emperor Qian long in the eighteenth century, and the encyclopedia compiled in the Ming dynasty under Yong le. It also contains books printed from tenth-century wood blocks and the earliest bound book, *Flowers from a Literary Garden*, dated 1260. The library also has a collection of magazines from both China and abroad.

Temple of Heaven (Tian tan)

The Temple of Heaven lies in the south-western corner of Peking. The tradition which required the emperor to come here to pray for good harvests and offer sacrifices to Heaven goes back further than Confucius. In the layout and construction of the temple can be seen the perfect marriage of geometry, magic numbers, propitious sites and majesty. The most dignified and important cere-

monies of the year were carried out here. Leave behind for a moment the knowledge that it was all superstitious pomp and circumstance, and try to imagine the atmosphere and the solemnity; as you visit the various parts of the temple, such as the Whispering Wall, you will realize what an acoustic masterpiece it was. Symmetry in design was felt to endow all things with meaning, purpose and harmony, providing the right atmosphere for the emperor to commune with Heaven.

There are three other temples in Peking – the Temple of the Sun (Ri tan, near the embassy quarter) in the east, the Temple of the Earth (Di tan, beyond Anding men), and the Temple of the Moon (Yue tan on Nan lishi lu) in the west of the city. Together they represented the firmament – the four elements with the emperor in his palace as the cardinal point. Sacrifices were carried out at the appropriate time of year at each temple, but the Temple of Heaven was the major one. All these temples have been opened as parks, with some remnants of their altars still remaining. The last time the ceremonies were performed here was in 1915 by the pretender Yuan Shikai.

The Temple of Heaven was first built in 1420 and consists of three major buildings – the Hall of Prayer for Good Harvest (Qinian dian), the Imperial Vault of Heaven (Huangqiongyu) and the Circular Sacrificial Altar (Yuanqiu). They are connected by a terrace – Danjie qiao or the Red Steps Bridge – which is 360 m long from north to south. The perimeter wall is 3,292 m long; on the south side it is straight, and on the north it is curved in keeping with the view held then that Heaven is curved and the earth is flat.

The Hall of Prayer for a Good Harvest is renowned for its blue roofs – triple-deckered, round, harmonizing with the blue of the Peking sky and the blue robes and livery associated with the ceremony, the hall is topped by a small gilded orb and erected on a three-tiered white marble terrace. During the reign of Guang xu it was struck by lightning and burnt down, but was rebuilt in 1899 in the former style. It is 38 m high and 30 m in diameter; it constitutes quite a feat of architecture since it is built solely of wood and has no cross beams or nails, but is supported by twenty-eight wooden pillars made from a type of cedar tree found in Yunnan in south-west China, and held together by mortice joints. The four central pillars are highly decorated and painted and represent the four seasons, while the outer circle of twelve pillars represents the twelve months of the year. The very outermost circle represents the twelve divisions of the day.

In the centre are a throne, a table and a screen where the Tablet to the Supreme Ruler of Heaven is placed. On the right is a similar layout where the emperor made offerings to his ancestors, and to the left is the throne where the emperor would sit after the ceremonies. The roof design of a dragon and a phoenix is echoed in the stone floor in the centre of the hall.

A walk along the Danjie qiao will bring you to the Imperial Vault of Heaven, which is enclosed by the Whispering Wall. This is where the ancestral tablets, brought out for the winter solstice, are kept, as well as the tablets of the gods of rain, the sun, the moon, the stars, the dawn, wind, thunder and lightning. The Imperial Vault of Heaven is smaller than the Hall of Prayer for a Good Harvest; it was built in 1530 and is a round building encircled by the Whispering Wall. Just in front of the entrance to the vault is the Thrice Echoing Stone which is at the centre of the complex; if you stand here and clap you should hear a triple echo.

Leaving the Imperial Vault of Heaven, continue southwards and you will reach, through a series of marble arches carved with wings and cloud designs, the Circular Altar. The altar is set on a three-tiered terrace of white carved stone. Everything in the altar is in multiples of nine: for instance there are nine steps on each level, the stones which form the floor of the altar are in multiples of nine, there are nine rows, and the balustrade round each terrace has posts in multiples of nine. Again there is an acoustic effect − if you stand on the central slab and speak quite softly the sound should rebound loudly.

The emperor used to come to the Hall of Prayer for Good Harvest at the first full moon of the year. He would come to the altar itself at the winter solstice to offer sacrifice to Heaven. The evening before the ceremony a great procession would leave the Forbidden City through the Front Gate. The emperor would pass the night fasting and preparing himself; he would pray first in the Imperial Vault of Heaven and then he would approach the altar, facing north, waiting on the middle terrace with the tablets arrayed around him. His court would be behind him and on the lower terrace, and the proceedings would be accompanied by traditional and ancient music on clay pipes. The emperor would mount the top terrace at the appointed time, offer prayer and return. Later on a bull calf would be sacrificed and eventually he would return to his pavilion. The solemnity of the occasion and the power it invested in the emperor was almost as vital as that of going up to Mount Tai.

Today around the foot of the Hall of Prayer for Good Harvest there are several shops selling carpets, ink stones and handicrafts. In the Zhai gong Temple, near the western entrance, the Marco Polo Commission Shop has been reopened; it sells a wide range of antiques and unusual handicraft goods.

Great Wall (Wanli changcheng)

Some people say that astronauts can see the Great Wall from the moon. However it is only 75 km from Peking, and it is something the first-time visitor to Peking really must see. Since earliest days the Chinese have built walls around their cities, and in the seventh century BC they began to build walls between rival states. Construction continued in the Warring States period, when the northern states built strategically placed walls to keep out the Xiongnu – the Huns and other nomadic tribes. The Emperor Qin Shi Huang had them joined together and extended as he unified the country; the work took ten years.

In the Han dynasty another wall was built to the north of the original one by Han Wu Di. The wall did provide a barrier and was kept well repaired and maintained as long as China felt threatened, but in the Tang dynasty, with the enormous growth of China's power and strength, the wall fell into disrepair. Major repairs were undertaken in the Ming dynasty when China was threatened by the Mongols and the Nuzhen. A tablet discovered near Ba da ling, and dated 1582, records the numbers of soldiers and civilians involved in the repairing of the wall. The wall visible today – and you will see sections of it on journeys through many parts of northern China – actually starts in Jiayu guan pass in Gansu Province, passes through Ningxia autonomous region, Shaanxi, Inner Mongolia and Shanxi to Shanhai guan on the coast of the Bo hai Sea in Hebei Province, a distance of 6000 km.

The original wall was built of earth and rock, and in desert areas of sand and rubble alternating with layers of reeds and branches. In the Ming dynasty it was faced with bricks and slabs of stone. The wall was wide enough for five horsemen to ride abreast along it, and it was around 6 m high. Fortresses were positioned at strategic spots, and watchtowers every few hundred metres enabled messages to be transmitted along the wall.

The section of the wall that people visit from Peking is at Ba da ling, 75 km north-west of Peking in the Juyong Pass, in the Yanshan mountain range. It can be reached by train or bus. The bus affords a close look at the countryside, and the sensation of leaving the plain and climbing up into the mountains. You will catch your first glimpse of the wall snaking over the hills, and see some of the sights of rural life such as oranges or persimmons drying on a roof. Often you take a lunchbox and have a picnic under the shadow of the wall in heated rooms; alternatively there is a snack bar shop selling coffee, other drinks and noodles. All year round the wall is windy and colder than the city, and though the climb to the top of it will usually make your blood circulate, warm clothes and a hat are a must in winter. At Ba da ling the wall is 800 m above sea-level at the highest point. It was restored in 1957 and is one of the national monuments under government protection. The wall has an east and a west section here and you can climb along its top to the summit of both hills, giving you a view into the plain which leads to Kalgan (Changjiakou). The Juyong Pass on the approach to the wall has been the gateway to Peking since the Han dynasty, and it was an important garrison during the Ming dynasty. The Yun tai is a curved white marble archway plinth carved with buddhas and sutras in several languages. Built in the Yuan dynasty in 1345, on a former site of a monastery and pagodas, it seems to be the place where the legendary woman general Gui Ying addressed her troops.

Ming Tombs

These tombs are 50 km to the north of Peking on the southern slopes of the Tian Mountains. The third Ming emperor, Yong le, chose this site for his tomb, and the other twelve emperors followed suit. Chinese geomancers declared the site to be a propitious one, which can well be appreciated as you approach the Valley of the Ming Tombs and see the gleaming yellow roofs of the tablet towers nestling in the crescent of wooden hills. This whole area, which covers approximately 40 km², was once strictly out of bounds to anyone not connected with the tombs and their upkeep.

The first two Ming emperors are not buried here – the first emperor is buried on Purple Mountain in Nanking, and no one knows the whereabouts of the remains of the second, who was usurped by Yong le. The only other Ming emperor not buried here was the seventh, who ruled by default as his brother was captured by the Mongols and later returned. Surprisingly enough the last Ming emperor, who hanged himself, also lies here. As Yong le was the first to build a tomb here the approach to the tombs area leads directly to his tomb, which is called Chang ling. He started building it in 1409 and finished it four years later.

After turning off the main road leading to the Great Wall you will come into the Ming tombs area. It is 7 km from the elaborate white stone archway built in 1540 to Chang ling – as with the Forbidden City, the builders were thinking on a grand scale. One kilometre further along is the main gate – a large red arched building with three doorways, the central one of which was used only to bring in the body of a dead emperor. After the main entrance comes the Tablet Pavilion, containing a 7-m high tablet on the back of a large stone tortoise, inscribed in honour of Yong le by his

successor, Hong xi. On the reverse side is another inscription, by Qian long, describing the repairs that he effected in 1785.

From here the visitor reaches the famous Sacred Way – a guard of honour of animals and officials characteristic of tombs since the Han dynasty. Twelve animals are placed on either side – one pair standing and one pair kneeling; there are lions, camels, elephants and horses as well as the mythical *xiezhai* – a kind of Chinese unicorn, and the *qilin* – an auspicious animal also rather like a unicorn. The officials consist of high-ranking soldiers and politicians and the Chinese equivalent of Knights of the Garter – there are four of each, all standing. After the Sacred Way you pass on the right the Ming tombs reservoir, built in 1958 and containing a hydro-electric power station.

Continuing straight ahead through another archway and over a bridge you will come to the largest and most complete tomb – Chang ling. The layout is typical of all the tombs – a kind of keyhole shape with a *ling'en dian* for offering prayers and sacrifices to one's ancestors. The one at Chang ling was built in 1427 and is similar in style to the Hall of Supreme Harmony in the Forbidden City, though it is in fact bigger, with pillars of sofora trees from south China. Behind this is a tower on a large square base containing the 'tombstone'. From the tower begins the so called Precious Wall which surrounds the tumulus.

The only tomb which has been excavated so far is Ding ling; to reach it, instead of continuing straight ahead after the Sacred Way take a left turn after the bridge. Ding ling is the tomb of Wan li (1573–1620) or Zhu Yijun as he is also called, who came to the throne when he was ten years old. He was the thirteenth Ming emperor and started to build his tomb when he was twenty-two. The tomb took eight years to build, and was an expensive and labour-intensive project.

After passing through the entrance to the tomb area you will see on the right rooms for picnics. You will pass through courtyards and terraces where once buildings stood, including the hall where the emperor would sacrifice to his ancestors. In the final courtyard, below the square tower are two exhibition rooms containing exhibits from the tomb, such as blue-and-white Ming china and some of the 'phoenix crowns', made from kingfisher feathers, worn by the empress. Behind the Square Tower (Fang cheng) is the entrance to the tomb itself.

The discovery of the entrance to the tomb was the result of archaeological detection work – all the tombs are 'hermetically sealed' and their exits and entrances were a carefully guarded secret. The search began in 1956, and by 1957 the tomb had been excavated. Loose stones were discovered in the wall surrounding the tumulus, and investigation revealed an earthen tunnel behind them and tablets detailing the size and direction of the vault or underground palace (Dixia gong) as it is referred to, which was found eventually 27 m underground. A staircase has now been built into the vault, and there are five chambers covering an area of 1195 m². The whole construction is entirely of stone, without any supporting beams.

The small ante-chamber, built in 1957, contains the Diamond Wall with its small triangular opening which was where the first and last bricks were sealed before and after the burial. From here you come to the entrance of the large outer hall with the first large marble doors, made of whole pieces of marble and carved with nail heads and a door knocker; each leaf weighs four tonnes. Just inside the door on the right you will find a stone called the Stone

Which Got There by Itself (zilai shi), which acted as a kind of extra lock on the door, preventing intruders from getting in. Various theories have been put forward as to how it was put into place as the tomb was left for the last time.

From here you enter the outer hall, with rectangular, arched ceilings 20 m long and 6 m wide. Graphs and pictures on the walls demonstrate what an extravagant piece of work it was, and how it exploited the ordinary people. Passing through another heavy door in the Central Hall you come to a chamber 6 m high and 32 m long, containing three large carved marble thrones – the front two were for the empresses and the last one for the emperor. In front of them are large blue-and-white pitchers which were supposed to have burnt the 'everlasting flame' – however when the archaeologists entered the chamber the pitchers were still almost full of vegetable oil. On small pedestals in front of the thrones were placed ritual objects used in funerals.

Branching off from the Central Hall are two smaller side chambers which were designated for the two empresses and had their own separate entrance. However in the end they were buried with the emperor. Placed horizontally across the end of the Central Hall is the Far Hall which contains copies of the three coffins of Zhu Yijun and his two wives, as well as boxes containing the funerary objects and treasures which were to accompany them into their next lives. No one is quite sure how the two empresses finished up in the same hall as the emperor, since one had died several years before the emperor, and the other a few months before him. It is thought that the funeral rites were carried out in some haste, possibly due to a peasant uprising.

After coming out of the somewhat chilly and eerie vaults climb up to the Stele Tower, which contains the 'stone' marking the site of Wan li's grave and provides a splendid view over the Ming tombs valley.

Summer Palace (Yihe yuan)

The Summer Palace was one of the Empress Dowager's final extravaganzas, for which she appropriated funds allocated for building a Chinese navy. In the north-west suburbs of Peking, it is a favourite spot for a Sunday outing among the Chinese. In summer you can row on the lake, in spring people fly their kites, and in winter many come skating here. The array of pavilions, courtyards, gazebos, temples and galleries is built along Longevity Hill, overlooking Kunming Lake.

Surrounded as the palace is by the Western Hills and Fragrant Hill, it is not hard to imagine how it has long been a favourite cool retreat from the heat of the city in the summer; in fact as long ago as the Jin dynasty in the twelfth century there was a summer palace here. During the Yuan dynasty, after some hydraulic engineering had been carried out the waters of the Jade Spring – famous for their freshness and coolness – were channelled into the lake. Today you can still look across from the Summer Palace and see a white pagoda – the Jade Spring Pagoda. During the Ming dynasty it continued to be the site of a temple and a summer palace. Under Qian long the palace was refurbished and extended to celebrate his mother's sixtieth birthday, at which time he renamed the hill on which it was built Longevity Hill, and the lake Kunming Lake.

In 1860 the Summer Palace was ransacked and burnt by the French and British armies. Ci xi built the present Summer Palace in 1880, though it was plundered again in 1900 by the Allied forces who came into China, with the Empress Dowager's connivance, to quell the Boxer Uprising; it was re-paired in 1903. In 1924 the palace was opened to the public.

The visitor enters by the East Palace Gate. The eastern section of the Summer Palace was where the court had its living quarters, where matters of state were attended to, and where entertainments were performed. You will visit first the Hall of Benevolence and Longevity (Renshou dian) where the emperor held audiences. To the right of the Hall of Benevolence and Longevity is the Courtyard of Virtue and Harmony (Dehe yuan), which contains an ornate stage jutting into the middle of the courtyard, with a viewing gallery on three sides. To the left of this and slightly below is the Palace of Jade Waves (Yulan tang), walled all round, where the Empress Dowager imprisoned Guang xu for ten years. From here follow the shores of the lake to the Empress Dowager's luxuriously appointed apartments – the Palace of Joy and Longevity (Leshou tang) – where bronze cranes stand guard. Here you may be informed about some of her excesses, such as the selection of porridges from which she could choose every morning.

From here you enter the Long Gallery, which is 728 m long and follows the line of the lake. The ceiling is painted with flowers and scenes from famous stories. From the lake the view across the shore is designed to give a harmonious ensemble of colour and nature, repeated by the reflection in the water. Halfway along the corridor is a complex of temples and belvederes built into the side of the hill, which in fact dominate the palace and lake. This is the site of the former Ming dynasty temple, and here Ci xi built a palace in which to celebrate her birthdays – the Palace Which Dispels Clouds (Paiyun dian). If you climb the steps behind you will reach the Belvedere of the Fragrance of the Buddha (Foxiang ge), a four-

Marble bridges in the Forbidden City

Left The Hall of Prayer for a Good Harvest in the Temple of Heaven. *Right and below left* The ceiling of the Hall of Prayer for a Good Harvest

Right Ceremonial arches leading to the sacrificial altar in the Temple of Heaven

The Temple of Heaven

The Empress Dowager's folly: the Marble Boat moored alongside pleasure craft on Kunming Lake in the Summer Palace

Each painting on the beams of the Long Corridor in the Summer Palace is based on a well-known legend

storeyed building housing the statue of Buddha. To the west of it is the Precious Cloud Pavilion (Baoyun ge), often called the Bronze Pavilion because it contains a bronze kiosk put there by the Jesuits in 1750. Behind the Palace of the Fragrance of the Buddha stands a building constructed entirely of green- and yellow-glazed bricks and with designs of buddhas on them: it is called 'the Sea of Boundless Wisdom' (Zhihui hai).

Continuing through the Long Gallery you come to the the Listening to Orioles Hall (Tingli guan), which was once a theatre and is now a restaurant which does an excellent line in sea cucumber, fish and deep-fried *mantou* (steamed bread). Leaving the restaurant and continuing to the end of the promenade you reach the famous Marble Boat, a real folly which resembles a showboat–paddle steamer.

You can often take a boat from here across the lake. Behind this are a bridge and a series of buildings in southern style which are often called Little Suzhou Street. The water continues on round to the back where once there were shops, temples and boat houses which are now in varying states of repair – an area which was never as important as the south side of the hill as it didn't command such a good view. On the way you will pass the Many Treasures Pagoda (Duobao ta).

If you have time to spare you can take a rowing boat and explore the lake. The West Dyke (Xi ti) divides it into the West Lake and South Lake; passing under the Jade Belt Bridge or the Mirror Bridge you come to the West Lake. On crossing the lake you reach South Lake Island, on which is the Temple of the Dragon King, joined to the mainland by the Seventeen-arched Bridge, at the end of which is a bronze ox. Coming back along the eastern shore you reach the Meeting Spring Pavilion (Zhichun ting). The Garden of Harmonious Interests (Jiequ yuan) is situated on the eastern side of Longevity Hill. Built round a lake with bridges, pavilions, twisting galleries and lotus flowers, it was modelled on the Ji garden in Wuxi after Qian long had returned from one of his visits to the south of China, enthralled with the style of architecture and gardens and eager to copy it in Peking. The Garden of Harmonious Interest is often referred to as 'the garden within a garden'.

Former Summer Palace (Yuanming yuan)

The ruins of the old Summer Palace can be found in Haidian village, near Qinghua University and Peking University in the north of the city. It was built by the Qing emperors in idyllic natural surroundings. Qian long had parts of the palace designed by Italian and French architects, and built largely of stone, but all that remains are a few carved ruins since the palace was invaded and destroyed in 1860, forcing the Emperor Xian feng and the young Empress Dowager to flee to Jehol.

Temple of the Sleeping Buddha (Wofo si)

Continuing on the road from the Summer Palace in a westerly direction you arrive at the Temple of the Sleeping Buddha, at the foot of Peaceful Longevity Hill (Shouan shan) and Incense Burner Peak (Xianglu feng) in the Western Hills. Entering through the main portico, decorated with yellow and green tiles, crossing a bridge to the Drum and Bell Tower and going past two halls which used to contain Buddhist statues, you come to a courtyard and darkened room containing a massive bronze statue of the sleeping Buddha, reclining on one elbow, with a serene smile on his face. As far back as the seventh century there was a temple here with a sandalwood sleeping buddha.

This particular statue and temple were begun in 1322 in the Yuan dynasty and completed ten years later, after interruptions. According to Yuan dynasty records it was made of 227 tonnes of bronze; the statue is more than 5 m long, and actually weighs only about 54 tonnes. The scene depicts Sakyamuni giving his last will and testament to his twelve disciples under a saul tree – a rare tree which originally came from India. Two of these trees are growing in the grounds of the temple. The correct name of the temple is the Temple of Universal Consciousness (Shifang pujue si). A short distance to the north-west of the temple lies a small valley called Cherry Valley (Yingtao gou), with a brook and exquisite natural surroundings of bamboo, flowers, pines, waterfalls, the remains of old temples, and stone tablets and rockeries. There used to be a temple here called the Black Gate Temple, surrounded by vegetable gardens and an orchard where many cherry trees grew – hence the name.

Temple of the Azure Clouds (Biyun si)

The Temple of the Azure Clouds is in the Western Hills, to the east of Fragrant Hill; built in the 'diamond pagoda' style, its five ornate steeples rise through the trees on the hillside. It was first built in the Yuan dynasty, and its history includes tales of princes and ministers who hoped to retire here from the ordeals of political life or to be buried here. The fearsome seventeenth-century eunuch, Wei Zongxian, chose this as his burial place, but his life ended in ignominy. It was also a favourite haunt of the Emperor Qian long, who had improvements carried out in 1748 and built the Hall of the Five Hundred Arhats and the Five-steepled Pagoda.

You enter the temple grounds across a white bridge, past cypress and pine trees and a pair of stone lions which date from the time of the eunuch Wei Zongxian, and a spring emanating from dragons' heads. Then you come to the Hall of the Heavenly Kings – the four guardian gods and Milo fo – the Laughing Buddha, and the Buddha's Hall.

Behind is Sun Yatsen's Memorial Hall; after his death in 1925 Sun Yatsen's coffin was placed here before being moved to Nanking. The Memorial Hall now contains some of his effects and the glass coffin presented by the Russians.

The highlight of the visit to the Temple of the Azure Clouds is the climb to the stupa, with its five pagodas on top, each with elaborate bas-reliefs on white marble depicting in Tibetan style scenes from the Buddhist scriptures. The name of the stupa in Chinese, Jingang baozuo ta, indicates that it is dedicated to Sakyamuni and probably contained a holy relic such as a tooth, which was removed by a monk when the temple was under attack and has now been lost.

The Hall of Saints (Luohan tang) to the left of Sun Yat Sen's Hall contains 508 statues. There are 500 arhats, seven sages and, perched on a beam, Ji gong, the arhat who arrived too late.

Fragrant Hill (Xiang shan)

Fragrant Hill, next to the Temple of Azure Clouds, was once the favourite hunting ground of emperors. The best time of year to visit it is October – it is famed for the red leaves of autumn, and the hills echo with the cries of children careering up and down some of the steep paths. The area combines unspoiled wilderness with temples and pagodas, and there is also a good restaurant here. It is of course attractive all year round, and Fragrant Hill in the snow is one of the eight wonderful sights of Peking. The highest peak is 557 m and the park covers an area of

160 ha. As early as the eleventh century there was a Fragrant Hill Temple here, a summer palace was built in the Qing dynasty, and by the mid-eighteenth century it was one of the best-known parks in Peking. Unfortunately it was ransacked and damaged by invading troops at the end of the nineteenth century.

There are two main entrances to the park – the northern gate, next to the Temple of the Azure Clouds, and the eastern gate. Going through the northern gate cross the bridge over Spectacles Lake, pass the quiet 'Looking into the Mind' studio and the Shao Temple, and you will come to one of the major landmarks of Fragrant Hill, the octagonal Glass Pagoda, seven storeys high, covered with green- and yellow-glazed tiles. The wooded part of the hill faces south and is referred to as Red Leaves Forest. Traces of the old temple can be found on the southern slopes. The stele praising this view in the snow is on the western side of the hill; so is the famous Incense Burner Peak.

Western Hills (Xi shan)

These have long been a favoured beauty spot with emperors and their courts, not to mention a quiet hideaway for the religious since they are so conducive to meditation. Today the area is still popular among the citizens of Peking, who came here on their days off, and on Sundays you will often chance upon families taking photographs of each other or budding artists capturing the autumn colours. Apart from Fragrant Hill, already described and the Jade Spring Hill next to the Summer Palace, do not forget to visit the Ba da chu – the eight great sites – to be found directly west of the city. It is an area dotted with temples, springs and pagodas in varying states of repair. This was also a popular area for summer villas.

The Lama Temple (Yonghe gong)

Situated in the north-eastern suburbs of Peking, close to Anding men, the Lama Temple is one of Peking's most impressive temples.

The Lama Temple was originally the residence of the Emperor Yong zheng, before he assumed the throne in 1723. As there was a restriction on using the vacated residences of the royal family for any purposes other than that of the royal family or as a temple, in the reign of Qian long in 1744 it became a proper lama temple. At the entrance to the temple there is an elaborate 'pailou' or ceremonial arch, which forms the approach to the five main halls, flanked by the drum and bell towers.

The first hall contains the kings of heaven – the guardian gods. There is an elaborate bronze cauldron, decorated with lions and dragons, which was presented to Qian long in 1747. Beyond this is a stone tablet inscribed in Chinese, Manchurian, Mongolian and Tibetan explaining the significance of Lamaism. The main hall contains statues of Sakyamuni, the Buddha of the Past and the Buddha of the Future, statues of the eighteen arhats and a wall relief depicting Guanyin. This leads into the Yongyou Hall (the Hall of Eternal Blessing). The Falun Hall (the Hall of the Wheel of Life) contains a large statue of the famous Lama thinker and reformer Tsong Kapa, who was born in Qinghai and lived from 1417–1478; also five statues depicting his various metamorphoses. There is also a bronze sculpture of the mountain of 500 arhats and copies of the Tibetan scriptures. The fifth hall is three storeys high and stands between two two-storeyed towers connected by 'heavenly bridges'. It contains the giant gilded sandalwood statue of Milo fo – the Maitreya Buddha or Buddha of the Future – which is 18 m high and was presented to Qian long by the 7th Dalai Lama in 1750. Side halls were used as meditation rooms and study rooms where medicine and philosophy were discussed. They contain astronomical instruments and are decorated with erotic murals on Buddhist themes engaged in love-making.

Fayuan Temple

Reopened in 1980, this temple situated in the southern suburbs of Peking is now the headquarters of the Chinese academy of Buddhism, which acts as a research centre, seminary and also a museum.

A temple has been standing on this site since AD 645 and it has been the scene of many significant events in Chinese history. The temple has long been famous for its ancient trees and many flowers. Services are held regularly in the Daxiong Hall with its resplendent carved beams and painted pillars. The Dabei Hall contains several statues of Buddha including one of the earliest in China – a pottery statue dating from the Eastern Han dynasty.

Marco Polo Bridge (Lugou qiao)

To reach the bridge travel through the busy southern suburbs of Peking towards Zhoukoudian in the direction of some of the important industrial areas, such as the iron and steel works at Shijingshan, passing the somewhat dilapidated Anning Temple – with its 'stone' pagoda and intricate carvings.

Around 40 km outside Peking cross Lugou Bridge over the Yongding River – it is the oldest bridge in the vicinity of Peking and the first bridge on the site was built in 1189. Marco Polo described it, hence it is known to foreigners as Marco Polo Bridge. The emperor Kangxi rebuilt the bridge in 1698. It was another of the sights of old Peking – the 'morning moon over Lugou Bridge' – recorded on a stele by the bridge in Qian long's hand. It was also the site of the Marco Polo Bridge

Incident which was the immediate cause of the outbreak of the Sino–Japanese War in 1937. The bridge is elegantly carved in white marble with numerous lions in different poses forming the railings, and the arches are shaped like elephants. The Marco Polo Bridge is the southern city limit for foreigners.

Zhoukoudian and Peking Man

Zhoukoudian, approximately 50 km south-west of Peking, is the home of Peking's oldest inhabitant – the 500,000-year-old Peking Man, known scientifically as *Sinanthropus pekinensis*, *Pithecanthropus pekinensis*, or *Homo erectus pekinensis*. Zhoukoudian does not usually form part of the tourist round in Peking, although archaeologists and other specialist groups can arrange a visit here.

Having crossed Marco Polo Bridge, a few miles further along the road past fields of corn or rape, you will reach the foot of the Western Hills where Zhoukoudian lies. The fossils were first identified on Dragon Bone Hill, where for years people had been finding bones. At the site is a reception room, where visitors are given an introduction to Peking Man, followed by a tour of the museum. Then visitors can inspect the original cave home of Peking Man and his more sophisticated descendant, Upper Cave Man.

This is an area of limestone and coal mining, and it was a couple of miners who discovered two teeth in the early 1920s. Systematic excavation by French and American specialists began in 1927. In 1929 the first skull to be identified as Peking Man was excavated; work was interrupted in 1937 by the Sino–Japanese War. All the remains which were discovered before Liberation have been lost. Most of the finds were stored in the American Hospital near Wangfujing; an attempt was made by the

Left The Great Wall at Ba da ling, north of Peking.
Right A view of Chang ling: the tomb of the 2nd Ming emperor, Yong le, in the Valley of the Ming tombs near Peking

The Sleeping Buddha, outside Peking

Left Boating in Peking. *Right* A shop-front in Peking

A bird's eye view of Tianan men Square in Peking. On the left is the Great Hall of the People and, in the centre, the Chairman Mao Memorial Hall. Tianan men Gate and Palace Museum are in the background.

A night view of Peking railway station

The Iron Bridge over Suzhou Creek in Shanghai

Left Practising Wushu: martial arts on the Bund in Shanghai. *Right* The streets of Shanghai

A street scene in the Old City of Shanghai

Americans to get them out of the country after Pearl Harbor and they were lost in the process. The mystery surrounding these priceless archaeological relics has fired the imaginations of several authors who have written novels on the subject. Work was resumed after 1949 and further discoveries were made, enabling scientists to construct a picture of a settlement of around forty people, as well as something about animals, vegetation, climate, diet, stone tools and the use of fire. Extensive finds have also been made which throw light on Upper Cave Man – Peking Man's descendant who dates back 200,000 years and had both a more developed social organization and physique than Peking Man.

The museum, built in 1972, follows the evolution of animals from invertebrates to vertebrates and mammals, showing us the development from ape to man worldwide. The relics of Peking Man discovered after 1949 are in storage and the exhibits shown are copies. Exhibits relating to Upper Cave Man include needle, thread and ornaments. There is also a display of dinosaur fossils and eggs, some from Sichuan Province.

Peking Man's Cave faced north-east, was 175 m long and 50 m wide. It was discovered under thirteen natural strata which reveal clues about the change in climate in the area; in the days of Peking Man it was cooler than it is today. Upper Cave Man was discovered at a higher level: a burial ground was found, with three skulls and the remains of eight people.

Peking Man was an ape-man of the Lower Palaeolithic period, a period lasting approximately one million years, but showed some of the characteristics of later *Homo sapiens*, such as erect posture, a large brain, and the ability to use tools and implements. The characteristics similar to those of an ape were a low skull vault, a thick skull wall, bony crests around the skull's horizontal rim and a receding chin.

Museum of Chinese History (Lishi bowu guan)

Peking has a wide variety of museums and exhibition halls. The Museum of Chinese History on the eastern side of Tianan men Square is the largest and most comprehensive museum in China. It covers the period from the beginning of man in China, i.e. 1 million years ago; and the primitive stage lasting up to 4000 years ago; continues through the stage in man's social development which socialist historians dub slave society (2000 BC to 500 BC); goes on to the feudal period from 500 BC to AD 1840; and finally deals with the semi-colonial stage between 1840 and 1919, the turning-point in the Chinese democratic revolution. The same sub-divisions are followed in other museums in China.

In the same building is the Museum of Chinese Revolution, covering the period from 1919 to 1949; temporary exhibitions are also held here. It can be visited during opening hours, without prior notice, for a small entrance fee.

The Military Museum (Junshi bowu guan)

Situated at the western end of Chang'an Avenue, the museum covers the military history of the Chinese Revolution from the founding of the People's Liberation Army on 1 August 1927 at Nanchang to the Korean War, ending in 1958. Visits are by special request only.

Cultural Palace of the National Minorities (Minzu wenhua gong)

Again situated on Chang'an Avenue, just west of Xidan, it is a distinctive, tall, white building with an ornate tiled roof of turquoise green. It contains an exhibition centre of national minority crafts, costumes and language, a library and a theatre. It also has a clubroom bar and dance hall, often used for foreigners, and a restaurant serving 'national minority cuisine' such as shashlik.

Gallery of Fine Arts (Meishu guan)

It stands at the crossroads of Wangfujing and Wenjin jie – the road which leads to the back of the Palace Museum. The gallery, an enormous building with a yellow-glazed tiled roof, houses different exhibitions throughout the year from Chinese arts and crafts to foreign publications.

Observatory

It is at Jianguo men, near the Friendship Store and International Club. One of the few remaining landmarks of old Peking was the observatory, a tower containing a fine assortment of ancient instruments silhouetted against the sky. Unfortunately part of the tower collapsed under a rainstorm in 1979 although efforts are being made to restore it.

There was an observatory on this site as early as the days of Khubilai Khan in the late thirteenth century. Many of the instruments were made under the direction of the Jesuit priest Verbiest, who was placed in charge of the observatory as head of the Imperial Board of Mathematics in the seventeenth century in the court of the Emperor Kang xi.

Agricultural Exhibition Hall (Nongye zhanlan guan)

Visitors usually pass this building, in the north-eastern suburbs of Peking on the north-east circular road, on the way from the airport. It contains an exhibition of machinery and techniques and is of interest largely to specialists. Overseas agricultural exhibitions are sometimes held here.

Peking Industrial Exhibition (Beijing zhanlan guan)

This is a permanent exhibition housed in an ornate Russian-designed building east of the Zoo on Xizhi men wai dajie. The centre is also used for overseas exhibitions and Chinese temporary exhibitions. It has a theatre and a restaurant serving western food.

Zoo

The Peking Zoo, one of the finest in the world, contains a panda house, elephants, and other animals from China and abroad. It is on Xizhi men wai dajie. Opposite the Zoo is a bus station (for the bus to the Summer Palace), a small taxi rank, and a modern planetarium and observatory.

Capital Sports Stadium

This is situated at the crossroads of Xizhi men wai dajie and Baishi qiao lu.

Lu Xun Museum (Fucheng men bei dajie)

Housed in one of the places where Lu Xun, the great modern Chinese writer, lived, this museum is of interest to students of Chinese literature. Visits are by appointment only.

Underground Railway

The Peking underground system consists of one line running from east to west beginning at Peking Station, passing beneath Chang'an Avenue, and going as far as Pingguo yuan in the west. The north–south line is presently under construction. Trains are clean and frequent, and you can travel any number of stops for 1 *jiao*.

Main Station

A distinctive building with a clock, a beaming portrait of Chairman Mao and green-glazed turrets, it was finished in the early 1960s, though a new station is already planned. The present one, off

Jianguo men nei dajie copes with all internal and international traffic.

Handicrafts Studio
Peking has many traditional handicrafts and in 1960 the small scattered craft shops were brought under the roof of one large arts and crafts studio in the north-west suburbs of Peking. The visitor will find here cloisonné enamel, jade carving, ivory carving, traditional painting, painting inside snuff bottles, lacquerware, paste (flour and water) figurines and filigree jewellery. There are also a separate jade carving factory and a carpet factory in Peking.

Underground Anti-aircraft Shelters (Didao)
For some time preparation for war has been central to Chinese foreign policy. These shelters are to be regarded not so much as anti-atomic bombs but more as part of China's tunnel warfare strategy which helped the country out in the Sino–Japanese War. Both remarkable and chilling, it is the intention of the central government to ensure that every major city is equipped with a network of underground tunnels and halls which will enable inner city inhabitants and workers to reach safety outside the city or at least to shelter until danger has passed. They contain very basic supplies and first aid facilities. Work units or neighbourhood committees are usually mobilized to dig the tunnels in spring. Often on the sides of the street you will come across concrete moulded arches which are connected with the building of these tunnels.

Shopping: General Information
Peking has shopping facilities rivalled only by Shanghai, from the main shopping street of Wangfujing to some of the alleys and side streets leading off the old entertainment quarter of Qian men.

Opening hours are generally 8.30–5.30 every day, unless otherwise stated.

Friendship Store (Tel.: 593531)
On Jianguo men wai, it is open from 9 am to 8 pm. It has an exchange counter and shipping facilities, and is situated close to the diplomatic quarter. The goods for sale include food, tea, plants, songbirds in cages, Chinese medicine, acupuncture needles, imported spirits and cigarettes, silk, brocades, cashmere cloth and clothing; embroidered goods, Chinese padded jackets, dressing-gowns, blouses, shoes, fur coats, leather goods, china and porcelain, jewellery, jade, ivory, carpets, furniture, tablecloths and cloisonné enamel. There is a tailor in the friendship store who generally needs three to four weeks to make up a garment.

Wangfujing
Wangfujing is the main shopping street and runs northwards from the Peking Hotel and Chang'an Avenue. Walking northwards along the west (left-hand side of the road), the shops on this side of the road begin after the offices of *People's Daily*. Below is a selection of the main stores:

Wangfujing
261 Chops or seals
255 Baihuo dalou, the main department store: open until 7 pm

231 Musical instruments
Walking northwards along Wangfujing on the east (right-hand side) of the street from Chang'an Avenue:

214 New China Bookshop: has section for foreigners with books in Chinese, dictionaries etc, also posters
210 Waiwen shudian (foreign-language bookshop): sells Chinese publications

in English, magazines (orders for subscriptions taken); open until 7 pm
Tel. 555140
200 Arts and crafts, with exchange facilities: open until 8 pm
192 Fur and leather goods
172 Toys and children's clothing
156 Shoes and hats
136 Pharmacy

Dongan men dajie
28 Peking Stamp Company: turn left at first major crossroads after the department store

*East Wind Market
(Dongfeng shichang)*
This is off Wangfujing and consists of an assortment of snack shops and restaurants and a department store.

Liuli chang
This small alley lies south of Chang'an Avenue and the New Peking Duck Restaurant, off Nan xinhua jie, is the traditional 'antiques alley' of Peking. Parts of it have recently been knocked down as part of a new improvement plan. However, several important shops still remain in the vicinity. On the west side you will find the famous woodcut studio of Rongbao zhai where you can purchase all kinds of prints and scrolls, cards for New Year, paintbrushes, paper, inkstones and inksticks – all the paraphernalia of the Chinese calligrapher – and see woodcuts being prepared. On the east side is a small shop selling copies of Tang dynasty three-colour-glazed horses and effective rubbings taken from bas-reliefs on ancient tombs, etc.

For the time being at least, the shops which were formerly in Liuli chang have been transported to the Temple of Heaven. Selling seals, antiques and paintings, they cluster round the foot of the plinth which forms the main part of the Temple of Heaven.

In the western part of the Temple of Heaven complex in the Zhai gong Temple is the Marco Polo Commission Shop, reopened very recently; it has a reasonably priced antique shop and slightly unusual new goods.

Qian men (Front Gate)
It runs southwards from Tianan men Square and is a bustling shopping street.

Dashalan
Just south of Tianan men Square, it is an alley running off Qian men with green- and red-painted fascias. It was the site of one of the earliest cinemas in Peking, and here you will find a clothes store, hat store, bookshop, fabric shop and one of the oldest Chinese pharmacies in Peking (Tongren tang).

Qian men
At No. 149 is the Jingde zhen porcelain shop, selling mugs, teapots and tea services from Guangxi and Hunan Provinces.

Xidan
This street runs northwards from Chang'an Avenue between the Telegraph Building and the Palace of National Minorities. No. 195 is the food market, No. 110 sells chopsticks and fans, and No. 120 is a department store.

Dongdan
To the east of Wangfujing, it runs northwards from Chang'an Avenue near the station and is a colourful area containing local shops and a food market.

Useful Addresses

Post Office
Dongdan bei dajie (for sending parcels). Otherwise all hotels have stamps and telegram facilities. Opening hours: 8.30 am–6 pm.

Telexes
Dianbao dalou, the Telegraph Building, is on West Chang'an Avenue, open twenty-four hours. A three-minute telex costs approximately 25 *yuan*, but it is not possible to receive telexes here.

Banks
All Peking hotels and many shops supplying foreigners have exchange facilities. The main branch of the Bank of China is on the west side of Tianan men Square, behind the Great Hall of the People; it is recognizable by its red roofs and clock tower. The address is: Zhongguo yinhang, 17 Xijiao minxiang. Opening hours: Weekdays, 9 am–5 pm; Saturdays, 9 am–12 noon. Tel. 338521.

Many of the big international banking organizations now have representative offices in Peking, but all financial transactions are made through the Bank of China.

Hospitals
The Capital Hospital (Shoudu yiyuan) is at 1 Shuaifuyuan. Travelling northwards along Wangfujing, it is the second turning on the right.

There is also a new clinic on Dongdan with excellent facilities: Dongdan menzhenbu.
Tel. 553731

Photo Service
Zhongguo tupianshe, in the south-west corner of Xuanwu men, has a photo library and processing facilities. Most of the hotels in Peking also have processing facilities, using Kodak equipment.

Churches
The Catholic church (mass celebrated every Sunday) is at 141 Qian men xi dajie, Xuanwu men. The Protestant church is at 21 Dongdan bei dajie, Meizha hutong. The mosque is in Nanheng jie, the Islamic centre in the southern quarters of the city.

Airline Offices
CAAC, the Chinese airline, is at 117 Dong si xi dajie, at the northern crossroads of Wangfujing and Dongsi. Tickets are issued only here.
Tel. *Flight Information:* 552515
International Flight Bookings: 556720/554415
Enquiries: 558341

As more and more carriers are flying to Peking, airline offices are opening. Their main function is liaison work as all tickets have to be issued or endorsed by CAAC at Head Office Dong sixi dajie. However you may need to visit an office to obtain permission to change a date or airline or to check onward flight reservations. The offices are manned by personnel from the airline concerned and Chinese staff. Most airline offices are situated in the large Foreign Trade Apartments (Waijiao gongyu), Building 2.2 in Jian' guomenwai, behind the International club.

Ethiopian Airlines: Tel. 523812
Iran Air: Tel. 523843
Japan Airlines: Tel. 523457
Pakistan International Airlines: Tel. 523972
Air France: Tel. 523894
Swissair: Tel. 523492
Yugoslav Airlines: Tel. 523486
Philippine Airlines: Tel. 523992
Aeroflot: Tel. 523581
Tarom (Romanian Airlines): Tel. 523552. The office is in the Romanian Embassy, Ritan dong erlu.
British Airways: All enquiries handled by CAAC
Panam: Tel. 521756/522043
Lufthansa: Tel. 522626/523588

China International Travel Service (Luxingshe)
The head office is at 6 Dong Chang'an Avenue (tel. 553121). The Peking branch is at 2 Chongwen men damen

(tel. 755124 and 757181). Use the south-facing door.

Embassies
There are two embassy quarters in Peking: the first is around Jian'guomen-wai near the Friendship Store and the other is at Sanli tun, further east on the road towards the airport.

Australia
15 Dongzhi men wai dajie
Tel. 522331

Austria
5 Xiushi nan jie
Jianguo men wai
Tel. 522061

Belgium
6 Sanlitun lu
Tel. 521736

Canada
10 Sanlitun lu
Tel. 521475

Denmark
dongwu jie No1
Sanli tun
Tel. 522431

Finland
30 Guanghua lu
Tel. 521753

France
3 Dong san jie
Sanli tun
Tel. 521331

Germany (DDR)
3 Dong si jie
Sanli tun
Tel. 521631

Germany (FDR)
5 Dongzhi men wai dajie
Tel. 522161

Greece
19 Guanghua lu
Tel. 521391

Ireland
Temporarily Peking Hotel, room 5042

Italy
2 Dong er jie
Sanli tun
Tel. 522131

Netherlands
10 Dong si jie
Sanli tun
Tel. 521731

New Zealand
1 Dong er jie Ri tan lu
Tel. 522731

Norway
1 Dong yi jie
Sanli tun
Tel. 522261

Spain
9 Sanli tun lu
Tel. 521967

Sweden
3 Dongzhi men wai
Tel. 521770

Switzerland
3 Dongwu jie
Sanli tun
Tel. 522831

United Kingdom
11 Guanghua lu
Tel. 521961

United States of America
17 Guanghua Lu
Tel. 522033

Hotels: General Information
Businessmen, delegations, conferences, exhibitions, performing troupes and tourists converging on Peking have all placed a strain on limited hotel facilities, however 1982 has already seen the opening of two new hotels, with a third planned for the autumn. The average rate for a twin-bedded room with bathroom is around 35 yuan. The new luxury hotels charge more, with prices starting at 120 yuan and rising to 260 yuan per day.

Friendship Hotel (Youyi binguan)
Haidian lu
Tel. 890621
It is situated some 15 km to the north-west of the centre of Peking, on the way to the Summer Palace and near to Peking University.

The Friendship Hotel was built in the 1950s to house Russian experts, and consists of a complex of four main buildings, and several annexes and flats which are reserved for the 'foreign experts' and teachers resident in Peking. Other amenities include a gymnasium and a swimming pool (in summer), a theatre, restaurants and shops. In winter the hotel is well heated. In summer there is air-conditioning in the main building and electric fans in blocks 2 and 3. Accommodation is chiefly in twin-bedded rooms, all with bathroom. The hotel also has a clinic in building No. 4. During the summer months there is a roof garden bar and in the winter dances and variety shows are often held in the main building. Exchange and post office facilities are, in the main building. There are also shops in the buildings and in the galleries leading to the restaurants. Tourist groups usually eat in the dining-rooms attached to buildings 2 and 3. There is a restaurant in the main building which also serves throughout the day until 10 pm, and has a bar service. Banquets and speech venues can be arranged by the friendly staff. The hotel has a taxi rank.

Peking Hotel (Beijing Fandian)
Dong Chang'an jie (East Chang'an Avenue)
Tel. 552231
Cable 6531
Excellently situated on the corner of Wangfujing, the main shopping street, and three minutes from Tiananmen Square, this is the largest hotel in Peking. It consists of three inter-connecting blocks, the middle one dating from 1917, the newest and tallest from 1974, and the west block from the 1950s. The lobby of the new block is laid out with shops and the bar is open from 10 am to 11.30 pm. A post office and exchange facilities will be found on the ground floor, and a hairdresser and masseur on the first floor. There is a telex room in the West Block.

The hotel has several restaurants. The main dining-room in the new-block, dominated by a mural of Guilin, is on the right of the lobby. There is a buffet service at lunch and breakfast, and an after-hours restaurant with a selected menu open all day until midnight. On the first floor of the new wing is a restaurant serving Japanese food, small and large banqueting rooms, and a dining-room used largely by groups. There is another dining-room reserved for groups on the ground floor of the west wing.

At the front of the lobby is a taxi rank, and the No. 1 bus, which stops opposite the hotel, will take you to the Friendship Store.

Front Gate Hotel (Qian men fandian)
Yong an lu
Tel. 338731
The Front Gate Hotel is located in the south-west corner of the city, five minutes' walk from Liuli chang, the antiques quarter, and within walking distance of Qian men Street, the shopping street south of Tianan men Square.

Shops, exchange, post office, hairdresser and masseur are all located on the ground floor. There is also a taxi-rank here. The restaurant on the left of the lobby serves Chinese food only; the restaurant on the right of the lobby serves western food and has a section for hotel guests which serves both western and Chinese food, and offers an after-hours service. The hotel was built in the 1950s and has a slight Soviet feel about it – the rooms are comfortable and the service is very pleasant.

Xinjiao Hotel
2 Dongxiao minxiang (Chongwen men)
Tel. 557731
Cable 5154
This hotel was built in 1954 and is famous for its cuisine, serving not only excellent Chinese and western food but also Pakistani food in its sixth-floor restaurant. It is centrally located close to Peking railway station, at the end of Dongdan, a major shopping area. It is within walking distance of Wangfujing (alternatively the No. 3 trolleybus will take you the three stops there), and on the No. 9 it is five stops to the friendship store. Post office, exchange, hairdressing and shops are situated on the ground floor, and there are bar facilities on the sixth floor. This hotel is generally not used by tourist groups, but more often by long-stay businessmen.

The Nationalities Hotel (Minzu fandian)
41 Fuxing men wai
Tel. 668541
Cable 8541
The Nationalities Hotel is a comfortable, airy hotel built in 1959, adjacent to the elaborate National Minorities Palace on Chang'an Avenue, with an excellent view from the back of the hotel over the city and Bei hai Park. Xidan shopping street is less than five minutes' walk away. The No. 10 or No. 1 buses will take you to Wangfujing and Tianan men Square; the No. 1 goes as far as the Friendship Store.

Exchange, post office, shops, restaurants and taxi hire are on the ground floor. There is a bar and billiards room on the tenth floor. This hotel is used largely by business delegations, and some overseas companies have offices here.

Huaqiao daxia
2 Zhushı dajie (north Wangfujing)

Tel. 558851
Opposite the CAAC offices and the Gallery of Fine Arts, this hotel is used by overseas Chinese.

Huadu Hotel
Close to Agricultural Exhibition Centre on Donghuan bei lu, this well-appointed hotel was opened in May 1982.

Yanjing Hotel
19 Fuxing men wai, Chang'an Avenue
Tel. 868721
This large new hotel is used largely by visiting businessmen, trade delegations and visiting sports teams etc.

Yanxiang Hotel
Jiangtai lu, Chaoyang District
Tel. 471131
Situated on the road to the airport, the hotel is comfortably appointed and is a new 'joint venture' hotel.

Jianguo Hotel
Jianguo men wai dajie
Tel. 595261/593661
This is Peking's most luxurious hotel. It was built as part of a joint venture between Luxingshe Peking and a Hong Kong company and is managed by the Peninsular Group. All fixtures and fittings have been imported from the USA, there is an in-house cinema, and minibars in most rooms. It is a short walk to the Friendship Store and the diplomatic quarter.

The Angler's Rest (Diaoyu tai)
Sanlihe
Tel. 668541 or 866152
Situated in the Western suburbs of Peking, close to the major ministries, this state guesthouse has only recently been open to foreigners. Situated in grounds with a lake, it consists of a series of villas appointed in the most luxurious Chinese fashion. The cuisine is excellent. In keeping with its role as a state guest house the hotel is somewhat isolated.

International Airport Hotel
Tel. 558341/522931
Adjacent to the airport, this hotel is well appointed and very convenient for those waiting for flights or in transit.

Heping Hotel
Jinyu hutong
Tel. 588841
Situated in an alley between Peking Hospital and East Wind Market on Wangfujing. Used mostly for overseas Chinese and some visiting delegations.

Xiang shan Hotel
Tel. 819244
Situated to the north-west of Peking, near the Summer Palace, this hotel is due for completion in late 1982.

Note
At the busiest times hotels outside the immediate Peking area will occasionally be used. They generally have a good standard of service and adequate facilities, their main drawback being the fact that it takes a drive of up to two hours to reach the centre of the city. There are also several hostels in Peking, which are mostly used for overseas Chinese and students.

Huilongguan
Beijiao
Tel. 275376
Situated to the north of Peking on the road to the Ming tombs, 20 km outside the city, this hotel is well situated for visits to the Great Wall, the Ming tombs and the Summer Palace.

Ji xian Guesthouse
Situated to the east of Peking in Tianjin municipality, with courtyard-style buildings, the service and cuisine of this guesthouse are highly recommended.

Zhuo xian Guesthouse
South of Peking in Hebei Province.

Restaurants: General Information
Peking has a wide selection of res-taurants, serving both local delicacies and the varied cuisine of every corner of China. If you wish to eat outside the hotel during your stay in Peking, since restaurants get extremely crowded it is best to book a table with the help of your local guide. The average price for a meal, including drink, is 25 *yuan*. The types of food you may expect to find are described on pages 75–7. Unless other-wise stated lunch is served from 11.30 am to 1.30 pm, and dinner from 5 pm to 7.30 pm. Below is a selection of Peking's most popular restaurants:

Peking Duck Restaurants (Kaoya dian)

Big Duck
24 Qian men dajie (behind Tianan men Square)
Tel. 751379
The oldest Peking duck restaurant.

Sick Duck
13 Shuaifu yuan (near Capital Hospital, off Wangfujing)
Tel. 553310

New Peking Duck Restaurant
Xuanwu men
Tel. 334422

Regional Variations

Donglaishun
At north entrance to East Wind Market
Tel. 551098
Mongolian hotpot, shashlik, Moslem-style food, Peking duck.

Sichuan fandian
51 Rongxian hutong
Tel. 336356
Hot peppery dishes in old Peking court-yard house setting.

Qinghai canting
555 Dong si bei dajie
Tel. 442947
Shish kebab, lamb spare ribs, 'winter worms chicken' – the 'worms' are a medicinal plant with excellent tonic properties, tasty and to be eaten in win-ter, shrimps with marrow.

Shoudu kaorouji
Shichahai (situated on lakeside near the Drum Tower; difficult to find)
Tel. 445921
Serves Mongolian-style food and barbecues, on balconies in the summer.

Cuihua lou (formerly Capital Restaurant)
60 Renmin lu (continuation of north Wangfujing)
Tel. 554561
Serves Shandong-style dishes – seafood, velvet chicken, crispy rice with shrimps.

Fengze yuan (Horn of Plenty)
83 Zhushikou xi dajie (south of Qian men)
Tel. 332828
One of the oldest and better restaurants in Peking; serves Shandong-style cuisine.

Bei hai fang shan
Bei hai Park
Tel. 442573
In an idyllic setting, serves food in the style of the court of the Empress Dowager. Fairly expensive.

Tingli guan (Listening to Orioles Pavilion)
Summer Palace
Tel. 281276/281936
Sea cucumber, deep-fried steamed buns.

Hongbing lou
Xi Chang an dajie (at intersection of Chang'an Avenue and Xidan)
Tel. 336461
Serves Mongolian hotpot and sea-food.

Zhenjiang fanguan
On south-west corner of Xidan and Chang'an Avenue crossroads
Tel. 662115
Yangzhou-style cuisine – spring rolls, fish maw, sea cucumber, crispy duck. Was frequented by poets and writers. Food served on china from Imperial Palace.

Ri tan Park
In Ri tan Park, close to embassy quarters
Tel. 592648
Serves full-scale meals and *jiaozi*. Open till 9 pm.

Shaoguoju
60 Xi si nan dajie
Tel. 663206
300-year-old restaurant, serves pork in Peking style and casseroles.

Western Food
All the hotels in Peking serve western food. However, if you are a long-term resident you may welcome a change of scene.

Exhibition Hall Restaurant (formerly Moscow Restaurant)
In Exhibition Centre, next to Zoo
Tel. 893713
Serves Russian-type dishes such as lemon tea, coffee, caviar, chicken Kiev, etc., in chandeliered splendour. Can also arrange banquets.

International Club
Jianguo men wai, near the friendship store and embassy quarters
Tel. 522254
Serves both Chinese and western food; mixed grill is good. Background music, piped and live, until 9 pm. Other amenities include a swimming pool (health certificate required), tennis court, banqueting facilities, Chinese films, dances at least once a week, taxi rank. The club is open to all foreigners, and some companies have offices here.

Entertainments
All foreigners' hotels in Peking now have a bar service. Dances are held regularly in the Palace of the National Minorities, the International Club and the Friendship Hotel, and there are many restaurants to choose from. Peking is also the cultural centre of China,

and you can see not only Peking Opera performed here but every kind of regional opera, the popular *kuaiban* – humorous rhythmic recitation, puppets, acrobats, and the newest plays. The new theatres are in the Palace of the National Minorities. The Capital Theatre in Wangfujing has been reviving old plays and putting on new ones, while old theatres include the Chang'an daxiyuan, where Mei Lan fang, the famous male interpreter of female roles in the Peking Opera, used to perform.

SHANGHAI

This is a city whose name evokes a racy past; today it is all gone apart from a skyline which recalls the 1930s. The skyscrapers which once housed international business concerns now house the local council and various administrative departments such as the Department of Agriculture or Foreign Trade. However, Shanghai does have a character all its own, which is apparent even to the visitor who has only been in China for a few days. The contrast with Peking is not unlike the difference between Milan and Naples.

Shanghai is south of the Yangtse River (Jiangnan), which is where climate, customs, dress and eating habits change, the dialects become even more incomprehensible, traditional architecture is different and rice becomes the staple diet as against wheat. Even the physiognomy of the people is different. Instead of the secretive courtyards of Peking you will find houses which front on to the street, with people standing in doorways eating a bowl of noodles, or knitting, and groups of men sitting playing cards. Washing is threaded on bamboo poles balanced between the trees which line the Shanghai boulevards. While the city is as flat as Peking the feeling of space and regularity is mis-

sing, and the vertical aspect is different – two-storeyed, balconied houses piled with baskets, the inevitable washing, evil-looking cabbage drying in the sun, not forgetting of course the skyscrapers of the early part of this century which dominate the skyline.

The long avenues of Shanghai crisscross the city, converging and parting, and changing names halfway along. The principle for naming the streets is that those running east to west are named after cities, those going north to south are named after provinces. The atmosphere is teeming and bustling. An accident in the street or an argument with a policeman becomes a matter of general interest as the crowd gathers to pass comment and assist.

People dress more flamboyantly than in rather conservative Peking. Even in the years when an excessive interest in one's appearance was frowned upon as being unrevolutionary, the Shanghainese wore better-cut clothes and leather shoes and their hair was stylishly coiffured – recently perms have become the height of fashion. The milder winters of the south obviate the need to wear the shapeless padded coat of the north; the silk jacket padded with camel wool or silk is standard wear, worn with a patterned 'dust' cover and a well-chosen scarf.

Shanghai is not a city of fine monuments and historical sites – it is the largest industrial city and port in China, with a population of over 11 million. It is a city lived in and to be lived in, and much more commercially minded than Peking: the shops are well stocked, and Nanking Road on a Sunday is more crowded than London's Oxford Street before Christmas. Of course you must take a stroll along the Bund – the promenade which gives on to the Huangpu River. Here young lovers stroll or sit behind umbrellas on rainy days, and families and visitors from the country come to take their photos against the backdrop of ocean-going liners, steamers, junks and barges which crowd the river.

Unlike Peking, it is not a city bound up with the imperial past of China. Its special geographical position in relation to the rest of the country gave Shanghai a history which is bound up with that of the rest of the world. In modern Chinese history its role was vital – it was here that the first Communist Part convention was held; some of the strikes which were to trigger off the Civil War took place in Shanghai; and in post-liberation times it has continued to be a political and industrial centre as well as a cultural one, setting the pace for the rest of the country.

The international airport is situated in the western suburbs of Shanghai, approximately 18 km from the city centre. It is served by air routes from all over China and from Japan. There are daily flights to Hong Kong and also flights to Osaka and Tokyo. There are also daily flights to Peking and Guangzhou, both taking approximately one and a half hours. Shanghai North Station is north of Suzhou Creek in the Hongkou district. The train journey to Peking takes 22 hours, to Guangzhou 36 hours. Passenger ships now operate between Hong Kong and Shanghai; the trip takes two and a half days. It is also possible to take a boat to Shanghai from ports in the north of China, such as Qingdao. Foreign cruise liners often berth at Shanghai.

Location

Shanghai has a unique position in relation to the rest of China, and its development has taken place as a result of a fortuitous change in physical circumstances. The city is approximately halfway down the eastern coast of China. Situated on a tributary of the Yangtse, the Huangpu, it commands a hinterland which includes the whole of the Yangtse valley as far west as Sichuan Province – approximately half the land mass of China, as well as the most densely populated areas. It is easily accessible to the sea and foreign trade, and in the fifth century it was even prey to Japanese bandits. In the days before railways Shanghai was at the hub of a network of waterways, natural lakes, rivers and canals which meant that all locally produced goods could readily be exported to the rest of the country, as could incoming goods from abroad. The foreign powers on the rampage in the nineteenth century were quick to realize the advantages of prosperous Shanghai over Guangzhou, the only port where foreign concessions were then allowed. The first British ship came to Shanghai in 1832, and by 1842 the British had attacked and laid claim to the city.

The geographical history of Shanghai is an intriguing one, for six thousand years ago the area was in fact under water. However, silt brought down by the Yangtse has caused the coast to spread constantly outwards. The two lakes to the west of Shanghai were formerly joined together, and even today the land to the west of Shanghai is lower than that to the east. The tendency to become silted up also influenced the path of those rivers which were tributaries of the Yangtse, and the growth of Shanghai itself.

Today the port of Shanghai stands on the Huangpu, which rises in Lake Tai and extends 83 km from Wusong in the north to Songjiang in the south. At its widest point it is 800 m wide. At the northernmost end of the Bund the Huangpu is joined by the Soochow Creek, which reaches a maximum width of 50 m.

The city of Songjiang was once the most important in the region, and in 780 the river of the same name was

8 km wide in places. However by the eleventh century the river had become silted up and the trading centre shifted northwards to a point where what is now the Huangpu and the Song jiang form a confluence. As the land became silted up to the east, the sea encroached, and through the centuries dykes have been built – the first one was constructed in the eighth century, while the most recent was built in 1906. Today the Huangpu only needs dredging from time to time. As a port Shanghai has all the advantages of being near the sea but none of the drawbacks: it is sheltered from the typhoons which threaten that part of the coast, it never freezes over, it is wide enough to take ships of some 10,000 tonnes, and is unimpeded by mist.

Since 1958 Shanghai has enjoyed a political and administrative status as a municipality reporting directly to the central government, and covers an area of 6000 km²; the urban area itself is 140 km.². The total population is 11.3 million of which half live in the city and half in the rural areas. The municipality occupies a triangular peninsula between the Yangtse and Hangzhou Bay; in the west it is bounded by Jiangsu and Zhejiang Provinces, and the distance from these boundaries to the sea is 100 km at the widest point. In the estuary of the Yangtse lie three islands which are also part of Shanghai. Formed by the silting process, they are largely agricultural; the largest, Chongming, is the most important fishing port in the area.

Agriculture

The rural area of Shanghai lies on an alluvial fertile plain, and the major problem facing the peasants is drainage, because of the relationship of the land to the sea. The communes around Shanghai are wealthy, and the peasants on the outskirts enjoy all the benefits of spacious homes, enough fresh vegetables from their private plots (the surplus has an ever-ready market) and easy access to the city. People living in the city itself, on the other hand, have to face all the daily problems of getting up early to go to the market to buy what is available that day, having to wait for a small flat, and possibly commuting to the other side of Shanghai to reach their place of work.

The important task of the communes around Shanghai is of course to provide food for the urban area. This is an enormous operation, and if you happen to be in Shanghai in the early hours of the morning you will see piles of vegetables in season being brought into the city by every available means of transport from barges piled high with cabbages to bicycle carts and even sheer manpower. Small tractors are used extensively for transportation; in and around Shanghai, unlike Peking, you will see very few horses used to draw vehicles.

There are 200 communes in and around Shanghai, with a total population of over 4 million. The workforce runs to more than 2 million and around 200,000 work in small factories. Quite a few people work in the city itself, in administrative posts related to agriculture or in factories. Apart from vegetables, the major crops are cotton, rice, wheat and rape. Communes here usually expect three crops a year.

Industry

Shanghai began to industrialize towards the end of the nineteenth century when the first cotton mill in China was opened there. Until then it had made its fortune as a port and by the production of cotton on an individual cottage industry basis. The city boomed at the beginning of the twentieth century, but despite the industries introduced by foreign powers 800,000 were unemployed in the 1940s. Today there are 2 million workers in industry and 8000 factories. Major industries include textiles, chemicals, shipbuilding, electronics, machine building, metallurgical industries, fertilizers, and petrochemicals; a new steel plant is being built at Baoshan. Most of Shanghai's industry is spread along the banks of the northern part of the Huangpu and along Soochow Creek.

Climate

The climate of Shanghai is more temperate than that of Peking. Its proximity to the sea and the weather conditions enjoyed by all of China south of the river give an average annual temperature of around 15°C. Shanghai also boasts one of the finest and most complete meteorological observatories in China, set up in 1873 by the Jesuits in Siccawei, which means that the idiosyncrasies of the Shanghai climate have been well charted. The inhabitants of Shanghai know this variability well, and with one sniff of the air can tell that brighter weather is on the way.

Winter begins quite late in Shanghai, at the end of November. The coldest month is January, and even then the temperatures rarely fall below freezing. Cold, dry winds blow down from the north-west, and three days of a cold stream and bitter weather will be followed by four days of milder weather. There is sometimes a little snow in January.

The end of March usually sees the last of the winter frost – there is usually no snow after 5 April, and no frost after 20 April, and the temperature rises from 9°C in March to 13°C in April and 17°C in May. As the winds veer round from north to south the weather tends to become changeable and showery, hence the local saying 'Spring is like the face of a child: it changes three times a day.'

June sees the onset of summer with the 'plum rains', the monsoons brought in by the southerly–easterly winds.

Within a period of thirty days a fifth of Shanghai's annual rainfall of over 1000 mm falls. The air becomes extremely humid and people walk around in shirtsleeves and plastic open sandals, with an umbrella or a wide hat at the ready. Clothes kept for too long in dark corners sprout mildew overnight.

By July and August the weather is drier, the monsoons have moved northwards and people take to the streets, stretched out on bamboo loungers, enjoying the relative cool of the evening. The average temperature is 27.4°C–33°C at the highest. Typhoons and rainstorms may be experienced at this time of the year, with Force 6–8 gales. September to November is probably the best time of the year, with little rain and much sun.

History

Archaeological evidence shows that the area was inhabited as long as five thousand years ago. Some of the most important finds have been at Maqiao commune to the south-west of the city proper, and at Songjiang, where pottery, necklaces and stone tools have been discovered.

During the Warring States period the area belonged to the state of Chu, and graves, pottery and jade have been discovered in areas to the north of present-day Shanghai. During the fourth and fifth centuries a fishing method was developed by which fish were caught on the incoming tide in bamboo palisades (known as 'hu' in Chinese) stretched across the estuary. The name of the town then was Hudu; nowadays the abbreviated name for Shanghai is still Hu, and Shanghai opera is referred to as Hu opera.

The sea was constantly encroaching, and in the eighth century a dyke was built just to the east of present-day Shanghai. In 751 the town of Huating-xian was established on the spot where

Songjiang now stands. In those days the river was very wide at this point, as already mentioned, and it soon became a very important port. Between the tenth and thirteenth centuries domestic and foreign trade flourished in the area, and there were salt fields around Songjiang. The first reference to Shanghai is in the eleventh century, for as the river became unnavigable at Songjiang a new port and customs post were established around the 'old city' and Shanghai village was set up on the tributary of the river, where ships were loaded and unloaded.

In the mid-thirteenth century local government was set up here – until then Shanghai had been under the jurisdiction of Songjiang. Overseas shipping offices and customs posts were opened, along with a mass of wine shops, hotels, schools, temples and shops, and in 1292 it became a county in its own right.

During the thirteenth and fourteenth century Shanghai experienced another important development – the cottage industry in weaving cotton. Before the Yuan dynasty a rather coarse cotton had been produced, but new methods were now introduced from Hainan Island. The story goes that a young girl who had run away to Hainan Island returned towards the end of her life armed with the knowledge of new weaving techniques learnt from the Yi nationality which inhabit the island. By the Ming dynasty this handwoven cotton was worn the world over.

At the beginning of the Ming dynasty another canal was constructed at Fanjiabang, and the Huangpu became larger and more navigable. Merchants brought sugar from the south in exchange for cloth, and Shanghai was fast becoming a prosperous city. After Japanese pirates beleaguered the whole area in 1558 a wall was built around the city. It was knocked down in 1912, but the original shape of the old quarter,

bounded by Renmin lu, can still be seen on any map.

In 1832, Lord Amherst was sent by the East India Company on a reconnaissance mission to Shanghai. Though the crew were allowed to land, they were told by the Chinese authorities that their trading was to be restricted to Canton. Other ships came to Shanghai after this, all bringing back reports of a flourishing city, a busy port, and marvellous trading opportunities. It wasn't until 1842, however, that the British were able to gain a foothold in the desirably situated city, when they captured it in the course of the Opium Wars. The Treaty of Nanking of that year gave the British the right to land and trade there, and by the end of 1842 eleven companies were established in Shanghai, as well as a consul, two missionaries and twenty-three foreign residences.

The population of Shanghai was then estimated at between a quarter and half a million, and the city exported tea, silk and cotton to the rest of China, receiving in return grain, pulses and medicinal drugs. Tea and silk from the hinterland of Shanghai were soon to constitute as much as 90 per cent of China's total exports. By the mid-nineteenth century it had become a city of commerce, new fields of trade and industrial development, somewhere to escape to, to get rich, to trade in opium and to open missions.

As many guidebooks of the late nineteenth and early twentieth century will tell you, when you stepped off the boat at Shanghai on the Bund you would think yourself in a European city. The confines of the international and French concessions were clearly marked, and the extent of the divisions was emphasized by the sign which once hung outside the garden now known as Huangpu Park, forbidding entry to 'dogs and Chinese'. A clause in the

Nanking Treaty allowed the foreigners 'extra-territoriality', which meant freedom from Chinese laws and permission to establish their own terms in contract making. To maintain their own low tariffs the British gained access to the Chinese customs.

In every treaty port clubs, a racecourse and a church could be found, and in the concessions the foreigners had their own police force and army. From small beginnings in an area on the bank of the river, the concessions were to spread westward and northwards into the area known as Hongkou. In the 1920s and 1930s the population of Shanghai was over 3 million, of whom around 40 per cent were foreign and included forty-seven nationalities – Russian, Italian, French, British, Japanese and Americans among them – all of whom have left their mark on the city.

Industry came to Shanghai, as mentioned above, towards the end of the nineteenth century. While the foreign traders there enjoyed more freedom than they had known in Canton with the restrictive *hongs* and their code of commerce, they had not been allowed to establish industries. In 1865 the Chinese government established the first arsenal and dockyard south of the river. Several attempts were made to establish filature factories in Shanghai by the Italians, who eventually succeeded in 1880. The cotton which the British brought in from India had an adverse effect on the Chinese cottage industry, and in 1890 the first cotton mill was opened. The Treaty of Shimonoseki was signed at the end of the Sino–Japanese War in 1895 and ceded many territorial and economic rights to the Japanese. It contained a 'most favoured nation' clause and was the signal for an industrial revolution in Shanghai and factories and mills sprang up along the waterways. The first rail-

way in China was built between Shanghai and Jiangwan in 1876 along the banks of the river.

In the Chinese quarters and particularly in the old city the inhabitants eked out a living in small workshops. The peasants had to contend with the influx of foreign competition and goods, their main contact being through middlemen – the so-called Chinese *compradores*. Their frustration erupted in movements similar to the Taiping Rebellion of 1850. While the Taiping government held its own in Nanking, the Small Knife Society – an underground organization with headquarters in the Mandarin Garden – led an armed uprising in 1853. They controlled many of the small centres in and around Shanghai and after an attempt by foreign troops to quell them they were eventually defeated by government troops in 1854. Although not directly connected with the Taiping Rebellion the causes and sentiments were the same – a strong sense of nationalistic indignation at the imperialists, disgust with their own weak government, and poverty and hunger caused by drought and poor harvests.

While such uprisings were all symptoms of a crumbling empire, Shanghai was to be the focus of events which were to shape the future of China. The first twenty years of this century saw a boom for certain sectors of the population of Shanghai, and the final collapse of the dynastic period in 1912 led to a new awareness among the ordinary people. Contact with the western world had been growing, and the eruption of the May Fourth Movement of 1919, begun in Peking, was echoed by a week of strikes in Shanghai when even the merchants closed down their shops. Its large international population made Shanghai, like the other treaty ports, a hotbed of new ideas. It also had one of the largest bodies of industrial workers in China. It was an important cultural centre containing the earliest cinemas and film studios, and large publishing houses. Important writers converged here, particularly in the 1930s. It had a teeming underworld of prostitutes and gangs, including the Green Gang which is said to have worked with Chiang Kaishek in the program against the Communists in 1927.

The Communist Party was officially founded in Shanghai in July 1921. There were thirteen people present from the small cells which had sprung up in China, plus two Comintern delegates. The first part of the congress was held in a girls' school in the French concession, which was closed for the holidays; it is just behind Huaihai lu and can be visited on request. However, the congress discovered a spy and were forced to move to a boat on South Lake in Jiaxing to continue their meeting in the guise of holidaymakers.

In 1927 a general strike was declared in Shanghai in response to the success of the northern expedition against the warlords. However Nationalist and Communist differences were becoming more irreconcilable, and the business sector was growing alarmed by the talk of land reform and the damage which strikes could cause. On 12 April 1927 the army opened fire on the strikers in their various strongholds; Thus began the White Terror, led by Chiang Kaishek and supported by the Shanghai business world. The actual attacks were made with the support of troops from the international concessions. The following day, as the people of Shanghai rallied in a peaceful unarmed protest, troops opened fire on a procession of men, women and children. Zhou Enlai had been participating in the organization of the strike and was able to escape.

The Nationalists and Communists remained at war until once more forced into uneasy alliance, against the Japanese. The Communist Party was forced underground or into Guangxi Province to establish the first soviets. In 1932 the Japanese attacked Shanghai, on the pretext of protecting their own people there, and in 1937 a bitter battle took place, which forced a large part of Shanghai's manufacturing upriver to Chongqing in the province of Sichuan.

In the early days of the Communist and resistance movements the missionaries, who had already established their own network of aid and education in the factories and workshops of Shanghai, provided an alibi and an outlet for many of the youthful idealists, in working for their country. After 28 May 1949 a big cleaning-up operation was carried out in Shanghai, directed against criminals, prostitutes and so on. Major slum clearance was begun, and today only Fangualong is retained as a reminder of the days gone by. Shanghai is still a very crowded city, but the people have a spirit and resilience of their own. In 1958 Shanghai was given the status of a municipality, to include ten counties.

In the Cultural Revolution Shanghai became the centre of the most radical activities. In 1967 Yao Wenyuan led the January storm which established the first revolutionary committees in China – the term which was to be given to the organizing body of every school, factory or commune for the next ten years. Today Shanghai leads the country in almost every field – educational, industry, commerce, and so on.

Culture

Shanghai is one of the principal cultural centres of China. It boasts four film studios, including one for dubbing foreign films, its own music conservatory and philharmonic orchestra, and a famous dancing school – near Shanghai Zoo and passed on the way to and from the airport – which produced the ballet

The White Haired Girl and has renewed interest in Western Classical Ballet. There are over thirteen theatre groups – ranging from a Peking opera troupe to groups performing in the local genres – Hu and Yue Opera and puppets. One of the most popular entertainments for foreigners is a visit to the acrobatics at 'Thunder and Lightning Acrobatics Circus', a modern round building on West Nanking Road. Shanghai also has colour television.

There are sixteen institutes of higher education – including the well-known Fudan University – medical schools and technical colleges, and Shanghai has a student population of around 30,000. There are 5500 schools in Shanghai, and over 2000 sports fields. Spring and autumn are traditionally the time for limbering up, and mass exercises take place along the Bund and in the main streets.

Shanghai is particularly well equipped with extra-curricular activities – houses which might once have belonged to some wealthy foreign merchant or diplomat now house eleven Children's Palaces, where children may come after school hours to participate in group activities – usually some kind of outdoor sport, such as basketball or football. There are also music classes, dancing classes, gymnastics, electronics, art classes and traditional handicrafts for children who show special talent. The famous club on the corner of Yan'an lu and Xizang lu – the Grand Monde, or Da shijie as it was known from the 1930s until the Cultural Revolution – has become a Youth Palace.

Local ballads on any topical subject – half sung and half chanted in local dialect, to the accompaniment of clappers, are also popular.

The Bund (Waitan)

This is a good setting-out point for a tour of Shanghai. There are fewer museums in Shanghai than in Peking, so they are dealt with here under their geographical area and not separately. Though there are few major monuments in the city, the varying architectural styles offer clues to the past of any particular area.

On the west bank of the Huangpu, the Bund is one of the recurring motifs of Shanghai. Its tall and varied nineteenth-century buildings once housed the customs – still an important point of reference in Shanghai; Jardine and Matheson, the Standard Chartered Bank and world-famous hotels, and it was on to the Bund that one alighted from a sea voyage. Today these buildings house the offices of Shanghai Municipal Council and the Women's Federation of Shanghai. Where once stood statues of such heroes as Sir Robert Hart now there are gaily painted placards depicting the national minorities of China or a topical exhortation to modernization.

From the Bund today, opposite the Customs Building, you can take a ferry to the other side of Shanghai – Chuansha, the industrial area – or a pleasure boat to sail northwards to the mouth of the Yangtse River (arranged through your Luxingshe guide and group leader). Following the Bund northwards to the point where it is joined by the Suzhou Creek, you come to the small Huangpu Park. Entrance is 2 *fen*, and as well as rockeries and flowers it contains modern-style pavilions with a view of the river.

The junction of Suzhou Creek and the Huangpu is particularly noisy as barges presage their arrival with loud blasts, ships sound horns and traffic control men in their booths shout urgent instructions which disturb the quiet of the nearby hospital and the Shanghai Mansions. In pre-1949 days the area around the Bund was largely British territory. Crossing the road from the park you enter a corner of the old British Empire, with perfectly kept lawns. It once housed the British consulate and is now the friendship store and the seamen's club. Also in the area are churches, the former Shanghai Boating Club, the Hong Kong and Shanghai Bank and the Standard Chartered Bank, which have maintained offices since 1949.

North Shanghai
From here you cross the Garden Bridge, or Baidu Bridge as it is now called. A familiar Shanghai motif, it is an iron girder bridge set against the background of the soaring Shanghai mansions; on the right is the former German consulate. The bridge was once the highest point in flat Shanghai, until the next bridge along was built, which joins north and south Sichuan lu. Here you will see peasants from the countryside dragging their loads with great difficulty over the bridge. On the north bank, with its distinctive clock tower, is the main post office.

The area north of Suzhou Creek (inner city) includes the districts of Hongkou, Chabei and Yangpu. Yangpu, which follows the Huangpu round to the Yangtse, was and still is largely industrial. Chabei was one of the Japanese quarters, and was destroyed during World War II. On Henan bei lu is Shanghai's major station – always a very busy and crowded spot, teeming with people and bundles and every mode of transport from bicycle carts to trishaws – three-wheeled taxis. Here eating houses and hotels abound. The trains go over a level crossing, holding up the traffic and providing ample opportunity for steam enthusiasts to ogle at passing engines.

In this vicinity is the Fangualong, where a few very dilapidated hovels are kept standing as a reminder of the slum conditions people once lived in. Much of this area consists of tenements which have been built in the last twenty or thirty years. Following through the winding, busy streets of this quarter, along Sichuan bei lu, you will arrive at Hongkou Park, in extensive grounds with a lake and boating in season. It also houses a monument to the writer Lu Xun. Built in 1961 to commemorate his eightieth birthday, it contains his tomb and a museum. Lu Xun lived nearby when he was in Shanghai in 1936.

Further north out of Shanghai are two of its major institutes of further education – Fudan University and Tongji University. Not far from Wujiao chang – Five Corners Place – are a stadium and swimming pool. The bus journey from Wujiao chang to the Bund takes twenty-five minutes.

Nanking Road
Returning to the centre of Shanghai, get off at the Bund and take a walk along Nanking Road, the shopping centre of Shanghai, stopping to gaze at the musical instruments, the silk shops and art shops. Fuzhou lu runs parallel to Nanking Road. Past the silk shops you will come to the tower blocks of department stores. The food market is worth a visit for its supplies of tea, cakes and various dried fruits and seasonings from all over China. At the end of the road is the massive building of the main department store, at the intersection of Nanking Road and Xizang Road. Here the road widens out into People's Square, where rallies are held and all important announcements made. This was formerly the racecourse. From here you can see the turrets of the Young People's Palace – the Grand Monde – where theatres and dance halls have been replaced by the socialist equivalent of shooting ranges and pinball machines.

Nanking Road continues as West Nanking Road where you pass the tall Park Hotel, the handicrafts shop, the

People's Park, the acrobatics circus, Shanghai's municipal library (reopened to the public in 1978), the television tower, and dozens of little shops. This area was once called Bubbling Well Road and was famous for its clothes shops, boutiques and residences. You also pass the Fine Arts Gallery which houses temporary exhibitions on topics ranging from cartoons about the Gang of Four to Chinese traditional painting.

Jingan Temple Area

Turning right at the end of West Nanking Road – Nanjing xi lu – you come to Jing'an Park – the Park of Quietude. There was formerly a very old temple here, and the buildings have been undergoing repairs for some years. If you stay in the Jing'an Hotel you can take a stroll here at the end of a busy day. At the far end the road joins Yan'an lu.

To the north of Nanjing xi lu, at 170 Anyuan lu, you come to the Temple of the Jade Buddha. In the midst of bustling, built-up Shanghai you suddenly step over a threshold through typical large wooden doors into a world of serenity where the smell of incense pervades the air, and while the bell no longer sounds at the appointed hour, an atmosphere of reverence remains, particularly as visitors are asked to remove their shoes on entering. You go in past the gaze of the customary fearsome guardian gods, the laughing Buddha, and the Goddess of Mercy with her entourage of eighteen arhats. As ever, they are decorated in rich red and gold. You continue through the abbot's quarters, where he would have held audience and given instruction to his novices.

Upstairs is the statue of the jade Buddha himself; like the one in Peking, it was presented by Burma in 1882. It was originally housed in a temple in Jiang-

wan lu, and this temple was only built in 1918. Other Buddhist sculptures are also on show here, including a jade Sleeping Buddha, and a brass mountain depicting the Buddhist Heaven. The room also contains 7240 volumes of Buddhist sutras – one of the most complete sets in China. The sutras are divided into three parts – the classics, that is the actual teachings of Sakyamuni; the precepts, which are rules and guidance for the ascetic life; and explanations of the classical sutras written by disciples, together with theses on Buddhism and interpretations and explanations.

Yan'an lu

This street formerly marked the boundary between the French and the international concessions, and was called Edward VII Avenue; on the corner stood a club with (reputedly) the longest bar in the world. Near to the Bund are two museums – the Natural History Museum, and on the left-hand side of the road the Shanghai Museum. The latter is well worth a visit and contains an excellent collection of pottery. The exhibits start with some very fine bronze ritual vessels and some of the earliest mirrors. There are some beautiful examples of the first Tang dynasty porcelain, a delicately inscribed neck cushion, celadon ware, Ming and Qing porcelain, and present-day artefacts. The museum also houses some fine paintings which are on display when the weather is not too humid.

Where Yan'an lu joins Xizang lu are the Young People's Palace and the Concert Hall. Over a mile down the road from them you will come to the ornate and majestic-looking Industrial Exhibition Hall, built by the Russians, which gives an overall picture of Shanghai's industry; some rooms house temporary and visiting exhibitions. Further along the road is the Yan'an lu entrance to

Jing'an Park. On the other side of the crossroads on the left-hand side is the Shanghai International Club, opened in 1977, which offers swimming, tennis courts and pingpong as well as an excellent restaurant. Opposite is one of Shanghai's many children's palaces.

The Huaihai lu Area
Huaihai lu is another of those long and seemingly endless avenues which runs parallel to Nanking Road. At the Bund end it borders the edge of the old city at Renmin lu. It was one of the major roads in the former French concession, and many Russians lived around here too. In the central part of the street are all the best clothes shops in Shanghai, as well as a selection of cake and sweet shops with marvellous dummy displays in the window.

Behind Huaihai lu is the site of the first congress of the Chinese Communist Party (see page 137). This too was the area where Sun Yatsen lived during his stay in Shanghai. Many of the houses along here were formerly grand mansions which have now either become educational institutions or have been divided into flats.

The Old City
The old city is a distinctive 'island' on the map of Shanghai, and was surrounded by a city wall until 1913. Today it is a mass of buildings and humanity packed together in a small space – you will see washing hanging over your head as you pass through the alleys and market stalls. The best way to get into the old city is through Anren jie from Yan'an lu.

As well as the shops around the former city temple there are silk shops, haberdashers, snack shops selling tasty *baozi* and steamed bread fashioned into seashell shapes, shops selling artists' materials, musical instruments, handicrafts, basketware and cane furniture,

fans and chops and hand-carved sticks. In the centre of this quarter is the Shanghai tea house; hovering over an ornamental pond and reached by a zig-zag bridge, it's a favourite meeting-place for the elderly. The tea house was formerly known as Wuxing ding and is now called the Pavilion on the Lake.

Opposite the tea house is the entrance to the Yu yuan or Mandarin Gardens. These were built between 1559 and 1577 and originally belonged to a wealthy bureaucrat's family. The gardens cover an area of 30 *mu* or more. They contain a wide assortment of artificial mountains, pavilions and lakes, and a small theatre. The outer wall is crowned by the curling body of a dragon which ends within the garden in the form of a head. It was here that the Little Knife Society organized its 1853 uprising in the Dianchun tang, and a small exhibition room tells their story. One fascinating exhibit is a grain of rice inscribed with a message, a case of the intricate art of the miniature serving the secret society. The garden was presented to the city in the mid-nineteenth century.

Usually visitors enter and leave by the Anren jie entrance, which is most easily accessible from the main road. The former Confucian city temple was situated in the south-west corner of the old city but is now closed.

South and West Suburbs
On the way to the airport is the Western Suburbs Park; it contains Shanghai's Zoo which, like all good Chinese zoos, boasts a pair of indolent pandas. A permanent agricultural machinery exhibition is housed opposite.

Turning southwards you will come to the extremities of Shanghai and Ziccawei or Xujiawei. It was here that the Jesuit missions established their observatory, schools, workshops and orphanages. Continuing south-westwards you come to a major roundabout and Shanghai's new and striking stadium. It was in this part of the city that Chiang Kaishek first established his base in the early 1920s. The Longhua Park contains the only pagoda in Shanghai, made of wood and recently restored; the Longhua Botanical Gardens have a display of bonsai trees, some over two hundred years old; they are also a research centre.

Songjiang

One hour from Shanghai by coach, at Songjiang, once so important, you may visit the brick Fang pagoda, built in the eleventh century, and admire some of the brick carvings. A visit to a commune – here they specialize in rice, grain and cotton – may be organized, and there is also an embroidery factory here, which you pass on the way to Hangzhou.

Factories and Handicrafts

Since Shanghai is China's leading industrial city a very wide range of factories can be visited, ranging from textiles to heavy machinery. Visits may also be arranged to the port area. In the handicrafts line you can go to an ivory carving factory, a carpet factory and see embroidery being made. The Shanghai Arts and Crafts Trade Fair is located in the east wing of the Industrial Exhibition Centre; it displays and sells high-quality goods.

Harbour Trips

Your Luxingshe guide will often arrange a leisurely boat trip along the Huangpu River as far as the mouth of the Yangtse.

Shopping

Shanghai's excellent shopping facilities are well known throughout China, for the shops are always well stocked with the most up-to-date goods in the country. The main shopping areas, as mentioned in the area-by-area tour above, are around Nanking Road and Huaihai lu. There are in fact 24,000 stores in Shanghai, of which 140 are open around the clock, and 1300 offer late-night closing or early opening. Most stores in Shanghai open at 8.30 or 9 am and close between 6 and 6.30 pm. The largest department stores remain open until 8 pm.

While most shops are state-owned, Shanghai has quite a few street sellers as well. These people have always lived a wandering life and buy from a central warehouse goods such as pencils, shoelaces, ponytail elastic and hair bands. There is a fixed price limit at which they can sell the goods. Nowadays small snack, repair and handicraft collectives are being encouraged to give employment to Shanghai's youth.

Friendship Store

On Zhongshan yi bei lu, at the northernmost end of the Bund, opposite the bridge, it is open from 9 am to 11 pm. It is very well stocked, with reasonably priced paintings and scrolls and a good selection of silks. The assistants are very accommodating and have an excellent command of many languages.

Nanking Road

Starting from the Bund even numbers are on the right-hand side and odd numbers on the left.

114 Musical instruments

190 Photographers' supplies, including 35 mm films

319 New China Book Shop: large selection of posters

388 Guangming tea shop; old-fashioned wooden counters, and walls stacked high with tea

422 Shanghai shuhuashe (also known as Duoyunxian): fine arts shop with a section for foreigners containing painted fans, old and new paintings, artists' materials

550 (right-hand side) Guohua ciqi shangdian: a wide variety of crockery, flasks etc., and section for foreigners

592 Shanghai Silk Shop (a must): sells raw silk and a wide selection of patterned silk by the metre (although price tags often give it by the foot)

720 Food store.

760 Pharmaceutical supplies shop, particularly good for Chinese medicine and acupuncture needles

780 Fan shop: all kinds of fans from simple paper ones costing a few pence to large silk, hand-painted or carved sandalwood ones.

830 Shanghai No. 1 Department Store, at crossroads of Nanking Road and Xizang lu: well worth a visit

West Nanking Road

190–208 (just past International Hotel): Shanghai Handicrafts Shop (Shanghai gongyi meishupin fuwu bu) is open from 9 am–9 pm.

There are several interesting shops along West Nanking Road selling everything from furniture to potted plants and underwear. There are a children's store and an antique shop (a branch of the friendship store).

Foreign Language Bookshop
290 Fuzhou lu

Commission Shops
1299 Huahai lu
1303 Yan'an lu
Here you may obtain antiques.

Antique Shops
694 West Nanking Road. This is the antiques and curios branch of the Shanghai friendship store.
218–226 Guangdong lu is the traditional site of Shanghai antiques stores.

Useful Addresses

Post Office
1761 Sichuan bei lu

Telexes
These can be sent from the Telegraph Office at the Bund end of the Nanking Road, adjacent to the Peace Hotel.

Banks
The Bank of China, 23 Zhongshan yi bei lu (on the Bund) will exchange your bank notes on six days a week (closed Sundays). There are exchange facilities in all hotels in Shanghai.

Hospitals
Should you become ill in Shanghai you will be taken to the Huadong Hospital – registration fee 2 *yuan*. Most of the staff have a limited command of a foreign language. You will also be required to pay for treatment and drugs.

CAAC Office
789 Yan'an zhong lu
Tel. 532255 (International)
535953 (Domestic)

Luxingshe
66 Nanjing dong lu/59 Xiangang lu
Tel. 217200

Hotels: General Information
The hotels in Shanghai were all built before 1949, although new ones are planned. The present ones all offer the comfort and style of days gone by, combined with gracious service which is among the best in China. The cuisine in the hotels is of the highest standard.

Peace Hotel (Heping fandian)
20 Nanking Road
Tel. 211244
Cable 3266
This hotel was built in 1923–6 by the Sassoons, a famous Jewish property-owning family. It is very conveniently sited on the corner of Nanking Road and the Bund, within easy reach of shopping centres and the friendship store. It is centrally heated in winter and has air-conditioning in summer. Its facilities include a shop, a bookstall with antique books and paintings, hair-

dressing facilities on the mezzanine floor, billiards, exchange facilities at reception, and taxi hire.

The restaurant on the eighth floor must be one of the most exciting-looking in China. It is called the Dragon and Phoenix dining-room on account of the ceiling, which bears a design of gold dragons and a phoenix in bas-relief on a red background. There is a larger banqueting room with an elegant, high-arched ceiling, and small banqueting rooms may be hired. The coffee bar on the ground floor, open between 4 and 11 pm, also serves drinks and cocktails and has a television and music. The annexe, on the opposite side of Nanking Road, has full facilities and its own dining-room.

Shanghai Mansions (Shanghai dasha)
20 Bei Suzhou lu
Tel. 246260
This hotel's twenty-two storeys make it one of the tallest buildings in Shanghai. It dominates the skyline on the north side of Suzhou Creek and is convenient for the friendship store and Nanking Road. It was built between 1930 and 1935 when it was known as the Broadway Building. It overlooks the river and the city, and has a viewing terrace on the eighteenth floor. On festive occasions the whole length of the hotel is hung with banners.

Its facilities on the ground floor include exchange at the service counter, a hairdresser, a post office, a shop with daily necessities and some books and paintings, and a coffee shop. The first floor dining-room is decorated in unmistakable 1930s' Art Deco style overlaid with modern Chinese pictures of the Welcoming Guest Pine. Most of the Chinese food is in the Yangzhou style – beancurd, eels' tails, and steamed and salted fish. Western food includes chicken Rossini, T-bone steaks and veal piccata. The bar make its own cocktails.

Jinjiang fandian
59 Maoming nan lu
Tel. 434242
Cable 7777
This hotel is in the former French quarter of the city, very close to Huaihai lu, Shanghai's second shopping centre. It was built in 1929 and was then known as the Astor. It has three buildings – the northern block is the main building; the southern block consists of luxury suites which are usually reserved for VIPs (Mrs Thatcher stayed here in 1977); and the new southern block, built in 1965, which has recently been renovated. In the centre is an attractive garden. The hotel has an excellent reputation for service. Opposite the Jinjiang Hotel is the Jinjiang Club, which is situated on the site of the former French Consulate.

The No. 42 bus from Shaanxi lu takes you to the Bund, and the No. 26 from Huaihai lu to Sichuan lu, just behind Nanking Road. The hotel is within walking distance of the Red House Restaurant (see page 146). The shops on Huaihai lu sell clothes, china and basketware, and there are also department stores here.

The hotel's main block has a ground-floor lobby reached by a sweeping staircase, a post office, exchange shop, hairdresser, lounge and bar, which is open from 4 to 11 pm. The dining-room, on the eleventh floor, specializes in Cantonese food. Most rooms have a bathroom en suite. The southern and new southern blocks have their own dining-rooms on the ground floor.

Jing'an binguan
370 Huashanlu
Tel. 563050
Cable 3304
A luxuriously appointed hotel, it is set in extensive grounds in one of the most attractive residential areas of Shanghai, behind Yan'an lu and the International

Club and within walking distance of the Park of Quietude and the Industrial Exhibition. An apartment block in the 1930s, it was refurbished as a hotel in 1978. It is ten minutes' walk to the No. 9 Department Store in Huashan lu. A No. 20 or 27 bus will take you from Yan'an lu to the No. 1 Department Store in Nanjing lu. Taxis can be ordered at reception; a post office, exchange shop, hairdresser and bookshop are also provided. Service counters on each floor can arrange film developing and minor repairs. The dining-room, on the eighth floor, serves Sichuanese food. The bar on the first floor remains open until midnight.

Heng shan binguan
534 Heng shan lu
Tel. 377050
Cable 5295
Situated in the south-west of Shanghai, this pleasant, fourteen-storey hotel was built at a five-way intersection in 1935 as a block of flats known as Picardy Mansions. It is a long way from the centre, but you can take the No. 42 bus to the Bund (Waitan) or the No. 26 to Sichuan lu – the terminus. Taxis are available from the hotel reception.

A post office, a bookshop with paintings, a hairdresser and exchange facilities are all on the ground floor. The dining-room on the fourteenth floor enjoys a good view over the city and serves Sichuanese-style food. Nearly all the rooms are suites, with separate bedroom, lounge and bathroom. Service is very gracious and the guest is always welcomed with steaming towels.

International Hotel or the Park Hotel (Guoji fandian)
170 Nanjing xi lu
Tel. 225225
Cable 1445
This twenty-four-storey Art Deco hotel is the tallest building in Shanghai. Conveniently situated, it overlooks the People's Park and has a very good restaurant and service.
Dahua binguan
914 Yan'an xi lu
Tel. 523079
At the junction of Yan'an lu and Jiangsu lu, this comfortable hotel is rather far from the city centre.

Shenjiang Hotel
740 Hankou lu
Tel. 275115
Well-appointed but rather far from the city centre.

Restaurants: General Information
For the long-stay visitor to Shanghai eating out is a very good proposition, for the city boasts not only excellent Chinese restaurants but also ones which prepare western food. The latter are very popular with the Shanghainese, who can be seen eating wiener schnitzel with chopsticks. As usual it is best to ask your guide to make a reservation beforehand. Lunch is served very early in Shanghai – it can start around 11 am and last orders will be taken just before 1 pm. In the evening meals are served from 4.30 to 7.30 pm. The cost of a meal will be around 25–30 *yuan*.

Chinese Restaurants
Yangzhou fandian
308 Nanking Road
Tel. 222779/225826
Probably the best Chinese restaurant serving food in the Yangzhou style, the most common cuisine in this part of China; excellent fish and soups are served here.
Sichuan fandian
457 Nanking Road
Tel. 222246
Serves the hot, spicy dishes of Sichuan.

Xinya caiguan
719 Nanking Road
Tel. 223636
Cantonese-style food.

Yanyun lou
755 Nanking Road
Tel. 226174
Peking-style food.

Huimin fandian
Fuzhoulu
Tel. 224273
A pretty restaurant opening on to a
balcony with green tiles. Serves Mos-
lem-style food.

Old Shanghai (Shanghai lao fandian)
242 Fuyou lu
Tel. 282782
In the old quarter, close to the Mandarin Gardens
This, the oldest restaurant in Shanghai,
has been in existence for over a hundred
years. Proud of its presentation of food:
specialities are excellent duck (Eight
Treasure Duck), fried prawns and crab.

Gongdelin Vegetarian Restaurant
43 Huanghe ku
Tel. 531313

Western Food

Donghai Café
143 Nanking Road
Serves coffee in glasses, soup, cakes and
sandwiches; always very crowded.

The Deda (the Great German)
Around the corner on Sichuan lu
Serves omelettes, goulash and schnitzel.

The Red House (Hong fangzi)
Shanxi lu
Tel. 565748
Formerly Chez Louis, serves French-
style cuisine with excellent onion soup,
filet mignon and baked alaska, which
should be ordered in advance.

TIANJIN

Tianjin, formerly spelt Tientsin, is one
of those cities to be found all over the
world, whose own character is overshadowed by its proximity to the capital, and which people often visit only if
they have to. Carl Crow's comments in
A China Handbook apply as much today as they did in the 1920s and 1930s.

> Tientsin holds little attraction for
> the occidental sightseer and com-
> paratively few tourists stop in
> Tientsin on the journey between
> Shanghai and Peiping [Peking]. Its
> foreign settlements are modern
> with well paved streets, handsome
> buildings and efficient administra-
> tions but in these features there is
> nothing that cannot be seen else-
> where. The businessman and stu-
> dent of industrial development
> however will find much of interest.

If you are resident in Peking, or only
visiting northern China during a short
stay in the country, then for you Tianjin
still retains the architecture and appearance of its days as a foreign concession
city. If Tianjin is suddenly inserted in
your itinerary, do not despair: time can
be used in visiting studios carrying out
some of China's most skilled traditional
crafts, such as carpet weaving, jade
carving and woodblock printing, or
even visiting the port, or one of Tianjin's famous hospitals or educational
establishments. For the businessman,
either visiting or resident in the city,
many of the trading corporations are
based here. There are excellent facilities
for conferences and easy access to Peking and scenic areas in the vicinity of
Tianjin, as well as a few choice restaurants, shopping facilities and the
Friendship Club with its swimming
pool, bowling alley and billiards tables.

The city has long served as the river
port for the old capital and an entry port
for the other northern provinces. The
old city south of the junction of the Hai
River and the Nanyun he, bordered by
Beima, Xima and Nanma Streets. Tianjin was ceded to foreigners after the

Opium Wars in the mid-nineteenth century, and at one stage the eight major powers all held concessions here, with the British, Japanese and French the most prominent. Li Hongzhang governed in Tianjin between 1871 and 1898 and effected many progressive reforms, particularly in the areas of education and the army. The railway to Peking was completed in 1897. During the Boxer Uprising the city was besieged for twenty-seven days. After the foreign concessions were relieved by the Allied troups a temporary city government was formed, consisting of an international commission. The city underwent many changes and thorough Europeanization during these three years; the walls of the old city, built in 1403, were knocked down and used to construct a new ring road.

Today Tianjin is China's third municipality and the third largest city in China, with a total population of over 7 million. It is situated near the Bo hai Gulf on the Hai River and is 137 km south-east of Peking. The city's port at Xin gang is the most important one in the north-east and it is one of China's industrial centres, with oil refining, iron and steel, cotton, flour milling etc., as well as being well connected to the industrial north-east, Peking and the northern inland provinces. The city was affected by the devastating earthquake at Tangshan in 1976 and an energetic reconstruction programme has since been initiated. The city still retains many of the buildings constructed by the foreign powers, and the riverside promenade winding through the city is a popular gathering place in the summer months. As you cross the bridge from the main railway station on arrival in Tianjin you will pass through the former French concession and into the British concession – indeed Racecourse Road still retains its former name in Chinese.

The train journey from Peking to Tianjin North Station takes two hours; the city is also on the railway line between Shanghai and Guangzhou. There is a good road between Peking and Tianjin. By air the city can be reached from Guangzhou and Shanghai; and the airport is considered a second one to Peking. In November 1981 direct flights to Hong Kong were established.

Park on the Water (Shuishang gong-yuan)

As the name suggests, this park, in the south-western suburbs, is built on and around a large expanse of water. It is modern, begun in 1950, but contains all the traditional features such as pavilions, viewing towers, long corridors and zigzag bridges. There are snack-shops, a children's playground with a miniature train and roundabouts, and in the south of the park a zoo. You can take boats out on the lake.

New Port (Xin gang)

The new port, 35 km south-east of Tianjin on the Bohai Gulf at Tanggu, is the largest man-made port in northern China. It was begun in 1939 and extended and developed after 1949. Now the port can accommodate 30,000-tonne vessels. Container terminals and international passenger ship berths are also planned. The port has its own living quarters, seamen's international club and friendship store for sailors from overseas.

Pan shan Mountains

Situated in Ji xian county to the north of Tianjin, this is a popular scenic area containing several historical relics, among them the Dule Temple (the Temple of Solitary Joy). Built of wood in the Liao dynasty, it is one of the oldest buildings of this kind in China.

Educational Institutions

Nankai University enjoys a reputation similar to Oxford or Harvard. Zhou Enlai attended the middle school attached to the university. Tianjin University is nearby. Both establishments lie south of the ring road. The city also possesses respected teaching hospitals, specializing in both traditional and western techniques.

Museums

The Zhou Enlai Memorial Museum records Zhou Enlai's life in Tianjin. The city also has two historical museums and an art gallery.

Museum of Art
77 Jiefang bei lu

History Museum
4 Guanghua lu

Handicrafts

The tradition of modelling and painting clay figurines has been handed down through several generations of the Zhang family for 140 years. Their present studio, situated near the International Club, was established in 1959. Here visitors can see the processes of modelling and painting, as well as buy the finished articles.

Several studios in Tianjin specialize in the production of wool and silk carpets; most are made for export and facilities for shipping can be arranged. The work requires an admirable amount of skill and concentration, and such a visit also gives an insight into the organization and management of light industry in China.

Yangliuqing New Year pictures can be bought at 111 Sanheli, Donglou (tel. 34843). Yangliuqing was originally a small village south-east of Tianjin, where the local people were renowned for their vivid New Year pictures with which country people liked to decorate their windows at the Spring Festival.

The studio now operates from the original distribution point, near to the International Club. All the stages from tracing through to carving, printing, painting and mounting are carried out here. The pictures are bright and full of propitious symbols for the New Year, such as images of baby boys holding fishes, pomegranates and all the traditional elements which the Chinese use to wish for a long life. Traditional-style paintings are also reproduced by the woodblock method.

Tianjin also has an excellent jade and ivory carving studio, and paper kites are another popular local product.

Hotels: General Information

Like Shanghai and Wuhan, Tianjin is well supplied with hotels, built in the era of foreign concessions, which have been well maintained.

City Guest House (Tianjin ying bin-guan)
337 Machang dao
Tel. 24010
Situated in the south of the city, in secluded grounds, the hotel consists of several villas and a conference hall. The service and cuisine are of the highest quality, and great attention is paid to detail – the bed linen is embroidered, for instance.

Tianjin Grand Hotel
Youyi lu
Tel. 39613
Situated in the very south of the city.

Tianjin fandian
219 Jiefang bei lu
Tel. 34325
Formerly the Astor Hotel, it is centrally located close to the river, the friendship store and the popular restaurants.

Friendship Hotel (Youyi binguan)
At the crossroads of Shengli Road and Hebei Road
Tel. 35663

A recently built hotel, centrally located.

Tianjin No. 1 Hotel
198 Jiefang bei lu
Tel. 36438
A centrally located hotel.

Restaurants: General Information
Tianjin cuisine has a high reputation, with a wide selection of local produce including pears, walnuts, chestnuts, dates, rice and prawns.

Friendship Club (Youyi julebu)
Hexiqu
Machang dao 268
Tel. 32465
Situated in attractive grounds in the south of the city the Friendship Club is a perfect period piece with carved wooden panels, gracious ballrooms, bars, a bowling alley and a swimming pool, as well as an excellent restaurant.

Kiesling's Restaurant (Qisiling canting also known as Tianjin fandian)
33 Zhejiang lu
It retains the name of the former Austrian owner who had a chain of patisseries in north China, and today is best known for its pastries and western-style dishes.

Tianjin Snackshop (Tianjin baozi pu)
97 Shandong lu – Heping chu
Tel. 23277
This unassuming restaurant is renowned for its *goubuli* dumplings, which first became famous in the nineteenth century.

Dengying lou Restaurant
94 Bingjiang dao
Famous for its Tianjin specialities and Shandong-style cuisine.
Tel. 23594

Shopping
The friendship store, at 2 Zhangde dao, off Jiefang lu (tel. 32513), offers friendly service with shipping facilities. There is an arts and crafts store at 234 Heping lu, the Tianjin Department Store is at 226 Heping lu, and the Foreign Language Bookshop is at 143 Binjiang dao.

Useful Addresses
Post Offices
141 Binjiang Road
153 Jiefang bei lu

The Bank of China
80 Jiefang bei lu.

Hospital
Tianjin Medical Hospital
178 Anshan dao
Tel. 22608

CAAC
61 Taier zhuang lu
Tel. 37014

Luxingshe
55 Chongqing dao
Heping District
Tel. 34881

ANHUI PROVINCE

This province is rarely found on the tourist's itinerary; however for those drawn by inspiring scenery it is famed for the scenic beauty of Huang shan (Yellow Mountain) and Jiuhua shan (one of the four Buddhist mountains), as well as being the home of the 'four treasures of the art studio' – the finest brushes, paper, ink and inkstones in China are produced here. In olden days Hui zhou in the south of the province was famous for a particularly astute breed of businessmen and bankers.

Anhui is an inland province surrounded by other provinces – Jiangsu and Zhejiang to the east, Jiangxi to the south and Hubei and Hunan and the foothills of the Dabie mountains to the west. The province is split economically and geographically by the Yangtse River – the area south of the Yangtse has a warm climate with ample rainfall, fertile soil, wooded hills and mountains, and yields double-cropped rice. In the north lies the North China plain with its problems of soil erosion, arid winters, and the tendency of the Huai River to flood – a threat which has been reduced by the assiduous introduction of dykes and flood control schemes. In the past the area was often devastated by alternating flood and famine, and even today it is still one of the poorest and most backward areas in the country. The population is 48.03 million.

The major cities of the province are served by railways and the Yangtse is of course a major means of transporting goods – particularly rice, lumber and iron ore to Shanghai and the east coast. The province is rich in minerals. Huainan, situated on the south bank of the Huai River, is at the centre of a massive coalfield which has been mined since the late 1920s. At Tongling on the Yangtse copper is mined (the name means copper mound), and at Maanshan, close to the border with Jiangsu Province and near the Yangtse River, is one of China's major iron and steel works, which were first developed by the Japanese during the Second World War. Rice, tea, cotton and wheat are the major crops of the province. Carl Crow records that in the 1920s Chao Lake and some of the wooded hills of Anhui were excellent wildlife areas, recommended for hunting.

Hefei
Situated in the north central part of the province, at the confluence of the Tungfei and Nanfei Rivers, Hefei became the provincial capital in 1950. Until then the capital of the province had been Anqing, an ancient city, famed for its great pagoda and unusual elevated position, founded in the Song dynasty on the northern banks of the Yangtse.

Hefei is an almost entirely new city whose population has expanded from 50,000 to 400,000 since the early 1950s. It was one of the focal points of the industrialization programme of those years. The total population, taking in the rural districts as well as the city proper, is 1.4 million. The city is renowned as an educational centre and contains the Hefei Institute of the Academy of Science and China's University of Science and Technology.

To the south of the city is Lake Chao, the largest lake in Anhui and a favourite beauty spot. To the west are Dashu Mountain and Shu Mountain Lake. Despite the rather new appearance of the city itself, the area abounds in legends of heroes of the ancient Three Kingdoms period, and there are several monuments of interest to visit. The museum also has some interesting fossils on display.

Xiaoyao jin Park
In the north-east of the city, this park combines traditional and modern features and was the site of one of the great battles of the Three Kingdoms period. It houses the rostrum where Cao Cao, Emperor of Wei, lectured his troops on the art of the crossbow. The Mingjiao Temple dates from the Tang dynasty; another temple here commemorates the good offices of the Song official Bao Zheng (999–1062).

Tourist Information

Travel
Hefei is 1107 km from Peking. It can be reached by air from Peking and Guangzhou, by train from Peking, and by train from Nanking.

CAAC
73 Changjiang lu
Tel. 3798
Luxingshe
68 Changjiang lu
Tel. 2221

Hotels

Daoxiang lou binguan
Tel. 4791

Jianghuai
68 Chang jiang lu

Wuhu

This major river port is situated on the southern bank of the Yangtse, some 80 km from Nanking, and is one of the ports of call on many tourist itineraries plying the lower middle reaches of the Yangtse. The town's origins reach back to the Warring States period, and it has been known as Wuhu since the Han dynasty – almost two thousand years. By the Ming dynasty it had become a commercial centre, and in the Qing dynasty was famed as one of the four great rice centres, along with Changsha, Jiujiang and Wuxi. It also played an important role in distributing lumber, cotton and flour. In 1877 Wuhu became a treaty port. Today it is still a major rice distribution centre and is renowned for its freshwater fish. It is accessible by river and rail from many parts of China.

The city is attractive, with all the atmosphere of riverside life and a backdrop of mountains both within the city itself and on the outskirts, where visitors will see Zhe shan Mountain topped by its brick pagoda. In this city is Mirror Lake – perhaps a reference to the Tang dynasty poet Li Bai, who, in a state of intoxication, is reputed to have drowned after falling into the lake as he tried to catch the reflection of the moon. The Mid-river Pagoda was built in 1669. Visible for 50 km, it has served as a beacon for shipping on the river since that time. The city is famous for its wrought ironwork, feather pictures and lacquer paintings. Both Jiuhua Mountain and Huang shan may be reached by road from Wuhu.

Jiuhua shan

Jiuhua shan or Flower Mountain is in Qingyang county, south of the Yangtse River, an area of densely wooded mountains with over ninety peaks, caves, springs and venerable old trees. Jiuhua shan is one of the four sacred mountains of Buddhist lore (the others are Emei Mountain in Sichuan, Putuo in Zhejiang, and Wutai in Shanxi). The region abounds in temples and the stories and legends of sages and Buddhist adepts. The earliest temples were founded in the fourth century AD, and by the Ming and Qing dynasties there were some three hundred monasteries here, the most famous of which were the Roushen, Zhiyuan, Baisui, Ganlu, Tiantai and Chandan. Today there are less than a hundred monasteries still standing, containing many fine relics such as sutras, seals, calligraphy and paintings.

The Roushen monastery was first built in the Tang dynasty, although the present building dates from the mid-nineteenth century and boasts such fine features as unusually carved and painted eaves and corridors. One of the most famous Buddhist adepts was Wu Xia, who came here to fast and meditate at the turn of the sixteenth century. He died at the age of 126 and his gold-plated mummified remains can be seen here. The Tang poet Li Bai is associated with the mountain, and gave it its name.

Huang shan

Huang shan or Yellow Mountain remained almost unknown as a scenic area until the seventeenth century because it is so remote and inaccessible. It is situated in the south of Anhui Province between Taiping and She counties. The scenery is epitomized by the combination of the 'sea of clouds' which engulfs steep, craggy peaks for a large part of the year, perilously perched pines and thundering waterfalls.

Huang shan has inspired a whole school of painters from the late Ming dynasty up to the present day, when people try to capture the atmosphere with their cameras. On Huang shan grows the original Welcoming Guest Pine whose painting graces every hotel foyer. The mountain is also famous for its rhododendrons, and there are many other examples of wild flowers and plants, bird and animal life to be found here.

The whole area comprises some seventy peaks and covers about 154 km². The entrance is announced by a decorative triumphal arch and visitors may follow the main road up as far as Cloud Valley Temple, although many prefer to stop earlier at the warm springs, where there are a guesthouse and facilities for taking the waters. To reach other parts of the mountain, you must then follow the mountain trail up to Jade Screen Tower, precariously perched on the steep mountainside. From here one may view or even climb up to the highest peaks – Tian du, and Lianhua, which is 1800 m above sea-level. Naturally every peak has a descriptive title, from the unusual Eyebrow Peak to the typical Nine Dragon.

At Bei hai – which means northern sea, extending the metaphor of the cloud formations resembling the sea – is another vantage point, and a guesthouse. Here visitors will find Lion Summit and Cool Platform; it is one of the best places to watch the sunrise. There are also old gnarled pines with names such as Recumbent Dragon and Black Tiger. The view of the mountains from the nearby Searing the Clouds Pavilion is compared to a jade carving.

The Chinese guide to the area carries some recommendations for the visitor to Huang shan which it would be wise to follow. Wear soft-soled shoes – not leather ones. Carry a stick, a water bottle, some dried food and a raincoat. As it is cool in the evening and morning you would be well advised to bring some kind of hooded anorak or windcheater, but you can also hire padded jackets at service centres on the mountain. Even in July and August the average temperature is 7°C, so all visitors are recommended to bring garments suitable for cold, damp conditions. The climb can be arduous, but cable cars are being built. As mentioned above, there are guesthouses on the mountain.

Although it is not possible to go all the way to Huang shan by rail, you can get there by good roads from Zhejiang, by rail and road from Nanking or Wuhu, and by road from Hefei. There are also local flights from Hefei to Dunxi, south of Huang shan.

FUJIAN PROVINCE

Fujian, formerly spelt Fukien, is the mountainous coastal province in southeast China which faces the island of Taiwan. It has always been of strategic importance because of its easy sea access to other parts of south-east Asia, and it enjoys an international reputation as the home of many overseas Chinese. Famous for its tea, lacquerware, and numerous thick dialects, it is visited mostly by returning overseas Chinese. However in the north the scenery of the Wuyi Mountains will delight visitors of any nationality, and its coastal resorts offer natural beauty and a number of fascinating ancient monuments.

The several excellent natural harbours have made the province a trade centre through the ages. The main rivers are the Min and the Han, which meets the sea at Swatow in Guangdong Province; the Wuyi Mountains form the border between Jiangxi and Fujian. The province has a population of 24.88 million.

The climate is sub-tropical, with plenty of rainfall and a year-round growing season. Where there is sufficient arable land three harvests a year can be achieved, and the many products include rice, tea, tobacco, sugar, rape, bananas, oranges and sweet potatoes. However the main problem in Fujian has long been overpopulation which has resulted in a flow of emigrants. The north of the province is largely given over to the lumber industry; camphorwood and varieties of bamboo are found here. In the south of the province the land is more intensively farmed.

Fujian was absorbed into the Chinese empire in the Tang dynasty. By the twelfth century it was a rich province – Fuzhou and Quanzhou were international ports – renowned for its culture, and local products were sent northwards and abroad. In the Ming dynasty the province was prey to Japanese pirates, and the late seventeenth century saw emigration to Taiwan and southeast Asia. Xiamen (Amoy) and Fuzhou were both opened to foreigners as a result of the 1842 treaty. Competition from Japanese-occupied Taiwan with sugar, and from Ceylon and India with tea, placed great strain on the province's two major sources of income and led to poverty and emigration. In 1955 the railway to Xiamen and Fuzhou brought the province in touch with the rest of China. Though industrial development has taken place, the province remains poor and backward. In 1979 Xiamen was declared a special economic zone, where overseas companies can establish joint ventures.

Fuzhou

The provincial capital is situated in the north-east of Fujian on the northern banks of the Min River; halfway between Shanghai and Guangdong, it is 48 km from the sea and a major port. The approach to the city from the sea is through narrow winding gorges. Today the main port area is at Mawei. The city now has a population of around 700,000. It may be reached by air, rail or boat and has the only airport in Fujian Province.

Fuzhou was probably established in the Tang dynasty; however it was during the Song dynasty that it first earned its name Three Hills, when the city wall was built to enclose Wushi Hill, Yu Hill and Ping Hill. It is also known as the city of banyan trees – some nine hundred years ago the local governor had many banyan trees planted.

Hot Springs
On the outskirts of Fuzhou are hot springs renowned throughout China for their beneficial effects on the skin, rheumatism, and hardening of the arteries.

Luoxing Pagoda
This pagoda, the 'lighthouse' of Fuzhou, can be seen from the sea as it has been for many centuries.

Drum Mountain (Gu shan)
Situated to the east of the city, this is a flat-topped hill 1000 m high. The Yongquan Temple was built here in 908; although the original building is no longer there, part of the later Ming building can still be seen. Outside the temple is the Thousand Buddha Pagoda – it is one of the few surviving porcelain pagodas in China and dates from the early Song (1082). The white jade Buddha inside the temple was presented by Burma, and many ancient and valuable manuscripts, dating from the Ming and Qing dynasties, are housed here. The hill has a fine view of the city and the sea; it is wooded, and has caves and pathways in true Chinese style, as well as many stone tablets bearing callig-

raphic carvings by the great literary figures of the Song and Ming dynasties.

Westlake (Xi hu)

This park, in the north-west of the city, has ancient origins. It is laid out with a lake and trees and has a small museum with 'boat coffins' from Wuyi Mountain (see below), a Han dynasty boat and silk from a Song dynasty tomb.

Products and Cuisine

Fuzhou is famous for its lacquerware which is made into screens, tea sets, containers, trays and so on. Its food is also renowned.

Useful Addresses

CAAC
Nanmendou
Tel. 31188

Luxingshe
Wu si lu
Tel. 33962

Wuyi Mountain

The mountain is a famous scenic area in Chongan county in north Fujian. It is also renowned for its Oolong tea (rock tea), wildlife and abundance of rare plants – 570 km² have been designated a nature reserve. Here are to be found deer, leopards, 140 different kinds of birds, many snakes and reptiles, and the bearded toad; also box, sarcandra, plum yew, beech and gingke trees.

One of the most enjoyable experiences in this area is a leisurely boat ride along the 7-km Nine Twist Stream, which winds its way between soaring, wooded peaks of an unusual club shape. The ruins of the villa where the neo-Confucian philosopher Zhu Xi lived are also passed. Today the area has a sanatorium, hotels, restaurants and shops.

An unusual feature is the wooden 'boats' which seem to be perched high in the cracks of the side of the mountain; they were even mentioned by Zhu Xi eight hundred years ago. Naturally

many legends surround the 'boats', but in recent years archaeologists have been able to establish that they are coffins which date back two thousand years.

Quanzhou

This, one of Fujian's ancient international ports, was described by Marco Polo and Ibn Battuta, an Arab explorer. It lies between Fuzhou and Xiamen on the Jinjiang River and is characterized by its ancient bridge and the twin pagodas which punctuate the skyline. The city is also renowned for its coral bean trees which were planted in the tenth century; only a few are now left.

It was from Quanzhou that the early fifteenth-century Hui Moslem explorer Zheng He set out on his fifth major voyage, and there is a tablet commemorating the spot where he came to burn incense before his journey. Many of the sights of Quanzhou relate to its cosmopolitan past, a tradition which has been maintained by the opening of the Overseas Chinese University. In 1974 a wooden ship was found in the bay; thought to be a merchant ship from the twelfth or thirteenth century, it contained herbs, cinnamon and tortoise-shell and is now an exhibit near the Kaiyuan Temple. Today the old port has been reconstructed; there are also dams, reservoirs and a certain amount of light industry in the area.

Stone Bridge

This ancient bridge spans the mouth of the Luoyang River. It was built over nine hundred years ago of massive stone boulders and is 83 m long and 7 m wide. It is still in use today, although heavy traffic is diverted to cross the nearby dam, completed in 1973.

Kaiyuan Temple

First built in 686 in the Tang dynasty, it was known then as the Lotus Flower Temple, and was later renamed the Kaiyuan Temple, Kaiyuan being the reign title of the Tang emperor Xuan zong. The building is of fine proportions and known particularly for its excellent carvings. In the Hall of One Hundred Pillars are carvings of musicians which have been incorporated into the structure. Outside the main hall are the octagonal, five-storey twin pagodas, carved with Buddhas; the eastern one details the life of Sakyamuni. The Zhongguo Pagoda (east) was built in 865 and the Renshou in 916; originally of wood, they were later reconstructed in stone.

Ling shan (Ling Hill)

Outside the eastern gate of the city is Ling shan, where merchants and travellers from overseas were buried. This tradition began with the burial of two moslems who came to Quanzhou in the seventh century when international trade was at its height in China. Two granite tombs with tablets chart their deeds: the middle tablet, lettered in Arabic script, was erected in 1323. Further evidence of Quanzhou's cosmopolitan past survives in the ancient mosque which was first built in 1010 and renovated in 1310. At the entrance is a gate tower in classic Moslem style based on that of a mosque in Damascus. At one stage there were some 10,000 Moslems living in Quanzhou.

Wu shan (Wu Hill)

Other religious influences are recorded in the statue of Lao zi, the founder of Daoism, on Wu shan, 3 km from the city. Previously there was a Daoist temple on this site, but this has long since disappeared; the statue was carved a thousand years ago. There are many caves on the hillside with tablets bearing religious inscriptions, though modernity intrudes in the form of a television transmission tower.

Wan shan (Wan Hill)

On Wan shan in the suburbs are the remains of a temple dedicated to the religion known as Manicheism, which came to China along the Silk Route in the seventh century. The temple was first erected during the Song dynasty and has since been rebuilt. There is also a bas-relief carving of a Manicheist figure.

Zhangzhou

Situated upstream from Xiamen, this is the home town of many overseas Chinese. It is famous for its narcissi, grown for the Spring Festival, and fruit such as bananas and lychees. A great deal of experimental work has been carried out in connection with agriculture and irrigation projects, and pepper and rubber plantations have been introduced.

Xiamen

Known formerly as Amoy, Xiamen is the major port in southern Fujian and has an excellent natural harbour which can berth 10,000-tonne vessels. Abroad it is known as the home of many overseas Chinese, as a centre of food packing and processing, and for its educational establishments.

The city has an illustrious past – Koxinga defended it against the Manchus from 1647 until they finally took over in 1680 as one of the last areas to fall to them. The Portuguese were here for a time in the sixteenth century, and in 1842 it became one of the five major concession ports. It was from Xiamen that the tea ship sailed which became the subject of the Boston Tea Party, which sparked off the American War of Independence in 1775.

One of Xiamen's famous figures was Tan Kah Kee (1874–1961), a great educationalist who spent much of his time overseas and in Singapore, and used the funds he had amassed to set up the Jimei primary and middle schools and the Overseas Chinese Museum. He is

155

buried behind the Jimei Liberation Monument in Aoyuan Park.

The city is actually built on a series of islands, although it has now expanded on the mainland at Jimei, to which it is connected by a causeway constructed in 1956. Foreigners who came to Xiamen took over the attractive island of Gulangyu. Many buildings with porticos and shady balconies and colonnades remain, giving an Italian atmosphere. The city enjoys a pleasant climate, particularly between October and February.

Wulao Hill

On the south-east of the city is Wulao Hill where stands the famous South Putuo Temple, first put up in the tenth century and later rebuilt. The style is typical of south Fujian, with highly decorated eaves and beams, especially in the Dabei Hall, where there are a jade buddha and a wooden statue of Guanyin with many arms. The temple is also famous for its vegetarian cuisine.

Other Places to Visit

Gulangyu is often called the Park by the Sea, and at the foot of Longtou Hill are a beach and park. On a seemingly unclimbable promontory stand the ruins of the fort which was Zheng Chenggong's base from which he set out to rout the Dutch from Taiwan in 1662.

Tourist Information

Travel

You can get to Xiamen by rail from Fuzhou, or by sea from Hong Kong and Canton and coastal resorts to the north. The time taken from Hong Kong is 24 hours.

Luxingshe
444 Zhongshan lu
Tel. 4286/2729

Hotels

Gulangyu Guesthouse
25 Riguangyanlu,
Gulangyu Island
Tel. 2052

Lujiang Hotel
54 Lujiang dao
Tel. 2212

Shopping

Antiques shop
211 Zhongshan lu

GANSU PROVINCE

This somewhat strangely shaped province, squashed between the sparsely populated provinces of the Ningxia-Hui Autonomous Region and Qinghai Province, was once on the Silk Route, when caravans passed through the Gansu corridor, stopping at oasis towns. It is rich in historical relics, such as the last pass on the Great Wall and the famous grottoes of Dunhuang. Throughout the history of China it has remained part of the empire, and after it fell into poverty during the Qing dynasty it was selected as one of the major centres of industrial development in the first Five-Year Plan because of its deposits of oil, coal and iron ore. The capital, Lanzhou, has become a major railway junction from which lines branch into Qinghai, Xinjiang, Inner Mongolia and Shaanxi.

Gansu divides roughly into two areas. In the Yellow River basin area and southwards the climate is relatively humid, and around the Yellow River basin itself it is very fertile; the area to the south is a continuation of the loess plateau of Shaanxi Province, rising into the South Gansu Highlands. Winter wheat is grown, as well as gaoliang and millet. In the vicinity of Lanzhou agriculture returns to the spring wheat belt.

156

The west of the province is charac- terized by the soaring Qilian Mountains rising to 3000 m on the Gansu–Qinghai border, with the Gansu–Hexi corridor to the north stretching westwards for some 1000 km. Beyond those moun- tains lies the desert area of the Alashan, which is largely inhabited by Mongo- lian herdsmen – about a quarter of the province is given over to cattle rearing. Along the Gansu corridor melting snow and ice from the Qilian Mountains pro- vide oases where excellent rice and fruit are grown. Land has been reclaimed by the planting of tree belts, often called the Green Great Wall.

The total population of the province is 18.94 million. There are several minority districts in the province: Mongolian banners in the northern grasslands, Chinese Moslems in the south-east, Tibetans in the south-west and Mongol Moslems, known as Dong- xiang.

The main mineral wealth of the prov- ince comes from the Yumen oilfields in the north-west, first discovered in the late 1930s. Production began with a single oil well; the total workforce is now 20,000, and annual production runs to 600,000 tonnes per annum. During the first Five-Year Plan it was China's only oilfield, where among others Wang Jinxi – the Iron Man of Daqing fame – worked. The field is connected by a pipeline to Lanzhou where the oil is refined.

Lanzhou

Lanzhou (formerly spelt Lanchow) sprawls in a disorderly fashion, quite untypical of Chinese towns and cities, along the banks of the Yellow River in the most fertile part of the province of Gansu. In centuries past it was a major strategic and commercial city on the Silk Route, a role which has taken on a modern guise with the completion of

the railway lines which meet here from north, south, east and west – Qinghai, Baotou, Longhai and Xinjiang – and the city's selection for modern indust- rial development under the first Five- Year Plan. It is a bleak city, subject to sudden sandstorms, with an industrial landscape and overshadowed by stony hills. Its chief interest to the visitor is as a point of access to the ancient sites of the Silk Route.

Today Lanzhou has a total popula- tion of 2.2 million, with a flourishing oil refining industry for which purpose it is linked by pipeline with Yumen oilfields. Other industries include machinery, metals and textiles, as well as an exten- sive light industry in products for daily use. Its situation on the Yellow River has been turned to advantage by the harnessing of hydroelectric power at the Liujia Gorge, west of Lanzhou. The Yel- low River Valley area is the most fertile area in the province, and Lanzhou is well known for its fruit. Nearly every brigade has an orchard or melon field. The area also grows several different types of tobacco. The climate, however, is characterized by alternating extremes of day- and night-time temperature; the rainfall is low and the land alkaline.

The Gansu Provincial Museum (see below) contains a vast collection of re- cently excavated objects which point to very early settlements in the area. The first city on this site was built during the Han dynasty as a fortified city protected by passes, forts and watchtowers. It was called Jinzheng and corresponded to the present western district of Lanzhou which is called Xigu. It was one of the first major stops on the Silk Route after setting out from Xi'an. During the Sui dynasty the prefecture of Lanzhou was established here in the late sixteenth century, and a network of roads radi- ated from the city. The Yellow River enabled furs and skins, herbs and cotton to be transported into the area.

Development took place only slowly for many centuries and the beginnings of industrialization came at the end of the nineteenth century with the building of an arsenal in 1870, and a woollen mill; the main output of the factories established here consisted of sabres, saddles, army blankets and wool. The city today is divided into four main sectors: in the far west is Xigu; south of the river lies Anning; north of it is Qili he; and south of the river, where it is wide and contains several islands, is the centre, situated around the railway station. The city is sheltered by hills and mountains on both sides of the river, which creates for the visitor attractive landscapes.

Lanzhou is 1813 km from Peking, from where it can be reached by train or by air; you can also get there by train from Xi'an or Baotou. The airport is two hours' drive from the city centre. The 1950s-built Lanchou Hotel is centrally situated; its food is recommended. The Friendship Hotel (tel. 30511), opposite the Provincial Museum, houses the local Luxingshe offices; the rooms are spacious and it is set in pleasant grounds. There is a Friendship Store here with pleasant staff, and in the hotel grounds is a traditional-style building containing an antique shop. As far as cultural activities are concerned, the Gansu Song and Dance Troupe are responsible for the innovative production *Rain and Flowers on the Silk Road*, inspired by the murals at Dunhuang (see below).

CAAC
46 Donggang xi lu
Tel. 23432

White Pagoda Hill (Bai ta gongyuan)

North of the river and the city centre is this seven-storey white pagoda, built in the fifteenth century in Indian Buddhist style. It has a distinctive large bronze bell. The rest of the area has been laid out as an attractive park.

Five Springs Park

This park is south of the city, beneath Gaolao shan from where Huo Qubing, the famous general of the Han dynasty, led many forays against the Xiongnu in an attempt to make the Silk Route safe. Huo Qubing stationed his troops here but could find no water for them; he is said to have pierced the ground with his stick, whereupon five columns of water shot up. Several ornate buildings, a bronze buddha and a bell are to be found here.

Museum

The Provincial Museum is well worth a visit. The famous bronze flying horse, dating from the second century AD, was discovered in Wuwei in 1969, and though the exhibit in the museum is only a copy other interesting bronze funerary objects are housed here; in addition a Han tomb from the area has been transported and reconstructed in the museum. The wall paintings are also of special interest, and some of the famous brick paintings from the tombs at Jiayu guan are on display.

Grottoes of Bingling Monastery

Situated to the south-west of Lanzhou in Yangjing county, the Buddhist grottoes and temple were in use here from the fourth century AD. Today there are 183 grottoes on the northern banks of the Yellow River.

Jiuquan

One of the major cities on the Gansu corridor, Jiuquan is 32 km east of Jiayu Pass and the end of the Great Wall; in the Han dynasty it was a military base and economic centre. The picturesque name of the town means Wine Spring, and to the east of the town is a park called Wine Spring Lake Park, where the source of the spring is said to be. Again there is a story connected with the legendary general Huo Qubing. During a feast celebrating a victory the wine ran low; he poured the remaining wine into the spring, and invited every one to drink from it. The quality of the water from the spring still makes excellent tea. The most famous product of this area is the 'night glow' cup, made of highly polished local jade sparkling with yellow spots. The bibber's ideal is a good wine drunk from one of these cups.

Jiayu guan

Standing between the Qilian and the Mazong Mountains, the fortress of the Jiayu Pass (often dubbed the "most strategic pass in the world") is indeed an impressive sight, as one imagines battles fought against marauding invaders, or Zhang Qian setting forth with his troops to visit the western regions. The fortress dates from 1372, when the Ming emperor Zhu yuanzhang supervized a nationwide wall and fortress building programme in his attempts to prevent invasion from the north. The fortress consisted of an inner and an outer city. The inner city was surrounded by a crenellated wall 11.7 m high and 73 m in circumference, with east and west gates, dominated by watchtowers with winged roofs. The building was so perfectly planned that at the end there was only one unused brick; it has been preserved in the watchtower. Several relics from the area are on show in the Jiayuguan Exhibition Hall. Best known are the brick paintings taken from Wei dynasty tombs, depicting scenes from daily life; they were discovered in 1972.

In a valley to the north-west of Jiayu guan is a cliff engraved and painted with figures which reflect nomadic life in north-west China. The modern city has a population of 100,000 and several small industries.

Dunhuang

This was one of the four main prefectures to be established along the Gansu corridor by the Han emperor Wu Di in the first century BC. It was an oasis from where the Silk Road branched westwards into present-day Xinjiang and southwards into India. Among the great legacies of the period are the earliest examples of Buddhist art in China, to be found at the Thousand Buddha Caves (Qian fo dong, or the Mogao Grottoes), the West Caves of the Thousand Buddhas and the caves at Anxi. Ruins of ancient garrison cities and passes can also be seen here.

The population of Dunhuang is 90,000, of whom 10,000 live in the township. Dunhuang is an oasis with less than 2.5 cm of rainfall per annum; temperatures range from 28°C in the summer to −18°C in the winter.

For the time being the best way to reach Dunhuang is by train from Lanzhou; after a twenty-four-hour journey you alight at Liuyuan in the north-west of Gansu, a storage and distribution depot for the area. From here it is a three-hour journey (130 km) by bus through the Gobi Desert along the foot of the Qilian Mountains to Dunhuang. Air connections are planned for the future.

Accommodation is of a basic nature in local guesthouses. The rooms have beds and basins, but the tap is usually in the courtyard, and there are public conveniences only. Again, a hostel built to higher standards has been planned. Take with you lavatory paper and instant coffee. Only Chinese food is available, so you may need supplies of chocolate or cereal bars, and a torch is a must for viewing the frescoes as the caves are not well lit. Photography is either forbidden or expensive. Peter Hopkirk's book *Foreign Devils on the Silk Road*, publisher John Murray, provides an interesting background to the area and the part that foreign explorers played in rediscovering the treasures of the area and removing them to the West.

Thousand Buddha Caves (Mogao Caves)

The grottoes are situated some 25 km south-east of Dunhuang. Follow the road between the Sanwei and Mingsha Mountains, through a tree-lined oasis, until you approach the caves, built into the side of the sheer cliff face and distinguished by a nine-storeyed tower with flying eaves. There are 492 grottoes which were painted and decorated between the Eastern Qin dynasty in the fourth century and the Yuan dynasty in the fourteenth century. In 1900 a hidden monastery library was discovered. The caves are accessible along wooden walkways, and in recent years the Dunhuang Cultural Research Institute has restored and reproduced many of the murals and statues. The themes are many and varied – religious, scenes from the Silk Road, and the gods and figures of the Chinese pantheon. From them much information can be gleaned concerning the dances, music and customs of different periods. During the Song dynasty the murals were protected and added to by the governor Cao Yiqin and his sons and grandsons. After the fourteenth century the caves were neglected as the Silk Route diminished in importance.

West Thousand Buddha Caves

Travelling south-west of Dunhuang, after about 30 km you will come to the West Thousand Buddha Caves. They stand on the former banks of the swift-flowing Tang River, which has destroyed many of them so that today only sixteen remain. The caves were decorated between the fourth and the tenth century AD. Planks have been erected to facilitate viewing. Further south, under the watchful eye of the ruins of a Han dynasty fire beacon, are the Tang River reservoir and power plant which supply the Dunhuang area with electricity and irrigate the farmland.

Other Sites

Continuing in a south-westerly direction you will pass the ruins of Han burial sites and come to the ruined city of Shouchang on the edge of the oasis. It flourished in the Tang dynasty; here now is the Nanhu commune, famous for its fruit and vegetables. Seventy kilometres south-west of Dunhuang are the valleys of the Yang Pass, which was established by Han Wu Di and remained a vital garrison on the Silk Road until the thirteenth century.

The Crescent Spring is situated 4 km from Dunhuang. You can walk for half an hour over the 'echoing sand dunes' – local legend has it that a whole army was buried by a sandstorm here in the Han dynasty, and that if you listen carefully you will still hear the sounds of drums and battle.

GUANGDONG PROVINCE

Guangdong (formerly Kwangtung), China's southernmost province, comprises a large area on the mainland, Hainan Island, the second largest island in China, and the many small islands between the coast of Guangdong Province and Malaysia in the South China

Sea. At the mouth of the Pearl River Delta are those small, useful contacts with the rest of the world – Macao and Hong Kong. The total population of the province is 56.81 million, and the total land area is 22,000 km².

To the north and west of the province the terrain is mountainous, becoming lower towards the coast. The coastline is the longest of all the Chinese provinces. The centre of the province is fed by the Pearl River and its tributaries the Xi jiang from Guangxi and the Bei jiang from the northern Nanling Mountains. The Pearl, China's fifth longest river, rises in Yunnan Province and is over 2000 km long. The Han River in the north-east feeds this area.

The climate of the province is tropical or subtropical. It has hardly any winter except in the northernmost areas, and the yearly average temperature ranges from 19°C in the north to 25°C in the south; in winter the average is 9°C in the north and 21°C in the south. The hottest month is July, when the average temperature over the whole province is 28–29°C. The monsoon season lasts from April to September, and between May and November the coastal areas are exposed to typhoons.

Natural vegetation is lush and semi-tropical. The Pearl River delta area is particularly fertile and criss-crossed with a network of man-made and natural waterways. The growing season is year-long, and Guangdong is one of the major rice growing areas in China; sweet potatoes, wheat, maize and sorghum are also grown. Cash crops include sugar cane, peanuts, jute and silk. Guangdong Province is known for its four famous fruits – pineapples, mandarin oranges, lychees and bananas – not to mention others such as mangoes. On Hainan Island and in the Leizhou Peninsula rubber, coffee, tobacco, sisal, cocoa and pepper are harvested. In the central part of the province tea, rosin and different kinds of edible oils are produced. Along the coast all kinds of exotic fish are caught, among them delicacies such as sea slugs, abalone, oysters, prawns and crabs. Pigs are bred for Guangdong and Hong Kong, and beef cattle are raised on Hainan Island. The province is rich in natural resources, among them tin, iron ore, lead, copper, tungsten, antimony and salt. Heavy industry is largely centred on Guangzhou (Canton); petrol is made from shale at Maoming, and food processing, sugar refining and canning are major industries.

The province was first annexed as part of China under the Qin dynasty, after which period it remained independent until the first century, during the Han dynasty. It immediately became a point of contact for China with Southeast Asia, although it was not until the Tang dynasty that Han Chinese grudgingly came and settled in the area, since it was regarded as provincial in the extreme and cut off from the sophistications of court life. A period of separation and independence took place before the Ming dynasty, but then there was another influx of Chinese and Hakka (Kejia) with their own customs and dialect. The population was to grow in the early, wealthy years of the Ming dynasty, and people emigrated to other southern provinces and overseas. The sixteenth century saw the first contact with the West as Portugal gained a foothold on the island of Macao, and in the seventeenth century began the trade with the merchants of Guangdong – the *cohongs*. Hong Kong was ceded to Britain in 1842.

Today Guangdong and Fujian provinces have been afforded a certain independence in establishing trade contacts and joint enterprises, particularly with Hong Kong. Many 'overseas Chinese' originated from Guangdong and are now welcome to visit relatives freely and assist with overseas know-how and contacts; they have traditionally assisted their country from abroad.

Guangzhou

The Guangzhouese (Cantonese) have traditionally been China's innovators and travellers, and it is often said in China that 'Everything new comes from Guangzhou.' Historically it has always been the city with the most links with the rest of the world, and today it is the home of the twice-yearly Guangzhou Trade Fair. It is the major port of entry for visitors from Hong Kong and maintains very close contacts with that island.

Guangzhou is the provincial capital with a population of 5.3 million people, of whom approximately 2 million live in the city proper in an area of 54 km²; the rest inhabit an area of 4300 km². The city stands on the northern corner of the Pearl River delta, with the Baiyun (White Cloud) Hills to the north, upriver from the port of Whampoa.

The old city formerly stood on the north of the river, and the river was home for many people. Nowadays few people live in boats; the southern bank has been developed with new housing for the former boat-dwellers, and as an industrial area. The city walls and narrow streets were demolished early this century, and by the 1930s it was a city of wide boulevards and streets, with cars a common sight.

Today Guangzhou presents the most modern and cosmopolitan aspect in China, from the moment you step out from the light and spacious, recently completed railway station. There are more cars than you will find anywhere else in China – even garish taxis and modern office blocks. The city is crossed from east to west by the long Zhongshan lu, some 15 km in length. The major commercial centre is around Zhongshanwu lu and Jiefang zhong lu. Haizhu Square and the bridge and riverside area are also important and busy shopping centres. Shamian – once a sandy flat which was conceded to the British after the Opium Wars – is an area of tree-lined boulevards and grand old houses in colonial style.

The people and countryside differ from the rest of the country. There is a tropical light in the air, the old people wear wide, baggy trousers in black or bright blue, and the large shady hats typical of Chinese headgear; huddled, whitewashed houses with curving gable ends, and water buffalo, complete the scene. In town the mood is faster: between the modern multi-storeyed blocks are small shops such as charcuteries hung with Guangzhouese sausage; moon-gates give on to alleys hung with washing, and the streets are shaded by Italian-style colonnades. The people are wiry and strong-looking; the soft sounds of the northern accent have given way to the strident word-endings of the Guangzhouese dialect, in which the four tones increase to a seemingly impossible eight. On the pavements are street sellers of such things as sugar cane or pickled vegetables; some of them will offer to cut out your silhouette in paper. Babies are attached to their mother's back by red-embroidered baby slings, and it was in Guangzhou that I first discovered the bicycle as the ideal mode of transport for a family of four – a young child in front, father pedalling, and mother behind with a baby strapped to her back.

Traditionally there has been much rivalry between the north and south over the relative merits of cuisine, customs and so on, and for many years Guangzhou was a place to be banished to. Today the Guangzhouese are still regarded as quirky – they are very health-conscious and have an extensive

The dragon-topped wall of the Yu yuan Garden in the Old City of Shanghai

A gaudy festival dragon in Guangzhou

The colonnades of Guangzhou

A European-style residence on
Shanmian Island in Guangzhou

pharmacopia of curious cures and medicines. The number of Guangzhouese abroad has left an impression of the Chinese as good, hard-working businessmen. The overseas Chinese certainly have maintained contact with their people and country, and in the early part of the twentieth century were often responsible for the good works and relative wealth of the city. In today's China they are welcome to come and go freely, and in Guangzhou Province there are also several overseas Chinese communes.

The countryside is rich and fertile. Rice is the major crop and fruit is also important: if you visit Guangzhou at virtually any time of the year you will be able to eat one or other of its exotic fruits – lychees in June, 'dragon's eye' (longyan) in July, pineapples in October, and oranges and bananas in November. The port of Whampoa continues to develop, and industry includes metallurgy, engineering, food processing, paper, textiles and light industry. Exotic plants, trees and flowers abound, and at the time of the Spring Festival a flower market is held. The climate is subtropical – between April and August there are heavy showers almost daily, and the air is dank and humid with temperatures rising to 30°C. October to March are the best months to visit Guangzhou.

History

A township has existed on the site of Guangzhou since the Zhou dynasty, around 860 BC. The legend of the founding of the city is as follows. There had been a great flood, after which out of the sky appeared five sages mounted on five goats, each goat carrying a stalk of rice in its mouth. The people were enjoined to live in peace and prosperity and the rice was presented to them. Thereafter they would have the means to plant rice; the water subsided and the

sages disappeared. The goats turned to stone and were for many years revered in the Temple of the Five Sages, one of the many temples in Guangzhou which now no longer exist. In the 1950s a larger-than-life model in a modern, realistic style of the five goats was made and now stands in Yuexiu Park. They are popular photographic subjects for Chinese families and their children. Guangzhou is sometimes even today referred to as Goat City, Five Goat City or Rice Grain City.

During the Three Kingdoms period, in the third century AD, the city was designated Guangzhou by the kingdom of Wu, and by the Tang dynasty it had become a truly international port with trade connections as far west as Persia and even Europe. Xiangyang xi lu was largely inhabited by foreigners, and the mosque probably dates from that period.

The Portuguese began trading in the sixteenth century, to be followed by the British a century later, and it was under the Qing emperor Qian long that all foreign trade was restricted to Guangzhou, controlled by the powerful merchant guild known as the *cohong*. The sorry story of the introduction of opium into China began here and Lin Zexu was the Chinese hero who succeeded in capturing the British supplies and burning them, after blockading the British quarter for a week. The anti-British uprising of 1841 is commemorated in a monument in the northern quarter of the town, in Sanyuanli. These events led to the Opium Wars and the eventual opening of the five treaty ports, taking away some of Guangzhou's monopoly.

Guangzhou remained one of the cities most open and susceptible to new ideas. Sun Yatsen and the Tongmeng hui (United League) plotted to overthrow the Manchu dynasty, leading to the uprising of April 1911. A memorial to the martyrs of this uprising can be found in the north-east corner of the city at Huanghuagang. Chairman Mao and the Communist Party played their part when they came to Guangzhou and taught in the Peasants' Military Academy. In July 1926 the northern expedition against the warlords set out from here. In 1925 there was a general strike of seamen and dock workers lasting sixteen months. The following year saw an uprising against Chiang Kai-shek's anti-Communist programme.

Yuexiu Park and Guangzhou Museum
Yuexiu Park is spread out over hills in the northern suburbs of Guangzhou. Entrances to the complex are on Jiefang bei lu, within easy walking distance of the Dongfang Hotel and the Guangzhou Trade Fair. One of the largest parks in Guangzhou, it covers an area of 928,000 m². Before 1949 the tree-covered hills were known as Guanyin Hill (Guanyin is the goddess of mercy in Buddhist lore). The park has many amenities: apart from three artificial lakes, there is a swimming pool complex with separate pools for children, beginners, proficient swimmers and divers. The stadium built into the side of the hill can hold up to 30,000 spectators. Flower shows are held in the park during spring and autumn.

The museum is housed in a building in the park, known as the Zhenhailou. One of the oldest buildings in Guangzhou, built in the early Ming dynasty in 1380, it is five storeys high and thus is also known as the Five-storeyed Tower (Wuceng lou). It is red, with wooden balconies and curving eaves, and was probably formerly used as some kind of lookout tower. By the twentieth century only the shell of the building remained but it has been refurbished as a museum with a very interesting ceramics collection, as well as extensive details of Guangzhou's history.

In the northern part of the park is a cenotaph to Sun Yatsen, built in 1939. The view from here is comparable with that from the Zhenhai lou. In the southernmost part of the park is the Sun Yatsen Memorial Hall, a late 1920s' building with deep blue-glazed tiles and an octagonal dome which is often used for meetings or concerts. Sun Yatsen was born in Zhongshan County, South of Guangzhou. Visits can be arranged from here or Hong Kong.

The other major attraction of the park is the enormous stone sculpture of the five goats which, as mentioned above, figure in the popular legend of the founding of Guangzhou.

Lanpu Orchid Nurseries
The orchid garden, to the west of Yuexiu Park, is open only to specialists, or at times of the year when the orchids are in bloom. It contains more than three hundred different kinds of orchids, as well as special kinds of bamboos and other trees.

Liuhua Park
This park is to the left of the Dongfang Hotel, entered from Xi cun gonglu. Again it is within very easy walking distance of the Dongfang Hotel and the Trade Fair. It is perhaps a more restful alternative to the Yuexiu gongyuan since there are no hills to climb; most of the park consists of a lake, where boats may be hired. It was laid out as a park in the 1950s by voluntary labour, and contains galleries, restaurants and snack bars. In the southern part is Guangzhou's only children's palace, which is often visited. Adjacent to the park is a small garden called West Garden, constructed in 1965, which specializes in potted miniature scenery – bonsai, artificial lakes, waterfalls and hills, and pavilions.

Cultural Park (Wenhua gongyuan)

Situated in the centre of the city, close to the waterfront and the Nanfang department store, this park is dedicated to various recreational activities. It contains several open-air theatres and cinemas, facilities for pingpong, basketball, skating and chess, shooting ranges, small shops and restaurants, reading rooms, eight exhibition halls which display local products, an aquarium, arts and crafts and lanterns, and house overseas exhibitions. Before 1949 it was known as Central Park. It is quite close to the Shamian foreign concession area and People's Bridge.

From the Cultural Park it is interesting to follow the promenade eastwards to the iron girder Pearl Bridge and Square. Along the promenade are several wharves for ferry boats and pleasure boats used for river trips.

Liwan gongyuan

Situated in the westernmost area of the city, this is a new park with a large lake.

Sanyuanli

In the north-western suburbs of the city, off Jiefang bei lu, is the memorial to the uprising against the British at Sanyuanli in 1841. It is passed on the way into the city from the airport.

Guang ta or Huaisheng Mosque

In Guang ta lu, off Haizhu zhong lu, this building contrasts traditional Chinese walls and curved eaves with the stark lines of its Islamic minaret. One of the oldest mosques in China, it has been in existence since the early seventh century.

Flowery Pagoda in the Temple of the Six Banyan Trees (Liu rong ta)

This temple dates back to the fifth century. The Song poet Su Dongpo came here in the eleventh century, wrote a poem in praise of the six banyan trees he found in the courtyard, and also the two characters *liu rong*. After Su Dongpo's visit it became known as the Temple of the Six Banyan Trees. It contains carvings of small buddhas as well as the traditional eighteen *luohans* and a pagoda.

National Institute of the Peasant Movement

Situated to the north of Zhongshan si lu, the institute was witness to the first uneasy alliance between the Communists and the Nationalist Party, leading up to the period of the Northern Expedition against the warlords. Originally a Confucian temple, it was taken over by the Nationalists and Communists as a training school for peasant cadres between late 1924 and 1927.

The background to this union is as follows. In 1923 the Third National Congress of the Communist Party was held in Guangzhou, at which a motion was passed favouring co-operation between the Nationalists – then led by Sun Yatsen – and the Communists. This was also the occasion of Mao's first election to the Central Committee. In 1924 the Nationalist Party approved the admission of Communists to their ranks, and Mao was made an alternate member of their Central Executive.

During the next couple of years the Peasant Movement and the active involvement of the peasants in the affairs of China began. Mao worked in his native province of Hunan until he was forced to flee to Guangzhou, and from May to September 1926 was deputy director of the Nationalist Peasant Bureau and the Peasant Movement Training Institute as well as leader of the political education organization. By this time Wang Jingwei was the Nationalist leader, and Chiang Kaishek had risen to power as the commander of the army. Other notables of the Communist leadership, for example Zhou Enlai, Peng Pai, Yun Taiying and Xiao Chunu, taught at the institute.

Three hundred students from some twenty provinces and regions throughout China came to study basic military and political tenets in 1926. This was the earliest recognition of the role of the peasants as active participants in their country's future. Lectures were given by Mao on Marxism–Leninism, geography, the problems of the Chinese peasantry, and rural education. Zhou Enlai specialized in the relationship between the military and politics. The students were also divided into study groups – investigating and drawing up statistics on the ownership of the land by different ranks of the rural population. During this period Mao published his analysis of class in Chinese society. By September that year the students had graduated and the Northern Expedition had begun.

A visit usually includes an inspection of the living quarters, students' dormitories and classrooms, and to Chairman Mao's own house. Adjacent to the institute is the Museum of the Chinese revolution, resplendent with sculptured flames on the roofs. The institute was set up as a permanent exhibition in 1953.

Huangpu Island Military Academy

This army officers' academy was founded in May 1924 and was run jointly by the Nationalist Party under Sun Yatsen and the Communist Party. Zhou Enlai ran the political section and Sun Yatsen was President. The academy's *raison d'être* was Sun Yatsen's belief in the need for a revolutionary army. The cadets trained here were to form the basis of the expeditionary armies against the warlords in Guangdong and later on in northern China.

Memorial Park to the Martyrs of the Guangzhou Uprising (Guangzhou qiyi lieshi lingyuan)

The Guangzhou uprising took place in 1927. It was the angry retort of the local people to the programme of arrests and persecution carried out by the Nationalists against the Communists, which had begun in Shanghai in 1927 and had been followed up in other towns throughout China, including Guangzhou. The uprising began early in the morning on 11 December. The insurrectionists gained control quickly and the Guangzhou commune was set up. The Nationalists with support from the foreign powers in Guangzhou, launched a counter-attack on the new government, which was defeated within three days. On the afternoon of 13 December the reoccupation of the city by the Nationalists was followed by the execution of at least 5000 people.

The park is situated on Zhongshan san lu, east of the Peasant Training Institute. The garden, built in 1950, covers an area of 260,000 m². The tomb itself consists of a grass-covered mound surrounded by a low wall, with lions standing guard. Near the entrance to the park, on a wall, is an inscription written by Zhou Enlai.

As well as a wide variety of flowers, bamboo and cacti, there is a boating lake and two pavilions commemorating the friendship of the Chinese and Korean people and the Chinese and Russian people. To the left of the path leading to the mound itself is a round hall which contains exhibits of the history of the Revolution in Guangzhou.

Lu Xun jinian guan

Lu Xun, the Chinese modern writer, lived and taught for a while in Guangzhou. His house, near Yananerlu, has been set up as a museum of his life.

Tomb of the Seventy-two Martyrs at Huanghua gang

On Xianlie lu, on the north-eastern periphery of Guangzhou, is another memorial to an earlier stage in the Revolution. Built with donations from overseas and patriotic Chinese in 1918, it commemorates the seventy-two people who gave their lives in the uprising of 1911 which led to the final overthrow of the Manchu government and the establishment of the first Republic, under the leadership of Sun Yatsen. If you continue northwards along the same road you reach Guangzhou Zoo.

Zoo

Established in 1958, it has 215 different species of animal, many of them rare indigenous ones such as the giant panda, golden-tailed monkey and red-headed crane. It also houses over forty kinds of snake and other reptiles from the subtropical zones of southern China. The zoo is at the end of the No. 16 and No. 6 bus routes in the northern suburbs.

White Cloud Mountain (Baiyun shan)

Baiyunshan is Guangzhou's favourite beauty spot, in the north-east of the city. Its tallest peak is 382 m above sea-level, the highest point in the vicinity. In the last thirty years an energetic reforestation policy has clothed the hill in pines and bamboo, and there are pavilions and tea houses all the way to the top, as well as the remains of small temples, villas for high-level government officials, lakes and reservoirs. The hilltop park gives a fine view of the city and river.

Culture

Apart from its many arts and crafts, Guangzhou has its own rich cultural traditions. The Guangzhou acrobatics team was for a long time the best known such group in China and the rest of the world. The local style of opera, called *Yueju*, is characterized by the typical soothing and relaxed sounds of the south. Guangzhou has its own symphony orchestra, and the Sun Yatsen Memorial Hall is often used as a theatre, as mentioned above.

Places of Interest and Contemporary Life

If you spend long enough in Canton it is worth trying to visit a commune. Factories you might ask to see include those making heavy machinery, bicycles, rattan articles and electronic instruments. The children's palace, nurseries and primary schools; the College of Science and Arts (Zhongshan daxue); Hua nan teachers' training college; and new residential quarters, including the Bingjiang jie for people who used to live in boats, may all be of interest to visitors.

Guangzhou Trade Fair

In keeping with Guangzhou's traditional role as the centre for international trade in China, the Fair has opened twice a year since 1957. Until 1974 it was housed in Haizhu guangchang, when it moved to its present site on Xi cun gonglu opposite the Dongfang Hotel and less than one kilometre from the spanking new railway station which was completed around the same time. The building consists of a four-storeyed, five-winged complex; the total floor space is 110,000 m², and total exhibition space 60,000 m². The scope of the Fair has increased since 1976, and the exhibition centre now often holds shorter, more specialist exhibitions.

The Fair, held in April and October, is sponsored by China's foreign trade organizations. These two periods are devoted to light and heavy industry respectively. During the Fair units from all over China display their wares and discussion rooms are set aside for negotiation.

Applications to attend the Fair may be made through the commercial department of the Embassy in your country, or directly to the relevant state or provincial corporation.

The main products cover the following areas: cereals; oils; foodstuffs; native products; arts and crafts; chemicals; metals; minerals; and machinery. Also represented are the Guoji shudian – the international publishing house – and the Philatelic Export Corporation. During the period of the fair extra transport facilities are available from and to Hong Kong.

Environs of Guangzhou: General Information

There are several very interesting and unique places to visit outside Guangzhou. They make a restful change from the bustle of city sightseeing and can often be arranged – given sufficient notice – if one's stay is more than two nights. They range from hot springs to beauty spots.

Fo shan (Hill of the Buddhas)

This is one of the most popular and worthwhile places to visit outside Guangzhou. Approximately 25 km south-west of Guangzhou, it is reached after a very pleasant ride through a countryside full of typical Chinese scenes such as bent figures in broad-brimmed hats planting rice. The total population, comprising the urban area, Shiwan township and three people's communes, is 240,000. A very old town with a long tradition as a busy commercial centre, Fo shan dates from the Tang dynasty. The main attractions for the visitor are the Ancestral Temple, the pottery and ceramics works, and the arts and crafts centre. The name Fo shan, meaning Hill of the Buddhas, is an allusion to the Buddhist figures which were found here in the Tang dynasty.

Lunch stops or overnight stays can be arranged at the Overseas Chinese Hotel.

Ancestral Temple (Zu miao)

The Ancestral Temple was first built between 1078 and 1085 in the Song dynasty; it was rebuilt at the beginning of the Ming dynasty in 1372. In principle and style it was a Confucian temple dedicated to the worship of the God of the North.

The temple consists of the Front Hall, the Main Hall, the Tower of Rejoicing in Immortality (Qingchenlou), the Pond of Splendid Fragrance (Qinxiangchi), and the Stage of Myriad Blessings (Wanfu tai). The adjacent area has been converted to a park and local museum of Qing artefacts. The style and architecture of the temple are typically ornate. Objects within the temple consist of locally produced Shiwan pottery, and there is an enormous bronze statue of the God of the North. Note the ornate and colourful bas-relief legendary scenes depicted over archways, and the roof ornaments typical of the south.

Shiwan Artistic Ceramics Factory

Situated approximately 3 km from the centre of Fo shan, are fourteen potteries. The Shiwan art pottery factory specializes in figurines, birds and animals, miniature landscapes and exquisite tableware, and has a shop where the products can be bought. The inspection tour includes the processes of moulding, casting, shaping, painting, glazing and firing. The wood-fired kilns, typical of the south, are known as 'dragon' kilns and are built into the side of the hill. The best-quality pottery comes from the highest step of the oven. The typical glaze is red.

Folk Art Institute
Here you may see some of the other traditional handicrafts of the area, including papercuts and lantern making, also masks and scrolls.

Silk Printing and Dyeing Mills
The area around Fo shan is a traditional silk producing area, and the Hongmian and Nanhai silk weaving mills may be visited.

Xinhui County
Xinhui is an attractive garden city south-west of Guangzhou. Here there is a museum with examples of Tang pottery and a well known bird sanctuary.

Conghua Hot Springs
Conghua is approximately 70 km north of Guangzhou; the springs themselves are a further 16 km away, and it takes 1¾ hours to get there by bus or car. The area provides an ideal place for convalescence, with the beneficial water and the luxuriant surrounding scenery, where lichees, plum blossom, orchids, cassia, pines and bamboo abound.

The resort is divided by Liuxi River and joined by a bridge. There is an old hotel on the west bank and a new one on the east bank, as well as some villa-type accommodation. Each room has a bath fed by water from the springs, as well as being coolly furnished with rattan and cane. The hotels have restaurants and shops where local products such as dried (fresh in season) lichees and honey may be bought.

There are hot springs all over China, and Guangdong Province boasts some 240 such areas. At Conghua there are eight springs – four have their source in the river and four come out of the cliff side. The water, varying in temperature from 30°C to 70°C, is particularly beneficial for skin diseases and chronic illnesses and has a high soda content. It is colourless, odourless and tasteless.

In the area are three waterfalls, and the Liuxi River has been dammed to form a source of hydroelectric power. The dam is called Liuxi heshui dianzhan. Another hydroelectric power station in the vicinity is known as the Young People's Hydroelectric Station.

Zhaoqing and Seven Star Crags (Qixing yan)
Seven Star Crags is a scenic spot near Zhaoqing, approximately 100 km west of Canton on the Western River. The shapes of the mountains and the inscriptions on the cave walls have earned the area the reputation of a lesser Guilin. The Seven Star Crags are seven largely limestone mountains arranged like the big dipper constellation. In Chinese fashion each peak has a name which makes the unattuned eye of the foreigner strain to see the resemblance.

The Seven Peaks are Langfeng (Lofty Wind), Yuping (Jade Screen), Shishi (Stone Chamber), Tianzhu (Pillar of Heaven), Chanchu (Toad), Shizhang (Stone Palm), and Apo (Hill Slope). Each mountain has its special feature in the form of either reconstructed pavilions or caves such as the one under Stone Chamber Hill, which is large, with an underground river which can be reached by boat. The cave walls are a veritable exhibition of inscriptions and poems in all styles of calligraphy, and there are stalactites in many different shapes. The caves beneath contain two small rivers. In 1955 the small lake in the area was enlarged to provide irrigation for the surrounding area and for fish breeding. A 22-km long embankment was built all around it, as well as new pavilions and bridges in Ming and Qing style. It was named Star Lake.

Zhaoqing has been known for a thousand years and is famous for its Duan inkstones (Duanzhou was the former name of the city). There is also an ivory carving factory here. The

169

Moon in the Water Palace is a former temple which has been restored as a museum and art gallery.

Xijiao shan

This is a scenic spot 80 km south-west of Canton in Nanhai County. The area comprises seventy-two peaks, of which the tallest, Dake, is 400 m above sea-level, with five characters carved in the side proclaiming it the No. 1 peak in Xijiao. The area also contains thirty-six caves, twenty-one crags and thirty-two springs!

Baiyun Cave is the best-known cave. Just before it is the entrance, Yunchuan-xianguan, whose name means 'cloud spring hall of the immortals'. In the inner part of the cave is one of the eight famous sights of Guangzhou, Xijiao yun bao, with descriptive characters reading 'a thousand foot waterfall' inscribed at the side. The volcanic formation of the range has left behind rocks in all shapes and forms.

The most famous well in the area is called the Leafless Well. The water should be drunk with the local Cloud Mist tea. The irrigation problems of the area have been helped by the installation of pumping stations and reservoirs. A visit to a local commune is often included in an itinerary that takes in this area.

Tourist Information

Most of the tourist traffic into China enters from Hong Kong via Guangzhou, and there are now several quicker and more efficient express services than the famous train which goes from Kowloon to Luowu and involves a walk across the bridge to Shenzhen, before boarding the train to Canton.

There are two through trains between Hong Kong and Guangzhou, with customs formalities in both places. The check-in time is one hour earlier than departure.

Departs	Arrives
Guangzhou	*Hong Kong*
8.30 am	11.26 am
10.10 am	1.07 pm
Departs	*Arrives*
Hong Kong	*Guangzhou*
1 pm	3.59 pm
2.55 pm	5.50 pm

Customs formalities at Guangzhou are fairly rigorous due to the large amount of incoming and outgoing traffic. Porters charge 2 *yuan* per piece carried. On arrival at Hong Kong you must fill in immigration forms and present your passport.

There are also frequent trains between Guangzhou and Shenzhen (Shumchum) on the Chinese border where you must alight, cross the border on foot and reboard the train at Luowu (Hong Kong new territories). Shenzhen makes a popular day trip from Hong Kong. It was declared a special economic zone in 1980 and there are many joint enterprises in the area.

The Hong Kong–Guangzhou hovercraft service runs three times a day. It takes approximately 2 hours 45 minutes, plus transfer by bus to Guangzhou from Whampoa. It currently costs 30 *yuan* and tickets can be bought from the China Travel Service office in Hong Kong.

Departs	
Hong Kong	
(Kowloon)	*Departs*
	Guangzhou
7.30 am	7.30 am
11.30 am	11.30 am
3.30 pm	3.30 pm

CAAC now operates three return flights per day between Hong Kong and Guangzhou, but the timetables are changeable, so confirm reservations.

Shopping

With its many local crafts Guangzhou is very good for shopping, either in the local shops or in the friendship store for more intricate and specialized types of goods. Among local products are household and craft goods made of bamboo and rattan; ivory carvings, particularly the well-known concentric ivory spheres; 'cool mats', used in the summer; porcelain from Foshan; and crochet and embroidery from Chaozhou – the latter consists of raised appliqué in bright colours, favourite subjects being phoenixes and peonies.

Zhongshan wu lu is the main shopping area of the city. Here you will find the Jiangnan tutechan shangdian (the South China Local Products Store). In Beijing lu are the foreign-language bookshop, a bank and major chemists. Behind the Guangzhou binguan in Taikang lu is the Taiqin Local Products Store, specializing in baskets and the famous broad-brimmed Guangzhouese hats. The Renmin dasha in Changti lu is also one of the main stores, as is the Nanfang dasha on the waterfront just past Renmin nan lu. In Wende lu, parallel to Beijing lu, is an antique store.

Most shops are open seven days a week from 9 am to 6 or 9 pm. The Friendship Store was opened in 1978 next to the Baiyun Hotel, and is open from 9 am to 9 pm.

A No. 1 bus takes you to the shopping centre – Zhongshan wu lu and Beijing lu. To reach Renmin nan lu take a No. 3 bus from outside the Trade Fair on Jiefang bei lu.

Useful Addresses
CAAC
181 Huan shi lu
Tel. 34079 (International)
     31460 (Domestic)

Luxingshe
179 Huan shi lu (adjacent to main station)
Tel. 33454

Bank of China
137 Changti lu

Hospital
Zhongshan Medical College
74 Zhongshan er lu
Tel. 78314

Hotels: General Information
The hotels in Guangzhou are more attuned than those elsewhere in China to the needs and requirements of foreign guests, due to many years of looking after them during the Trade Fair. While this means that such details as directions within the hotel and amenities are clearly advertised, it has also tended to render the service more impersonal than you will find in other areas.

Dongfang Hotel (Dongfang binguan)
Xi cun gonglu
Tel. 69900
This enormous hotel (2000 beds) is directly opposite the Exhibition Hall of the Trade Fair, in the northern quarter of the city close to the station and the airport, and within walking distance of Liuhua Park and Yuexiu Park. It consists of the old wing, built in 1961, and the new one, completed in 1973. The hotel has recently been refurbished, air-conditioning has been installed, and there is an American-style steak bar on the ground floor, as well as other restaurant facilities.

The hotel has on the ground floor all its amenities, which are often open until nine or ten in the evening. They include post office, telex and telegraph facilities, and a selection of shops. There is also a clinic in the hotel.

The main dining-room is on the ground floor; there is another on the eighth floor, and on the eleventh floor of the new block which is largely used for banquets. Guangzhouese cuisine and local specialities such as salted chicken, beancurd and goose are served; northern-style and Sichuan dishes are also available. There is a 20% surcharge for room service. The hotel has a roof garden with a view over the city, games rooms, electronic games machines and a sauna.

White Cloud Hotel (Baiyun binguan)
Tel. 67 70 0
Cable 06 82

The newest and tallest building and hotel in Canton, it has thirty-three floors altogether. It is situated in the north-eastern suburbs near the Overseas Chinese New Village Housing Estate and adjacent to the friendship store, in a newly developing quarter of the city, and looks out at the White Cloud Mountain area itself. It is also near Huanghua gang and the Zoo.

The entrance to the hotel includes a covered walkway. The spacious lobby is furnished with chairs and tables and an electronic tourist map of Guangzhou; a cool effect is given by the décor of marble, bamboo and tiles. All facilities are on the lobby floor, and there are lifts at the back. Two restaurants can be reached by a covered gallery at the right of the lobby, built round an ancient enormous banyan tree and a rockery. The restaurants serve western-style food on request, and the Chinese dining-room specializes in Guangzhouese-style sweet and sour pork. A bar and a snack service can be found on the left of the lobby. The bedrooms, though air-conditioned and all with their own bathrooms, are somewhat spartan.

Guangzhou bingguan
Haizhu guangchang
Tel. 61 55 6

This hotel, centrally situated next to the Haizhu Bridge and the Agricultural Exhibition Hall, is within walking distance of the shopping area around Renmin nan lu and Nanfang dasha (the large department store); it is also within reach of the Cultural Park. It consists of a west wing (five storeys), and an east wing (twenty-seven storeys) which was completed in 1968.

Amenities are normally open at the times of day when guests are in the hotel. During the Trade Fair, as in most other Guangzhou hotels, post office facilities remain open until late at night. The restaurants, on the first and second floors, specialize in Guangzhouese and Japanese-style cooking. There is a bar on the fourth floor which serves iced drinks and snacks from 9 pm to 12 pm. The rooms are simply furnished and supplied with electric fans in the summer.

Liuhua binguan
Renmin bei lu
Tel. 68 80 0

Situated right next to the station, this hotel is simply furnished and is used by overseas Chinese and European tourist groups.

Other Hotels

There are a few other hotels, such as the Overseas Chinese Hotel in Haizhu Square and the Friendship Hotel near the river front, which are reserved for overseas Chinese on the whole. The Nanhu Hotel, situated in beautiful surroundings on the outskirts of the city, has recently been opened.

Restaurants: General Information

Guangzhou has many excellent restaurants: many are in attractive garden surroundings, while others trade on their exotic fare. The Guangzhouese are the gourmets of China, and special consideration is given to the nutritional value of various foods, although some of the dishes which tempt the Guangzhouese are regarded with horror by people in other parts of China. Some of the best-known specialities include *shahemian* – noodles made of rice flour and water, *dimsum* – sweet and savoury pastries and dumplings, roast sucking pig, and sweet and sour pork. The Cantonese know fifty ways to cook chicken.

The lush tropical
vegetation and the gilded
decoration which are
typical of Guangdong
Province

Gaudy plaster
sculptures, used as roof
ornaments, also typical
of Guangdong: depicted
here is a domestic scene
in an official family,
dating from c. 1900

Reflections of Guilin

Picturesque scenery in Guilin

Dog meat restaurants can be found, but for the truly exotic there is little to beat the snake dinner – the snake is selected alive by the diner, killed and skinned in the restaurant. It can be prepared in up to thirty different ways, and the snake's gall bladder, soaked in spirit, is said to be an excellent cure for rheumatism.

The tea house tradition is strong in Guangzhou. The time to go is very early in the morning for a pot of tea and a selection of *dimsum*. The most popular tea houses are Panxi, Beiyuan, Guangzhou jiujia and Taotao ju.

Panxi jiujia
Xiangyang yi lu
Tel. 85 65 5
Built overlooking a small lake near Liwan Park. Specializes in *dimsum*.

Beiyuan jiujia
Dengfeng bei lu
Tel. 33 36 5
One of the oldest restaurants in Guangzhou.

Nanyuan jiujia
Qianjin lu
Tel. 50 53 2
Specializes in *Chaozhou* and Guangzhouese-style food.

Guangzhou jiujia
Xiuli er lu
Tel. 87 13 6

Datong jiujia
Yanjiang lu
Tel. 86 39 6

Dongjiang fandian
Zhongshan si lu
Tel. 35 56 8

Beixiu fandian
Jiefang lu
Tel. 35 94 1

Shewangman
Jiangwan lu
Tel. 22 51 7
A snake restaurant.

Dongfeng lou
Xiuli san lu
Tel. 85 76 9

Taotao ju
228 Xiuliyilu
Tel. 87306

GUANGXI-ZHUANG AUTONOMOUS REGION

This autonomous region was constituted in 1958 and expanded in 1965 to include the coastal area and the port of Bai hai. Many of the Zhuang nationality, of whom there are 7 million in China, are concentrated in this region. The total population is 34.70 million. The Zhuang are one of the ethnic groups which have most readily absorbed Chinese customs and language, which probably accounts for their survival in such numbers. Modern Chinese literature makes much of the fact that they were among the earliest rice planters, and they also played an important part in the early years of the Taiping rebellion. Since the Qin Empire the Chinese have established their rule here – at least indirectly through the efforts of local chieftains. Also represented here are the Miao and Yao ethnic minorities, who have in the past assimilated Chinese rule and customs less readily.

Guangxi is surrounded by mountains, high in the north-west as they join the Yunnan–Guizhou plateau, but becoming lower towards the south-east. Half of the province is covered with limestone, making this one of the most extensive karst regions in the world, with the extraordinary scenery characterized by Guilin. Geologists think that the area used to be under water, that the earth's crust threw up limestone, and that the weird shapes have been formed by erosion both underground and above ground.

173

The Xi River and its tributaries flow through the province. The climate is temperate: around Guilin January temperatures average 9–10°C and July ones 26°C. Annual rainfall is 1100–2800 mm. Agriculture is hindered in many areas by thin soil and hilly ground, as well as the extreme porosity of the rock. Efforts have been made in water conservancy by the creation of underground reservoirs and irrigation work. Double-cropped rice is grown in the paddy fields in the south-east of the province. Other crops in the hilly areas include maize, sweet potatoes, sugar cane, peanuts, tobacco, jute and a cornucopia of fruit: oranges, bananas, pineapples, lichees and longans. The area also specializes in star anise, fennel oil and *Cassia lignea*. Forestry plays an important role in the northern hills of Guangxi, where sandalwood, pine and cedar are cropped. From the coastal areas in the south tropical crops are obtained such as rubber, coffee and pepper. Deposits of manganese, tin, coal and iron ore are to be found in the province. Industry is based on food processing, canning, sugar refining and agricultural implements. The region is well served by a natural network of waterways and railways connecting it with neighbouring Guizhou, Hunan and Guangdong. At Bingxiang the railway, now temporarily closed, passes from Guangxi into Vietnam.

Nanning

This city has been the cultural and administrative capital of the province since 1912 and is a river port standing on the banks of the Yu River in the south of Guangxi. The completion of the railway in the early 1950s made Nanning an important regional centre. With a population of 500,000, it is a pleasant town set in exotic surroundings of tropical vegetation. It is the regional educational centre and also has its own Nationalities Institute where members of the different nationalities come to study. Its walking tractors are well known, and it has developed a food processing industry as well as producing a local brand of watches. There are several parks within the city and a visit to one of the local communes is well worthwhile. Near the city is a hydro-electric power station at Xiqin.

Yiling Cave

Twenty kilometres north-west of Nanning is the Yiling Cave with a marvellous display of stalactites and stalagmites; it is over 1 km long and 45 m deep.

Wuming

This is a scenic spot to the north-west of Nanning on the Wuming River.

Binyang

To the north-east of Nanning, this town is particularly famous for its pottery.

Guiping

On the confluence of the Qian and Yu Rivers, this town lies just east of the Dateng Gorge, north-east of Nanning; there are hot springs in the area and a sugar refinery. To the north is the village of Jintian (Gold Field) where the first battle of the Taiping Rebellion took place; many of the sites of interest are closely connected to the history of that movement. Guiping can be reached by rail as far as Gui xian, from where you take the road to Guiping.

The Taiping Rebellion developed from a number of causes in this area. In the early half of the nineteenth century there had already been peasant rebellions, the area was poor, resentment was felt against the Manchus and the influx of foreign ideas and missionaries via Guangdong Province. Hong Xiuquan had failed the officials' entrance examinations; then he came into contact with the missionaries and the Bible and found renewed enthusiasm. He began lecturing to disaffected coolies and peasants, and gathered around him the five men who were to be the movement's leaders. By 1845 a militant and rebellious society of God-worshippers had formed, incorporating all the floating outcasts of society. They sought a new order of equality and neighbourly love – not the traditional aim of the secret societies, which was the restoration of the old Han dynastic order. By 1850 Hong Xiuquan and his followers had established their camp at Jintian, won victories against the imperial soldiers, and proclaimed the Kingdom of Heavenly Peace. In 1852 they took the fortified town of Yongan and in April moved northwards into Hunan Province, eventually making their way into the Yangtse River valley and Nanking.

Liuzhou

Set in attractive natural surroundings, Liuzhou lies on the banks of the Li River. It is here that one should come to die, as the old saying goes, for the cedar wood found in the area is of a particularly fine quality for coffin making. Tradition apart, it is an important transhipment port for the distribution of timber and a railway junction where the lines from Hunan and Guizhou meet.

Until 634 the city was known as Kunzhou, and in the Tang dynasty, when the south was still considered a barbarous and foreign land by the high society of the north, it was a place where out-of-favour officials were given posts. Liu Zongyuan was sent here as governor in 815; like so many officials he was a poet, and his poems have often been republished in modern China for the way they reflect sympathy with the sufferings of the ordinary people. Today you can still visit the temple built in his memory and the grave where his hat and gown are said to be.

Maan shan gives a view of the city and the river wending its way through it, and nearby is the scenic spot of Liyu Peak and the Small Dragon Pool in Yufeng shan Park. The pool figures in the local legend of a Zhuang nationality girl, Liu Sanjie, famed for her singing about the sufferings of the ordinary people, who was threatened by local landlords. She eventually jumped into the Dragon Pool, but two carp jumped out of the pool, one carrying her on its back, the other bearing the Liyu Peak which crushed all the landlords.

Local handicrafts include stone carving, and local industry building machinery and transistors. In the suburbs is Tuluo Cave.

Guilin

In the Reed Flute Cave near Guilin (formerly Kweilin) is a rock stalagmite called the Old Scholar. He is said to have come to Guilin many years ago; enchanted by the scenery, he started to write a poem, but never got beyond the second line, 'I'd like to praise it but find it difficult to describe.' He turned into stone before he had finished the poem. Others were more fortunate in their search for words – Han Yu described Guilin thus: 'The river is a turquoise gauze belt, the mountains like a jade clasp.' For my part I recall the extraordinary limpidity of the waters, the reflections of the mountain pinnacles, the flatness of the paddy fields contrasted with the sudden rising of the mountains, the bamboo groves along the river banks, and the timelessness of a bamboo punt containing a solitary fisherman in a wide-brimmed hat.

Modern Guilin is a clean and spacious town, where factories and modern red- or grey-tiled buildings with whitewashed façades nestle under the watchful protection of Duxiu Mountain or Diecai shan. Since the Qing dynasty it has been a vital communications centre, and was severely damaged during the Sino–Japanese War. Until 1912 it was the provincial capital; today it has a population of 400,000 with food processing industries and machine tool factories, cement works, chemical plants and thermal generators nearby. Nowadays most of its income comes from tourism, providing a developed service industry for the many foreign and Chinese visitors. It is a relaxing town for the visitor, and compact enough to walk around in.

The name Guilin means Forest of Cassia – the tree blossom between mid-August and mid-October. The city is built on the banks of the Li River, with the Taohua (peach blossom) River joining it to the south. The built-up area is on the western banks of the Li jiang, and the remains of a moat describe the former shape of the city walls. The railway, which was completed in the early 1950s, aesthetically skirts the city's perimeter, with stations at the northern and southern end. The main thoroughfare, Zhongshan zhong lu, runs north–south through the city. The Ling Canal, constructed in 214 BC, is to the north of Guilin and is well worth a visit.

You can get to Guilin by plane from major cities in China; from Guangzhou the flight takes fifty minutes. There is a rather long rail connection from Guangzhou via Changsha. The airport is 16 km north-east of the city. Shortly after your arrival in Guilin you will almost certainly visit one of the two peaks near the city centre, for a general introduction to the Guilin scenery.

Duxiu feng

'The peak of unique beauty' dominates the city centre from a park to the north of Jiefang zhong lu. You will feel the steep climb has been worthwhile as you gaze eastwards to the Li River and the Seven Star Park on the opposite banks, north to Piled Silk Hill and south to Elephant Trunk Hill. To the west are

Old Man Hill, the Western Hills and Hidden Hill. Duxiu Peak is especially beautiful at sunset, when it seems to wear a 'purple gown and a golden belt'; characters carved into the hillside proclaim 'a pillar of the southern heaven' and 'purple and gold mountain belt'.

Piled Silk Hill (Diecai shan)

It takes its name from the numerous peaks, and lies in the north of the city on the banks of the Li River. There are several attractive pavilions on the mountain, with the Nayun ting (Grasping Cloud Pavilion) at the very top, and stone benches and stools where you may surprise a group of young boys playing cards or chess, or where elderly men gather to gossip and drink tea on cane chairs. Again there are characters carved in the rock face, and you can visit the well-known Wind Cave (Feng dong) where even on the hottest and stillest days an icy current of air whips through. On the side of the hill are tablets bearing poems by Zhu De and Xu Deli.

Fubo shan

Fubo Hill overlooks the Li River between Duxiu Peak and Piled Silk Hill. At the foot of the hill is an arch proclaiming 'the outstanding scenery of Fubo'. After this there is a small flower garden and two relics – a big cauldron and an iron bell – of the Dingao Temple which stood in the vicinity in earlier years. In the sides of the hill are bas-reliefs and stone tablets of Buddhist figures or paintings of bamboo. In the mountain is Huanzhu Cave, which overlooks the Li River; inside it is the famous Shijianshi – the sword testing stone – where a hanging rock appears to have been cut away from its base. On the cave walls are tablets bearing poems, names of earlier visitors and figures of dragons and buddhas.

Elephant Trunk Hill
Standing on the south of the confluence of the Taohua River and the Li jiang, its shape is like that of an elephant drinking from the water. Local legend has it that this was originally the elephant of the Jade Emperor who did not want to return to Heaven – the pagoda on top of the hill is said to be the handle of the sword which pierced the sacred elephant. South of Elephant Trunk Hill is Southern Creek Hill.

Seven Star Park
To reach Seven Star park cross the recently built Jiefang (Liberation) Bridge to the eastern bank of the Li River, and then walk over the picturesque Flower Bridge, a covered bridge with a tiled roof, palisades and arches to regulate the flow of water; the first bridge was built here some 500 years ago. Here the park spreads before you, with trees, tea houses and pavilions. In recent years some 900,000 cassia trees have been planted in Guilin, and from August to October their scent pervades the air.

To the right is Crescent Hill (Yueya shan) and the pagoda which takes its name from the hill. In the past artists would climb the hill to paint the surrounding scenery, and the pagoda became known as the Painters' Pagoda (Hua ta); now it is climbed by eager photographers. On the south side of the hill at the foot is the famous Hidden Dragon Cave (Yinlong yan), which derives its name from the markings on the cave ceiling which seem to depict a dragon struggling to get out. On the rock face in and around the cave is the oldest and most numerous collection of tablets written by admiring visitors from the Song dynasty onwards. It is called 'a forest of tablets in a sea of cassias'.

Beneath Seven Star Hill is the Seven Star Cave which has been a popular site for over a thousand years. It takes an hour to work your way through the cave, with the singsong tones of the guide introducing the various highlights of the stalagmite formations – monkey stealing the peaches, the old fisherman spreading the nets, or the spacious chamber which has been named the 'sports ground'. When you emerge from the cave you come face to face with Camel Hill (Luotuo shan), whose shape even the most unimaginative visitor will have no problem in recognizing. Nearby is a small garden with a fine collection of bonsai and potted rockeries, and in early spring, around the time of the Spring Festival, the first narcissi; there is also a small zoo nearby. Looking south from Crescent Hill you will see the distinctive Pagoda Hill, whose pagoda seems to grow out of the hilltop.

Reed Flute Cave (Ludi yan)
Ludi Cave is 6 km to the north-west of the city on the banks of the Taohua River. The existence of this cave was kept a closely guarded secret by the local inhabitants, to be used as a hideout in times of war and so on, until it was opened to the general public in 1958 and turned into a beauty spot with all the amenities of transport, tea houses, landscaping and tree planting. The natural beauty of the stalactite and stalagmite formations in the cave is enhanced by coloured lighting and the fact that the Chinese eye has as usual appointed a name and story for each rock. This is where you will find the poet who was lost for words, the crystal palace (home of the dragon king), a rustic scene of paddy fields and so on.

From Guilin to Yangshuo
The boat ride to the picturesque village of Yangshuo, south-east along the Li River, is the high-light of a visit to Guilin. Often likened to the unrolling of a painted hand scroll, this 80-km boat ride takes seven hours and must remain one of the indelible memories of a lifetime. One word of warning: if you visit

177

Guilin in the very early spring or winter you may have to forego the whole boat ride as the water may be too low, and there are many sandbanks and rapids. If so, take the bus to the environs of Yangshuo (1½–2 hours; 65 km) and enjoy a shorter boat ride in the vicinity of the village.

Passing southwards through Guilin you will see the Writing Brush Peak (Danbi feng), then the Cap Peaks (Kuan yan), where the peaks resemble hats. Now in Yangshuo county, you go past Goat Hoof Mountain, the communes of Goat's Hoof, Double Streams, Wave Stone (Lang shi) and the Drum and Bell rapids (after the sounds of the water), then the famous Mural Hill (Hua shan) where you will discern the shapes of nine galloping horses. As you travel south the waters become calm and smooth; there are many fishing boats and the river banks are fringed with feathery bamboo. Finally you will float past the ancient village of Xingping, with the Five Finger Mountains in the background, known as far back as the Three Kingdoms period; nearby is a thousand-year-old banyan tree.

Yangshuo
The village itself is extremely picturesque, with pavilions and galleries overlooking the river, open shop fronts and curving rooftops. At the foot of Azure Peak Mountain (Bi feng shan) rise the roofs of the Jian shan Tower and the Meeting of the River Turret, with its six windows each framing a complete and different scene; there are rock carvings in the hillside. The ferry crossing point is at Baisha tan from where one can see the 'romantic pavilion' and 'rock of Western youth and Jade maiden peak' – commemorating the story of two brothers and a beautiful local girl.

Handicrafts
Carved wooden cigarette holders,

Zhuang woven bags, batik, bamboo boxes, square bamboo walking sticks, brush holders and basket ware can be bought. See also below.

Cultural Activities
These include a local theatre group and a children's acrobatic group. Visits can be made to schools and the teachers' training college; also to the local arts and crafts studio, where stone and jade carvings, traditional painting and bamboo goods are produced.

Shopping
There is a Friendship Store (119 Zhongshan zhong lu) and many souvenir shops, and the atmosphere the nearest to that of a resort I have seen anywhere in China. The commercial area is around Liberation Street and Zhongshan zhong lu; the shops are generally open between 9 am and 9.30 pm.

Useful Addresses
CAAC
144 Zhongshan zhong lu
Tel. 3063

Luxingshe
14 Ronghu bei lu
Tel. 3870

People's Hospital
Wenge lu
Tel. 3767

Hotels

Li jiang Hotel, Shanhu bei lu
Tel. 2881/3050
Completed in 1976, it is modern, well-equipped, centrally situated, close to Jiefang lu and Bin jiang lu.

Ronghu or Banyan Lake Hotel
Tel. 3811/
Next to Rong hu and Shan hu lakes, it is a villa-type hotel in attractive grounds with shops and good restaurant.

Dangui (Osmanthus) Hotel
Zhongshan Road
Tel. 3576
On the banks of the Taohua river, three minutes from railway station, this hotel has been extensively refurbished.

Jia shan Hotel
Lijun lu
Tel. 2249
Prefabricated Motel outside City centre.

Local Cuisine Specialities
Exotic game such as lynx, bamboo rat, partridge, citrus fruits including pomeloes and tangerines, bamboo shoots, *hong dou* – red beans, water chestnuts, Sanhua wine, cassia wine, sweets and tea.

HEBEI PROVINCE

Hebei is the northern province which embraces the independent municipalities of Peking and Tianjin, and so to many travellers to China it is little more than the somewhat bleak and in winter arid landscape passed through on one's way to Peking. The historical and cultural links between the province and the two cities are very close, and their separation is merely an administrative requirement; the capital of Hebei Province is now at Shijia zhuang in the southwest of the province. Naturally the geographical and climatic factors which influence the province are those which also apply to Peking and Tianjin, as described earlier, since they are all situated on the North China Plain. The total population of the province is about 51 million and its classical name is Ji – a name which was first recorded in the ancient *Book of Shang* as one of the Nine States. There are many sites of historical interest in the area including the bridge at Zhaozhou, the terminus of the Great Wall at Qin huang dao, the mini potala at Chengde, and the seaside resort of Bei dai he.

In the Tang dynasty, during the seventh century, it was first called Hebei (meaning north of the Yellow River), and after this, during the Jin dynasty under the Khitans from the north, it became the area in which the 'southern capital' was situated.

In 1952, during the first stages of administrative reorganization, it was expanded to include the northern province of Chahar and Jehol (whose former major cities were Kalgan and Jehol). To the north the province borders on Inner Mongolia and Liaoning Provinces. To the west it meets Shanxi and the Taihang Mountains.

Much of northern Hebei is mountainous. The Taihang Mountains, which were important bases during the war against the Japanese, sprawl in an arc across the north of Hebei, meeting the Yan shan range, across which winds the Great Wall, to end up in the Bo hai Sea which bounds Hebei to the east. The Taihang Mountains are 1000–2000 m above sea-level, and the Yan shan mountains are 1000 m above sea-level.

North of Zhangjiakou (Kalgan) begins the plateau which stretches into Inner Mongolia, an area of interior rivers prone to sandstorms, and of cattle and livestock breeding. The Hebei plain covers 40 per cent of the province and is well irrigated with rivers which flow into the sea around Tianjin – the main river is the Hai he, which has five major tributaries, and in recent years flood prevention work has been carried out.

This is one of the major cotton producing areas of north China; other crops include wheat, maize, millet, peanuts, sesame, beans and tobacco. The average number of harvests is three every two years. The province is also renowned for its fruit – pears from Tianjin, peaches and grapes – also chestnuts and medicinal herbs, the latter from Anguo xian to the north-east of Shijia zhuang, where they have been grown since the Song dynasty.

Other farming includes cattle rearing in the north, rabbits, chickens, furs and skins, and around the icefree Bo hai Gulf fishing is an important source of income. The major natural resources are coal, iron ore and salt, with some copper, lead, asbestos and fireclay. Major coal mining areas are along the slopes of the Taihang Mountains, at Kailuan, Jingxing and Feng feng. Salt comes from the Bo hai Gulf and the North China Plain. Phosphorus is also present, and oil prospecting has been carried out in the Gulf area. Major industries are coal mining, textiles, electrical power, iron smelting, machine tools, chemicals, building materials, foodstuffs, medicinal herbs, paper and pottery.

Winters are very cold, harsh and dry. The temperatures, ranging between 10°C, call for all the paraphernalia of padded clothing; heating is turned on in public places from 15 November. All the cabbages that you may see piled in the streets of Peking in early November are in the countryside put into underground pits for storage. One local prewinter custom is to hang decorative papercuts against the windows. The summers are hot and most of the rainfall is in late June, July and August.

As mentioned above, the cultural links with Peking are strong: the dialects are related – that of Hebei has a more rustic burr; the comic diologue, also known as *xiangsheng*, which originated in Peking is very popular here, as are puppetry – both string and shadow puppets, particularly in the Tangshan area – and the Hebei bangzi, the local opera. Other traditional local crafts include bamboo and grass weaving, papercuts, ceramics, leather, kites, jade carving, carpets, clay figures and gold leaf work.

Shijia zhuang

The provincial capital of Hebei Province, 283 km south-west of Peking, Shijia zhuang lies at the crossroads of the Peking–Guangzhou and Taiyuan–Dezhou railways, with the Taihang Mountains to the west. In fact the city really only came into existence at the beginning of this century with the advent of the railway. Its aspect is essentially modern with wide boulevards and a square which is a pale imitation of Tianan men Square in Peking. The area encompasses good farming land; wheat and cotton are the major crops. There are coalmines at the foot of the Taihang Mountains, and since 1949 a machine tool and chemical industry have been developed. The cotton mills are the biggest employer. The city's population is now 850,000, and its industry is concentrated in the north-east and south-east.

Shijia zhuang is linked with the Canadian doctor Norman Bethune, who worked in China during the Sino–Japanese War and eventually died of septicaemia. His memorial statue and tomb are situated in the Memorial Park to the North China Revolutionary Martyrs. In the north of the city, on Zhongshan lu, is an exhibition of his life and works. The PLA hospital in Shijia zhuang has also been named after him.

Anji Bridge

This bridge, also known as Zhaozhou Bridge, is in Zhao county south-east of Shijiazhuang. The bridge, over the Jijiao River, was built in the Sui dynasty, in the late sixth century, by Li Chun, and is one of the oldest remaining bridges in China. A single-span arched bridge, one of its special features are the beautifully carved railings. Since 1949 the bridge has undergone extensive renovation and strengthening. Thorough dredging of the lake has revealed many artefacts from the Sui and Tang dynasties, which are now on display in an exhibition room in the park adjacent to the bridge.

Longxing Temple
To the north-east of Shijia zhuang, in Zhending County, it was built at the end of the Sui dynasty and is one of China's oldest temples.

Xibaipo
This is a revolutionary site in Pingshan county to the north-west of Shijia zhuang, from where the revolutionary leaders conducted their northern campaigns in the Civil War. It was here also that they convened the Second Plenary Session of the Party's Seventh Central Committee.

Qinhuangdao
On the north coast of the Bohai Gulf, some 250 miles from Peking, Qinhuangdao is reached by train via Tianjin and Tangshan. It is an icefree port and therefore often serves as a secondary port if Tianjin is frozen in winter; it also receives international traffic and is connected by pipelines to the Daqing oilfields. The city records go back to the Shang dynasty, and the name, which means 'The Qin Emperor's Island', commemorates a visit by the Qin Emperor in 215 BC – since that time it has often played a strategic role and acted as an important lookout post for many of the great figures of Chinese history. It became a concession port in 1898, and according to Carl Crow it is where the allied troops landed to march on Peking. He also records that at the fall of the Ming dynasty Wu Sangui commanded the local garrison and called on the Manchu troops for assistance in 1644, for this was the border between China and Manchuria. Modern Qinhuangdao has a precast bridge works and a major

glassworks, honey and seafood are prized local products.

Bei Dai he
A favoured seaside resort south-west of Qinhuangdao, until the end of the nineteenth century Bei Dai he remained a small, out-of-the-way fishing village; then it was discovered by foreigners and wealthy Chinese in Peking as an ideal place to escape from the torrid heat of the cities. Sheltered by the Lianpeng Hills, part of the Yan Mountains, the south-facing, sandy beach stretches for several miles from the Dai River to Hawk Rock. There are good swimming and fishing, and Tiger Rock, halfway along the beach, acts as a natural breakwater. In recent years the resort has been used in the summer by members of the diplomatic community in Peking and leading Chinese officials – even Chairman Mao came here and was inspired to write a poem – and there are also sanatoria here. Accommodation is often in villa-style hotels. There is a branch of Kiesling's bakery here, and the seafood is excellent – particularly prawns and crabs in autumn.

Shanhai guan
Situated to the north of Qinhuangdao, this is the point where the Great Wall meets the sea – the name means 'Pass between the Mountains and the Sea', and in the past it gave access to the north-east. The area has always had great strategic significance. At the end of the Ming Dynasty, Li Zicheng's uprising was echoed here, but General Wu Sangui called for the assistance of the eagerly waiting Manchus.

During the Ming Dynasty the Great Wall was strengthened and rebuilt, and nine major garrison areas were established along its length – the area between Shanhai guan and Juyong guan came under the jurisdiction of the Ji garrison. In the 1920s it was the scene of battles led by the warlord Feng Liangxi, and in 1933, when the Japanese established their state of Manzhoukuo, it was the border post between China and Manchuria.

The Wall merges into the sea at Laolongtou – a rocky promontory meaning 'Old Dragon Head'. The city itself is a walled structure with a moat and four gates, the most impressive of which is the eastern gate tower with the sign proclaiming 'The First Pass under Heaven'. The base is pierced by a gate which in the past was open and shut at dawn and dusk, surmounted by a two-storey tower pierced by sixty-eight arrow windows. From here one may look out to sea or inland to the Great Wall winding along the Yan shan Mountains, interspersed with beacon towers. The tower was completed in 1381.

Meng Jiang Temple

On Phoenix Hill overlooking the sea is a temple dedicated to a model of wifely piety – Meng Jiang. The origins of the temple are ancient and disputed – the most popular version is that the temple was built to commemorate a wife who came to look for her husband who had been conscripted by Emperor Qin Shihuang to build the Great Wall. She travelled a great distance to bring him some warm clothing for the cold weather, only to learn he was dead.

She cried so many tears that part of the Wall collapsed. Commander Zhang Dong, who supervised the rebuilding of the temple at the end of the sixteenth century, suggests that she might have been the wife of two ancient heroes – one of whom is mentioned in the Spring and Autumn period, the first half of the Zhou dynasty, 770–476 BC – a long time before Qin Shihuang built the Wall. Local records indicate that a temple had stood here since before the Song dynasty. Whatever the legend, the story of Meng Jiang, and honouring her

with a temple, was a reminder to all women of the importance of fidelity to one's husband.

The temple is approached by a steep climb of 108 steps – on passing through the entrance you will come to an antechamber containing a statue of Meng Jiang attended by a boy and girl. The hall behind this originally contained a statue of Guanyin. Behind this is the so-called Searching for My Husband Stone and a hexagonal pavilion, the Zhenyi ting (Shaking Clothes Pavilion).

Sandao guan (Three Roads Pass)

If you come out of Shanhai guan through the east gate, and follow the road north-east to the foot of the Yan Mountains, you reach the valley of the Sandao guan or Three Roads Pass. This narrow, precipitous valley afforded excellent natural protection in the past and today is considered a fine beauty spot with waterfalls, pine trees and birds.

Past Three Roads Pass is Yellow Ox Mountain with its weirdly shaped rocks. Here is the entrance of Suspended Sun Cave, so named because deep inside the cave natural light enters via a gap in the cave roof.

Nearby is Yansai Lake, a reservoir created since 1949 from the diverted waters of the Shi he or Stone River. The reservoir is attractive and in places resembles other parts of China such as the Yangtse Gorges or Guilin.

Qing Imperial Tombs

If time allows, a visit to one of the Qing tomb complexes, such as the one below or Xi ling on p. 183, makes an interesting comparison with the Ming tombs north of Peking.

The Dong ling or Eastern Tombs are in Zunhua county, to the north-west of the county town and 125 km east of Peking. They are surrounded by mountains and a natural wall of trees; the complex itself is enclosed by a wall and moat. Here are buried Shun zhi (1644–62), Kang xi (1662–1723), Qian long (1736–96), Xian feng (1851–62), Tong zhi (1862–5), as well as Ci xi – the Empress Dowager herself, Ci an, fourteen empresses and over 100 concubines.

From the southern entrance runs a long approach road. First you pass the ceremonial arch, a procession of stone figures of animals and beasts, then go through the imperial gate, across bridges and past stele halls; side roads lead to the other tombs. The largest tomb is that of Shun zhi, although the most impressive are generally thought to be those of Qian long and Ci xi. Each tomb is encased in a wall, with a tower (*minglou*), two halls and a tumulus and an underground hall. The tombs are ornate and often gilded. Also on show are the imperial seals, and in the tomb of Ci xi there are many Buddhist figures – she was known to be a devout Buddhist.

Handan

This town in the south of Hebei Province has a varied history. Its origins go back to the Warring States period, when it was the capital of the state of Zhao, and there are many stories connected with the heroes of this epoch. The city is particularly well known for its unique, richly patterned porcelain called Cizhou ware, which has been produced in the area since the beginning of the Song dynasty. The Martyrs' Mausoleum commemorates those from North China who died in the cause of revolution; there are also related exhibition halls.

One of the most interesting sights in the city is the Cong Terrace of the Duke Wu Ling. Between 325 and 299 BC the Duke watched singing and dancing or reviewed his troops from here. The terrace was renowned in every state for its

unique structure and has been extended; it now forms a park with a lake.

Ancient City of the Zhao Dukes

Traces of the ancient city remain to the south-west of the modern city; it was the scene of rivalry between the states.

Xi ling – The Western Tombs

Situated to the west of Yi xian, approximately 30 km from Liangge zhuang in Baoding county, Xi ling is more modest in proportion than Dong ling (above). Fewer emperors are buried here, and their tombs are scattered, but more individuality is displayed in the building of each tomb.

Set against an arch of wooded hills are four tombs. That of Yong zheng (1723–36) is the earliest and biggest. Situated on a high ridge, with a ceremonial arch and yellow-tiled roofs, it is approached across a marble bridge and down a long sacred way. Jia qing's (1796–1821) tomb is built of yellow stone, while Dao guang's (1821–51) is pale grey. The pitiable Guang xu (1875–1908) is buried in a natural setting of mountains, pines and streams.

Chengde (Jehol)

Chengde lies 250 km to the north-east of Peking in Hebei Province; it was the favourite summer haunt of the Manchu emperors and was known in Manchu as Jehol.

The Manchu emperor Kang xi was the first to recognize the area's natural beauty and potential. The name Jehol comes from Re he meaning 'warm river', denoting the hot springs to be found there, and the surrounding wooded hills made ideal hunting grounds. Kang xi began to construct the palace and lay out the grounds in 1703, and his successor Qian long continued his work. In fact Chengde became more than a summer retreat and was regarded as the second political centre of the Manchu emperors. It was here that the first British emissary of King George III, Lord Macartney, was received by Qian long in 1793.

Today the resort lies to the north of the city of Chengde. It is surrounded by a 10 km long red wall which encloses a palace complex, lakes, hot springs and the uncultivated expanse of the Imperial park with its many strange rock formations. The other feature of the resort is the Eight Outer Temples.

At the entrance to the grounds of the palace, in front of the Meridian Gate, hangs the sign written by Emperor Kang xi, 'Summer Retreat'. The first group of buildings comprises the Front Palace where the emperor and his entourage lived during the summer months. The main hall is the Nanmu Hall – the special fragrance of the Nanmu wood which was imported from Sichuan and Guizhou pervades the air, and the ceilings and walls are carved with the traditional symbols of longevity and good luck.

The Lakeside area is to the north-east of the palace: the amenities include boats for hire, exhibition halls and a tea house. The lake Centre Pavilions can be identified by their double eaves. The House of Mists and Rain – which used to be the emperors' study – stands on another small islet. Other buildings to be found in the lakeside area include the Wenjin ge Library: this used to contain a collection of all the extant writings up to the eighteenth century, but war and time have taken their toll and only a small selection remains. The remainder of the grounds consist of uncultivated woodland and hills, many of which are named after the special shapes or rocks which stand on them – the most distinctive of these are the 'club-shaped' rock, Luohan Hill, Frog Rock and Twin Pagodas Hill.

The Eight Outer Temples (Ba wai miao)

The Eight Outer Temples were built in the Qing period at the time when the emperors were seeking to consolidate their relationships with the border peoples – particularly Tibet, Inner Mongolia and Xinjiang. Today only five of them are still standing and each one reflects a different aspect of Chinese architecture.

Puning si

The Puning Temple is dominated by the impressive five-storeyed Mahayana Chamber: this contains the many-armed statue of Buddha, which is 22.2 m high. The vestibule and forecourt of the temple were built in Han style while the Main Hall and the red and white terraces which flank it are in Tibetan style.

Putuo zhongsheng si

Modelled on the Potala at Lhasa, the temple has a large terrace and houses the statue of the Propitious Heavenly Mother which is mounted on a horse – she was renowned for subduing the forces of evil and traditionally people came to pray to her at New Year.

The Xumi fushou Temple

This temple emulates the Zhashen lunbu Temple at Shigatse. It is crowned by the Longevity Pagoda which is decorated with glazed porcelain tiles and was built to commemorate the visit of the Panchen Lama who visited Qian long to offer his congratulations on his birthday.

The roofs of the temple are extravagantly gilded and on the roof of the Hall of Profound Solemnity there are the writhing lifelike statues of eight dragons, looking poised for flight. There are also two carved stone elephants at the Glazed Memorial Arch.

The Anyuan Temple

This temple is modelled on a temple at Yili in Xinjiang. Its most unusual feature is the roof which is covered with black glazed tiles.

The Pule Temple

The exterior of the main building of the Pule Temple recalls the Hall of Prayer for Good Harvest in the Temple of Heaven. The interior is extravagantly and intricately decorated with gilded murals and bas relief, with the imperial dragons playing with a pearl as the centrepiece of the ceiling.

Tourist Information

Hotels

There are two hotels in Chengde for use by foreign visitors. The City Guesthouse in the centre of the town is convenient and well appointed, while the Resort Guesthouse is located close to the Old Summer Palace Resort and the Outer Temples site.

HENAN PROVINCE

This province is an archaeologist's paradise, for it is around these lower middle reaches of the Yellow River – the literal translation of Henan is 'south of the river' – that the earliest records of Chinese civilization have been found. From the earliest Shang dynasty until the Yuan dynasty in the thirteenth century the capital was almost constantly in this area, in the cities of Luoyang, Zhengzhou and Kaifeng; for the remainder of the time it was at Xi'an, further to the west. It was the gradual encroaching of the 'barbarians' from the north which was to force China's capital southwards. For centuries Henan was known as the 'central province' as it was at the heart of the Chinese Empire. As the focus of the empire's activities Henan drew all the talent and brains of China. It used to be said that 'the wind and rain from six directions meet in the central province'.

Henan, always a strategic province in times of war, is today a vital communications centre and since 1949 has been redeveloped as an industrial centre. One of the smaller provinces, covering an area of 600,000 km², it has a population of 71.89 million and is divided into ten districts, fourteen cities and 110 counties.

From earliest times Henan has produced some of China's most colourful characters. During the Three Kingdoms period Cao Cao had his capital here. Talented Henanese women enjoyed positions of importance – from the young lady who continued writing the history begun by her father, to the women generals of the Yang family and the wife of Zhou Enlai, Madame Deng Yingchao. In the arts the province produced the poets known as the 'scholars of the bamboo grove' and the lively local opera, the Yu Opera and the Henan bangzi.

The Yellow River runs along the north of Henan and the Huai River flows in the south. Henan is surrounded by mountains on three sides, and in the east it forms part of the North China Plain. In the north-west of the province are the Taihang Mountains, on average 1500 m high, forming a natural border between Henan and Shanxi. Flood control work has been carried out in the area of the Huai River and it is the major agricultural area in the province, which is known as the granary of China. Access from the mountainous west is via narrow passes and gorges such as the Sanmen Gorges.

The climate is typical of the north, with long dry winters and north-westerly winds bringing sandstorms in spring. Most of the rainfall comes in the summer months and ranges from 600 mm in the north to 900 mm in the south. Summer temperatures average 27–28°C and the coldest winter temperatures fall below freezing. Autumn is the best season with clear days and most sunlight; winter begins in November.

Climate and soil mean that Henan has an average of three harvests every two years. It is one of the major wheat-growing areas; other important crops are maize, gaoliang and sweet potatoes. Tobacco, cotton, sesame and peanuts are major cash crops. Some rice is grown and silk is produced – the oracle bones at Anyang provide evidence of silk in this area more than 3000 years ago. Other local products are tea in Xinyang and medicinal herbs, melons from Kaifeng, honey, dates and apples. There are forestry projects in the mountain regions. Industry has been concentrated along the south of the Yellow River; natural resources comprise coal, aluminium and iron ore. Henan is now a major textile producer, and at Anyang there is an iron and steel works.

The Yellow River, or 'Calamity' river as it has been dubbed, has its source at the northern foot of the Bayankara Mountains in Qinghai Province. After passing through the loess plateaux of the west it reaches the North China Plain where it widens and slows down, depositing silt on the river bed to such an extent that in several places it travels above the surrounding countryside. Ever since the fifth century BC dams and dykes have been constructed in efforts to tame the river, and in 2500 years of recorded history the capricious river has changed course twenty-six times, has breached its dykes 1500 times, 900 of these times in Henan. The mouth of the Yellow River is at the Bo hai Gulf, and the river is 5464 km long.

In June 1938, when the Japanese had taken Kaifeng, Chiang Kaishek ordered one of the dykes to be breached near Zhengzhou to cover their retreat; this expensive defence weapon cost lives and homes and rendered much of the area unfarmable for almost ten years. In 1952 Chairman Mao established the Yellow River as a priority area. Following his mandate 700 km of dykes were reinforced in Henan alone, locks and irrigation canals were constructed, paddy fields were established, and the dykes were planted with trees and grass to strengthen them. At Sanmen Gorge in the west of Henan province an ambitious dam and hydroelectric project was begun with Russian aid, and state fish breeding farms were established. In Huayuankou the people built their own electrical pumping station. In 1972 a pumping station was built at Mang shan, 40 km north of Zhengzhou, to bring water to the industries there via a two-tier pumping system; the project includes 40 km of trunk canal, six tunnels, two aqueducts and two silt-precipitating pools.

Zhengzhou

Today Zhengzhou is the provincial capital of Henan, a role which it took over from Kaifeng in 1954 because of its situation at the vital junction of the Peking–Guangzhou Railway and the east–west Longhai Railway. It lies approximately 28 km south of the Yellow River. It is almost entirely a modern city, which has been expanding steadily since 1949 and now has a resident population of 1.2 million. It was one of the areas selected for industrial development in the first Five-Year Plan and is now the centre of light industry in Henan. You will probably hear Chinese guides tell you that before liberation there were only five factories and 400 workers in Zhengzhou, and now there are 600 factories and 200,000 workers. As cotton is grown in Henan, the major industry is related to textiles.

The first impression is of long, wide, tree-lined avenues of which the people of Zhengzhou are justly proud, as the trees provide some protection against the sandy winds of the early spring months – early this century visitors described the province as the most treeless in China. Most buildings are several-storeyed red brick. The town has grown up around the railway junction, and is crossed by the Jin shui River. The city now has several parks, a provincial stadium, gymnasium and cultural palace. The commercial centre is at Erqi Square – Seventh February Square – which commemorates the uprising of the railway workers in 1923. The people of Zhengzhou have a ruddy, tanned look reflecting the harshness of the winds.

While Zhengzhou is a modern city with little to offer by way of temples and traditional Chinese sites, excavations during the last thirty years have shown that it was probably one of the major towns of the Shang dynasty; it gradually faded in importance as Kaifeng and Luoyang grew, only to increase again in importance with the building of the railway line between Peking and Guangzhou at the beginning of this century. Its major interest today is to archaeologists; the well-filled provincial museum (see below) contains tracings of ancient cities. It is also a point from which to visit Kaifeng to the east and Luoyang to the west, as well as some of the other sites of historical interest in Henan.

Zhengzhou is 695 km from Peking, and 1618 km from Guangzhou, from both of which cities it can be reached by train. It also has a small airport.

February Seventh Monument
Between 1921 and 1923 the workers began to organize themselves into unions, assisted by the recently founded Communist Party. Clubs were formed among railway workers and charters were drawn up demanding improved conditions of work. They even found support among some of the warlords. However, when the workers on the Peking–Hankou railway line sought to establish a United Syndicate of Railway Workers, Wu Peifu objected on the grounds that such an organization might pose a threat to his proposed

troop movements on the line. The workers struck in response and he sent in his troops to break the strike up. Several workers were killed. This massacre was followed by a nationwide clampdown on labour organizations and strikes which was to last until 1927.

Henan Provincial Museum
Situated on Jin shui Road, near the hotel in Zhengzhou, this is an excellent museum containing almost 100,000 objects – many of which are still in storage, with particular emphasis on the Neolithic period. The museum contains the plans and the finds of the Shang dynasty at Zhengzhou, also two of the oldest examples of bronze 'ding' and a porcelain wine vessel, both discovered in Zhengzhou in 1974. There is evidence that porcelain was made in Henan from deposits of kaolin 3500 years ago – 2000 years earlier than previously thought. There are tools made from human bones, and maritime artefacts – proof of extensive early trade. Musical instruments from the second half of the Shang dynasty are on display. They include gongs and whistles and a kind of oka discovered at Anyang. Also on show are lacquer ware and early examples of writing on bamboo strips, bronze vessels and jade ceremonial discs, pictures of some of the ancient pagodas and temples of Henan, examples of Tang porcelain and horses, Song dynasty bricks with bas-reliefs of acrobatics and theatres, examples of the fine local pottery – *ru* and *jun*, funerary figures from Yuan dynasty graves and Ming funerary objects from officials' houses. A further exhibition hall is planned to display more than a thousand carvings and other finds excavated from Han tombs.

Yellow River Exhibition Hall
A visit to the Exhibition Hall, situated at the junction of Jin shui lu and Renmin lu, is usually combined with a visit to the

Yellow River and the Mang shan pumping station 28 km north of Zhengzhou. The exhibition is presented in four sections: (1) a short film describes the source and route of the Yellow River in Qinghai province and its progress through nine provinces, and describes attempts made through history to tame the river; (2) photographs, diagrams and maps catalogue the disasters wrought by the river, the recurring cycle of drought, flood and famine, and the effects of erosion and the changes of course; (3) Mao and his programme for taming the river; (4) plans for the future and work still to be done.

Mang shan Pumping Station

After a drive through the countryside to the Yellow River you may see the two major bridges over the Yellow River serving the Zhengzhou area. The original railway bridge, built in 1919, was superseded by another railway bridge completed in 1960. The first sight of this legendary river is an extraordinary experience; depending on the time of year the water will be sluggish and low or turbulent and high, retaining the brownish ochre colour which has earned it its name – the colour is caused by the heavy load of silt which it carries.

It was in the area of the Mang shan pumping station that Mao first stressed the importance of harnessing the Yellow River. The station was built between 1970 and 1972 with funds accumulated by the Zhengzhou city council and with the help of a workforce from communes, factories, schools and the army, diverted from their usual tasks. The station provides water for daily consumption in the city by industry and for domestic use, and irrigates more than 9000 *mu* of land. The hills around the station have been terraced and planted with fruit trees, and there are plans to turn it into a recreational centre with pavilions, tea houses and an exhibition site.

From the Mang shan pumping station, time permitting, you may also be taken on a visit to the Huayuankou commune on the southern bank of the Yellow River, one of the areas devastated by the deliberate breaching of the river in 1938 and which became an 'alkali desert', but which now cultivates rice among its many other enterprises.

Drama

The Henan bangzi and Yu-style plays are loved for their peasant qualities – they originate in the Ming dynasty and were at first performed in country areas; much later on they became established in the cities.

Arts and Crafts Workshop

This workshop specializes in jade carving.

Medical and Educational Establishments

Zhengzhou has four institutes of higher education and seventy-five secondary schools. The People's Hospital is famous for its development of acupuncture anaesthesia.

Shopping

The Friendship Store, antique store, department store and bank are all on Erqi Road, near the main square.

Hotels

Zhongzhou Hotel, Jin shui lu
The hotel is situated on the outskirts of Zhengzhou, overlooking the Jin shui River, in the administrative and residential quarter of the city; it is near Dongfang hong Park, the Yellow River Exhibition Centre and the Museum. At Huayuankou lu there are some local shops and a department store which closes at 8 pm.

Grandiose in appearance, with a

fountain and shrubbery in the spacious forecourt, it was built in 1961 for Chinese officials. The airport is 5 km east of the hotel, and the station is in downtown Zhengzhou, about 6 km away. From the front desk taxis may be hired to go to the city centre. Exchange facilities are available.

Food, Drink and Restaurants
The staple diet in Henan is wheat-based; the various types of steamed bread and noodles are very popular, and local peasant women are expert in quickly turning out hair-fine noodles. Most of the vegetables associated with the north are available here, and also some specialities such as 'monkey's head' (*houtou*) a fungus shaped as its name suggests, which is served with meat and fish or other vegetables. The most popular fish is Yellow River carp, praised by poets such as Wang Wei, which is served steamed or steamed and fried or with a sweet and sour sauce and a 'quilt' of fine noodles (*yubei mian*). Stuffed chicken and Henan roast chicken are also popular.

Henan is the home of the legendary *Dukang jiu* wine which has been drunk for two thousand years by great Chinese poets and statesmen. Zhu Geliang from the Three Kingdoms wrote the lines 'How can I release my sorrow, there is only Dukang wine'. For the 'scholars of the Bamboo grove' it was a key to immortality, and there is a stock of stories about their ruses to cheat their wives of money to buy this wine. Henan also produces a special type of tea called Before-the-Rain Tips, it comprises the youngest, most delicate tips which are picked in April, shortly after the Qing-ming Festival, before the rains begin.

The Restaurant on the Water, built on the Jin River, within Renmin Park on Jinshuilu, is the best restaurant in Zhengzhou and serves the local dishes mentioned above.

Xinxiang
Lying some 80 km north of Zhengzhou, Xinxiang is one of the main centres of communication in northern Henan and has a textile and machine tool industry; the sixteen counties (xian) in the vicinity are major producers of cotton and grain.

North of Xinxiang is Jiyuan County, home of the legend of the Foolish Old Man who Moved the Mountain – a story retold by Chairman Mao as an example of what the will of ordinary people could achieve in the building of socialism, how the masses could remove the mountains of feudalism and imperialism. This was the theme of his concluding speech at the end of the Seventh Party Congress on 2 June 1945. The slogan 'The Foolish Old Man Who Moved the Mountain' can often be seen in China, painted on a rock face where large-scale building projects are being carried out. The area formerly suffered from drought and since 1949 an irrigation scheme has been implemented. On the outskirts of Xinxiang, on Phoenix Hill, a spring has been dug which now irrigates the surrounding area.

Qiliying
En route for Xinxiang you will pass Qiliying Commune – the first commune to be established in China in 1958, which earned the Mao seal of approval: 'People's Communes Are Good.' It is on the former bed of the Yellow River and was a backward and barren area affected by alternating drought and flooding from the river. In 1952, with state aid, an irrigation canal was built here using the waters of the Yellow River, and after 1958 a further 300 small ditches were constructed, establishing a network of wells and ditches over the whole area. Today Qiliying is one of the most advanced and mechanized communes in China.

Gong xian

This town lies 82 km west of Zheng-zhou, at the confluence of the Luo and Yellow Rivers, and can be reached by train or bus. It boasts a comfortable new hotel and several extremely interesting sights. South-west of Gong xian there are eight Song dynasty tombs, with excellently preserved brick carvings, stone murals and a sacred way, as well as other tombs built for members of the Song imperial family. At the Caves Temple are Buddhist caves which are smaller, earlier versions of the Longmen grottoes, completed in the sixth century, and a cave with natural stalactite and stalagmite formations.

Gong xian has much to offer from the artistic point of view. It was the home of the famous Henanese actress Chang Xiangyu, who ran her own drama school here. It was closed down during the Cultural Revolution, although the last couple of years have seen her re-emerge as a star. Huiguo zhen People's Commune enjoys a reputation for the high standard of cultural performances given by its children.

Jiaozuo

This town, at the foot of the Taihang Mountains, is not on the tourist route since it has little of scenic or historic interest. However it is the third largest city in Henan Province and is known as the 'black peony' of China because it is one of the most important coal mining areas in the country. Other industries include iron and steel, aluminium, concrete and fertilizers.

Hui xian

On the south-eastern slope of the Taihang Mountains, some 20 km north-west of Xinxiang, this was formerly an area of bare, stony mountains, poor soil and communications and constant drought. Although there were underground sources of water the people didn't have the knowhow to use them. However since 1949 the enormous 4000 km² Chengjiayuan Reservoir has been built, with an irrigation canal 200 km long and an electrical pumping station, as well as a series of underground reservoirs and extensive terracing of the mountainsides. After 1970 communications were improved with the completion of roads and bridges, small railway tracks and tunnels. There is a small and simple hotel at Hui xian. Warm springs can be found at Bai quan (A Hundred Springs) near the Taihang Mountains, with a complex of traditional-style pavilions and buildings. Also in the vicinity are the tombs of a Ming prince and his wife.

Yuxian

Eighty kilometres south of Zhengzhou, as well as a water conservancy project there is an orchard with some seventy types of apple – significant, because this was an area where little fruit was previously grown.

The Jun type of porcelain is produced at Yu xian. During the Song dynasty it was one of the five major porcelains of China and was an essential commodity in aristocratic households. Some was exported to Europe as early as 700 years ago. It is very similar to the Shiwan pottery of Foshan and is said to have been taken to Foshan by a master worker who was discovered using the porcelain, which was meant only for the imperial house.

Deng feng and Song shan Mountain

This scenic and historic area lies between Luoyang and Zhengzhou, approximately 70 km south-west of Zhengzhou. Once the favoured resort of emperors, poets and recluses, the area is rich in historical relics and within a 15-km radius of Deng feng you will find temples, pagodas, steles and much evidence of China's past.

The Song shan, to the east of Deng feng, was one of the five sacred mountains of Chinese lore. Situated as it was in the central province of Henan, it was also referred to as the Central Peak (Zhong yue) and elaborate Zhong yue miao is one of the oldest Daoist temples in China first built in the Qin dynasty. Temple fairs are held here in Spring and Autumn.

Growing here are ancient cypress trees, at least two of which are said to date.back almost two thousand years. When the Emperor Wu of Han saw them he likened one to a general and dubbed the nearby tree 'the second in command', which so upset the tree that it bent over in shame, and has retained this shape to the present day.

In the valley to the south of Song shan was the site of the four famous imperial academies. Songyang Academy, founded in the fifth century, was a centre for various religious sects until it became an imperial academy during the Song dynasty. It fell into disuse during the Yuan and Ming, to be revived by the Qing Emperor Kang xi.

In another part of the Song shan valley lies one of the oldest pagodas in China, in the grounds of the Song yue Temple. It was in fact one of many pagodas built during the northern Wei dynasty at the beginning of the sixth century. It was put up in AD 520 and is unusual by virtue of both its great age and structure. Made entirely of bricks, it is fifteen storeys high and twelve-sided as opposed to the usually octagonal shape.

Shaolin Temple and the Forest of Stupas (Talin)
This famous old temple in idyllic surroundings of mountains and bamboo was first built in 495 and is one of the earliest temples in China. It was also a major religious centre and one of the places where *chan* (Zen) Buddhism was first established. On a more secular level the branch of *taijiquan* (shadow boxing) known as *Shaolinquan* was developed here – it has been said that alone in the mountains the monks were easy prey for bandits and had to learn self-defence. The temple contains many steles – historically important examples of fine calligraphy showing the relationship between Japanese and Chinese Buddhism. To the south-west of the temple is an area where the abbots were buried over a period of a thousand years between 791 and the Qing dynasty. There are some two hundred stupas here, which have earned the area the name of the Forest of Stupas.

At Shicong he, a famous scenic spot, are many tablets carved with the appreciative poems of famous poets. Among them is the Empress Dowager of the Tang dynasty, Wu Zetian, who came to the area often and received guests here; she was the first to call the area Deng-feng. Sima Guang wrote his history of the Song dynasty here. Here is one of the largest steles in China – 9 m high × 2.4 m wide and 1 m thick, it contains an essay written by Li Linpu, an infamous, two-faced prime minister, and carved by the calligrapher Xu Hao.

Sanmen xia (Three Gate Gorge)
The Three Gate Gorge and the city of the same name lie in the west of Henan Province on the banks of the Yellow River. The city was formerly an insignificant hamlet on the Lunghai Railway, which has now been built up into a sizeable industrial centre. Archaeological finds contemporaneous with Peking Man have been discovered in the area, as well as several Yangshao sites which date back six or seven thousand years.

The name 'Three Gate Gorge' derives from the fact that at the entrance to the gorge, approximately 250 m wide, are two islands with channels between them providing three routes for ships. The islands were known as Devil's Gate Island and Spirit Gate Island, and in decreasing order of danger the channels were the Devil's Gate, the Spirit's Gate and the Man's Gate. The gorge was rendered even narrower by promontories, and as a consequence the water was very swift-flowing and turbulent and many ships perished here. At either end of the gorge were granaries and storehouses, and the Tang Emperor Xuan zong attempted to divert some of the water through a safer passage, Kai yuan xin he, but to no avail. Even Da Yu, the great tamer and regulator of the waterways of China, was unable to tame the Three Gate Gorge. In the days when the capital was at Xi'an, to the west of the gorges, it was almost the only major route through the mountains between east and west. It was a great problem bringing supplies from the east or from Shandong, so a secondary capital was established in Luoyang.

In 1957 the Chinese embarked on a joint project with Russian experts to build an enormous, kilometre-long dam and to make an enormous lake in Shanxi Province where the waters of the Yellow River could be diverted and serve for irrigation. Construction was completed by 1960; however the problem of the silt level of the Yellow River had not been reckoned with, and the scheme had drawbacks. By 1965 work had been done to reduce the silt and disperse it. While the plans may not have been realized in the same dramatic way as intended, the reservoir can be used in flood control and to irrigate fields and supply the cities, as well as for a low-level hydroelectric station; and the area around the gorges is now far safer to pass than ever before.

Anyang
Situated in the north of Henan Province, with the Anyang or Huan River flowing to the north, this town has long been a relatively fertile area. Its major points of interest are the Shang dynasty excavations and the discovery of the oracle bones; however today it is also an important industrial and handicraft centre. With a present population of 500,000, since 1949 it has built up a sizeable industry based on metallurgy, textiles, machine tools and food processing, and during the Great Leap Forward established its own iron and steel industry. On the arts and crafts side it produces colourful basketware woven from wheat stalks, hand-cut carpets in Peking style, with the traditional cluster of dragons as the centrepiece (arrangements can be made for shipment abroad), and carving in jade from nearby Dushan.

Wengfeng Pagoda
It is situated in the old quarter of the city, in the Tianning Temple. Built during the Five Dynasties period in AD 952, it is unusual in form, being smaller at the base than at the top. The base is lotus-shaped and there are five octagonal storeys, with a bronze bell on each corner and surmounted by the 'chianti bottle' structure associated with Tibetan religious buildings. It stands 38 m high altogether.

The Yin Ruins
The discovery of the Yin ruins in and around Anyang is among the most vital archaeological finds in China, as these ruins were among the first to establish that the Shang was more than a mythical age. The main sites are to the northwest of Anyang, on the banks of the Anyang or Huan River, at Xiaotun, Wuguan cun and Houjia zhuang, spread over an area of 24 km². They span a period of 273 years between the fourteenth and eleventh century BC. The Shang dynasty is thought to have had seven capitals – in the area of northern Henan, for instance, the site at

Zhengzhou is thought to have been the capital Ao, and the site at Anyang was the capital Yin. It was the seat of twelve kings from Pang Geng to Di Xin, and this period is therefore often referred to as the Yin dynasty. As early as the *Shi Ji* – the historical records compiled by Sima Qian in the first century BC – there is a reference to the Yin ruins (Yin xu), concerning a battle fought at this site at the end of the Qin dynasty. The Yin dynasty was eventually defeated by the incoming Zhou dynasty and the last king is thought to have been burnt to death; the capital was moved and Yin fell into ruins.

Although as early as 1899 the importance of the site had been recognized, after the discovery of oracle bones intensive excavations were carried out between 1928 and 1937. They were halted by the Sino–Japanese War, but since 1950 almost constant excavation work has revealed Neolithic or New Stone Age sites of the Yangshao and Longshan period.

North of Xiaotun village palace foundations have been discovered – the largest being some 40 m long – as well as traces of stone pillars, dwellings, and bone and bronze workshops on the periphery. Other pits and storage cellars revealed over 5000 objects – pottery, bronze, jade, bones and enormous bronze *ding* – ceremonial vessels. The capital, lying on either side of the river, was 3–4 km from north to south and 5–6 km from east to west. There is no trace of a city wall. North of the river, at Houjia zhuang, was the burial ground of the royal family – two cross-shaped graves of the Shang kings of Yin buried together in mass graves with horses, other animals and slaves. Evidence suggests this was already a highly structured society.

The oracle bones themselves were first discovered in 1899 at Anyang, and many further examples have been found. These bones, either the shoulder bones of oxen or tortoise shells, were used in divination about sacrifices, the stars, agriculture, war and hunting. The shaman would scorch the bones until cracks appeared, and the shape of the cracks would provide the necessary 'information'. The answers were often scratched on to the bones, and they constitute the first written record of Chinese history. In 1971 archaeologists discovered a grave of the Northern Qi dynasty AD 550–577, containing examples of early glazed porcelain.

Lin xian

Lin xian is in the north-west corner of Henan Province at the foot of the Taihang Mountains. For hundreds of years it was a poor, barren, drought-ridden area. In 1942 1700 people died of starvation here during the Sino–Japanese War. It was a communist base area, and in 1944 the first plans were conceived to irrigate the area adequately and a start was made at digging dry wells, harnessing springs, and building small reservoirs and some irrigation canals.

However this proved inadequate, and in 1958 a more ambitious project was begun to redirect the waters of the Zhang River, which had its source in the south-west of Shanxi Province, and was separated from Lin County by the Taihang Mountains. Controversy raged at the time as to whether such a project wasn't a waste of money and effort, but the people set to work flattening mountain tops, drilling 180 tunnels and 3000 reservoirs, canals and aqueducts – 1500 km in all – through fifty cliffs and mountains, and finally subdivided into countless small irrigation canals within Lin xian, enabling the people in the area to grow wheat and fruit trees. Now there are fifty hydroelectric power stations in the area and small agriculture-related industries have been established.

At the same time the steep and dangerous mountain paths were widened and made safe. The project was completed in 1969.

Kaifeng

This town lies 64 km east of Zhengzhou on the Longhai railway, and south of the Yellow River on the open plain. It has its own centrally located hotel, the Kaifeng Guesthouse, although it can readily be visited for a day from Zhengzhou. Today it has a population of one million and an industrial base in machine tools and textiles.

It was one of the ancient capitals of China, one of the stops on the eastward shift of political focus. As early as the Warring States period (476–221 BC) it was the capital of the state of Wei and was called Daliang. Then in the Five Dynasties period, following the Tang dynasty, it was the capital of the Later Liang, Jin, Han and Zhou dynasties, and it was the last emperor of the Later Zhou, Shi Zong, who laid extensive plans for the expansion of the city, moving the burial grounds to the outskirts and widening the main streets. In the Song dynasty, from 960 to 1127, it was to enjoy a period as a great metropolis, until the encroaching Nuzhen tribes from the north forced the emperor to move to Hangzhou and set up his own Jin capital there.

Extensive records have been left about Kaifeng in the Song dynasty – or Bianjing or Bianliang as it was known then. Perhaps the best known is the painting by Zhang Zeduan called *The Qingming Festival on the River* which depicts a bustling scene of a commercial city, with details such as a barber, a busy restaurant, people carrying goods, and boats navigating their way under bridges. The scroll can be seen in the museum in Peking in October only, when climatic conditions are right. Facsimile editions are available.

There is also abundant written detail, with descriptions of the imperial way leading to the palace '300 metres wide', with arcades on either side for trading and barriers allowing the emperor and his entourage to pass. There was extensive trade between Kaifeng and the east and south-east; agricultural goods were brought by waterway and road from Shandong and the lower Yangtse valley. This was the era of the first paper money. The period was leisured, with the gentry gaining new importance, and in 1105 some 260,000 households were recorded – i.e. a total population of about a million. Services such as fire prevention were well established, and when the capital moved to Hangzhou everything was done to build the new capital with all the amenities and grandeur of Kaifeng.

In the same way as the other cities along its bank, Kaifeng was subject to the temperament of the Yellow River. It already flowed above the level of Kaifeng and was subsequently known as the 'hanging river', and between 1194 and 1887 it flooded Kaifeng fifty times. The worst occasion was in 1642, during the rebellion led by Li Zicheng, when the banks of the Yellow River were deliberately breached by defenders of the Ming dynasty, taking the lives of many people and causing extensive damage to many of the traditional sites of Kaifeng.

Among those affected was the small Jewish community who had lived in Kaifeng for many years, supporting a synagogue and reading the scriptures in Hebrew; many of their manuscripts were destroyed in this flood and the synagogue had to be rebuilt. However by the end of the nineteenth century the teachers were dead, no one could read Hebrew, and the number of Jewish clans had been reduced from seventy to seven. By the 1920s there were some 200 Jews left in Kaifeng; they had large-

The 'lesser Potala' at Chengde in Hebei Province

A view of the unique architecture of the ancient Yueyang Tower which overlooks Dongting Lake in Hunan Province

Suzhou Canal

Suzhou Bridge near the Mountain Temple

ly intermarried with the Chinese, although they still didn't eat pork. At this stage the former site of the synagogue was still known, and there were three steles commemorating the history of the Jewish community.

Xiangguo si (Monastery of the Protector of the Country)

This monastery, on the south of the city, was built in AD 555 in the Northern Qi dynasty. It became one of the Buddhist centres and is mentioned in many of the popular novels such as *The Water Margin* and *Monkey*. It was destroyed by the flood of 1642 and rebuilt in 1766; then it gradually fell into disrepair and became the haunt of fortune tellers and shady businessmen. It was restored after the liberation. The monastery contains several interesting stone carvings from the Ming and Qing dynasties, as well as a statue of the Buddha with a Thousand Arms and Eyes, carved from a gingke tree. Exhibition rooms for fine arts and calligraphy have been built. The calligraphy of Henan was renowned and several styles of script were refined at Xiangguo Temple. A small shop sells scrolls and paintings as well as embroidery.

Tie ta (The Iron Pagoda)

This pagoda is so named because the glazed tiles used to decorate it resemble iron. Built during the Song dynasty in 1049, it is octagonal and has thirteen storeys – it stands over 50 m high. It is said to have been cemented with a mixture containing glutinous rice, and has withstood floods, fire and earthquakes. The top stories were damaged by a Japanese bomb and the pagoda was restored in 1957. Again examples of calligraphy and embroidery can be bought here.

Long ting (The Dragon Pavilion)

The Longting, on the north-east of the city on the previous city walls, is thought to be on the original site of the palace of the Northern Song emperor and was built in the Qing dynasty. Inside is a cube carved with dragons – probably the site of the throne. It is built on a raised dais with a double roof, yellow-glazed tiles and red pillars and walls. On either side of its approach is a lake.

Yu Wang tai (Terrace to Emperor Yu)

Set among pines and cypress trees, the Yu Wang tai commemorates Emperor Yu, who controlled the waters of China. It was rebuilt in the Ming dynasty; before that it had been known as the Ancient Music Terrace (Guchui tai) after the musician Shi Guang of the Eastern Zhou dynasty. It was frequented by many poets, including Li Bai and Du Fu.

Po ta or Fan ta

This somewhat dumpy hexagonal pagoda was built in the Song dynasty in the south-east of the city.

The Teachers' Training College

This is a well-known institution with an excellent library.

Embroidery Institute

Bian embroidery was very well known; the tradition developed out of supplying the Song dynasty emperors with their finery. When the capital moved to Hangzhou the style of embroidery went too, so that the two styles are very closely related. Lifelike animals are typical subject matter.

Luoyang

The ancient capital of nine dynasties and the city of peonies is today a city with a largely modern face, the centre of heavy industry in Henan Province. To the south lie the famous Longmen grottoes. The city stands in the centre of a fertile basin, south of the Yellow River, with the Mang Mountains to the north. It is surrounded on the remaining three sides by mountains, with narrow passes to the east and west, which early on gained it a reputation as a place of great strategic significance. In the historical records it is stated as being one of the most populous areas of the earliest dynasties, and it is fed by four rivers – the Yi, the Luo, the Jian and the Li. It is well placed for communications since the Longhai Railway passes through and branch lines connect it with the south of the province. Luoyang is about 120 km west of Zhengzhou, from where it may be reached by train or plane.

When the city was liberated in 1948 the population was 80,000. The city proper covered an area of 4.5 km², and industry was restricted to a hand-worked open mine near Longmen and some handicrafts. Luoyang was chosen as one of the key cities in the first Five Year Plan; new streets and factories were planned and erected, and full use was made of the area's natural deposits of coal, iron and copper. Today the city covers an area of 79 km² and has a population of about half a million. Many people from Shanghai and Guangzhou have settled in Luoyang and there are now four hundred factories here, of which the machine tool and building industry is the most important; the well-known Dongfanghong tractor plant, the ball-bearing works and mining equipment plants were all established in the first Five-Year Plan. Other major products and industries include rolled steel, glass, cement and clay, building materials, textiles, fuel, metallurgy, food processing and chemicals.

The city has expanded to the West. Zhongzhoulu, 11 km of tree-lined boulevard, is the main commercial and administrative area. The new residential quarters are to the south. The main industrial area is now in Jianzi, to the west of the city, and new bridges have been built over the Luo River.

The major agricultural produce of the area around Luoyang includes grain and fruit – grapes, apples and pears. Luoyang is also the city of tree peonies. The peony has long been used in Chinese medicine, and was given extensive coverage in the Chinese *materia medica Ben Cao* over 1400 years ago. Today over a hundred varieties are grown in Luoyang, and the best time of year to see them is in April in Labour Park. They range from the rare black peony to such exotic varieties as Twin Sisters – flowers of different colours on the same branch. In the Tang dynasty the poet Bai Juyi wrote, 'For twenty days between which the flowers bloom and fall, the entire city is in ecstasy.'

History
There is evidence of Neolithic settlements in the west of Luoyang from over five thousand years ago. It first became a capital or royal city at the end of the Shang and beginning of the Zhou dynasty, in the eleventh century BC, when there was a rebellion against the Shang. The Zhou emperor moved in, and though his capital was at Xi'an he established a secondary capital at Luoyang – a walled city where he could survey and control the restive Shang. Invasion on the western front enforced the removal of the capital to Wang cheng, the royal city of the eastern Zhou, in 770 BC under King Ping. In 1954 the site of the walls of this city was discovered, and it is now enclosed in Labour Park. Many other discoveries were made during the development of the new industrial area, and the government insisted on archaeologists excavating an area before building was allowed to proceed.

From 770 BC onwards Luoyang was to be the capital of nine dynasties – their individual characteristics and relative importance in regard to the other dynasties of the period would not be exhausted by a lifetime's research.

770–256 BC Eastern Zhou
AD 25–220 Eastern Han
AD 220–65 Cao-Wei
AD 265–316 Western Jin
AD 386–534 Northern Wei
AD 581–618 Sui
AD 618–907 Tang
AD 907–23 Later Liang
AD 923–36 Later Tang

The end of the tenth century saw the beginning of the decline of Luoyang, as the centre of China's political activity shifted from the Yellow River area to the north-east and Peking; the small area which constitutes the old city today dates from this period. It was rebuilt in the Ming dynasty, and Luoyang did not really experience further expansion until the twentieth century. However, during the first thousand years AD it was a vitally important city culturally and commercially, sharing the status and importance of Chang'an (Xi'an) to the west.

One of the most prosperous periods in Luoyang's history was the Han dynasty, from AD 25 until 534. It is described at this time as a city of noble palaces and dwellings and trees; it was an important cultural centre, where the first imperial university was established in AD 29 – a tablet can be seen in the museum, describing how students came from all over the country to attend the college. It was in Luoyang that the famous intellectuals of the Han dynasty carried out their work. Pan Ku wrote the first dynastic history, *The Han Shu*; Zhang Heng, the court astronomer, worked at the Lingtai Observatory where he developed his armillary sphere, seismoscope and the Chinese calendar; and the physician Hua Tuo used the first anaesthetic. The city saw a decline towards the end of the Northern Wei as the country was racked by war. The ruins of the city wall of the Han and the Wei can still be seen from the train as you approach from the east, near the pagoda of the White Horse Temple.

The next period of ascendancy for Luoyang came in the Sui and Tang dynasties. This city lay west of the former Han city, had a circumference of 27.5 km, and covered the modern day 'downtown' and southern suburbs of Luoyang. This change in the city's fortunes coincided with the reunification of the country under the Sui emperor Wen and his son Yang, who was responsible for building the famous Grand Canal. During the Sui and Tang dynasties the capital was often at Chang'an, moving eastwards in times of food shortage. During the reign of the Empress Dowager Wu Zetian (690–705) 100,000 families moved to Luoyang, and the total population is recorded as 1 million. One of the more interesting finds of recent years has been the discovery in 1971 – ironically in preparation for building warehouses – of underground granaries, which were 'damp-proofed' with the result that much of the grain was still preserved. Dating back to the Tang dynasty, these were the stores of the imperial household. An exhibition hall has been built over the site, and further granaries have since been discovered. Luoyang was also an eastern depot on the Silk Route, and a centre for the development of Buddhism; the legacy of this period is the Longmen Grottoes.

Longmen Grottoes
The Longmen or Dragon Gate Grottoes are a colossal example of religious art lying 12 km south of Luoyang, in a forested area with springs and pavilions. They are built on either bank of the Yi River at a point which has long been of strategic significance and was referred to as the Yi River Watch Tower, as well as being praised for the impressive beauty of the sheer sides.

197

The two mountains on either side of the river are called Fragrant Hill and Dragon Gate Hill. A bridge, built in 1962, is a copy of the Zhaozhou Bridge built in Hebei Province in the Sui dynasty, characterized by the length of span and the relatively slender arch.

The complex was begun in the northern Wei dynasty (386–534) and added to over the next four hundred years until the Tang dynasty. The Northern Wei were a non-Han people; they were the Tobas who had their first capital at Datong, where they constructed the Yungang Buddhist grottoes. They were a very religious people – even their emperors were ardent followers of Buddhism – and as they moved southwards, encroaching on Chinese territory, they gradually assimilated much of Han culture. Consequently the aspect of the grottoes at Yungang in the north is rather austere and spiritual, while the sculptures at Longmen are more benign and humane.

The difference is apparent also between the earlier and later statues. The features of the statues of the Wei have longer noses, wider eyes, thinner faces and slender necks, reflecting a possible Greek influence, whereas the statues of the Tang have the flatter, fuller faces characteristic of the Han.

There are 1352 grottoes, 750 niches, forty carved pagodas or *stupas*, and 100,000 statues ranging in length from 17.4 m to 2 cm; there are also 3600 steles and tablets relating to the construction of the Buddhist image, among which are some prime examples of the art of calligraphy. Parts of the grottoes were vandalized by visiting archaeologists – for instance, the historically important statues showing the emperor and empress paying homage to Buddha. The largest temple grotto is the Fengxian si, peopled with characters from Buddhist lore – the Vairocana Buddha, the Attendant Kasyapa, the gently reverent Ananda, the solemn Boddhisattvas, the wrathful Deva Rajas, the heroic Viras, and the powerful and awe-inspiring Dvarapalas.

Longmen is now one of China's major protected monuments, with a special office for maintenance and protection. The pneumatic tool factory at Luoyang has developed a special kind of steel rod which can be inserted into statues to reinforce them, and high-polymer chemicals are used to restore eroded areas.

Luoyang Museum
The museum is centrally situated, near the Laodong renmin gongyuan; the exhibits include a fossil of elephant tusk dating back more than half a million years, Neolithic pottery, bone and stone tools, bronze wine vessels and weapons from the Spring and Autumn period, iron tools from the Warring States period, and fine examples of Tang three-coloured glaze pottery (some pieces excavated from the site of Wu Zetian's Palace, for example a cup in the shape of a dragon's head). Other pieces of pottery reflect the life of the Silk Route and its cosmopolitan influence. From the Tang dynasty there is a bronze mirror inlaid with mother of pearl from the reign of emperor Ming huang (712–42).

Workers' Park (Laodong renmin gongyuan)
This park is famous for its myriad varieties of peony, and also contains the ruins of the old city wall.

White Horse Temple (Baima si)
The White Horse Temple, on the eastern outskirts of Luoyang, was the earliest temple established in China after the introduction of Buddhism. Stories, legends and interpretations of how the temple came to be built and named the White Horse Temple abound –

Luoyang was at the end of the Silk Route and visitors from India had already brought news of Buddhism. Emperor Ming di of the Eastern Han sent two monks to collect the *sutras*; they returned with them on white horses and lived in the place where the emperor himself had studied, translating the *sutras*. The emperor built a temple here in AD 68 as a memorial to them. There is also a square pagoda, thirteen storeys high, called Jiyun ta – 'massed clouds pagoda'. The temple has been rebuilt and repaired several times and reflects Indian influence; the entrance is flanked by two white horses. These are situated near the White Horse Temple.

Han Tombs

Two have recently been excavated and may be visited.

Zhou Gong miao (Temple of the Duke of Zhou)

West of the city, this is said to be the place where the first Zhou ruler established his dynasty. There is also a street called Dingding lu, which refers to the ceremonial tripod – the sign of power and rank; the new Zhou ruler brought nine of them here. Behind the temple are several steles dating from the Tang dynasty.

The Luoyang Arts and Crafts Experimental Studio

Luoyang has long been renowned for its arts and crafts – in the Western Han dynasty there was a saying, 'copper is produced in Xuzhou, whereas master craftsmen are from Luoyang'. The studio produces facsimiles of the grey pottery of the Han, the white, glazed porcelain of the Sui and Tang, and palace lanterns and silk flowers of the Ming and Qing dynasties. During the Tang Dynasty a new process of producing tri-colour glazes by means of minerals and metallic oxides was discovered and this studio specializes in reproductions using the same techniques.

The East is Red Tractor Plant

This is one of the major tractor plants in China and covers an area equivalent in size to the old city. A visit to this plant provides a picture of industrial production but also one of Chinese contemporary life, including welfare, nursery and leisure facilities. There is in the same area a ball bearings factory where visitors are often taken.

Hotels

Friendship Hotel (Youyi binguan)
Dongfang hong lu
Tel. 2139/2159
Situated in the western suburbs of Luoyang, this hotel is somewhat dingy. Another hotel is planned.

HUBEI PROVINCE

The middle reaches of the Yangtse River wend their way through the south of Hubei Province towards the sea some 1500 km distant. The name of the province means north of the lake – referring to the Dongting Lake which borders the south of the province; indeed much of the southern half of the province is made up of an almost solid network of old lakes and waterways, and in the early twentieth century provided excellent guerilla territory. In the north and west the Dabie Mountains and the Wuding shan and Wu shan ranges shelter the province from cold northern winds. The Han River flows southwards through the centre of the province from the south of Shaanxi Province to meet the Yangtse at Hankou – literally the mouth of the Han.

The extensive and fertile Yangtse–Han shui plain has been settled for three thousand years and is the major agricultural area of the province; water conservancy projects built in the early 1950s have reduced flooding in the area. In the north and north-west of the province the major crops are wheat and sesame; the central area is a major rice producer – in the eleventh century it was exporting rice to the rest of the country. Cash crops include cotton, ramie, tea, tong oil and lacquer, particularly from the hilly south-east; there is some forestry in the north-west; and the Yangtse–Han shui plain is renowned for its fish breeding and exports the fry of several well-known fish to the rest of the country.

Though agriculture is the chief occupation of the province, at Daye, south of Hanyang there are vital deposits of iron ore. The climate is subtropical and along the Yangtse the temperature in summer is often higher than in Guangzhou; this is usually attributed to the fact that the whole of the lower and middle reaches of the Yangtse and the bordering plain are surrounded by hills, forming a heat trap. The population of the province is 46.33 million.

Wuhan

Wuhan, the capital of Hubei Province, is an amalgam of the three cities of Wuchang, Hankou and Hanyang on the banks of the Yangtse, where the Han shui joins the Yangtse 960 km from the sea. It has a total population of 3.83 million.

It is not hard to understand why Wuhan is often referred to in China as the 'crossroads of nine provinces' as you approach the distinctive skyline by river from Sichuan or Shanghai, or as you slide into the spacious Wuchang Station coming north from Guangzhou, or Hankou Station coming south from Peking. For the visitor to China who has no time to visit Shanghai, Wuhan

affords a very good second choice combining its European aspect and a very Chinese pace of life. The city has a strong industrial base and is fairly prosperous, and offers a number of interesting scenic spots.

The origins of the city are in the Han dynasty. By the Tang it was a major trade and shipment centre – indeed today it is China's first inland port. The city flourished in the Ming dynasty and the names of the streets bear testimony to the handicrafts and variety of trades carried out here.

Hankou, formerly a small fishing port, is probably remembered by many foreigners as an important foreign concession area, first opened to foreign trade in 1858. The British, French, Japanese, Germans and Russians all had concessions along the northern banks of the Yangtse. By the mid-1920s all except the French had given up their rights to territories here. Today the area is a commercial centre, and the place where the majority of tourist hotels and facilities are to be found.

Hanyang, connected to Hankou by a bridge over the Han River completed in 1954, was the location of the first major iron and steel works in China. Built at the end of the nineteenth century under the progressive Viceroy, Zhang Zhidong, it also housed a governmental arsenal. Today it is a predominantly industrial area.

Wuchang is the ancient city – there has been a city here on the south bank of the Yangtse since AD 221. Until the early twentieth century there was a city wall with Snake Hill at the centre and the renowned Street of a Thousand Shops, and Wuchang was the administrative seat of local government. Beyond Wuchang lies the eastern lake with its universities and museums. On this side of the river are the iron and steel works, which were reconstructed between 1956 and 1959 and are now the largest in China. Other industry is concentrated for the most part in the Qingshan and Goujin areas of Wuchang and includes machine and ship building, chemicals, textiles, cigarettes, aluminium and glass. Local agricultural produce includes bamboo, the famous Songfeng – Pine Peak tea, cassia flowers which are used in wine, sweets and cakes, freshwater fish – particularly crabs in October, lotus root and seeds, cherries, monkey head fungus, oranges, rice, cotton and rape seed. Before Wuhan was industrialized in the late nineteenth century it was an important trading centre for the distribution of bamboo, wood, edible oil and tea, rivalled only by Jiangling further up the river.

Spring and autumn are the best times of year to visit the city. The coldest time of year is for approximately fifteen days in February, when icy winds blow down from Siberia. The rainy season begins in June, preceded by the damp season of Mei yu – 'the plum rains'. Wuhan in the summer is one of China's 'furnaces', with temperatures rising well into the thirties Centigrade; almost every type of shop keeps a stock of ice lollies, and people sleep outside at night.

Wuhan played a part in the 1911 Revolution. The railway from Peking to Hankou was completed in 1906 while controversy over the building of the Hankou–Chongqing railway raged, encountering increasing pockets of resistance. It was while half the Hubei army was away from Wuchang quelling troublemakers inland that government troops decided to mutiny. While they were not supported by the Guangzhou-based Tongmen hui (Revolutionary League) their aims were similar and they were anti-Manchu.

The rebellion was hastened by the accidental explosion of a bomb at the plotters' headquarters. The police moved in very quickly, some of the group leaders were injured or fled, and the remainder decided to mutiny the following day before the police had time to begin any drawn-out programmes of repression. On 10 October 1911 the rebel troops attacked and took over government buildings and appointed new heads to their proclaimed provisional government; reprisals were taken and fighting continued for some six weeks, razing much of Hankou. However, by the beginning of 1912 a new Republic was announced at Nanking, with Sun Yatsen designated President.

The years following the May Fourth Movement saw an increase in spontaneous and organized strikes, with the Communists already working in Wuhan by 1920. They organized the rickshaw workers into trades unions and saw them hold their first strike in 1921; in the following years there was a round of factory closures, economic crises and strikes. In 1923 the warlord Wu Peifu ordered the suppression of the Unified Syndicate of Railway Workers. They were told at their opening meeting that he wanted the railway lines kept open for the movement of his troops in battle against other warlords. The Peking–Hankou railway workers refused to disband and Wu Peifu's troops attacked. This was followed by a period of harsh suppression of all trades union organizations. In the late 1920s Mao and his comrades continued peasant cadre training work here. In 1938 Wuhan was taken by the Japanese. After 1949 it was chosen as one of the major cities for industrial development in the first Five-Year Plan.

You can get to Wuhan by train from Guangzhou or Peking, or by boat from Sichuan or Shanghai, or from Nanking. The present airport is 25 km south-east of Hankou, but a new one is planned. Hankou Station is centrally situated on Jinghan Street.

Yangtse Bridge

Designed in 1957 by Mao Yisheng with a small amount of Russian aid, this was the first bridge to be built across the Yangtse, between Hanyang and Wuchang. Wide avenues sweep up to the bridge, which is 1670 m long (span of 1156 m), built on eight pillars. It is two storeys high, with the upper storey for road and pedestrian traffic and the lower one for trains. Before this bridge was built people travelling north to Peking from Guangzhou had to cross the river by ferry to make their onward train connections. This bridge was followed by the Nanking Bridge, and further bridges are scheduled at Chongqing and Jiujiang.

Near the Binjiang Park (Riverside Park) on Hankou is a monument commemorating the last flood, in 1954. Since then extensive water diversion and dyke work have been carried out and there have been no major floods.

Revolutionary Monuments

The Monument to the Martyrs of the 7 February General Strike is situated in Hankou, at the eastern end of Jiefang lu.

The Central Peasant Movement Institute was established at the period when the Communist Party was working to involve the peasants in the Revolution. Mao moved here with his wife Yang Kaihui between 1926 and 1927 and wrote his document on the peasant movement in Hunan.

The Monument to the Nine Heroines (Jiu nü dun) on the western shore of the East Lake is built in cubist style commemorating the death of nine girls from the Taiping Army in April 1855 at the hands of the Qing armies. There is a tablet written in 1955 by Guo Moruo and Mrs He Xiangning, commemorating their heroism.

A bronze statue of Sun Yatsen stands on the parade ground of the revolutionary army headquarters. Other sites such as those commemorating the efforts of Sun Yatsen and the early Nationalist period are under restoration.

Tortoise Hill and Snake Hill

These twin hills face each other across the Yangtse. The former lies on Hanyang and the latter on Wuchang; both are passed as you approach the city by train from the south. Tortoise Hill is 87 m high, and from a rock – resembling a tortoise – projecting over the river you will get the best view of the Yangtse.

Near to Yuehu Lake is the site of the legendary Guqin tai Pavilion where there is a natural rock resembling a zither stand. The famous musician Yu Beiya felt that no one understood the feelings expressed in his playing, until a hermit called Zhong Zhiqi heard his music; one of the strings of the zither broke and Yu Beiya became aware that somebody was listening to his music. When he asked Zhong Zhiqi's opinion, he replied: 'When you reached the climax it was like a high mountain; when the music was subdued it was like water.' The two became firm friends; several years later Yu revisited the spot to find that Zhong had died, whereupon he broke his zither.

On Wuchang is the former site of the Yellow Crane Pagoda, commemorated in many poems, where a sage seated on a yellow crane is said to have passed, playing the flute. A pagoda stood here for over a thousand years but it was burnt down in 1884; there are plans to rebuild it in Ming style. Snake Hill used to divide the old city in half. Also here is the grave of Chen Youliang, leader of a peasant uprising at the beginning of the Ming dynasty.

East Lake

In Wuchang, this is a natural freshwater lake and a favourite spot with the people of Wuhan; it has pleasure boats and swimming pools, and is also used for breeding fish and growing lotus plants. In these idyllic surroundings are set the University of Wuhan and other colleges, sanatoria and the History Museum. The History Museum displays some excellent finds from the Han tombs in the province, and at different times of the year flower shows are held in the exhibition halls around the lake. South-east of the lake are Moshan Hill and the Botanical Garden. The west of the lake has been set up as a scenic area with the Reciting Poetry Pavilion commemorating Qu Yuan, the founder of Chinese popular poetry, famous for his poignant ballad 'Li Sao'. During the Cultural Revolution it was renamed the Red Flag Pavilion. To the north of the monument to the Nine Martyrs are a picture gallery, Lake Centre Pavilion and the Changtian Tower.

Guiyuan Temple
This temple, in Hanyang, was first built at the end of the Ming dynasty, some four hundred years ago, in the decorative southern style. It is famous for its hall of 500 arhats – said to have been carved over a period of nine years by two artisans. The temple contains a jade Buddha presented to China by Burma in 1935; it also has a collection of sutras. The five hundred luohans had the role of patron saints, and the ordinary people would come to pray to different ones for special needs; there was also a system of counting luohans to tell your fortune.

There is a vegetarian restaurant here, and halls to the Guardian Gods, the Earth God, the Weiduo God and the Goddess of Mercy. Practising monks can be observed at the temple.

Iron and Steel Works
Few people have any idea of the operation of an iron and steel works, and a half-day spent here can be an illuminating experience particularly if you feel saturated with Buddhist temples. The works are on the outskirts of Wuchang and employ some 300,000 people. They began operation in 1958 and are one of the major steel suppliers in China.

Food and Drink
Steamed dishes are very popular in Hubei, such as the dumplings called shao mai, made from wheat flour. Also very popular is Hubei weitang soup served in pottery dishes – a meal in itself usually eaten with two pancakes. Eight Treasure Rice (babao fan) comes from this area, as do san xian dou pi – Three Fresh Bean Curd Skin (popular with Mao) and fish – particularly carp and the famous wawa fish from the west of the province. Tortoise is also cooked, and there are several famous local spirits.

Culture
The local opera is called Chu Ju – after the classical name of Hubei or Han Ju. The acrobats from Wuhan are particularly well known for their chair-balancing acts, and indeed the Wuhan troupe is the most exciting I have seen in China.

Educational Institutions
Wuhan houses a university, the Central China School of Engineering, Teachers' Training College, Wuhan Sports School, Geology Institute, Research Institute of Marine Biology, and three medical colleges, including one which specializes in Chinese medicine.

Shopping
The principal commercial area in Hankou is along Zhongshan Avenue and Jiefang lu, long avenues which run parallel to the river. The friendship store is at Jiefang dadao (Liberation Avenue).

Local souvenirs include household and decorative products made from bamboo, carving, feather- and shell-work, embroidery from Hong Lake, and the greenish semi-precious Lüsong stone found only in Songzi County.

Hotels: General Information
Wuhan has a legacy of comfortable hotels in Hankou.

Shengli (Victory Hotel)
11 Siwei lu
Tel. 22531/21241
Situated within easy walking distance of the Riverside Park and the flood monument in the former French concession area, the hotel is comfortably appointed, with air-conditioning to counteract the summer heat. The service and food are both of the highest standard.

Xuangong fandian
Jianghan yi lu
Tel. 24404
Centrally located close to Zhongshan Avenue, the antiques store and arts and crafts store.

Jianghan fandian
Shengli Street
Tel. 23998
Also a centrally located and well appointed hotel, with an excellent reputation for its cuisine.

Hong shan Guest House
At Wuchang, this large hotel is used mainly for overseas Chinese. You may well stop here for lunch when visiting the iron and steel works.

There is also a guest house at the iron and steel works, used for foreign technicians who may be working there. A new hotel is planned for Hanyang.

Restaurants
Xiao tao yuan (Little Peach Garden)
Hankou
Specializes in soup

Laotongcheng canguan
1 Dazhi Road, Hankou
Tel. 21562

Famous for its snacks and dumplings (*doupi*)

Yeweixiang canguan
76 Yingwu dadao, Hanyang
Tel. 41198
Specializes in wild game

Wuchang or Dazhonghua canguan
188 Pengliuyang Road, Wuchang
Tel. 72029
A fish restaurant in Wuchang where Mao evidently once ate.

Useful Addresses
CAAC
209 Liji bei lu
Hankou
Tel. 51248

Luxingshe
1395 Zhongshan da dao
Hankou
Tel. 25018

Yichang

This town, the first stop in Hubei coming from Sichuan, was formerly a riverside port used by foreign ships and had a British concession. Today it is still a busy riverside port with some industry. It was the scene of several battles during the Three Kingdoms period. It houses a temple which dates from the Han dynasty called Yu quan si (Jade Spring Temple) and an Iron Pagoda. It also has an important hydroelectric power generator, producing 3 million kilowatts, and the Gezhouba dam project. It can be reached by plane, boat or bus.

Shashi

Further down the Yangtse lies this small town with a population of some 180,000. The major industry is textile production (cotton, silk and wool) and food processing also takes place. Some 5 km to the west is the ancient capital of

Jiangling, an important city up till the Ming dynasty, and the capital of Chu in the Warring States period. Among interesting sights here are the excavations of a Han tomb, a group of tombs dating back to the Warring States period, the old city and the Museum of Archaeology. It can be reached by bus, plane or boat.

Also near Shashi is the Red Cliff, the site of the famous battle between Cao Cao and Liu Bei in the Three Kingdoms period. The name Red Cliff derives from the colour of the flames burning the boats from which the battle was fought.

Xiangfan

In the north-west of the province, 400 km and nine hours by train from Wuhan, this was an ancient waterways junction. A railway was built here in 1965, and since 1978 the Xiangfan–Chongqing line has been opened. It was the home of the Prime Minister Zhu Geliang and the famous Song painter Mi Fei – there is a pagoda in his memory and stone carvings of his work. At nearby Dan jiang is a hydro-electric power station and in the Wu dang Mountains there are buildings in the style of the Imperial Palace in Peking – famous for their golden roofs.

HUNAN PROVINCE

South of Lake Dongting, Hunan is the sister province of Hubei; in fact in the Yuan and Ming dynasties the two provinces were one administrative area called Hukuang, and between them provided China with rice and grain, shipped northwards to the Grand Canal. Hunan is a province of rich red earth, of country houses with flying buttresses, and of Chairman Mao's birthplace; in the local dialect 'h' becomes 'f', and the cuisine is characterized by hot, spicy dishes.

The province is surrounded on the east, west and south by mountains; the fertile Dongting plain lies to the north and the remainder of the terrain is gently hilly. Four major rivers drain into the lake – the Xiang jiang (after which the province is sometimes called 'Xiang'), the Li, the Yuan and the Ze, and water transportation is vital. The Guangzhou–Peking railway runs through the province and there are also lines into Guangxi, Guizhou and Jiangxi (from Shanghai). The climate affords a long growing season, ranging from eight months in the north-west of the province to ten months in the south-east, with plentiful rain and hot summers. Rice is the major crop, and the cash crops are rape seed, ramie, cotton, tong oil and tea oil (used for cooking) and tea – green, black, and red. The area is also very important for forestry, particularly cedar wood, and wood is rafted down from Xue feng and Nan ling Mountains in the west and south, along the major rivers into Lake Dongting and on down the Yangtse. The pigs raised in Hunan are renowned throughout the country. The province contains natural deposits of antimony, lead and zinc and in recent years coal seams have also been worked.

The total population of the province is 52.23 million. In the west and south of the province are several national minority areas – the Tujia autonomous district, the Tong Autonomous County and the Yao Autonomous County.

Changsha

The provincial capital, built along the eastern bank of the Xiang River, takes its name, which means 'long sand flat', from Orange Island which occupies the middle of the river opposite the city. The streets are wide and many of the houses built of wood; the total population of the city is 2.63 million. Changsha has a long-standing reputation for producing men of high calibre – in fact Carl Crow records that many temples and ceremonial arches had been erected in their honour, and Hunan was one of the first places where revolutionary ideas took root.

Changsha has been settled since the Warring States period, when it was the seat of power for the state of Chu. Afterwards it was absorbed into the unified Empire of Qin, but was long to retain its own distinctive southern culture. The fortunes of Changsha grew with those of the rest of the province; however, by the mid-nineteenth century the effects of over-population, a corrupt official class and shortage of land, as well as the long-standing mistrust of the Manchu Imperial House, were fuel for a succession of peasant rebellions and the organization of numerous secret societies. The Taiping Rebellion was, however, kept out of Hunan by the governor, General Zeng Guofan, who recruited Hunanese to his armies and created a war fleet based on Lake Dongting, where he defeated the able Taiping leader Shi Dakai. Zeng Guofan had the wholehearted support of the large and powerful gentry class of the province. There were to be other risings during the century, and it was the Boxer Rebellion which eventually allowed foreigners access to Hunan Province, and the Standard Oil Company to set up shop in Changsha; the foreigners established their homes on Orange Island.

The province was one of the radical forerunners in advocating new standards of education: reforming intellectuals from the gentry class, such as Chen Baozhen, established cultural centres, and their own newspaper and current affairs college in 1897; these were to be influences on the future leaders of the Chinese Revolution. During the unsettled period following the overthrow of the Manchus, Tan Yankai was appointed governor, supported by the local gentry; however there was a great deal of fighting in and around Hunan. The May Fourth Movement inspired new magazines and critical stances all over China, not least in Changsha where the Hunan Students' Association, of which Mao was by this time a member, published the *Xiang River Review*. In early 1920 and 1921 there was a demand for Hunan to become an independent autonomous state within China; the warlord Zhao Hendi proclaimed independence and was supported by the gentry, intellectuals and workers alike – including Mao, who in an interview with Edgar Snow described it as a very appealing way of bringing progress to Hunan. However, co-operation among workers, students and warlord was short-lived, and Zhao Hendi used repressive measures against their organizations and strikes. Attempts by the Chinese Communist Party to organize a peasant army in Hunan initially met with failure, and eventually the Jinggang Mountains were to become the stronghold for the Communists on the border of Jiangxi and Hunan.

During the Sino–Japanese War in, 1938, in their attempts to flee and dislodge the Japanese, the Guomindang had Changsha set on fire. This tactic had a somewhat tragic outcome, as the population of the town was at that time swollen by an enormous influx of refugees. As a consequence most of the buildings in Changsha are relatively modern.

Changsha is 1587 km from Peking, and 726 km from Guangzhou. There are both train and air services from Shanghai, Guangzhou, Peking and Guilin.

First Normal School of Hunan Province
Many of the places to visit in Changsha, including this one, are closely linked to the activities of Mao Zedong. The somewhat Florentine-looking building with its shutters and arches was where the young Mao came to study and later to teach. He took the examinations here in the spring of 1913, when he was twenty, and graduated in 1918. During his time at the school he seemed a lively and critical student who took an interest in Western philosophy, and his classroom contains photographs of his books. In the summer vacation of 1917 he took a walking holiday in the local countryside, visiting villages. Behind the school is the well or pond where Mao would come every day for a cold dip; he always considered physical exercise of great importance, and wrote an early essay about it. Also during his time here he became involved in various revolutionary activities. In summer 1918 he went to Peking, where he worked in a library.

Today the school is still a teachers' training college; it was rebuilt in the mid-1960s, having been burnt in the fire of 1938. It accommodates some 1300 students and 170 teachers. At the entrance is Mao's slogan: 'To be a teacher of the people, one must first be their pupil'. The school is close to Jiang-xiang Road, just south of Laodong lu.

Qingshui tang (Clear Pools)
This is the original site of the Xiang (Hunan) district committee of the Communist Party, opposite the Martyrs' Memorial Park. This was where Mao lived in 1921 with his wife Yang Kai Hui, from where he founded the Hunan Area Party Committee and directed the strike of 1922.

Orange Isle (Juzi zhoutou)
From May First Street continue westwards to the Xiang River and the seventeen-arched Xiang jiang Bridge, completed in 1972. From here you can reach Orange Isle, 4.75 km long, and between 45 and 140 m wide; oranges grow here, and it has long been a favourite beauty spot, particularly for students. It is also possible to take a boat to the head of the island, where on the sandy shore stands a pavilion with a tablet recording Mao's poem 'Changsha', written in 1925.

Yuelu Hill
On the west bank of the Xiang jiang is the ancient beauty spot Yuelu Hill, also called Lushan, which has a long-standing educational tradition for it was the site of one of the four great academies – the Lushan Academy. The Song neo-Confucian philosopher Zhu Xi taught here, and the tradition has been continued, for on the lower southern slopes are the Hunan University complex and other colleges, first established in 1925.

Behind the university, halfway up the hill, is the famous Love Dusk Pavilion (Aiwan ting), another haunt of the young Mao Zedong and his fellow students; it houses a tablet inscribed with Mao's calligraphy. The first Love Dusk Pavilion was built in 1792 and called the Maple (Hongye) Pavilion. Since the days of the Tang poet Du Mu who had written a poem in praise of the maple in autumn, this has been a famous scenic spot. The present pavilion was erected in 1952.

Hunan Provincial Museum
Dongfeng lu
The main features of this museum are the exhibits taken from the no. 1 Han Tomb at Mawangdui. Mawangdui is 4 km from the city centre and, in late 1971, while construction work was being carried out, two Han tombs were discovered. Between January and April 1972 the first of these tombs was carefully excavated. It was established that the tomb belonged to the wife of the

Marquis of Dai who had lived in the western Han dynasty in the first century BC.

The museum relates the progress of the excavations, displaying the massive wooden structures which formed the outer containers for the sarcophagus; the principle of the tomb construction was that of a series of 'Chinese boxes'; one inside the other. Inside the coarse outer containers there were beautiful lacquer coffins, all luxuriously designed. Articles of silk clothing, food such as lychees, lacquer dressing-table ware, funerary figures, writing on bamboo strips, musical instruments, bronze mirrors, pottery and bamboo baskets were all preserved intact. Over the innermost coffin was draped an elaborate painting, a T-shaped hanging depicting the Han cosmos – from the heavens to the netherworld – at the centre of which is the figure of an elderly woman, the wife of the Marquis of Dai together with her attendants.

Within the coffin, wrapped in silk, archaeologists discovered the magnificently preserved body of a fifty-year-old woman: her skin still retained its elasticity and all the limbs could be bent. Pathologists were called upon to give a thorough autopsy – her entrails were removed and are now neatly displayed in glass jars.

The museum also has several articles from the Zhou Dynasty on display and a small shop.

Hunan Ceramics and Chinese Paintings Museum

This museum contains displays of local ceramics and paintings.

Local Culture

The local Xiang Opera, accompanied by drums, is well known for its relaxed, light-hearted liveliness. The area is known for its shadow puppetry, dancing, folk songs and humorous love songs.

Handicrafts

Hunan is famous for its embroidery and porcelain. The Xiang embroidery uses bold colours and exciting subject matter – lions and tigers – and you can visit the studio where it is made. The porcelain is blue and white, and light in the hand. There are factories and studios in Changsha itself, and outside the city to the south-east, is the Liling Ceramics Centre, where deposits of kaolin were found in the Qing dynasty by a Guangzhouese potter who set up a temple to his old pottery master. He produced blue-and-white folk-style porcelain with underglaze decoration. The factory closed in the 1930s and was reopened after 1949.

Changsha is also renowned for its umbrellas.

Shopping

In the vicinity of May First (Wuyi) Square and Road are an arts and crafts store, a foreign-language bookshop, a large department store and a branch of the Bank of China.

Hotels

Hunan Bin guan
Yingbin Road (compound on outskirts of city)
Tel. 26331
Has a shop and post office

Xiang jiang binguan
Zhongshandong Road
Tel. 26261
More centrally located and recently built, with a friendship store and a post office

Food

Hunanese food is hot, and the staple diet of ordinary people is rice and fish. The local spirit, in a gourd-shaped bottle, is made from spring water and called *baisha jiu*.

Hengyang

The second largest city in Hunan Province, it lies south of Changsha on the junction of the Peking–Guangzhou and Hunan–Guilin railways, on the banks of the Xiang and Zheng Rivers. It is a major distribution centre for the south of the province and has mining equipment and building material plants.

Heng shan

One of the five sacred peaks whose praises have been sung by the famous bards of China's past, this is the 'Nan yue' or southern peak. The peaks can be reached from Heng shan, a small stop between Changsha and Hengyang. The range consists of some seventy-two peaks running over 80 km; the highest peak is 1290 m above sea-level. It was once a Daoist and Buddhist retreat.

In modern times it was here that Chiang Kaishek came in 1938, after his retreat from Changsha, in the hope of reaching some settlement with the Japanese. The mountain is connected with the mythical Zhu rong – accredited with the discovery of fire, the art of smelting iron, engineering and music – who is said to be buried on the highest peak and is the guardian of the mountain. In the past the most popular time for pilgrims to visit was at the time of the autumn festival, when local wooden handicrafts were sold: abaci, toys and violins. The mountains are lush, tree-covered and often shrouded in mist, and there are waterfalls. Along the 15-km road to the Zhu rong Peak stand temples, pavilions and commemorative tablets written by the many poets of antiquity who came here. At the foot of the hill is the Nan yue Temple. There is also a memorial hall, similar to Sun Yatsen's mausoleum at Nanking, built to commemorate the martyrs of the Sino–Japanese War.

Xiangtan

This is a newly industrialized city on the way to Mao's birthplace, Shaoshan. It was renowned for its herbal medicines and is also the birthplace of the famous painter Qi Baishi, born in 1863.

Shaoshan

The birthplace of Chairman Mao, in Xiangtan county, lies 100 km southwest of Changsha from where it can be reached in two and a half hours; a railway branch line was specially built to connect with this small village. For details of Mao's childhood his interview with Edgar Snow in *Red Star over China* (see Bibliography) provides a background. Mao's family house was large, with several rooms, and had a pond in front of it. Signs indicate the places where Mao used to swim, play, help his mother dry the corn, and where his neighbours lived. In the nearby village is a memorial hall showing the life and history of his family. There are also a hotel/reception centre and shop.

Shaoshan Irrigation Project

Often visited during an afternoon or full-day visit to Shaoshan, this project was begun in 1965 when Hua Guofeng was Party Provincial Secretary. The intention was to divert the Lian River to irrigate the basin in the centre of the province and the six counties of the area. An extensive network of reservoirs, intakes and distribution channels, aqueducts and pumping stations has provided the region with hydroelectric power and an extended fisheries area, and improved yields of tea, oranges, and grain as well as reducing flood and drought risk.

Lake Dongting

Forming a natural barrier between Hubei and Hunan, this is the second largest freshwater lake in China, and in summer when the water is high it covers an area of 4200 km². In ancient times the lake covered a much larger area but it gradually became silted up, leaving a fertile farming area with a tendency – now much reduced – to flooding. As well as being a rich agricultural area the lake abounds in colourful tales and legends of famous personalities of the past, and there are several notable scenic spots accessible by train and road from Changsha.

In the high summer the lake is covered with acres of lotus flowers, and you can take a boatride on the lake to pick the lotus fruit *(ou)* and the flowers.

Dragon Boat Festival at Miluo
In June 1980 the Dragon Boat Festival was revived in all its excitement and colour for the first time in more than ten years. The festival commemorates the death of the poet and state adviser Qu Yuan (340–278 BC), who drowned himself in the Miluo River on hearing that his state of Chu had been over-run by the enemy in the era of the Warring States. The local people threw rice and other food into nearby Lake Dongting to stop the fish and turtles from eating his body – hence the custom of eating *zongzi*, glutinous rice wrapped in bamboo leaves, on the 'Double Fifth', the date in the lunar calendar when he is supposed to have died. The Dragon Boat race is rowed over 2000 m in boats which carry forty-five oarsmen. There is still a temple to Qu Yuan in the area, containing tablets depicting scenes from his life; there used to be even more monuments to him, but they have now fallen into disrepair.

Yueyang

This port is in the north of the province, at the junction of the lake and the Yangtse River, and was one of the first areas in Hunan to open to foreign trade in the nineteenth century. Today it is a major river port, the gateway to Hunan, and a centre for rice and timber. During the Warring States period the Prince of Ba from Sichuan used to march on Chu, and after a battle would bury his dead here. During the Three Kingdoms period General Lu Su of the Kingdom of Wu reviewed his troops here.

It is renowned above all for the unique Yueyang Tower, built near the west city gate overlooking Lake Dongting and Jun shan Island.

The first tower was built in AD 716 in the Tang dynasty, on the south side of Mount Tian – the name Yueyang means 'on the sunny side of the peak'. It quickly became the haunt of some of the famed Tang poets and there are many legends associated with Lu Dongbin, a scholar and Daoist of the Tang dynasty. The tower was restored in 1045 in the Song dynasty, and again damaged by flood and war. It was last rebuilt in 1867 on the burial ground of the Ba soldiers.

INNER MONGOLIA
(NEI MENGGU)

Beyond the Great Wall on the borders of Hebei and Shanxi provinces lie the extensive steppelands of the Inner Mongolian Autonomous Region, an area formerly considered unfarmable by the Chinese. When the Great Wall was rebuilt during the Ming Dynasty it was generally on the boundaries between arable and non-arable land, and as a result this area has always been inhabited by nomadic and semi-nomadic peoples, whose main form of subsistence is from cattle rearing, sheep herding and horse breeding. While loose-knit commune settlements have begun to replace the nomadic life of the *yurt* community – the *yurt* (*menggu bao* in Chinese) is the warm and adaptable tent home traditional to the Mongolians, made from layers of stretched skins over a wooden frame – the area is still the largest one for animal breeding in the whole of China, and incorporates all the related industries such as leather tanning. Today the people of Inner Mongolia are renowned for their sporting and cultural traditions – wrestling, horse riding, acrobatics and a style of singing which seems to carry across a concert hall with the strength of a lone voice carried with the wind across the grasslands.

The history of the area is long and complex, since it has been peopled by different tribes alternately gaining ascendancy over one another, and at times over the whole of China. In earliest times the area was inhabited by the Xiongnu – the Huns – and by the tenth century the Khitan people established the Liao dynasty from here. During the twelfth century the Mongolians were building up their power and by the latter half of the thirteenth century their influence extended over the whole of China and the Yuan dynasty was established. When the Ming re-established Han sovereignty, one of their first actions was to strengthen the Great Wall, a symbolic as much as a practical gesture designed to keep the invaders out. The Mongols were driven out of China in 1368 and until 1470 they were united under Dayan Khan. On his death in 1470 Mongolia was divided into small states among his sons. During the Ming dynasty relations with Mongolia were erratic: Chinese troops were stationed near the borders, but there were raids from the west. In 1689 the Congress of Dolon Nor brought the whole of Mongolia under Chinese rule and the Manchus organized the Mongolians into banners under hereditary chieftains.

Banners were grouped into tribes and tribes into leagues, with commanders approved by the imperial government. The area which corresponds to modern Inner Mongolia was under the Peking Colonial office, while Outer Mongolia was administered locally. At the end of the nineteenth century Russia was threatening Mongolia and the Chinese introduced a policy of colonization by encouraging Chinese people to emigrate there and take up farming. This continued until around 1912. In 1915, in a tripartite agreement signed by China, Russia and Mongolia, Mongolia was made autonomous but was still a part of the Republic of China. By 1921 the Mongolian People's Republic had been formed. In the 1920s the Peking–Baotou railway was constructed and Inner Mongolia became part of a special administrative area comprising Jehol, Chahar and Suiyuan. When the Japanese invaded Manchuria in the 1930s they gave Inner Mongolia its own prince.

In 1945 the Communists gained control of the area and in 1947 the first autonomous region was established. Until 1969 the region followed the borders of Outer Mongolia as far west as Xinjiang and as far north as the Amur River. Then in 1969 it was reduced in size. To the west it was defined by the borders of present-day Ningxia-Hui Autonomous Region, and to the east areas were absorbed into the northeastern provinces and the south-east borders of Shanxi and Hebei.

The main religious influences in Mongolia are Lamaistic Buddhism and Islam. Lamaism was introduced from Tibet after the death of Khubilai Khan in 1295 and until 1664 the religious centre was Kuku-Khoto – the Blue City (Guihua cheng) – after which it was moved to Urga (present-day Ulan Bator). Mohammedism was introduced in the tenth century.

The total population of Inner Mongolia is 18.52 million. The Mongolians live on the borders and plateaux, their traditional tribal units of leagues and banners having been absorbed into the current administrative system. The banner, *qi*, corresponds to the administrative level of the county, while the league, *meng*, has jurisdiction over the banner and counties and cities where applicable. Most Han Chinese live in the industrial and arable belt along the Yellow River or in the important border towns such as Erlian – where the railway built in 1955 passes into Outer Mongolia on its way to Moscow, and the towns follow the Chinese system of administrative divisions.

North of the Yellow River, which loops through the south of Inner Mongolia, the terrain consists largely of plateaux some 1000 m above sea-level, much of it grassland given over to grazing by sheep, cattle, camels and horses. The Yin shan range in the south-west of the plateau is a rich source of minerals – above all iron ore and coal, as well as mica and asbestos.

The Hedao, Baotou and Huhehot plains are the main centres of population and agriculture and have adequate irrigation systems. Major crops in the area are spring wheat, gaoliang, some hardy rice, oats and millets; cash crops are soya beans, hemp, rape seed, tobacco, medicinal plants such as licorice, and sugar beet. The Ordos region, south of the Yellow River and bounded by the Great Wall as it makes its way through Shaanxi Province, is stony and sandy and has been planted with a tree belt to prevent erosion. The winters are dry and very cold; temperatures may fall to −30°C and rainfall is a maximum of 300 mm, with less in the west.

Hohhot

The capital of Inner Mongolia stands on the Peking–Baotou railway, north of the Dahei he – the Great Black River, a tributary of the Yellow River – and south of the foothills of the Daqing Mountains. The name means Green City. Hohhot dates back to the Ming dynasty and used to be called Guihua. When in the late eighteenth century Chinese settlers came here to farm they set up their city, north of the present one, which has a population of 1.1 million. Local industry includes tanneries, woollen textiles, iron and steel and chemical plants, tractor and diesel engine factories and sugar refining. In 1957 the first university in the region was established here, as well as medical and veterinary colleges.

The Peking–Baotou railway runs through the north of the city. In the north-east corner is the old quarter, where part of the former city wall still stands. Here you will find shop signs written in both Chinese and Mongolian, and colourful local costumes are worn. On sale are horse saddles, whips, felt carpets, boots, knives, headgear and snuff boxes. In the bookshops the Mongolian-language books reflect the rich oral tradition of story telling and songs.

There is a daily plane service to Hohhot and Xilinhot from Peking. The train journey from Peking takes ten hours, and you change at Jining.

The modern commercial centre with shops, banks and theatres is along Zhongshan lu, which runs from the south-west to the north-east and joins Xinhua dajie. Along Xinhua dajie is the seat of the local government.

White Pagoda
This pagoda, in the old city, is also called Wanbu huayan ta, which means 'the Huayan Pagoda which contains volumes of the sutras'. It is octagonal in shape and seven storeys high, and one may climb it for a view across the city and surrounding plain. It was built during the Liao dynasty (983–1031) in the region of Shengzong. Inside are inscriptions in Chinese, Khitan, Nurchen and Mongolian from the Jin, Yuan and Han dynasties.

Museum

The new museum with its statues of white horses on the rooftops is in Xinhua dajie. It contains interesting finds of pottery brought from all over China during the Yuan dynasty, and examples of some of the art of the Xiongnu, which demonstrate that China and the warring border tribes have inextricably linked fates. There are also copies of tomb paintings from the Han dynasty.

Five Pagoda Temple (Wuta si)

Built during the reign of Qian long (1736–95) in distinctive Tibetan style, it consists of five *stupas* 6.62 m high on a square brick base 7.82 m high, glazed and carved with scenes from Buddhist lore and nature.

Zhao Jun mu (Tomb of Princess Zhao)

The Tomb of Princess Zhao lies 9 km south of the city centre, on the south bank of Dahei River in beautiful natural surroundings, and is a grassy tumulus where tradition and records have it that the Han Princess Zhao Jun is buried. She was given in marriage to a tribal chieftain Hu Hanxie of the Xiongnu and became his chief wife. Dong Biwu, the veteran vice-chairman of the Communist Party, came here in 1963 and gave his seal of approval, saying that writers were wrong to portray this as a tragic story of exile among an uncivilized people, but that it should be interpreted as a sign of the friendship between the Han and the Xiongnu.

Ethnic Traditions

It is possible to arrange to visit the steppeland and spend a night in a *yurt*. If you visit Inner Mongolia in late May or early June this will coincide with the Nadum, the annual games, when all the nomads converge near the city and engage in every aspect of Mongolian sportsmanship – horse racing, acrobatics, horse taming, singing and dancing in local style, and wrestling. There are also opportunities for camel- and horse-riding.

In Hohhot, visits may be arranged to the University where interesting work on the Mongolian language is being carried out. It is also possible to visit the school of fine art, whose workshop produces local goods – boots, knives and hats etc – as well as schools, hospitals and a mosque.

Shopping

Hohhot has a Friendship Store. Local handicrafts on sale include carpets, knives, buttons, hats, boots and leather.

Food

The Mongolians are renowned for their hospitality and their capacity for drink, and you will be plied with brick tea, lamb and beef hotpot, and sesame seed cake.

Hotels

Hohhot Guesthouse
Xinhua Avenue, Yingbin lu

Xilinhot

In the north-east of the province, this frontier town can be reached by train as far as Suniteshi banner, then by road to Xilinhot. There are also air connections from Hohhot. Set amidst bleak pastureland this town, the administrative seat of Abahanaer banner, lies against a backdrop of distant hills, and is a mixture of functional new and decorative old, such as the famous Lamaist Bailing Temple. Today it has a population of 60,000 with electricity, coal mines, machine building, tanning, wool and textiles, paper making, cement and dairy products its chief sources of wealth.

Baotou

The iron and steel centre of Inner Mongolia is one of the five major suppliers of these commodities to the whole of

China. It stands on the railway between Peking and Lanzhou, close to the Yellow River and north of the Ordos region, and was formerly a frontier trading city which the Japanese wanted to develop. The iron ore is taken from Bayinobo, and the coal from Shikuaigou. The steel works began operation in 1958 and the city's population has grown to 700,000. Other industries have developed, such as blast furnaces, railway girders and rolling stock, aluminium, chemicals, fertilizers and cement.

JIANGSU PROVINCE

This compact and densely populated province has a population of 58.92 million distributed over more than 405,000 km². It stretches north and south of the Yangtse and is bounded on the east by the Yellow Sea. Much of the province consists of a flat alluvial plain, on average 50 m above sea-level, with mountainous regions in the north-west and south-west. The area is crisscrossed by a network of waterways – natural lakes and rivers, and man-made canals from the historic Grand Canal to post-1949 irrigation projects – and is intensively cultivated; much of the land to the east has been reclaimed by the sea. The north is markedly poorer than the area south of the Yangtse, and has none of the glamorous history associated with cities such as Nanking, Yangzhou or Suzhou, not to mention the favourable conditions for agriculture and a relatively strong industrial base.

The northern part of the province has long, fairly cold and dry winters, characteristic of north China, with a period of heavy rainfall during July and August which often causes flooding. The Huai River runs through this part of Jiangsu and in the past often flooded – it is now a priority area for irrigation.

The most important crops are winter wheat, millet and gaoliang, with cash crops of sweet potatoes, peanuts, soya beans and now some cotton. The only port on this part of the coast, where the water is extremely shallow, is Lianyungang, a city of the 1930s which is also the terminal of the east–west Longhai railway. The other major town of the area, also a communications hub, is Xuzhou. It was formerly an important trading post on the Grand Canal and is today an important railway junction. Coal mining began in the area around Xuzhou.

South of the Huai River the area along the coast has long been one of the salt fields of China, and in fact the merchants of Yangzhou achieved their fame and fortune through the shipment and handling of salt from this area. Rice is grown in the westernmost parts, where lakes and marshes abound, and cotton is produced in the central plain. The staple, though, is grain with cash crops of jute, oil seeds, rape, indigo and cotton. Major cities of the area include Yan cheng – literally Salt City, Qingjiang, and Yangzhou and Nantong, which are both on the northern banks of the Yangtse.

The tale south of the Yangtse is a more illustrious one; the area is known as the 'land of fish and rice', the epithet used in China to characterize a fertile area. The climate is temperate, with a longer growing season, enabling much of the area to produce three crops per year – the pattern being two crops of grain such as wheat, rice, and one of the fertilizer crops such as alfalfa or rape seed. The fields glow with yellow and purple during the spring months. Cotton is grown in the south and other cash crops include silk – this is one of the major centres of production in China, tea, fruit and freshwater fish from Lake Tai. Water transportation is used more frequently than any other.

The history of the region reflects its

independent development, far from the capitals in the north. It was sometimes a place to be banished to, while at other times it maintained its independence and flourished while the north was over-run by foreign invaders. Until the second century BC, when it was absorbed into the Qin empire, Jiangsu developed separately as part of the Yue state, and in the times of the Warring States as part of the state of Wu which covered half the country. The brief periods of union were followed by a split into the tiny state of Wu-Yue. During the Tang dynasty Jiangsu was exporting rice to the rest of China, and by the Song dynasty – when for a short while the capital was in nearby Hangzhou – it was the most economically flourishing area in the country. When the Ming dynasty succeeded in routing the Mongols the capital was at Nanking, until the third emperor moved it back to Peking at the beginning of the fifteenth century. Even though from then on the political capital was in the north, the area still continued to prosper, and gained a reputation for attainments in the arts. Cities such as Suzhou were favoured by the gentry as retirement places.

Northern Jiangsu

Northern Jiangsu is somewhat neglected touristically, but ecstatic reports have been received of the welcome afforded in such cities as Xuzhou.

Situated in the north-western corner of the province, Xuzhou has a population of 700,000. The Grand Canal passes to the north-east and the old course of the Yellow River skirts the northern limits of the city. The city is also at the junction of the Longhai/Peking/Shanghai railways. There are many places to visit which give an insight into contemporary institutions in China – an old people's home, a kindergarten, colleges, communes etc. There is

a park and a monument commemorating the Martyrs of the Huaihai Campaign of the 1930s, Han tombs, and a museum.

235 km south-east of Xuzhou is Huainan – the birthplace of Zhou Enlai. Lianyun gang is on the coast, the only port in northern Jiangsu and the terminus of the Longhai railway which reaches westwards as far as Xinjiang Autonomous Region. The city has a population of 350,000. There are many areas of scenic and historic interest including beaches, hot springs, mountains, stone carvings from the Han dynasty and the Flower Fruit Mountain and the Water Curtain Cave which Wu Cheng'en incorporated into his novel *Journey to the West* (also known as *Monkey*).

Nanking

Nanking (also known as Nanjing) was first given the seal of approval as a city fit to be a capital by the famous political adviser of the Three Kingdoms period, Zhu Geliang; on seeing it for the first time he described Nanking as 'a curling dragon and a crouching tiger', an epithet which has remained with the city right down to modern times, when Mao echoed it in his poem written after the taking of Nanking in 1949. The western eye and imagination have to stretch themselves to see the dragon and the tiger in the low-lying, wooded hills which surround Nanking. Nonetheless, lying on the southern bank of the Yangtse, with its wide, tree-lined boulevards to provide protection against the scorching summers, the town has a serene and easy-going atmosphere.

The position of Nanking is favourable – close to all important communications and able to make use of the natural wealth of the surrounding countryside. While no longer the capital of the whole country, it remains the capital of Jiangsu Province and houses all the relevant administrative offices. Parts of the old and somewhat irregular city wall still remain, and even the wide Zhonghua Gate still stands. It is 380 km from the sea.

For the inhabitants of the city as much as for the visitor, the environs of Nanking are crowded with places to visit and cool hills and shady woods where you may escape the fierce heat of summer, for the city is known as one of the three ovens of China – temperatures reach the mid-thirties centigrade in June, July and August, with a typical monsoon climate at this time of overcast skies and short, sharp bursts of rain. Winter temperatures rarely fall below zero, and in the autumn Nanking is often on the edge of typhoons. The area is excellent for agriculture and an adequate system of dykes and irrigation ditches has removed the threat of flooding. The area produces three crops annually – winter wheat is harvested in May, followed by two crops of rice. It is also an important cotton producing area, and other cash crops include sweet potatoes, gaoliang, soya beans and vegetables.

The total population of both the inner city area and suburbs is almost 3.5 million. Nanking is one of the leading centres for electronics, has its own petrochemical plant, and coal, gas and lorries are produced here. It also boasts its own chemical fertilizer plant.

For the first-time visitor to China Nanking is a city with a historic feel about it. Since it is situated on the Yangtse there is much to see. It has a rural atmosphere combined with the advantages of a large town, and lies within easy reach of other interesting towns.

The administrative centre of Nanking is at Gu lou guangchang (Drum Tower Square). The downtown area, called Xinjiekou, is where most Nanking people go to shop and eat. At Drum Tower Square stand the offices of the Nanking Civic Administration, housed in a building in 1950s' Chinese style, surmounted with the three red flags which symbolized the spirit of the Great Leap Forward (the General Line, the Great Leap Forward, and People's Communes). In the centre of the square is an island of flowers which can be moved to accommodate a rally. The building after which the area is named lies behind the square.

History

The history of Nanking, whose name means southern capital, dates back over 2400 years to the Warring States period, when the state of Wu used the area for munitions works. In 473 BC Yue took over from Wu and the first city walls of Nanking date from this time. During the Three Kingdoms period the kingdom of Wu established its capital there and began the construction of the Stone City Wall. It remained capital of the southern dynasties between the third and the seventh centuries when China was reunited under the Sui and Tang.

During this period the north was ruled by the Huns or alien dynasties. The southern Jin dynasty was set up in 317 by a former prince of the northern Jin, whose country had been over-run by northern invaders, on a site adjacent to Nanking. Many northern Chinese moved to the south, particularly the gentry, slowly integrating with the native inhabitants of the region and the earlier settlers from the north. The fourth and fifth centuries were in fact a period of great civilization and wealth, marred only by rivalry between cliques and powerful families based in Nanking or Wuhan. During the Song dynasty the Toba tribesmen moved nearer from the north, while the emperors and court of this period were quite dissolute.

During the following Qi dynasty the fighting between north and south continued. The Toba were finally defeated by the south – and following the usual pattern of things, the victor was in a position to make himself emperor, so the Liang dynasty was established. The first emperor of the Liang dynasty took the name of Wu Di – the martial emperor. He ruled from 502 to 549 and was known even in the West for his love of culture, literature and Buddhism. He strengthened the Stone City walls the remnants of the massive fortified walls and ramparts which protected the people of Nanking from the northern marauders, and can today be seen in the western part of the city.

The final dynasties of this period were weak and divided, and as the Toba were gradually driven out of China the south became reabsorbed into the Sui dynasty. Although during the Tang dynasty the capital was at Chang'an – present-day Xi'an – nonetheless the area was still culturally and economically important.

Nanking was to have a brief period as capital at the beginning of the southern Song dynasty, in the early part of the twelfth century. In 1356 the peasant leader Zhu Yuanzhang captured Nanking from the Mongols and set up a local administration for the Yangtse area. Twelve years later, when he had conquered the north, he was in a strong position to establish the Ming dynasty and have his capital at Nanking. The Ming palaces were in the eastern quarter of present-day Nanking. They were burnt down in the power struggle after his death, and Yong le moved the capital to Peking for reasons of national defence. However the city wall – much of which can still be seen today – dates back to this period. During the Qing dynasty Nanking was a major textile and cultural centre. The famous Qing dynasty novels, *The Scholars* and *The Dream of the Red Chamber*, are both set in Nanking.

Until 1842, when the Opium War advanced northwards and British gunboats threatened Nanking and the mouth of the Yangtse, the only previous foreign visitors had been the Portuguese in 1519 and the Manchus who had captured Nanking in 1645. The Qing government gave in to the demands of the British, and the Nanking treaty, which opened up five treaty ports along the east coast of China, was signed on a ship outside Nanking. Nanking itself, however, was not established as a treaty port until 1858 and it actually began operation in 1859.

In 1853 Nanking acquired the title of the capital of the Heavenly Kingdom of Great Peace (Taiping tianguo) when during the Taiping Rebellion it was taken after an eleven-day siege. Hong Xiuquan, the rebel leader, had his headquarters in the centre of Nanking, around Xinjiekou, and much of the surrounding area was used for garrisons. Between 1853 and 1856 their rule was stable until internal disagreements led to the collapse of the government, and by 1864 government forces were able to retake Nanking. Many of the fine buildings and monuments for which Nanking was famous were destroyed during this period, among them the renowned Porcelain Pagoda, built in the early Ming dynasty.

In 1911 Nanking became the capital for a while when, at the fall of the Manchu dynasty, the Republicans assembled in Nanking to elect Sun Yat-sen President. Nanking was to become capital under Chiang Kaishek from 1927 onwards. During this time much rebuilding was carried out: Zhongshan lu, which makes its way from north to south across Nanking, was built then. Chiang Kaishek took up residence in the former palace of the Taiping leader Hong Xiuquan, near Xinjiekou. Nanking remained the nominal capital until 1949, although the invasion of the

217

Japanese forced the Generalissimo to remove the government offices first to Wuhan and then to Chongqing in 1937. Between 1940 and 1941 Wang Jingwei led the puppet government of the Japanese in Nanking. Between 1946 and 1947 a delegation of the Communist Party continued negotiations with the Nationalist Government to try and reach a peaceful accord, and eventually in 1949 the Communist-led forces took Nanking.

Since 1949 Nanking has been restored to its place as a leading cultural centre. It contains many colleges of further education, a school of traditional medicine and an observatory. One of the major achievements in the bringing together of north and south was the completion of the Nanking Bridge in 1969.

Drum Tower

It was built in 1382 by the first Ming emperor, Zhu Yuanzhang, who is said to have stood here beating a drum in preparation for a battle against rebels; thereafter the watch would be sounded seven times a day. This was the former city centre. Reached by winding paths and flowering shrubs and trees, a tower has stood on this spot since the end of the eleventh century. One of the early Protestant missionaries took refuge here during 1867 when anti-foreign feeling ran high.

Bell Tower

On the north-eastern side of the square in Daqing lu stands the sister Bell Tower, built in 1388. Its bell is one of the largest in China and the people of Nanking like to recount a legend of emperors, blacksmiths, virgins and ultimatums – the emperor ordered his blacksmith to make a bell with an alloy of iron, gold and silver. This combination would only fuse, so the story goes, with the blood of a virgin, and the penalty was death if the job was not

completed. The blacksmith's three daughters threw themselves into the cauldron and out flew three bells – one flew off to settle in the Imperial Palace, one went to the river and the third to this very spot. The emperor was so pleased he ordered a tower to be built, but the tower collapsed and its ruins became a propitious shelter for female beggars.

Yangtse River Bridge

If you follow the road north-westwards from Drum Tower Square along Zhongshan bei lu, past buildings which were formerly consulates and government offices, past the university and most of the hotels, you eventually reach the approach to the bridge which is the symbol of modern Nanking. The bridge joins Nanking and a suburb called Pukou, and the area surrounding the approach has been made into a park. It is a two-tier bridge: the upper tier is a road bridge and the lower one is for trains, and it is a bridge of superlatives – 120 trains pass over it every day.

It was begun in 1960 and after many political disruptions was completed in 1968. The design team consisted of about a hundred people led by the great Chinese bridge designer, Mao Yisheng. The original plan had been to use Russian steel, but after the breakdown in Sino–Soviet relations in 1960 the Chinese devised their own immensely strong steel at the Anshan steelworks in Liaoning Province. The important basis of such an operation was the unity between technicians, workers and leading cadres. A workforce of 5000 was engaged in the major building works, and in the months nearing completion as many as 50,000 worked voluntarily to complete the bridge.

The dimensions are as follows. The railway bridge is 6772 m long and 14 m wide, while the road bridge is 4589 m long and 19.5 m wide. There are nine

A stupa in front of the Thousand Buddha Grottoes in Nanking

Left Linggu Pagoda near the Linggu monastery in Nanking. *Right* A guardian on the Sacred Way leading to the tomb of the first Ming emperor in Nanking

Sun Yatsen's
mausoleum in
Nanking

Typical garden
scenery in Wuxi,
Jiangsu Province

piers and ten arches. At this point the water is 35 m deep and the piers are 17 m below ground. From the base to the top of the bridge is 120 m. The bridge took 100,000 tons of steel. In the towers on the Nanking side of the bridges there are lifts and viewing platforms, as well as spacious lounges and facilities for tea.

Until the bridge was completed there was a ferry service across the river, but now only two boats are in operation. Whole trains used to be ferried across the river – the Shanghai–Nanking railway was opened in the early part of this century. The bridge is 380 km from the sea, and downstream from it is a small shipyard. If your only encounter with the Yangtse River Bridge at Nanking is to be crossing it on your way to or from Shanghai, it will be announced with a great fanfare of martial music, followed by information relayed over the train's public address system about the construction and dimensions of the bridge.

Xuanwu Lake

Situated in the north-east corner of the city, just outside the old city wall, Xuanwu hu is a natural lake. It is Nanking's version of Loch Ness, for the meaning of Xuanwu is Black Dragon, and a black dragon was said to emerge from the water from time to time. The lake is connected to the Yangtse by a small tributary, and the Song dynasty Emperor Xiao wu is said to have reviewed his navy here in 463. When the park was first opened to the public in 1911 it was called Five Continents Park, after the five connected islands in the lake. It is on these that the main features of this park are arranged with stages – including one floating stage for festive occasions, a Tang-style tea house and restaurant, exhibition pavilions for flower shows, a small zoo, and boating facilities. On the eastern banks of the lake stands Jiuhua Pagoda; there is a swimming pool on the north-west bank and from Liangzhou Island it is possible to take a ferry to the station, entered from Xuanwu men.

Mochou Park

Travelling north on Zhonghua lu, you take a left turn along Mochou lu, to Shuixi Gate and Mochou Park, whose name can best be translated as 'sans-souci'. You will also cross the Qinhuai River, a tributary of the Yangtse much written about by early poets.

One of the oldest parks in Nanking, it has many legends surrounding it. The lake covers an area of 500 *mu* and the park 200 *mu*; the lake is full of lotus flowers and offers boating facilities, and from the park you can look across to the ruins of the Stone City built into the corner of Qingliang Mount. The park is a harmonious arrangement of galleries, hexagonal windows, courtyards, pavilions and willows, and is named after a beautiful and talented peasant girl from Luoyang, who was given in marriage to a wealthy, high-ranking family in Nanking in the fifth century. She lived a comfortable and luxurious life with the Lu family, but, longing for her childhood sweetheart, she eventually died of a broken heart. A small courtyard contains her statue, built around a hundred years ago, a poem engraved on a tablet in the wall, attributed to the emperor Liang Wu di, and another by the ubiquitous Guo Moruo, written in 1964, comparing the plight of Mochou with the freedom of the modern Chinese woman.

Adjacent to the courtyard with the statue of Mochou is the Winning at Chess Pavilion. The downstairs room is arranged as a canteen, while the upstairs one is arranged in perfect Qing style, with high-backed carved wooden chairs and paintings from Yangzhou, as well as paintings by the brother of the last Qing emperor. At the beginning of the Ming dynasty Zhu Yuanzhang, the first emperor, used to come to this lake to play chess, challenged by one of his generals, a certain Xu Da. Since the general allowed the emperor to win the emperor gave him his lake, which remained in the family until 1958, when the municipal government bought back much of the lake, extended it, and opened it to the public.

Zhonghua Gate

Returning from Mochou Park you will come to Zhonghua lu. Follow it southwards until you reach the southern wall of the city with the Zhonghua Gate, which consists of three enclosures capable of holding 3000 men; each enclosure has its own gate. It was built in the early years of the Ming dynasty and is the biggest city gate in China.

Yuhua tai (Terrace of the Rain of Flowers)

Beyond the gate is another park area, known as Yuhua tai – a beauty spot where previously you could find brightly coloured stones lying on the side of the hill (they are now on sale in Nanking and are usually displayed in bowls of water to show off their colours to best advantage). The hill takes its name from a legend: a monk once recited his *sutras*, it is said, and moved the gods to tears which, when they fell, turned into flowers and then into coloured stones.

There is also a monument here to the People's Revolutionary Martyrs, since between 1927 and 1949 this was the execution ground of the Guomin dang and over 100,000 people lost their lives here.

There are also streams and wells here, and formerly there were temples and the previously mentioned Porcelain Pagoda.

Taiping Museum

Retracing your steps northwards along Zhonghua Road you will come to the Exhibition Hall of the History of the Taiping Rebellion. Set in beautiful grounds with fountains and rockeries, it was formerly the residence of the Taiping leader's assistant. Under the Guomin dang it was used as a ministerial building, and was later converted for use as police headquarters. In 1959 it became a museum tracing the beginnings of the Taiping Rebellion, showing details of their life and laws.

Meiyuan xin cun (Plum Blossom Garden New Village)

Continuing northwards along Taiping lu into the residential quarter of Nanking, you reach No.17 and No.3 Meiyuan xin cun, where the Communist Party had its headquarters in 1936. It is usually only visited by those who have a particular interest in the history of the Chinese Revolution, and for political reasons remained closed until 1979. In this small street were the office and living quarters of the delegation of the Chinese Communist Party between May 1946 and March 1947, the period during which the Communists, Chiang Kaishek and the United States tried to achieve a *modus vivendi*. At No.30 are the office, reception room and bedroom of Zhou Enlai and his wife Deng Yingchao, in No.135 the office and bedroom of Dong Biwu and Liao Zhengzhi. No.17 contained the offices from which foreign affairs, military affairs, information, women's work, advisory and telecommunications groups operated, and where press conferences were held. The windows from which the Guomin dang spied on Communist Party activities are also pointed out. The visit round the houses is completed by a pictorial exhibition of the progress of the Chongqing negotiations. *Xinhua ribao (New China Daily)* was started here and is still published in Nanking. The exhibition room documents the history of the agreements and struggles between the Communists and the Guomin dang.

In *Changjiang lu* is the site of the former residence of the Taiping leader, Hong Xiuquan, and later of Chiang Kaishek. The grounds are most attractive and there is a 'marble boat'.

Nanking Museum

The museum is housed in a purpose-built pink-walled Tang-style 1933 building at the eastern end of Zhongshan dong lu, just inside the city gate. It consists of a permanent exhibition which covers the history of the area from 600,000 years ago to the May Fourth Movement. A further room to the left of the entrance and main building holds specialist exhibitions throughout the year.

The exhibits begin with pieces dating back to the period of Lantian Man. The earliest discoveries from the Nanking area date back some 5000 years and were excavated at Yinyangying in 1956; they include stone tools, pottery, burnt rice, jade, jewellery, as well as evidence of early weaving methods and the beginnings of domestication of animals.

From 4000 years ago artefacts are displayed which belong to the beginning of the Bronze Age, for example the first oracle bones and vessels with characters inside delineating property and rank. Most of the population then lived in the north of the province. From the Warring States period there is bronze ware – not only the usual ritual vessels but also decorative bronze deer and mirrors.

One of the best-known exhibits is the Jade Princess; discovered in Xuzhou in the north of Jiangsu in 1970, the princess dates back 1800 years to the Han dynasty and wears a suit made from 2600 pieces of jade. The figure is often on loan to other museums. Also from the Han dynasty there are exhibits which are associated with Hua Tuo (141–203) the surgeon from Xuzhou who was responsible for the early use of anaesthetics.

Maps show the various sites of Nanking and its reign as capital from the Six Dynasties (229–589) and the southern Tang dynasty (937–75), when it was known as Jinling, to the beginning of the Ming dynasty when it was called Nanking for the first time (1368–1409) and the eleven years under the Taipings when it was known as the Heavenly Capital (1853–64). Maps show how the city was connected to Persia and the Middle East during the southern and northern dynasties via the Silk Route, and many funerary objects excavated from tombs of this period are on display.

There is a feature on the nearby town of Yangzhou, which was a major international trade and cultural centre during the Tang dynasty. Porcelain and copper mirrors are on show. Among other exhibits are a description of the construction of the Grand Canal from Peking to Hangzhou, begun during the Warring States period and continued in the Yuan and Sui dynasties; a display relating to the monk Jian Zheng, who took Chinese culture, architecture, music and medicine to Japan from Yangzhou in the eighth century; examples of Song dynasty lacquerware and of major scientific discoveries such as block printing, the compass and gunpowder; examples of the famous terracotta pottery from Yixing near Lake Tai, the pottery capital which first became important in the Ming dynasty. There are funeral objects taken from the grave of a general buried outside Zhong hua men, Yangzhou lacquerware, Qing pottery and porcelain, a picture of the rich life of Suzhou in the eighteenth century, and historical sketches of Qing dynasty doctors and writers – among them Cao Xueqin, author of the *Dream of the Red Chamber* – and examples of Suzhou embroidery. The exhibition introduces the Opium Wars, the Taiping Rebellion, the Xinhai Revolution and the May Fourth Movement and the protagonists such as Li Dazhao (founder member of the Communist Party) and Lu Xun, who both studied in Nanking for a while.

Jiangsu Provincial Gallery

This gallery, in Chang jiang lu, houses temporary exhibitions.

Zijin shan (Purple Mountain)

Perhaps the most famous spot in Nanking is the area to the east of the city known as the Purple Mountain. Here are the famous observatory, the monument to Sun Yatsen and the tomb of the first Ming emperor, as well as the oldest temple in Nanking. The luxuriantly wooded hills provide a popular escape from the heat of the city.

Zijin shan Observatory

The Observatory is situated on one of the three peaks which form Purple Mountain, on a site where the Taiping troops once had a stronghold. As well as affording a panoramic view over the city, the Observatory is attached to the Chinese Academy of Sciences. There are six observatory towers containing reflecting and refracting telescopes for observing and photographing satellites. The staff are engaged in various forms of astronomical research. The unit also lays claim to its own 'short period comets' sighted in 1965 and named after the Mountain, as well as some asteroids.

As well as the modern side of astronomy, the Observatory also contains an open-air exhibition of China's early astronomers and their instruments. The major exhibits are as follows:

First, the celestial globe – the surface of the globe is a model of the sky marked with the constellations. It was invented 1800 years ago by Zhang Heng (98–138) from Henan Province, during the eastern Han dynasty. He was a scholar and satirist and became involved in the controversy which already existed at that time over whether the world was round or flat. He is also responsible for the seismoscope which can be seen in Peking Museum.

Second, the armillary sphere: a primitive viewer for observing and charting the stars, it consists of concentric rings which indicate the relative positions of principal arches of the celestral sphere. It was first developed in 104 BC, but this particular copy was reproduced 500 years ago; it was plundered by the Germans, but returned after the Treaty of Versailles in 1919. It is held up by four dragons which form the stand.

There is also a second, simplified version of the armillary sphere, developed in the Yuan dynasty by Guo Shoujin. It was copied 500 years ago and taken by the French to their own embassy.

The gnomon, developed 3000 years ago, is perhaps the most interesting instrument because of its combination of simplicity and sophistication. A vertical shaft with a hole in the top throws a shadow on a horizontal beam, enabling the astronomer to establish the altitude of the sun.

Zhongshan ling (Sun Yatsen's Mausoleum)

Sun Yatsen's tomb, which dominates the southern slope of Purple Mountain, is on the site of the decisive battles that overthrew the Manchus; it was Sun's wish to be buried here. The blue roofs of the mausoleum can be seen from the city and the tomb itself is reached by an imposing white stone stairway of 392 steps, lined with dark evergreens; it is approximately 158 m above sea-level and 73 m above flat ground.

Sun Yatsen died in 1925; the construction of the mausoleum began in

1926 and was completed in 1929. It was designed by a young architect called Lu Yanzhi, who died before it was completed at a cost of over 2 million dollars. There is a ceremonial arch at the bottom of the steps carved with the characters 'bo ai', meaning universal love.

After a climb of 229 steps you reach the memorial hall, containing a white marble statue of Sun Yatsen; around the plinth are bas-relief scenes from his life with his manifesto for the Republic, 'General Programme for National Reconstruction', carved in gold on black marble. The highest building contains the coffin of Sun Yatsen in the burial chamber, a prone stone effigy of Sun Yatsen and a sign bearing the phrase 'Tianxia wei gong', which embodied Sun Yatsen's principle – 'Everything under heaven is for everybody'.

Ming Xiao ling (Tomb of the First Emperor)

Also on Purple Mountain is the tomb of the first Ming Emperor, Zhu Yuanzhang, who elected to be buried here in 1398. As with the early Han tombs and later with the Ming and Qing tombs, the approach to the tomb should really be straight, but this one makes a detour around the tumulus of Sun Quan – emperor of the Eastern Wu. The Ming emperor was given the choice of mowing the approach straight through the mound, but he elected to keep Sun Quan as a guardian. The tomb itself has now fallen into disrepair, as have all the buildings around it, although at the end of the tomb avenue traces of pillar bases may still be found. The sacred way with the ranks of animals and officials, is intact, although the style is coarser and the statues bigger than in Peking.

Linggu Temple

This temple is past the spot where Sun Yatsen's Mausoleum stands. It still houses practising monks, has been here for 600 years, and was originally on the site of the Ming Tomb.

Beamless Hall

To the left of the temple is the Beamless Hall (Wuliang dian) built between 1376 and 1382. It has no central beam, but the bricks form a self-supporting arch; the mortar is an exotic concoction of lime and glutinous rice. The building was originally used for storing Buddhist *sutras*. During the Taiping Rebellion it was used as a garrison and under the Nationalists it was where the party commemorated its dead.

Linggu Pagoda

Behind the Beamless Hall, through a garden and two side gates – the charm of this whole area derives from its lack of cultivation and genteel dilapidation, giving a greater sense of the past than the carefully manicured areas of Peking – is the Linggu Pagoda. There has been a pagoda in this area since the Liang dynasty (fourth century AD). It was removed to make room for the Ming Tomb, was rebuilt later in the Ming dynasty and again in 1929. A spiral staircase takes you to the top of the nine storeys; the pagoda, hexagonal with balconies, is 60 m high.

Other Sites of Historical Interest

Nanking abounds in historical relics which are only gradually being brought to the attention of the public. These include tombs of the emperors of the Six Dynasties, with vivid guardian statues, and foundations of the Ming dynasty palace.

The Thousand Buddha Grottoes

These date from the Qi dynasty (479–502). In front of them is a stupa containing Buddhist relics, dating from the Sui dynasty and carved with tales from the life of Sakyamuni, the founder of Buddhism.

Southern Tang Tombs

There are two tombs belonging to the first and second Tang emperors who ruled from 937–975. These feature some well-preserved murals and bas reliefs.

Downtown Nanking

Following Zhongshan lu southwards from Drum Tower Square, you approach Xinjiekou (new crossroads), the downtown area of Nanking. Here you will find the post office, bank, antique store and local department stores. To the west of this area is the Wutai shan Sports Stadium, Qingliang shan (Cool Mountain), and the ruins of the Stone City. Following the road westwards from Xinjiekou you come to the medical centre of Nanking, containing the Institute of Traditional Medicine, one of the best in the country, and the school of General Medicine.

Theatre

Jiangsu province boasts several different kinds of local opera – the Yangzhou opera is the best known. Nanking has its own Peking Opera Troupe and acrobatics team; its Little Red Guards are known all over the country for their performances and have even played in Romania.

How to Get There

Nanking is 1157 km from Peking. You can get there by rail or air or river boat from Sichuan and the Upper Yangtse, and there are also direct flights from Hong Kong. The airport is 13 km south-east of the city and the main railway station is on the northern side of the city; a larger new one is planned.

Useful Addresses

CAAC
76 Zhongshan dong lu
Tel. 43378

Luxingshe
313 Zhongshan bei lu
Tel. 85153

Post Office
25 Zhongshan lu

Bank of China
Xinjiekou
Zhongshan dong lu

Hospital

If you fall ill in Nanking you will be in very good hands as it is a major medical centre. The hospital for foreigners is the Gongren yiyuan in Guangzhou lu.

Shopping

The main shopping area is around Xinjiekou, where you will find the department store, the Bank of China and main post office; there is an antique store in Hanzhong lu. Most shops are open seven days a week; they often close for lunch at midday and reopen between 2 and 8 pm. For those staying in hotels in North Zhongshan Road there are some shops around Shanxi lu Square.

The friendship store is at 360 Daqing-lu, opposite the Bell Tower. On the first floor is a material shop. The store has a very extensive jewellery selection selling jade and agate charms, also ivory and porcelain. The main product of Nanking, figured velvet, can be bought here.

Arts and crafts shop: 199 Zhongshan lu
Antique shop: 7–11 Hanzhong lu
Department store: 71 Zhongshan nan lu

Hotels

(Hilltop Hotel) Dingshan bingguan
Zhongshan bei lu
Tel. 85931

As the name suggests, this hotel is situated on a hill in the north of the city, 6 km from the centre and overlooking the river and the bridge. It consists of one modern eight-storey block and three annexes. Taxis are available; otherwise you can take a ten-minute walk to the bus stop. Amenities include a shop, clinic, barber's and coffee shop. The dining-room is on the ground floor. South-facing rooms have verandahs and mosquito-proof netting on the windows. Everything in the hotel is made in the province. The cooks grow vegetables popular with western visitors.

Shuangmen lou bingguan
Zhongshan bei lu
Tel. 59313
This, the former British Consulate, consists of several buildings – three were built in 1973, set in a garden, and one was more recently completed. You can take a No. 31, 32, or 34 bus to Xinjiekou (seven stops) or Gulou guangchang (five stops). The first block inside the entrance has a post office and shop facilities; the former is open between 7.30 am and 9 pm, and you can make long distance telephone calls from here. The shop is opened at hours when guests are present – i.e. lunch and supper. Taxis can be called. The dining-room is in a large hall and serves Yangzhou, Wuxi and Suzhou dishes. In summer mealtimes are earlier: 7–8 am for breakfast, lunch starts at 11.30, and dinner at 6 pm. In winter these times are half an hour later. There is a small bar in the entrance to the hall, extending on to the lawn in summer. The rooms are spacious and comfortable, if slightly dingy. The service desk in each block can provide adaptors, ironing board and iron.

Nanking Hotel (Nanjing fandian)
Zhongshan bei lu 259
Tel. 34121
The hotel has two main blocks: one dates back to the 1930s and was originally the International Club, while the other, built in 1955 adjacent to a school, has a beautifully kept garden with its own nurseries and team of gardeners. There is a small shop inside the entrance in the driveway. The dining-room is reached from the main block via a covered gallery curving round a rockery; it serves food in the Yangzhou style. A snack bar on the first floor of the new (main) block gives on to a verandah.

Shengli fandian
75 Zhongshan lu
A small basic hotel in downtown Nanking; near to the Xinjiekou, it is used mostly for overseas Chinese and students.

Jinling fandian
This hotel was completed in 1982. Situated on the north-west corner of Xinjiekou Square, it is in the heart of the commercial centre. It is 37 storeys high with a revolving restaurant on the 36th floor and all modern amenities.

State Guest House (Dongjiao binguan)
When Nanking's hotels become overcrowded the State Guest House is used. Situated in the eastern suburbs en route for the Ming tombs, the cuisine at Dongjiao binguan is highly recommended.

Restaurants
Nanking is best known for its *guotier* – stuffed fried dumplings – and is a centre for the best in Yangzhou- and Lower Yangtse-style cuisine.

Jiangsu jiujia
126 Jiankang Road
Tel. 23698
Serves dishes in local style.

Sichuan jiujia
171 Taiping nan lu
Tel. 42243
Recommended for its Sichuanese-style dishes.

Dasanyuan
38 Zhongshan lu
Tel. 41027

Yangzhou

This ancient city lies north of the Yangtse downstream from Nanking, and is bordered to the east by the Grand Canal. It is a picturesque city of canals, hump-backed bridges, elegant gardens and pagodas, famed through the ages for its peonies, beautiful women, cuisine, sophisticated opera and handicrafts. It was popular with poets and was the centre of the Qing School of Painters known as the Eight Eccentrics (Ba da guai). From its origins in the Spring and Autumn period in the fifth century BC it grew to be a wealthy trade centre, situated at the hub of an extensive waterways network, distributing grain and salt. The Emperor Yang di of the Sui used to visit Yangzhou on his way from Luoyang via the Grand Canal, and in the thirteenth century Marco Polo was an honorary governor of Yangzhou.

The city can be reached by several routes from Nanking. Travel by bus or train to Zhenjiang and take the ferry across to the northern banks of the Yangtse. From here it is a two-and-a-half-hour bus ride to Yangzhou. It is also possible to take the boat from Nanking. For some years a railway has been planned along the northern shores of the Yangtse.

Wenfeng Pagoda
The pagoda, in the south of Yangzhou, was built in the Ming Dynasty 400 years ago. It is a seven storied pagoda in southern style.

Fajing Temple and the Memorial to Jian Zheng
On the north-west of the city, on Shugang Hill, is the Fajing Temple, first built in the fifth century. The temple has been rebuilt and renamed several times during its history – the name Fajing dates from a visit of the Emperor Qianlong in 1765, who interpreted the original name, Da Ming, as an indirect way of praising the former Ming Dynasty; since it had been usurped by his own dynasty, the Manchus, he suggested the new name. The temple still has Buddhist monks living in it.

Behind the temple is the Memorial to Jian Zheng, built in 1974 in the style of the chief wall of the Tōshōdai Temple at Nara in Japan. The story of the Monk Jian Zheng is a fascinating one, linking the cultures of Japan and China. He was born in 688 in Yangzhou; at the age of fourteen he had become a monk, and by twenty-six was abbot of the Da Ming Temple. Yangzhou was a cosmopolitan city in the Tang dynasty, and in 742 two Japanese monks came at the behest of the emperor to invite him to Japan. Between 742 and 748 he made five attempts to cross the perilous seas. On the fifth attempt the boat was caught in a typhoon and some of the crew died; he himself became ill and was left blind, but was still determined to reach Japan. He spent ten years in Japan before he died, and was buried there. His legacy to Japan was the beginning of a new branch of Buddhism in Japan known as the Ritsu sect, as well as other aspects of Chinese culture and science such as medicine, literature, architecture, calligraphy and painting. The Tōshōdai Temple of Nara was built to his design. Before his death a lacquer statue was made of him which is one of Japan's treasures; in 1980 it was returned to China for an exhibition.

To the west of the temple is the Old Hall of the Immortals or Flat Mountain Hall (Pingshan tang); it was built in the northern Song dynasty. The poet Ouyang Xiu was governor here, and in later years his pupil, the famous poet Su Dongpo, also held an administrative position in Yangzhou and came to the same spot.

Wenchang Pavilion
This pavilion, in one of Yangzhou's

main streets, was built in 1585 as a symbol of Yangzhou's literary and cultural traditions.

Stone Pagoda and Other Tang Relics
The Stone Pagoda is the oldest in Yangzhou and was built in 837 during the Tang dynasty. Other Tang relics include the site of the Guanyin Temple on Shugang Hill, which was also the site of the Tang city; several objets d'art have been excavated and are on display in the city museum.

Lesser West Lake (Shouxi hu)
Situated in an extensive park to the west of Yangzhou, it has been a scenic area since the Tang dynasty. A poet of the Qing dynasty compared it to the West Lake at Hangzhou, and ever since the name 'Lesser' West Lake has remained. Major landmarks include the Five Pavilion Bridge (also known as the Lotus Flower Bridge), built in 1757; a gazebo called Chui tai, with three moon gates framing a different scene; and a White Dagoba, similar to the one in Beihai Park in Peking, built in 1751 to satisfy the whim of Emperor Qian long during one of his visits to Yangzhou.

Other Gardens
The Yechun Garden, in the northern part of the city, is where the Qing poet Wan Yuyang used to come to recite poems. The pavilion overlooking the lake is thatched and the park is particularly attractive at night. The Heyuan Garden is a complex of rockeries and fish ponds in the south of the city. The Xiaopangu Garden is nearby.

Jiangdu Water Conservancy Project
Near to Yangzhou is the site of the ambitious Jiangdu water control project, aimed at lessening the flood risk from the Huai River and redirecting the waters of the Yangtse to the north of Jiangsu Province. It was begun in 1961 and includes a network of pumping stations, locks and sluices.

Yangzhou's Handicrafts
The crafts of Yangzhou include paper cuts, lacquerware, jade carving, wheatstalk work, bonsai trees, wood block printing and book binding.

Accommodation
Xiyuan fandian
Guang xu men wai
This hotel is situated in beautiful grounds in the northern quarter of Yangzhou, close to the Yechun Garden and the Yangzhou Museum. It houses the Yangzhou branch of Luxingshe.

Zhenjiang
An ancient city on the south bank of the Yangtse, which you pass on the Shanghai–Nanking railway, one hour away from Nanking, at the junction of the Yangtse and the Grand Canal, Zhenjiang was always of great strategic importance during periods of civil war and was formerly a provincial capital referred to as 'the gate of the Yangtse'. It was opened to foreign trade in 1861. There are many scenic spots here: best known is the Jin shan (Golden Mountain or Island) in the Yangtse to the north-west of the city. Both the Qing emperors Kang xi and Qian long visited the island, leaving their marks and impressions in poems engraved on steles.

In the north-east of the city is Jiaoshan Isle, covered in pines and bamboo, with a tower where people would go to watch the rising sun; here also is the ancient Dinghui Temple, originally built more than 1700 years ago and rebuilt in the Ming dynasty.

Beigu (meaning Fortified North) Hill is on the eastern outskirts of the city. It has three peaks and is closely associated with the personalities of the Three Kingdoms. Sun Quan, King of Wu, used it as a vantage point in battle and the Ganlu (sweet dew) Temple recalls the marriage arranged between his sister and Liu Bei of Shu during their alliance against Cao Cao. Carved on to a stele in the temple are the words of praise pronounced by Emperor Liang Wudi when he visited the temple: 'the best view in the world'. Various famous poets have also left inscriptions there. There are several pavilions on Beigu Hill and a restored Song dynasty pagoda.

Jin shan juts into the Yangtse River to the north-west of the city. On the top of the hill is a temple dating from the Eastern Jin, a copy of which was built at Chengde. This site is linked with the fairytale of the White Snake Goddess who fell in love with a mortal, young Xu Xian, who was an aspiring scholar. Xu Xian was tricked into coming to the island by the wicked monk Fa Hai who sought to thwart their love affair. There is a spring on the hill recommended for the excellent cup of tea it produces.

Zhenjiang has an ancient library containing 80,000 manuscripts, and it is also renowned for its azaleas. It has a wide range of local products, the most exotic and best known being pickles and vinegar. There are also small white carved stone screens, jade carvings, gold and silver jewellery, embroidered pillow cases, palace style lanterns and caps! The city is also an important centre for research into silkworm breeding.

Changzhou

Another ancient city on the railway between Shanghai and Nanking, it has recently developed light industry, particularly electrical components, and it also has its own industrial exhibition. Red Plum Flower Park contains a pagoda of the same name (Hongmei ge) built between 1341 and 1368 to commemorate the planting of red plum flower trees from Yunnan. There is also a pagoda which dates back to the tenth

century; however the steps inside were destroyed by the Japanese. Local products include delicately carved wooden combs, largely made for export, bamboo carving and 'fine carving' (xike) in which as many as 100–200 characters are carved on a piece of ivory the size of a grain of rice.

Suzhou

Whether you approach Suzhou (formerly Soochow) from Nanking or from Shanghai, you will pass through the closely cultivated land of the Yangtse delta area, crisscrossed with canals and irrigation ditches. Clusters of white peasant houses rise from fields of yellow rape oil seed or purple alfalfa, and then the pagodas of Suzhou loom into view. The city streets are narrow enough for the trees to form a continuous leafy bower, with shadows dappling the passers-by below. Most of the houses are traditional in style, single-storied or sometimes two-storied, largely whitewashed or with a wooden fascia. Doors open on to cool, dark rooms, and beyond there is often a courtyard. Many houses give on to canals, which have earned Suzhou the sobriquet 'Venice of the East'. Small humped-backed bridges characterize the town, and somewhere along many of these streets are discreet doorways – perhaps only discernible from the bicycles parked outside and a small ticket kiosk, which lead to the restful gardens which have long been the pride of Suzhou, each one a mirror image of the style of bygone days.

The climate is typical of the region – the winters are dry, and the temperature rarely falls below freezing, except in January ($-5°C$) when snow may fall. Spring and autumn are the most temperate times of the year, with a mean average temperature of $18°C$. Summers are hot and humid. Needless to say the gardens of Suzhou bring the artists out in all weathers – to paint chrysanthemums in autumn, azaleas in spring, snow scenes in winter.

Today the city depends on light industry and agriculture, with silk and textiles still the most important sources of wealth. Modifying its former role as supplier to the imperial court, Suzhou has a wide range of handicrafts – embroidery, sandalwood and fans, and mahogany furniture. The population of Suzhou is half a million: the municipality extends to the edge of Lake Tai and enjoys the benefits of the fish harvest and the rich soil. A commune visit is of interest if you want to observe fish farming and silk production.

The history of Suzhou was recorded in 150 volumes, begun by the scholar Fan Wenzheng in the Song dynasty. It was constantly updated and added to, and the last edition was published in 1824, with an addendum written in 1882 recording the events of the Taiping Rebellion, when during the worst fighting three-quarters of the city was destroyed and 70 per cent of the inhabitants were killed.

The beginnings of Suzhou go back to 500 BC and the Warring States period when He Lü the Prince of Wu, by then a powerful state, ordered his prime minister to build him a capital city. Suzhou was designed on a grand scale with gates and walls. The town grew steadily and thrived for a few hundred years, although apparently it fell prey to bandits and robbers and was removed for a while to another site during the early part of the sixth century.

However, during the Sui and Tang dynasties it saw a tremendous growth in wealth and reputation, and it was at this time that the phrase 'Above is Heaven, below are Suzhou and Hangzhou' was coined. The main source of its wealth was silk production. The city expanded and there is still a stele in Suzhou with a plan of the city during the Song dynasty.

During the Ming dynasty the city was more important than Shanghai. During the Song it had been known as Pingjiang fu, and in the Ming dynasty the name Suzhou was restored to it; the city walls have now been demolished, but during the Ming they were strengthened. In the early seventeenth century an uprising was staged by silk workers against their employers.

Throughout its history Suzhou has been renowned as a cultural centre; it had an extraordinary success rate in the imperial examinations, and ex-luminaries of the court would retire here to commune with nature and each other. Bai Juyi, the famous Tang dynasty poet, lived here, and during the Ming dynasty the Wu School of Painters were the most admired in the land. It was a stronghold of the Taiping Rebellion in the mid-nineteenth century. Although Suzhou was never a concession city, several missionaries made their homes here, setting up schools and so on.

Suzhou is on the railway between Shanghai and Nanking; the journey takes about one and a half hours from Shanghai. There is a small airport between Wuxi and Suzhou which is used mainly for VIPs. Suzhou is 1376 km from Peking, 219 km from Nanking, and 95 km from Shanghai.

Gardens: General Information
The gardens of Suzhou are the main attraction of the city. Six of the original hundred have been preserved and restored for public enjoyment, and each reflects the styles of a different period.

These gardens were originally built by retired court officials, self-made merchants or landowners who chose Suzhou as an attractive and fashionable retirement resort. They built houses with gardens which were retreats from the rigours of court life and where everything was designed to harmonize and aid the contemplative life; they have been called 'microcosms of nature' in harmony with man. The gardens were often small and the entrances discreet. They were built by individuals, designed by famous artists or patrons, and often passed from hand to hand – if a family fell on hard times then they would be sold to someone else; many were neglected.

The main elements of these gardens are pavilions, water, rocks, trees and flowers, laid out to create *trompe l'oeil* effects of depth or perspective in a confined area or to reflect a 'natural' scene. Many of the gardens used to contain animals; now only a few have fish or ancient turtles. Dragon or cloud walls weave their way round the garden, lattice windows focus the eye on some particular scene, moon gates lead to bamboo groves, and galleries zigzag around the water's edge. There are tea houses with old and young drinking iced drinks in summer or huddled over a mug of tea in winter.

Humble Administrator's Garden (Zhuozheng yuan)

The Humble Administrator's Garden is sometimes referred to as the Plain Man's Politics Garden. This strange title contains an allusion from a poem of the Qing dynasty, and can perhaps be interpreted as a quiet joke on the part of the demoted mandarin Wang Xianchen, who retired to Suzhou and had this garden built in 1513 in the Ming dynasty. This garden, generally considered the finest in Suzhou, is an elegant example of the Ming style and one of the four gardens in China afforded the special protection of the state. The Humble Administrator's Garden is in the north-east corner of Suzhou, past the North Temple Pagoda at the end of Beisitalu in Dongbei Street.

Visitors enter the garden from the eastern section, built in 1955. A carved mahogany screen – produced in Suzhou – gives a plan of the garden, and this is the section where you will find tea houses and snack shops. The major scenic effects come from the relationship between the pavilions, bridges, trees and shrubs and the expanses of water – reminiscent of the watery landscapes of the countryside south of the Yangtse.

The central section of the garden is the oldest part of the original garden. Here stone-latticed windows focus the eye on clumps of bamboo or shrubs. A view of the North Temple Pagoda looking as though it is part of the garden is a *trompe l'oeil* effect known as 'borrowed scenery'. A pavilion overlooking the water with three moon gates affords three distinctive views. The Hall of Distant Fragrance (Yuanxiang tang), leads on to the gallery known as the Little Rainbow Bridge (Xiao feihong). Discreetly placed mirrors give an illusion of depth to a small pond. The harmony of a two-storied pavilion with the surrounding scenery is not disturbed by an unsightly staircase, but a covered ramp 'grows' out of the rockery to join the upper storey. The Loquat Garden is an inner garden where the patterns of the lattice windows are echoed in the paving stones.

In the western section of the garden a curved jutting rock becomes the platform of a fan-shaped pavilion with fan-shaped windows and doors in the shape of 'flat' fans. This section of the garden was extended after the Taiping Rebellion. The Yiliangting, (the Pavilion of Clarity and Magnificence), gives a view of both the western and central parts of the garden. A small nursery is run by a master gardener whose family have tended the rows of potted scenery *(penjing* or bonsai) for generations, and in season you will find azaleas here.

The Mandarin Duck Hall, overlooking a small pond and glazed with blue and clear glass, was once a small theatre for listening to the delicate southern *kunqu*-style opera, with small antechambers for actors and musicians to use as dressing-rooms. Note how the narrowness of the garden has been disguised by the rockeries which are just high enough to mask the surrounding wall.

Tarrying Garden (Liu yuan)

The Liu yuan is on the north-western edge of the city in Liu yuan lu, just beyond the former city wall. The garden was originally built in 1525 by a Ming dynasty official, Xu Shitai, and was twice rebuilt during the Qing dynasty, the last time in 1876 when it was given the name 'tarrying garden' – another Chinese pun, as the common surname Liu and the word for tarrying are pronounced the same. The garden is another of the four protected gardens in China, and covers 3 ha. The separate sections are unified by a 70-m gallery which traverses the garden, following lakesides and curving around hillsides. In one part of the gallery are some 300 stone tablets in the wall, each an outstanding example of Chinese calligraphy. In the south-east corner the main feature of the gallery becomes a series of latticed windows, each offering a different scene.

However, the garden is best known for its fine example of Qing-style residential buildings, laid in the eastern section of the garden in a series of studios and lounges. Here you will find the Returning to My Reading Place Pavilion (Huan wo dushu chu) and, most famous of all, the Hall of the Immortals of the Five Peaks (Wufeng xian guan), more commonly known as the Nanmu Hall and the Mandarin Duck Hall. Both are constructed from the rich red *nanmu* wood, exquisitely carved and furnished with palace lanterns and the fashionable furniture used by a wealthy family in the Qing dynasty. In the middle of this sumptuousness stands the tallest rock from Lake Tai, which has been in the garden for 400 years; called the Cloud Capped Peak, it is 6.5 m high. Climb to the top of the Cloud Capped Pavilion for a view over the whole garden, with the pagoda of Tiger Hill in the distance.

By way of contrast, in the northern quarter of the garden is a rustic scene in Another Village (Youyi cun) of grape trellises, potted flowers and trees, cassia and peach trees. In the central part of the garden you will discover a harmony of mountains and water scenery, and in the west pavilions nestle in a canopy of maple trees which are especially beautiful in the autumn.

Lion Grove Garden (Shizi lin)

The Lion Grove Garden (also sometimes called the Rock Lion Garden) is in the north-east of Suzhou, on the southern side of Bei si ta lu, not far from Zhuozhengyuan. It is the oldest garden in Suzhou and was built during the Yuan dynasty, around 1350. The abbot of the Bodhi Orthodox Temple built it in the eastern part of the grounds to commemorate his guru; the guru had lived on Lion Crag on Tianmu Mountain, and so the abbot named the garden Lion Grove. Many of the great painters of the day assisted in the design of the garden, whose main feature is the winding mazes and rockeries where ancient trees grow in the crevices. The garden also contains stone tablets inscribed with the work of great calligraphers. On visiting the garden on one of his southern tours, Emperor Qian long described the scene as 'fascinating', which has been recorded in the Genuine Delight Pavilion (Zhenqu ting). Among other attractions are a small zigzag bridge, a stone boat and mid-lake pavilions.

West Garden (Xi yuan)

Xi yuan is situated at the western end of

Liuyuan lu, and combines the Monastery of Discipline (Jie zhang lü si), and the Fangsheng Pond Garden. A temple has been on the site since the end of the thirteenth century in the Yuan dynasty. During the Ming dynasty it was first known as the West Garden – the Tarrying Garden being referred to as the East Garden. The present building dates from 1892 (the earlier one was destroyed during the Taiping Rebellion). The temple has a Hall of Arhats – made from clay and gilded, there are 500 of them together with the statue of the popular Jia Dian, whose face wears a severe or friendly expression depending on the side he is viewed from. The garden to the west of the temple consists of the Pond for Setting Captive Fish Free, with a mid-lake pavilion from which you can watch the fish.

Garden of Ease (Yi yuan)

This garden is in the city centre off Renmin lu and south of Guanqian jie. It is the newest and smallest of Suzhou's gardens, constructed in the late Qing dynasty in 1870 by a retiring official. The style is somewhat eclectic as it takes both ideas and artefacts from other gardens in the city. The garden is divided into east and west by a promenade; on the east side are man-made structures, while the western side comprises natural scenery.

Finally, as you wend your way southwards down Renmin lu to Youyi lu, where the hotels of Suzhou are peacefully situated, you will come to two more gardens – Canglang ting and Wang shi yuan.

Garden of the Master of the Nets (Wang shi yuan)

This garden lies just off the south side of Youyi lu between the two hotels. The name is another allusion to the desire of court officials to retire from court life. It was originally built in 1140 as the Rich

Collection Hall; in the mid-eighteenth century it was rebuilt and renamed. The garden is compact – less than half a hectare – and the east of the garden is the residential area. In the centre are a small pond, rockeries and a covered promenade. The western sector is an elegant arrangement of rocks and plants, and in the north stands the Hall for Staying Spring (Dian chun yi), built in the Ming Dynasty.

Gentle Waves Pavilion (Canglangting)

Gentle Waves Pavilion is past the intersection between People's Road and Friendship Street. It is the oldest garden in Suzhou, having originally been constructed in the Song dynasty in 1044, and was the home of General Han Shizhang. The garden is surrounded by water and must be reached by crossing a bridge. The first half is largely taken up by an artificial hill. Pavilions include the Viewing the Mountain Pavilion, and Looking at the Water Pavilion; the garden is famous for its sculpted bricks, the Room of the 500 Sages, which contains portraits carved in stone and the poem by Su Zimei bestowing the name 'Gentle Waves Pavilion'.

City Centre Landmarks

The centre contains several notable landmarks. As you travel southwards along Renmin lu from the station in the north, the famous Bei si ta (North Temple Pagoda), built in the sixth century, will loom into view. The most impressive pagoda in Suzhou, it is nine storeys high and attached to an ancient monastery.

Around the corner on Bei si ta Street, going towards the Plain Man's Politics Garden, is the local museum housed in the house of the former Taiping leader.

Guan qian jie means 'the street in front of the temple', and here stands what was once the largest Daoist Temple (Xuanmiao guan) in the city. It is some 800 years old and was the site of a busy market where paintings and scrolls were sold. The main hall was originally dedicated to the Three Pure Ones – the Great Original, Lao zi and the father of the Pearly Emperor; smaller side temples were dedicated to all those lesser godheads who deal with the lowly problems of daily life. The commercial traditions of this temple, which even in the 1930s, according to Mrs Nance's records of Suzhou, was used more as a market than as a temple, have been continued, as the local branch of the New China Bookshop was housed here while a new shop was being built.

On the eastern side of the city, near Ganjiang lu stand the famous Twin Pagodas or Pen Pagodas. They were near the former Examination Hall of Suzhou and supposedly had a propitious influence on the candidates. The nearby Bell Tower, now a ruin, was built to complement them and was nicknamed the Ink Pagoda. The twin pagodas are now used as a school.

Tiger Hill (Hu qiu)

On the north-west periphery of the city, this is not like the tidy, compact gardens found elsewhere in Suzhou. It has its own leaning pagoda and is thought to be the burial ground of the founder of Suzhou – everybody in Suzhou will tell you that you can't visit Suzhou without going to Tiger Hill. The park is built on uneven terraces planted with shrubs and trees; a tea house overlooks the garden, and every rock and stone has several legends attached. Fu Zhai, the son of He Lu, founder of Suzhou, built a tomb for his father here; it is called Tiger Hill because it is said that the tomb was protected by a white tiger.

The Thousand Men Rock is so named for its size. Nearby is the Third Spring under Heaven – Lu You, author of *The Tea Classic*, pronounced the water here the third best in the world! The Sword Pool is where some people say the King of Wu was buried in 500 BC with an armoury of swords as burial objects – others say it is so named for its narrow slope. Formerly there was a small pavilion near the Thousand Men Rock called the True Maiden's Grave (Zhenniang mu), after a virtuous girl who killed herself rather than allow herself to be sold as a concubine. There is a flat, cleft stone called the Testing Your Sword Stone; legend has it that He Lu tested a sword on the rock and split it in two.

The leaning pagoda of Cloud Rock Temple dominates Tiger Hill. While it was being strengthened in 1956 several relics of ancient times were discovered, including *sutras* wrapped in silk which are now on display in the Suzhou Museum. The pagoda, built in AD 961, is octagonal, seven storeys high and constructed entirely of brick. At the foot of Tiger Hill is the Tang Rivulet, constructed by the famous poet Bai Juyi during his period of office in Suzhou.

Precious Girdle Bridge (Baodai qiao)

This bridge, 7 km south-east of the city, has fifty-three arches – the three middle ones being raised to allow boats to pass. It was built over a thousand years ago, spans a small lake called Yantaihu, and is 100 m long.

Lake Tai

If you are staying more than a couple of days you may visit one of the communes on the shores of Lake Tai and inspect fish farming, silkworm breeding and tea growing (Biluochum tea is renowned) and visit orchards of arbutus, chestnuts and oranges. *En route*, travelling in a south-westerly direction from the city, you will pass Tianping shan (Sky Flat Mountain), so called because the mountain top is flat; here are sites commemorating illustrious visitors through history, and the Lingyou Hill (Immortal Cliff Hill).

Cold Mountain Temple (Han Shan si)

To the south of the Xi yuan and Liu yuan runs Fengqiao lu at the end of which, at the intersection of two canals, stands the ancient and renowned Han Shan (Cold Mountain) Temple, next to Feng qiao (Maple Bridge). It has long held an important place in the hearts of Buddhist adepts in China and Japan.

It was built between 502 and 519 during the Liang dynasty, when it was called the Universal Enlightenment Temple. The name Han Shan probably comes from the eminent Buddhist monk Hanshan, who resided here with Shi De during the Tang dynasty. Their memory has been immortalized on a stele depicting them as two large merry monks who were to become the patrons of marriage. Situated on a busy waterway, the monastery did excellent trade in local products; the temple was also well known for its bell, which inspired the Tang poet Zhang Ji to write the famous quatrain 'Mooring at Maple Bridge at Night', recorded on a stele in the temple:

The moon goes down, the birds cry and frost fills the air. On the river at Maple Bridge the lamps of the fishing boats flicker mournfully at each other. Outside the city of Suzhou at Han Shan Temple, At midnight the bell chimes, reaching the traveller's boat.

The bell in the temple was cast in 1898; the Tang original is thought to be in Japan. There are many engraved tablets and steles bearing the work of great poets and scholars as well as the *sutras*. The Flower Basket Tower affords a fine view over the surrounding area and was built in elaborate style on the site of the Maple Tower in 1954.

Embroidery Research Institute

The Institute was formed in 1957 and has a staff of around 200 people. Suzhou has been famous for its embroidery for more than a thousand years; there is an old saying that 'Every household breeds silkworms, everybody can embroider', and sutras have been found wrapped in embroidered cloth. The Institute concentrates on developing new designs in embroidery and handwoven silk tapestry. Other factories and workshops around the city produce embroidered children's clothes and household goods such as pillowcases. The Institute produces masterpieces which act as state gifts or are displayed in public buildings. Recent years have seen the development of new kinds of stitches, goldfish embroidered on to a fine silk gauze which forms a screen which can be viewed from either side, and an irregular kind of cross stitch which gives an uneven texture with the effect of an oil painting from a distance.

In Suzhou the main type of embroidery is 'Su' embroidery – the subject matter is traditionally cats, fish, birds and flowers; modern themes are also depicted, such as important political figures or famous revolutionary sites. The style is discreet, and subtle colours and the finest threads are used.

Mahogany Studio

Suzhou is no less famed for its mahogany furniture – some of the gardens contain fine examples of it, and there is a studio in Suzhou which produces mahogany furniture in traditional styles. The mahogany is imported from Hainan Island and Guangxi Autonomous Region, while boxwood comes from neighbouring Zhejiang Province. Major products from this factory are lacquerware inlaid with silver wire; carved lacquer screens; bookshelves; lacquer inlaid with shell made into tables; desks; sideboards; chopsticks; three kinds of mahogany furniture in the comfortable Ming style (Qing furniture was notoriously stiff and uncomfortable); and small, beautifully finished articles such as cigarette boxes and ornamental boxes in the shape of aubergines or pomegranates. The use of lacquer in Suzhou is rather special – the lacquer is made from the raw sap of trees grown in Fuzhou and is heat-resistant; the base is carved from mahogany and then seven layers of lacquer are applied, usually coloured by mineral dyes.

The mahogany passes through eighteen complex processes of seasoning and preparation, and joints and dowels are used in preference to nails, as the wood is very brittle. There is a 700-strong workforce and apprenticeship lasts three years. During this period an apprentice receives living expenses and one new set of clothes; after three years he receives a basic salary of 38 *yuan*.

Souvenirs may be purchased on the spot and it is sometimes possible to place orders.

Fan Studio

In a tiny, traditional house near the centre of Suzhou are produced some of the finest sandalwood fans in China. Delicate lace-like patterns are produced by fretwork, and designs are superimposed by a wood-burning pen. Hand-painted flat fans are also produced here.

Tourist Information

Shopping

The main shopping area is in Guan qian Street. The friendship store, at 92 Guan qian Street, is open between 8 am and 6 pm and has money exchange facilities. Local products include antiques and paintings, fans, embroidery, wood carvings, silk, acupuncture needles and Yixing pottery.

On the corner of Renmin lu and Ganjiang Street is a shop selling the products of Suzhou from household goods to cups and embroidery.

Lovers of Chinese food will look in food shops for sesame cakes and prawn egg oil. At 35 Guan qian jie is the world-famous Daoxian cun cake and candy store.

There is an arts and crafts shop at 274 Jingde lu.

Hotels

Suzhou has two major hotels for foreign visitors. They are both situated in a quiet avenue in the southern suburbs of the city, where you may step out from the hotel grounds and come into immediate contact with the daily life of Chinese people.

Nanlin Hotel
20 Gunxiufan
Tel. 44 41
This is a delightful modern hotel set in beautifully kept grounds; it is only three stories tall. There is also an annexe consisting of five small villas which are being repaired and refurbished. The hotel is reached by crossing a driveway over a canal. From the back you can see the North Temple Pagoda and the roofs of traditional-style houses. The hotel is at least half an hour's walk from the city centre; bus Nos 1, 2 and 4 from the end of the road will take you to the centre. Taxis can be hired from reception. The station is 5 km away.

Amenities include a shop selling local products, hairdresser, telephone kiosk for long distance calls, currency exchange from reception, and a post office.

The dining-room, in an adjoining block, has a stage, well furbished with Suzhou mahogany lanterns and Chinese landscape pictures. The coffee shop is opposite the reception with gramophone supplies, drinks, fruit juice and local specialities. A picture window looks on to bonsai trees and an ornamental rockery.

The rooms are air-conditioned with bathroom, wooden parquet floors, delicate wallpaper, and paintings by local artists.

Suzhou Hotel
115 Youyi lu
Tel. 46 46
The main block, built in 1958, is set in spacious grounds and has a flower-bedecked entrance. A new block has recently been completed. The No.4 bus stops outside the hotel and will take you to the main shopping area. Taxis can be ordered from the service counter in reception where you can also send telegrams, make long distance calls and buy stamps.

In separate wings of the old block there are hairdressing facilities and a shop. The restaurants are on the ground and first floors and enjoy an excellent reputation for their presentation of local dishes (boned duck, phoenix tail fish, and mud-baked chicken). There is a bar on the first floor.

The new wing consists of nine stories; all rooms are twin-bedded, with air-conditioning, clinic, shop, exchange facilities, barber and post office.

Gusu fandian
Tel. 4646
This is located in the grounds of Suzhou Hotel and is a small joint venture motel built with imported fittings.

Restaurants
Songhe lou caiguan (Pine and Crane Restaurant)
141 Guan qian jie
Tel. 20 66
Squirrel-fish, crab, eel, and prawns

Xinqu feng
Renmin lu
Tel. 37 94
Local-style cuisine

Useful Addresses
Luxingshe
115 Youyi lu

Wuxi

Wuxi (or Wusih) is a burgeoning township on the northern shores of Lake Tai. Its main attraction is as a lakeside resort, with all the natural scenery provided by the lake – at sunrise, in spring, as the backdrop for square-sailed fishing boats, or where the Chinese eye and hand have echoed nature in the planning of lake shore gardens. While the lake is surrounded by gentle hills the town itself, situated a little way inland, is flat. Many canals, including the Grand Canal, run through it and there is a small wharf. The streets are a motley crowd of bikes, people and carts, where traditional buildings jostle with new utilitarian blocks. The total population of Wuxi and the surrounding area is 650,000, with an equal rural and urban population.

The area around Wuxi is intensively cultivated under the three-cropping system, yielding two crops of rice and one of wheat a year. Wuxi also produces silk and typical of the area are the baskets where the silkworms feed, airing in the sun. The silkworms breed five times between May and October. Large areas on the periphery of Lake Tai have been cordoned off to allow for intensive fish farming; the fish from the lake is renowned throughout China, and cultured pearls are also produced here. The area produces a cornucopia of exotic fruits such as kumquats, loquats, apples, pears, seedless tangerines and – most famous of all – the white-skinned peaches, red and juicy inside, which ripen in August and September. Many of the seventy-two islands on Lake Tai are given over to fruit orchards. Excellent tea is produced on the slopes in the area. Today Wuxi lays claim to some 500 factories; silk filature and cotton weaving are the major industries. A small coal mine was established during the Cultural Revolution, and there is a small steel plant. Chemical fertilizers, machine tools, electric cables and air compressors are also manufactured here, and light industry produces household goods such as enamelware, and bicycles and watches.

The history of Wuxi is long – it first came to the notice of a Zhou dynasty prince almost 3000 years ago; he made it the capital of the small state of Gouwu (his tomb and remains of a temple still exist in Mei cun – Plum Blossom Village). During the Spring and Autumn periods the capital was moved to Suzhou, and Wuxi was caught up in the inter-state wars of the era. The name Wuxi actually means 'without tin'; the story goes that during the western Han dynasty in the second century BC tin was discovered and mined in Hui Mountain and the area was called Youxi – literally 'has tin'. However, when people came to the area in search of tin in the early half of the first century the deposits had been exhausted, and with wry humour people began calling it Wuxi – without tin.

From then on the history of Wuxi is unpretentious, though it produced some famous painters during the Yuan dynasty. People lived largely from the land and the water. In the sixteenth century it was referred to as the 'cotton wharf', an allusion to its importance as a textile centre. Towards the end of the Ming dynasty the East Wood Library was renowned throughout the land – not least for its political ideas.

The climate is typical of the area. The coldest months are January and February. The rainy season comes at the end of June, and July is the hottest month. Late August and September enjoy the best weather.

Wuxi is essentially a lakeside resort, where the object of the visit is to relax and drink in the scenery. Several organizations have established sanatoria around the water's edge. Apart from enjoying the natural beauty of the lake from the shore, a boat trip on the lake is a must and there are several attractive gardens in the area. A visit to a commune can be a rewarding experience.

Lake Tai (Tai hu)

Covering an area of 2250 km², the lake is the fourth largest freshwater lake in China. Its southern shores border on Zhejiang Province and there are seventy-two islands in the lake. Most of the year the lake is a calming sight of square-sailed fishing boats shifting in the breeze, against a backdrop of pastel hills, although at other times the water can become quite rough and choppy.

After boarding the boat – usually a pleasure boat with glassed-in sides – on the jetty south of Tai hu Hotel, the first stop is Turtle Head, a small promontory said to resemble a turtle's head; more than a million years ago this was a rocky platform in the sea. The modern writer Guo Moruo described Turtle Head peninsula as the best place from which to view the lake. You cross the Changchun qiao (Bridge of Everlasting Spring), which is particularly attractive when the cherry blossom is out. The name 'Turtle Head Peninsular' and 'Turtle Point in the Spring Waves' are carved in characters on the cave face. On another cliff face ancient characters proclaim '[Lake Tai] embraces Wu and Yue' – an allusion to the days when one side of the lake was in the state of Wu and the other in the state of Yue. There is also a bridge called the Bridge of Ten Thousand Waves. In the first half of this century it was the site of summer homes of the wealthy and of ancestral temples; later it became the haunt of bandits. Today young people swim in the coves, and winding paths shaded by pines and willows lead to tea houses from where one may gaze at the lake or at the locals enjoying a game of cards.

From Turtle's Head Point it is a short

ride across to one of the sanatoria around the lake; the patients are often seen in the vicinity first thing in the morning jogging or doing *taiji*.

Three Mountain Island is in the centre of the lake, and seen from Turtle Point resembles a brush stand. In the past it was a bandits' lair. At the highest point it rises 50 m above the lake; today you may stroll around the headland, where the breeze is most invigorating, or climb to the hilltop tea house. The two smaller islands are connected by a five-arched bridge and the islands have been planted with trees; paths, stairways and viewing pavilions have been constructed.

Plum Garden (Mei yuan)

Mei yuan is an extensive park on the slopes of Mount Xi (Xishan), some 7 km west of the city centre. The park is dominated by the curving roofs of Plum Blossom Pagoda, from which visitors can view the main attraction of the park, which is the sea of plum blossom in spring time. In the autumn the scent of the sweet osmanthus flowers fills the air; the flowers are gathered and used to produce the popular local delicacy, honeyed plums. In the centre of the garden are arrangements of four rocks taken from Lake Tai, and there is also an elegant lounge called 'Fragrance Bower'.

Li yuan Park

The Li yuan Park is built on the edge of Lake Li, a small lake within Lake Tai. The lake was named some 2400 years ago after King Gou Qin of Wu's chief advisor Fan Li, although the park was first built in 1930 by a family who rented the land from the original landlord, who was very envious of the end result of their efforts. You enter the park through a moon gate, following a narrow rockery maze of strange, sponge-like shapes fished from the depths of the lake itself. Then you go into the section of the park which is built largely round water, traversing dykes and bridges to the centre. The Four Seasons Pavilion is built in a square around water, with a pavilion at each corner — moulded stone flowers stick jauntily out of the edges of the eaves, and peach trees and willows form a border for the lake. From here you come to the Long Corridor. The wall side is pierced with windows, each with a different stone trellis design; here are tablets containing poems by the Song writer Su Shih, and the side which overlooks the water is lined with a bench. From the Long Corridor you can admire the Five Storied Pagoda, which seems to have been built in the water; eventually you emerge in the grounds of the villas of Li hu Hotel.

Xihui Park

This park is about 3 km from the city centre and takes its name from the two mountains which have a very close connection with Wuxi's past — Xi refers to the Tin Mountain already mentioned, and Hui to the mountain associated with the clay figurines for which Wuxi is famous. From the top of Hui shan and the stone pagoda you can look down on to the city and the park, following the spine of the wall which winds its way around the garden and ends as a fountain in the form of a dragon's head, giving on to a pond.

At the foot of the Hui shan is the 'Second Spring under Heaven' as it was acclaimed by Lu You in the Tang dynasty, the expert tea taster who wrote the *Cha jing (The Tea Classic)* – the expert's guide on how to plant and drink tea. The excellent local rice wine, *erquan jiu* (second spring wine) also uses this water. In the tea house on Hui shan they serve a very popular savoury pastry made with sesame oil, onions, lard and flour.

Jichang Garden

This is a garden within a garden in Xihui Park. This Ming Dynasty garden is said to have been Qian Long's model for the Garden of Harmonious Interests in the Summer Palace at Peking. Although the garden is small it makes deceptive use of the surrounding area – making Huishan and Xishan appear part of the garden, which consists of pavilions, rockeries, galleries and ponds.

Factories and Communes – Local Produce

It is well worth visiting a commune, in Wuxi where you will be able to see the commune system in operation in the most favourable conditions and inspect some of the more specific types of Chinese types of farming, from the rice growing process to fish farming and silk production. If you visit Wuxi between May and October you will almost certainly be able to observe silkworm breeding and learn something about the very delicate care of silkworms. You may also visit silk reeling and filature and weaving factories.

Huishan Clay Figurine Works

For four hundred years making clay figurines was a cottage industry of the poor. About one metre below the earth around Huishan is a dark clay, which if left exposed to the sun for a few days becomes hardened. The figures were traditionally of chubby, rosy-cheeked children – a kind of talisman, perhaps, or a reflection of people's aspirations. Today the figurines are characterized by a similar vividness and liveliness; fat babies are still popular, but other figures include characters from modern and classical novels. Now the range has been expanded to include plaster models made from moulds. The figurines were traditionally peddled around the foot of Huishan as a way of life one step away from selling firewood or begging.

This particular factory was formed in 1954 as part of the policy of keeping alive the popular folk arts. There is a small shop where you can buy models, as well as an exhibition room of the best work.

Travel Information

The journey to Wuxi by train takes 3 hours from Nanking and 2 hours from Shanghai. The railway station is to the north-east of the town. It is now also possible to take an excursion boat along the Grand Canal between Wuxi and Suzhou – the journey takes half a day. The sub-branch of the Luxingshe office is at 7 Xinsheng Road.

Shopping

Dongfang hong shangchang, the local main department store, is on the corner of Renmin lu and Zhongshan lu. There is an antique store in Zhongshan lu. The local shops are open between 8 am and 7.30 pm.

Hotels: General Information

Since the main attraction is the lake most of the hotels are situated around the water's edge, away from the bustle of the city.

Hubin fandian (Lakeside) Hotel
Tel. 2940/1
Situated next to Liyuan Lake and Park, this is the newest hotel in Wuxi and is ten storeys high. All rooms have a shower, air-conditioning and heating. There is a ground-floor concourse with post office, exchange facilities, coffee bar, shops and recreation room. The restaurant is in an extension. The hotel also houses a swimming pool and theatre. There are also three small villas which are sometimes used as annexes.

Shuixiu Hotel
Tel. 26591
This is in the grounds of Hubin fandian and is a joint venture hotel.

Wuxi Hotel
Ximen, Gongnongbing Square South
In the western suburbs of the town, it is used mostly for overseas Chinese and students.

Tai hu fandian,
Mei yuan, Houwanshan
Tel. 3931
A long yellow building which overlooks the Lake, it is approximately 13 km from the city centre. It is built on a small hill within a garden of exotic trees and plants, small ponds, pavilions and bridges. A wisteria-covered gallery joins an annexe to the main building; gardenia, oleander, camphor, evergreen, plum and peach trees provide flowers and colour all year round. There are three annexes. The atmosphere is comfortable but utilitarian, as the hotel was once a school. The hotel has a friendship store – open around main meal times – stocked with silk, agate, jade jewellery, ivory carvings and clay figurines. The dining-room is on the ground floor of the main block at the back of the lobby. You can walk to the side of the lake from here through the nearby village. There are plans to re-build the hotel in part.

Food and Restaurants
Wuxi's specialities are Wuxi spare ribs *(paigu)*, which have been popular in the area for almost 900 years; *heyeju ji* – chicken wrapped in lotus leaves and cooked for several hours; and *mianjin* – prawns or minced pork wrapped in a thin 'skin' made from flour.

The excellent fish includes shrimps and prawns from Lake Tai, freshwater perch, whitebait, *guiyu* (mandarin fish), and crabs between October and December.

These dishes may be sampled at some of the local restaurants:

Liangxi fandian
Zhongshan lu
Tel. 2951

Zhongguo fandian
Tongyun lu
Tel. 5623

Jiangnan fandian
Tel. 3651

Yixing
A small town on the western shores of Lake Tai, Yixing is about 120 km from Wuxi, from where it can be reached by bus. It is best known for the 'purple' terracotta pottery ware which you will find all over China; it has been produced in the area since 700 BC and its golden age was during the Ming dynasty, at the time of the master potter Gong Chun. The special clay comes in brown, yellow and red. The finished product is heat-resistant, absorbent and airy and makes the best cup of tea; it also keeps the tea fresh – you never scrub a Yixing teapot! Apart from the characteristic small brown teapots, vases, plant pots and casserole dishes are produced; prices range from less than 1 *yuan* to 20 or 30 *yuan* for an individually crafted piece, and these pots are some of the best Chinese souvenirs.

There are also two multi-storey caves here, formed from karst: Shanjuan dong and Zhanggong dong. Shanjuan dong is entered via the middle level to the Hall of the Elephant and Lion, where the rocks are in the shapes of these animals. On the upper level is the Hall of Mist and Clouds, where impressive stalactites form lifelike pictures – it is warm in winter and cool in the summer. Two hundred steps lead down to the lower cave which contains a waterfall; here you make take a canoe trip which brings you into the lake, past stalactites in the roof including one which looks like a moored boat. Zhanggong dong is also a multi-storey cave; one of its main features is the hole in the cave roof which gives you the sensation of being inside a volcano.

The local cuisine is excellent and a small hotel is being built.

JIANGXI PROVINCE

This province lies south of the lower middle reaches of the Yangtse. It is agriculturally rich and holds an important place in modern Chinese history because of its role as the scene of the Nanchang Uprising, from where the founding of the Chinese People's Liberation Army dates; and it was from their base in the Jinggang Mountains in the west of the province that the fathers of the Chinese Revolution established their first soviets. In the north-east of the province is the porcelain capital of Jingde zhen, and in the north Lake Poyang, the riverside port of Jiujiang and the mountain resort of Lu shan.

The province is surrounded on three sides by mountains, with passes and valleys providing access through the Wuyi Mountains to the neighbouring province of Fujian to the east, through the Dayu and Jinlian Mountains in the south, and through the Luoxiao Mountains to Hunan in the west. To the north Jiangxi is bounded by the Yangtse River and Lake Poyang. The Gan River, from which the province takes its simple Chinese name, flows from south to north along the full length of the province, into Lake Poyang and the Yangtse. It used to be one of the main thoroughfares between Guangzhou and Peking – Lord Macartney and his entourage passed through here at the end of the eighteenth century on their way to the court of Qian long.

Lake Poyang is the largest freshwater lake in China, with an area of 5100 km² at high water. The area was for a long time a favourite summer resort, combined with the mountain area of Lu

shan to the west. The river port of Jiujiang in the north was opened to foreign trade in the 1860s, and many foreigners visited the nearby resort of Guling. The climate is sub-tropical, with heavy rainfall in the summer. Temperatures in the winter rarely fall below 4–5°C, and are in the high twenties throughout the summer.

The main crops are rice – often double-cropped – and spring wheat; Jiangxi is one of the main rice-exporting provinces of China. The area around Lake Poyang is fertile and well irrigated, and flood prevention work has been carried out. Eighty per cent of the land is given to rice; other crops include rape, sugar cane, tea and hemp. The Nanfeng oranges are famous – small, sweet and seedless, they used to be sent as tribute to the imperial court. The mountain areas are rich with timber, from bamboo to cedar, camphor and horsetail pine. Coal has been mined at Pingxiang in the west of the province since the 1890s, when it was shipped across to the iron and steel works at Hanyang, and since the 1950s an important mine has been developed at Fengcheng in the centre of the province. The province also has some deposits of iron ore, and textile and machine building industries. The total population is 32.29 million.

Lu shan (Mount Lu)

While Lu shan is not classed among the sacred peaks of China, it is nevertheless an area long associated with Buddhism; its slopes, covered with temples and shrines, are a favourite site for pilgrims in autumn. An area of great beauty, it is almost continuously shrouded in mist and there is a saying: 'The real face of Lushan is rarely seen.' The highest peak is 1426 m above sea-level. It is the favourite scenic spot of the province, situated near the shores of Lake Poyang and south of Jiujiang.

The mountain has a wealth of legends

and history surrounding it, connected as so often with the great literati of China's past. Here are the pagoda and hot springs where the Jin dynasty poet Tao Yuanming (365–427) used to live, the peach blossom-lined path described by Bai Juyi, the Tang dynasty poet (772–846), and the academy established by the neo-Confucian philosopher Zhu Xi (1130–1200) next to the White Deer Cave. And of course there are many grottoes, waterfalls and sheer faces with the gnarled silhouette of a pine in the true style of Chinese painting.

Other sights are the Five Old Peaks – said by some people to look like five old men – in the south-eastern part of the mountain; others have compared it to a golden lotus flower, along the lines of its description in a poem by Li Bai. Some 1000 m above sea-level protrudes the Dragon's Head Cliff, and there are winding paths and steps past countless ancient pines. Black Dragon Pool with its waterfalls is another famous place on the mountain.

Perhaps best known of all the attractions on Lu shan, however, is the Cave of the Immortals (Xianrendong), to the west of Guling and set in one of the cliff faces. Legend has it that one of the eight immortals lived here in retreat. There is also an Imperial Stele Pavilion commemorating the visit of the Ming emperor Zhu Yuanzhang (1328–98).

Lu shan and the summer mountain resort of Guling are accessible by rail and road from Nanchang or Jiujiang on the Yangtse. There are several hotels on the mountain: the Lulin Hotel, Lu shan Guesthouse and Yunzhong Guest House.

Jinggang shan

I have long aspired to reach for the clouds,
Again I come from afar

To climb Jinggang shan, our old haunt
Past scenes are transformed . . .

So went Mao's poem on returning in 1965 to Jinggang shan in the south-west of Jiangxi Province, where the Communists first made progress in establishing soviets and waging guerilla warfare against the Guomin dang. The area is approximately 300 km south-west of Nanchang, situated in the centre of the Luoxiao Mountains, which were relatively inaccessible and strategically located between Jiangxi and Hunan Provinces. Jinggang shan is a long and difficult drive from Nanchang, but it is sometimes possible to fly there in a small plane.

After their abortive attempts at taking Changsha and Wuhan in 1927 the Communists withdrew here to build up their base in the countryside and seize the cities by a gradual process of encirclement, it was here that the principles of the Revolutionary Army were founded, where soldiers learnt self-respect and respect for others in the famous Three Main Rules of Discipline and Eight Points for Attention, which forbade looting, raping and the other excesses to which armies are prone. Principles were established whereby captured soldiers who did not wish to stay with the Communists and guerillas were given their fare to go home; the support of the peasants was gradually won and the agrarian revolution begun. By 1929 two-thirds of the province was pro-Communist and a central soviet-type government was set up in Ruijin in the south of the province.

Maoping

This is the mountain village where the headquarters was located for a time, where two base party congresses were held and where Mao wrote *Why Is It that Red Political Power Can Exist in China?*, his theories concerning the importance of small base areas. He lived in the Octagonal Building – named because of its octagonal skylight.

Sanwan
A stream flows through this village and there is a circle of trees under which Mao used to give talks. The army was re-formed here.

Longshi
South of Sanwan where Mao, Zhu De and Chen Yi joined forces, this area is now called Ninggan county. They first met at the Longjiang Academy on 28 April 1928; that meeting is commemorated at the Joining Forces Square. They held a big rally and formed the Fourth Army with Zhu De as commander, Mao as party representative, Wang Erzhuo chief of staff and Chen Yi director of the political department; the following guerilla tactics were laid down – the enemy advances, we retreat; the enemy camps, we harass; the enemy tires, we attack; the enemy retreats, we pursue.

Longyuankou
North-east of Longshi, this is where the Red Army won an important battle against the enemy in June 1928, leading to the enlargement of the base area.

Huangyangjie
Here, 1800 m above sea-level, is a tablet bearing a poem by Mao called 'Jinggang shan', describing the battle which took place in this, one of the five major passes in the area. The five passes protect a circumference of 275 km, and in this well protected area the army kept their stocks of grain and had their hospital and arsenal. In July 1928 the peasants in the area supported the Red Army in their battles against the Nationalist Party.

Ciping
This attractive new hamlet 27 km south of Huangyangjie is where Mao, Zhu De

and others lived. In winter 1928 new attacks were launched on the Reds; Peng Dehuai stayed here to defend the area and Mao plunged southwards to Fujian Province to establish new base areas.

Nanchang
Jiangxi's provincial capital stands on the eastern bank of the Gan River. An ancient city, its origins lie in the Han dynasty over 2000 years ago. In the late 1920s Carl Crow described it as a conservative town, surrounded by a high wall which had remained impenetrable even to the Taipings, protected by the city god – the Universal Lord of Happiness; although Crow's book came out in a fifth and thoroughly revised edition in 1933 there is no reference to the uprising or the activities in the soviets.

Modern Nanchang is a pleasant and prosperous city with a growing industry, places for recreation, and many historical sites connected with the Nanchang Uprising. If there is not enough time during your stay to visit Jingdezhen, where porcelain is made, the local museum and fine arts exhibition will give an indication of the quality of the products. Historical sites include the Plum Fairy Temple, which dates back to the western Han dynasty, and the Hundred Flower Islet, which is in the Bayi Park and dates back to the Song dynasty.

Jiangxi Provincial Museum
The museum was established in 1952; exhibits date from the earliest times. The porcelain and pottery section is the best, tracing their development in Jiangxi from the earliest pottery 6000 years ago to the Ming dynasty blue-and-white porcelain. It is situated at the crossroads of Ganzhou lu and Bayi dadao.

Jiangxi Arts and Crafts Exhibition
The main exhibits include typical local arts and crafts – porcelain, bamboo, wood carving, weaving and embroidery, Qinghua porcelain, jade carving, stone and ivory carving, and lacquerware.

The Nanchang Uprising: History and Sites
The founding of the People's Liberation Army dates from the Nanchang Uprising which took place on 1 August 1927. Up to 1949 it was known as the Red Army. 1 August is commemorated as 'Army Day', and in Nanchang the main street is called 'Eight First' i.e. First of August Street (Bayi dadao). The People's Liberation Army flag carries the characters for eight and one in gold on red. The park containing the Hundred Flower Islet has been renamed First of August Park. One of the best accounts of the early years of the formation of the Liberation Army and the background to the uprising can be found in Zhu De's biography by Agnes Smedley, *The Great Road*.

The main sights of interest relating to the uprising are its headquarters; the residence of Zhou Enlai and others during its planning; the site of the officers' training corps, founded by Zhu De; the site of the Eleventh Army headquarters; and the Museum of Jiangxi Revolutionary History.

The headquarters of the uprising are in Zhongshan lu, one of Nanchang's busiest thoroughfares; in 1927 it was a hotel where soldiers preparing for the uprising were billeted. This was a period of co-operation between the Communist and Nationalist forces, who had set out on the Northern Expedition against the warlords. However in April 1927 Chiang Kaishek instigated the 'white terror' against Communists and affiliated groups and parties. The August Uprising in Nanchang marked an independent stance and the establishment of an army based on Communist principles. At this time General Zhu De was as renowned as Mao Zedong – in fact the two were often confused, or thought to be one person referred to as 'Zhu Mao'. Workers' and peasant movements had already been established in the province; there were some 30,000 troops with Communist sympathies and only 10,000 Nationalist troops in Nanchang.

Ye Ting and He Long were stationed at Jiujiang with the twenty-fourth and twentieth divisions of the northern expeditionary army under their command. It was Ye Ting's men who became known as the 'iron contingent'. He Long and Ye Ting were suddenly summoned to Lu shan for a council of war with the Nationalist Zhang Fakui, as part of a plot to strip them of their military status. Ye Jianying intercepted them and they proceeded to Nanchang; Zhou Enlai also arrived in Nanchang to direct the uprising. This period also saw the first signs of the coming split in the Chinese Communist Party, when Zhang Guodao sent cables from Shanghai urging caution.

The news of the uprising was leaked to the Guomin dang and the time was brought forward to 2 am. Zhu De, as head of the officer training corps and of the municipal security bureau, was respected by all sides. The evening before the uprising he held a dinner for two regimental commanders and other officers; afterwards while they were playing majong, they were surrounded, and by daybreak the People's Army held Nanchang. As the other side's forces reacted Zhu De and his army moved southwards to Guangdong Province, met with many losses and eventually returned to the Jinggang Mountains to fight a guerilla war and begin their education of the peasants, as well as meeting up with Mao Zedong.

244

Travel Information

Nanchang can be reached by train from Shanghai or Guangzhou (overnight journeys); the railway station is in the south-east of the city. Planes go to Nanchang from Guangzhou, and there are also local flights between Nanchang and Jingdezhen and Jinggang shan. The airport is to the south of the city.

CAAC
26 Zhanqian lu
Tel. 62348

Luxingshe
Jiangxi Guesthouse, Bayi lu
Tel. 62571

Shopping

The commercial centre of Nanchang lies around Bayi dadao, which sweeps from the Bayi Bridge in the north-west southwards through the city and crosses Zhangshan lu – on the east–west axis. The friendship store is located in Bayilu. The Nanchang Emporium is at the crossroads of Bayi lu and Zhangshan lu, and the Nanchang Porcelain Shop is in Shenglilu.

Hotels

Most of the hotels in Nanchang are situated along Bayi lu.

Bayi fandian
Tel. 64207

Jinggang shan fandian
Tel. 63592

Jiangxi binguan
Near Bayi Park
Tel. 64861

Jiangxi fandian
Tel. 63624

Nanchang fandian
Zhangqianlu
Tel. 63595

Jingde zhen

The porcelain capital of China lies to the east of Lake Poyang. High-quality pottery was produced here as far back as the Han dynasty, and by the Tang dynasty they were making the well-known pale green celadon ware. However, it was in the Jing de period (1004–7) of the northern Song dynasty that the emperor sent a member of his court to supervise the production of porcelain for the imperial household, and all goods produced at this time had to be marked with the name of the reign title, 'Jing de'. The name stayed and the town became known as Jingde zhen (*zhen* means town).

The area has all the necessary resources for producing the high-quality porcelain: *kaolin* – named after the village of Gaoling 50 km east of Jingde zhen: feldspar and quartz, as well as minerals for producing glazes and the fireproof moulds and equipment for the kilns. It is renowned for its blue-and-white underglaze porcelain, the blue-and-white 'rice'-patterned porcelain, an enamel overglaze which produces a soft Chinese design against a strong-coloured background, and coloured glazes fired at high temperatures producing mottled effects and rich colours. Today there are fourteen state-run and many collective kilns employing some 50,000 people.

Jingde zhen can be reached by air from Nanchang and also by train.

MANCHURIA (DONGBEI)

The area referred to as Dongbei – the north-east or Manchuria – in modern China comprises the three northernmost provinces of Heilongjiang, Jilin and Liaoning. It is an area characterized by a bitter cold climate, great rivers, rich soil and mineral resources. Sparsely populated, it is nonetheless the industrial heart of China, with a dense network of railways, and it is of vital strategic importance because of its proximity to the Russian border. For the visitor the area offers winter scenery and landscape, and an insight into China's major industrial base and its potential.

Outside the short summers life cannot be easy – houses and dwellings are kept warm with the *kang*, the traditional heated bed/platform. Food is of necessity heavy; the staple is maize, often made into the conical *wowotou* or corncakes and banquet dishes with exotic delicacies such as 'bear's paw'.

For many hundreds of years Manchuria lay on the periphery of the Chinese empire, inhabited by Tartars and barbarians who encroached southwards into Han territory and finally succeeded in establishing the Manchu or Qing dynasty. During the Qing the Chinese were discouraged from settling here in order to preserve the purity of the Manchu strain.

The region's rich natural resources and strategic position were to render it the stage for Russian and Japanese greed and rivalry. The Russians wanted a more southerly access to their eastern-sea board, while for the Japanese it was a natural area for expansion. In 1899 the Russians obtained the lease on Port Arthur (Dalian) and built a railway connecting the area to the Trans-Siberian Railway. During the Russo–Japanese War of 1904–5, in which many non-combatant Chinese were killed, the Japanese took over the south of Manchuria and the Russians were pushed northward to Changchun. Eventually the Chinese were to regain nominal government, although the Russians and Japanese retained fiscal control of the railways, their own settlements and mines.

In 1932 the Japanese set up the puppet state of Manzhouguo with the deposed Emperor Puyi as nominal head. Gradually Chinese resistance to the Japanese grew, and by 1933 the North-east People's Revolutionary Army was formed from pockets of Communist and Nationalist Party members as well as semi-bandit groups. In 1936 it was re-formed into the North-east Anti-Japanese Forces, and by 1943–4 extensive areas had been liberated. In 1945 the Russian Army entered Manchuria and began dismantling heavy plant which they had originally installed; they withdrew in 1946. The importance of the area was re-emphasized during this period of civil war. The Nationalists airlifted troops to Mukden (Shenyang) but were gradually encircled and pushed back by the Communists until the latter had full control in 1948. Today many national minorities inhabit the north-east, particularly Mongolians, Koreans, Manchus and Uighurs.

HEILONGJIANG PROVINCE

The province takes its name from the Black Dragon River which forms the northern boundary between China and the USSR and is often referred to in the West as the Amur River. The river rises in the People's Republic of Mongolia and flows into the Sea of Okhotsk. The Treaty of Nerchinsk in 1689 established the Chinese border as far as the river's mouth; however the territory was little used by the Manchu government of the time and between 1858 and 1860 the Russians annexed the area to the north of the river and the coast as far south as Vladivostok, which gave them icefree access to the east. Heilongjiang is one of China's largest provinces, with an area of 460,000 km² and a population of 31.69 million. Since the 1953 census the population has almost trebled, due to migration from other parts of China. The province was first incorporated into the Chinese empire under the Liao dynasty in the early tenth century; central control weakened under the Ming and revived with the Manchu dynasty.

Apart from the Heilong River which flows along the northern boundary, the two main rivers which flow through the area are the Sungari (or Songhua) and the Nen. The north and west of the province are bounded by the Great and Lesser Xing'an ling mountain range, and most of the east is hilly. The climate is extremely harsh, with average winter temperatures ranging from −20°C in the south to −27°C in the north and large areas of permafrost. The summer season is short and steamy, with temperatures ranging from 20 to 24°C. The growing season lasts for 160–165 days and during this period some 500 mm of rain falls.

There are large areas of steppe and natural forest; lumbering is one of the major occupations of the area, which provides 40 per cent of China's timber, which is used for papermaking and building. The Valleys of the Sungari and Nen rivers are characterized by rich black soil where maize, gaoliang, millet and soya beans are grown; flax and sugar beet are major cash crops, and there is some animal husbandry and dairy farming. Many state farms have been established here and a large number of young people have come from other parts of China to help establish them.

The province has deposits of coal, iron ore and gold, and at Daqing is the great oilfield of China.

Harbin

The name of the provincial capital is Manchurian for 'the place to dry fishing nets', and until the beginning of the twentieth century Harbin was a small fishing village on the Sungari River. Today it has a population of 2.1 million.

The city grew up as a result of the construction of the Chinese Eastern Railway at the beginning of the twentieth century, after the Russians had obtained the lease on Dalian. The railway connected the Trans-Siberian route via Manzhouli on the Sino–Russian border with Vladivostok, and Harbin quickly became a major junction for people from Japan or America making their way into China. Though Russian supremacy in the area was eventually lost to the Japanese Harbin remained a refuge for many White Russians after the 1917 revolution, and today the Russian influence can still be seen in the cupolas of Orthodox churches. After the establishment of the state of Manzhouguo by the Japanese the atmosphere was fraught with tension and many bandits operated in the area. However, the Japanese contributed in some small part to an armaments industry. Some fifteen countries had consulates here.

Modern Harbin is a major centre for the production of heavy machinery, particularly turbines, boilers and power-generating equipment, as well as tractors and precision tools. Sugar beet refining, flour milling and fertilizer manufacture are also carried out here.

During the winter Harbin is a winter sports centre. From November onwards ice skating is possible and in January ice-lantern exhibitions are held in the parks: chunks of ice are carved into exotic lanterns, animals and flowers, and illuminated from inside. In summer the city comes to life, and people congregate in the Riverside Park which has been laid out along the Sungari River; here they can go boating, or make use of the sports centre, youth palace and open-air cafés. In the centre of the park is a monument to the flood of 1957, when the river rose 3 m above street level and the local people were instructed to build a dyke to protect the city.

Another popular resort area is Taiyang dao or Sunny Island, north of the river, which contains many sanatoria and rest houses built by factories and colleges. Here you can swim in the river.

The city fathers have emphasized the recreational side of life in their reconstruction of Harbin by laying out many parks. Particularly popular is the Children's Park, which has a miniature railway run by children under thirteen. Apart from winter sports the area is a centre for hunting.

You can get to Harbin by air or train from Peking, 1388 km away, or by rail from the USSR via Manzhouli. The city has branches of all the major import and export corporations and research institutes specializing in petrochemicals and natural resources. Local delicacies include braised bear's paw, moose's nose and grouse.

Hotels
China International Travel Service Hotel
124 Dazhi jie
Nangangqu
Tel. 33001
Exchange and Post Office facilities

Harbin Hotel
129 Zhongyang dajie
Daoli District
Tel. 45846

Heping cun Hotel
109 Zhongshanlu
Nangangqu
Tel. 32093

Friendship Palace
57 Youyi lu
Daoli District
Tel. 46146

Beifang dasha (North Mansions)
115 Huayuan Street
Nangangqu
Tel. 33061
Exchange and Post Office facilities

Harbin Guest House
Tel. 30846

Restaurants
Beileishun
113 Shangzhi dajie
Daoli District
Tel. 45673
Local cuisine.

Huamei canting
142 Zhongyang dajie
Daoli District
Tel. 47368
Western-style food.

Jiangbin fandian (Riverside Restaurant)
15 Xishisandaojie
Daoli District

Shopping
Friendship Store
93 Dazhi jie
Nangangqu

Antiques Store
50 Hongjun jie
Nangangqu

Northern Arts and Calligraphy (Beifang shuhuashe)
133 Diduan jie
Daoli District

Fur Shop (attached to Harbin Fur Factory)
88 Zhongyang dajie
Daoli District

Useful Addresses
CAAC
86 Zhongshan lu
Tel. 52334

Luxingshe
124 Dazhi jie
Nangangqu
Tel. 31441

Bank of China
90 Beidi dajie
Daowai

Daqing
Probably one of the major reasons for visiting Harbin is to get to the famous oilfields of Daqing to the north-west.

Daqing has been upheld as an example to industry and a model of revolutionary zeal and hard work, hence the slogan 'In Industry Learn from Daqing'. The oilfields were first developed in 1959; production began in 1962, and since 1965 Daqing has supplied a large proportion of China's oil. Oil is refined locally or transported to Dalian or Jinzhou in Liaoning Province. Where once there was nothing in this inhospitable area, there now exists a sizeable, almost self-sufficient township surrounded by farmland which has been developed largely by the families of those who came to work on the wells. A wealth of modern legend has grown up, centred round such heroic figures as 'Iron Man Wang', who blocked a burst pipe with his own body.

Mudanjiang

The city of Mudanjiang stands on the Peony River (Mudan jiang) in the south-east of the province. It is a lumbering centre, with paper mills. To the south-west is Lake Jingbo, a scenic spot with waterfalls and a source of hydroelectric power.

JILIN PROVINCE

The province of Jilin or Kirin borders Heilongjiang and Liaoning to the north and south respectively, and North Korea to the east; indeed in east Jilin there are several autonomous areas peopled mainly by Koreans. The south-east of the province is mountainous and forested, while the north-west is a continuation of the north-east plain of China, dry and subject to sandstorms, although efforts have been made to create a wind protection belt through tree planting. The province is fed by the Sungari and Liao rivers. Lake Songhua, with its Fengman dam, is a reservoir and hydroelectric power station.

The climate is milder than in Heilongjiang – the coldest winter temperature is around −16°C and summer temperatures range up to 23°C. The growing season lasts 170 days; rainfall is from 1000 mm in the east to 400 mm in the north-east. In the fertile Changchun plain maize, gaoliang, soya, sugar beet and millet are grown, and where conditions are favourable some rice is cultivated. Three other treasures are also associated with Jilin Province – ginseng, deer antler and sable. The population of the province is 21.84 million.

Changchun

The provincial capital stands in the centre of the Changchun plain on the Yitong River; the city's name means 'long spring'. It first grew in importance with the completion of the railway in 1905, and today has a population of 1.6 million. In 1932 it was declared capital of Manzhouguo and renamed Xin jing (new capital).

Today the city is characterized by long, tree-lined avenues and planted roundabouts. In winter the local population wraps itself in every conceivable piece of padded clothing and ice sculptures are created in the parks. The city contains the provincial university and a college of Geology as well as an impressive gymnasium. A favourite local beauty spot is South Lake, south of the city; also on the outskirts is the Xinlicheng reservoir.

The two things for which Changchun is best known today are Liberation brand lorries and cars, and the film studios, to which visits can be arranged. The lorry works are in the south-west of the city and first began production in 1956. Other important industries include food processing, diesel engines, tyres and pharmaceutical products.

Changchun is 1146 km from Peking and you can get there by train or by air via Shenyang.

Shopping
The commercial centre lies north of Renmin Square and includes a No.2 Department Store.

Hotels
Changchun Guest House
128 Changchun dajie
Tel. 26772
Near to the centre, Renmin Square and Renmin Park

Nan hu Guest House
On the edge of Nan Lake and Park

Chunyi Hotel
Tel. 38495
In the north, close to the station

Useful Addresses
CAAC
2 Liaoning lu
Tel. 39772

Luxingshe
2 Stalin Street (Sidalin lu)

Jilin

Built on a bend on the Sungari River east of Changchun, the city today has a population 3.7 million. It is surrounded by the foothills of the Changbai Mountains. There are several parks, the best known being Beishan Park on the western outskirts, with its Moon Pavilion, and Jiangnan Park, south of the river park with the Jilin Exhibition Hall close by.

On the eastern outskirts of the city you may visit the deer farm at Longtan Hill; deer are bred for the medicinal qualities of their antlers. Ginseng is cultivated in this area, and ermine are farmed. Formerly a market town and lumbering centre, in the 1930s Jilin became the base of the Japanese war industry. Now it is a centre for sugar refining and chemical and fertilizer plants. Local agricultural products in-clude soya beans, rice, flax and tobacco.

There is an exhibition of meteorites in the city. Its natural hilliness and the winter snow and ice give Jilin great potential as a winter sports centre.

South-east of Jilin is Lake Songhua, resembling a Scottish loch. The reservoir and hydroelectric system were built in 1942 by the Japanese.

The city of Jilin can be reached by train from Peking and Changchun.

Hotels
Jilin fandian
139 Chongqing lu
Tel. 2974
North of Jilin Bridge, overlooking the Sungari River, it is within walking distance of the commercial centre

Xiguan Guest House
On the southern outskirts of the city, overlooking the river

LIAONING PROVINCE

Railway building by the Russians and Japanese established the province's importance early in the century and it was the first area to come under Japanese control after the Russo–Japanese War. Like Jilin it rapidly became industrialized in the cause of the Japanese war effort, and by 1945 had a relatively dense railway network, sources of hydroelectric power, coal and iron, heavy industry and an urban population. The population now stands at 34.43 million.

Shenyang

Standing on the Shenyang Fushun plain, Shenyang is the capital of Liaoning Province; with its population of 4 million it is the most important industrial city in the north-east. Its Manchurian name was Mukden, and it has also been called Fengtian. It was from Shenyang that the Manchus built up the power base that was to enable them to take the rest of China. Nurhachi, the famed Manchu leader, established his base here in 1625, making loose alliances with local tribes, and from here waged his campaigns against the Chinese until it was possible to establish the capital at Peking in 1644.

People began to emigrate here from other parts of China, particularly Shandong, in the nineteenth century. The Japanese took Shenyang in 1905 and developed their power here. In 1945 the Russians took the area; the city was liberated in November 1948, and it was from here that the People's Liberation Army was to win the rest of China.

Shenyang is a major producer of heavy machinery, and as well as the coal mines at nearby Fushun and iron and steel works at Anshan there are a large transformer plant, steel mills and factories producing switchgear, pneumatic tools, wires and cables as well as light industry such as flour milling, textiles, furniture, clothing, paper, leather, electronics, chemicals, soap and bicycles. For some years foreign students have been attending Liaoning University in Shenyang.

The city is 841 km from Peking. You can get to Shenyang by rail or air; the station is close to the commercial centre in Zhonghua lu, and the airport is in the east of the city.

Imperial Palace
Situated in the centre of old Shenyang, this was the palace begun in 1625 by Nurhachi, continued and completed by his son and successor Chong de in 1637, and later expanded and renovated by the emperors Kang xi and Qian long. It can be divided into four parts – Daqing men, Chongzheng Hall, Phoenix Tower and the living quarters. Near the front of the Great Qing Gate, at the spot where formerly people dismounted

from their horses, is a tablet inscribed in Chinese, Manchurian, Mongolian, Uighur and Tibetan. Inside the gate are the Flying Dragon Turret and the Phoenix Tower. The Chongdian Hall is where the emperor used to hold discussions with his officials. You can climbe to the top of Phoenix Tower for a view of Shenyang. The living quarters of the emperor and his entourage are behind the Phoenix Tower; many of the rooms are now used as exhibition halls for artefacts from the Qing dynasty. The palace reflects the fusion of the Manchu and Han styles.

Other Sites
There are also some temples and pagodas in Shenyang which are being restored. There was formerly an active church here, as well as a large mission.

Bei ling
Situated 10 km north of Shenyang is the tomb of the Qing emperor Tai zong (Huang Tai Ji), also known as Zhao ling. Nearby is the tomb of his wife Poerjijide, built between 1643 and 1651. The tombs are set in attractive wooded surroundings. On the approach to the tombs themselves you first pass the Pavilion of Holy Merit and the Tablet of Sacred Virtue; on either side of the approach road stands a line of animals carved from stone, which form the sacred way. The grounds occupy 4.5 km², and the main halls and tombs are surrounded by a wall 7 m high. In the Ling'en dian (Hall of Bounteous Favour) in the Square City is the place where sacrifices were offered; behind this is the Bao ding (Precious Mound) where the Emperor and his wife are buried.

Dong ling
Some 20 km east of the city is the tomb of the first Qing emperor Nurhachi, who was buried in 1629. Behind are the Tianzhu Hills and in front the Yun

River. Two of the scenic spots of Shen yang are 'Tianzhu Hills in the Clouds' and 'Yun River in the Evening Glow'. The approach road to the mounds is flanked by stone animals and a small, two-storied pavilion.

Shopping
Friendship Store
Zhongshan lu West

Fine Arts Shop
Taiyuan jie

NB Taiyuan jie is the main commercial and shopping centre and the location of an antique store, a bookshop and a department store.

Hotels
Liaoning dasha
Huanghe jie
Tel. 62546
Close to Beiling Park, north of the city centre on Beiling lu. Soviet-style

Youyi binguan (Friendship Hotel)
West Side of Beiling Park
Tel. 62822

Liaoning binguan
Hongqi guangchang (Red Flag Square)
Tel. 61292
Downtown, close to the commercial centre and People's Square, opposite the People's Department Store

Useful Addresses
CAAC
31 Dongfeng dalu
Sanduan
Tel. 33705

Luxingshe
Nanzhan (Southern station)
Tel. 34653

Post Office
Taiyuan jie

Bank of China
Zhonghua lu

Fushun

The mining town of Fushun, built around an extensive coal field, is 50 km north-east of Shenyang. It was worked as early as the twelfth century by Koreans, although the Manchus are thought to have stopped mining for reasons of geomancy, and work was not taken up again until 1902, when the Russians and Japanese were quarrelling over Manchuria's natural resources. The town has a population of 1 million and some 15–20 million tons of coal per year are mined. There are also copper mines in the vicinity, and artificial rubber is produced.

Anshan

This city, 90 km south-west of Shen-yang, houses one of China's major iron and steel works. The steel industry was established here by the Japanese in 1917; by 1945 it was the major source of iron and steel in China but it was dismantled by the Russians as war booty in 1945. It was reconstructed by the Chinese very soon after 1949, and has since been the mainstay of Chinese industry as well as being of political significance. There are guest house facilities here.

Dalian

Situated at the tip of the Liaodong Peninsula, Dalian is 1238 km from Peking and one can get there by rail, air or ship. It is also known as Dairen (Dalny in Russian) and includes the municipality of Port Arthur (Luda). It is an attractive seaside resort, with beach areas to the south and east of the city, as well as a major national and international ice free port where ships of up to 10,000 tonnes can dock. Since 1976 it has been China's most important oil port.

Until 1898 when the Russians obtained the lease, it was a small fishing port. The Russians created an attractive city with long avenues. In 1905 they were forced to cede the city to the Japanese.

The city has expanded rapidly in the last 30 years, and the population is now 4.4 million. Industry includes machine tools, petrochemicals, smelting, ship-building, and electrical goods. The area is famous for its apples – over 50 varieties – the fishing industry is highly developed, and the local people have a reputation for being keen on football. The city has little to offer in the way of ancient monuments.

Xinghai Park is 5 km to the south-west of the city centre. This is an attractive park area with pavilions over-looking the sea. One can reach the beach through a natural cave and not far from the cave entrance is the star stone from which the park takes its name. The beach here is 800 m long and has amenities such as changing-rooms and boats for hire.

Laohu tan gongyuan (Tiger Beach Park)
Tiger Beach is to the south-east of the city centre. There is a park giving on to the beach and an attractive pavilion with double eaves containing a tablet inscribed with the words 'Tiger Beach'. Legend has it that a tiger once appeared on the beach and attacked the local fishermen. From the beach it is possible to take a pleasure steamer along the coast to Ginseng Island.

Laodong gongyuan (Labour Park)
Labour Park is a large park in the city centre, south of Qing niwa qiao (one of the old names of Dalian was Qing niwa, meaning dark mud). This park is famous for its cherry blossoms which can be seen in May, and it also has a sports ground and theatre.

Tourist Information

Hotels
Dalian binguan
7 Zhongshan Square
Tel. 23111
Built in 1905, this guesthouse has all amenities and is renowned for its sea-food – red cooked prawns, snowflake fish, and clear soup with sea cucumber.

Dalian fandian
6 Shanghai lu
Tel. 23171
Situated in the city centre, this is used mostly for overseas Chinese.

Dalian Friendship Hotel
137 Stalin Street
Tel. 23890
This is situated above the friendship store and is used mostly for business-men and sailors.

Nanshan binguan
56 Fenling jie
Tel. 25103
This is situated in extensive, beautifully cultivated grounds and has all ameni-ties. It serves both Western and Chinese food.

Bangchui dao Guesthouse (Ginseng Island)
Tel. 25131
This hotel is situated on the sea front facing Ginseng Island, south-east of the main city. Built in 1959, it has a post office, exchange facilities and shops.

Restaurants
Dalian is renowned for its seafood.

Dalian Seafood Restaurant
85 Zhongshanlu
Tel. 27067

Huibin canting
3 Jinbujie
Tel. 35362
Peking cuisine

Shopping
Tianjin jie is the main shopping area and also has a china shop and a foreign

253

languages bookshop. Visits to a glass-ware workshop, a shell-carving studio and handicrafts studios can be arranged.

Friendship Store
137 Stalin Street

Dalian Antiques Store
229 Tianjin jie

Dalian Department Store
199 Tianjin jie

Culture and Recreation
Dalian Natural History Museum
3 Yantai jie

Dalian Zoo
This is situated on the western side of Qing niwa Bridge and species exhibited include the north-eastern tiger.

International Seamen's Club
1 Changjiang lu
Tel. 23181
Built in 1976, this houses theatres and restaurants.

Useful Addresses
Bank of China
8 Zhongshan Square

CAAC
20 Changtong jie
Tel. 35884

Luxingshe (sub-branch)
56 Fenglin jie
Tel. 25103

SHANDONG PROVINCE

The Shandong peninsula is where the Yellow River flows out to the sea. It is the birthplace of the philosopher Confucius and Mencius, and the great sacred mountain of Tai shan stands here. Modern Shandong is characterized by the seaside resort and port of Qingdao, the port of Yantai, and the Shengli (Victory) oilfields.

During the Spring and Autumn period, when the fulcrum of Chinese civilization was around the middle reaches of the Yellow River, the Shandong peninsula – whose name means 'east of the mountains' (ie, the Taihang Mountains) – comprised the distant and somewhat troublesome state of Qi and Lu. Provincial identity is very strong in China and Shandong has its own recognizable characteristics – its people are said to be particularly tall, and to be good businessmen – for a long time they grew a larger proportion of cash crops than any other province. The population of the province today is 72.32 million; density of population is second only to Jiangsu, and size second only to Sichuan. Much of Shandong is on a peninsula lying between the Bo hai Gulf to the north and the Yellow Sea to the south, while to the west the province adjoins the northern plain of Hebei and Henan, and to the south it borders on Anhui and Jiangsu.

The peninsula itself is somewhat hilly, with a sheer coastline and natural harbours. The 'neck' of the peninsula is formed by the fertile and densely populated Jiaolai plain between Laizhou bay to the north and Jiaozhou bay to the south, and fed by the Jiaolai River. The central plateau of Shandong ranges from 500 m to over 1000 m in height and includes the Tai shan range; the area has suffered from deforestation and erosion.

The western part of the province consists of plain, where the Yellow River emerges into the Bo hai Gulf. The capricious Yellow River has in fact only followed this outlet since 1852 when it changed course after neglect of the dykes – amidst enormous devastation – from its former outlet into the Yellow Sea. It was the alternation of floods and drought combined with population explosion which gave rise to emigration from Shandong Province to the border

Left The Steps to Heaven on Mount Tai in Shandong Province. *Right* Confucius Temple at Qufu

Tianzhu Temple on Mount Tai in Jin'an Province

Excavations at the tomb of Qin Shi Huangdi in Lintang County in Shaanxi Province

Left A terracotta warrior from Qin Shi Huangdi's tomb. *Right* Scenes of old China: the curving eave, the stone tablet and the gnarled tree (Shaanxi Province)

areas of Inner Mongolia and Manchuria, and made Shandong a centre of the Boxer Rebellion. In places the Yellow River is higher than the surrounding land and rigorous efforts have been made in flood control and dam and reservoir building. The northern section of the Grand Canal, constructed in the Yuan dynasty in 1293, passes through the west of the province from Tianjin on its way southwards to the Huai and Yangtse River areas.

The main agricultural produce consists of wheat, sweet potatoes and tobacco; three crops are harvested every two years. Cash crops include cotton in the north-west, peanuts, and between Qingdao and Ji'nan, tobacco. The area also produces the famous *tussah* or pongee silk from silkworms which feed on a dwarf oak leaf. Shandong is also renowned for its fruit – peaches from Feicheng, pears from Caiyang, and apples and grapes from Yantai. The climate is less dry than the rest of northern China, enjoying 500–900 mm average rainfall per year, with six to seven frostfree months; winter temperatures rarely fall below 4°C, and summer ones are in the region of 24–27°C. The mountainous central plateau contains deposits of coal and iron ore, and there are also salt fields in the coastal areas of the Jiaolai Plain. The Shengli oilfields were first drilled in 1965 – China's first 1000 tonne per day oil wells – and are situated near the Bo hai Gulf, south of the Yellow River. The British, Germans and Japanese played a part in the early establishment of industry and railway facilities in the area as they fought over control of the choice sea ports of Yantai, Qingdao and Weihaiwei.

Ji'nan

The provincial capital of Shandong lies some 10 km south of the Yellow River and north of Taishan on the railway line between Tianjin and Shanghai – the bridge and railway were completed at the beginning of the twentieth century and connected to Qingdao. Today the Ji'nan administrative area has a population of 3.2 million.

Tradition has it that a town has existed here since the time of Da Yu, some four thousand years ago. Earliest records show that this was the capital city of Ji 2600 years ago during the Spring and Autumn Period. It was later renamed Ji'nan – meaning south of the River Ji; the course of that river corresponded roughly to the present course of the Yellow River, and Carl Crow records that residents used to point out a spot just inside the city wall where there is a well dug by the emperor Shun. He also comments that Ji'nan was a conservative city going about its own business until after the Boxer Rebellion. It was opened to foreigners in 1906 and soon became a centre for missionary work, with schools and hospitals and wide avenues. A picturesque willow-lined moat still marks the position of the former city wall. The city has much expanded in recent years and now boasts major machine building industries, locomotive production and food processing. Jinan has been famous since Ming times for its theatre.

Ji'nan, the 'city of springs', is above all renowned for its natural springs, of which the traditional number is seventy-two though there are really over a hundred. They have not only made the city attractive but provided water for agriculture and industry. Liu E, in his famous nineteenth-century travelogue *The Travels of Lao Can*, describes it thus: 'I came to Ji'nan, and on entering the city, every house has its own spring, every family a willow, even more interesting than the scenery of southern China.' There are four springs feeding the moat, the lake, and the Xiao qing River.

The train journey from Peking takes about nine hours; the station is in the west of the town. There are air links from Peking, Nanking and Hefei to the airport on the western outskirts of Ji'nan.

Daming Lake
The lake lies north of the old city, has a circumference of 6 km, and is fed by the clear green Precious Pearl Spring. The lake was once the pleasure ground of the wealthy who came in their canopied boats to meet their friends, and today people still congregate to go boating. In spring the lake is admired for the green haze of the newly budding willows; in summer come the lotus and hibiscus; in autumn the reeds; and in the winter the frost turns everything silver. The Lixia ting Pavilion was where the Tang poets Li Bai and Du Fu met and drank together; it now contains paintings of them and of the calligrapher Li Yi. On the north-east of the lake is the Beiji Pavilion; built in the Yuan dynasty, it often contains small exhibitions. Nearby is the memorial temple to the scholar Zeng Gong who was governor in Ji'nan in the Song dynasty.

Bubbling Spring Park (Baotu gongyuan) and Golden Thread Spring
Situated in the south-west corner of the moat and former old city, near to the Provincial Museum, the Bubbling Spring Park is the site of the major spring in Ji'nan. You can hear it bubbling away even before you see it, although it is said not to bubble as vigorously as in days gone by, since it has been directed to serve industrial needs.

Nearby is the Golden Thread Spring which comes out into a rectangular pond, and when the sun is reflected on it appears to be golden.

Black Tiger Spring (Heihu quan) and Five Dragon Springs (Wulong quan)
In the south-east corner of the city moat is the Black Tiger Spring, whose water is black and thunders from the mouths of three carved stone tiger heads.

The Five Dragon Springs are also very popular.

Thousand Buddha Cliff and Other Sites
Ten kilometres south of the city is the Qianfo ya, the Thousand Buddha Cliff, where the Buddhist figures sculpted on the mountainside date from the Sui and Tang dynasties.

Further south, on the slopes of Qinglong Mountain approximately 56 km from Ji'nan, are such landmarks as the Four Door Pagoda – a square, one-storied edifice with four semi-circular doors dating from the late sixth century; the pillars and beams are of stone, and Buddhist figures are carved on the central pillar. Here too stand the Dragon and Tiger Pagoda (Longhu ta) and the Nine Tip Pagoda (Jiuding ta), both dating from the Tang dynasty.

Shopping
The main shopping streets are Weisi lu, near the Ji'nan hotel, and Quancheng lu within the old city. The local products to look for are mineral water and embroidery.

Hotels
Ji'nan fandian
372 Jingsan lu
Tel. 35351
Centrally located, this hotel consists of two buildings, one of which was once the German Consulate

Nanjiao binguan (Southern Suburbs Hotel)
2 Maan shan lu
Tel. 23931

Food and Restaurants
The cuisine of Shandong has influenced

the north Chinese and is particularly famed for its sauces and seafood. Try the Huichuan restaurant near the moat, and the Chufengte near the hotel.

Useful Addresses
Luxingshe
372 Jingsan lu
Tel. 35351

Tai shan

Of the five sacred peaks in China, Tai shan is traditionally the most sacred. Emperors came here in the past to perform sacrifices and as proof of their holiness in the steps of the legendary sage – emperor Shun. There are many sayings in the Chinese language which mention Tai shan – 'He had eyes, but didn't see Tai shan' is the Chinese equivalent of 'There's none so blind as those who will not see.'

The highest peak of Tai shan stands in Taian County and is 1524 m above sea-level; it can be reached from Taian, some 50 km south of Ji'nan. Throughout the centuries pilgrims of all denominations – Buddhist, Confucian and Daoist – used to come here between February and May in their thousands; the wealthy were borne to the summit by agile chair-bearers. In the traditions of geomancy, if a house was built in an inauspicious spot a stone from Tai shan inserted in the building with the words 'Tai shan accepts responsibility' would ward off evil. Tai shan has only recently been opened to foreign visitors; the Chinese come here in spring and autumn, and one of their rituals is to get up early enough to watch the sun rise.

The area abounds in historical and cultural relics. At the foot of Tai shan is the Tai shan Temple, built in the Han dynasty and expanded during the Tang and Song, with its pines, stone tablets, pavilions and towers. The most noteworthy building is the Main Hall – double-eaved and of magnificent proportions, with yellow tiles and vermilion walls, it ranks with the Hall of Supreme Harmony in the Forbidden City in Peking and the Confucian Temple in nearby Qufu as an outstanding example of palace-style architecture. There is also a mural which dates back to the Song dynasty and depicts the god of Mount Tai and his entourage.

In one valley a massive rock face is covered with the text of the Diamond Sutra – it is 3000 m² in extent, and each character some 50 cm high. Near the summit of the mountain is an essay written by the Tang emperor Xuan zong, recording his visit to Tai shan in AD 726.

The climb usually begins near the southern foot of the mountain at the Daizong archway. About 1 km later you will reach the temple of the Celestial Pool of the Queen of the Immortals, where the emperor would rest during his ascent of the mountain; there are two springs here. Halfway up is the Toumugong – a Buddhist convent; from here you can see a waterfall and nearby is a primary school for the local children. Several spectacular waterfalls can be seen on Mount Tai, and as witness to the changing times there are also several recently built reservoirs at its foot. Trees form an integral part of the Tai shan scenery, from the lonely mountain pine to the cypress tunnel which lines the approach and forms a shady avenue, or the *wutaifu* pines – honoured with an official title by the first Qin emperor when he took shelter here against the rain. Each peak has its own name and story – from the Heavenly Candle peaks to the place where a Han dynasty peasant leader, Fan Zhong, had his stronghold.

The Southern Gate to Heaven is the entrance to the summit. Seemingly endless steps wind steeply to the top to the Azure Cloud Temple (Bixia si) with its bronze and iron roof tiles, and the Emperor of Heaven Temple.

Qufu

The birthplace of Confucius lies to the east of the main Shanghai–Peking railway and Yanzhou Station. It is said that the original line was intended to pass much closer to Qufu, but a descendant of Confucius objected and the railway was built further away.

Qufu itself is a small rural town which has changed very little in recent years, and it is dominated by the memory of Confucius. One can travel there by train or by coach and accommodation may sometimes be allocated in the grounds of Confucius's residence. The town has one antiques shop. There are three main areas of interest – the Temple of Confucius, his family seat, and the burial ground of the Kong Clan.

The temple is situated in the main part of Qufu, near the southern gate. It was first established in 478 BC, a year after the death of Confucius, when one of his relatives decided to consecrate the buildings where he had lived and worked. The present temple was first erected in 1104 and rebuilt in 1724. It consists of several hundred halls, pavilions and altars, and the grounds are surrounded by red walls, ancient cypresses, pines and carved railings.

The main hall is one of the great examples of Chinese palace-style architecture. It is called the Dacheng dian – the Hall of Great Achievement. It is 32m high, 54m long and 34m wide, and the roof is supported by marble pillars which are carved with dragons and other motifs. The hall used to contain statues of Confucius which were lost during the Cultural Revolution, but there is now a painting of him instead. The Dacheng dian also contains ceremonial vessels and musical instruments of the type which might have been used for performing traditional ceremonies.

At the back of the temple is the Chengji dian – the Hall of Holy Works. It was built in 1592 and contains an engraving of Confucius and 120 panels depicting his life, from the time of his birth to the visit of the first Han emperor to pay homage to him.

On either side of the Dacheng Hall are two covered corridors containing stone tablets and figures. These date from the first to the fourteenth century and are a vital source of historical information: as well as recording official events they reflect developments in calligraphy. Of particular interest are the Han dynasty tablets recording scenes of daily life.

The Confucius Woods are 1 km to the north of Qufu. The burial grounds of the Kong clan cover some 30 hectares and contain over 1000 tombstones as well as stone-carved guardian figures and larger tombstones commemorating a particularly important clan member. In the north-west of these grounds are the tombs of Confucius, his son and his grandson. Such a concentrated collection of tombstones provides interesting source material for the study of genealogy.

Qingdao

This resort, whose name means 'Green Isle', is built on a promontory facing the Yellow Sea on the south of the Shangdong peninsula and the edge of Jiaozhou Bay. Its great charm lies in the fact that it is one of the few seaside resorts in China with a recognizable promenade, long sandy beaches and piers like those at Brighton but with Chinese influence reflected in the pier head building. Other visual attractions are the white sails of the recently established Qingdao Sailing Club and the pleasant, tree-lined streets. Many buildings have a German aspect, reflecting the city's colonial past, with shuttered windows, neo-Gothic turrets and red roofs; the railway station is quite distinctive.

Modern Qingdao is the largest city in Shandong province with a total population of 3 million (of which 1.04 million are concentrated in the city centre). It has an icefree harbour and is a major national and international port. Its industry includes steel, diesel locomotives, tractors, machine tools, generators, television sets, wristwatches, cameras and precision equipment; one other product which has acquired particular fame is Qingdao beer.

Qingdao was originally a small fishing village with an excellent natural harbour, which developed in the commercial age of the Song dynasty as a transportation centre. It was one of those important sites on the eastern seaboard whose potential was quickly recognized by foreigners, ever increasing their foothold in China. It was speedily thrown into the twentieth century with the completion of railways and establishment of modern industry. In 1891 a fortress was built here by the Chinese. The Germans had long had their eye on Qingdao as a suitable naval base. After a seemingly engineered incident in an area where anti-missionary feeling was strong, in which two German missionaries were killed, the Germans landed troops and acquired a ninety-nine-year lease on the port. They set about establishing a naval base, built a new pier and dock, and a railway to Ji'nan. Thus they displaced the role of the Chinese transport system and by working with imported cotton yarn put out of business the cottage industry in spinning and weaving.

The Japanese too had designs on Qingdao, and at the beginning of World War I demanded that it be given over to them – one of the triggers of the May Fourth Movement was indignation at the fact that cities such as Qingdao had not been returned to the Chinese after the Treaty of Versailles but were kept by the Japanese. Eventually Qingdao was returned to the Chinese in 1922 by the Washington Conference, although an overseas community contrived to thrive there.

While Qingdao is above all a seaside resort, the town itself is pleasant. Much of the architecture reflects German influence: the station, the church and various other buildings were built with elaborate detail, similar to the Baroque style. There are many miles of beach around Qingdao, parts of which have been specially prepared for bathing.

To the south of the main street, Zhongshan lu, is the 440m pier which leads to the Huilan pavilion overlooking the sea and the small island with a lighthouse known as Little Qingdao. To the east of the pier is the Lu Xun Park, originally laid out in 1930, but renamed after 1949. The park is thickly wooded and there are many pavilions; open air concerts and shows are staged there in the summer. Also in the grounds of the Lu Xun Park is a large building reminiscent of a fortress – this is the Qingdao Aquarium (Qingdao haichan bowuguan). Qingdao is one of the major centres in China for the study of oceanography.

Zhongshan Park, set back from the seashore, is the largest park and was originally a nursery. Part of the park is still used as such and there is also a temple – the Zhan shan Temple.

There are about 200 sanatoria in the Qingdao area, to the east of the main bathing beach. The roads where they are situated are all named after famous Chinese passes and the area is called the Eight Great Passes Sanatoria District.

While in Qingdao beer drinkers may arrange to visit the Qingdao brewery, and it is also possible to visit handicraft studios in the area.

Laoshan

The mineral water produced here is the most famous water in China. Situated 75 km east of Qingdao, Lao shan (Lao Mountain) itself is a beautiful scenic spot with woods and waterfalls and springs overlooking the sea. There is a bottling plant, and the water is also used in brewing Qingdao beer. The local granite is used in building. There are several old buildings, the oldest being the Taiping Palace which dates from early Song. There is also a large Daoist temple.

Jimo Hot Springs

75 km north-east of Qingdao, the water and mud here are considered to be beneficial for many skin and bone complaints. The average temperature of the water can be as much as 90°C, but it is usually maintained at 37°C.

Tourist Information

You can get to Qingdao by train from Jinan or by boat from Shanghai and Dalian. There are good rail connections to and from all major cities via Jinan. As mentioned above, international cruise ships also berth here.

Useful Addresses
Luxingshe (sub-branch)
9 Nan hai lu

Hotels
Huiquan binguan
9 Nan hai lu
Tel. 25216
This was completed in 1979 and overlooks No. 1 beach. It has all amenities.

Zhanqiao Guesthouse
31 Taiping lu
Tel. 27402
This is a small hotel on the sea front near to the station.

Ying binguan
45 Long shan lu
Tel. 26120
This was built in 1906 and has all amenities.

Qingdao Hotel
Qufu lu
Tel. 26747
This incorporates the friendship store and the seamen's club and is close to the harbour area.

Bada guan binguan
Shanhai guan lu
Tel. 26800

Overseas Chinese Hotel
Hunan lu
Tel. 27738
This is close to the railway station.

Restaurants
Haibin fandian
Guang xi lu
Tel. 24447
Peking- and Sichuan-style cuisine.

Chunhe lou
Zhongshan lu
Tel. 27371
An old restaurant serving Peking and Tianjin food.

Qingdao Restaurant
Qufu lu
Tel. 26747
Shandong-style cuisine.

Shopping
The main shopping street is Zhongshanlu where you will find an arts and crafts shop, an antique store, a department store, and a branch of the famous Peking pharmacy Tongren tang. Local handicrafts include carved shell pictures, embroidery, feather pictures and carpets.

Yantai

This sea port on the northern coast of the Shandong peninsula, opposite Dalian, was connected to Qingdao by railway in 1955 and today is used as a port of call for visiting cruise ships. It is best known to foreigners as Chefoo – the name of one of the local villages. Indeed before 1863, when it was opened to foreigners, it was a small fishing port, and fishing is still one of its mainstays. It began to be used as a summer resort by foreigners and a summer station for the US fleet based in East Asia at the end of the nineteenth century. It is well known for its wines and spirits made from local grapes and fruit, and has a canning and a watch industry. Local handicrafts include hemp embroidery and lace crochet.

Places of interest include Yantai Mountain, Song temples and Penglai Tower.

Zibo

On the railway between Qingdao and Ji'nan, Zibo is an agglomeration of several small towns which has developed as a mining centre. It is also important for its ceramics and glass industry, and for petrochemicals. It covers the towns of Boshan, Zichuan, Jinlingzhan and Zhangdian. Boshan is the centre of the Shandong school of snuff bottle painters. Zibo has a small guest house.

SHANXI PROVINCE

To the north of Shanxi the Great Wall wends its way between the hills, making a border with Inner Mongolia. To the east lie the lower slopes of the great Taihang mountain range, on average 2000 m above sea-level; they divide Shanxi from Hebei and were the scene of guerilla warfare during the war with the Japanese. North-east of the province are the sacred Wutai and Heng shan mountain ranges. The name

Shanxi means west of the mountains – in this case the Taihang Mountains. The Yellow River forms the western boundary with Shaanxi Province, before turning eastwards along the north of Henan Province.

Much of Shanxi consists of loess plateau, on average 1000 m above sea-level, dissected by ridges and valleys. The Fen River flows through the province from north to south, joining the Yellow River in the south-west corner. Most of the area drained by the Fen he has been intensively cultivated for centuries. In the mountain areas in the west and east of the province forestry and stock breeding are important. The climate is very cold and dry in the north, becoming warmer and wetter in the south. The main crops are cotton and winter wheat – two crops are grown in the south, but only one in the north – also millet, gaoliang and maize. The province is rich in coal deposits, which have been increasingly exploited since 1949. The population is 24.47 million.

Shanxi was one of the early seats of Chinese civilization and one of the major bastions against the incursors from the north. From the third to the sixth centuries, during the northern Wei dynasty, it was under Toba rule; they established their capital at Datong in the north of the province. Later, in the Tang dynasty, the province was of vital importance in the struggle against Turkic power. During the Ming and Qing dynasties Shanxi gained a reputation for its banking system and trading methods.

During the early twentieth century the province was dominated by the warlord Yan Xi shan, who modernized the province with idiosyncratic ferocity, forbidding the growth and use of opium, and foot binding, and establishing schools. His interest was the retention of his personal power, and he assumed an ambivalent role in the Sino–

Japanese War. The province became accessible by rail at this time and Yan Xishan was responsible for connecting by rail the two major cities, Datong and Taiyuan. The eastern part of the province was a strong guerilla base in the Sino–Japanese War.

The main attractions in Shanxi are the Yungang Buddhist Grottoes in the northern city of Datong, and the Song sculptures at the Jin Ancestral Temple in Taiyuan.

Taiyuan

The capital of Shanxi Province, Taiyuan has a population of one million and is a modernized, heavily industrial city, specializing in iron and steel, the production of heavy machinery, chemicals, fertilizer, plastics, aluminium, textiles and food processing; it has its own thermal generating plant. The city is built along the banks of the Fen River in the north central part of the province, where it has always been on the main route between Shenxi and Hebei. In the fertile Fen valley winter wheat, gaoliang, millet, cotton and hemp are grown.

Earliest records show there was a city here in 497 BC, called Jinyang. During the eastern Han dynasty the capital of Bing zhou prefecture was at Jinyang, and today Taiyuan is sometimes called Bing. The city known as Taiyuan dates from the Song dynasty and grew in importance as a commercial centre during the Ming and Qing dynasties. Until the early part of this century it was laid out in traditional style – walled, with eight gates, and wide symmetrical avenues cutting through the city. Carl Crow records that missionaries were killed during the Boxer Rebellion and the indemnity exacted was used to build a modern university. The railway reached here in 1907.

The first half of the century saw the dominance of the warlord Yan Xishan.

After 1949 it was one of the key areas for industrial development, on the base left by Yan Xishan and by the Japanese during their occupation.

You can get to Taiyuan by train from Peking or Hohhot via Datong (overnight journey); there is also a new line from Zhengzhou. A limited plane service flies from Peking. The station is behind May First Square, and the airport is south-east of the city.

Sights: General

The Shanxi Province Museum is in two traditional buildings – the first in Wuyi Square and the second on Ying Boulevard. Yingze Park and lake with the lakeside conference hall, and the People's Cultural Palace, are in Yingze dajie. Although many of Taiyuan's temples have long been put to other uses, in the east of the city is the Zhong shan Monastery with its Thousand Armed Buddha, and at the end of Twin Pagoda Street is the Shuangta si (Twin Pagoda Monastery). The local opera is called Jinju.

In the environs of the city are the Xuanzhong Monastery; Apricot Blossom Village, home of the famous *fen jiu* wine; the Memorial Park to the young female revolutionary martyr Liu Hulan; and the Jinci Ancestral Temple.

Jinci Temple

While Taiyuan may seem to have little to offer, the temple known as Jinci makes the visit worthwhile, since some fine examples of Song dynasty and local architecture and sculpture are exhibited here. The Jinci lies 25 km south-west of Taiyuan at the foot of Xuanweng Mountain; it is estimated to be at least 900 years old and is a state-protected monument.

Jin is the classical name for Shanxi, and the term *ci* denotes that the temple was primarily an ancestral one; it was built to commemorate Prince Shu Yu, son of Wu wang, founder of the Zhou

Dynasty. Prince Shu yu reigned in the area of present-day Taiyuan, then the principality of Tang. After his death it was renamed Jin after the nearby river; later it became the province of Shanxi and Jinyang became the name for Taiyuan.

The date when a temple to Shu yu was first erected at the source of the Jin River is uncertain; the earliest records suggest that there was a temple on this site in the fifth century, already called the Jinci. In later years the area became a summer retreat for members of the royal family. The name of Prince Shu yu was constantly honoured and he was often awarded posthumous titles. Tablets commemorate the visits of emperors throughout the Wei, Qi, Sui, Tang and Song dynasties. It was in the Song dynasty that the Shengmu dian (Temple of the Holy Mother) was built in honour of the mother of Prince Shu yu. She was attributed with many powers and became the main focus of the temple. The Jinci Temple is an extensive complex of rooms, pavilions, streams and bridges; in China it is famous for three things – the eternal springs, Song sculptures, and ancient cypress trees.

On entering you find yourself in a spacious courtyard with the Terrace of the Mirror of the Water (Shuijing tai), which was built in the Ming dynasty as a theatre. The style of the roofs is quite unique – a low-level curved roof stands in front of a higher, pointed one, and there is a gallery on three sides. From here you walk across to the Huixian Bridge (Meeting the Immortals) over the Zhi Bo Canal – a branch of the Jin River, named after the man who is thought to have built it in the Spring and Autumn period – passing a cluster of exhibition halls on the left. After crossing the bridge you come face to face with four fierce guardian gods on the Jinrentai – literally Gold Man Terrace. In fact the figures, more than 2 m high,

are made of cast iron. They have been standing here since 1097, in the time of the Northern Song dynasty.

You pass the Duiyue fang (screen wall), where on either side are the drum (left) and bell tower (right). In front is the Xian dian – the Temple of Offerings where the sacrificial gifts were displayed. It is a kind of annexe to the Shengmu dian, originally built in 1168 and reconstructed in 1955. After passing the Moon Terrace (Yue tai) and a pair of iron lions cast in 1118, among the oldest in China, you come to the unique structure of the Flying Bridge (Fei liang), built over a square fish pond and the second source of the Jin River. The bridge is cruciform and stands on thirty-four octagonal columns. There is mention of a Flying Bridge in records of the northern Song dynasty; this one dates from that dynasty and was repaired in 1955. It is flanked by carved stone lions in a prone position, dating from the Song dynasty.

Opposite the Jinci is Jinci Park, containing lakes and flower gardens, an ancestral temple and caves.

The centrepiece of the temple is the Shengmu dian, the Temple of the Holy Mother, with the Xuanweng Mountain for a backdrop, the Flying Bridge before it, and to the left and right the Nanlao quan (Eternal Spring) and the Shanli quan (Beneficent Spring). It is the oldest building here, dating back to 1023–32 and rebuilt in 1102. A wide verandah encircles the building, which has double eaves and is supported by sixteen wooden carved pillars. The building marked an important development in Chinese architecture and the understanding of laws of stress, for there are no supporting pillars in the temple itself.

The interior displays the main feature of the temple – the sculptures. First is the statue of Yi Jiang, the mother of Shu yu, followed by forty-two clay statues of her ladies-in-waiting. The statue of Yi Jiang is enthroned in a shrine while the others are arrayed in the main body of the hall; each of the ladies-in-waiting is holding something, as if to present it to her. The sculptures are admired for their expressiveness, and are the only extant examples of the costume and customs of the Song dynasty.

The Eternal Spring (Nanlao quan) is set in front of a charming, octagonally roofed pavilion, the chief source of the Jin River. The Tang poet Li Bai compared the flowing water of the Jin to jade; the temperature of the water in the spring is 17°C and it is used for local irrigation. Behind is the Shuimu lou (Temple of the Mother of the Water). Built in the Ming dynasty in 1563, it has two storeys: the lower one contains a bronze cast image of the Mother of the Water, while above is another shrine to the Mother of the Water, attended by eight ladies-in-waiting. The style is different from that of the Shengmu dian – the statues seem more robust than those of the Song. One of the walls is covered with a bas-relief mural giving the story of the Mother of the Water's life.

In the Zhen guan bao chao Pavilion is the stone tablet written by Li Shimin, the founding emperor of the Tang dynasty, who visited the temple in AD 646 and wrote a eulogy of Wu wang and Shu Yu and their policies in a 1200-character essay whose style reflected his own political intentions. The tablet is one of the earliest examples of *xingshu* – running hand script.

To the right of the Flying Bridge is a cedar tree, said to have been planted in the Zhou dynasty over two thousand years ago which grows at an angle of 40 degrees; there is also an oak tree which dates from the Sui dynasty. In the northern end of the Jinci is the complex of halls dedicated to Prince Shu yu, next to the Beneficent Spring. In the main hall stands a statue of Prince Shu yu and twelve life-size statues of ladies-in-waiting, all holding musical instruments and probably sculpted in the Ming dynasty. The only pagoda in the Jinci is in the southern end of the grounds. Called the Sheli shengsheng ta, it is seven storeys (38 m) high and octagonal in shape. First constructed in the Sui dynasty, it was reconstructed in the Song and again in the Qing, in 1751.

Shopping
The main commercial centre is on Jiefang lu, which runs north–south, and around Wuyi (May First) Square, in the south-east of the city at the eastern end of Yingze dajie and the southern end of Wuyi lu. Department stores will be found here.

Taiyuan was famous for its glazed tiles which it supplied to the Imperial household. Today there is a lacquer ware studio.

Hotels
Yingze binguan
Yingze dajie

There is also a guesthouse near the Jinci Temple, outside the city centre.

Local Food and Drink
Fen jiu wine, one of the most renowned wines in China, is produced in Xinghua cun (Apricot Blossom Village), immortalized in the Tang Dynasty poem by Du Mu. It is in Fenyang county, south-west of Taiyuan. The wine is produced with time-honoured care and attention to the quality of the water, yeast, vessels and other implements; it contains gaoliang.

Useful Addresses
CAAC
Yingze dong dajie
Tel. 27182

Datong
Situated in the north of Shanxi Province, between the inner and outer Great Walls and in the fertile San'gan River

basin, Datong contains several important sites. For lovers of art, history and sculpture there are the famous Yungang Grottoes, and for train enthusiasts it has locomotive works where steam engines are still built, though production is soon to be run down.

The Datong municipality covers some 2000 km² and has a total population of 800,000. From a map the former square which was the city wall can be discerned quite readily, although by now the city has sprawled far beyond these confines. The area is very rich in coal, and mining is one of the major industries. There is also a cement works, a food processing factory, and a woollen and tanning industry using hides and wool from Inner Mongolia.

In AD 398 the Wei or Toba, a non-Han people, established their dynasty with the capital at Datong. They brought Buddhism to the area and ruled here for a hundred years. In later years Datong became an important frontier trading town. There are several sites of contemporary interest to visit: the locomotive factory, carpet factory, pottery works, mines, and industrial exhibition hall.

Datong is a seven- to eight-hour train journey from Peking; alternatively it is the first stop after the border from Erlian. The station is in the north-east of the city. Datong can also be reached by air from Taiyuan, though not from Peking.

Yungang Grottoes

Situated 16 km north-west of Datong, the Yungang Grottoes have been carved into the southern face of Wuzhou Mountain and stretch for almost one kilometre along the cliff face. The grottoes contain more than 51,000 sculptures and engravings on Buddhist themes, set out in fifty-three caves ranging from 17 m down to a few centimetres in height.

The grottoes predate those at Luoyang and Dunhuang by a hundred years, and reflect the growing influence of Buddhism as an instrument of rule and power. They were constructed during the reign of the Tóbas, whose fortunes fluctuated and were subject to many revolts. In the fifth century the capital was moved to Pingcheng – present-day Datong – and a great deal of traffic came through the Wuzhou Pass; the emperor of the Northern Wei came here to pray, and the mountain became a sacred area. Before the ascendancy of the Northern Wei the neighbouring province of Northern Gansu, on the Silk Route, had become a centre of Buddhism. In 439 the capital, Liangzhou, was captured and monks, local officials and their families were brought to Pingcheng, influencing the spread of Buddhism. They also formed the basis of the workforce for the Yungang Grottoes.

The first Northern Wei emperor established the precedent of involving Buddhists in affairs of state – Buddhism had until then been essentially an apolitical creed. The emperor Tao Wu had a monk, Fa Guo, declare that the emperor was the living Buddha, and monks were made tutors to the princes of the royal household.

The caves were begun in 460 by the emperor Wen Cheng. In his efforts to restore the dynasty he sought to revive Buddhism and appointed Tan Yao to supervise the construction of the caves as a place of silent meditation and worship. He was responsible for the construction of five caves with a large Buddha (today known as caves 16–20). The major characteristic of these first caves is their oval shape. Their walls are carved with Thousand Buddha images and they contain statues of the three generations of Buddha – past, present and to come: Buddha, Sakyamuni and Maitreya. Significantly the statues of the buddhas are sculpted in the likenesses of the Wei emperors.

The second period of construction began with Xiao wen, who came to the throne in 471. Contemporary writings describe a thriving religious community with temples, pavilions and nuns all wreathed in incense smoke. Under Xiao wen the seventh and eighth caves were begun, and by 494 nine more caves (9, 10, 5, 6, 2, 11, 12, 13 and 3) were completed. The style reflects a growing Chinese influence and also the fact that the religion was reaching the ordinary people; the themes are more secular and decorative, and concerned with Buddhist love. The caves are polygonal, with an ante-chamber and back chamber, tunnels run along the back wall; the ceiling is decorated with rectangular designs; and the walls are sectioned.

The late period of construction continues into the first quarter of the sixth century; by now the caves had become smaller and more numerous and were commissioned by ordinary people as an offering to the souls of the dead or in the hope of influencing the fortunes of the living. Later the grottoes were repaired, the Lingyan monastery was established, and in 641 the three colossal figures of cave 3 were constructed.

During the eleventh century, when the Liao dynasty was under the rule of the Khitan Tartars, ten monasteries were built into the side of the rock face. These were later destroyed by fire in the fight for supremacy between the Liao and the Jin.

Reconstruction work began in the twelfth and thirteenth centuries. The name 'Yungang Caves' was first used in the Ming dynasty, according to records, and in 1651, at the beginning of the Qing dynasty, the monastery by caves 5 and 6 was built which still exists today. Repairs were carried out, and the monks owned large tracts of land and much property.

Jiulong bi (Nine Dragon Screen)
The largest and most impressive of the three dragon screens of China, it was built in the early Ming dynasty. It used to stand in front of the residence of the Viceroy in Datong and is now situated close to the city centre.

Huayan si
This centrally located monastery is divided into an upper and a lower section. The first building was erected in the fifth century, but during the twelfth century the temple was rebuilt. It contains five Buddhist figures, guards and gods. Most of the site was restored during the Qing dynasty.

Wutai shan (Five Peak Mountain)
This sacred mountain area in the northeast of the province, between Datong and Taiyuan, is a Buddhist centre set in beautiful natural surroundings. The first records of Buddhist activities date back to AD 58 and between the Tang and Song dynasties there were some 360 temples on the mountain. The best-known temples are the Nanchan and Foguang Temples, and there are nuns, lamas and monks practising in the area. The Foguang si is one of the oldest buildings in China, dating from the Tang dynasty.

Dazhai
Established as a model commune in the mid-1960s, Dazhai is situated in the rocky and unfriendly terrain of the lower slopes of the Taihang Mountains. It is accessible by train as far as Yangyuan, a major coal mining town. Every agricultural unit was told to take Dazhai as a model of hard work and political zeal and one of the commune leaders, Chen Yanggui, was promoted to the State Council and Politburo. However, such singling out is incompatible with the pragmatic mood of China today, and doubt has been cast on the veracity of some of the claims of the Dazhai brigade.

Hotels
Datong binguan
Xinjian lu
Tel. 2704/2607
The Datong branch of Luxingshe has its office in this hotel. The hotel is situated in the southern suburbs of the city, 6 km from the station.

SHAANXI PROVINCE

Entering Shaanxi Province by train from Henan, visitors become aware of a timeless part of China, for the land is tilled with the same implements that have been used for centuries. The people of Shaanxi are renowned for several idiosyncratic traditions – they make noodles as wide and as long as belts; they live in 'half houses', houses which have sloping roofs on one side only; the traditional head-dress of peasants in the fields is a towel; and they evidently prefer to squat rather than sit on chairs. It is steeped in history – to the west of Xi'an, the present-day provincial capital and former capital of all China, lies Xianyang, the capital city of the Qin, which was the first state involved in the unification of China. In Shaanxi are the ancient burial grounds of the Qin emperors and of the later Tang imperial family. Some of the earliest traces of man were found at Lantian. Modern Chinese history is represented by Yan'an in the north of the province, where the Communists established their first base at the end of the Long March.

The province has a population of 28.07 million. Geographically it divides into three – the northern loess plateau, the Wei River valley and the Hanzhong basin. To the north the Great Wall divides Shaanxi from Inner Mongolia; on the eastern boundary the Yellow River turns suddenly northwards, forming a natural barrier between Shaanxi and Henan; to the south the waters of the Han River flow in from Hubei Province and mountains separate it from Sichuan Province; while on the west the province is bounded by Gansu Province, and Ningxia-Hui Autonomous Region.

The most densely populated area is along the Wei River valley – traditionally the route followed by the silk traders, and even today the one best served by communications. The first railway to Xi'an was built in 1934, and extended westwards to Baoji in 1937. Extensions into Gansu Province and southwards into Sichuan Province were built much later, in the early 1950s. Branch lines were also built as far north as the coal-producing town of Tongchuan, but the fertile south and the loess-covered north remain poorly served by anything other than a system of roads.

The Wei and Jing Rivers form a large alluvial plain; the Wei River area was the site of the earliest irrigation network in China, built in the third century BC, which has since been extended. The growing season lasts around 240 days and the annual rainfall is 500–600 mm. The main crops are rice in the irrigated areas, winter wheat, tobacco, cotton, millet, maize, barley and gaoliang; oats, millet and buckwheat are grown on higher ground. The area is subject to drought, particularly at the beginning of the year.

The area to the north is rich in coal, although due to poor communications the only area where it has been extensively mined is around Tongchuan. The terrain in the north consists of plateau approximately 1000 m above sea-level. The deposits of loess soil have allowed the wind to carve a landscape of sheer cliff faces and ravines, into the side of which are built cave homes such as those in Yan'an. The climate is harsh – the growing season is short, ranging from 190 days in the very north to 220 days in the south of the area. Rainfall is low, from 300 to 500 mm. The major crops are spring wheat and millet, and the extreme north-west is given over to grazing land for sheep and cattle.

South of the rugged Qinling Mountains (2500–3500 m), the southernmost part of the province enjoys a different climate and better growing conditions. It is fed by the waters of the Han River and separated from Sichuan by the lower Dabashan range. The Qinling Mountains act as a natural barrier against the harsh weather of the north and the climate is semi-tropical. Rice is the major crop; maize, winter wheat, tea, tong oil and citrus fruits are also cultivated; however this fertile area is disadvantaged by extremely poor communications.

Xi'an

If you arrive in the provincial capital by train the station tells you a lot about the city. Bearing in mind that the railway did not reach Xi'an until 1934, it is a building in Chinese style, combining Ming with Qing, embodying red pillars with ornate eaves, and gives visitors an inkling of the mixture of old and new which await them.

Modern Xi'an is the major industrial centre of the north-west. A glance at the city map reveals a chessboard city, and Xi'an is one of the few cities in China whose city walls still stand. Built in the Ming dynasty, they were much reduced from the extensive dimensions of the Tang city, when Xi'an was one of the largest and most cosmopolitan cities in the world. Today the crenellated walls and soaring city gates rival the towers of the telecommunications building, Sturdy modern blocks and office buildings stand next to one-storied courtyard-style houses, wineshops for the thirsty traveller, and corner shops. The people here look hardy and weather-beaten.

The city lies south of the Wei River; to the east are the Li Mountains and to the south the Qinling Mountains start. The coldest winter temperatures fall to −6°C and snow falls. Spring and autumn are the pleasantest and driest times of the year, with temperatures in the region of 18°C. In the summer months the temperature hovers in the thirties, although the evenings are cool and rain brings respite from the heat. In the flat, intensively cultivated areas around Xi'an the main crops are wheat, millet, cotton and fruit, including pomegranates.

In 1934 the Longhai Railway was extended to Xi'an, making it more accessible from the rest of China. Industrial suburbs have been built in the east and west; the east concentrates on machine tools and textiles, while the western quarter has developed an electrical industry manufacturing transformers and electrical transmitters. There are large coal deposits in the Xi'an area. Xi'an is now one of the major textile centres producing silk (farmed in the southern part of the province), velvet, cord and woollen knitwear from the sheep of the north. In the south of the city are most of the institutes of further education.

Xi'an is 1165 km from Peking, from where there is a plane service. You can also fly to Xi'an from Guangzhou and other cities. There are regular rail services from Peking and Shanghai and from Xi'an westwards to Xinjiang.

History

In and around Xi'an are traces of the earliest settlements in China – from the 600,000-year-old remains of Lantian Man to Xianyang city to the north-west of Xian, which was the capital of the Qin emperor Qin Shi Huang Di, the first emperor to unite China. Today the province is still referred to as Qin, and the plain in which Xi'an lies is often referred to as the Eight Hundred Li

Valley of Qin. Since 1100 BC the city of Xi'an has been a major one, rivalled in this region only by Luoyang and Kaifeng further to the east.

From 206 BC to AD 8 it was the capital of the Western Han dynasty. The ruins of the Han city wall can be found in the north-west, approximately 7 km from the city centre. Records show that the Han city wall was 22 km long, with twelve gates. A system of long, straight avenues crossed the city, and in the Provincial Museum you can see examples of the pottery drains which were used. A raised platform in the south-west corner of the Han city remains marks the site of the Imperial Palace (Weiyang gong), where affairs of state were conducted. From this ancient capital, then called Chang'an (Eternal Peace – Xi'an means Western Peace), the intrepid General Zhang Qian set out to establish peaceful conditions for the traders and merchants using the Silk Route, and during the Han dynasty special offices were set up for the reception of foreign guests and emissaries. All kinds of foreign delicacies were on sale in Chang'an, and the strains of Persian music and entertainment could be heard in the streets. At the end of the Han dynasty war and invasions from the north forced the capital eastwards to Luoyang.

Chang'an's heyday was the Tang dynasty (618–907), when China was powerful, prosperous and peaceful. The population rose to more than one million, and the city was seven and a half times bigger than it is today; the city wall was 36.7 km long. The city centre was at the crossroads of present-day Xi dajie and Guangji jie, three blocks west of the Bell Tower. The royal family's quarters were in the north of the city; today only a few traces of the Daming Palace remain, several blocks north of the station. The seat of government was in the south, and the east and west were the residential and commercial quarters of the city. The layout was precise – avenues were tree-lined and drained, and in fact Chang'an became a model of urban planning for other cities in China, and even for other countries, notably Japan. The western quarter was where most foreign trade was carried out – in silk, jewellery, medicinal herbs and handicrafts. Theatres and cabarets abounded.

Chang'an was the city of the Tang, of poets and music, of emperors and their concubines, and of rebellions. Unfortunately little remains today apart from the occasional stele, a couple of pagodas and tombs in the environs.

The walled city within modern Xi'an represents the Ming and Qing city, while the sprawling suburbs are post-1949. The rebel leader Li Zicheng made this one of his first stops at the end of the Ming dynasty. The area was plagued by warlords in the first half of the twentieth century, and during the 1930s it was the scene of a battle between the Communists and the Nationalists – the Communists had already established their base in the north of the province, at Yan'an. Xi'an was the scene of the incident in which Chiang Kaishek was captured by his own generals and threatened with death if he didn't form a united front with the Communists against the Japanese. The incident is well recounted by Edgar Snow in his book *Red Star over China*.

Bell Tower

The focal point of the city is the Bell Tower, first built in the early years of the Ming dynasty in 1384. In 1582 it was moved from its original site west of the Drum Tower at the crossroads of Guangji jie and Xi dajie. It was repaired in 1739 and 1959. During the 1930s and early 1940s it was used as a garrison by the Guomin dang – prisoners were kept on the lower floor and the troops were stationed above. Traditionally the bell in the upper storey of the Tower was rung in the morning and the drum beaten at night. The Tower reveals several important features of Ming architecture – for instance the *trompe l'oeil* effect of the façade which suggests that there are three storeys, whereas in fact there are only two; also, no nails are used in the entire construction – the building is supported by a system of beams and bracket supports, which become firmer the more pressure is exerted on them. From the Bell Tower there is a view towards the north and south gate towers, and looking southwards you can see the Hua Pagoda. The Drum Tower is situated on the left on Xi dajie – Western Avenue.

Other Sights in Central Xi'an

Partly as a result of its cosmopolitan traditions there has always been a large Moslem community in Xi'an. Off Bei guangji jie is the mosque – Qingzhen si – which was built in the Tang dynasty in AD 742 and has recently been restored.

The area around the Bell Tower is the commercial centre, containing shops and department stores and telegraph offices. New City Square is north-east of the Bell Tower at the end of South New Street (Nan xin jie), opposite the provincial administration offices, and not far from the People's Mansions Hotel.

There are several small parks within the old city walls. The Children's Park lies just inside the western city gates, off Western Avenue. Lian hu Park (Lotus Lake Park), on Lian hu lu, offers boating and swimming in the summer and a lake full of lotus flowers. Revolutionary Park (Geming gongyuan), on the north side of Western Fifth Avenue, contains a modern pagoda.

Eighth-Route Army Headquarters

This building is north of the Revolutionary Park, off New North Street.

Before the Xi'an Incident there was a Red Army liaison office here, which assumed the new name of Eighth Route Army in early 1937 and played a leading role in popularizing the United Front against the Japanese.

The complex consists of a series of adjoining courtyards and rooms. Some of the rooms have become exhibition rooms detailing the history of the formation of the Eighth Route Army and the work they carried out from this post – propaganda, education and the publication of the *Xinhua ribao*, the *New China Daily*. The office was also in close radio contact with Yan'an. Zhou Enlai, Dong Biwu, Ye Jianying, Zhu De and Deng Xiaoping all lived and worked here at different times. Bai Qiuen (Norman Bethune, the Canadian doctor who was sympathetic to the Communist cause) also lived and worked here for a while.

Shaanxi Provincial Museum and Forest of Steles

Near the south gate of the old city, off Boshulin jie (Cedar Wood Street) and Sanxue jie, this fascinating museum is situated in a former Confucian temple – visitors enter through the archway which was the original entrance to the temple, and on the left is the traditional ceremonial arch, the *paifang*. The main exhibition halls were rebuilt in the 1960s in Ming and Qing style. The three main exhibition halls display objects from prehistoric times up to the Tang dynasty, as well as a room of recent finds such as the horses unearthed from the Qin tomb in Lintong County in 1974, coloured pottery from the Spring and Autumn period, silk, and bronze ritual vessels. One renowned piece is a stone drum dating to around 770 BC, which describes in great detail life and structure in the Zhou dynasty. Also on display are Han dynasty moulds for making coins, and engraved bricks from

Nine Dragon Pool at the Huaqing Hot Springs. Xi'an, with Li Mountain in the background

The 7-storey, 64-metre high Dayan Pagoda, a famed cultural relic in Xi'an. Built in AD 652 it is symbolic of the high architectural and sculptural level of the labouring people in the Tang dynasty.

The terraced loess terrain of Shaanxi

the Western Han. From the Tang dynasty there are examples of three-coloured glaze, and black porcelain from Tongchuan.

The exhibition of stone carvings consists of early carvings often used as tomb guardians. The early Han examples of whales, horses, lions and tigers are simple and follow the natural shape of the stone. Also from the eastern Han dynasty there are lively bas-relief designs carved on door jambs and entrances to tombs. There is a child's coffin from the Sui dynasty (589–618) and the famous horses from the tomb of a Tang dynasty prince, as well as Buddhist-influenced carvings from the Sui and Tang dynasties.

The value of the stele (stone tablet) as a historical document in China cannot be underestimated. In a culture where the written word was so important, but perishable on bamboo or paper, the words of great emperors and poets and the works of great artists have been preserved for posterity and are to be found all over China. The collection in the Provincial Museum referred to as the Forest of Steles (beilin) is the finest in China. It was begun in 1090 and contains about a thousand tablets.

At the entrance to the hall stands a column commissioned by the Tang emperor Xuan zong, who wrote down the whole of Confucius' discourse to his disciples on filial piety.

The first room contains 114 steles carved with the thirteen classics, including the first dictionary, the *Analects* of Confucius, the history of the Spring and Autumn period, and further steles carved with commentaries on the classics. There are also steles recording the work of the best calligraphers of the Tang dynasty and the different styles of calligraphy from Qin Shi huangdi's small seal characters, the first universal script to be used throughout China, and the different cursive and grass scripts.

Of great interest to foreign visitors is the stele which dates from 781 and records in Syrian and Chinese script the presence of Nestorian Christianity in China during the period when Xi'an was a cosmopolitan city at the start of the Silk Route. Other steles are pictorial – the subjects include monks and religious scenes, while one shows a plan of the Daxing Palace, now a park on the edge of the city, where the concubine Yang Guifei lived.

Centres of Higher Education
Passing through the south gate you come to the new part of Xi'an where you will find the arts school, the colleges of medicine, the provincial acrobatics theatre, the drama and dancing school, and the provincial sports stadium. Here also are two of the only remaining buildings of the Tang dynasty, the Great and Small Wild Goose Pagodas.

Great Goose Pagoda and Temple of Benevolence (Da yan ta and Da zi'en si)
This building stands at the southern end of Heping lu and Yan ta lu. Enter the temple through the main gate and go past a small garden, the Drum and Bell Tower and ticket kiosks to the main hall. Originally erected in 652, the temple was rebuilt during the Ming dynasty and is particularly interesting for the simplicity of the style of the figures within it – no gaudy gold-plated affairs here. There are three statues of Sakyamuni, blue and red paintings and *arhats* – again simple in execution, but each one different, reflecting the characteristics of mankind. There is also a famous tablet of Xuan Zang carrying the *sutras* from India; he set out around AD 630 for India, and on his return lived in this temple for eleven years translating the *sutras* he had brought back with him. He died around 664, and his grave is at the Xingjiao Temple outside Xi'an. The pagoda itself may be climbed and provides an excellent view

of the surrounding countryside, which used to be a favourite retreat of poets and emperors because there was a lake here (unfortunately it has long since dried up), and they often used to visit the pagoda afterwards.

It is called the Great Goose because Xuan Zang came back from India much impressed with the style of pagodas there and wanted the Emperor Gao zong to build a similar one – they were usually of stone, five storeys high, and with wings protruding from the second storey. The emperor deemed this arrangement impractical and expensive, so the pagoda was built in the traditional square, seven-storied style – 64 m tall. Outside the temple is a commemorative tablet written by a Tang minister and calligrapher.

Small Wild Goose Pagoda (Xiao yan ta)
This is situated off Nan guan zheng jie, just south of the southern gate on Youyi xi lu. It stands in the grounds of Xianfu Temple, dedicated to Guanyin, and is a brick pagoda fifteen stories high, built in 707. The monk Yi Jing set out for India in 671, returned in 695, and translated fifty-six sets of scriptures which were stored here. An earthquake caused cracks in 1555, and the pagoda was repaired in 1965. In between it was used for a time as a Nationalist Party garrison.

Xingqing Park
The park is just outside the south-east corner of the Ming city walls; the entrance is on Xianning lu, opposite Xi'an Communications University. The origins of the park date back to the Tang dynasty: it was here that the Tang emperor Xuan zong grew up with his brothers, and where he came in later years with his favourite concubine Yang Guifei. The park, which had fallen into total disrepair, was rebuilt in 1958.

It consists of a large lake where you may take a boat ride, and pavilions. The Peony Bridge joins the mainland to the Island of the Pavilion of Deep Fragrance (Shenxiang ting) where the emperor Xuan zong came with his concubine to admire the peonies. The Tang-style pavilion is still called by its original name – it was first built of *garu* wood, which is scented; tree peonies have been replanted here.

The lake is now called Eastern Lake, although in the time of Xuan zong it was known as Dragon Pool; the emperor would watch dragon boat races here. On the western shores of the lake a restaurant has been built on the site where Xuan zong came every year for a reunion with his three brothers. This was the place where the emperor had grown up with his brothers, and though he was only the third eldest he had been made emperor by virtue of his talent for leadership and the skill he had shown in quelling rebellions. This annual reunion at their childhood home was a diplomatic gesture aimed at dispelling resentment or sniffing out potential rebellions which would threaten the emperor's position, and might be instigated by resentful elder brothers who felt that they had a greater right to the throne. The name of the restaurant is Hua xiang hui lou – a four-character phrase which compares the interdependence of a flower and its calyx, and by extension came to be used to describe the help given by a younger to an elder brother. Near the main gate are the remains of the emperor's office where he received foreign envoys, particularly Japanese ones, and where he watched cock-fighting and played polo, an import from Persia which was very popular in the Tang dynasty.

Li shan and Huaqing Pool
In Lintong county, 30 km east of Xi'an, the mountain called Li shan means Black Horse Mountain – viewed from the site of the Emperor Qin's tomb it is

said to resemble a recumbent black horse. The park and hot springs lie at the foot of the mountain, and the legends connected with it have survived from the Zhou and Tang dynasties.

To reach this spot you follow a road north-east of the city, crossing the Chan and Ba Rivers. This was formerly the site of a bridge built in the Han Dynasty and the people of Xi'an welcomed the rebel leader Li Zicheng there at the end of the Ming Dynasty. You pass through the open countryside – wheatfields and small villages built of mudbrick – and you can see the characteristic walls and winged archways which create the 'half house' effect of the Shaanxi-style house.

The hot springs were discovered in the Zhou Dynasty and Lishan was thereafter a favourite resort of Qin, Han and Tang royal families. The peak above the park is still called Fenghuotai to commemorate the fires which the Zhou Emperor You used to light to make his recalcitrant concubine Pao Si smile – a ruse which worked on her, but later turned against him when his vassals no longer heeded the constant false alarms and the enemy invaded. This site is also associated with the story of the Tang Emperor Xuan Zong and his concubine Yang Gui Fei. The story is well known in China, partly as an example of how women can destroy governments, and partly because their love story has been immortalized in the 'Song of Everlasting Sorrow' – a ballad poem by the famous Tang poet, Bai Ju Yi, who refers to the Hua Qing Pool and the 'Flying Frost Palace', built by Xuan Zong for himself and Yang Gui Fei. The emperor neglected affairs of state for Yang Gui Fei and a rebellion led by one of his brothers-in-law flared up – the Anlushan Rebellion. Xuan Zong was forced to see his concubine put to death. Today the Flying Frost Pavilion is used as a reception room for visitors.

The main pool near the entrance to the park is called Nine Dragons Pool. It has a gallery winding round its edge, a marble boat and nine dragon head fountains. If you follow winding paths through the trees by the lake you come to the Huaqing Pool and behind it the source of the spring, whose temperature is 43°C. There is also a special pavilion which has been built on the spot where Yang Guifei used to bathe; privileged guests may now bathe there and wonder what it was like to be a Tang emperor's concubine. There are also public baths where you may wash – the water is good for the skin. The area became a popular spa resort at the beginning of this century and there are several sanatoria in the vicinity.

The park is also the scene of a major event in China's modern history: behind the Flying Rainbow Bridge a path leads up the hillside to The Capturing-Chiang Pavilion. Chiang Kaishek lived in a villa here in the mid 'thirties. On 12 December 1936 he was warned that Zhang Xueliang was coming to arrest him. He escaped from his bedroom window without his false teeth and wearing only a thin pair of pyjamas, to be caught cowering halfway up the hill. The eventual outcome of this event was an uneasy coalition between the Nationalists and Communists against the Japanese. In 1946 a Romanesque pavilion was erected to commemorate Chiang's bravery, and after liberation in 1949 it was renamed The Capturing-Chiang Pavilion.

The Neolithic Site at Banpo

Directly east of Xi'an on Changle lu, 10 km away on the other side of the Chan River, is the site of Banpo Museum. The first important discoveries in this area were made in 1953, extensive excavations were carried out in 1954–7, and by 1958 an exhibition hall had been built on the site. The site dates back to the Yangshao or coloured pottery period 6000 years ago, when social organization was matriarchal and based on clan communities. There are now exhibition rooms giving a background to the area and its significance in relation to other similar sites in China, and a giant dome covers the actual site of the settlement.

It seems from the archeological discoveries that this area previously had a warm climate, and that the animals were forerunners of deer, badger and rat. Small pots containing millet and cabbage were discovered, and tools such as axes and hoes made of stone and bone. Grinding stones and pottery, knives for harvesting, arrows, bones and stone spheres attached to the end of pieces of twine for hunting have also been found. Banpo was close to a river and fishing hooks and weights for nets have also come to light.

The second exhibition room contains a model showing the village surrounded by a moat for defence from wild animals, and different-shaped houses – some semi-underground, others round or square. Among other exhibits are a communal cooking stove, woven material, pots, which give evidence of 'professional' potters from the markings on the bottom, paintings on pots executed with red iron ore and showing the development from representational to symbolic design, steamers and other cooking utensils, jewellery, hairpins, water canteens.

Exhibition room no. 3 shows the site of the village and its layout, indicating where houses were reconstructed, children's graves dug etc. Adult graves were further away outside the settlement. People were buried along with objects representing the village/community in which they were born. If they were buried face down or on the side this indicated punishment.

Lantian

At Lantian, some 40 km south-east of Xi'an, in 1963 and 1964 fossilized parts of an ape-man's skull were discovered, near the Ba River. Lantian Man lived in the indeterminate period before Peking Man (600,000 years ago) and had a smaller brain than Peking Man. Stone tools used by Lantian Man have been found, but no habitation sites.

Xianyang

A satellite town 15 km north-west of Xi'an on the northern banks of the Wei River; a city was first built here during the Warring States period as a capital for the increasingly powerful state of Qin, eventually to become the capital of a united China under the first Emperor of Qin, Qin Shihuang di. The sites of the former city and palace were discovered in 1961, and archaeologists have established that it was an enormous complex of buildings reflecting the style of each newly annexed state. A summer palace was built on the outskirts. Objects unearthed include bricks and tiles, drainage pipes, iron and bronze nails and hinges, jade ornaments, silk, murals and earthenware. In 206 BC the city was invaded and destroyed by a peasant army led by Xiang Yu. During the Tang dynasty Xianyang was a post on the Silk Route. Today it is a major textile centre.

Han Tomb at Maoling

In Xingping County, 40 km north-west of Xi'an, this is the grave of the famous Han Dynasty General Huo Qubing, who had many successes against the Xiongnu, and of the Han dynasty emperor Han Wudi. Some of the stone carvings from here are on display in Shaanxi Provincial Museum.

Qian County Tombs

Here, approximately 90 km north-west of Xian, are tombs of members of the Tang royal family. On the side of Liang Mountain are the tombs of Empress Wu

Zetian, who reigned between 684 and 705, and her husband Emperor Gao zong, neither of which have been excavated. On the approach to the two unexcavated graves are sixty-one life-size statues in varying states of repair, representing the different dignitaries who attended the imperial funeral. Their names are carved on the back of each statue, and the different facial characteristics and costumes reflect the cosmopolitan life of the Tang court. Three of the tombs have been excavated and there is an exhibition of the finds. One of the tombs belonged to the young Princess Yong tai who met an untimely death at the hands of Wu Zetian and had to wait five years for a decent burial. When excavated in 1964 her tomb revealed detailed murals depicting her attendants, a stone sarcophagus, glazed and unglazed pottery tomb figures, as well as evidence that the tomb had already been robbed some time in the past.

At Zhao ling 20 km from the county town of Liquan, north-west of Xi'an, is the tumulus of the second Tang emperor, Li Shimin, who came to the throne in 626 and died in 649. The tomb stands on one of the peaks of Mount Jiuzong, and spread over an area of 300,000 *mu* there are 167 tombs of members of his court and the imperial family. About half of the tombs have been identified but only fourteen have been excavated – artefacts from them are on display in the Zhao ling Museum and include murals, crowns, sculptures and a forest of steles. The funerary figures are often glazed and are extremely lifelike and accurate. The tombs were excavated in the course of road building and land reclamation for agricultural purposes.

Tumulus and Terracotta Army of the First Emperor

One of the most exciting archaeological finds of recent years has been the terracotta armies which form part of the Qin Shihuang di's massive burial complex in Lintang county, east of the Huaqing hot springs and at the foot of the Lishan Mountains. Before he succeeded in uniting China under the short-lived and rather harsh Qin dynasty in 221 BC, Qin Shihuang became king of the state of Qin at thirteen, and began ambitious projects for constructing palaces and his future tomb at the age of fourteen. The projects were supervised by his Chancellor Li Si and General Zhang Han from the capital Xianyang, and took ten years to complete.

For a long time all that was known of Qin Shihuang's tomb was the grassy windswept tumulus, marked by a stone tablet recording the difference between past and present dimensions. The tumulus itself has yet to be excavated, and it is now thought to have been surrounded by a series of rectangular walls and occupied a total area of some 250,000 m². In 1974 traces of funeral ditches containing armies of warriors made from terracotta were first discovered by peasants sinking a well. These 'garrisons' were east of the tumulus and beyond the surrounding walls, and by analogy with the living world can be seen as a sentinel force for the 'Imperial City' – in other words the emperor's tomb.

Three major burial pits were discovered; the largest has been covered over as a permanent exhibition centre, which was opened in October 1979. The three ditches contain some 8000 figures and cover a total area of 20,000 m². The pits were rectangular and constructed from earth. Tree trunks about 3 m high were used as supports, and the floor was made from bricks.

The statues themselves are life-size – the average height is 1.9 m – and lifelike; the facial characteristics of some are those of the people of the Wei River valley – the faces have large foreheads, thick lips and moustaches; others, however, are of different nationalities, from the north-west. The soldiers are arranged according to rank: the foot soldiers wear a short shift or plain armour, with their hair in a 'chignon' or soft hat; their officers sport chest armour and boots; and high-ranking officers wear chain mail armour, have long beards and stand at the rear of their armies. There are also charioteers, archers and mounted cavalry. The statues were fired in kilns close to the tomb site and were originally painted. The horses are 1.5 m high and 2 m long and resemble animals from Hetian (Khotan) in Xinjiang. Various metal weapons and the remains of chariots have also been discovered in the burial pits.

Several theories have been put forward as to the role of this terracotta army. They seem on the alert, ready to do battle, perhaps reflecting the precariousness of the Emperor Qin Shihuang's mandate to rule.

Huxian County
This area lies 50 km south-west of Xi'an. Cao tang Temple, dating from the early Tang dynasty, is south of the county town, at the foot of the Qinling Mountains, in natural surroundings of tall grass and bamboo and encircled by a brick wall. It is said that Jiumoluoshi (Kumārajīva), who was born in modern-day Kuchi in Xinjiang in AD 344, came here in 401 to teach Buddhism and translate the Buddhist scriptures. He translated seventy-four of them and was influential in spreading Buddhism in China. In the courtyard of the temple stands a small shrine containing his relics.

En route, in Zhouzhe xian county, is a pagoda which was part of the Nestorian Daqin Temple, built in the Tang dynasty with the agreement of Emperor Tai zong (599–649) by the Nestorian monk Aluoben from Persia. Only this pagoda remains.

Huxian county is also the source of the world-renowned peasant naive paintings which have become popular in recent years, and at two commune brigades you may meet some of the painters.

Chang'an County
Directly south of Xi'an is Chang'an county, which you pass through on the way to Xingjiao si; dedicated to the monk Xuan zang, the pagoda, built in 669, contains his remains. On the way you pass two pagodas from the former Huayan Temple, which was important in developing one of the branches of Buddhism.

Shopping
The main commercial centre of Xi'an is around the Bell Tower on Dong dajie (Eastern Avenue), and Nan xin jie (South New Street), where you will find the department stores, handicrafts shops, bookshops and the new friendship store. There is an antique shop in the Drum Tower.

The best buys are silk, enamel, stone rubbings, inlaid lacquer screens, ivory carvings, walking sticks carved in a local temple, tri-colour glazed and Song-style porcelain, and traditional musical instruments.

Hotels
People's Mansions (Renmin dasha)
Xi xin jie
Tel. 25111
The hotel is well situated within the so-called Ming city, close to the New City Square and the main shopping street of South New Street (on the right as you come out of the hotel) and Jiefang lu (Liberation Street; to the left as you leave the hotel).

The hotel has two main blocks and is in the early Liberation style with mock Ming-style roofing and pavilions. Both the front and back blocks are used for visitors, although the front one is in poorer condition. Much of the accommodation is in the form of suites.

It is 5 km from the station at the north of the city walls and 8 km from the airport which is south-west of Xi'an. It has a clinic, shop and post office open from 8 am to 8 pm and a public telephone for long distance calls. The dining-room, at the end of the west wing on the fourth floor on the rear block, serves hot, salty food. The hotel is somewhat dingy and badly lit, and the plumbing is erratic.

Xi'an Guesthouse
Nan xiaomen wai
Tel. 51351
This was opened in 1982 to cope with Xi'an's ever increasing number of visitors. It is situated south of the city wall and has all amenities.

Shengli Hotel
Heping men wai
Tel. 23184
This is situated outside Heping gate in the south-east of the city. Only rarely used for foreigners.

Xiaozhai Hotel
Xiaozhai
Tel. 52131
Situated south of the main South Gate off Chang'an Road. Only rarely used for foreigners.

Food and Restaurants
Dishes in Xi'an tend to be hot and spicy and include a lot of chilli sauces – the saying is that the people of Shaanxi eat hot sauce and nothing else. The noodles are excellent, particularly served with kidneys; try also steamed dumplings, and hot lamb and beef *niuriu paomo*.

The local spirit is *xifeng jiu*. There is also a light, milky rice wine which has been produced since the Tang dynasty.

Xi'an fanzhuang
Dongdajie
Local dishes

Wuyi fandian
Dong dajie 2
Local dishes

Chuan caiguan
Jiefang lu
Sichuan cuisine

Useful Addresses
CAAC
296 Xi shao men
Tel. 21885

Luxingshe
Renmin dasha (People's Mansions)
Tel. 25111

Yan'an
A small town in the north of Shaanxi Province, it has risen to the status of a national shrine since it was here that the Communists established their base in 1935 at the end of the Long March. The symbol of Yan'an is the Bao Pagoda, built in the Song dynasty, which stands on Precious Pagoda Hill overlooking the city. Yan'an can be reached by air from Xi'an or overland by coach, which takes the best part of a day. It has a small hotel called the Yan'an binguan.

Apart from the attraction of being in a very unspoiled part of China, there are several communes to visit, such as the Liuling brigade, from where Jan Myrdal wrote his *Report from a Chinese Village*, and Nanniwan, 40 km from Yan'an, one of the first places to be farmed and turned into a co-operative by the Communists. 'If we all lend a hand,' ran their slogan, 'there'll be enough to eat and wear.'

There are silk, carpet and radio factories here, but the main feature of interest is the quarters where the leading members of the Communist Party lived and directed their guerilla war against the Nationalists and the Japanese. These include the Date Garden, the cave quarters, the assembly hall, the site where Mao gave his Yan'an forum on art and literature to mend the growing ideological rift, and the quarters of the Eighth Route Army. Edgar Snow was one of the few foreigners to reach Yan'an, and his book *Red Star over China* provides an excellent background to the atmosphere of those times.

SICHUAN PROVINCE

With its enormous landmass equivalent in area to France, its population of 97.74 million, its mineral wealth and fertile soil, throughout history isolated Sichuan has had all the potential of an independent state. The Tang poet Li Bai, speaking of the province's isolation, once said 'The road to Shu [Sichuan] is more difficult than the road to Heaven!' The talented people who have come from Sichuan reflect an independence of spirit unlike the natives of other provinces in China. The Chinese connect Sichuan with hot food, silk bedcovers, giant pandas and bamboo, and indeed for its natural wealth the basin around Chengdu has been described as 'Heaven's storehouse'.

To the foreign visitor Sichuan offers the old and the new – from the ancient provincial capital of Chengdu to the recent history of Chongqing. Mount Emei in the south of the province is both a scenic area abounding in exotic plant life and wild monkeys as well as being a historic Buddhist site. You can visit the ancient irrigation scheme engineered by Li Bing, or take a journey along the Yangtse through the famous Gorges. Sichuan also has long-standing traditions in the crafts, from the cultivation of bonsai trees to fine silk and filigree work or bamboo household objects.

The province as it is today was constituted in 1955 by incorporating the mountainous plateau of Sikang and the Red Basin area. It is surrounded on four sides by mountains, which in the west and south-west rise to a height of 7000 m, and in the east rise to 3000 m with the chain of the Daba and Wu Mountains broken only by the narrow gorges and the Yangtse River.

The western highlands begin to the west of Chengdu. The area is mountainous and sparsely populated by Tibetans, Yi and Hui minority groups and is divided into three autonomous districts – Abei, Ganze, and Liangshan. Communications are poor and the growing season is short; livestock herding and lumbering are the main activities. The mountains rise from 3000 m to over 7500 m where they become the Great Snow Mountains; it was this difficult terrain, and the torrential Dadu River, which the Red Army crossed during the Long March.

However in the Sichuan Basin – also referred to as the Red Basin because of the characteristic red soil – is one of the most densely populated and intensively cultivated areas in the world, where even early this century the area was described as more like gardens than farmland, and where groups of family houses nestle in bamboo groves. The area is fed by the four main tributaries of the Yangtse River, which has probably given the province its name, which means 'four streams', the Jialing, the Min jiang, the Tuo jiang and the Wu jiang. The area enjoys warm winters, an early spring, hot summers and up to eleven frostfree months. It also has a tendency to be foggy, and the saying goes that when the sun comes out the dogs bark. It is hottest along the Yangtse, while the Basin enjoys a milder climate; the area is also sheltered from the harsh winds from the north.

The Basin is one of the major producers of rice in the country and has been irrigated and terraced since the second century BC. The main crops are rice, wheat, maize, sweet potatoes and soya beans; rice is double-cropped, and many areas have three crops per year. Cash crops include cotton, rape, sugar cane, silk, tea, tong oil, hemp, camphor, lacquer, bamboo, rare medicinal herbs and oranges. Salt wells around Zigong, Wutongqiao and Yanyuan have made Sichuan one of the major providers of salt and taxes used to be paid in this commodity. The province has an enormous coal field, as well as supplies of natural gas and oil in the centre of the province.

Today the Yangtse is still the major artery of communication with the rest of China. A railway line from Shaanxi Province was completed through to Chengdu in 1956 and extended to Yunnan and Guizhou. There is also a line from Chongqing to Chengdu. However, construction of a railroad between Wuhan and Chongqing has been a major political issue since the beginning of the century. There are regular flights to and from Sichuan.

From Zhu Geliang to Deng Xiaoping Sichuan has provided some of the most colourful characters in Chinese history. Other modern notables include the writer and historian Guo Moruo, Marshal Zhu De and the writer Han Su-yin. Sichuan was first incorporated into China in the fourth century under the Qin dynasty. In the ensuing Three Kingdoms period it was the powerful state of Shu, led by the famous Liu Bei and Zhu Geliang. Both the great Tang Dynasty poet Li Bai and the Song poet Su Dongpo came from Sichuan. The province grew in wealth until the Yuan dynasty, when it suffered at the hands of the Mongols. At the end of the Ming and beginning of the Qing dynasties there was a great deal of opposition to the alien Manchus and much of the population was wiped out or forced to flee, to be replaced by an influx from south and central China.

Opposition to the Manchus from Sichuan eventually helped bring them down, and in the early part of the twentieth century Sichuan was divided by warlords, who quarrelled among themselves, uncontrolled by the central government, until that government was forced to move to Sichuan as it fled the Japanese. It has long been said of Sichuan that in times of peace it is the first province to erupt, and in times of resettlement and restoration it is the last to become peaceful. It remained closed to foreign visitors until 1978, due largely to the chaos of the Cultural Revolution period which saw severe factional fighting, and eventually the army intervened to restore a semblance of order. Almost as in pre-Liberation days, the province was dominated by individuals. Production fell, and at one stage even rice had to be imported into the province.

Today there is a new production drive; the pragmatic Zhao Ziyang, the new Premier, was until recently head of the Provincial Party Committee, free markets among peasants are encouraged, and efforts are being made to modernize this potentially rich area, with foreign companies making direct approaches to the relevant corporations in Sichuan.

Chongqing
In days gone by, after an arduous upstream climb, boats would arrive at Chaotian men (Gazing at Heaven Gate) and look up at the city thankfully, for Chongqing built on a rocky promontory at the confluence of the Yangtse and Jialing Rivers, is one of the few Chinese cities built on a hill. While sedan chairs no longer carry you into the city proper a stairway will bring you to the city, and there is a funicular operating from one of the wharves. The city has expanded in the last thirty years and today has a population of some 6 million. The oldest quarter of the city is to be found on the promontory on the

northern banks of the Jialing, where it meets the Yangtse River.

The city was devastated by Japanese bombs and even today as you wend your way into it you will see entrances cut into the sides of the hills for bomb shelters. Many of the buildings are new red brick, while a few of the old 'Tudor'-style jettied houses remain, with protruding upper stories and the ground floor opening on to the street to display workshops and stores. There is a noticeable absence of bicycles in Chongqing due to the hills, and people of all ages will be seen dragging heavy loads to their destination. The pace is leisurely – in the hot summer months Chongqing is one of the furnaces of China; shops remain open until nine o'clock, and the residents sit outside in the relatively cool evenings.

The old name for Chongqing was Yu, which is still used as an abbreviation; the name was changed in the Song dynasty when a local prince became emperor – the present name means 'twice blessed'. Chongqing was first opened to foreign traders in 1891, after the efforts of Archibald Little to bring steamers up the Yangtse. Missionaries also made their way upstream in junks, and it was a point for carrying out trade with Tibet.

In the 1930s the Sino–Japanese War drove the Nationalist government upstream to establish their capital here. They brought not only their government departments and the universities: whole factories were moved up the Yangtse to continue manufacturing in Chongqing, which was in many ways to provide a base for Chongqing's industrial development. Today the city produces iron and steel as well as machine tools, chemicals, fertilizers, buses and lorries, textiles and nylon.

Modern Chongqing also boasts a university specializing in technical subjects, a teachers' training college, a fine arts school, a school of architecture and a foreign languages institute. It is also renowned for its mists and fogs, which engulf the city from the end of October until the end of February. The warm climate and humidity ensure an all-year-round growing season. The fields around the city are intensively cultivated and you will come across such delightful sights as children making lotus leaves into hats and babies carried in bamboo baskets slung across their mother's back.

There are several flights a week from Peking (2252 km away) and Guangzhou, and regular connections to Chengdu. Chongqing has recently become accessible by train, but it is always by an indirect route. The Xiangfan–Chongqing railway was completed in 1978, providing access from northern Hubei Province. The distance between Chongqing and Chengdu by rail is 504 km. The Yangtse River is the most straightforward route to the east coast of China: from Chongqing to Wuhan takes three days by boat, and there are daily departures with stops at small towns along the river. The upstream journey from Wuhan takes several days.

Sights: General
The centre of Chongqing, at the confluence of the Jialing and Yangtse, is said to resemble the head and neck of a goose. E Ling Park – whose name means 'goose neck' – is situated at this point, just outside the city off Chang jiang yi lu. It used to belong to a landlord; apart from a lake and pavilions and a monument to Russian soldiers it has a very good selection of bonsai trees. The people of Chongqing seem particularly fond of potted plants – all over the city you will see cactus plants and bonsai trees balancing on windowsills.

As you make your way into the city you pass the hilltop stadium and the Cultural Palace off Zhongshan lu, and then on your right you come to Loquat Hill Park (Pipa shan gongyuan). Reached up a winding path, it is the highest point in the city, and people come here in the summer evenings as it is reputedly some two or three degrees cooler than in the city. The infamous warlord Wang Lingji used to occupy this hill; his stronghold was beneath the Red Star Pavilion, from which you are invited to enjoy the view. After 1949 it was used for municipal offices and when they moved in 1955 it was opened as a park; an entrance fee is charged. On special occasions the city is lit up and can be viewed from here. You can also see on to the opposite bank of the Yang-tse; below is the sandy flat which was used as a landing strip during the war.

Jiefang bei in the commercial centre is the Liberation Monument, commemorating the Sino-Japanese War. The People's Hall, used for conferences and meetings as well as a hotel and guest house, overlooks the Jialing River. Chongqing also has a zoo in its western suburbs which contains five giant-pandas.

Chongqing Museum of Arts and Crafts through the ages

Many of the exhibits in this museum are taken from all over China; however there are a few which have special reference to Sichuan and make the visit worthwhile, such as early examples of boats made by the Ba tribe, thought to be early settlers in Sichuan. The history of ceramics in China is traced up to the characteristic large brown pickle jars – the salted vegetables of Sichuan are re-nowned. (The jars can be bought very cheaply in the shops and make excellent storage jars at home providing you don't mind carrying them.) There are some brick carvings from the western Han dynasty, many from around Chengdu; also stone buddhas un-earthed during construction of the new

railway station at Chongqing, and funerary figures from the Ming dynasty. The pride of the museum are the Ming and Song paintings, which include the works of local painters, with a characteristic style of sweeping strokes and using wash as a medium. There are also examples of the coveted Sichuan *bei-mian* – brocade quilts – and jade and ivory carving.

Natural History Museum

The Natural History Museum is on the road to the Northern Hot Springs (see below). It is well known that Sichuan has particularly rich fauna, and China itself has a long record of natural history research and classification. The exhibition includes an overview of the ecology of China and then gives a local breakdown from the many kinds of fish found in the Yangtse to the forty-two species of snake in Sichuan – not omitting instructions on dealing with snake bites. Giant pandas are still found in the northern part of Sichuan and the south of Gansu Province, as well as the golden-haired monkey, leopards and the lesser panda. The museum also con-tains the 14-m-long skeleton of a dino-saur, discovered in the area around Zigong in 1974.

Northern Hot Springs

If you follow the Jialing River some 50 km upstream you reach the area of the Northern Hot Springs (Bei wen quan). Set in wooded surroundings overlooking the Jialing River are temple buildings which date back to the Ming, Qing and Tang dynasties. The Tang one is referred to as the Iron Tile Hall; the others are ornate and have recently been repainted with decorative eave orna-ments. Bonsai trees and decorative plants have been trained into the shapes of dogs and other creatures. There are also caves, pathways and bamboo groves. One of the caves is known as the Milk Flower Cave. There are stalagmite formations and the cave alternately widens and narrows so that only one person may pass at a time. There are unusual fish to be found here, such as the Black African Carp, and the Five Pools Which Mirror the Moon are each a different colour due to the differing depths of the water. In three open air swimming pools or baths visitors can enjoy the benefits of the spring water. Nearby is the summer resort of Jinyun Mountain and a temple. Lion Peak is 1000 m high and its dense forest contains some rare plant species.

Southern Hot Springs

The Southern Hot Springs are some 30 km south of Chongqing on the northern banks of the Yangtse, reached by bus and ferry. Here there are waterfalls, swimming pools and caves, and you can also row in the Huaxi River, a small tributary of the Yangtse. There is also a sanatorium and the so-called Fairy Cave. Legend has it that a child-bride was so ill-treated by her mother-in-law that she ran away to this cave. She bathed in the spring, her bruises were healed, and she changed into a fairy and flew off to heaven. The waterfall represents her towel and the Flowery Stream was named after the flowers which fell from her hair. There is a modern statue of her in the cave.

Dazu Buddhist Caves

Dazu county is 160 km north-west of Chongqing and may be reached by coach on a one-day excursion. The Dazu Grottoes were created between the end of the Tang dynasty (ninth century) and the end of the Song (thirteenth century). Consisting of over 50,000 sculpted figures, there are two main sites – Bei shan (North Hill) and Baoding shan (Treasure Peak Mountain). Bei shan's outstanding feature is the Buddha Crescent – a 250-m-long gallery of Buddhist carvings from the Tang and Song. It is also the site of an intricately carved stone pillar called the Wheel of the Universe. Art historians have discovered that within the pillar was a revolving tablet representing the cycle of man's life. At the same spot there is a beautifully executed statue of Puxian, one of the Bodhisattvas, and another of Guanyin, the Goddess of Mercy.

At Baoding shan all the carvings were created between 1179 and 1249 following a model conceived by a monk. The sculptors of these figures used a number of devices to create a feeling of depth and movement. A giant sleeping Buddha reclines along 31 m. One of the reasons for the relatively good state of preservation of these caves is the hidden drainage system, which is an underground conduit. While most of the themes are religious there are also secular images – of animals and rural life, for example. There is a series known as 'parental love' which, in eleven cameos, follows the stages of childhood, from the future parents praying to Buddha for a child, and the birth, to the child growing up and finally going off into the world.

Red Crag Revolutionary Museum

During its period as capital Chongqing was the scene of the major power struggles and controversies of the day. From here the Nationalists and Communists buried their differences to fight the Japanese, and in the historic Chongqing negotiations worked towards a *modus vivendi* after the end of that war. Several sites in and around Chongqing have been preserved under the auspices of the Red Crag Revolutionary Museum, including the offices of the left-wing newspaper *New China Daily*.

No.13 Red Crag Village stands on the banks of the Jialing River, 10 km from the city centre. This was where the Communist Party set up its 'southern bureau' of the Central Committee between 1938 and 1946, and where members of the Eighth Route Army had their quarters. Zhou Enlai lived here with his wife Deng Yingchao; so did the leading party figures Ye Jianying and Dong Biwu. During this period of co-operation between the Communists and Nationalists they attended the National Parliament. The land was rented to them by a sympathetic farmer whose children later went to Yan'an, and who after Liberation became a member of the Consultative Conference.

No.50 Zengjiayan was Zhou Enlai's house in the city. Both this and No.13 Red Crag Village were spied on by the Nationalists.

On 28 August 1945, after many invitations from Chiang Kaishek, Mao Ze dong arrived in Chongqing. The Japanese had been defeated and it now remained to solve the differences between the Communists and the Nationalists and re-establish a stable government. During his stay in Chongqing Mao stayed at the Cassia Garden, the home of General Zhang Zhizhong who was one of the Guomin dang.

On the outskirts of Chongqing was the site of the Sino–American Special Technical Co-operative Organization, where forces were trained by US army officials to fight the Japanese. After the war it was used by the Nationalists as a prison and training ground for spies. Today an exhibition has been mounted to remind people of the events of the time.

Culture and Contemporary Life
The Sichuanese theatre has its own unique characteristics – the style of Chuanju. Apart from being performed in the local dialect it is also humorous, colourful and employs the technique of 'prompters' behind the stage, who in high, reedy tones voice the thoughts of the central characters in the drama. The Chongqing acrobatics troupe is among the best in China. Among places you

may choose to visit are the school of fine arts, a lacquer factory, a glass factory and a people's commune.

Tourist Information

Shopping
There are friendship stores in the hotels, and also one in the main department store. The commercial centre is around Jiefangbei. Local products include bamboo scrolls, bamboo utensils, woven bamboo, inkstones, household ceramics such as typical brown pickle jars, and many Chinese medicinal herbs, particularly *yiner* fungus which is renowned for its excellent tonic properties.

Hotels
Renmin Hotel
Renmin lu
Tel: 53421

Yuzhou binguan
Panjiaping
Tel. 51486
This is a small guest house on the outskirts of the city, near the Chongqing medical college.

Food and Drink
Apart from the hot spicy favourites such as *dandan* noodles and beancurd in chilli sauce, other notable dishes include steamed fish from the Yangtse, chicken stuffed with salted vegetables and with a crispy skin, and duck stewed in herbs. The best local spirit comes from Luzhou, upstream from Chongqing, and is called *daqiu jiu*.

Useful Addresses
CAAC
Zhongshan san lu
Tel. 52643

Luxingshe
Renmin lu
Tel. 51449

Chengdu

The provincial capital of Sichuan was first ruled by the legendary figure Can Chong, a chieftain of the Shu tribe in the eighth century BC. In the Qin dynasty 2200 years ago Li Bing, the great irrigation engineer, set up the Dujiansyan irrigation system in the plain outside Chengdu which was to ensure its development as a wealthy agricultural area. In the Three Kingdoms period it emerged as the capital of Shu when Liu Bei declared himself emperor and plotted with his trusted minister Zhu Geliang to defeat his rivals in the Kingdoms of Wu and Wei.

Always a centre for the fine arts, it became known as Hibiscus City in the tenth century after a local overlord planted hibiscus along the city walls. Much of the Ming city was destroyed during a peasant uprising at the end of the Ming dynasty; in the Qing it was renowned for its fine architecture and layout, including a wide city wall used as a promenade by its citizens until it was destroyed in 1949. During the Han dynasty Chengdu became famous as the city of brocade. Silk washed in the river which flowed south of Chengdu seemed to take on special lustre. Today this river is still called the Brocade River (Jin jiang), and Chengdu has often been referred to as the Brocade City.

Modern Chengdu has multiplied in size; it has a population of 3.8 million, and a wide boulevard lined with shops and government offices runs from north to south. Still one of the cleanest cities in China, it has the typical Sichuan 'mock Tudor' timber-framed houses still standing in many quarters, a riverside promenade, and streets which carry on their traditional trades. It is the major industrial base of south-west China with textiles, electrical engineering, machine tools, steel tubes and electronics. Following the tradition of its long-standing reputation as an erudite city – the first state-run school was founded in Chengdu in the second century BC – there are many universities, colleges and research institutes here. Sichuan University is particularly renowned for its Chinese language and literature faculty.

The atmosphere is leisurely and the tea house life flourishes. Throughout the year many local festivals are enjoyed, such as the Flower Festival in February and the Lantern Festival.

Du Fu's Thatched Cottage
(Du Fu caotang)

One of the great poets of the Tang dynasty, Du Fu was admired through the ages for his melancholy poetry which reflected his sensitivity to the sufferings of mankind. He was a minor official in the court at Chang'an until in 759, tired of the vagaries of court life, he went into retirement in Chengdu. He was to spend four years there; at first he took up residence in a local temple, and later sought a peaceful nook on the outskirts of the city where he built a small thatched cottage near the Wanhua stream. While here he wrote some 240 poems.

In the tenth century the poet Wei Zhuang located the original spot where his cottage had stood and had it rebuilt in the great poet's honour. In later years a temple was built in his memory, gardens were laid out, and tablets inscribed with his poems. Today these have been preserved and the area is now a small park with bamboo groves, galleries, lattice windows and a museum with a collection of Du Fu's works, from an early hand-copied, wood block edition to modern ones. It has recently become a research centre for his life and works. The Thatched Cottage can be reached by following the road westward from Xin xi men.

Temple of the Marquis of Wu
(Wu hou ci)

Situated south of the former city gate on the south bank of the Jin jiang, this temple was built in honour of the famous strategist Zhu Geliang (181–234), chief advisor to Emperor Liu Bei. The temple was built during the Tang dynasty, and a tablet dating from 809 lists Zhu Geliang's attributes and achievements. To the west of the temple is the tomb of the emperor Liu Bei. Although the temple has been built several times the present building dates from the Qing dynasty, and the ancient cypress trees are said to have been planted by Zhu Geliang himself. There is a statue of him and three bronze drums bearing designs.

River View Pavilion (Wangjiang lou)

Outside the east gate of the city a four-storied pavilion in ornate southern-style architecture overlooks the Jin River. In its grounds are reminders of another figure from Chengdu's illustrious past – the Tang poetess Xue Tao (768–831). In one corner is the well from which she would draw water to make the pink paper on which she wrote her poems; that paper is still made in Chengdu today. Xue Tao was also fond of bamboo, and of the 200 varieties found in Sichuan some 130 grow in the grounds of the River View Pavilion.

Dujiangyan Irrigation System

Fifty kilometres north-west of Chengdu, this feat of water conservancy engineering was built in the Qin dynasty 2200 years ago by Li Bing and his son. The Min River flowed down from north Sichuan, and on reaching the plain would cause alternately flood and drought. Li Bing directed the construction of bamboo and pebble dykes which diverted the waters of the Min into an inner and outer section, ensuring a year-round water supply. It contributed to the wealth of the area through the ages and today irrigates almost 7 million ha of land. The waterways are crossed by a series of covered wooden bridges and frail suspension bridges. The Lidui Pavilion (Mouth of a Treasure Bottle) is the spot from where the flow of water on to the plain is controlled; there are also temples to the memory of Li Bing, such as the Erwang miao, the Two Kings Temple. The system includes dams designed to reduce the level of silting; the whole undertaking was repaired and expanded between 1950 and 1952, and is now regularly maintained.

Emei shan

Emei shan and Le shan (below) are two beauty spots about 150 km south-west of Chengdu on the Chengdu–Kunming railway. Emei shan is one of the sacred mountains of Buddhist lore, enveloped in mist and sunlight and known as the retreat of poets and hermits. The mountain rises 3099 m above sea-level and is as much of interest for its natural and scenic surroundings as for the religious buildings – you will find monkeys, rare trees such as the dove tree, and plants. At the foot of the mountain is the Baoguo Temple and from here you follow a road 60 km up the mountain. From Double Wells it is a further 11 km or so on foot to the summit, where you can gaze on the rivers of Sichuan or across to the snowy mountains which have for centuries protected the province.

Other interesting sites on the mountain include the Elephant Bath, where the Bodhisattva Samantabhadra, the first disciple of Sakyamuni, used to bathe his elephant, the Xianfeng Temple, and caves where sages used to shelter. At Hongchunping Monastery there are carved Buddhist statues, a 2-m high bronze lamp, dragons and lotus carvings, a ravine and bridge over a crystal-clear stream called A Strip of Sky, and the Qingyin Pavilion, in an idyllic natural setting. The Wannian Temple was built in the Ming dynasty during the reign of Wan li. There is a famous 9-m-high bronze image of Samantabhadra seated in his lotus on an elephant.

Le shan

This ancient city, dating back to the Tang dynasty, stands on the confluence of the Qingyi, Min and Dadu Rivers, and it is a main junction for water traffic to southern Sichuan. Nearby are the scenic spots of the Lingyun and Wuyou Hills. Carved into the side of Lingyun Hill is a 70-m-tall statue of the Buddha; here you may climb the Staircase with Nine Turnings to the Buddha's head. This magnificent statue, built in AD 713, was suggested by a monk as a way to tame the river; it can be reached by motor launch from the city. There are guardians on either side, carved into the rock face. A suspension bridge joins Linyun Hill to Wuyou Hill with its fan-shaped pavilion and monastery, which dates back to the Tang dynasty and has on exhibition calligraphy paintings, Buddhist *sutras*, and stone tablets with poems by Su Dongpo.

To visit Emei shan or Le shan the traveller must allow a minimum of one overnight stop before returning to Chengdu, or continuing his journey. Both areas were only recently opened to foreigners and guest house facilities are simple, particularly on Emei shan (where stout walking shoes are essential). However the natural surroundings will almost certainly compensate for any deficiency in luxury.

Tourist Information

Travel

Chengdu is 2048 km from Peking. One can either fly there from Peking, Shanghai or Guangzhou, or go by rail from Chongqing. From Chengdu it is possible to travel by rail to Kunming, a journey which is highly recommended as it reveals the splendour of many little-known parts of China and affords the opportunity to see Miao minorities in their native surroundings.

Hotels

Jin jiang Hotel
Renmin nan lu
Tel. 4481
Overlooking the Jin River, this hotel stands east of Nan renmin lu and south of Binjiang lu. It is well appointed with air-conditioning in each room and central heating. There is a foreign exchange, a post office, some small shops and a bar.

Dongfeng fandian
Dongfeng lu
Tel. 7012

Shopping and Local Products

Apart from the excellent food, brocade, and bamboo 'silk' woven around a ceramic base or for flask covers, Chengdu's traditional crafts include silver filigree work and lacquer ware. Visits may be made to factories and studios producing these items.

Friendship store
Shengli zhong lu

Antique shop
Nanjiao Park

Arts and Crafts shop
Chun xi lu

Useful Addresses

CAAC
31 Bei xin jie
Tel. 3038

Luxingshe
Jin jiang Hotel
Renmin nan lu
Tel. 5914

Yangtse Gorges

The time-honoured route, at least for leaving Sichuan, is to set out from Chongqing early in the morning while the infamous mist still hangs over the city for the downstream trip to Wuhan via the Yangtse Gorges. Travelling in the wake of the Tang poet Li Bai you will pass through ancient countryside where many of the legendary heroes of the Three Kingdoms period fought their battles. The downstream journey takes three days and two nights to Wuhan.

The river has been tamed in the last thirty years by rock blasting; buoys mark the safe channels, arrows indicate the direction of the gorge, and traffic regulations give priority to downstream traffic. Nonetheless the currents are still swift, and in the summer rainy season the waters can rise 30 m. *En route* the boat passes historic and legendary sites, many relating to the Three Kingdoms period, such as cliff faces with Chinese characters engraved on them. It will stop off at small towns to pick up or put down passengers, for while it is a romantic journey to the foreign visitor it is also the major route linking towns and villages along the Yangtse River. Listed below are the main landmarks and ports of call.

Before steamships ever began to ply the Yangtse, the upstream journey was a perilous one, accompanied by many prayers and sacrifices to the river gods. Today you pass ancient pagodas built on either bank to ward off evil spirits. Outside Chongqing there used to be a Buddhist temple where it was customary to stop and give thanks for a safe arrival. A still common sight are the 'trackers', often bent double pulling their bamboo rope along narrow riverside paths – the people of Sichuan make no secret of the fact that manpower still rules.

The Yangtse River is 6300 km long and has its source in the mountains of Tibet. Today it is navigable by steamers over 1000 tonnes upstream from Chongqing to Luzhou, a town famous for its spirits. The Yangtse cleaves its way through the Daba Mountains at the eastern extremity of Sichuan Province into the plain of Hubei. Two hours after leaving Chongqing, the first two stops *en route* in the morning are Changshou and Fuling. The river is around 400 m wide at this point, and the riverside towns sprawl along a gently sloping bank.

Fengdu

Here, five and a half hours downstream from Chongqing, is an ancient temple which can be seen from the boat. It is said to have been founded by two Han scholars, and is now used as a school.

After seven and a half hours you pass Chong xian and after nine hours Shibaozhai (Precious Stone Stockade). Instantly recognizable, the latter is a steep cliff with a temple and a pagoda built into the cliff face, from where a bridge used to run across to the walled city. Each storey contains tablets and at the top there is said to be a stone with a hole in it – the story goes that the hole was once smaller, but enough rice miraculously appeared through it to feed the temple monks. When they became greedy and tried to make the hole bigger the supply of rice stopped.

In the early evening the first stop is Wan xian, where the boat moors until dawn in order to negotiate the Gorges in daylight. You will now have travelled 327 km downstream from Chongqing.

Wan xian

This small but important riverside town, shortly before the entrance to the Yangtse Gorges, is typical in that you climb a flight of stairs to the city gates. This is the only place where there is enough time to disembark on the journey between Chungking and Wuhan.

The total population including the city and nine county districts along the river bank is a quarter of a million, but it is a one-street town with a People's Park on the western outskirts and a clock tower built in 1932 by the warlord Yang Sen. Near Wan xian is the so-called Li Bai Cliff, where the famous Tang poet is said to have studied. The name Wan xian means the 'county with 10,000 products', reflecting the natural wealth of the area. It was given its name in the Qing dynasty, and the local industries and produce include pig bristles, meat, fruit and vegetable canning, leather goods, silk and textiles, rice, wheat and maize, oranges and orange wine, and longans – a smaller version of lychees whose skin is used for a tonic.

Wan xian is also the scene of the blockade of the British frigate *Cockchafer* in 1926. The larger British steamships on the Yangtse had often caused the frail local junks to capsize. Yang Sen, the local warlord, commandeered two ships docked at Wan xian and placed troops on them, threatening the *Cockchafer* with immediate action if any attempt was made to free the boats. Aid was sent from Yichang and the rescue was almost peaceably complete when a stray shot was heard 'on board one of the ships' and firing and shelling began. Extensive damage was done to the city, and the captain blamed the advice given to Yang Sen by some interfering third party (possibly non-Chinese) for the escalation of the incident. It was followed by an anti-British boycott, and ships anchored there had difficulties procuring food and supplies. The incident is now merely referred to with a smile.

Leaving Wan xian at first light, the first stop is the small, picturesque town of Yunyang; on the opposite bank is the Zhangwang Temple. Zhang Fei was one of the brotherhood of the Three Kingdoms period. When one of their number had died and mourning was called for, the capricious and irascible Zhang Fei ordered the local monks to provide white mourning clothes. The monks did not finish them quickly enough and he lost his temper. The local people in turn were resentful and killed him; his head was removed and later brought back and buried here. The temple dates from the Song dynasty.

Fengjie (formerly Guizhou fu) is the last town before the beginning of the Gorges. A steep stairway leads up to this medieval-looking town which seems to grow out of the river bank. Opposite is a mountain, thought to resemble a peach and so named. Nearby are the remains of the Summer Palace of Liu Bei, where his wife died. At the top of the stairway you can still see the ancient arch of the city gate. Before 1949 this was a guerilla base area, and Zhang Jie, a female guerilla leader, came here from Chongqing to find the head of her husband, who was political commissar of the area, hanging outside the city gate. The wharf is very active: queues of people get on and off and the locals come to sell the passengers apples and pomeloes. Further down river are a series of stones in the river, referred to as Bazhentu (Eight Pattern Stones). Their origin and meaning are uncertain, they are set out symmetrically and may have had something to do with ancient forms of worship. Perhaps dragons were believed to lurk beneath them, or maybe Zhu Geliang used them as a form of blockade for enemy ships. There are also salt wells beneath the water.

The Three Yangtse Gorges

A mood of excitement pervades the ship on the second morning of the journey as you approach the famous Gorges, which have long been regarded as one of the most romantic sights of China. The Tang Poet Li Bai immortalized the special feeling of emotion, in his qua-train written over a thousand years ago when the Gorges were more treacherous than they are today:

Day dawns, we leave White Emperor City towering in the mist, it will take one whole day and a thousand li to reach Jiang Ling, monkeys chatter ceaselessly on the river banks, as my frail craft scuds past soaring mountains.

White Emperor City (Bai Dicheng)

After his defeat by the Kingdom of Wu, Liu Bei came here to die, entrusting the care of his son to Zhu Geliang. The name is thought to date back to the Han dynasty when a local duke with delu-sions of grandeur saw a dragon-like mist emanating from the White Goose Well. Taking this as an omen that he was to be the new emperor, he called himself the White Emperor and gave the city the same name. There is also a temple here dating from the Tang dynasty, and a pavilion where Zhu Geliang consulted the stars about Liu Bei's death.

White Emperor City marks the begin-ning of the first gorge – the Qu tang Gorge, which is 8 km long and in places no more than 100 m wide. Stone tablets warn of the dangers of the gorge, which has very sheer sides. You pass the Lad-der of Mang Liang, where ladder-like steps seem to have been hewn out of the face of the gorge. The legend is that the Song general Mang Liang had died at the summit of the cliff and his men tried to scale the cliff face to be near him. A more modern explanation is that the footholds were made by local people looking for medicinal herbs. You now pass through swift-flowing rapids to the Wind Box Gorge. If you gaze upwards to the right as you travel downstream (binoculars are useful) you may see stone-like shapes resembling bellows or wind boxes, which seem to be lodged high in a crevass. Nearby are rock formations resembling a sword and a copper incense burner.

Daixi

Black Stream is the translation of the name of a small village in a delightful rustic setting at the end of the Qutang Gorge, where a small tributary enters the Yangtse. It takes about a quarter of an hour to travel downstream through Qutang Gorge.

Mistaken Gorge (Cuokai xia)

Before reaching the next gorge you pass the Mistaken Gorge, which leads no-where. The formation of the gorges is attributed to the mythical Emperor Da Yu, who in the creation of China played an important role in taming the water-ways and preventing floods by opening new waterways wherever he went to redirect flood water. The Mistaken Gorge was apparently started in error!

Wu xia Gorge

The Wu xia Gorge begins shortly after the hamlet of Wushan xian, just beyond the point where the Daning River joins the Yangtse on the northern bank. Both the winding Wuxia Gorge and the Qutang Gorge are under the jurisdic-tion of Wan xian municipality.

The Chinese describe this gorge as a picture gallery. The first feature encoun-tered is the soaring, mist-swathed twelve peaks known as the Shennu feng – the Fairy Peaks. The legend is that when Da Yu was taming the waters of China the Queen of Heaven agreed to send twelve of her entourage to earth to assist him; when their work was com-pleted the twelve decided they would stay on earth and stood on the twelve peaks on either side of the river to watch over the sailors and ships passing up and down the river. They eventually turned to stone, and each peak is named after one of them. In the poem written after his famous swim across the

Yangtse at Wuhan Chairman Mao refers to the 'Twelve Fairy Peaks', wondering whether they would recognize the new world.

The next landmark is the Kong Ming Tablet – Kong Ming was another name for Zhu Geliang – containing an article on policy and the strategy of uniting with the weaker generals and kingdoms against the strongest aggressors. The gorge ends at Guandukou, and on the south bank of the river you reach Badong, the first village in Hubei Province.

Zigui

One hour downstream from Badong, Zigui is the birthplace of the poet Qu Yuan, famous for his collection of verse known as *Li Sao (Encountering sorrow)*. Qu Yuan was advisor to the Emperor of the State of Chu during the Warring States period and, finding his counsel falling on deaf ears, he drowned himself. Legend has it that he was swallowed by a fish in Lake Dongting and brought back to his birthplace. A commemorative temple stands here, but unfortunately it cannot be seen from the river.

Fragrant Stream

Here a green, crystal stream enters the whirling yellow waters of the Yangtse. It cuts through limestone and carries no silt, which is why it is so clear.

Xiling Gorge

Fragrant Stream marks the beginning of the Xiling Gorge. It is 76 km from Fragrant Stream to Nanjin guan at the end of the gorge. Here you first pass the Book of Strategy and the Precious Sword Gorge – the bluff resembles a sword and a hole in the rock face seems to contain a book, Zhu Geliang's advice on military strategy. The style of buildings begins to change from grey tall medieval riverside hamlets to lower houses with curving eaves. The Qing tan (Black Rapids) are

some of the most treacherous rapids in the river. Then you reach the Ox Liver and Horse Lung Gorge. Konglingtan are another set of rapids, also known as Devil's Gate Pass. Huangling Temple, on the south bank of the Yangtse, is said to have been built by Zhu Geliang; it rises above the village amidst orange trees and bamboos. From here you pass Lantern Shadow Gorge, which has peaks which resemble the characters from the saga of *Monkey* – Monkey himself, Pigsy and Sandy. This can be seen particularly clearly when the sun rises and casts its shadow. At Nanjinguan the gorges widen suddenly and you will come into the Hubei plain at around 5 pm.

It has taken about twelve hours to negotiate the gorges and the first stop is the city of Yichang. Towards midnight you reach Shashi. While the remainder of the journey has none of the grandeur and excitement of the gorges, the wide shores have their own peace and the traveller has the sensation of returning to the orthodox centre of China.

On the third morning you pass the historic Red Cliff, scene of one of the great battles of the Three Kingdoms period, between Cao Cao of the Northern Kingdom of Chu and Liu Bei of the Kingdom of Shu, aided by his ingenious advisor Zhu Geliang.

General Information on the Trip

The most interesting way to travel along the Yangtse is on one of the scheduled passenger boats. This is usually a steamer of 2500 tonnes, with four decks and accommodation for up to 800 passengers. The boat leaves daily from Chongqing, and has soft-class cabin facilities for twenty passengers; these cabins have a washbasin and two beds, and there is no price differential between inner and outer cabins. Sometimes, due to overbooking, overseas passengers will be accommodated in eight-berth cabins. There is a first-class viewing lounge on the deck just below the bridge. Catering facilities are adequate, but usually only Chinese food is available.

Several specially constructed charter cruise boats now ply this route. Carrying only overseas passengers, they have more flexible schedules and make stops at places such as Bai di cheng (White Emperor City). Although these boats are more luxurious, the passengers have less contact with the riverside life. The downstream journey takes three days at a speed of 32 kph. It is sometimes possible to disembark at Yichang and continue one's journey to Wuhan by land, giving one night and two days on board ship. The upstream journey from Wuhan takes four nights at a speed of 18 kph.

At the moment there is only one boat in the luxury category, the *Kunlun*, which has berths for some thirty guests. The disadvantage is that you get less of a feel of riverside life, although the boat can make more stops *en route*.

The best time to take the trip is between April and October; at other seasons the river is covered in mist. Between April and October the weather is generally somewhat 'Scottish' – it is cooler than on land, windy and often overcast, so take a windcheater or similar clothing. Binoculars are extremely useful. You may also want to take a pack of cards or a book to pass the time in between the famous sights.

TIBET

This region has sent a *frisson* of excitement through every traveller down the ages, because of its renowned inaccessibility. Well described by its oft-repeated epithet, 'the roof of the world', its physical situation has reinforced its political status, keeping Tibet remote and aloof from the rest of the world. In few cultures have the religious and political elements been so absolutely intertwined: the Dalai Lama was both the spiritual and temporal leader, and in almost every family one of the sons was chosen to enter a monastery at an early age. Even today a certain effort is required to reach Tibet – there is no railway, a road journey would take at least a week from any of the major Chinese cities, and even flights are subject to the vagaries of the rising and setting of the sun and mist.

Tibet is above all mountainous – part of the Qinghai–Tibet plateau which covers one-quarter of China's total landmass, and which is on average 4000 m above sea-level. The plateau is considered by geologists to be rather young – some 40 million years ago it was still under the sea. Tibet can be divided into three major regions: the northern Tibet plateau is bounded by the Kunlun Mountains, rising up to 7000 m. It is a barren, desert-like area where cultivation is almost impossible and which has only two months of warm weather a year. In eastern Tibet, known as the Chamdo area, there is more rainfall; the Salween, Mekong and Yangtse Rivers rise here. Southern Tibet, the most densely populated area, is bordered by the Himalayas. It consists of a series of high valley basins; the climate is milder and the land can be readily cultivated. Here are the sources of the Brahmaputra and Sutlej Rivers. Mountain barley is the major crop, which is pounded into flour and mixed with tea and yak's butter to make the *tsampa* beloved of the Tibetans. Sheep, yaks and horses are bred.

History
The origins of Tibet as a political and cultural unity are usually traced to King Songtsang Kampo, who unified the

country in AD 640, at the height of the Tang dynasty in China. He established a Tibetan alphabet based on Sanskrit, and his alliance with the Tang court was formalized and strengthened by his marriage to Princess Wen cheng, the adopted daughter of Emperor Tai zong. He also had a Nepalese wife and a Tibetan one. Princess Wen cheng is accredited with bringing Buddhism to Tibet, where it became invested with some of the Animistic features of the indigenous Bon religion. In 779 Buddhism was recognized as the official creed.

Under Songtsang Kampo and his successors Tibet was an aggressive power conducting raids against the surrounding countries. Tibetan influence extended northwards into Yunnan, Sichuan, Gansu and Qinghai (people of Tibetan origin are still found in these areas today), as well as southwards into Burma, Sikkim, Bhutan and Kashmir. With the nobility engaged in war, the power of the monasteries grew and the local form of Buddhism assimilated features of Hinduism and Tantraism.

Tibet first became part of the Chinese empire in the late thirteenth century under the Yuan dynasty. The leader of the Red Hat (Sakya) sect, Basba, went to Peking where he impressed the court and also worked out an alphabet for the Mongolian language. He was rewarded with power extending as far as Lake Kokonor in Qinghai.

During the fourteenth century the 'church' had become a corrupt organization and there were many power struggles between leading families; under Tsong Kapa a clean-up campaign was launched. Celibacy became prerequisite of the priesthood, and a kind of mitre worn by members of his sect probably gave rise to the name of the Yellow Hat sect. Celibacy meant that there was no natural heir to the throne – a problem which was solved by the system of finding the Dalai Lama. The Dalai

Lama (whose name means 'sea of wisdom') was the reincarnation of the Bodhisattva – one who had achieved enlightenment and returned to earth to help. The soul of the Dalai Lama was declared to pass into the body of a baby born at the moment of his own death, so massive searches would be made and clues would come from the high priests' dreams.

The Dalai Lama always came from a family of lowly origins. In 1578 Sonam Gyatso was named Dalai Lama during a visit to Mongolia. The titles of first and second Dalai Lama were posthumously conferred. Under the fifth Dalai Lama the building of the Potala was begun. The seventeenth century was a period of strife between sects which were eventually resolved by awarding land and power to the Panchen Lama. The fifth Dalai Lama dreamt that his tutor was the reincarnation of Amitabha Buddha (Opame). In the Buddhist hierarchy Opame is higher than Chenresi, the Buddhist god of mercy, but from the point of view of temporal power the Dalai Lama held the balance with influence over 109 counties, while the Panchen Lama's influence extended to only ten. The Dalai Lama's seat was at Lhasa, the Panchen Lama's at Shigatse.

In the reign of the Manchu emperor Kang xi, Tibet was invaded from Dzungaria. Kang xi's army was requested to assist: a Chinese Viceroy was sent to Lhasa and the seventh Dalai Lama was instated in 1720. In 1751 there were uprisings against the Chinese and although the Dalai Lama was recognized as the ruler of Tibet his executive powers were curtailed. Peking decreed that all major appointments should be approved by the court and a cabinet was set up with a Chinese Viceroy at its head. A copy of this Imperial edict and the urn used for casting votes for the cabinet members were placed in the uppermost rooms of the Potala Palace and once a year the Dalai Lama was obliged to make obeisance to this symbol of Chinese sovereignty.

In 1789 the Ghurkas invaded Tibet from Nepal. Chinese troops came to Tibet's aid and also sent troops into Nepal and established borders with India.

Within Tibet the nineteenth century was peaceful apart from further conflicts with Nepal in 1854–56. However Tibet was now to become the focus of rival interests between the British and the Russians who saw the area as a buffer zone between British interests in India and expanding Tsarist Russia. British diplomatic and exploratory missions had been coming to Tibet since the end of the eighteenth century. By 1876 there was open diplomatic conflict between Russia and Britain; by 1890 Britain had annexed Sikkim; and in 1904 a military expedition led by Colonel Younghusband reached Tibet and the 13th Dalai Lama was forced to flee to Mongolia. By 1910 the Chinese had regained partial control of Tibet, forcing the Dalai Lama to flee once more. 1911 saw a further uprising of the Tibetans against the Chinese and the Dalai Lama achieved shortlived independent rule. At the Conference of Simla held in 1913–14 between the British, Chinese and Tibetans, Britain argued for an independent Western Tibet. There were also discussions about borders between Tibet and India and the Macmahon line was drawn up; however the talks ended inconclusively without being ratified by the Chinese party. Following this the British maintained a mission in Lhasa until 1947 when India gained independence. Eastern parts of Tibet were then absorbed into the Chinese empire and internal preoccupations in China meant that the Tibet question was ignored until the accession to power of the Communists in 1949. On receiving news of the impending arrival of the Chinese Army in 1950, the Dalai Lama fled as far as Sikkim, but then returned to Lhasa, where he was still acknowledged as titular leader of Tibet. Freedom of religious belief and practice was guaranteed and former nobles were allowed to leave Tibet safely. In 1951 the People's Liberation Army began their extensive reform programme: schools were opened, there was a new health care system, industry was developed and main roads were constructed, linking Tibet to the rest of China. In 1954 the Dalai Lama and his entourage were invited to Tibet where they were hosted by the Chinese Government and discussions were held on future relations. In 1959 there was an uprising of the Tibetans, but the Chinese army moved in and stricter controls were introduced. The Dalai Lama fled to India and in 1965 Tibet was formally declared an Autonomous Region.

In the ten years following the Cultural Revolution it suffered from the same excesses as other parts of China – religious worship became impossible and little account was taken of the natural conditions and customs of Tibet. The Han Chinese assumed an excessive role in the administration of the region at this time.

Today many of the Han cadres are returning to China, and Tibetans are taking up all the administrative posts at district level and 80 per cent of them at county level. The Tibetan language is assuming greater importance again and much decision making is taking place at local levels, in keeping with the rest of China. Free markets and local crafts may flourish once more, and monasteries have re-opened. The present population of Tibet is 1.8 million.

One of the great debates in modern Tibet is the future role of the Dalai Lama. Born in Qinghai in 1935, he came to Lhasa at the age of two. His life in the Potala is recorded very vividly by Heinrich Harrer in his book *Seven Years in Tibet*. Today the Dalai Lama lives at Dharamsala in India, in the foothills of the Himalayas, heading a community of forty monks and a kind of government-in-exile of the many exiled Tibetans. Unlike the previous Dalai Lamas he has a wide knowledge of the world, is much respected and has sent several delegations to Tibet and Peking. His picture has reappeared in many Tibetan households, and many long for his return. He is the fourteenth Dalai Lama, and it was predicted long ago that there would only be fourteen Dalai Lamas.

Lhasa

The name Lhasa automatically conjures up that soaring edifice the Potala Palace, former 'home' of the Dalai Lama, containing thousands of rooms and chapels. The city stands 3600 m above sea-level on a tributary of the Yalongzangpo River, the Lhasa. The total population is 80,000. While parts of the city remain quite unchanged, the new quarters have the unmistakable straight lines and leanness of any modern Chinese city.

Potala

The earliest Potala dates from the reign of King Songtsang Kampo in the seventh century. The name 'potala' is a word of Sanskrit origin meaning 'Buddha's Mountain'. The present Potala was rebuilt in the seventeenth century by the Great Fifth. The external elevation consists of the main part of the palace (the White Palace) and the two wings of the Red Palace – so named for the colour of the walls. The building is thirteen storeys high and is built into the side of a hill for 110 m. The palace is approached by sweeping staircases and halfway up you reach a platform where religious ceremonies were held; at this level are a seminary and the halls and lodgings of the 154 lamas.

The East Main Hall is the largest in the Potala, with sixty-four elaborate pillars, and was the place where the ceremonies for the consecrating of the Dalai Lamas, were held. The West Main Hall is the Hall of Sacrifice and contains the embalmed remains of the fifth and the seventh to the thirteenth Dalai Lamas; their *stupas* are all covered with gold leaf and jewels. Before the *stupas* are incense burners and the butter lamps whose distinctive aroma pervades the Potala.

At the top of the White Palace are the lofty living quarters of the Dalai Lama – from here the young Dalai Lama used to gaze on the city of Lhasa through a telescope. The oldest rooms in the Potala are the living quarters of King Songtsang Kampo in the Red Palace, where there is also a statue of him. Also in the topmost rooms of the Potala is the tablet proclaiming long life and reign to the emperor Qian long, written in Chinese, Tibetan, Mongolian and Manchu.

The stone foundations were strengthened with molten copper, while the upper storeys of the palace are wooden structures with sweeping eaves and bells. Many of the walls are lavishly decorated and painted with religious scenes and secular tales. The Potala also contains volumes of *sutras* and seals.

Norbu Lingka (Jewel Park)

The Dalai Lama's summer palace, it consists of a walled garden with rare trees, flowers and chapels. Now opened as a park, it also exhibits many of the seals and artefacts of the Dalai Lama.

Drepung Monastery

This monastery, 12 km east of Lhasa, was the largest in the world and there were once 10,000 monks here – now there are only 240. The other great monasteries were the Ganden, which

Left The Twelve Fairy Peaks are one of the landmarks of the Wuxia Gorge (Sichuan).
Right Morning mist over the Wuxia Gorge on the Yangste River

The Big Buddha at Le shan in Sichuan Province

View of the Potala Palace in Lhasa

Scenic spot at Xinjiang's Heavenly Lake

was razed during the Cultural Revolution, and the Sera.

Zuglakang Temple (Jokhang)

The Temple is one of the major landmarks of Lhasa, visited by every pilgrim to the city, who would then move around its perimeter prostrating himself along the Barkhor, the street approaching the temple. It was built by Songtsang Kampo in honour of his Chinese wife Wen cheng, who brought Buddhism to Tibet. Its Tibetan name, Zuglakang, means Temple of Sakyamuni, for Wen Cheng is thought to have brought a statue of Sakyamuni with her from Xi'an. A withered willow tree in front of the Temple is said to have been planted by her. Tablets in Han and Tibetan proclaim early alliances between Tibet and the Chinese empire.

In the fifteenth century Tsong Kapa, founder of the Yellow Hat sect, carried out extensive work of the Temple. The monastery contains some 300 Buddhist statues, the most magnificent of which is the bronze one brought by Wen Cheng. There are statues of Songstang Kampo, Wen Cheng and his Tibetan and Nepalese wives. The walls are covered with delicate, detailed murals showing scenes from daily life in Tibet, also murals showing Princess Wen Cheng's journey from Chang'an and the building of the Zuglakang Temple, which combines features of Nepalese, Indian, Tibetan and Chinese architecture. It has undergone extensive repairs since the early 1970s.

Shigatse (Xigaze)

Tibet's second city, the former seat of the Panchen Lama, is some 337 km west of Lhasa. The journey takes ten hours and is as interesting as the destination, as one travels down the new highway along the banks of the Lhasa River, the best cultivated areas in Tibet. At Qushui you will see the Yalongzang-po, Tibet's major river, whose name means 'mother'. It has a very steep drop and flows very swiftly, which make it an excellent source of hydroelectric power.

After Qushui there is a steep climb up to the Kamba la Pass, almost 5000 m above sea-level. Below the pass lies Lake Yamzhog Yumco, the largest lake in Tibet (678 km²); set in unique mountain scenery, it is renowned for its scaleless fish!

The next major attraction is Gyantse; one of Tibet's ancient cities, it stands on the Nyang River, a tributary of the Yalongzangpo. There once stood an impressive fort and monastery here. South of the city is fertile farmland. Gyantse is also famous for its carpets.

Shigatse itself is 90 km from here. The Panchen Lama's seat, the Tashi lumpo Lamasery, is a golden-roofed building with a 27-m gilded Buddha, overshadowed by a fort. There were once 3700 monks here, but this number has now dwindled to 100.

Tourist Information

Travel

There are daily flights from Chengdu to Lhasa. A railway is planned between Qinghai and Tibet, but as yet the only other means of access to Tibet is by road.

Accommodation

At present the development of tourism to Tibet is very slow. Only very small groups are allowed to visit and the tour cost is high, due to the fact that all the daily necessities of life are brought in by air from Chengdu. The accommodation is basic, and it is difficult to find interpreters with a command of Tibetan, Chinese and English. There is a guesthouse in the centre of Lhasa.

People travelling to Tibet are recommended to undergo a thorough medical examination beforehand, because of the high altitude. On arrival in Lhasa visitors are asked to rest in order to become acclimatized. Oxygen bags are readily available.

XINJIANG-UIGHUR AUTONOMOUS REGION

The name of this region (also called Sinkiang) means the 'new territories', and comprises one-sixth of China's total landmass it is the larges autonomous region in China, but has a sparse population of 12 million. The Xinjiang–Uighur Autonomous Region was constituted in 1955; the Uighurs are one of China's largest nationality groups – they are Moslems of Turkic origin. There are some thirteen nationalities in Xinjiang – the majority comprise 45 per cent Uighurs, 41 per cent Han Chinese, 6 per cent Kazakh, and 1 per cent Mongolian. By law all publications must be printed in the four languages of the region. During the Cultural Revolution local customs and the right to follow one's religion were suppressed, but these constraints have now been removed. There are new figures in the regional administration, and the minority nationalities are exempt from the rigid family planning programme which applies to Han Chinese.

For the visitor, a journey to Xinjiang offers a new experience – a glimpse of Chinese Turkestan, of different nationalities with their non-Chinese physique, languages and customs, of geographical extremes from the alpine scenery of the Tian Mountains to the Turfan Depression and Oasis, and the edges of the Taklamakam Desert. It is also a region rich in the relics of the Silk Route, for it was through this unfriendly terrain that the merchants passed to and from the west. Ruins of ancient cities, tombs, beacons and Buddhist grottoes await the visitor.

Xinjiang is separated from Tibet to the south by the soaring Kunlun Mountains. The Tian mountain ranges stretch from east to west across the region, dividing it into two, with the Dzungari Basin to the north and the Taklamakam Desert and Tarim Basin to the south. The word *taklamakam* means in Uighur 'once you go in, you never come out' – a sinister name for this massive, impassable area of uninhabited desert, the second largest in the world. It divided the old Silk Route, and travellers would be forced either to pass from oasis to oasis on the south of the desert, along the foothills of the Kunlun Mountains, passing such centres as Hetian (Khotan), famous for its carpets, or to follow the northern route, leaving the oasis of Hami to cross the Tian Mountains and the Yili River and continuing westward to the Black Sea.

Other stops on the northern route, to the north of the Tarim Basin, were the city of Korla with the famous Iron Gate Pass, which since 1980 has been connected to Turfan by rail. Further west is the city of Kuche (Kuqa, formerly known as Qiuci); during the western Han dynasty it was a large city state on the Silk Road. A Han princess was married to the Prince of Qiuci, and by 60 BC Qiuci was under the jurisdiction of the Hans. In the Tang dynasty the governor's office was moved here from Turfan. Qiuci became a great centre of Buddhism, the home of thousands of nuns and priests, where lavish ceremonies were held. Kumarajiva, the son of an Indian father and a local mother, was born here and spent a long time in Changan translating the scriptures. The music and dancing of the area were influential in central China. In the vicinity of Kuche is the westernmost example of Thousand Buddha Grottoes in China, at the Kizil Grottoes on the slopes of the Muzat River. There are some 236 caves which are under state protection. They were decorated between the fourth and fourteenth centuries; characteristic of the caves are the diamond-shaped pictures, each containing a different scene from the life of Sakyamuni. Today Kuche is the second largest county in Xinjiang, with a population of 300,000.

Yining was for a long time the exit for the direct route westwards. It is close to the USSR border and in fact the Yili River on which it stands flows into Lake Balkhash. The fertile Yili region was famous for its horses, 'the heavenly steeds of the Western Han', which were first presented to the Han emperor when General Zhang Qian came here in 119 BC; the relationship was further cemented by marriage between the Wusun and Han royal families. Today the area is inhabited by Mongols and Kazaks – nomadic peoples who are a hybrid of the early Wusuns, Turks, Khitans and Mongolians. The area has many ancient tumuli, Silk Route remains and Turkic stone figures which date from the early Tang. There are also the remains of the Tang dynasty Crescent City – north-east of the present-day city of Yining. Lin Zexu was banished here by the Qing government after the Opium War in 1842, and supervised water conservancy and land reclamation projects.

Other major cities to the south-west of Yining are Aksu and Kashgar. Apart from the capital, Urumchi, and the Turfan Oasis, these other areas have not yet been opened to visitors. The lakes and rivers of the Tarim Basin region are fed by mountain springs and drain mostly into Lake Lopnor to the east of the Taklamakam Desert.

In the northernmost part of the region, around the Dzungari Basin, the climate is damper. The area is inhabited mostly by Kazakhs and Torgut Mongols; grass grows over the sandy soil, so the area is used for cattle breeding. At Kelamayi there is a major oilfield.

One of the most unusual features of the region are the Turfan and Hami Depressions in gaps in the Tian Mountains. They are very hot in summer, and are both some 150 m below sea-level. Turfan is famous for its grapes, and Hami for its melons.

The agricultural priorities in Xinjiang are improved methods of animal husbandry, water conservancy and reforestation projects. There are large, mechanized state farms, and communes around the oases. The Xinjiang Production and Construction Corps of the People's Liberation Army made efforts to expand arable land areas, construct water conservation projects and build state farms. Industry is closely linked to agriculture – sugar refineries for processing the beet grown in the north of the area, and cotton and woollen mills. North of Urumchi there are coal fields and iron ore deposits, as well as oil from Kelamayi. Railway links between Urumchi and the rest of China were first established in 1963 when the Lanzhou–Urumchi railway was completed. Recently a line has been built as far south as Korla, and further railway links with Qinghai are planned.

History
The history of the area is characterized by alternating tension and tolerance between the Han Chinese and the Turkic peoples, and the western regions have for centuries been of great strategic importance. During the Han dynasty the Chinese first sent emissaries to the western regions to establish good relations and a safe passage for their merchants travelling westwards. During the Tang dynasty the confines of the empire extended to Lake Balkhash (now in the USSR) and it was in this area that the famous poet Li Bai was born. The Uighurs settled here in the ninth century, when they were forced westwards from Mongolia. They gradually gained

297

ascendancy in the area, and during the eighteenth century the Manchus conducted campaigns and garrisoned the army here to work on new farming projects.

Between 1863 and 1873 there were Moslem rebellions led by Jakub Beg, since the Manchu government seemed prepared to see the area lost to the Russians, while the British had other interests in maintaining the area as a buffer state. The rebellions were quelled by General Zuo Zongtong, and in 1885 the founding of Xinjiang, the New Territories, was announced. The Russians also had access to the mines, and had their own consul in the area. Rebellions broke out during the early part of the twentieth century, and the warlord Sheng Shicai flirted with the Communists and the Japanese. In 1942 he turned on his advisors, among them the brother of Mao Zedong, and joined forces with Chiang Kaishek. In 1944 Uighur autonomists created the Republic of Eastern Turkestan – led by Sai Fu Din. They established their base at Yili and were the first to welcome the Communists in 1949. Sai Fu Din was the main secretary of the local Communist Party until 1980. The setting up of the Xinjiang–Uighur Autonomous Region was proclaimed in 1955.

Shihezi

This town lies on the southern rim of Dzungari Basin in the Gobi Desert, 150 km east of Urumchi. After Xinjiang was settled under Qian long in the eighteenth century, soldiers were sent here to reclaim and farm the land. The new city was developed by the reconstruction unit of the People's Liberation Army, who built factories and reclaimed farmland. The urban population is 100,000, although 780,000 people come under the Shihezi municipal administration. Reservoirs and irrigation canals have been built, so that now fruit, cotton and grain are grown. Local industry includes canning, flour milling, sugar refining, machinery and oil pressing.

Urumchi

Urumchi is 3000 km from Peking and you can travel there by air (a journey of 4 hours) or by rail via Lanzhou (36 hours). There are local unlisted flights to other cities in Xinjiang. CAAC international flights sometimes stop at Urumchi so it can be used as a port of entry. The airport is half an hour away from the city.

The regional capital is also known as Wulumuqi. The primary name originates from Dzungar Mongolian, and means 'beautiful pastures'. The city, spread along the banks of the Urumchi River, north of the Tian Mountains, has a population of 850,000. It is very hot and dry in summer, and very cold, dry and windy in the winter.

Though by no means a beautiful city, it contains an interesting mix of modern Han and Uighur-style building – there are boulevards lined with administrative offices as found all over China, but the signs are written in Uighur script. The Han population has increased to 76 per cent, 10 per cent are Uighurs and 10 per cent Hui. The city has its own university and technical colleges. Industry includes oil refining, cement, thermal power, chemicals and cotton, and there are coal and iron deposits to the north.

There are few interesting sites in the city itself, but the fascination of the place lies in the different customs, peoples and costumes. Several arts and crafts factories produce Uighur artefacts such as the famous embroidered caps, as well as jade carving, musical instruments and carpets, and an evening meal in a local restaurant is well worth experiencing.

The museum contains many artefacts from tombs and the Silk Road. The office of the Eighth Route Army was where Mao Zemin, the brother of Mao Zedong, operated from, and gives a background to revolutionary history in Xinjiang.

In the north of the city there is the People's Park, situated on the western banks of the Urumchi. There is a boating lake there and several Chinese-style pavilions and willow trees.

Further to the north is Hong shan (Red Hill), a rocky promontory which affords a fine view over the city, surmounted by the Red Pagoda which is nine storeys high and was first built in the Tang dynasty.

There are two interesting journeys to be made out of town, as well as an overnight journey to the Turfan Oasis.

Tian chi The Heavenly Lake
The Heavenly Lake is situated in the Tian Mountains to the east of Urumchi. The journey there takes at least two hours and passes through the bleaker industrial quarter of Urumchi, gradually coming into pasture land where you may see herds of camels and *yurt* settlements. You then make your way into the mountains, past waterfalls and wild flowers, birds, horses and the occasional sight of a *yurt* being erected or dismantled. The climb is hair-raising and the road very basic. The Heavenly Lake is 1990 m above sea level and from here you can see the Bogda Peak which is 5400 m above sea level and snow-capped all year round. The scenery is Swiss in flavour. You can take a boat ride on the lake, or sample a meal of barbecued lamb in one of the rest houses. It is advisable to take warm clothes for this expedition as the temperature is often several degrees cooler than in the city. In winter people come here for winter sports.

The Southern Mountains
This is a mountain resort to the south of the city. The journey is more pictures-que than the road to Heavenly Lake, passing through fertile valleys where there are impressive waterfalls.

Tourist Information

Useful Addresses
CAAC
Fanxiulu
Tel. 2536

Hotels
Kunlun Hotel
Tel. 3901
This is a standard Soviet-style hotel with friendly service. There are post office and banking facilities, and food shops and gift shops on the ground floor in the lobby. There is an antique shop on the second floor.

Ying binguan
Fanxiu lu
Tel. 2351

Shopping
The main department store is in the downtown area. Urumchi is well known for its embroidered caps, musical instruments, and carpets.

Food
The local specialities are barbecued lamb, yogurt, and pasties with lamb fillings.

Turfan Oasis
After travelling through miles of Gobi desert, the green pointed poplars which mark the perimeter of the Turfan Oasis shimmer into view. Turfan was once an important station on the Silk Route, and many of the sites in the area are connected with the Silk Route and the powerful city states which thrived here. Turfan lies at the foot of Huoyan shan (the Flaming Mountains), described in *Monkey*. The oasis covers 50,000 km^2 and, at its lowest point in the centre of Lake Aydingkol, is 154 m below sea level. There is hardly any rainfall and

between June and August the temperature often reaches 40°C. However the oasis is irrigated by the *karez*, a system of underground wells and channels which carry down the snow which has melted from the nearby mountains. The edge of the oasis is protected from the encroaching desert by a system of wind- and sand-breaks formed from rows of poplar trees – in Chinese this is known as Wu dao lin, the 'Five Row Forest'. Turfan is famous for its grapes which grow in endless rows in the luxuriant Grape Valley; every courtyard seems to have its own vine offering shade from the heat. Other fruits include melons and apricots. Cotton is also grown in the oasis. The people are not wealthy but they are both kind and curious, and if you have the chance to visit the home of a Uighur family you will be plied with tea, fruit and the traditional bread made from threadlike strands of dough, while sitting on a raised dais.

The style of architecture is typical of central Asia – low mud-baked houses designed to be as cool as possible. There are several sites of historic interest in the area.

Jiaohe

Between the second and fifth centuries this was the capital of the state of Cheshi. During the Tang dynasty it became the centre of local administration for the Anxi area. The city stands on a natural fortress formed by two rivers passing at its foot. The main street, city temples and niches for Buddhist statues are still distinguishable. Jiaohe is 10 km west of the district town of Turfan.

Gaochang

This town is 40 km south of Turfan in the Flaming Mountain commune. It was a walled city – the wall was 5 km in circumference and 11 m high, and the exterior, inner and palace complexes are still distinguishable. In 640 it became the seat of the prefecture of Xichang, and in the ninth century it was taken over by the Huihus – forerunners of the Uighurs. The city flourished until the fourteenth century, when it was abandoned.

Astana

On the site of the ancient city of Astana are over four hundred tombs, which date from AD 273 to 772. Archaeologists have excavated silk destined for export, murals and skeletons.

Yimin Pagoda

The mosque was built in 1776 of mud, and is now almost abandoned. The main feature is the 44-m-high pagoda or tower which is constructed in Uighur style and decorated with many different patterned motifs.

Grottoes

For students of Buddhist art the grottoes at Bezeklik are a two-hour drive from Turfan.

Tourist Information

Travel

You can travel to Turfan by rail getting off at Daheyan or by bus from Urumchi, this latter option involving a four-hour journey through the desert.

Accommodation and Food

Lodging is in the Turfan reception centre in the county seat of Turfan. By no means luxurious, the rooms are cool, with stone floors. They are supplied with electric fans, basins and flasks of water. There is a communal tap in the courtyard, as well as a shower house and public conveniences. The complex includes a small shop. The courtyard is shaded by a vine where local people sit and play cards and where your host will welcome you. Often in the evening it is transformed into a stage, when the local song and dance troupe will come to entertain visitors in true Uighur style.

Only Chinese or Uighur-style food is available here. It is well prepared, and you can buy the local wine and packets of raisins. The reception centre is well located, and you can easily visit the colourful local market.

YUNNAN PROVINCE

The name of this province means 'south of the clouds', for it is situated in the far south-west of China, bordering on Burma, Laos and Vietnam. In China it is associated with the many national minorities – around twenty-one – which have long inhabited the area. These peoples, living in autonomous districts and counties, constitute a third of the total population of over 31.35 million. The most numerous nationalities are the Yi, Bai, Hani, Zhuang, Dai and Miao, and recently another small nationality has been recognized – the Jino. In the south-west of the province the Xishuangbanna Autonomous District is open to foreign visitors; it is an area of lush vegetation and picturesque landscape, and inhabited largely by the Dai peoples.

Yunnan is a mountainous province – part of it is formed by the Yunnan–Guizhou plateau averaging 1300 m above sea-level and rising to 5000 m in the north-west. The province is drained by major rivers which pass through Indo-China – the Salween, Mekong, Red and Black Rivers. In the north of the province the upper reaches of the Yangtse – here called the Jinsha or Golden Sand River – form the border with Sichuan Province.

Like all China's border provinces it was for a long time an independent kingdom. Under the Han dynasty it was the state of Dian – the province's classical name which is still used today. By the eighth century Dali in the west of the province was the capital of the Nanchao dynasty, whose influence was felt in Burma, Thailand and Vietnam.

The area was finally assimilated into the Chinese empire in the thirteenth century. The area is rich in mineral resources, and copper was mined extensively in the seventeenth and eighteenth centuries. In the nineteenth century Yunnan was the scene of a series of Moslem uprisings, and then gradually became prey to warlords and the vagaries of opium. In the early twentieth century the French completed their narrow-gauge railway from Haiphong to Kunming and established themselves in the province, building hospitals and other amenities of modern life in the major cities. Memoirs written by American and British visitors are somewhat damming about French behaviour and their treatment of the Chinese, but one wonders whether this is not the result of pique at their own countries not having established their influence earlier.

During the war against the Japanese between 1937 and 1945, when the government retreated to Chongqing, many enterprises and universities also came to the south-west and set themselves up in Kunming. Roads were built from Sichuan and Guizhou, and the Burma road became a route for refugees. Kunming was also on the air route from India, from where supplies were brought. Although much of the industry returned to northern China at the end of the war, the government made efforts to establish an industrial foundation for the province. The spectacular Chengdu–Kunming railway completed in 1970 also brought the province closer to the rest of China.

The climate is tropical in the south, cooler in the mountainous north, and has copious rainfall. Rice, wheat and maize are grown, and rape, tobacco, cotton, tea and sugar cane are the major cash crops. Lush plants, fruit and colourful wildlife abound – particularly peacocks and other birds.

Kunming

This city is the provincial capital; before its original name was restored the city was known for a time as Yunnan fu. The French built many administrative buildings here. As mentioned above, the city enjoyed an important role as a refuge for industry and universities during the war against the Japanese. Today it has a population of one million and a developing industry. Known as the spring city because of its year-round spring-like weather, the city has much to offer the first-time visitor by way of historic and scenic attractions. It has temples, lakes and hot springs; to the south-east of the city is the Stone Forest at Lu'nan; and from Kunming you may visit the more remote areas of Dali, famous as an early Buddhist centre, and the Xishuangbanna Autonomous District, home of the Dai nationality.

Kunming is 3179 km from Peking, and can be reached by air from there as well as from Guangzhou. Two flights a week go to Rangoon. There are rail connections to Hanoi, Taiphong (closed at present), and Chengdu.

Green Lake Park

Situated on the western slopes of Wuhua Hill, the lake was a marshy flat beyond the city walls until in the Qing dynasty a local governor constructed a pavilion on the island in the middle of the lake and cleared the lake. The lake is crisscrossed by two causeways planted with willows, and these, together with the green of the lotus flowers in the lake, have given it its name. The Haixin Pavilion is used to house exhibitions, and the grounds have been planted with the exotic flora of Yunnan Province. There is also a guest house in the grounds.

Yuantong Temple and Zoo

In the north of the city; a temple has stood on this site since the early days of the Yuan dynasty. The Temple is situated at the foot of Chignon Hill – the highest point in Kunming and worth the climb for the view over the city. Among the Temple's interesting features are the gaudy painted figures characteristic of the south, and the supporting beams carved with dragons.

There is a zoo in the grounds where animals typical of the province are kept.

Black Dragon Pool

The Black Dragon Pool lies on the northern outskirts of Kunming in the Wulao Hills. Legend has it that in ancient times ten dragons were terrorizing the local populace. One of the eight deities, Lu Dongbing, overcame nine of them and had them safely buried under a pagoda. The smallest and blackest of them was allowed to live in this very pool, on condition that he perpetrated only good deeds. Historical records suggest that there was a temple by Black Dragon Pool as early as the Han dynasty; however the Black Water Temple which stands there today dates from the Qing.

Other attractions include the Dragon Fountain Temple, first built in the Ming dynasty. In the temple courtyard grows the Tang plum tree, reputedly planted by a monk in the Nanchao Kingdom in the Tang dynasty; to this day blossom still appears in springtime, although the main trunk has withered. Shading the temple courtyard is the Song cypress, a tree of enormous girth and height. Nearby is the camellia garden, a riot of colour at the time of the spring festival. In a Ming dynasty tomb the scholar Xue Erwang is buried; he lived in the last years of that dynasty and drowned himself and his family rather than surrender to the encroaching Qing. The Yunnan Botanical Gardens are also situated here.

Golden Temple (Jin dian)

On the northern outskirts of Kunming, the Temple nestles among the forested slopes of Ming feng Hill. Much of the temple complex has been cast in brass, hence the name. To reach it you must climb many steps, passing through the three gates to Heaven, until you come to the Taihe Palace, the Palace of Great Harmony. Here there is a chamber cast entirely – pillars, walls and screens and balustrades – out of brass and engraved.

The building was first put here in 1602, then moved to Dali in the west of the province, and finally returned to be reconstructed in 1672, during the reign of the Emperor Kang xi, by the well-known Qing personality Wu Sangui. At the side of the Golden Temple is the famous butterfly wing camellia tree, which has been here for some five hundred years and whose beauty has often been praised by poets; it is always visited at the time of the spring festival when it is in full bloom.

Bamboo Temple (Qiongzhu si)
Set in tranquil wooded surroundings to the north-west of Kunming, the Bamboo Temple is one of those Chinese temples whose founding is related to stories about the appearance and disappearance of ethereal beings from nowhere, and sticks planted in the ground which flourished and became bamboo groves. In the Nanchao Kingdom, during the Tang dynasty, it was one of the earliest Buddhist temples in the Kunming area.

The main hall contains 500 life-size statues of Buddhas made during the reign of Guang xu between 1883 and 1890. The statues are vivid portrayals of Bodhisattvas, each adopting striking lifelike poses and painted in accurate detail. The Temple houses a tablet dating from the fourteenth century, written in both Chinese and Mongolian script; known as the Emperor's Edict, it has been a valuable historical source for Yunnan's past.

Anning Hot Springs and Caoxi Temple
Dong Biwu declared the Anning hot springs 'the best spa in the world' when he came here in 1962. The spa is south-west of Kunming, nestling among luxuriant wooded hills. The temperature of the water is around 42°C and it is beneficial in the treatment of dyspepsia and rheumatism. The spring was discovered over a thousand years ago. The grounds contain villas for visitors.

About 2 km from the spa is the Caoxi Temple. Built in the Song and Yuan dynasties, the buildings and the wooden statue of Buddha are among the finest examples of early Song architecture in China. A hole in the roof called Silver Moon in the Sky captures the beams of the mid-autumn moon once every sixty years, illuminating the statue of Buddha. In the grounds of the temple are plum and canna trees dating from the Yuan dynasty. Nearby is the Pearl Fountain – a natural spring.

Dian Chi (Lake Dian) and Environs
Dianchi Lake, the sixth largest freshwater lake in China, covers an area of 340 km². South of Kunming, it is a highland lake with all the clarity and blueness of the lakes of the European Alps. The countryside surrounding the lake is fertile and prosperous, and many buildings of historical interest stand on the shores of the lake. A guest house has been opened for visitors on the shore and a boat-ride is an essential part of your visit here. On the north-eastern shores there are bays suitable for sunbathing and swimming.

At the northern tip of the lake is the Daguan Pavilion. When built in 1696 it was called the Buddha Temple; extensive renovations were carried out under the provincial governor in 1866, creating an area of willows, bridges, galleries, lotus flowers and causeways. The park is dominated by the pavilion, from which there is a fine panorama of the lake and which contains tablets inscribed with paeans of praise for the lake written by poets through the ages.

Other temples on the lake shore include the sumptuous Taihua Temple and the Huating Temple, which was built in the eleventh century and by the twentieth century was the biggest temple in Kunming, with five magnificent buildings.

Sanqing Pavilions and the Dragon Gate Caves

Perched on the sheer cliffs of Buddha Hill in the Western Hills are the Sanqing Pavilions, which were built for the Prince of Liang in the Yuan dynasty as a summer palace to overlook the lake and the city of Kunming. From here you may climb up stone steps to caves painted and carved with murals and statues on Buddhist themes. Passing through a tunnel in the cliff face you cross the Dragon Gate to reach the Sky Scraping Cave, with its stone statues of gods from Buddhist lore.

Tourist Information

Hotels

Cui hu binguan (Green Lake Hotel)
6 Cui hu nan lu
Tel. 3514
Situated opposite Cui hu Park, this is one of the best appointed hotels in Kunming and has all amenities.

Kunming fandian
145 Dong feng dong lu
Tel. 5286
Situated to the east of the main commercial area of Zhengyi lu. All amenities.

Shi lin binguan (Stone Forest Hotel)
Lu'nan County
Tel. via long-distance operator
Situated in the scenic Stone Forest area, the amenities are simple but adequate.

Xiyuan fandian
Kunming xijiao (Kunming West Suburbs)

Overlooking Dianchi Lake, this is a small, villa-type hotel.

Restaurants

Yunnan guoqiao mixian
Nantong jie
Tel. 2610
Local cuisine and rice noodles.

Shopping

The main commercial centre is on Zhengyi lu and Dong feng dong lu. Close to the intersection you will find the foreign language bookshop, the antiques shop, the National Minorities Arts and Crafts shop and a department store.

Useful Addresses

CAAC
123 Dong feng dong lu
Tel. 4270

Luxingshe
68 Hua shan xi lu
Tel. 4992

Stone Forest (Shi lin)

The Stone Forest is one of the major and most unusual sights in Yunnan Province. Situated 126 km south-east of Kunming in Lu'nan county, it merits an overnight stay and there is a small guesthouse here.

Legends give many accounts of the formation of the Stone Forest. However the scientific account suggests that over 220 million years ago the Stone Forest was under water, and a thick deposit of limestone was left here. A great deal of movement of the earth's crust caused the sea to subside, and rainwater seeped into the cracks between the remaining stones, eroding them and widening the cracks. Continuous weathering eventually formed stone sprouts which grew into pillars.

The Stone Forest covers an area of 400,000 *mu* and is sometimes referred to as the greatest spectacle on earth. For grandeur and natural magnificence it can be compared with the Grand Canyon, although the stark karst scenery is relieved by graceful bridges and pavilions. In every pinnacle and peak there is a shape and a story, such as Lion Arbour and Sword Peak Pond. Nearby is a magnificent waterfall.

Xishuangbanna

Its exotic plant life gives Xishuangbanna Autonomous District in the south-west of the province an air of the Garden of Eden. The largest nationality group in the area is the Dai, and the name of the region means 'Twelve Districts' in their language. The population numbers 620,000 and several other nationalities live here. The capital of the prefecture is Jinghong (Yungjinghong).

Perhaps the best time to visit Xishuangbanna is in April, for the weather is warm and the air full of the fragrance of a myriad varieties of flowers. On 14 April the Dai New Year is celebrated with dragon boat races, peacock dances and the famous 'water splash' ritual – a rumbustious way of chasing away the dirty old year and bringing in the new.

The Dai people are generally Buddhist and the area contains ornate temples reminiscent of those in Burma. Houses are built on stilts from wood and bamboo, with storage space for boats underneath them. Rice is often eaten with the fingers. The costume of the Dai women is a colourful combination of turban, silver jewellery and slim, ankle-length skirts.

The tropical climate and fertile soil produce many exotic fruits and cash crops, from excellent tea to rubber, teak oil, palam, cinnamon, pepper, mangoes, pineapples, bananas, grapefruit, and a pharmacopia of medicinal herbs. In the local forests can be found peacocks, wild buffalo, elephants, panthers and monkeys.

ZHEJIANG PROVINCE

A small but wealthy coastal province south of Shanghai, it has a population of 37.92 million. The northern area forms part of the fertile Yangtse River delta, and to the south it adjoins mountainous Fujian Province. Zhejiang contains the scenic and cultural city of Hangzhou, with its West Lake; Shaoxing, home of writer, Lu Xun and famous for rice wine; the ancient commercial port of Ningpo; and Wenzhou, renowned for its oranges and the breathtaking scenery of the Yandang Mountains.

The Shanghai–Guangzhou railway passes through the province, and apart from this and the minor branch lines the major form of transport is via the many rivers and waterways – indeed the Grand Canal terminates at Hangzhou. The major river of the province is the Qiantang, which was also known as the Zhejiang – hence the name of the province. Historically, the northern part of the province was part of the state of Wu in the Warring States period, while the south and east belonged to Yue. The province began to grow in importance in the sixth and seventh centuries, after the completion of the Imperial Canal.

Between Shaoxing and Ningpo, in the area south of the Hangzhou bay, the plain is surrounded by hilly uplands. Rice is grown in the valleys, and wheat and barley on the uplands; tea, cotton, jute, rape, ramie, timber and silk are major cash crops, with fisheries and salt on the coast. The upper basin of the Qiantang River consists of an upland area with wooded hills less than 1000 m high; rice is double-cropped here, and maize, wheat, barley and some sugar cane are also grown. One of the major developments is the hydroelectric power schemes based round the upper reaches of the river and its tributaries;

they are connected to the Shanghai and Hangzhou grids.

The south-east of the province is the highest and most rugged area. Where cultivation is possible rice, green fertilizer, wheat, barley, rape and sweet potatoes are grown; cash crops are sugar cane, jute, ramie, cotton, citrus fruits and tea. The area is also important for timber and wood oils. The major local port is Wenzhou on the Ou River. The rugged mountains provide some fabulous scenery.

The climate of the area is sub-tropical – warm and damp. The January temperature ranges from 4°C in the north to 7°C in the south; in July it is 28–29°C all over the province. Rainfall is 1200–1800 mm, falling between April and September. The area is subject to the vagaries of flooding and drought, and major work has been carried out to regulate these threats. Most of the province can guarantee three crops per year, and it is one of the major producers of jute, large bamboo and silk. Natural resources include coal, lime, zinc, alum, iron ore and brimstone.

Hangzhou

Traditionally one of the favourite scenic spots of the Chinese, Hangzhou is a town of great wealth and splendour. At its peak in the Song dynasty, it retained its popularity with the emperors of the Qing dynasty and with the rich in the early years of the Republic. Even today it is regarded as one of the most romantic cities in China, the one where young couples should go for their honeymoon. It is best known for the scenery of West Lake – Xi hu. The town is built on the eastern shores of the lake and the remaining shores contain a host of legendary scenic spots, surrounded by gentle wooded hills revealing temples, gardens, all kinds of flora and fauna, cool bamboo groves and springs.

Hangzhou, the provincial capital, lies on the eastern shores of the lake. It is approximately 100 km from the sea and was built on a silt ledge formed between the West Lake and the Qiantang River. The Imperial Canal terminates here, and this was a major contributory factor to Hangzhou's early growth.

The climate is not too harsh – in the coldest month the temperature rarely falls below 5°C, and the occasional light snowfall only enhances the beauty of the lake. Spring and autumn see the mildest weather, with temperatures around 18°C, although the rainy season begins in April. In the summer months the temperature is in the high twenties, though the air is rarely cloying but rather suffused with sweet fragrances. The peach blossom comes out in spring; in June and July the lake is covered in lotus flowers; while August and September bring the fragrance of the osmanthus and cassia trees.

The land around Hangzhou is fertile, and famous for its tea and silk. People used to say that Hangzhou was just 'West Lake and scissors', but today the city has developed industry, which does not, however, encroach on the place's scenic beauty. It has an iron and steel mill, machine tool factories, a paper mill, a chemical fertilizer plant, one of the largest jute works in China, and oxygen generators. The paper mill is particularly well known for its resourcefulness in the processing of waste for fertilizer.

Many traditional handicraft enterprises flourish in Hangzhou, and the brocade is among the best in China. A popular saying recommends that one should be born in Suzhou because the women are beautiful, and should be clothed in Hangzhou for its fine silk. Scissors, bamboo weaving, Chinese herbal medicine and western medicine are also produced in Hangzhou. The city also has a university and a school of fine arts.

Zhejiang University specializes in engineering and the sciences, while Hangzhou University's specialities are art, and classical painting in particular. The Shanghai Railway Workers' Sanatorium deals with chronic non-infectious diseases, combining western and Chinese medicine.

The population of Hangzhou and the surrounding area is just over a million. The town is a mixture of old and new residential quarters in the Jiangnan style of whitewashed lower storeys with wooden-fasciad upper storeys. The shop fronts are open to the street. Some of the oldest areas in the city still retain names such as the Fish Market or the Rice Market, which indicate their chief trade in the Song dynasty. The oldest and quietest area is around the foot of Wu shan on the southern edge of the city.

Some of the old parts of Hangzhou still contain some very interesting neighbourhoods – such as the quarter where one of the Taiping generals had his garrison and headquarters. It also happens to be a quarter which was praised by Chairman Mao for its cleanliness.

You can get to Hangzhou by train from Shanghai, Peking, Guangzhou or Changsha; the station is in the eastern suburbs. There are plane services from Guangzhou and Peking. A new airport, approximately 24 km from Hangzhou, was built in 1972 for President Nixon's visit.

History

Although Hangzhou and Suzhou have been associated in the epithet 'Above is Heaven, below are Suzhou and Hangzhou', at certain periods in their history they were at war with each other. The history of Hangzhou does not stretch quite as far back as Suzhou's – indeed in the Han dynasty it was probably still under water. Emperor Qin Shihuang, who first unified China, is said to have moored his boat on what is now the northern shore of West Lake. By the fourth century a silt barrier had formed across the bay separating the lake from the Qiantang River and forming the area where Hangzhou would be built.

The Imperial Canal was completed as far as Hangzhou at the end of the sixth century, in the Sui dynasty, and Hangzhou began to come into its own. The first city wall was built by Yang Suo, who also carried out some dyke work at the end of the sixth century. The original settlements were probably around Wu shan and Fenghuang shan, south of the modern city, and during the Tang dynasty it was a thriving centre. In the tenth century Hangzhou was the capital of the state of Wu Yue, and more land reclamation work was carried out. During the first part of the Song dynasty the famous poet Su Dongpo was governor.

The second half of the Song dynasty gave rise to the second golden age of the city. With the southward encroachment of the Tartars the capital was moved from Kaifeng to Hangzhou, which became an international trading centre for silk. Most of the imperial buildings, which have long since been destroyed, were in the southern half of the city. The city was ravaged by the Mongols, but by the time that such travellers as Marco Polo and the German Friar Odoric visited it in the fourteenth century it was once more flourishing.

In the Ming and Qing dynasties the city walls were rebuilt and the Tartar city was established. The ubiquitous emperors of the Qing dynasty, Kang xi and Qian long, did much for the reputation of the place by making it one of their favourite summer retreats and building palaces here. In the Taiping Rebellion the city was largely destroyed, although in the 1920s Carl Crow was able to report that considerable progress had been made since the founding of the Republic, that the Tartar city was one of the finest in China, that it had good road communications and broad streets and was one of the favourite resorts of the wealthy; it also had the most famous fan shop and Chinese medicine store in China.

Wu shan (Wu Hill)

Time permitting, one of the best ways to get an idea of the layout of the city is to visit Wu shan, a hill between West Lake and the Qiantang River on the southern edge of the city. To the north and east sprawls the city, built on the flat plain to the east of the lake; to the west the lake is surrounded with its crescent of gentle hills; and to the south-east you can glimpse the Qiantang River. In a lounge furnished with carved, straight-backed chairs in Qing style you can eat the famous *wushan youbing* – a delicious flaky pastry covered with icing sugar. To reach the top of the hill you pass through the picturesque old quarter of the city. The hilltop theatre, formerly a temple, is a favourite meeting place for old men who bring their song birds in small bamboo cages to sing in chorus.

West Lake: General Information

One of my fondest memories of China is of West Lake at night in early July. It was balmy, with a gentle breeze, a few lights shone around the shores and I heard a lone Chinese voice singing exuberantly somewhere along the western shores. The lake is not so massive that you don't have a sensation of the whole as you stand on any of its shores. It covers an area of some 5.6 km² and has a circumference of 15 km; it is 3.3 km from north to south and 2.8 km from east to west. It is crossed by two causeways, built many years ago from the silt dredged from the lake, and there are three man-made islands and one natural one. A boat trip on the lake is a must, and is possible at most times of the year;

there are several landing stages around the edge.

The lake is fed by spring water from the hills surrounding the lake. Dredged and cleared in 1957, the lake is on average 1.8 m deep and is good for boats, irrigation and fish breeding. Trees were planted around it and the free park areas were expanded.

Past visitors to the lake, from emperors to poets, have admired and immortalized ten scenic spots in four-word epithets. Six of the attractions still remain; the others have fallen into disrepair or have collapsed, as for instance the famous Lei feng Pagoda which used to stand on the western shores but which collapsed in 1924. The legend surrounding this pagoda was one of the most popular of the Qing dynasty, and even now it is retold in operas and story books how, against the background of the West Lake, a young student married the White Snake Goddess (in human form), but their happiness was disturbed by a wicked monk who eventually locked the spirit of the goddess beneath the pagoda.

Bai Causeway and The Melting Snow on the Interrupting Bridge

The Bai Causeway starts in the northeast corner of the lake at the Interrupting Bridge (Duan qiao) and continues round the foot of Solitary Hill to Xiling Bridge, dividing West Lake into the outer and inner lake. The causeway's correct name is the White Sand Causeway (Baisha ti), but the romantic people of Hangzhou prefer to call it after the famous Tang poet Bai Juyi, who was governor here between 822 and 825. He was responsible for building a dyke in the lake as part of a water conservancy project, but it has now disappeared.

The Broken Bridge or Interrupting Bridge (Duan qiao) is thought to date back to early Tang days. It was here that Xu Xian met White Girl in the famous

Hangzhou story, 'The White Snake Goddess'. It is one of the ten attractions of Hangzhou and is known as The Melting Snow on Duan qiao – as the bridge is hump-backed, it is one of the first places where the snow melts.

Su Causeway and The Spring Dawn on Su Causeway

The Su Causeway runs from Southern Screen Hill at the southern end of the lake to Yeast Courtyard in the north, and is some 2.8 km long. There are six bridges along it, and the area to the west of the dyke is known as the inner lake. In spring it makes an impressive sight lined with willows and peach trees, and like the Bai Causeway it is wide enough for traffic to pass along it. The time to view the Su Causeway is in the spring dawn, another of the ten sights of Hangzhou (The Spring Dawn on Su Causeway). It is named after the poet Su Dongpo, governor here in 1089–91. When he arrived he found the lake dirty and silted up, so he ordered extensive dredging and clearing work to be carried out, which enabled the surrounding land to be irrigated; the silt was used to build a dyke.

The Fragrant Breeze of the Distillery Courtyard

The Su Causeway finished at the Yeast Courtyard, the site of the imperial distillery in the Song dynasty. Later it became an ornate garden famous for its lotus flowers. The 'fragrant breeze' is an allusion to the perfume of the lotus flowers, and it was another of the ten scenic spots. Today there only remains a small garden, within walking distance of the Hangzhou Hotel.

The Three Pools Reflecting the Moon and Xiaoying Island

Near the middle of the lake are three obelisk-shaped markers, first erected here by Su Dongpo to mark the deepest parts of the lake. Near this point in the

Ming dynasty a circular embankment was built, creating a lake within a lake called Xiaoying Island – today the island is adorned with lotus flowers, a zigzag bridge, a tea house and ornate windows set in the walls.

At The Three Pools Reflecting the Moon, during the mid-autumn festival when the sky is clear and the moon full, candles are lit in the towers; the five holes are covered with paper and the light seems to reflect fifteen moons on to the water's surface. With the moon and its reflection there are seventeen moons altogether. Each tower is placed in such a way that if you stand in the correct position you can see through the holes to the other two.

There are two other islands in the lake, both much smaller. The Pavilion in the Centre of the Lake was once the site of a Buddhist monastery. Ruangong islet, to its left, was built 100 years ago on the completion of dredging work. However it is too soft to bear any buildings and has been left in a natural state.

Listening to Orioles Among the Willows Park

On the north-eastern shores of the lake is a narrow lakeside park, an attractive tree-lined promenade adjacent to the main streets of Hangzhou, from where you may take a boat across the lake. Further down the lake is the evocatively named Listening to Orioles Among the Willows Park (Liulang wenying), which after the twentieth-century ravages of war and invasion was marked only by a rubbish dump and a stone tablet. In 1951 reconstruction work was begun, and new gardens and hills were laid out and planted with trees; it now contains a children's park. Formerly it housed a temple to Jian Liu, founder of the Wu-Yue Kingdom (893–975), who was responsible for a great many water conservancy and lake-clearing projects as well as being the founder of Hangzhou's reputation as a cultural centre. There were also tablets inscribed with the poems and writings of Su Dongpo.

Solitary Hill (Gu shan)

Solitary Hill is at the north of the lake, joined to the mainland by the Bai Causeway and Xiling Bridge. It was here that Qian long built his summer palace, and the area contains several interesting parks and buildings.

Pavilion of the Autumn Moon on the Calm Lake

Another of the ten famous spots around West Lake, the Pavilion juts out over the lake at the south-eastern corner of Gu shan. As early as the Tang dynasty a pavilion stood here for viewing the lake, and in 1699 the Qing emperor Kang xi built another in the same spot. The name refers to the fact that the best time to view the lake is under the moon of the autumn equinox. Opposite the pavilion is the Zhejiang Agricultural Exhibition Hall.

Zhejiang Provincial Museum

Following the road around the foot of Gu shan you come to the Zhejiang Provincial Museum which was founded in 1929. Many exhibits were destroyed during the war years, and the opening hours of the museum are erratic. In the grounds is the building known as the Hall of Flourishing Literature (Wenlan ge), built by the emperor Qian long as part of his project of collecting and editing all the great books of Chinese literature and history; he established seven libraries, one of them in Hangzhou. The building and many of the books were destroyed in the Taiping Rebellion. Later rebuilt by the Emperor Guang xu, the hall still contains some of the original books.

Adjacent to the Museum is the Sun Yatsen Park and Zhejiang Library, one of the largest in China; also on this stretch is the Academy of Fine Arts.

Sun Yatsen Park

The emperor Kang xi once had an imperial lodge in this small park, which was opened after 1911 to the public and later renamed in honour of Sun Yatsen. The park is natural in aspect with many small pavilions, rockeries and plants; climb to the top of the park for an excellent view over the lake. On the other side of the hill are several sights of interest which can be reached from the park or from a road around the back of the hill.

Tending Crane Pavilion (Fanghe ting)

In the Song dynasty a famous poet and painter, Lin Heqing (967–1028), made his home at the foot of Solitary Hill at a time before it had been cultivated. An eccentric and recluse, he tended three hundred plum trees and a crane with such loving care that people used to say that his trees were his wife and the crane his son, and that when he died the trees and crane died too. A temple and pavilion were built in his memory during the Yuan dynasty; it was rebuilt in 1915, and after 1949 the plum trees were replanted and the pavilion was restored.

Xi Ling Seal Society

Facing the outer lake, the Xi Ling Seal Society keeps up the tradition of one of China's most ancient crafts. It was first set up in 1903, but since the Ming dynasty the reputation of the Zhejiang seal engravers had come to rival that of Anhui Province. The area comprises a cluster of workshops and pavilions nestling behind trellis in bamboo groves and reached by a precarious zigzagging path. There is a small pagoda nearby with an interesting carved base and in the workshops, time permitting, you may have your name engraved on a seal, or buy some stone rubbings and calligraphy equipment.

The unique rock formations of the Stone Forest at Lunan near Kunming

View of the Su Causeway on West Lake, Hangzhou

Figure of Sakyamuni in a Buddhist temple in Zhejiang Province

The entrance to the Temple of Yue Fei in Hangzhou

The courtyard of a temple in Zhejiang Province

Ceiling detail in the
Temple of Yue Fei in
Hangzhou

View over the West
Lake, Hangzhou

Precious Stone Hill (Baoshi shan)

Here, on the northern shores, are more historic beauty spots, as well as two of Hangzhou's major hotels for foreign visitors. The Needle Pagoda (below) overlooks Hangzhou and the West Lake. To the north-west of the lake is the campus of the Provincial University.

Needle Pagoda (Baoshu ta)

The major feature of Baoshishan is Baoshu ta (literally Protecting Shu Pagoda), which was first built in 968. The last king of the Wu-Yue Kingdom, Qian shu, had been summoned to the capital after a very long absence. There was no news of his return, so his prime minister had the pagoda built to protect him in his travels – hence its name. It originally had nine storeys, but when it was rebuilt in the Yuan dynasty it was reduced to seven. Its slim silhouette has earned it the name of the Needle Pagoda.

Several famous personages were reputedly buried here, for instance Su Xiao, a historic beauty of the fifth century; and Wu Song, the hero of the *Water Margin* saga, who killed a tiger single-handed. These are both legendary figures, but among real people Qiu Jin, the first woman revolutionary, had her tomb near the Hangzhou Hotel, and Yue Fei, the great Song general, is buried here.

Yue Fei's Tomb and Temple

The tomb of Yue Fei is approached from Huan hu bei lu at the foot of Xixia Ridge on the north-west corner of the West Lake. Yue Fei (1103–42) was a Song dynasty general born in Henan Province, who fought back the Jin Tartars. However, Yue Fei's success and popularity threatened the prime minister Qin Hui's own plans, and Yue Fei was imprisoned and executed at the age of thirty-nine.

In 1162 the Song emperor Xiao zeng rehabilitated Yue Fei. His body was found with the help of one of the prison warders, who had secretly buried it in expectation of this moment, and he was given a hero's burial at Hangzhou, the Song capital.

In 1221 a temple was built called King Yue's Temple; he represents absolute patriotism. In the main hall is a new statue of Yue Fei in full battle dress, and the ceiling is decorated with cranes – the symbol of steadfastness. The burial mound lies outside the main hall, surrounded by pines and with a stone guard of honour of six officials and six guards. Before the tombs are the kneeling iron figures of the prime minister Qin Hui, his wife and two accomplices who murdered Yue Fei. Nearby is the tomb of Yue Fei's adopted son, Yue Yun (1120–42), who was also imprisoned and murdered.

In the grounds of the Temple there are stone tablets recording poems and articles copied and written by Yue Fei, his successes against the Jin Tartars, and tributes to his character. Another pavilion contains ancient fossilized remains of a pine tree said to have been discovered near his death cell.

Geling shan

Adjacent to Baoshi shan is Geling shan, one of the highest points in the area (166 m), from where you can see over the lake and the city to the Qiantang River. It is also a favourite place to watch the sunrise from the Sunrise Terrace (Chuyang tai). In the fourth century the Daoist Ge Hong is reputed to have mixed the elixir of life here.

Zhixia Ridge, the next hill, has several famous caves and was renowned for its peach blossoms. The Purple Cloud Cave, on top of the ridge, has a temple at the opening and inside are purple, cloud-coloured rocks – whence the name. There are three Buddhas at the rear of the cave and a spring at the bottom of the hill. Some fifteen minutes' walk away is the Yellow Dragon Cave, set in a bamboo grove; there is a spring here which falls from the mouth of a carved dragon.

West and South Areas of the Lake

On the western shores are several sanatoria, and on the southern shores more of the famed scenic spots of the West Lake.

Watching Goldfish in a Flowery Pond (Huagang Park)

On a promontory adjoining Su Causeway in the south-west corner of the lake is the largest park in Hangzhou, which gives on to the shores of the lake. Here, by a pond crossed by a zigzag bridge, you will find a crowd of people gazing at the numerous goldfish and silver carp for which the park is renowned – the fish are tame, greedy and enormous. There is also a peony garden planted with every kind of peony, tree peony and azalea. Following the southern shores eastwards you come to two of the remaining beauty spots of the lake.

On another promontory jutting into the lake is Sunset Hill, where once stood the famous Leifeng Pagoda, about which the epithet was uttered 'Thunder Peak Pagoda in the Sunset Glow'. The pagoda, one of the classical pagodas of Hangzhou, was built by one of King Qian shu's concubines. It was rebuilt and repaired several times, and even withstood burning by Japanese pirates in the Ming dynasty, but eventually in September 1924, as mentioned above, it collapsed. Buddhist scriptures written on silk scrolls were found in the hollows of the bricks and were sent to the Zhejiang Museum.

Opposite Sunset Hill at the foot of Southern Screen Hill is the site of the Temple of Pure Compassion (Jingzisi). In earlier days visitors admired the sound of the monastery bell resounding through Southern Screen Hill in the evening. The monastery was first built by the King of Wu-Yue, Qian Hongshu, in the tenth century, and was later rebuilt. It has three main halls and was the second most important temple after Lingyin si; it is now used as an office.

Jade Spring (Yu quan)

North-west of the West Lake, Jade Spring can be reached by following the road which borders the north of the lake and continues into Yu quan lu. There is a natural spring here which erupts into a rectangular pool, containing clear jade green water. Since the fifth century a temple had stood on this sight. In 1964 the area was refurbished and laid out with gardens and corridors reminiscent of Suzhou, tea houses and a restaurant. There are enormous vats where goldfish are bred – popular tradition has it that Hangzhou was the first place in China to breed them. Adjacent to the Jade Spring is an extensive botanical garden containing many ancient and rare species of tree, a thousand different medicinal herbs, many types of bamboo and a maze.

The range of hills running from the east of the Jade Spring to 5 km south of it is dominated by the Twin Peaks Which Cleave the Clouds (Shuangfeng chayun), another scenic spot. The north and south peaks are over 300 m high; their peaks are often shrouded in cloud, and between them in the low-lying hills are some of the best-known points of interest in the vicinity of Hangzhou.

Temple of the Soul's Retreat and the Peak that Flew Over (Lingyin si and Feilai feng)

The temple and hill grounds are to the south of the Northern Peak and nestle among the hills west of the lake. They can be reached by a No. 7 bus or along Lingyin lu. The area is wooded and a stream runs through it. A cable car has recently been constructed behind the temple to give a view of the lake and the city.

The area has long been an important Buddhist centre – tenth-century records show that there were over 3000 monks here and that the temple was a massive complex consisting of some seventy-three halls and small buildings. The temple was first established in approximately AD 326, during the eastern Jin dynasty, when an Indian Buddhist by the name of Hui Li came here – the hill reminded him so much of one in his own home country that he exclaimed at the similarity, saying it looked as though 'it had flown over'.

The cliff face is covered with countless figures from the Buddhist canons; the Chinese clamber over them to have their photos taken on the arm of the Laughing Buddha. There are also caves, the most famous being the Longhong Cave with the story of Xuan Zang's pilgrimage to India to collect the Buddhist scriptures engraved on the inside; Yixiantian (One Thread of Heaven) – through a tiny opening in the roof of the cave you can see the sky; and the Cave of Green Woods (Qinglin Cave). Many of the carvings date from the tenth century and were added to up until the seventeenth century. Some damage was caused during the Cultural Revolution.

While no longer having the proportions of the tenth-century building, when Buddhism flourished, the main hall of the Temple of the Soul's Retreat is one of the largest and most impressive of its kind in China. There has been a temple on this site since the fourth century. The main hall was built in 1644–61, and is 33.6 m high. Many of the buildings were burnt or damaged during the war, and in fact the main roof of the temple collapsed and damaged the statues in 1949. It was rebuilt by 1956, and a new 19.6-m-tall statue of Sakyamuni, gaudily painted and made from camphorwood was erected.

In the approaches to the main hall stands the familiar figure of the Buddhist temple, the Laughing Buddha; the Four Guardians, Hui Tuo, carved from one piece of camphorwood 800 years old; and Sakyamuni, surrounded by his disciples. Behind him is an ornate collection of relief sculptures of Guanyin as Queen of the Fairy Isle (Xian dao). Outside the main hall are two 1000-year-old pagodas.

The Temple was also known as Yunlin si – Temple of Clouds and Woods – possibly due to an error of the emperor Qian long, who, when tracing the characters for the temple 'sign', made a mistake, and therefore changed it to as close a rendering as he could achieve.

South of the Lake and the Way to the Qiantang River
Following the lakeside road southwards to the Qiantang River and the Pagoda of Six Harmonies you pass several places of interest in varying states of repair or put to other uses such as sanatoria or offices. Following Hangfu lu southwards on the left you pass the Jade Emperor Hill (Yu huang shan), some 300 m high, where you may follow a paved path to the top where once you were rewarded with a view over what was once known as the Bagua tian, the Eight Diagrams Field – the distinctive octagonal form that has become familiar to those in the West interested in the 'Book of Changes' (the *Yi jing*). The fields were said to have been cultivated and dug by the Song emperors.

Halfway to the top is a cave known as the Zilai Cave, which can be approached by following Yuqing lu at the south-east corner of the lake to the foot of Jade Emperor Hill, and then following the footpath.

Turning right off Hangfu lu, facing Jade Emperor Hill, you may follow Manjuelong to the famous Dragon Well, after which the tea was named. The tea is grown in communes and

313

farms around the Shifeng Hill and is one of the four famous teas of China. At Dragon Well itself you will find a spring and the site of a temple which has been here since the tenth century.

In the hills approaching Dragon Well are three famous caves containing many stone carvings. Yanxia Cave (Cave of Morning Mist and Sunset Glow) is the highest. The others are the Water Music Cave – so named for the sound of the water falling on the rocks in the cave – and the Stone House Cave, whose dimensions are similar to those of a house.

Returning to the main road, Hangfu gonglu, continue southwards to the zoo and the pathway leading to Hupao, the Hill Where the Tigers Ran Away. It is in one of those delightfully cool green spots that abound in the environs of Hangzhou, a cool, shady retreat from the summer's heat, and with a temple and legend in keeping with the humour of Chinese traditions. The story goes that in the Tang dynasty two monks came here and wanted to set up a temple; however they couldn't find a spring to supply them with water. During the night one of them dreamt he saw two tigers digging the ground until water came out. The next day he went with his fellow monk to this spot, dug, and sure enough he found water. They named it Tiger Spring. Later they built a stone tiger here; today you will see a gaudily painted plaster tiger, with children climbing on to it to be photographed. A temple has stood on the site since the ninth century and in the tea house here you can sample the unique flavour of Tiger Spring water and Dragon Well tea. The spring is sometimes referred to as the Third Spring under Heaven, and the water is rich in minerals with a specific gravity and surface tension that allow coins to float on the surface, and you may actually fill a bowl beyond the rim without it overflowing!

Continuing southwards, you will pass a modern memorial to a young boy who sacrificed his life when he removed an obstruction from the railway bridge over the Qiantang River as a train was approaching.

Six Harmonies Pagoda (Liuhe ta) and the Qiantang River

The Liuhe ta is an impressive red pagoda, built primarily to ward off evil spirits and to appease the river god. The Six Harmonies refers to Buddhist precepts of comportment and cultivation, and can also be seen to refer to the six directions – north, south, east, west, above and below.

The pagoda was first built in 970 by the Wu-Yue Prince Qian Hongshu. It was rebuilt in its present form in 1156, although it has undergone complete reconstruction several times since. The base of the structure is wide and it is built of wood and stone. From the outside it appears to be thirteen storeys high, but inside there are in fact only seven storeys. Bells hang from the eaves and the inside walls and ceiling are covered with faded paintings. The view looks over the river at boys swimming, boats and the road and rail bridge which was built in 1934–7 and designed by Mao Yisheng.

The Qiantang is renowned for its bore, which in days gone by would often wreak destruction in the area as water gushed from the Hangzhou bay into the funnel shape of the river. The best time to see the bore is after the mid-autumn festival in September; people come from Shanghai and surrounding areas to view it.

Continuing along the north banks of the river you reach the beauty spot known as Nine Creeks and Eighteen Rivulets, and on route to Meijiawu tea brigade is the famous Trail in a Bamboo Grove at Yunqi; the well-known sanatorium here specializes in combining

Chinese herbal medicine with western techniques.

Traditional Industries

Some of Hangzhou's factories and workshops make an interesting visit.

The Hangzhou All-purpose Silk Production Factory covers every aspect of silk production from the cocoon to spinning, weaving, printing and dying.

It was long said that all Hangzhou had to offer was 'West Lake and scissors'. The scissors are still among the best in China, with handles which make cutting very comfortable.

Hangzhou is traditionally one of the best producers and purveyors of Chinese herbal medicines. In the No.2 Chinese Medicine Factory modern, scientific methods of production are used with a high standard of hygiene. You should get a chance to sample some of the tonics and such delicacies as royal jelly.

Bamboo is grown extensively in Zhejiang Province, which is one of the largest producers in China. At the West Lake Bamboo Factory you can follow all the processes from first preparing and splicing the bamboo; everything is made here, from woven dishes to bamboo furniture. On the streets of Hangzhou you will see street sellers selling bundles of coloured baskets – a traditional example of private enterprise.

The Red Flag Paper Mill, first established in 1932, is well known for its recycling of waste for fertilizer and cinder blocks. It once had a front-page mention in *People's Daily*.

There are three brigades in the West Lake commune where you can go to see tea production methods – Longjing, Shuangfeng and Meijiawu. Tea is also produced on a state farm. Longjing tea was once served to the emperors.

Mogan shan

This is a mountain resort two hours north-west of Hangzhou by bus in the Tianmu range, famous for its bamboo groves and views. It was early established by missionaries as a summer retreat from the heat of Shanghai. Today guests stay in some of the refurbished villas and hotels.

Xin'an jiang Water Conservancy Project

Xin'an is in the west of Zhejiang Province, south-west of Hangzhou, and accessible by train – change at Jinhua, famous for its ham. The Xin'an River rises in Anhui Province, and in Zhejiang joins the Lan and Fuchun Rivers. In 1957 a project to build China's first Chinese-designed and -built hydroelectric power station was started. Built in the spirit of self-reliance and the Great Leap Forward, it took only three years to complete. Its main role is to generate hydroelectric power which serves the Shanghai, Nanking and Hangzhou area, but it also serves to control flooding which is one of the major hazards of this river, and is also used for navigation, irrigation and fisheries. The reservoir itself has become something of a beauty spot and is of particular interest to hydraulic engineers.

Entertainment

Hangzhou has its own song, dance and music groups, and there are four major theatres in the city. Opera is in the local Shaoxing style – Shaoju or Yueju.

Shopping

Many different kinds of souvenirs can be bought in Hangzhou – silk and brocades, woven pictures, silk umbrellas, cushion covers, tablecloths, boxwood carved walking sticks, scissors, bamboo chopsticks, and in fact anything made from bamboo. The major shopping area is situated around the crossroads of Yan'an lu and Jiefang jie, near Hubin Park. On Hubin lu there is an antique store, and at No.31 a printing and calligraphy store. On Yan'an lu are a silk shop, porcelain store, local department store and tea shop, where you can

315

purchase the latest harvest of famous Dragon Well tea as well as chrysanthemum tea, which is drunk in the summer and is very refreshing. There is also a pharmacy and scissors shop. Ham is a renowned local product.

Hotels: General Information

Hangzhou has four hotels for foreigners and a new one is planned. The best known and furbished are the Hangzhou Hotel and the Xiling hotel.

Hangzhou Hotel
Yuefen jie
Tel. 22921

The hotel is well situated on the northern shores of the river, near Yue Fei's tomb. Built in the mid-1950s, the style is recognizably Chinese, with pillars and balustrades leading up to the cloud-design entrance of the hotel in the style of the Forbidden City, and the Chinese key design on the balconies. From the front of the hotel you can see the lake and Solitary Hill, and it is two minutes' walk to the local shops and department store, Xihushangdian, the lake and the area known as the Distillery Courtyard.

In the lobby are a post office and taxi hire facilities, and on the mezzanine floor a shop and exchange facilities. The dining-room is on the second floor in the east wing. Bedrooms are comfortable, and mosquito nets are provided in summer.

Adjacent to the hotel is a big theatre and conference hall, built in three months in the flurry of the Great Leap Forward in 1959.

Xiling Hotel
Address and telephone number as for the Hangzhou Hotel.

This pistachio-green hotel is east of the Hangzhou Hotel and in fact in the same grounds. It was built in 1962 to accommodate state guests and is under the same management as the Hangzhou Hotel.

It consists of a main V-shaped block and an annexe built around a small courtyard. The hotel is named after the bridge which joins Solitary Hill to the mainland. It has its own sweeping entrance and a rather modern feel. In the lobby there is a floor-to-ceiling mural in bas-relief of the scenic spots in the vicinity of Wenzhou.

For shop, exchange and bar facilities walk through the grounds to the Hangzhou Hotel – take a small stairway and path at the side of the entrance to the Xiling Hotel. The Xiling's rooms are light and airy, with parquet floors. The restaurant is on the seventh (top) floor.

Huagang Hotel
Huanhu xi lu
Tel. 24001

In the south-west corner of the lake, next to Huagang Park, the hotel is set in beautiful grounds. It was built in the mid-1950s and the Chinese architectural tradition can be seen in the towers at the sides; it was formerly used as a sanatorium. There are a shop and hairdressing facilities on the ground floor, and several dining-rooms on the first floor. The bedrooms are comfortable but simple – the plumbing is not very good and there are public bathrooms on upper floors. It is due for renovation.

Liutong binguan
Faxianggang
Tel. 26354

Approximately ten minutes' walk from Huagang Park, this is a small guest house set in the countryside which you pass through a small village to reach. It has a pleasant forecourt with benches and trees, and though there are no facilities such as shops the food is fresh and excellent. All rooms have bathrooms – formerly another sanatorium, it is not used very often for foreign visitors.

Overseas Chinese Hotel
92 Hubin lu
Tel. 23100

Situated in downtown Hangzhou, near

the lake, the hotel is reserved for overseas Chinese visitors.

Food and Restaurants
The food in Hangzhou hotels is excellent – always fresh and varied. Specialities include beancurd, fish, prawns, bamboo shoots and chicken. Some of the dishes are *zhaxiangling* – fried crispy beancurd roll; *longjing xiaren* – prawn cooked in Longjing tea; *sanbei ji* – Three Cups Chicken, cooked in a marinade of wine, soya sauce and oil; and *xiangsu yazi* – crispy duck or chicken. West Lake fish is served in sweet and sour sauce.

Among Hangzhou's restaurants, try the following:
Hangzhou jiujia
132 Yan'an lu
Tel. 23477
The speciality here is Beggar's Chicken.

Louwailou caiguan
2 Wai xi lu
Tel. 21654
With a view over the lake, this is one of Hangzhou's oldest restaurants. Its name comes from a poem by Su Dongpo, accusing the rulers who took no notice of the impending ruin as the Jin Tartars moved into China.

> *Mountains upon mountains,*
> *towers upon towers.*
> *When will the singing and dancing*
> *on West Lake cease?*

The wine to drink is the yellow wine from nearby Shaoxing, and the speciality is vinegar fish.

Shopping
Friendship store
302 Tiyuchang lu

Useful Addresses
CAAC
304 Tiyuchang lu
Tel. 24259

Luxingshe
10 Baochu lu
Tel. 22921

Shaoxing

A picturesque rural town south of Hangzhou, Shaoxing is famous for its wine, opera, tea, canals, boats rowed with the feet and felt hats, and has several illustrious sons and daughters. Indeed there used to be a saying in China: 'There are three things to be found everywhere in the world: beancurd, sparrows and men from Shaoxing.' In former times they were found in every echelon of the civil service. From here came the Song poet Lu You, the Ming calligrapher and painter Xu Wei, the female revolutionary Qiu Jin, the ancestors of Zhou Enlai, and Lu Xun – China's great modern writer.

Legend dates the founding of the city to 2000 BC, when the mythical Emperor Da Yu settled here after taming the waters of China – his legacy is supposed to be the canal system in and around Shaoxing. A tomb was built in his honour at the foot of Mount Kuaiji in the Han dynasty, and in the sixth century a temple was built. A temple is still on the site today, and the present one contains a statue of Da Yu and many engraved tablets.

The city was actually founded in the fifth century BC during the Warring States period, and was the capital of the Kingdom of Yue under King Gouqian. Today, on Wolong Hill to the west of Shaoxing, stands the Seaview Pavilion – the lookout post of Gou Qian's army – and at the foot of the hill the terrace from which he issued orders.

The modern city has a population of 100,000, and is crisscrossed with canals and 2,000 bridges. South-west of it is the extensive Lake Jian, both a scenic spot and vital to local agriculture. Near the city is the East Lake – Shaoxing's answer to West Lake – where you can go boating. Apart from the famous rice wine, other industries include textiles, tea, pottery, power, metal goods, chemicals and machine building.

Shaoxing is 64 km south-east of Hangzhou, on the Hangzhou–Ningpo railway.

Qiu Jin

This revolutionary leader (1879–1907) was born here and worked from Shaoxing to organize an armed uprising against the Manchus. She helped edit one of the first magazines for women and was a prolific poet. Eventually she was executed for her anti-government activities and her former home has been turned into a museum chartering her life and with many of her original works on display.

Lu Xun

The famous modern writer (1881–1936) was also born here, and many of his works provide interesting cameos of life in Shaoxing in the late nineteenth century. Today you can visit his house and the nearby Three Flavour Study, where he was given a traditional Confucian education. In 1953 an extensive Lu Xun Museum was established, tracing his life and works.

Opera

Shaoxing opera is particularly renowned throughout China. It incorporates the reedy gentle characteristics of southern-style opera.

Tea and Wine

The Changwang brigade outside Shaoxing is renowned for its tea plantation and is often praised as a model brigade. They have also carried out extensive irrigation work.

However Shaoxing is perhaps best known for its wine – made from rice and served warm it is often called 'yellow wine' or *huang jiu*. Shaoxing used to have, so they said, three wine shops for every ten houses. Traditionally, when a baby girl was born into a household the local peasants would brew the wine and store it until she came of marrying age, when it was brought out for the wed-

ding feast. During the Tang dynasty production became centralized into a brewery which supplied the imperial court.

The main ingredients are glutinous rice and yeast, and the spring water from Lake Jian. First the rice is soaked, steamed and left to ferment in enormous open vats. Then the resulting mash is pressed and the liquor sealed in jars for 100 days. The ideal length of time to mature the wine is between three and five years.

In the past Shaoxing wine has won prizes in both national and international competitions. In former days it used to be bottled in pitchers elaborately decorated with flowers; nowadays it is sold in brown-glazed pitchers. There are four kinds of Shaoxing wine: *yuanhong* – 'champion's' red which is brewed with a special kind of yeast; *shanniang* made by adding old wine instead of water; *jiafan*, made by adding an extra quantity of rice; and Fragrant Snow *(xiangxue)*, to which spirits from the *jiafan* mash are added instead of water. A visit to the winery provides interesting photographic possibilities and generally a wine-tasting session is included.

Local Products and Souvenirs

Tea, rice wine, porcelain, jewellery, and felt hats as worn by the peasants.

Hotel

Shaoxing fandian
Longshan jiaoxia
Tel. 3483
The hotel is located in an old courtyard-style house.

Ningpo

A major coastal port on the south of the Hangzhou bay, the name Ningpo means 'calm waves'. Its overseas connections date back centuries: even in the Tang dynasty it was a major foreign trade centre. Many overseas Chinese in south-east Asia originated from Ningpo, and it was one of the concession ports of the 1842 treaty. Ningpo also enjoys a certain reputation as a city of bankers and merchants. The present city dates from the Ming dynasty, and on a hill above the Yong River are the remains of a fort from which general Qi Jiguang routed Japanese pirates who plagued the coast in the Ming dynasty.

Today the city has a population of 900,000. The docks have been extended and new terminals built – it is a port for both ocean-going and coastal traffic, and a major distribution centre for Zhejiang's products, which are rice, cotton and fish. It has a modern manufacturing industry, and is particularly well known for its food processing and canning industry which exports the Maling brand of canned foods worldwide.

Ningpo can be reached by sea from Shanghai and by rail from Hangzhou.

Sights
In the middle of Lake Yue is the picturesque Moon Island Park, and on the western shore stands the oldest library building in China – the Tianyi ge (the Heavenly Pavilion), which was originally started as the private collection of a Ming dynasty official. It contains manuscripts which date back to the eleventh century and a major set of local chronicles from the Ming dynasty. Today the library has some 300,000 volumes. Set in extensive grounds at the foot of the Taibai Mountain is the Children of Heaven Monastery (Tian tong si). The Japanese monk Dogen studied here in 1223, and returned to Japan to found the Sōtōshu branch of Buddhism.

Nearby, on Yuwang Hill, stands the fifth-century King Asoka Monastery, one of the eighteen extant *stupas* in the world which still contains relics of Sakyamuni, the founder of Buddhism.

Some 15 km west of Ningpo, on Biaoqi Mountain, is Baoguo Monastery. Built entirely of wood, it dates from the eleventh century, and the kind of joints used in the construction make it a building of major architectural significance.

Souvenirs
Local arts and crafts include lacquerware and embroidery.

Putuo shan
This island off the coast of Zhejiang Province is a Buddhist centre for the cult of the Goddess of Mercy – Guanyin. Until 1949 there were some 4000 monks and nuns on the island, but there are now about 100 monks left. A Buddhist association was set up in 1979. There are three major monasteries on Putuo shan – the oldest is the Puji Monastery, built in 1080; the Fayu, the second largest, in the south of the island, is built on several levels to blend in with the terrain; and the Huiji is on Foding Peak.

Wenzhou
A port at the mouth of the Ou River on the south-east coast of Zhejiang Province, Wenzhou is responsible for the shipment of tea, timber and fruit to other parts of the country. It is particularly renowned for the quality of its oranges, and has some paper mills and food processing and a porcelain industry. Apart from sea communications with Shanghai, a railway is projected. Approximately 60 km north east of Wenzhou are the Yandang Mountains, a scenic area famous for soaring peaks, clear waters and waterfalls. Each peak has a name and a story, and there is a famous nine-storied temple built into the mountainside. One of the crafts of this area is bas-relief work called Ou jiang sculpture.

Glossary

Arhat/Luohan A Buddhist disciple or saint.

Bodhisattva A holy person destined for Buddhahood, but who has chosen to live among mortals to help them.

CAAC The Chinese National Airline whose full title is General Administration of Civil Aviation of China.

Cadre In its strictest sense the term cadre is applied to activists in the Communist Party. More generally it applies to people in the professional and managerial classes or civil service.

Chan Buddhism Known as Zen Buddhism in Japan, this branch of Buddhism was founded during the seventh century. The main tenet is that 'enlightenment' should be achieved through meditation.

CCP Chinese Communist Party.

Chop Seal made from semi-precious stone, ivory, or even plastic, with the owner's name or company inscribed on it. The seal has been significant in Chinese society for many years: obtaining the imperial seal gave the right to rule. The style of engraving used on seals is an art form in its own right. Seals can be obtained quickly and cheaply during a short visit to China.

Dagoba A Buddhist building in Indian style, often compared to a peppermint-bottle or Chianti-bottle shape.

Gaoliang (Kaoliang) Sorghum, a type of millet grown in north China.

Gobi Shale-type desert to be found across North-West China.

Guomin dang (Kuomintang) Nationalist Party, founded originally by Sun Yat Sen in 1921. Jiang Kai Shek later became leader and the Nationalists and the Communist Party were chief protagonists in the civil wars prior to 1949.

Jiangnan South of the river; used to denote that part of China which is south of the Yangtse.

Karma Buddhist concept of destiny.

Karst Limestone rock formation typified by the scenery of Guilin. The name is taken from an area in Yugoslavia where the rock formations are similar.

Lacquerware The resin of the lacquer tree *(rhus vernicus)* is found in south-east China. Layers of the resin are worked onto a thin wooden mould and allowed to harden. Lacquer is traditionally red or black and it can be carved intricately.

Lamaism Branch of Buddhism developed in Tibet and disseminated through to Mongolia, combining Buddhist beliefs and animism. Each family would try to send a male to become a lama or monk, so that they could benefit vicariously from his proximity to heaven and enlightenment. Prayer wheels and flags inscribed with prayers are part of the paraphernalia of the devotee, all contributing to his relative holiness.

Loess Fertile alluvial soil of the Yellow River Valley, prone to rapid erosion.

Manchu/Qing Name of the northern tribe which came to rule China from 1644 to 1911.

Pictograph Pictorial symbol. In their early form most Chinese characters were pictographs.

Pinyin System of romanization for Chinese characters approved and used in all translated government documents and taught in schools.

Politburo The policy-making body of the Chinese Communist Party.

Revisionism/ist One who tries to change the principles of Marxist–Leninism, and therefore one whose ideas are contrary to government policy.

Shaman High priests of the Shang court who, through methods of divination, advised the emperor.

Sheng Province.

Shi City.

Sino/Sinicization/Sinologist The prefix sino- denotes a person or thing connected with China. A sinologist is a specialist in Chinese studies. Sinicization is making something Chinese, as in the case of the foreign tribes who ruled northern China.

Stele Stone tablet to be found everywhere in China from earliest times and an important historical document.

State Council The government 'cabinet'.

Stupa Buddhist reliquary.

Sutra Buddhist scriptures or writings, often stored in pagodas and temple libraries.

Xian County.

Useful Phrases

The following section contains a list of phrases given in Chinese characters, in pin yin, and in English translation. By no means exhaustive, they may prove of assistance in obtaining the little comforts of life:

Hello/How are you?	*ní hǎo (ma)?*	你好(吗)？
I'm well	*wǒ hén hǎo*	我很好
Thank you	*xièxie*	谢谢
Goodbye	*zàijiàn*	再见
How much is it?	*dūoshǎo qián?*	多少钱？
2.55 *yuan*/10 cents	*liǎngkùai wǔshi wǔ/yì máo*	二块五毛五/一毛
Please bring . . .	*qǐng lái . . .*	请来…
A bottle of beer/wine/ mineral water	*yì píng píjiǔ/pútao jiǔ/lǎoshān shǔi*	一瓶啤酒/葡萄酒/崂山水
Ice	*bīng kùai (r)*	冰块
Cold water	*lěng kāishǔi*	冷开水
Boiled water	*kāishǔi*	开水
A glass of milk	*yìbēi niúnǎi*	一杯牛奶
A cup of coffee	*yìbēi kāfēi*	一杯咖啡
Tea (black)	*hóng chá*	红茶
Jasmine tea	*huā chá*	花茶
Green tea	*lù chá*	绿茶
Ice cream	*bīng qí lín*	冰琪淋
Orangeade	*júzi shuǐ*	桔子水
Orange juice	*júzi zhī (r)*	桔子汁
Fork, knife, spoon	*chāzi, dāozi, sháozi*	叉子, 刀子, 勺子
I want a taxi to . . .	*wǒ yāo yiliàng chūzū qìchē dào . . .*	我要一辆出租汽车到…
Please wait	*qíng nǐ děng yi děng*	请你等一等
What's your name?	*nín gùi xìng?* (polite)	您贵姓？
	nǐ jiào shénmo mingzi?	你叫什么名子？
My name is . . .	*wǒ jiào . . .*	我叫…
Where is the toilet?	*cèsǔo zài nǎr?*	厕所在哪？
Where is the friendship store?	*yǒuyìshāngdiàn zài nǎr?*	友谊商店在哪？
Where is the Museum of History?	*Lìshǐ bówùguǎn zài nǎr?*	历史博物馆在哪？

322

Where is the service desk?	*fúwùtai zài năr?*	服务台在哪?
Where is the bank?	*yínháng zái năr?*	银行在哪?
Where is the White Cloud Hotel?	*Báiyún bingŭan zài năr?*	白云宾馆在哪?
Where is the Peking Hotel?	*Bĕijing fàndiàn zài năr?*	北京饭店在哪?
Hotel	*fàndiàn/bīngŭan*	饭店/宾馆
Restaurant	*fàndiàn/cāngŭan*	饭店/夕馆
I want to make a (long distance) telephone call	*wŏ xiăng dă yīge (chángtù) diànhùa*	我想打一个(长途)电话
I want to buy . . .	*wŏ xiăng măi. . .*	我想买
some stamps	*yóupiào*	邮票
some postcards	*míngxin piàn*	明信片
Silk	*síchóu*	絲绸
I want to send a telegram/telex	*wŏ yāo fā yīge diànbào/diànchúan*	我要发一个电报/电传

The negative is formed in two ways: with *méi* and *bù:*

Have you got any ice?	*ní yŏu bing kuài(r) ma?*	你有冰块吗?
	ní yŏu méi yŏu bing kùai(r)?	你有没有冰块?
Yes, we have	*yŏu*	有
No, we haven't	*méi yŏu*	没有
Do you want any more rice?	*nĭ hái yào fàn ma?*	你还要饭吗?
No, thank you	*wŏ bù yào xìxie*	我不要,谢谢
Is Mr Li there?	*Li xiànsheng zài ma?*	李先生在吗?
No, he isn't	*(Tā) bù zài*	(他)不在

Numbers

1 *yī* 一	5 *wŭ* 五	9 *jĭu* 九	13 *shí sān* 十三
2 *er̆* 二	6 *liù* 六	10 *shí* 十	14 *shí sì* 十四
3 *sān* 三	7 *qī* 七	11 *shí yī* 十一	etc.
4 *sì* 四	8 *bā* 八	12 *shí er̆* 十二	

20 *er̆ shí* 二十   21 *er̆ shi yī* 二十一   22 *er̆ shi er̆* 二十二 (etc.)
100 *yì băi* 一百   105 *yì băi líng wŭ* 一百零五 (etc.)   112 *yìbăiyìshíer̆* 一百一十二
130 *yì băi sān shí* 一百三十

1000 *yī qiān* 一千

10,000 *yī wàn* 一万 (the Chinese count in units of 10,000, so 100,000 is *shí wàn*, and 200,000 *er̆ shí wán*)

1,000,000 *yī yì* 一亿

*For 2 the Chinese also often use *liăng* as an adjective, eg 2 cups of coffee – *liăng bei kafei* (not *er bei kafei*)

Forms of Address

Comrade	*tóngzhi*	同志	⎫ all placed
Miss	*xiǎojie*	小姐	⎪ after the
Mr	*xiānsheng*	先生	⎬ name, eg Wang
Mrs	*fūren*	夫人	⎭ Xiansheng

NB When Chinese women marry they keep their own surname, so *furen* is usually used for foreign women.

Xiǎo (young) and *laǒ* (old) are usually used together with the surname between colleagues and students, depending on respective seniority: *xiǎo Yáng* (to school-friend or colleague of the same age), *laǒ Wàng* to neighbours, superiors, and all those older than yourself.

Chinese names usually consist of the surname first, followed by a two-character given name, eg *Sūn* (surname) *Wúkōng* (given name). There are a few exceptions such as a double-barrelled surname, or a one-character given name.

Who's Who

A brief introduction to some of the characters that may come up in conversation during your visit to China.

Bethune, Norman (Bai Qiuen)
Canadian doctor who worked in China during the Sino–Japanese War and died of septicaemia. He is commemorated by a hospital in Shijia zhuang.

Chiang Kaishek (Jiang Jieshi)
Born in 1887 died in 1975. Chiang Kaishek was the soldier and general who emerged as leader of the Nationalist party after the death of Sun Yatsen. He held the balance of power in China until he was fifty and was president until he was forced to flee to Taiwan, where he died in 1975. He married Song Meiling, daughter of a wealthy banking family and sister of Song Ch'ing-ling.

Deng Xiaoping (Teng Hsiao-p'ing)
Born 1904 in Sichuan Province. He went abroad to study, and during his stay in Paris joined the Communist Youth League and in 1925 the Chinese Communist Party. He was a veteran of the Long March and political commissar of the Eighth Route Army, working with Liu Shaoqi. He has been a member of the Politburo since the Liberation, and also held important military and political positions in the south-west of China. By 1953 he was acting premier. In 1962 he came in for criticism at the Eighth Party Congress, when in defence of his drive towards increased production and modernization he made his famous statement 'It doesn't matter if it's a black cat or a white cat as long as it catches mice.' From 1966 to 1973 he was out of public life, making a comeback with Zhou Enlai's new pragmatic policies, and often took the role of acting premier for him. In 1976 he was criticized once more for his policies on modernization. He was rehabilitated in 1977, and was at last strong enough to implement his modernizing and liberalizing reforms as vice-premier. He has chosen to withdraw slightly – to make way for younger blood, by resigning from the post of Vice-Premier and chief of staff, and taking up a position on the new Central Advisory Commission.

Deng Yingchao
Born 1903. The much loved and revered wife of Zhou Enlai holds positions in the Central Committee and Politburo. She played an active role in all activities prior to Liberation. They met in France, and never had any children.

Gang of Four (Siren bang)
Arrested by Hua Guofeng in October 1976, the Shanghai gang were 'radicals' who held the balance of power in the final years of the lives of Zhou Enlai and Mao

Zedong. They were Jiang Qing (see separate entry), Zhang Chunqiao, Yao Wenyuan and Wang Hongwen.

Zhang Chunqiao was the most experienced politician of the four: he was already active in Shanghai in the 1930s and was mayor of Shanghai and vice-premier before his arrest. Wang Hongwen made a meteoric rise from factory floor to vice-chairman in 1975. When he was less than forty he was in charge of the organization of the People's Militia. Yao Wenyuan wrote the article against Wuhan's play which sparked off the Cultural Revolution. He later became chief of the Politburo's propaganda department and had control of the media which contributed greatly to the success of the Gang in the '70s. At their trial in 1980 they were accused of 'counter-revolutionary crimes' and given suspended death sentences and long-term prison sentences.

Guo Moruo (Kuo Mo-jo)
Born 1892 and died in 1978. He was an early member of the Creation Society – a group formed by intellectuals seeking to radicalize written forms and their society – and active in the May Fourth Movement. In many ways Guo Moruo was a member of the old-style literati. He held many positions of importance in the cultural sphere, including president of the Academy of Sciences, and has written extensively on archaeology, history and literature. His name and quotations have been affixed to many ancient and modern sights in China.

Hu Yaobang
Born 1915 in Hunan, he ran away at fourteen to join the Red Army. He joined the Chinese Communist Party in 1935, was active in the first soviets in Jiangxi, and was a veteran of the Long March. His special sphere of influence has long been the Communist Youth League. He held important provincial posts in Sichuan and Shaanxi, was made a member of the Politburo and at the Eleventh Party Congress was given charge of day-to-day affairs. In June 1981 he became Party chairman. Hu is a protégé of Deng Xiaoping and in favour of party reform.

Hua Guofeng (Hua Kuo-feng)
Born 1920 in Shenxi. Designated Mao's successor in 1976 after the demise of Deng Xiaoping. He first came to prominence for his work in Hunan Province, ending up with responsibility for the Bureau of Public Security. His bona fides were questioned concerning the Tianan men Incident, and he was considered too Maoist for the new pragmatism in the party. By 1981 he had ceded his posts as premier and chairman to Zhao Ziyang and Hu Yaobang respectively.

Jiang Qing (Chiang Ching)
Born in Shandong Province in 1914, Jiang Qing made her way to Shanghai where she became an actress and film star. She tried to gain admission to the Communist Party, and eventually made her way to Yan'an via Chongqing. At Yan'an she met Mao and became his fourth wife. She kept out of politics until 1960, when Mao gave her work in the cultural field reforming the traditional Peking Opera and devising her famous ballets. By the time of Mao's death it was thought that she aimed to become his successor, and after her arrest with the rest of the Gang of Four she was unflatteringly compared with ambitious Chinese women rulers of the past. At the trial of the Gang of Four, her manner was the most defiant of the four and she was given a suspended death sentence.

Kang xi (Kang Hsi)
Reigned 1662–1723. One of the Manchu (Qing) emperors, he supervised the restoration of peace to China, suppressed the vestiges of Ming opposition and encouraged Manchus to study the Chinese language and culture through his patronage of the arts and the compilation of many great encyclopedias.

Lei feng
Born in 1940, died in 1962. A 'people's hero' from the People's Liberation Army, whose diaries were discovered after his untimely accidental death and revealed the life of a model revolutionary soldier who was held up as an example for all in selflessness and revolutionary ardour, particularly during the Cultural Revolution.

Lin Biao (Lin Piao)
Born 1908 in Hubei, died 1971. He trained at the Whampoa military academy and joined the Red Army in 1937. An excellent tactician, he commanded the First Red Army Corps, and detachments from the Eighth Route Army. His major success was in the north-eastern campaigns of 1946. He was also successful in the Korean War. After Liberation he followed a generally radical line, wrote on the 'people's war', and as army commander was important during the Cultural Revolution, working with Jiang Qing, organizing the *Little Red Book* and the deification of Mao. He was designated Mao's successor, but was toppled and after an abortive *coup* was killed in a plane crash while escaping to the USSR.

Liu Shaoqi
Born 1898 in Hunan, died 1969. One of the early members of the Chinese Communist Party, he was active in workers' organizations; from 1945 to 1966 he was vice-chairman of the Central Committee. In 1946 he wrote his seminal work *How to Be a Good Communist*, which was reprinted in 1980. After 1958 he replaced Mao as chairman, then after 1966 he was criticized as the Chinese Khrushchev. He was imprisoned, and died. He was rehabilitated in April 1980, when memorial services were held. He favoured pragmatic policies which would modernize China and improve living standards.

Lu Xun (Lu Hsün)
Born 1881 in Shaoxing, Zhejiang Province, died in 1936 in Shanghai. The Chinese Gorky, his country's greatest modern writer and essayist was towards end of his life politically active in Shanghai. Among his works are *Diary of a Madman, The True Story of A. Q.* and *The New Year's Sacrifice*.

Mao Zedong (Mao Tse-t'ung)
Born 1893 in Shaoshan, Hunan Province, died 1976. When he attended teachers' training college in Changsha Mao first became politicized. He went to Peking where he met Li Dazhao, and worked under him at Peking University where he was introduced to Communism. He was one of the founder members of the Chinese Communist Party. He met his second wife, Yang Kaihui (his first wife had been a child bride and the arranged marriage was never consummated) and married her in 1920. From 1924 he was a member of the Politburo and came to prominence in 1929 as chairman of the Front Committee. From 1934 until he died, Mao was chairman of the Communist Party. After Liberation he was State chairman until 1959 when he was replaced by Liu Shaoqi. His third wife was He Zicheng, whom he divorced at Yan'an; he married Jiang Qing in 1940.

Qin Shihuang di (Ch'in Shih-huang ti)
The first Qin emperor (221–206 BC), who united China and is buried in Lintong county near Xi'an.

Qian long (Ch'ien lung)
Reigned 1736–96. Extravagant Qing emperor who built and rebuilt many fine buildings, attaching his signature to many of the great scenic spots of China. He presided over the expansion of the Chinese empire, trade with the west and border wars. Uprisings by the White Lotus Society were a symptom of instability at this time.

Song Qingling (Soong Ch'ing-ling)
Born 1893 in Shanghai, to one of the wealthy families of China, she received a western-style education both at home and abroad. In 1915 she married Sun Yatsen. Although she never joined the Communist Party, she played an important role before Liberation in obtaining support for China, and afterwards held many posts. She founded the magazine *China Reconstructs* and played an important role in supervising welfare, relief and Red Cross missions, and the Women's Federation. Before her death in 1981 she was made honorary president of the Republic.

Sun Wukong
Monkey hero of the Buddhist novel *Journey to the West*, written by Wu Cheng'en in the sixteenth century. His name Wukong means 'aware of vacuity' and was given him by his guru.

Sun Yatsen (Sun Zhongshan)
Born 1866 at Cuiheng village, Guangdong Province, died 1925. Sun Yat Sen studied abroad before returning to China to found the Resurrection Society and the Revolutionary League, which helped to bring about the downfall of the empire. He became the first President of the Republic in 1911. His main theories were the three People's Principles, which were also the political basis for the Nationalist Party. After his death he was buried near Peking and then moved to a specially commissioned mausoleum at Nanking.

Wang Guangmei (Wang Kuang-Mei)
Wife of Liu Shaoqi, she has held positions in the Politburo and has recently returned to public life. She is Director of Foreign Affairs in the important Academy of Social Sciences.

Wu Zetian (Wu Tse-t'ian)
A concubine of the Tang emperor Gao zong, she became empress in 655, one of three women in Chinese history to wield such power. She established her own Zhou dynasty between 690 and 701, but the Tang line was restored by Xuan zong in 713. She died in 705 and her tomb is near Xi'an.

Zhao Ziyang
Born 1919 in Henan Province, Zhao joined the Chinese Communist Party in 1938 and was active in the Sino–Japanese War. He worked in Guangdong, Inner Mongolia and finally Sichuan, where he came into close contact with Deng Xiao-ping and supervised the economic liberalization of the late 1970s. Under Deng's tutelage he has become premier.

Zhou Enlai (Chou En-lai)
Born 1898, died 1976. During his studies in Paris, Zhou Enlai was one of the founding members of the Communist Youth League in 1920–1. Active in the Long March, he gained respect for the Communists by his abilities as an able diplomat. After the founding of the People's Republic he became Prime Minister and Foreign minister. He managed to retain his posts during the Cultural Revolution, and was instrumental in bringing China back into the United Nations. Mourning of his death was suppressed by the media, although today he is referred to with affection and respect as 'our dear premier' and is seen as the force of good and moderation since 1949.

Zhu De (Chu Te)
Born 1886 in Sichuan, died 1976. One of the founders of the People's Liberation Army, this warlord turned Communist soldier directed many campaigns and his prestige rivalled Mao's. He was chairman of the National People's Congress and came in for criticism during the Cultural Revolution.

THE CHINESE DYNASTIES

XIA   c21st–16th century BC
SHANG   16th–11th century BC
WESTERN ZHOU   11th century to 771 BC
SPRING AND AUTUMN PERIOD   770–476 BC
WARRING STATES   475–221 BC
QIN   221–207 BC
HAN   206 BC–220 AD
THREE KINGDOMS   220–265
WESTERN JIN   265–316
EASTERN JIN   317–420
SOUTHERN AND NORTHERN DYNASTIES   420–581
SUI   581–618
TANG   618–907
FIVE DYNASTIES AND TEN KINGDOMS   907–960
NORTHERN SONG   960–1279
YUAN   1271–1368
MING   1368–1644
QING   1644–1911

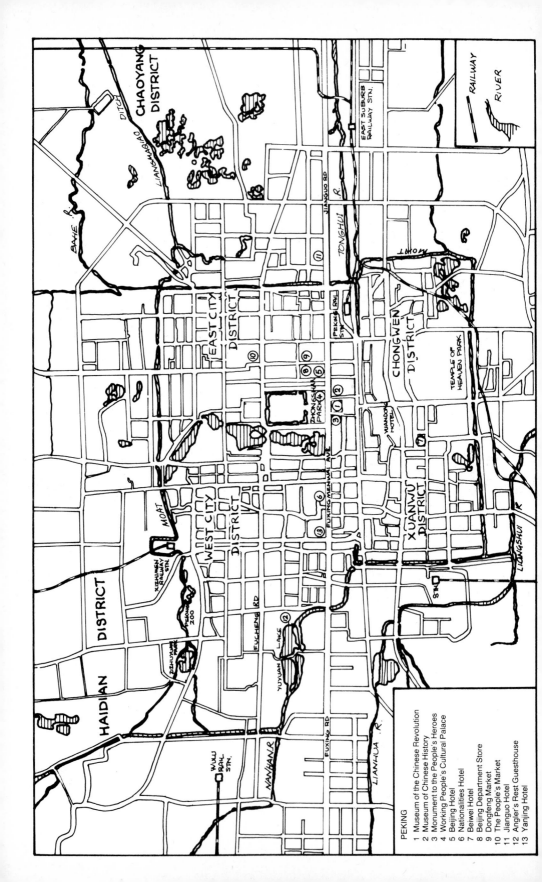

PEKING

1 Museum of the Chinese Revolution
2 Museum of Chinese History
3 Monument to the People's Heroes
4 Working People's Cultural Palace
5 Beijing Hotel
6 Nationalities Hotel
7 Beiwei Hotel
8 Beijing Department Store
9 Dongfeng Market
10 The People's Market
11 Jianguo Hotel
12 Angler's Rest Guesthouse
13 Yanjing Hotel

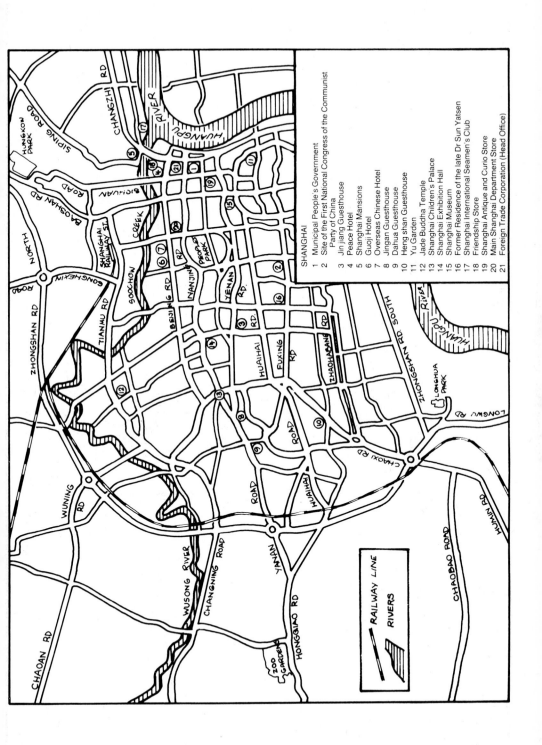

SHANGHAI

1 Municipal People's Government
2 Site of the First National Congress of the Communist
   Party of China
3 Jin jiang Guesthouse
4 Peace Hotel
5 Shanghai Mansions
6 Guoji Hotel
7 Overseas Chinese Hotel
8 Jingan Guesthouse
9 Dahua Guesthouse
10 Heng shan Guesthouse
11 Yu Garden
12 Jade Buddha Temple
13 Shanghai Children's Palace
14 Shanghai Exhibition Hall
15 Shanghai Museum
16 Former Residence of the late Dr Sun Yatsen
17 Shanghai International Seamen's Club
18 Friendship Store
19 Shanghai Antique and Curio Store
20 Main Shanghai Department Store
21 Foreign Trade Corporation (Head Office)

RAILWAY LINE

RIVERS

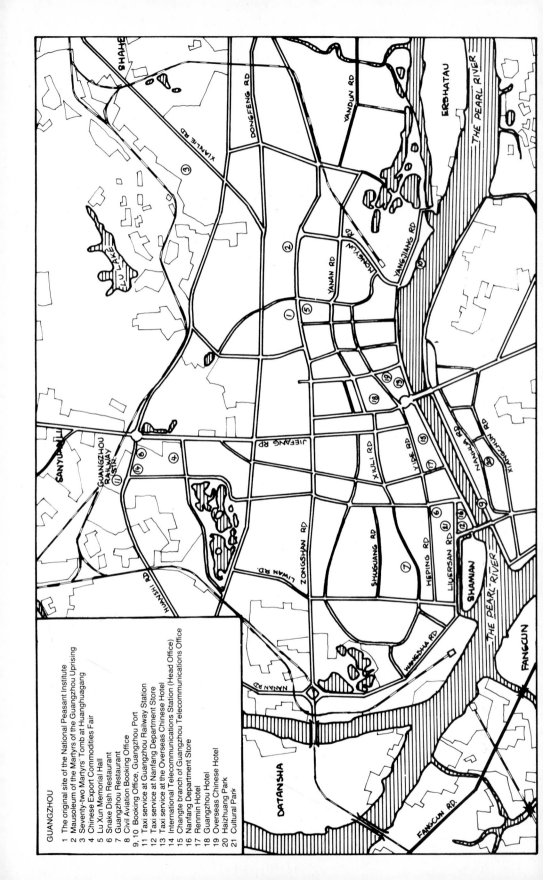

GUANGZHOU

1 The original site of the National Peasant Institute
2 Mausoleum of the Martyrs of the Guangzhou Uprising
3 Seventy-two Martyrs' Tomb at Huanghuagang
4 Chinese Export Commodities Fair
5 Lu Xun Memorial Hall
6 Snake Dish Restaurant
7 Guangzhou Restaurant
8 Civil Aviation Booking Office
9,10 Booking Office, Guangzhou Port
11 Taxi service at Guangzhou Railway Station
12 Taxi service at Nanfang Department Store
13 Taxi service at the Overseas Chinese Hotel
14 International Telecommunications Station (Head Office)
15 Changte branch of Guangzhou Telecommunications Office
16 Nanfang Department Store
17 Renmin Hotel
18 Guangzhou Hotel
19 Overseas Chinese Hotel
20 Haizhuang Park
21 Cultural Park

Bibliography

This reading list includes books which are easily available and readable, as well as those dealing in depth with specialist topics. Some of the books listed are out of print and may only be found in libraries, but are nonetheless worthy of inclusion, either as important documents of the time, or because they are among the few books ever written on a particular topic.

The Foreign Languages Press (FLP) is the state publishing house which issues all foreign language publications in China, publishing in English, Japanese, French, Spanish and Esperanto, as well as other less well-known languages. In China, its main outlets are the Wai Wen Shudian (Foreign Language Bookshops) which are to be found in most cities. Books and magazines may be ordered from overseas through the Guoji Shudian, P.O. Box 37, Beijing, the People's Republic of China.

ARCHAEOLOGY
Chang, Kwang-Chih, *The Archaeology of Ancient China*, Yale University Press, 1968
Rawson, J., *Ancient China, Art and Archaeology*, British Museum Publications, 1980
Watson, W., *Ancient Chinese Bronzes*, Faber, 1977
Watson, W., *China before the Han Dynasty*, Thames & Hudson, 1961
Watson, W., *Early Civilisation in China*, Thames & Hudson, 1966
   Archaeological finds in China since 1949 – a series of titles published by the Foreign Languages Press.

ART
Gascoigne, B., *The Treasures and Dynasties of China*, J. Cape, 1973
Keswick, M., *The Chinese Garden*, Academy Editions, 1978
Palludan, Ann, *The Imperial Ming Tombs*, New Haven and London, Yale University Press, 1981
Sickman & Soper, *The Art & Architecture of China*, Penguin, 1971
Sullivan, M., *Arts of China*, Thames & Hudson, 1973
Tregear, M., *Chinese Art*, Thames & Hudson, 1980
Watson, W., *Art of Dynastic China*, Thames & Hudson, 1981

DIRECTORIES
The China Phone Book and Address Directory, Hong Kong, China Phone Book Co Ltd., annual
Telephone and Address directory for China's major cities, H. K. China Tourism Press

GEOGRAPHY
China – a General Survey, FLP Peking
The Geography of China, FLP Peking
The Times Atlas of China, Times Books, 1974

HISTORY
Eberhard, W., *A History of China*, Routledge, 1977
Gernet, J., *Daily Life in China on the Eve of the Mongol Invasion 1250–1276*, Allen & Unwin, 1962
Fitzgerald C. P., *China – A Short Cultural History*, 4th ed. pub. Barrie, 1976
Loewe, M., *Everyday Life in Early Imperial China 202BC–220AD*, Batsford, 1968
Myrdal, J., *Silk Road: A Journey from the High Pamirs & Ili through Sinkiang and Kansu*, Gollancz, 1980
Wiethof, B., *An Introduction to Chinese History*, Thames & Hudson, 1975

19TH CENTURY
Chesneaux, J., *China from the Opium Wars to the 1911 Revolution*, Harvester Press, 1977
Schurmann F. & Schell O., *Imperial China, China Readings 1*, Penguin, 1968
Spence, J., *The Gate of Heavenly Peace*, Faber & Faber, 1982
Fleming, P., *The Siege at Peking*, (o/p)

20TH CENTURY
Belden, J., *China Shakes the World*, Monthly Review, 1970, with new introduction to 1949 edition
Chesneaux, J., *China: from the 1911 Revolution to Liberation*, Harvester Press, 1977
Fitzgerald, C. P., *The Birth of Communist China*, Penguin, 1970
Han Suyin, *A Many Splendoured Thing*; *Destination Chungking*; *A Mortal Flower*; *Birdless Summer* (All pub. by Cape)
Schiffrin, H. Z., *The Reluctant Revolutionary – Sun Yat Sen*, Little, Brown & Co.
Schurmann, F. & Schell O., *Republican China, China Readings 2*, Penguin, 1968
Snow, E. *Red Star Over China*, Gollancz, 1969
Smedley, A., *The Great Road: Life and Times of Chu Teh*, Monthly Review, 1972

POST 1949
Bonavia, D., *Chinese*, Allen Lane, 1981
Broyelle, C., *China, A Second Look*, Harvester Press, 1980
Broyelle, C., *Women's Liberation in China*, Harvester Press, 1977
Chelminski, R. & Bao Ruo Wang, *Jean Pasqualini, Prisoner of Mao*, Penguin
Chesneaux, J., *People's Republic of China, 1949–76*, Harvester Press, 1977
Chi Hsin, *The Case of the Gang of Four*, Cosmos Books, H. K., 1977
Chi Hsin, *Teng Hsiao Ping*, Cosmos Books, H. K., 1978
Fraser, J., *The Chinese Portrait of a People*, Fontana, 1981
Garside, R., *China after Mao – Coming Alive*, André Deutsch, 1981
Van Ginneken, J., *The Rise & Fall of Lin Piao*, Avon
Hinton, W., *Fanshen: A Documentary of Revolution in a Chinese Village*, Monthly Review, 1966
Hinton, W., *Hundred Days War at Qinghua University*, Monthly Review, 1972

Leys, S., *Broken Images: Essays on Chinese Culture and Politics*, Allison & Busby, 1979
Leys, S., *The Chairman's New Clothes*, Allison & Busby
Leys, S., *Chinese Shadows*, Penguin, 1978
Naisingoro, Pu Yi, *From Emperor to Citizen*, FLP Peking
Schram, S., *Mao Tse Tung – a Biography*, Penguin, 1970
Schram, S., *Mao Tse-Tung Unrehearsed*, Penguin, 1974
Schurmann, F. & Schell, O., *Communist China, China Readings 3*, Penguin, 1968
Snow, E., *Red China Today*, Vintage, 1962
Terrill, R., *800 Million – the Real China*, Heinemann, 1972
Terrill, R., *Future of China: After Mao*, Deutsch, 1978
Wilson, D., *Mao Tse Tung in the Scales of History*, Cambridge University Press, 1977
Witke, R., *Comrade Chiang Ch'ing*, Weidenfeld & Nicholson, 1977

LANGUAGE
Newnham, R., *About Chinese*, Penguin, 1971
Peking Reader in Chinese, FLP Peking
de Francis, J., *Beginning Chinese* (Pinyin only), Yale University Press, 1976

LITERATURE
Ba Jin, *Family*, Pub. in translation, FLP Peking
Birch, C., *An Anthology of Chinese Literature*, Penguin, 1967
Cao Xueqin, *Dream of Red Mansions*, (Trans. Gladys Yang), FLP Peking
  also: *Story of the Stone*, (Trans. D. Hawkes,) 3 vols, Penguin, 1973
Lu Xun, *Selected Stories*, Published in translation by FLP Peking
Luo Guangzhong, *Tales of the Three Kingdoms*, (Trans. Moss Roberts), Pantheon
Mao Dun, *Midnight*, Pub. in translation by FLP Peking
Shi Nai An, *The Water Margin*, (Trans. J. H. Jackson), pub. H. K.
  also: *All Men are Brothers* (Trans. P. S. Buck), John Day
Wu Cheng En, *Monkey* (Trans. Arthur Waley), Penguin, 1973

PHILOSOPHY
Creel, H. G., *Chinese Thought from Confucius to Mao*, Chicago
Confucius, *Analects* (Pub. in translation), Penguin, 1979
Lao Tzu, *Tao Te Ching*, (Pub. in translation), Penguin, 1969
Lau, D. C., (Trans.) *Confucius. Analects.* Penguin, 1979
Lau, D. C., (Trans.) *Lao Tzu. Tao te ching.* Penguin, 1963
Lau, D. C., (Trans.) *Mencius.* Penguin, 1970
Mencius, *Works*, (Pub. in translation), Penguin, 1970
Liu Shaoqi, *How to be a Good Communist*, FLP Peking
Mao Tse Tung, *Selected Works*, Volumes 1–5, FLP Peking
Needham, J., *The Shorter Science & Civilisation of China*, (Abridged by C. Ronan) Cambridge University Press, 1978
Collected Works of Marx, Engels & Lenin, FLP Peking

TRAVEL AND TRAVELOGUES
Secondhand bookshops are often an interesting source of books about China written by the many foreign residents of the late 19th and early 20th centuries.

Such books are often extremely personal, but nonetheless revealing, accounts of life in China in those days.

Bonavia, D., & Bartlett, M., *Tibet*, Thames & Hudson, 1981
Bonavia, D. & Griffiths, P., *Peking*, Time Life, 1978
Crow, C., *Handbook for China*, Kelly and Walsh, Shanghai, 1933 (o/p)
Fisher, L., *Go Gently Through Peking*, Souvenir Press, 1979
Fleming, P., *News from Tartary*, Allen & Unwin, 1962
Hopkirk, P., *Foreign Devils on the Silk Road*, John Murray, 1980
Harrer, H., *Seven Years in Tibet*, (o/p)
Trevor-Roper, H., *The Hermit of Peking*, Macmillan, 1979
15 Cities in China, FLP Peking
60 Scenic Spots in China, FLP Peking
Nagel's Guide to China
Polo, Marco, *The Travels*, Trans. & pub. Penguin, 1965

PERIODICALS AND NEWSPAPERS IN ENGLISH

Peking Review – A weekly giving all the latest political news
China's Foreign Trade – A showcase of products
China Pictorial, China Reconstructs – Monthly magazines providing excellent illustrations and articles on history, contemporary events, places to visit. Minimal political content
China's Screen – Quarterly on films
China's Sports – Monthly
Chinese Literature – Monthly
Chinese Medical Journal – Monthly
Social Sciences in China – Quarterly (Academy of Social Science revived and supported by Deng Xiaoping. A window on currents of thought)
Women of China – Monthly
China Daily – New English Language publication, printed and distributed in China

HONG KONG

Newspaper articles in Hong Kong often are very revealing about events in China. The *South China Morning Post* is the best known daily newspaper. There are also glossy magazines printed in Chinee about places of touristic interest such as *Zhongguo luyou*, written partly in Chinese and sometimes very erratic English.

Index

Entries in italics refer to illustrations in the section between the pages specified.

Xianbi, 17
Xiang River, 206
Xiang Yu, 274
Xiang Zhongfa, 27
Xiangfan, 205
Xiangguo si, 195
Xiang jiang, River, 205, 209
Xiangtan, 209
Xianyang, 267, 268, 274
Xiao Chunu, 166
Xiaoqing River, 255
Xiao Wen, Emperor, 265–6
Xiao Wu, Emperor, 219
Xiao Zeng, Emperor, 311
Xiaotun, 192
Xie He, 35
Xigaze, (Shigatse) 295
Xi jiang, River, 161, 174
Xi jiao shan, 170
Xi ling, 183
Xiling Gorge, 290
Xilinhot, 213
Xinhai Revolution, 24, 222
Xinan, 315
Xingang, 147
Xingang ling, Mountains, 246
Xingjiao si, 276
Xingping, 178
Xingxiang, 189
Xingzhong hui, 23
Xinjiang (Sinkiang), 55, 211, 215;
    agriculture, 50; geography, 5, 6; history,
    21, 22, 297–8; Moslems, 43;
    population, 8, 9; tourist guide, 295–300;
    294–5
Xinyang, 186
Xiongnu (Huns), 12, 16, 17, 113, 211, 213,
    274
Xiqiao Mountain, 169
Xishuangbanna Autonomous District, 301,
    302, 305
Xixia, 19
Xu, Mount (Xu shan), 238, 239
Xu Beihong, 37, 71
Xu Da. 220
Xu Deli, 176
Xu Hao, 191
Xu Shitai, 231
Xu Wei, 317
Xuan tong, Emperor, 104
Xuan Zang, 42, 43, 271–2, 276, 313
Xuan Zong, Emperor, of the Tang dynasty
    18, 155, 192, 198, 257, 271, 272, 273
Xuanweng Mountain, 262

Xuanwu Lake, 219
Xue Erwang, 302
Xue Muqiao, 56
Xue Tao, 285
Xue feng, Mountains, 205
Xuzhou, 82, 214, 215, 221

Yalongzangpo River, 295
Yamzhog Yumco, Lake, 295
Yan, 15, 19
Yan Mountains, 98, 113
Yan Xishan, 25, 62, 261, 262
Yan'an, 29, 51, 68, 267, 269, 277
Yancheng, 214
Yandang Mountains, 305, 319
Yang Di, Emperor, 17, 226
Yang family, 185
Yang Guifei, 18, 272, 273
Yang Jian, Emperor, 17
Yang Suo, 307
Yang guan, Pass, 160
Yangsen, 287, 288
Yangshao, 191
Yangshao culture, 13–14, 193, 196, 273–4
Yangshuo, 177–8
Yangtse Gorges, 182, 278, 286–91
Yangtse River, 8, 150, 175, 301;
    agriculture, 200; boat trips, 280,
    286–91; bridges, 202, 218–19; delta,
    12, 132, 305; geography, 6, 7; history,
    12, 14, 20, 27; Red Basin, 278; at
    Shanghai, 132–3; source, 291
Yangzhou, 36, 77, 82, 214, 221, 225–7
Yansai Lake, 182
Yang shan, Mountains, 179, 181, 182
Yantai (Chefoo), 254, 255, 260–1
Yanyuan, 278
Yao, 9, 173
Yao, Emperor, 13
Yao Autonomous County, 205
Yao Wenyuan, 31, 32, 68, 137
Ye Jianying, 244, 270, 282
Ye Ting, 26, 244
'Yellow Emperor', 13, 63
Yellow Hat sect, 292, 295
Yellow River, 157, 185, 186, 254, 261;
    agriculture, 158; exhibition, 188; floods,
    22, 28, 194; geography, 6–7; history,
    11, 12, 13, 14; hydroelectricity, 55; in
    Inner Mongolia, 212; irrigation projects,
    192; in Shaanxi, 267
Yellow Sea, 214, 254, 258
Yellow Turban Uprising, 16
Yenshi, 14